Lecture Notes in Computer Science

Lecture Notes in Artificial Intelligence   14126

Founding Editor

Jörg Siekmann

Series Editors

Randy Goebel, *University of Alberta, Edmonton, Canada*
Wolfgang Wahlster, *DFKI, Berlin, Germany*
Zhi-Hua Zhou, *Nanjing University, Nanjing, China*

The series Lecture Notes in Artificial Intelligence (LNAI) was established in 1988 as a topical subseries of LNCS devoted to artificial intelligence.

The series publishes state-of-the-art research results at a high level. As with the LNCS mother series, the mission of the series is to serve the international R & D community by providing an invaluable service, mainly focused on the publication of conference and workshop proceedings and postproceedings.

Leszek Rutkowski · Rafał Scherer ·
Marcin Korytkowski · Witold Pedrycz ·
Ryszard Tadeusiewicz · Jacek M. Zurada
Editors

Artificial Intelligence and Soft Computing

22nd International Conference, ICAISC 2023
Zakopane, Poland, June 18–22, 2023
Proceedings, Part II

Springer

Editors
Leszek Rutkowski ⓘ
Systems Research Institute of the Polish
Academy of Sciences
Warsaw, Poland

Marcin Korytkowski ⓘ
Częstochowa University of Technology
Częstochowa, Poland

Ryszard Tadeusiewicz ⓘ
AGH University of Krakow
Kraków, Poland

Rafał Scherer ⓘ
Częstochowa University of Technology
Częstochowa, Poland

Witold Pedrycz ⓘ
University of Alberta
Edmonton, AB, Canada

Jacek M. Zurada ⓘ
University of Louisville
Louisville, KY, USA

ISSN 0302-9743 ISSN 1611-3349 (electronic)
Lecture Notes in Artificial Intelligence
ISBN 978-3-031-42507-3 ISBN 978-3-031-42508-0 (eBook)
https://doi.org/10.1007/978-3-031-42508-0

LNCS Sublibrary: SL7 – Artificial Intelligence

This Springer imprint is published by the registered company Springer Nature Switzerland AG
The registered company address is: Gewerbestrasse 11, 6330 Cham, Switzerland

Paper in this product is recyclable.

Preface

This volume constitutes the proceedings of the 22nd International Conference on Artificial Intelligence and Soft Computing, ICAISC 2023, Zakopane, Poland, June 18–22, 2023. The Conference was organized by the Polish Neural Network Society in cooperation with the Department of Intelligent Computer Systems at the Częstochowa University of Technology, the University of Social Sciences in Łódź, and the IEEE Computational Intelligence Society, Poland Chapter. The Conference was held under the auspices of the Committee on Informatics of the Polish Academy of Sciences. At ICAISC 2023 the invited lectures were presented by the following outstanding researchers: Luís A. Alexandre, Aleksander Byrski, Włodzisław Duch, Zbigniew Michalewicz, Witold Pedrycz, Jerzy Stefanowski, Wenying Xu and Shaofu Yang. Previous conferences took place in Kule (1994), Szczyrk (1996), Kule (1997) and Zakopane (1999, 2000, 2002, 2004, 2006, 2008, 2010, 2012, 2013, 2014, 2015, 2016, 2017, 2018, 2019, 2020, 2021 and 2022) and attracted a large number of papers and internationally recognized speakers: Lotfi A. Zadeh, Hojjat Adeli, Rafal Angryk, Igor Aizenberg, Cesare Alippi, Shunichi Amari, Daniel Amit, Plamen Angelov, Sanghamitra Bandyopadhyay, Albert Bifet, Piero P. Bonissone, Jim Bezdek, Zdzisław Bubnicki, Jan Chorowski, Andrzej Cichocki, Swagatam Das, Ewa Dudek-Dyduch, Włodzisław Duch, Adel S. Elmaghraby, Pablo A. Estévez, João Gama, Erol Gelenbe, Jerzy Grzymala-Busse, Martin Hagan, Yoichi Hayashi, Akira Hirose, Kaoru Hirota, Adrian Horzyk, Tingwen Huang, Eyke Hüllermeier, Hisao Ishibuchi, Er Meng Joo, Artur Luczak, Janusz Kacprzyk, Nikola Kasabov, Jim Keller, Laszlo T. Koczy, Tomasz Kopacz, Jacek Koronacki, Zdzisław Kowalczuk, Adam Krzyzak, Rudolf Kruse, James Tin-Yau Kwok, Soo-Young Lee, Derong Liu, Robert Marks, Ujjwal Maulik, Zbigniew Michalewicz, Evangelia Micheli-Tzanakou, Kaisa Miettinen, Krystian Mikołajczyk, Henning Müller, Christian Napoli, Ngoc Thanh Nguyen, Andrzej Obuchowicz, Erkki Oja, Nikhil R. Pal, Witold Pedrycz, Marios M. Polycarpou, José C. Príncipe, Jagath C. Rajapakse, Šarunas Raudys, Enrique Ruspini, Roman Senkerik, Jörg Siekmann, Andrzej Skowron, Roman Słowiński, Igor Spiridonov, Boris Stilman, Ponnuthurai Nagaratnam Suganthan, Ryszard Tadeusiewicz, Ah-Hwee Tan, Dacheng Tao, Shiro Usui, Thomas Villmann, Fei-Yue Wang, Jun Wang, Bogdan M. Wilamowski, Ronald Y. Yager, Xin Yao, Syozo Yasui, Gary Yen, Ivan Zelinka and Jacek Zurada. The aim of this conference is to build a bridge between traditional artificial intelligence techniques and so-called soft computing techniques. It was pointed out by Lotfi A. Zadeh that "soft computing (SC) is a coalition of methodologies which are oriented toward the conception and design of information/intelligent systems. The principal members of the coalition are: fuzzy logic (FL), neurocomputing (NC), evolutionary computing (EC), probabilistic computing (PC), chaotic computing (CC), and machine learning (ML). The constituent methodologies of SC are, for the most part, complementary and synergistic rather than competitive". These proceedings present both traditional artificial intelligence methods and soft computing techniques. Our goal is to bring together scientists representing both areas of research. The proceedings are divided into four parts:

- Computer Vision, Image and Speech Analysis
- Various Problems of Artificial Intelligence
- Bioinformatics, Biometrics and Medical Applications
- Data Mining and Pattern Classification

   I would like to thank our participants, invited speakers and reviewers of the papers for their scientific and personal contribution to the Conference. Finally, I thank my co-workers Łukasz Bartczuk, Piotr Dziwiński, Marcin Gabryel, Rafał Grycuk, Marcin Korytkowski and Rafał Scherer, for their enormous efforts to make the Conference a very successful event. Moreover, I would like to appreciate the work of Marcin Korytkowski who was responsible for the Internet submission system.

June 2023   Leszek Rutkowski

Organization

ICAISC Chairpersons

General Chair

Leszek Rutkowski — Systems Research Institute, Polish Academy of Sciences, Poland

Co-chair

Rafał Scherer — Częstochowa University of Technology, Poland

Technical Chair

Marcin Korytkowski — Częstochowa University of Technology, Poland

Financial Chair

Marcin Gabryel — Częstochowa University of Technology, Poland

Area Chairs

Fuzzy Systems

Witold Pedrycz — University of Alberta, Canada

Evolutionary Algorithms

Zbigniew Michalewicz — Complexica, Australia

Neural Networks

Jinde Cao — Southeast University, China

Computer Vision

Dacheng Tao   University of Sydney, Australia

Machine Learning

Nikhil R. Pal   Indian Statistical Institute, India

Artificial Intelligence with Applications

Janusz Kacprzyk   Systems Research Institute, Polish Academy of
                                Sciences, Poland

International Liaison

Jacek Zurada   University of Louisville, USA

ICAISC Program Committee

Hojjat Adeli   Ohio State University, USA
Cesare Alippi   Polytechnic University of Milan, Italy
Rafal A. Angryk   Georgia State University, USA
Robert Babuska   Delft University of Technology, The Netherlands
James C. Bezdek   University of Melbourne, Australia
Bernadette Bouchon-Meunier   Sorbonne University & LIP6, France
Aleksander Byrski   AGH University of Krakow, Poland
Juan Luis Castro   University of Granada, Spain
Yen-Wei Chen   Ritsumeikan University, Japan
Andrzej Cichocki   Systems Research Institute, Polish Academy of
                                Sciences, Poland
Krzysztof Cios   Virginia Commonwealth University, USA
Ian Cloete   Stellenbosch University, South Africa
Oscar Cordón   University of Granada, Spain
Bernard De Baets   Ghent University, Belgium
Włodzisław Duch   Nicolaus Copernicus University, Poland
Meng Joo Er   Dalian Maritime University, China
Pablo Estevez   University of Chile, Chile
Tom Gedeon   Curtin University, Australia
Erol Gelenbe   Institute of Theoretical and Applied Informatics,
                                Polish Academy of Sciences, Poland
Hani Hagras   University of Essex, UK
Saman Halgamuge   University of Melbourne, Australia

Yoichi Hayashi	Meiji University, Japan
Tim Hendtlass	Swinburne University of Technology, Australia
Francisco Herrera	Granada University, Spain
Kaoru Hirota	Tokyo Institute of Technology, Japan
Hisao Ishibuchi	Southern University of Science and Technology, China
Ivan Izonin	Lviv Polytechnic National University, Ukraine
Mo Jamshidi	University of Texas, USA
Nikola Kasabov	Auckland University of Technology, New Zealand
Okyay Kaynak	Bogazici University, Turkey
James M. Keller	University of Missouri, USA
Etienne Kerre	Ghent University, Belgium
Frank Klawonn	Ostfalia University of Applied Sciences, Germany
Robert Kozma	University of Memphis, USA
László Kóczy	Budapest University of Technology and Economics, Hungary
Józef Korbicz	University of Zielona Góra, Poland
Rudolf Kruse	University of Magdeburg, Germany
Adam Krzyzak	Concordia University, Canada
Věra Kůrková	Czech Academy of Sciences, Czech Republic
Ivan Laktionov	Dnipro University of Technology, Ukraine
Soo-Young Lee	Korea Advanced Institute of Science and Technology, South Korea
Simon M. Lucas	Queen Mary University of London, UK
Luis Magdalena	Technical University of Madrid, Spain
Jerry M. Mendel	University of Southern California, USA
Radko Mesiar	Slovak University of Technology in Bratislava, Slovakia
Zbigniew Michalewicz	Complexica, Australia
Kazumi Nakamatsu	University of Hyogo, Japan
Detlef D. Nauck	British Telecom, UK
Ngoc Thanh Nguyen	Wrocław University of Science and Technology, Poland
Witold Pedrycz	University of Alberta, Canada
Leonid Perlovsky	Northeastern University, USA
Marios M. Polycarpou	University of Cyprus, Cyprus
Danil Prokhorov	Toyota Tech Center, USA
Vincenzo Piuri	University of Milan, Italy
Sarunas Raudys	Vilnius University, Lithuania
Marek Reformat	University of Alberta, Canada
Imre J. Rudas	Obuda University, Hungary
Norihide Sano	Shizuoka Sangyo University, Japan

Rudy Setiono	National University of Singapore, Singapore
Jennie Si	Arizona State University, USA
Peter Sincak	Technical University of Kosice, Slovakia
Andrzej Skowron	Systems Research Institute, Polish Academy of Sciences, Poland
Roman Słowiński	Poznań University of Technology, Poland
Pilar Sobrevilla	Barcelona Tech, Spain
Janusz Starzyk	Ohio University, USA
Jerzy Stefanowski	Poznań University of Technology, Poland
Vitomir Štruc	University of Ljubljana, Slovenia
Ron Sun	Rensselaer Polytechnic Institute, USA
Johan Suykens	KU Leuven, Belgium
Ryszard Tadeusiewicz	AGH University of Science and Technology, Poland
Hideyuki Takagi	Kyushu University, Japan
Vicenç Torra	Umeå University, Sweden
Burhan Turksen	University of Toronto, Canada
Shiro Usui	RIKEN Brain Science Institute, Japan
Roman Vorobel	National Academy of Sciences of Ukraine, Ukraine
Deliang Wang	Ohio State University, USA
Jun Wang	City University of Hong Kong, China
Lipo Wang	Nanyang Technological University, Singapore
Bernard Widrow	Stanford University, USA
Kay C. Wiese	Simon Fraser University, Canada
Bogdan M. Wilamowski	Auburn University, USA
Donald C. Wunsch	Missouri University of Science and Technology, USA
Ronald R. Yager	Iona College, USA
Xin-She Yang	Middlesex University London, UK
Gary Yen	Oklahoma State University, USA
Sławomir Zadrożny	Systems Research Institute, Polish Academy of Sciences, Poland

ICAISC Organizing Committee

Rafał Scherer
Łukasz Bartczuk
Piotr Dziwiński
Marcin Gabryel (Finance Chair)
Rafał Grycuk
Marcin Korytkowski (Databases and Internet Submissions)

Contents – Part II

Computer Vision, Image and Speech Analysis

A Novel ConvMixer Transformer Based Architecture for Violent Behavior
Detection 3
  Andrea Alfarano, Giorgio De Magistris, Leonardo Mongelli,
  Samuele Russo, Janusz Starczewski, and Christian Napoli

Speech Emotion Recognition: Recent Advances and Current Trends 17
  Soundes Belkacem

A Smartphone-Based Computer Vision Assistance System with Neural
Network Depth Estimation for the Visually Impaired 26
  Mykola Beshley, Pastukh Volodymyr, Halyna Beshley,
  and Michal Gregus Jr.

Hybrid Learning Model for Satellite Forest Image Segmentation 37
  Clopas Kwenda, Mandlenkosi Victor Gwetu,
  and Jean Vincent Fonou-Dombeu

Adaptive Pruning for Multi-Head Self-Attention 48
  Walid Messaoud, Rim Trabelsi, Adnane Cabani, and Fatma Abdelkefi

Fast Visual Imperfection Detection when Real Negative Examples are
Unavailable 58
  Patryk Najgebauer, Rafał Scherer, Rafał Grycuk, Jakub Walczak,
  Adam Wojciechowski, and Ewa Łada-Tondyra

Vision-Based Mobile Robots Control Along a Given Trajectory 69
  Jan Rodziewicz-Bielewicz and Marcin Korzeń

Text Guided Facial Image Synthesis Using StyleGAN and Variational
Autoencoder Trained CLIP 78
  Anagha Srinivasa, Anjali Praveen, Anusha Mavathur,
  Apurva Pothumarthi, Arti Arya, and Pooja Agarwal

Application of Object Detection Models for the Detection of Kitchen
Furniture - A Comparison 91
  Benjamin Stecker and Hans Brandt-Pook

Support Learning Vovinam Exercises Based on Computer Vision   102
   Pham Son Tung, Thai Thanh Do, Pham Hong Giang, and Phan Duy Hung

Semantic Segmentation Neural Network in Automatic Weapon Detection   112
   Michał Wieczorek, Jakub Siłka, Martyna Kobielnik, and Marcin Woźniak

Various Problems of Artificial Intelligence

An Application of Fuzzy Techniques to Predict the Polymorphism
of Selected Microsatellite Sequences   123
   *Adam Kiersztyn, Krystyna Kiersztyn, Grzegorz Panasiewicz,
   and Martyna Bieniek-Kobuszewska*

Monte Carlo Tree Search with Metaheuristics   134
   Jacek Mańdziuk and Patryk Walczak

Phishing Attack Detection: An Improved Performance Through Ensemble
Learning   145
   *Benjamin McConnell, Daniel Del Monaco, Mahdieh Zabihimayvan,
   Fatemeh Abdollahzadeh, and Samir Hamada*

Removing Ambiguity in Natural Language for Generating Self-Join
Queries   158
   Pradnya Sawant and Kavita Sonawane

Predicting Churn Rate in Companies   170
   Magdalena Scherer

Training Set Preparation for Deep Model Learning Inpatients
with Ischemic Brain Lesions and Gender Identity Disorder   176
   Ana Starcevic, Boris Vucinic, and Ilona Karpiel

From Simulated to Real Environments: Q-Learning for MAZE-Navigation
of a TurtleBot   192
   Tobias Weiss, Simon Reichhuber, and Sven Tomforde

Bioinformatics, Biometrics and Medical Applications

3D Reconstructions of Brain from MRI Scans Using Neural Radiance Fields . . .   207
   Khadija Iddrisu, Sylwia Malec, and Alessandro Crimi

Exploring Target Identification for Drug Design with K-Nearest
Neighbors' Algorithm 219
   Karina Jimenes-Vargas, Yunierkis Perez-Castillo, Eduardo Tejera,
   and Cristian R. Munteanu

Computational Models for COVID-19 Dynamics Prediction 228
   Andrzej Kloczkowski, Juan Luis Fernández-Martínez,
   and Zulima Fernández-Muñiz

Electrochemical Biosensor Design Through Data-Driven Modeling
Incorporating Meta-Analysis and Big Data Workflow 239
   Martsenyuk Vasyl, Klos-Witkowska Aleksandra, and Semenets Andrii

A New Method of Verification of Dynamic Signatures Changing over Time
with Decomposition and Selection of Characteristic Descriptors 251
   Mateusz Mastalerczyk, Tomasz Szczepanik, and Marcin Zalasiński

Impact of the Pre-processing and Balancing of EEG Data
on the Performance of Graph Neural Network for Epileptic Seizure
Classification 258
   Szymon Mazurek, Rosmary Blanco, Joan Falcó-Roget,
   Jan K. Argasiński, and Alessandro Crimi

A New Rebinning Reconstruction Method for the Low Dose CT Scanners
with Flying Focal Spot 269
   Piotr Pluta and Robert Cierniak

Data Mining and Pattern Classification

Advancing Singular Value Decomposition Techniques for Enhanced Data
Mining in Recommender Systems 281
   Mykola Beshley, Olena Hordiichuk-Bublivska, Halyna Beshley,
   and Iryna Ivanochko

An Experimental Analysis on Mapping Strategies for Cepstral Coefficients
Multi-projection in Voice Spoofing Detection Problem 291
   Rodrigo Colnago Contreras, Monique Simplicio Viana,
   and Rodrigo Capobianco Guido

Mining Correlated High-Utility Itemsets Using the Cosine Measure 307
   Huynh Anh Duy, Huynh Anh Khoa, and Phan Duy Hung

Bayesian Inference in Infinite Multivariate McDonald's Beta Mixture
Model 320
   Darya Forouzanfar, Narges Manouchehri, and Nizar Bouguila

Cannabis Use Estimators Within Canadian Population Using Social Media
Based on Deep Learning Tools 331
Doaa Ibrahim, Diana Inkpen, and Hussein Al Osman

On the Bayesian Interpretation of Penalized Statistical Estimators 343
Jan Kalina and Barbora Peštová

Synthetic Data for Feature Selection 353
Firuz Kamalov, Hana Sulieman, and Aswani Kumar Cherukuri

ML Support for Conformity Checks in CMDB-Like Databases 366
Szymon Niewiadomski and Grzegorz Mzyk

An Improvement of Graph Neural Network for Multi-behavior
Recommendation 377
Nguyen Bao Phuoc, Duong Thuy Trang, and Phan Duy Hung

Binary Matrix Factorization Discretization 388
Georges Spyrides, Marcus Poggi, and Hélio Lopes

Combining Linear Classifiers Using Score Function Based on Distance
to Decision Boundary 402
Pawel Trajdos, Robert Burduk, and Andrzej Kasprzak

Author Index 413

Contents – Part I

Neural Networks and Their Applications

A Novel Approach to the GQR Algorithm for Neural Networks Training 3
Jarosław Bilski and Bartosz Kowalczyk

On Speeding up the Levenberg-Marquardt Learning Algorithm 12
Jarosław Bilski, Barosz Kowalczyk, and Jacek Smoląg

Reinforcement Learning with Brain-Inspired Modulation Improves
Adaptation to Environmental Changes 23
Eric Chalmers and Artur Luczak

Multi-Agent Deep Q-Network in Voxel-Based Automated Electrical
Routing 35
Tizian Dagner, Rafael Parzeller, and Selin Kesler

The Analysis of Optimizers in Training Artificial Neural Networks Using
the Streaming Approach 46
Piotr Duda, Mateusz Wojtulewicz, and Leszek Rutkowski

Training Neural Tensor Networks with Corrupted Relations 56
Tristan Falck and Duncan Coulter

Application of Monte Carlo Algorithms with Neural Network-Based
Intermediate Area to the Thousand Card Game 68
Łukasz Gałka, Paweł Karczmarek, and Dariusz Czerwinski

Learning Representations by Crystallized Back-Propagating Errors 78
Marcus Grum

Fuzzy Hyperplane Based K-SVCR Multi-class Classification with Its
Applications to Stock Prediction Problem 101
Pei-Yi Hao

Dynamic Hand Gesture Recognition for Human-Robot Collaborative
Assembly 112
Bogdan Kwolek and Sako Shinji

Transfer of Knowledge Among Instruments in Automatic Music
Transcription 122
    Michał Leś and Michał Woźniak

The Geometry of Decision Borders Between Affine Space Prototypes
for Nearest Prototype Classifiers 134
    M. Mohannazadeh Bakhtiari, A. Villmann, and T. Villmann

An Interpretable Two-Layered Neural Network Structure–Based
on Component-Wise Reasoning 145
    M. Mohannazadeh Bakhtiari and T. Villmann

Viscosity Estimation of Water-PVP Solutions from Droplets Using
Artificial Neural Networks and Image Processing 157
    *Mohamed Azouz Mrad, Kristof Csorba, Dorián László Galata,
    Zsombor Kristóf Nagy, and Hassan Charaf*

Pruning Convolutional Filters via Reinforcement Learning with Entropy
Minimization 167
    Bogdan Muşat and Răzvan Andonie

Unsupervised Representation Learning: Target Regularization
for Cross-Domain Sentiment Classification 181
    Michał Perełkiewicz, Rafał Poświata, and Jakub Kierzkowski

Decentralized Federated Learning Loop with Constrained Trust Mechanism ... 193
    *Dawid Połap, Katarzyna Prokop, Gautam Srivastava,
    and Jerry Chun-Wei Lin*

Learning Activation Functions for Adversarial Attack Resilience in CNNs 203
    Maghsood Salimi, Mohammad Loni, and Marjan Sirjani

Federated Learning for Human Activity Recognition on the MHealth
Dataset 215
    Sergio Sanchez, Javier Machacuay, and Mario Quinde

Image Classification Through Graph Neural Networks and Random Walks 226
    William S. M. Silva, Priscila T. M. Saito, and Pedro H. Bugatti

Bus Route Classification for Rural Areas Using Graph Convolutional
Networks 236
    *Timo Stadler, Sandra Weikl, Simon Wein, Peter Georg, Andreas Schäfer,
    and Jan Dünnweber*

Expansion Rate Parametrization and K-Fold Based Inference with U-Net
Neural Networks for Multiclass Medical Image Segmentation 251
  Roman Statkevych, Yuri Gordienko, and Sergii Stirenko

Transfer Learning from ImageNet to the Domain of Pigmented Nevi 263
  Grzegorz Surówka

Towards Detecting Freezing of Gait Events Using Wearable Sensors
and Genetic Programming 274
  Adane Nega Tarekegn, Faouzi Alaya Cheikh, Muhammad Sajjad,
  and Mohib Ullah

CNN-LSTM Optimized by Genetic Algorithm in Time Series Forecasting:
An Automatic Method to Use Deep Learning 286
  Eder Urbinate, Fernando Itano, and Emilio Del-Moral-Hernandez

Authorship Attribution of Literary Texts Using Named Entity Masking
and MaxLogit-Based Sequence Classification for Varying Text Lengths 296
  Tomasz Walkowiak

Gates Are Not What You Need in RNNs 304
  Ronalds Zakovskis, Andis Draguns, Eliza Gaile, Emils Ozolins,
  and Karlis Freivalds

Generating Image Captions in Polish Using Transformer Architecture 325
  Michał Żebrowski and Jacek Komorowski

Evolutionary Algorithms and Their Applications

An Hybrid NSGA-II Algorithm for the Bi-objective Mobile Mammography
Unit Routing Problem 339
  Thiago Giachetto de Araujo, Puca Huachi Vaz Penna,
  and Marcone Jamilson Freitas Souza

Controlled Refresh of the Population in Differential Evolution
for Real-World Problems 352
  Petr Bujok, Martin Lacko, and Patrik Kolenovský

A New Hybrid Particle Swarm Optimization and Evolutionary Algorithm
with Self-Adaptation Mechanism 363
  Piotr Dziwiński and Łukasz Bartczuk

Data Mining Car Configurator Clickstream Data to Identify Potential
Consumers: A Genetic Algorithm Approach 375
   *Juan Manuel García-Sánchez, Xavier Vilasís-Cardona,
   Álvaro García-Piquer, and Alexandre Lerma-Martín*

Multi-population Algorithm Using Surrogate Models and Different
Training Plans 385
   Daniel Kucharski and Krzysztof Cpałka

Multi-population-based Algorithms with Different Migration Topologies
and Their Improvement by Population Re-initialization 399
   Krystian Łapa

Machine Learning Assisted Interactive Multi-objectives Optimization
Framework: A Proposed Formulation and Method for Overtime Planning
in Software Development Projects 415
   Hammed A. Mojeed and Rafal Szlapczynski

Improved Barnacles Movement Optimizer (IBMO) Algorithm
for Engineering Design Problems 427
   *Syed Kumayl Raza Moosavi, Muhammad Hamza Zafar,
   Seyedali Mirjalili, and Filippo Sanfilippo*

Evolutionary-Based Generative Design for Electric Transmission Towers 439
   Hugo Moreno, Pablo S. Naharro, Antonio LaTorre, and José-María Peña

Ehnanced Grey Wolf Optimizer 451
   Radka Poláková and Daniel Valenta

Artificial Intelligence in Modeling and Simulation

Security Intelligence for Real-Time Security Monitoring Software 463
   Aneta Poniszewska-Marańda, Radoslaw Grela, and Natalia Kryvinska

Examining Effects of Class Imbalance on Conditional GAN Training 475
   Yang Chen, Dustin J. Kempton, and Rafal A. Angryk

Stochastic Model for Wildfire Simulation Based on the Characteristics
of the Brazilian Cerrado 487
   *Heitor F. Ferreira, Claudiney R. Tinoco, Luiz G. A. Martins,
   and Gina M. B. Oliveira*

Test Case Generator for Problems of Complete Coverage and Path
Planning for Emergency Response by UAVs 497
   Jakub Grzeszczak, Krzysztof Trojanowski, and Artur Mikitiuk

Application of Artificial Neural Networks in Electric Arc Furnace Modeling ... 510
  Maciej Klimas and Dariusz Grabowski

Profiling of Webshop Users in Terms of Price Sensitivity 522
  Eliza Kocić, Marcin Gabryel, and Milan Kocić

Learning Bezier-Durrmeyer Type Descriptors for Classifying
Curves – Preliminary Studies 530
  Adam Krzyżak, Wojciech Rafajłowicz, and Ewaryst Rafajłowicz

Prediction Accuracy of Direction Changes with ELM, MLP and LSTM
on the Example of Exchange Rates 542
  Jakub Morkowski

Child Tracking and Prediction of Violence on Children In Social Media
Using Natural Language Processing and Machine Learning 560
  M. K. Nallakaruppan, Gautam Srivastava, Thippa Reddy Gadekallu,
  Praveen Kumar Reddy, Sivarama Krishnan, and Dawid Polap

Adequate Basis for the Data-Driven and Machine-Learning-Based
Identification 570
  Marcel Rojahn, Maximilian Ambros, Tibebu Biru, Hermann Krallmann,
  Norbert Gronau, and Marcus Grum

Author Index 589

Computer Vision, Image and Speech Analysis

A Novel ConvMixer Transformer Based Architecture for Violent Behavior Detection

Andrea Alfarano[1], Giorgio De Magistris[1], Leonardo Mongelli[1],
Samuele Russo[2], Janusz Starczewski[3], and Christian Napoli[1,4(✉)]

[1] Department of Computer, Control and Management Engineering,
Sapienza University of Rome, Via Ariosto 25, 00185 Roma, Italy
{alfarano,demagistris,mongelli,cnapoli}@diag.uniroma1.it
[2] Department of Psychology, Sapienza University of Rome,
Via dei Marsi 78, 00185 Roma, Italy
samuele.russo@uniroma1.it
[3] Department of Computational Intelligence, Czestochowa University of Technology,
al. Armii Krajowej 36, 42-200 Czestochowa, Poland
janusz.starczewski@pcz.pl
[4] Institute for Systems Analysis and Computer Science, Italian National Research
Council, Via dei Taurini 19, 00185 Roma, Italy

Abstract. Nowadays most of the streets, squares and buildings are monitored by a large number of surveillance cameras. Nevertheless, these cameras are used only to record scenes to be analyzed after crimes or thefts, and not to prevent violent actions in an automatic way. In few cases there may be a guard who checks the videos manually in real-time, but it is a very inefficient and expensive process. In this paper we proposes a novel approach to Violence Detection task using a recent architecture named ConvMixer, a simple CNN which uses patch-based embeddings in order to obtain superior performance with fewer parameters and computation resources. We also use an interesting technique that consists in arranging frames into super images to encode the temporal information into the spatial dimensions. Our tests on popular "Real Life Violence Situations" dataset highlight a remarkable accuracy of 0.95, placing our proposed model at the second position of the leader board on the same dataset.

Keywords: ConvMixer · SuperImage · Violence Detection · Action Recognition

1 Introduction

The increase of violent episodes in cities has led to questions about the efficiency and effectiveness of surveillance cameras. Most of these systems are simply used to record videos of public and private areas and the recordings are weekly/monthly checked only in case of a report of violence or thefts. In few cases some guards are employed to monitor the real time video cameras but in

L. Rutkowski et al. (Eds.): ICAISC 2023, LNAI 14126, pp. 3–16, 2023.
https://doi.org/10.1007/978-3-031-42508-0_1

general both the approaches are ineffective in preventing violence. The presence of cameras does not stop criminals to commit violence because there is no way to rapid request help to the police, who always intervene when the violent people have already fled. The analysis of the recorded videos is time-consuming, and it does not always allow to identify the criminals. Therefore the necessity of an automatic system for detecting real time violence actions and notify it to the authorities.

For these reasons, many researchers have been interested in this task. In early experiments CNN models such as C3D, ConvLSTM showed the ability of extract spatio-temporal features from videos but require a high energy consumption to replicate state-of-the-art performances. Other architectures as VGG, ResNet, DenseNet and InceptionV3 have been used, reaching optimal results [33,39].

It is a well known fact that CNNs have become the dominant architecture for vision tasks for plenty of years. Although recently new Transformers based architectures, called Vision Transformers (ViTs), showed to be competitive (often better) compared to state-of-the-art convolutional networks while requiring substantially fewer computational resources to train and evaluate. The application of transformers to images requires some kind of embedding: it is not possible to apply transformers directly to a pixel's image, due to quadratic cost of self-attention layers which will lead to dramatic computational complexity. Several attempts have been made to apply transformers to computer vision, until the introduction of embedding by dividing images in pixel patches [6,11].

In this paper we propose a novel approach using a recent architecture named ConvMixer. This model tries to replicate transformer behavior using only CNNs. The basic idea that inspired the ConvMixer architecture is that superior Transformers capabilities mainly depend on patch based embedding approaches. In the ConvMixer original paper [42] it is shown how this approach allows to overcome classical object classification CNNs architectures, being competitive also with ViT but with dramatically less computational resources. Our contribution in the field of violence detection can be summarized in the following points:

- Until now ConvMixer was applied only in Object Classification and Medical Image Segmentation tasks. We are the first who have applied this novel architecture in the Violence Detection task;
- Two different datasets have been used. UCF101 is an action recognition dataset of realistic action videos, collected from YouTube, having 101 action categories [38]. It is used to pre-train the model to recognize human movements. Instead, Real Life Violence Dataset is a Violence Detection dataset which contains 1000 violent and 1000 nonviolent videos, both representing real life actions, and it is used to train and test the model to detect the presence of violence or not;
- We used a Super Image technique which consists in extracting frames from videos, resizing and combining them into a super image that encodes both spatial and temporal information;

– Multiple experiments have been conducted to find the best possible configuration of the network and the best dimension of the super images, leading to impressive results on both Action Recognition and Violence Detection tasks.

2 Related Work

This section reports relevant related works both in the general field of action recognition (Sect. 2.1) and in the more specific field of violence detection (Sect. 2.2).

2.1 Action Recognition

The detection and recognition of human actions from real-time CCTV video data streams is a popular task [46]. Humans easily recognize and identify actions in video but automating this procedure is challenging. Human action recognition in videos is of interest for applications such as automated surveillance, elderly behavior monitoring [10], human-computer interaction, content-based video retrieval and video summarization [34].

Human Action Recognition (HAR) can be also applied in sports. It is used to identify players and track their actions during both training and matches. The goal of Action Recognition is to identify the person performing an action in an unknown video sequence and categorize the action itself. It is well known that actions can vary in complexity. Simple actions can often be detected in a single image or frame, while complex actions may require a series of consecutive frames over a longer period to be accurately recognized.

Conventional techniques for recognizing 3D actions often utilize hand-crafted features, such as HON4D [30] and HOPC [2], to gather spatial-temporal information. These methods typically involve two phases: extracting features and reducing dimensionality and then classification. Features commonly used in HAR include Optical Flow for extracting motion information but also Histogram of Oriented Gradients (HOG) [5,13]. Classification can be then performed using machine learning techniques such as Support Vector Machine (SVM) [32] or K-Means algorithm [16].

On the other hand, deep neural networks such as Convolutional Neural Networks (CNNs) have emerged as a superior option for image related tasks. In [44], authors present a novel method called "Three-channel deep convolutional neural networks (3ConvNets) + Weighted Hierarchical Depth Motion Maps (WHDMM)", which utilizes sequences of depth maps as inputs to the ConvNets. In [19], the authors propose a 3D Convolution Neural Network 3D (CNN) to extract spatial and temporal features from videos to capture the motion information. In [24], the authors introduce a Robust Non-Linear Knowledge Transfer Model (R-NKTM), a deep fully connected neural network, to transfer knowledge of human actions from an unseen view to a shared high-level view by finding a set of non-linear transformations that connect the views. Other studies, such as [21] and [12], represent spatio-temporal information of skeleton sequences as "joint distance maps" (JDMs) and use CNNs to extract invariant features. Popoola and Wang [31] conducted a survey for detecting abnormal contextual human behavior in surveillance applications. Ke et al. [20] reviewed various methods for recognizing human activity using both static and moving cameras. Aggarwal and Xia [3] conducted a survey on human activity recognition based on 3D data, using RGB and depth information. Finally, Presti et al. [23] provided a review of techniques for recognizing human actions based on 3D skeletons.

The action recognition task is important in our project in order to train the model better. ConvMixer without a pre-training on action recognition task led to very bad results, with an incredible huge overfitting. On the other hand, by pretraining on a more general Action Recognition task, we noticed that the model focuses on detecting human movements rather than looking at the environment on the background of each image. In fact, many frames extracted from videos have the same background so, applying only Violence Detection task, the model just understand the environment and not the behavior of the humans in the scene.

2.2 Violence Detection

As in the case of Action Recognition, also in Violence detection there are multiple projects that aim to detect violence from videos and CCTV footage. Different approaches have been used:

In [40], researchers have used InceptionNet as image classifiers to detect violence in every frame of sports videos and movies, but this approach has resulted in poor generalization, slower inference, and loss of temporal information [25]. To preserve temporal information, some researchers have used ConvLSTMs to detect violence in CCTV footage [35, 37]. Also pre-trained models such as ResNet50 [35] and VGG16 [37] have been used to extract spatial features from video frames and concatenate them with latent features from the LSTM model [4].

Chen et al. [8] use the encoded motion vectors from MPEG-1 video data as features to detect the presence of blood as a sign of violence by building a classifier that represents data components with high motion intensity. Hassner et al. [17] develop the violent flows (ViF) descriptor, which calculates the statistics of how the flow vectors magnitude changes over the time to detect violent activities and classifies using a linear SVM classifier. In [47] the Gaussian Model of Optical Flow (GMOF) is used to extract spatiotemporal features from candidate locations using the Orientation Histogram of Optical Flow (OHOF). Gao et al. [14] introduce the oriented violent flows (OViF). In [43], the authors use a CNN model to detect objects, then pass the frames with individual detection to a 3D CNN to extract spatiotemporal features. These features are then classified using a softmax classifier. Peixoto et al. [29] utilize two deep neural network frameworks to learn spatial-temporal information in different scenarios, and then trained a shallow neural network to aggregate the information.

Differently from the previous approaches, our method consists in training ConvMixer first using a dataset for Action Recognition. Once the model is able to recognize human movements, we train again the network using a Violence Detection dataset. In this way ConvMixer is able to better classify violent and nonviolent actions, also avoiding false positives generated by friendly behaviors or fast movements such as hugs, small hits, claps and high fives (see Fig. 1).

Fig. 1. A general overview of Violence Detection.

3   Method

This section describes the proposed method, and in particular Sect. 3.1 outlines the datasets that we used to train our model, while Sects. 3.2 and 3.3 describe the two main components of our model, respectively the Super Image technique and the ConvMixer.

3.1   Dataset

In Table 1 there are some datasets used for action recognition and violence detection tasks. Among those, we selected UCF101 to pre-train the model on Action Recognition task for its wide variety of actions and its small size (only 7 GB with respect to the 720 GB of Kinetics400).

UCF101 contains 13,320 realistic action videos collected from YouTube and divided into 101 action categories. It gives the largest diversity in terms of actions and it also has large variations in camera motion, object appearance and pose, object scale, viewpoint, cluttered background, illumination conditions, etc. For these reasons it is one of the most challenging dataset available [38].

For the Violence Detection task instead, we used the Real Life Violence Situations Dataset. In this case the selected dataset is the biggest among the proposed ones because we want to train and test the model in as many conditions and situations as possible. It contains 1000 violence and 1000 non-violence videos collected from YouTube. Violence videos contain many real street fights situations in several environments and conditions while non violence videos represent many different human actions like walking, dancing, sports, etc.

Both the datasets are splitted into training (about 4/5) and evaluation (about 1/5). The selected datasets are the best ones because they contain good quality videos, represent human actions and behaviors, have differences in the backgrounds, in motions and poses while the majority of the other available datasets have drawbacks as small scale, reduced diversity, and low image resolution. Moreover, other datasets with high image quality contain videos taken from movies, which are not close enough to real-world scenes [9].

Table 1. Comparison between possible dataset

Task	Dataset	Videos
Action Recognition	Kinetics400/600/700	650,000 video clips that cover 400/600/700 human action classes
Action Recognition	UCF101	13,320 videos from 101 action categories
Action Recognition	HMDB51	6,766 video clips from 51 action categories
Violence Detection	SCVD	248 non violent and 112 violent videos from CCTV cameras
Violence Detection	RWF-2000	2,000 videos captured by surveillance cameras in real-world scenes
Violence Detection	Real Life Violence Situations	1000 Violence and 1000 non-violence videos collected from YouTube
Violence Detection	AirtLab	350 video clips labelled as "non-violent" and "violent"

3.2 Super Image Technique

The approach used to deal with videos is named Super Image. It is a technique that consists in extracting and resizing frames from videos and combining them into a super image that encodes both spatial and temporal dimensions [4]. In this way the number of images given to the model is less than the real number of frames.

For each video in the dataset, we divided them into frames, resized to 224×224 dimension and arranged them in such a way that the super images are formed by 9 frames. The super images have dimension 3×3 frames and are only composed by frames of the same video. Frames are arranged in such an order that the temporal information is not lost, in particular the first frame of the temporal sequence is at top left of the super image while the last frame is at the bottom right (see Fig. 2).

Fig. 2. Super Image structure.

For training the model, we decided not to use all the possible frames for each video but we selected only few frames per video in order to avoid repetitions of same scenes. In fact, giving all the frames as input to the model resulted in high over-fitting.

3.3 ConvMixer Model

For many years, Convolutional Neural Networks (CNNs) were the primary models used in computer vision. However, with the advent of Vision Transformers (ViTs), this has changed. Unlike CNNs which process pixel arrays, ViT splits the images into visual embeddings. These embeddings are then split into fixed-size tokens and processed by a transformer encoder, which includes positional embedding as an input. Essentially, it represents an image as a series of word embeddings (patches).

The ConvMixer is a straightforward model that combines ideas from the Vision Transformer (ViT) and MLP-Mixer. It takes image patches as input, separates the mixing of spatial and channel dimensions, and maintains consistent resolution and size throughout the network. However, it uses only standard convolutions for the mixing steps and batch normalization instead of layer normalization. Despite its simplicity, in some circumstances the ConvMixer showed better performances than ViT, MLP-Mixer, and also classical vision models such as the ResNet [42].

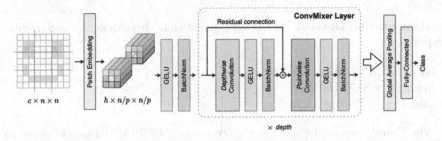

Fig. 3. ConvMixer architecture.

Architecture. The ConvMixer model (see Fig. 3) is composed of a patch embedding layer and multiple repetitions of a basic fully-convolutional block. The patch embedding layer is a convolutional layer with kernel size and stride that match the patch size, and c input channels and h output channels. This is followed by an activation function and a post activation batch normalization.

$$z_0 = BN(\sigma(Conv_{c \to h}(X, stride = p, kernelsize = p)))$$

The main ConvMixer layer is repeated h times and it consists of a residual block containing a depthwise and pointwise convolution. In depthwise convolution each channel is convolved independently with its own set of filters, while the pointwise convolution is used to aggregate the information from different channels by convolving the input with 1×1 kernels. After the h blocks, the prominent features are selected using max-poling and a final linear layer give in output the prediction vector.

$$z_l' = BN(\sigma(ConvDepthWise(z_{l-1}))) + z_{l-1}$$

$$z_{l+1}' = BN(\sigma ConvPointWise(z_l'))$$

More details of the model architecture can be found in Table 2

Table 2. ConvMixer architecture details

ConvMixer		
Parameter	Value	Description
embedding dimension	1024	Number of channels in the embedding layers
depth	20	Number of ConvMixer layers
patch size	2	the number of patches in which the image is subdivided, both kernel size and stride of the convolution in the embedding layer are equal to the patch size
kernel size	9	the kernel size of the depthwise convolutional kernel in the ConvMixer layers (the stride is 1)

Implementation Details. All the experiments have been done in the following environment:

- GPU = 1 AMD firepro s9300x2;
- Memory = 8 GB HBM ;
- Libraries = Pytorch Lightning.

The ConvMixer model has been pretrained on UCF101 dataset in order to allow the network to recognize human motions, movements and actions. For this task we used AdamW optimizer with a learning rate of 1e−5 without scheduling, while the number of epochs was 20.

Then the model was trained and tested on Real Life Violence Dataset to classify each video as violent or non violent. In this case we used the same parameters of the previous task but, at the end of the experiment, we noticed that the model stopped learning after some epochs. So, in order to introduce more stability, we augmented by a factor 4 the batch size and decreased the learning rate by 10 times and we also introduced a variable learning rate. With this configuration we were able to achieve extremely good results (0.95 of accuracy).

We also tested different Super Images configurations. In many experiments we adopted squared super images but we found that there is not a significant different in performance between the use of a 3×3 and 4×4 super image. We decided to use a 3×3 super images because it achieved the highest accuracy but also because we wanted to avoid repetitions of very similar frames.

4   Results

This section illustrates the results that the proposed model obtained in the action recognition task (Sect. 4.1) and in the violence detection task (Sect. 4.2), in which our model scores second in the Real Life Violence Situations Benchmark.

4.1 Results on Action Recognition

In the Action Recognition task we reached a top accuracy of 0.91 after 20 epochs of training.

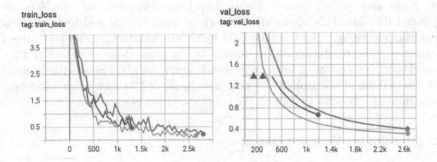

Fig. 4. Training and validation loss for the Action Recognition task with three configurations: 1) (orange curve) frames resolution 224×224, super images dimension 3×3, batch size of 96; 2) (grey curve) frames resolution 224×224, super images dimension 3×3, batch size of 144; 3) (green curve) frames resolution 224×224, super images dimension 4×4, batch size of 144. (Color figure online)

Figure 4 shows the results under the following three configurations. From the figure it emerges that the third configuration (gray curve) is better than the others, because the train loss is more stable and the valuation loss is smaller. It also emerges that super images dimension 3×3 lead to better performances than the 4×4 ones.

Our ConvMixer model ranks at the top of the leader board of the UCF101 Benchmark:

- C3D [41] reached an accuracy of 0.823;
- Two-Stream + LSTM [27] reached an accuracy of 0.886;
- ActionFlowNet [26] reached an accuracy of 0.839;
- HalluciNet (ResNet-50) [28] reached an accuracy of 0.7983.

Our model performances are also quite near to the ones of top models of the State-of-the-Art:

- SMART [15] reached an accuracy of 0.9864;
- Two-Stream I3D [7] reached an accuracy of 0.978;
- BubbleNET [18] reached an accuracy of 0.9762;
- I3D-LSTM [45] reached an accuracy of 0.951.

To make some comparisons, in SMART [15] the approach consists in using two streams. The first stream is used to classify singularly each frame of a video in relation of its utility while the second looks at the entire video and uses an attention and relation network. The resolution of the frames is the same as the one that we used in our work but they trained over 200 epochs, with a batch size of 128, a mini-batch stochastic gradient descent with a momentum of 0.9 and a learning rate of 0.0001 reduced by 10 times after every 25 epochs.

In Two-Stream I3D [7] the authors introduced a new type of network called Two-Stream Inflated 3D ConvNet(I3D) that is based on 2D ConvNet inflation: filters and pooling kernels of very deep image classification ConvNets are expanded into 3D. This allows the network to learn spatial and temporal features from videos by using the successful ImageNet architecture and pre-trained parameters. The resolution of the frames is the same that we used but they trained over 5000 epochs, using a larger batch size, a standard SGD with momentum set to 0.9 and a learning rate that is reduced of 10 times when validation loss saturated. We refer to Table 3 for a more detailed comparison.

4.2 Results on Violence Detection

Also in the second task on Violence Detection, we evaluated different configurations of learning rate and batch size, epochs and we obtained a top accuracy

Table 3. Comparisons between models on Action Recognition.

Model	#Parameters	#Iterations	Accuracy
ConvMixer	23.5M	2.6K	0.910
C3D	34.8M	1.9M	0.823
ActionFlowNet	-	40K	0.839
Two-Stream I3D	25M	5K	0.978

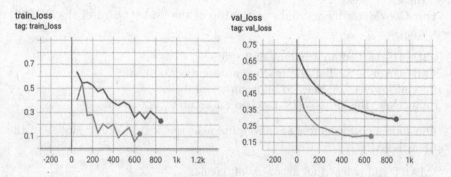

Fig. 5. Training and validation loss over Violence Detection task. The BLUE curve represents the loss using learning rate equal to 1e−5 and batch size 144 while the RED curve with learning rate equal to 1e−6 and batch size 384. (Color figure online)

Table 4. Metrics for the Violence Detection Task.

Accuracy	precision	recall	f1-score
0.95	0.96	0.93	0.95

of 0.95 after 20 epochs of training (see Fig. 5), using a multi-step learning rate scheduler (see Table 4 for the other metrics).

This result placed our model in the second position of the Real Life Violence Situations Benchmark:

– DeVTr [1] reached an accuracy of 0.9625;
– Temporal Fusion CNN+LSTM [22] reached an accuracy of 0.91;
– CNN+LSTM [36] reached an accuracy of 0.888.

To make some comparisons, in DeVTr [1] authors introduced a method for learning spatio-temporal features in videos using a data-efficient video transformer(DeVTr) and used a pre-trained 2D-Convolutional Neural Network (2D-CNN) as an embedding layer for the input data. The resolution of the frames is 200×200, they used an Adam optimizer with learning rate equal to 0.0001 and batch size of 16.

In CNN+LSTM [36] the authors used a pretrained VGG-16 on ImageNet as spatial feature extractor followed by Long Short-Term Memory (LSTM) as temporal feature extractor and sequence of fully connected layers for classification purpose. The resolution of the frames is the same as the one we used in our work but the learning rate is 0.02 and the number of epochs are 400.

5 Conclusions

In this paper we introduced a novel approach to detect violence from videos. We obtained state-of-the-art results in the Violence Detection task by pretraining a ConvMixer model on Action recognition and then training on the task of Violence detection. The proposed model showed also an impressive ability in classifying human actions and movements. The lightweight size of the proposed model combined with its ability to process a video using just 9 frames make it a good candidate for fast and automated violence detection systems.

References

1. Abdali, A.R.: Data efficient video transformer for violence detection. In: 2021 IEEE International Conference on Communication, Networks and Satellite (COMNET-SAT), pp. 195–199 (2021). https://doi.org/10.1109/COMNETSAT53002.2021.9530829
2. Aggarwal, J., Cai, Q.: Human motion analysis: a review. In: Proceedings IEEE Nonrigid and Articulated Motion Workshop, pp. 90–102 (1997). https://doi.org/10.1109/NAMW.1997.609859
3. Aggarwal, J., Xia, L.: Human activity recognition from 3D data: a review. Pattern Recogn. Lett. **48**, 70–80 (2014). https://doi.org/10.1016/j.patrec.2014.04.011
4. Aremu, T., Zhiyuan, L., Alameeri, R.: Any object is a potential weapon! weaponized violence detection using salient image (2022). https://doi.org/10.48550/ARXIV.2207.12850. arXiv:2207.12850
5. Calandre, J., Peteri, R., Mascarilla, L.: Optical flow singularities for sports video annotation: detection of strokes in Table Tennis, October 2019

6. Carion, N., Massa, F., Synnaeve, G., Usunier, N., Kirillov, A., Zagoruyko, S.: End-to-end object detection with transformers (2020). https://doi.org/10.48550/ARXIV.2005.12872. arXiv:2005.12872

7. Carreira, J., Zisserman, A.: Quo Vadis, action recognition? A new model and the kinetics dataset (2017). https://doi.org/10.48550/ARXIV.1705.07750. arXiv:1705.07750

8. Chen, L.H., Su, C.W., Hsu, H.W.: Violent scene detection in movies. Int. J. Pattern Recogn. Artif. Intell. **25**(08), 11611172 (2011). https://doi.org/10.1142/S0218001411009056

9. Cheng, M., Cai, K., Li, M.: RWF-2000: an open large scale video database for violence detection, pp. 4183–4190, January 2021. https://doi.org/10.1109/ICPR48806.2021.9412502

10. De Magistris, G., et al.: Vision-based holistic scene understanding for context-aware human-robot interaction. In: Bandini, S., Gasparini, F., Mascardi, V., Palmonari, M., Vizzari, G. (eds.) 20th International Conference of the Italian Association for Artificial Intelligence. Advances in Artificial Intelligence, AIxIA 2021, Virtual Event, Revised Selected Papers, 1–3 December 2021, vol. 13196, pp. 310–325. Springer, Cham (2022). https://doi.org/10.1007/978-3-031-08421-8_21

11. Dosovitskiy, A., et al.: An image is worth 16 × 16 words: transformers for image recognition at scale (2020). https://doi.org/10.48550/ARXIV.2010.11929. arXiv:2010.11929

12. Duan, H., Zhao, Y., Chen, K., Lin, D., Dai, B.: Revisiting skeleton-based action recognition (2021). https://doi.org/10.48550/ARXIV.2104.13586. arXiv:2104.13586

13. Efros, A.A., Berg, A.C., Mori, G., Malik, J.: Recognizing action at a distance. In: IEEE International Conference on Computer Vision, Nice, France, pp. 726–733 (2003)

14. Gao, Y., Liu, H., Sun, X., Wang, C., Liu, Y.: Violence detection using oriented violent flows. Image Vis. Comput. **4849**, 37–41 (2016). https://doi.org/10.1016/j.imavis.2016.01.006

15. Gowda, S.N., Rohrbach, M., Sevilla-Lara, L.: Smart frame selection for action recognition (2020). https://doi.org/10.48550/ARXIV.2012.10671. arXiv:2012.10671

16. Gupta, A., Karel, A., Sakthi Balan, M.: Discovering cricket stroke classes in trimmed telecast videos. In: Nain, N., Vipparthi, S.K., Raman, B. (eds.) CVIP 2019. CCIS, vol. 1148, pp. 509–520. Springer, Singapore (2020). https://doi.org/10.1007/978-981-15-4018-9_45

17. Hassner, T., Itcher, Y., Kliper-Gross, O.: Violent flows: Real-time detection of violent crowd behavior, pp. 1–6, June 2012. https://doi.org/10.1109/CVPRW.2012.6239348

18. Igor L. O., B., Victor H. C., M., Schwartz, W.R.: BubbleNET: a disperse recurrent structure to recognize activities. In: 2020 IEEE International Conference on Image Processing (ICIP), pp. 2216–2220 (2020). https://doi.org/10.1109/ICIP40778.2020.9190769

19. Ji, S., Xu, W., Yang, M., Yu, K.: 3D convolutional neural networks for human action recognition. IEEE Trans. Pattern Anal. Mach. Intell. **35**, 495–502 (2010). https://doi.org/10.1109/TPAMI.2012.59

20. Ke, S.R., Thuc, H.L.U., Lee, Y.J., Hwang, J.N., Yoo, J.H., Choi, K.H.: A review on video-based human activity recognition. Computers **2**(2), 88–131 (2013). https://doi.org/10.3390/computers2020088. www.mdpi.com/2073-431X/2/2/88

21. Li, C., Hou, Y., Wang, P., Li, W.: Joint distance maps based action recognition with convolutional neural networks. IEEE Sig. Process. Lett. **24**(5), 624–628 (2017). https://doi.org/10.1109/LSP.2017.2678539

22. Lima, J., Figueiredo, C.: Temporal fusion approach for video classification with convolutional and LSTM neural networks applied to violence detection. Inteligencia Artif. **24**, 40–50 (2021). https://doi.org/10.4114/intartif.vol24iss67pp40-50

23. Lo Presti, L., La Cascia, M.: 3D skeleton-based human action classification: a survey. Pattern Recogn. **53**, 130–147 (2016) https://doi.org/10.1016/j.patcog.2015.11.019. www.sciencedirect.com/science/article/pii/S0031320315004392

24. Much, A., Pottel, S., Sibold, K.: Preconjugate variables in quantum field theory and their applications. Phys. Rev. D **94**(6), 065007 (2016). https://doi.org/10.1103/physrevd.94.065007

25. Mumtaz, A., Sargana, A.B., Habib, Z.: Violence detection in surveillance videos with deep network using transfer learning, pp. 558–563, December 2018. https://doi.org/10.1109/EECS.2018.00109

26. Ng, J.Y.H., Choi, J., Neumann, J., Davis, L.S.: ActionFlowNet: learning motion representation for action recognition (2016). https://doi.org/10.48550/ARXIV.1612.03052. arXiv:1612.03052

27. Ng, J.Y.H., Hausknecht, M., Vijayanarasimhan, S., Vinyals, O., Monga, R., Toderici, G.: Beyond short snippets: Deep networks for video classification (2015). https://doi.org/10.48550/ARXIV.1503.08909. arXiv:1503.08909

28. Parmar, P., Morris, B.: HalluciNet-ing spatiotemporal representations using a 2D-CNN (2019). https://doi.org/10.48550/ARXIV.1912.04430. arXiv:1912.04430

29. Peixoto, B.M., Lavi, B., Martin, J.P.P., Avila, S., Dias, Z., Rocha, A.: Toward subjective violence detection in videos. In: 2019 IEEE International Conference on Acoustics, Speech and Signal Processing, ICASSP 2019, pp. 8276–8280 (2019)

30. Pham, H.H., Khoudour, L., Crouzil, A., Zegers, P., Velastin, S.A.: Video-based human action recognition using deep learning: a review (2022). https://doi.org/10.48550/ARXIV.2208.03775. arXiv:2208.03775

31. Popoola, O.P., Wang, K.: Video-based abnormal human behavior recognition - a review. IEEE Trans. Syst. Man Cybern. Part C (Appl. Rev.) **42**(6), 865–878 (2012). https://doi.org/10.1109/TSMCC.2011.2178594

32. Rahmad, N., As'ari, M.A.: The new convolutional neural network (CNN) local feature extractor for automated badminton action recognition on vision based data. J. Phys: Conf. Ser. **1529**, 022021 (2020). https://doi.org/10.1088/1742-6596/1529/2/022021

33. Ramzan, M., et al.: A review on state-of-the-art violence detection techniques. IEEE Access **7**, 107560–107575 (2019)

34. Shabani, A.H., Clausi, D.A., Zelek, J.S.: Improved spatio-temporal salient feature detection for action recognition. In: British Machine Vision Conference, August 2011, University of Dundee, Dundee, UK (2011)

35. Sharma, M., Baghel, R.: Video surveillance for violence detection using deep learning (2020)

36. Soliman, M.M., Kamal, M.H., El-Massih Nashed, M.A., Mostafa, Y.M., Chawky, B.S., Khattab, D.: Violence recognition from videos using deep learning techniques, pp. 80–85, December 2019. https://doi.org/10.1109/ICICIS46948.2019.9014714

37. Soliman, M.M., Kamal, M.H., Nashed, M.A.E.M., Mostafa, Y.M., Chawky, B.S., Khattab, D.R.: Violence recognition from videos using deep learning techniques. In: 2019 Ninth International Conference on Intelligent Computing and Information Systems (ICICIS), pp. 80–85 (2019)

38. Soomro, K., Zamir, A.R., Shah, M.: UCF101: a dataset of 101 human actions classes from videos in the wild (2012). https://doi.org/10.48550/ARXIV.1212.0402. arXiv:1212.0402
39. Sumon, S.A., Goni, R., Hashem, N.B., Shahria, T., Rahman, R.M.: Violence detection by pretrained modules with different deep learning approaches. Vietnam J. Comput. Sci. **7**(01), 19–40 (2020)
40. Szegedy, C., et al.: Going deeper with convolutions (2014)
41. Tran, D., Bourdev, L., Fergus, R., Torresani, L., Paluri, M.: Learning spatiotemporal features with 3D convolutional networks (2014). https://doi.org/10.48550/ARXIV.1412.0767. arXiv:1412.0767
42. Trockman, A., Kolter, J.Z.: Patches are all you need? (2022). https://doi.org/10.48550/ARXIV.2201.09792. arXiv:2201.09792
43. Ullah, F.U.M., Ullah, A., Muhammad, K., Haq, I., Baik, S.: Violence detection using spatiotemporal features with 3D convolutional neural network. Sensors **19**, 2472 (2019). https://doi.org/10.3390/s19112472
44. Wang, P., Li, W., Gao, Z., Zhang, J., Tang, C., Ogunbona, P.: Deep convolutional neural networks for action recognition using depth map sequences (2015). https://doi.org/10.48550/ARXIV.1501.04686. arXiv:1501.04686
45. Wang, X., Miao, Z., Zhang, R., Hao, S.: I3D-LSTM: a new model for human action recognition. IOP Conf. Ser. Mater. Sci. Eng. **569**(3), 032035 (2019). https://doi.org/10.1088/1757-899X/569/3/032035
46. Yang, W., Lyons, T., Ni, H., Schmid, C., Jin, L.: Developing the path signature methodology and its application to landmark-based human action recognition (2017). https://doi.org/10.48550/ARXIV.1707.03993. arXiv:1707.03993
47. Zhang, T., Yang, Z., Jia, W., Yang, B., Yang, J., He, X.: A new method for violence detection in surveillance scenes. Multimedia Tools Appl. **75**(12), 7327–7349 (2016). https://doi.org/10.1007/s11042-015-2648-8

Speech Emotion Recognition: Recent Advances and Current Trends

Soundes Belkacem[✉][iD]

LAMIE Laboratory, Department of Computer Science, University of Batna 2, Batna, Algeria
s.belkacem@univ-batna2.dz

Abstract. Speech emotion recognition has become an important endeavor in Human-computer-Interaction. Emotion recognition and understanding by computer are used for medical diagnosis, decision-making systems, and public security. In this paper, we investigate and analyze current technologies and research progress in speech emotion recognition. Methodology and experiment results related to phases of the SER system. Five aspects are described including emotional speech datasets, data enhancement and augmentation, feature extraction, emotion classification and recognition. Finally, we discuss research progress trends and give further research directions and scopes.

Keywords: Human-Computer Interaction · Speech Emotion Recognition · Speech Preprocessing · Deep Neural Network

1 Introduction

Human-computer interaction refers to adjusting the computer's responses to more intelligent and human-like perceptions, thinking patterns, and behavior [1]. Robots' responses have to be accurate and emotional [2]. Human communication depends on its emotional state, naturally and commonly expressed using speech [3]. Speech has considerable advantages (a) direct, convenient, and efficient [1] (b) contains paralinguistic and linguistic information, and (c) being less private than other data. Speech emotion recognition (SER) systems recognize human emotion based on features extracted from the speech signal. Recognition results can be used in robotics, medical fields, mental diseases diagnosis, distance learning, online learning, and working environment [4,5].

SER system involves two aspects: processing steps merged in a model and a dataset used to train the model. Processing steps include: preprocessing, feature extraction, classification, and recognition. SER is a challenging task due to (a) difficulties to define emotion precisely, (b) leak of available data, (c) selection of silent features subset, and (d) accurate classification.

Emotion recognition based on speech characteristics has been an active research area for the past 20 years. However, SER become crucial and requires more studying and investigation with the growing interest in Human-machine interaction and robotic affective communication.

In this paper, we present and investigate recent research in the field of SER within the last few years and state current technologies used in each step of the SER systems. Emotion models and recently used datasets are listed with referred works. In recent works the preprocessing step receive increased interest; techniques for data augmentation and noise removal are described. Since SER system performances are strongly related to recognition accuracy to feature extraction effectiveness. Recently, the selection of accurate and relevant features using efficient methods has received special attention. Several techniques are given and analyzed. The use of machine learning and deep learning algorithms with and without fusion in the classification is detailed in the description of the performance. Studying recent trends may reveal the future of SER by outlining limitations and gaps in existing solutions, hence, considering the ability for performance enhancement.

The rest of the paper is organized as follows. Section 2 discusses emotion models and the most used database for speech emotion recognition. In Sect. 3, an overview of the SER systems is presented including preprocessing techniques, feature extraction methods, and classification algorithms. Recent works on SER are shown and discussed in Sect. 4. The Paper is concluded with future research directions in Sect. 5.

2   Emotional Speech Datasets

The used dataset is a crucial aspect of SER systems. Collected data has to capture salient features with appropriate emotion. Speech emotion databases are either acted, spontaneous if recorded during real and natural conditions, or elicited if speech emotions are artificially evoked.

Emotion can be expressed in many modalities, however, automatic recognition has to be described with a precise and appropriate model is required. Emotions description models are grouped into two categories: (a) Categorical emotion and (b) dimensional emotion. Categorical emotion models also referred to as discrete models describe emotion manifestation independently from other emotions: anger, fear, disgust, sadness, fear, and surprise. Dimensional emotion models describe emotion in valence-arousal-dominance emotional space (Table 1).

Amharic Speech Emotion Dataset (ASED) [6] is a recent database for the Amharic language with four dialects: Gonder, Wollo, Gojjam, and Shewa, while, considering five emotions: sad, angry, neutral, fearful, and happy. ASED contains 2,474 recorded sound samples of 2 to 4 s duration of 65 participants' native speakers of Amharic (volunteers). The database experimented with VGGb, LSTM, RESNet50, and AlexNet. VGGb gives the best accuracy of 90.73%.

3   Speech Emotion Recognition Systems

3.1   Preprocessing

Preprocessing is an important step that affects feature extraction and recognition performances. It involves data augmentation, noise removal, and speech processing techniques: sampling, normalization, and windowing (Fig. 1).

Table 1. Currently used SER Datasets

Dataset	Language	Type	Size	Emotions	References
EMO-DB [8]	German	acted	10 speakers, 535 utterances	fear, disgust, neutral, sadness, anger, happiness,	[2,3,8–14]
SAVEE [15]	English	acted	04 speakers, 480 utterances	Surprise, fear, disgust, neutral, sadness, anger, happiness	[2,10]
ASED [7]	Amharic	acted	65 speakers, 2,474 s utterances	sad, angry, neutral, fearful, happy	[7]
JTES [16]	Japanese	acted	100 speakers, 20,000 utterances	joy, sadness, anger, neutral	[5]
CASIA [22]	Chinese	acted	4 actors, 9,600 utterances	Angry, scared, happy, neutral, sad, surprised	[1]
RAVDESS [18]	English	acted	24 actors, 1440 utterances	Disgust, calm, anger, neutral, happiness, sadness, fear, surprise	[10,13,14,19]
IEMOCAP [20]	English	Natural	10 actors, total duration 12 h	Neutral, sadness, frustrate, excitement, happiness, anger	[3,4,6,10,11,20]

In the SER system, classification performance is strongly related to the input data and extracted features. As discussed in the previous section available datasets are limited and generally of limited size. Data augmentation techniques have been used to enrich the database with more training samples to achieve better recognition performances. In [5] Generative Adversarial Networks (GAN) and Vision Transformers (ViT) are combined. GAN's generator network is trained with English IEMOCAP and JTES to generate synthetic samples of emotional speech. The discriminator network decides if generated samples are accepted as real or not based on given real samples. 2000 CycleGAN-transformed samples have been used to improve emotion recognition accuracy from 74.5% to 77.0% over RAVDESS database and from 60.6% to 63.32% over JTES database. Suppose Databases have imbalanced data the synthetic minority oversampling technique (SMOTE) can be used [2]. A novel data augmentation technique has been proposed in [9] Additional samples are created by adding noise fractions to the original samples. The noise ratio is obtained using 0,005 × max value in the speech signal to ensure not to corrupt the utterance content.

Environmental noise removal from speech signals is part of the speech enhancement process. In [8] a noise mask is generated using a trained DBN network. First, the fractional Delta-Amplitude Modulation Spectrogram (FD-AMS) features are extracted and used to train the DBN network. Then, to remove noise the delta feature vector and the fractional calculus are applied to the speech signal. Speech signals are referred to as I(u), and expressed as follows:

$$V = \{I(u); 1 \leq u \leq U\} \tag{1}$$

where: U is the total data samples within the input signal, and I(u) referred to each emotion from the total emotions contents M. Enhanced signal is $E(u)$.

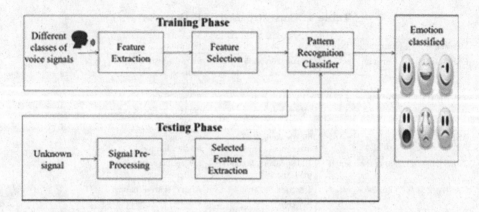

Fig. 1. Framework of SER system [4].

3.2   Feature Extraction

Emotional feature extraction affects speech emotion recognition accuracy [1]. Speech signals integrate two types of features paralinguistic acoustic features and linguistic features. Acoustic features include low-level descriptors, High-level statistical functions, and a combination of both [21]. Commonly used acoustic features are Mel-frequency cepstral coefficients (MFCC) and energy.

Mel-frequency Cepstral coefficients (MFCC) are the most commonly used feature for SER [11,13]. Zhiyou et al. [1] use thirty-nine-dimensional MFCC parameters for emotion recognition over CASIA database. MFCC features have been used to train machine learning classifiers: K-Nearest Neighbor Classifiers [4], and LSTM network classifier for spontaneous speech emotion recognition in a three-dimensional model (arousal, dominance, and valence) [20]. Wavelet packet coefficients are used for multi-resolution time-frequency feature extraction [12]. Cross-correlation techniques are used for feature selection from first and second-order differences of WPC.

Phase-based spectral features (PBCC) and statistical features are combined with the classifier gradient boosting machine-based for emotion recognition average recognition rate of 97% on the BanglaSER and SUBESCO datasets [13]. AMSNet [3] uses a connection attention mechanism to complementary fuse multi-scale features with frame-level features and utterance-level. PBCC features-based algorithm is proposed in [13].

Efficient emotion recognition is strongly related to feature description and extraction efficiency. Commonly used speech features are Mel frequency spectral coefficient (MFCC) features, pitch, formant, shorter energy, and filter Bank. However, varieties in emotion definition and expression, culture, and language make the selection of the most relevant features a hard task. Features fusion may be a solution but require information integration of extracted features.

Table 2. A summary of the studied SER systems

Paper	Used Dataset	Method	Classifier	classified Emotions	Experimental results
[1]	CASIA	39-dimensional MFCC features are used to train a simple structure broad learning network	Broad Learning network	disgust, Neutral, anger, happy, sadness, boredom, fear,	- Accuracy: 100% - Testing time: 0.194 s
[2]	EMO-DB SAVEE	A multi-lingual SER is tested and evaluated over cross corpus using a majority voting technique based on an ensemble learning of utilizes J48, SMO, and RF classifier	Ensemble learning	binary valence; positive or negative emotions	Cross-corpus accuracy is increased up to 15% when training in Urdu and testing on other languages
[3]	EMO-DB IEMOCAP	Temporal and spatial frame-level and utterance-level features are fused based on a connection attention mechanism	Attention-based long short-term memory (LSTM)	Neutral, sad, angry, happy	- IEMOCAP: WA = 69.22% UA = 70.51% - EMODB WA = 88.34%, UA = 88.56%
[4]	IEMOCAP	MFCC, MFCC Δ, and MFCC ΔΔ features	Fine KNN and weighed KNN classifiers	Boredom, sadness, fear, anger, neutral, happiness, disgust	- FKNN accuracy = 62.8 % - WKNN accuracy = 88.9%
[7]	ASED	MFCC features are used to train a four-layer version of VGG	A variant of the VGG model	Neutral, sad, fearful, angry, happy	Accuracy = 90.73%
[9]	EMO-DB	Multiple Kernel Mel Frequency Cepstral Coefficients (MKMFCC) and the spectral flux parameters	Taylor series-based Deep Belief Network	Calm, fear, happy, anger, sad	Accuracy = 97%
[10]	EMO-DB IEMOCAP RAVDESS SAVEE	The log Mel-spectrograms feature is extracted from 3 s speech utterance. Hyper-parameters optimization using stochastic fractal search (SFS)-guided whale optimization algorithm (WOA)	CNN-LSTM	Emotions in dataset	EMO-DB Acc = 98.13% IEMOCAP Acc = 99.76%, RAVDESS Acc = 99.47% SAVEE Acc = 99.50
[5]	IEMOCAP JTES	Emotional data augmented using one-direction cycle Generative Adversarial	Networks Vision Transformer (ViT)	Four classes classification and Eight classes classification	- IEMOCAP: *4 classes = 77.0% *8 classes = 63.5% - JTES *4 classes = 60.6%
[11]	EMO-DB IEMOCAP	Multi-type features representation model of speech emotion. Through merging different speech features are: acoustic, temporal, and image information.	CNN-DNN-LSTM	Sad, angry, neutral, happy	- EMO-DB Acc = 91.25% - IEMOCAP Acc = 72.02%
[12]	EMO-DB	Cepstral Coefficient (MFCC)	CNN-LSTM	Fear, anger, sadness, disgust, neutral, happiness, boredom	Accuracy = 85%
[13]	EMO-DB RAVDESS	The speech emotion feature vector is constructed using 2n Wavelet Packet Coefficients (WPC)	KNN, RBF-SVM	fear, disgust, neutral, sadness, anger, happiness.	EMO-DB KNN Acc = 89.71% RAVDESS *KNN Acc = 60.93%
[19]	RAVDESS SUBESCO	Speech and song features of the Bangla language and language independents are extracted transfer learning for cross-lingual classification is evaluated	Deep CNN-BLSTM	Emotions of data-set	- RAVDESS WAcc = 82.7% - SUBESCO Wacc = 86.9%
[6]	IEMOCAP	Increase dimension in the 3-dimensional space emotional space to nine levels. The relation between dimensional emotions and categorical emotions is investigated	LSTM-SVM	Dimensional emotions: dominance, valence, arousal.	- Accuracy for 4 categorical emotions = 71.92 % - Accuracy for 7 categorical emotions = 55.64%
[14]	Emo-DB RAVDESS	Long-term dependencies of SE extracted using Mel Frequency Cepstral Coefficient (MFCC)	Hybrid LSTM-Transformer Encoder	Neutral, happiness, sadness, calm, anger, fear, disgust, surprise.	- Emo-DB Acc = 85.55%, - RAVDESS Acc = 75.62

3.3 Classification and Recognition

Classification in SER systems uses machine learning and deep learning methods for accurate speech-emotion recognition [12]. In [4] the K-Nearest Neighbor Classifiers are used for SER over the Berlin database. MFCC features are extracted and used with five KNN classifiers: Fine KNN, Medium KNN, Cosine KNN, Cubic KNN, and Weighted KNN. Classifiers' performances are up to 85% training rates and 50% testing rates, where, the highest accuracy is given by fine KNN and weighed KNN classifiers. KNN is combined with multi-class Support Vector Machine(SVM) classifiers in [12] for emotion classification using two datasets RAVDESS and EMODB (Table 2).

A combination of two or more classifiers may increase accuracy. Hence, recent research introduces networks, and fusion-based models, with performance improvements. Sadia et al. [18] uses three Classifiers: a deep convolution neural network (DCNN) and a bidirectional LTSM and a time-distributed flatten (TDF) layer. In comparison to other CNN-based models, experiments show better accuracy 82.7% over RAVDESS datasets. HD-MFM framework [10] three-dimensional fusion of blocks: image-dimension features extracted by spectrogram-CNN, speech statistic-dimension features by HSF-DNN Block, and speech time-dimension features by MFCC-LSTM. Fusion is based on separate and merge strategies. Performance results of HD-MFM are 72.02% over IEMO-CAP, and 91.25% in EMODB. SER system based on CNN-LSTM and MFCC is proposed in [11] classification accuracy is 85% over EMODB database. LSTM is combined with Transformer Encoder to extract the feature's temporal dependencies from frequency distributions in speech [13]. The hybrid classifier is trained using the MFCC feature extracted from three datasets: language-independent, English, and German with a recognition accuracy of 72.49%, 75.62%, and 85.55% respectively (Fig. 2).

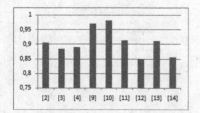

Fig. 2. Comparison of speech emotion recognition on Emo-DB Dataset

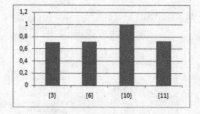

Fig. 3. Comparison of speech emotion recognition on IEMOCAP Dataset

Authors in [9] propose an optimized CNN-LSTM-based algorithm for SER. LSTM network creates four blocks based on local features and correlations in the log Mel-spectrogram. The whale optimization algorithm is used to optimize two hyperparameters based on stochastic fractal search. In experiments, model recognition accuracies are 99.47% using RAVDESS, 99.76%, over Emo-DB, 99.50% in SAVEE, and 98.13%, with IEMOCAP databases.

4   Comparative Study and Analysis

Human emotional expression is strongly related to the speaker's age and gender, used language, and culture. Then recent research focus on the use of datasets of a single language. In fact, 64% of the current SER systems study the English language using the IEMOCAP dataset while 63% focus on the German language using the Emo-DB dataset. Figure 3 compares the accuracy results of ML-based methods on the two commonly used datasets. From the comparison results, it can be observed that different classifiers provide different results for different datasets. The Hybrid LSTM models provide the highest accuracy compared to other classifiers and show the highest accuracy of CNN-LSTM up to 98.13% over the Emo-DB dataset.

To understand the performances of CNN-LSTM, Fig. 4 shows the comparison of accuracy results for individual emotion classification of CNN-LSTM-based SER systems applied on IEMOCAP and Emo-DB datasets. CNN-LSTM model achieves higher accuracy over IEMOCAP. This is mainly due to the fact that emotions are more intense and naturally expressed. The lower classification performance is provided over the neutral emotion on the Emo-DB dataset. In fact; acted emotions are less expressive and discriminate description ability.

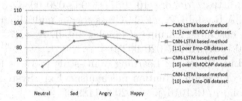

Fig. 4. Accuracy results for individual emotion classification using CNN-LSTM classifier on the Emo-DB and IEMOCAP datasets.

The studied SER systems present a variety of challenges for accurate emotion classification. Existing challenges for SER systems identified through the comparative analyses are summarized as follows: 1) Absence of precise emotion definitions and interpretation due to variety in emotion expression with different languages; 2) Accurate selection, extraction, and fusion of relevant features of speech, 3) Acted datasets can represent less accurate emotion representation. Hence, the classifier can perform better on a spontaneous dataset. 4) Dataset language can strongly affect the classification results. The same classifier may exhibit varying performance across different languages. Employing a cross-lingual approach is a possible solution to address this problem. 4) Machine learning-based models can be optimized by reducing the computational cost and decreasing model sensitivity through audio preprocessing for noise removal, 5) Archived performances can be improved with.

5 Conclusion and Future Works

Speech emotion recognition has been an active research area for the last decades and has received increasing interest in the past two years. This paper presents, analyzes, and compares recent solutions based on various machine learning and deep learning techniques for the SER. Hybrid deep-learning algorithms CNN-LSTM and DNN achieved the best performances. However, existing solutions performances are strongly related and conducted over acted datasets EMO-DB and IEMOCAP where speakers are native speakers of English or German languages.

Based on the studies SER systems. Future research directions for the recognition efficiency enhancement can be summarized as follow: 1) investigation in natural data creation. Creation has to consider human diversity and has to cover other languages. 2) Features extraction and fusions can be done according to data characteristics with dimension reduction using parameter optimization techniques. The recognition rate can be increased with the integration of two or more classifiers. The recognition rate can be increased with the integration of two or more classifiers and using deeper deep learning models.

References

1. Yang, Z., Huang, Y.: Algorithm for speech emotion recognition classification based on Mel-frequency Cepstral coefficients and broad learning system. Evol. Intell. **15**, 2485–2494 (2022). https://doi.org/10.1007/s12065-020-00532-3
2. Zehra, W., Javed, A.R., Jalil, Z., et al.: Cross corpus multi-lingual speech emotion recognition using ensemble learning. Complex Intell. Syst. **7**, 1845–1854 (2021). https://doi.org/10.1007/s40747-020-00250-4
3. Chen, Z., Li, J., Liu, H., et al.: Learning multi-scale features for speech emotion recognition with connection attention mechanism. Exp. Syst. Appl. **214**, 118943 (2023). https://doi.org/10.1016/j.eswa.2022.118943
4. Venkata Subbarao, M., Terlapu, S.K., Geethika, N., Harika, K.D.: Speech emotion recognition using K-nearest neighbor classifiers. In: Shetty D., P., Shetty, S. (eds.) Recent Advances in Artificial Intelligence and Data Engineering. AISC, vol. 1386, pp. 123–131. Springer, Singapore (2022). https://doi.org/10.1007/978-981-16-3342-3_10
5. Heracleous, P., Fukayama, S., Ogata, J., Mohammad, Y.: Applying generative adversarial networks and vision transformers in speech emotion recognition. In: Kurosu, M., et al. (eds.) HCI International 2022 - Late Breaking Papers. Multimodality in Advanced Interaction Environments, HCII 2022. LNCS, vol. 13519, pp. 67–75. Springer, Cham (2022). https://doi.org/10.1007/978-3-031-17618-0_6
6. Wang, H., Zhao, X., Zhao, Y.: Investigation of the effect of increased dimension levels in speech emotion recognition. IEEE Access **10**, 78123–78134 (2022). https://doi.org/10.1109/ACCESS.2022.3194039
7. Retta, E.A., Almekhlafi, E., Sutcliffe, R., et al.: A new Amharic speech emotion dataset and classification benchmark. ACM Trans. Asian Low Resour. Lang. Inf. Process. **22**, 1–22 (2022). https://doi.org/10.1145/3529759

8. Burkhardt, F., Paeschke, A., Rolfes, M., et al.: A database of German emotional speech. In: 9th European Conference on Speech Communication and Technology, pp. 1517–1520 (2005)

9. Valiyavalappil Haridas, A., Marimuthu, R., Sivakumar, V.G., Chakraborty, B.: Emotion recognition of speech signal using Taylor series and deep belief network based classification. Evol. Intell. **15**, 1145–1158 (2022). https://doi.org/10.1007/s12065-019-00333-3

10. Abdelhamid, A.A., El-Kenawy, E.S.M., Alotaibi, B., et al.: Robust speech emotion recognition using CNN+LSTM based on stochastic fractal search optimization algorithm. IEEE Access **10**, 49265–49284 (2022). https://doi.org/10.1109/ACCESS.2022.3172954

11. Xu, X., Li, D., Zhou, Y., Wang, Z.: Multi-type features separating fusion learning for speech emotion recognition. Appl. Soft Comput. **130**, 109648 (2022). https://doi.org/10.1016/j.asoc.2022.109648

12. Manohar, K., Logashanmugam, E.: Speech-based human emotion recognition using CNN and LSTM model approach. In: Bhateja, V., Satapathy, S.C., Travieso-Gonzalez, C.M., Adilakshmi, T. (eds.) Smart Intelligent Computing and Applications, Volume 1. Smart Innovation, Systems and Technologies, vol. 282, pp. 85–93. Springer, Singapore (2022). https://doi.org/10.1007/978-981-16-9669-5_8

13. Kawade, R., Bhalke, D.G.: Speech emotion recognition based on Wavelet Packet Coefficients. In: Kumar, A., Mozar, S. (eds.) ICCCE 2021. LNEE, vol. 828, pp. 823–828. Springer, Singapore (2022). https://doi.org/10.1007/978-981-16-7985-8_86

14. Andayani, F., Theng, L.B., Tsun, M.T., Chua, C.: Hybrid LSTM-transformer model for emotion recognition from speech audio files. IEEE Access **10**, 36018–36027 (2022). https://doi.org/10.1109/ACCESS.2022.3163856

15. Haq, S., Jackson, P.J., Edge, J.: Speaker-dependent audio-visual emotion recognition. In: AVSP, Vol. 2009, pp. 53–58 (2009). https://kahlan.eps.surrey.ac.uk/savee/

16. Takeishi, E., Nose, T., Chiba, Y., Ito, A.: Construction and analysis of phonetically and prosodically balanced emotional speech database. In: 2016 Conference of the Oriental Chapter of International Committee for Coordination and Standardization of Speech Databases and Assessment Techniques, O-COCOSDA 2016, pp. 16–21 (2017)

17. Tao, J., Liu, F., Zhang, M., Jia, H.: Design of speech corpus for Mandarin text to speech. In: The Blizzard Challenge 2008 Workshop (2008)

18. Livingstone, S.R., Russo, F.A.: The Ryerson audio-visual database of emotional speech and song (RAVDESS): a dynamic, multimodal set of facial and vocal expressions in North American English. PLoS ONE **13**, e0196391 (2018). https://doi.org/10.1371/journal.pone.0196391

19. Sultana, S., Iqbal, M.Z., Selim, M.R., et al.: Bangla speech emotion recognition and cross-lingual study using Deep CNN and BLSTM Networks. IEEE Access **10**, 564–578 (2022). https://doi.org/10.1109/ACCESS.2021.3136251

20. Busso, C., Bulut, M., Lee, C.C., et al.: IEMOCAP: interactive emotional dyadic motion capture database. Lang. Resour. Eval. **42**, 335–359 (2008). https://doi.org/10.1007/S10579-008-9076-6

21. Wani, T.M., Gunawan, T.S., Qadri, S.A.A., et al.: A comprehensive review of speech emotion recognition systems. IEEE Access **9**, 47795–47814 (2021). https://doi.org/10.1109/ACCESS.2021.3068045

A Smartphone-Based Computer Vision Assistance System with Neural Network Depth Estimation for the Visually Impaired

Mykola Beshley[1,2]([✉]) [iD], Pastukh Volodymyr[1] [iD], Halyna Beshley[1,2] [iD], and Michal Gregus Jr.[2] [iD]

[1] Department of Telecommunication, Lviv Polytechnic National University, Lviv 79013, Ukraine
{mykola.i.beshlei,halyna.v.beshlei}@lpnu.ua
[2] Faculty of Management, Comenius University in Bratislava, 82005 Bratislava, Slovakia
michal.gregus3@uniba.sk

Abstract. We propose a smartphone-based computer vision system for visually impaired people that uses a neural network to classify objects and estimate image depth to improve spatial orientation in the environment. For this purpose, we have developed and implemented a spatial orientation algorithm with a recursive function for calculating the sum of image array values to estimate depth. The advantage of this algorithm is the low complexity of calculations, which ensures its high performance in real-time. Our system is designed to be easy to use, portable, and affordable, making it accessible to a wide range of users. The proposed system utilizes a smartphone camera and computer vision algorithms to analyze the user's environment and provide real-time feedback through audio and haptic feedback. The neural network depth estimation model is trained on a large dataset of images and corresponding depth maps, which allows it to accurately avoid various objects in the user's field of view.

Keywords: Computer Vision · Depth Estimation · Neural Network · Visually Impaired Person · Recursive Function

1 Introduction

According to the World Health Organization, approximately 2.2 billion people globally suffer from visual impairment, with 1 billion experiencing vision loss that could have been prevented or is yet to be addressed [1]. For visually impaired individuals, spatial orientation in their environment is often challenging, limiting their independence and mobility. To solve this problem, various auxiliary technologies have been developed, including computer vision systems that can recognize objects and estimate their distance to them [2]. However, these systems can be expensive, require specialized equipment, and are often inaccessible to the general population [3]. Simpler systems exist, but they are limited in terms of image processing speed [4].

L. Rutkowski et al. (Eds.): ICAISC 2023, LNAI 14126, pp. 26–36, 2023.
https://doi.org/10.1007/978-3-031-42508-0_3

The problem we are addressing is the limited accessibility of current assistive tech-nologies for visually impaired individuals, as well as, the lack of real-time feedback in many existing systems. Our system aims to address these challenges by providing an affordable and portable solution that can be easily used by a wide range of users. By utilizing a neural network to estimate image depth, our system also provides more detailed information about the user's environment, which can greatly improve their spatial orientation and mobility.

2 Designing the Architecture of the Navigation and Spatial Orientation System

The proposed system in this paper is presented as a universal application that performs various functions and supports a convenient interface for communication with visually impaired users. The application is deployed on a Smartphone running the Android oper-ating system, but it can be ported to other environments provided that certain additional software and hardware support is described further in this section. The list of func-tions implemented in the system is not final and may include new features in future development.

The proposed architecture is universal and can be implemented on various platforms, with a clear separation of computational components into logical layers (Fig. 1):

- the data layer organizes the retrieval, storage, and conversion of data from hardware components of the system or third-party services;
- the data processing layer includes all complex business logic and computations;
- the presentation layer contains the functionality for system-to-user communication through accessible interfaces available on the platform.

The main data processing modules are presented in the data layer:

- The image processing module is a computational module that includes sets of algorithms, autonomous neural network models, and communication interfaces for processing a stream of graphic data.
- The navigation module is a software implementation of navigation based on open maps and data about the device's location and surroundings. This module deploys the functionality of full user navigation across available terrain, calculates routes, trajectories, and movements.
- The sensor data module is a direct and closed-tuned interfaces for obtaining data from hardware components of the system: sensors, communication interfaces.
- The analytics module is a set of built-in and third-party components for data storage and analysis: a database, and analytics. Analytics and data collection are required both at the initial stages of system development and during further development to increase accuracy and reliability.
- The network module is a communication interface in the network with the server and various cloud services.

The domain logic layer includes a dynamic number of use cases, which in turn are logical operations with data obtained from other layers of the system. In this architecture,

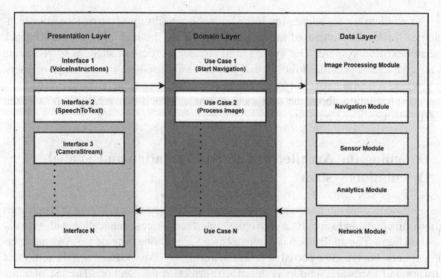

Fig. 1. Computer vision assistance system architecture diagram.

one use case is considered as an atomic simple operation that is configured and simplified based on the computing capabilities of the system's multithreading. Examples of such operations include image processing and matching it with data from accelerometers and gyroscope sensors to determine the user's motion pattern and predict their next steps in space.

The presentation layer is highly dependent on the platform and environment where the system is deployed but is organized with a clear structure of interfaces that contain the logic of communication between the user and the system. These interfaces include device audio output, vibration signal, display, and communication with peripherals.

Each of these layers operates independently, including a set of logically distinguished modules. Interaction between the layers is not direct but through implemented communication interfaces. Each layer operates on its own entity data types, which are prepared and limited for the current work area to ensure integrity and security. In the future, such an architectural approach enables easy system expansion, migration, and module unification, as well as the implementation of cross-platform solutions.

3 Development of Algorithms for the Proposed System with Fast Neural Network Image Depth Estimation

Based on the requirements and functionality of the system, an architecture and its separate modules have been proposed, and an algorithm for the navigation and spatial orientation system has been designed in the form of object classification of the user's environment and communication with the system. The algorithm of the navigation and spatial orientation system is depicted in Fig. 2. The main advantage of this algorithm is the correct distribution of computational work in a multi-threaded execution environment, which is reflected in the corresponding element of the algorithm flowchart.

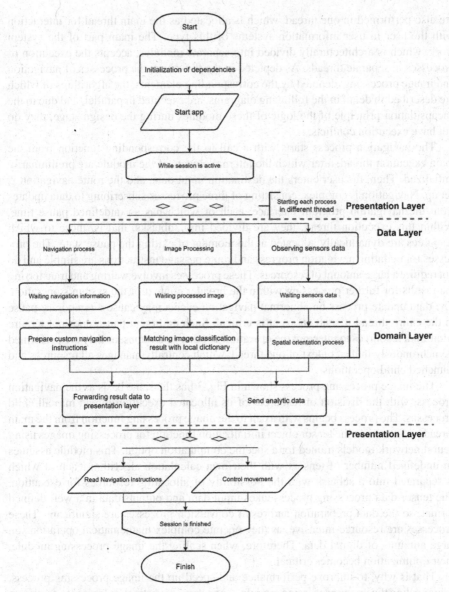

Fig. 2. Algorithm of navigation and spatial orientation system for visually impaired people based on smartphone and computer vision.

Not all processes can be executed in parallel, due to the impracticality of using separate threads or resources of a separate thread for asynchronous execution on simple tasks. Among such tasks is the initial initialization of necessary dependencies and modules, which will give a slight gain in time when executed asynchronously, taking into account the costs of conflicts accessing shared resources, which may occur. The start of the main functionality session of navigation and spatial orientation and its completion are also performed in one thread, which is allocated as the main thread for interaction with the user in user information systems of this type. The main part of the system work, which is architecturally divided into separate modules, accepts the execution of processes in separate threads. As depicted in the flowchart, the processes of navigation and image processing, denoted by the corresponding elements, the algorithms of which are described in detail in the following diagrams, are executed in parallel, and due to the encapsulation principle of the logic of these modules during the design stage, they do not have execution conflicts.

The navigation process starts with a call to the corresponding function from the main execution thread, after which the internal objects of the module are preliminarily initialized. Then, the user enters the destination input data, and the route navigation is set up. Navigation is complex, consisting of three processes subscribing to data updates from the navigation program interface, each of which has an undefined pause time. Within this execution thread, they are divided into subtasks, that is, those to which resources are dynamically allocated at the moment of exiting the pause state. The processes for updating navigation progress and route passage instructions are simple and do not require a large amount of resources. These processes involve waiting and transferring the results for further processing within the broader context of the system's operation. The data update process on abnormal navigation events may cause a temporary pause in the entire thread if such an event is critical. Such an urgent pause does not require additional resources to interrupt the operation of other operations, as they are performed asynchronously in the context of one thread, which centrally manages all resources and launched child operations.

The image processing process shown in Fig. 3 has the same basis as the navigation process, with the division of resources of its allocated execution thread into all child processes. The process begins with a call to the image processing function from the main thread and moves to the tensor object initialization function for processing images using neural network models trained for a specific computation option. This module assumes an undefined number of tensors with their own calculation algorithm, each of which is separated into a subtask with the possibility of allocating resources for execution. The tensor data processing process takes input data and outputs data in a well-defined format, so the data preparation and result conversion processes are significant. These processes are resource-intensive, as they operate complex mathematical operations on large amounts of digital data. Therefore, when scaling the image processing module, their optimization becomes critical.

That is why, to improve performance and speed up the image processing process, when scaling the image processing module, we propose to abstract its logic into a separate executable submodule, and to allocate each option for converting input or output data into a separate asynchronous subtask. It is important to continue monitoring and optimizing these processes as the system scales to ensure efficient and effective image processing. Currently, the system implements two options for processing video stream frames in accordance with the defined functions.

Object Classification in Image (MobiNet3).
On one of the tensors, the neural network model MobiNet of the third version is deployed, which is trained to classify popular objects. The input of the neural network is a processed

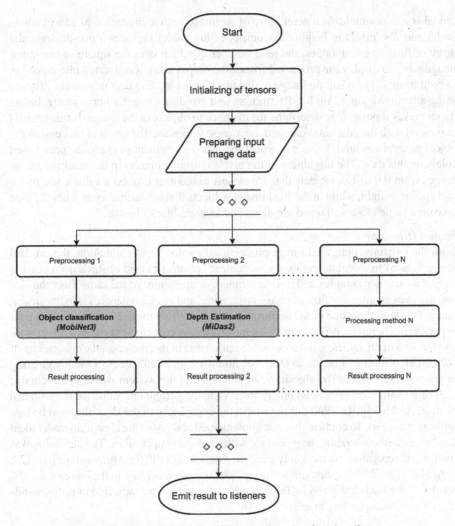

Fig. 3. Detailed algorithm of image processing functionality.

pixel array of an image with a dimension of 512 pixels in width and 512 pixels in height. The output of this model is a dictionary of integer values up to a floating-point value, which means a unique number of the classified object from the results file to the percentage value matching with it. The value with the highest percentage of matching is determined as the final result for the processed frame and is voiced to the user.

Depth Estimation with MiDaS 2 Neural Networks Model.
The MiDaS 2 Lite neural image depth estimation model is based on the tensor [5], which is characterized by working with simple images obtained with a camera. The model is trained on 10 datasets with different data and has a large number of improved versions, but currently, a publicly trained model of the second version is used. The input of the

model is a two-dimensional pixel array of an image with a dimension of 256 pixels in width and 256 pixels in height. The output of the model provides a one-dimensional array of floating-point values, the total number of which is in the square of the initial image size. To display the processed frame, the output array is converted into an object in bmp format. The resulting image is also used for controlling user movement in space using a recursive algorithm for determining and avoiding obstacles horizontally. Image depth makes it possible to determine the distance to objects in the image. If this value is compared with the accelerometer and gyroscope values and the result of processing the object recognition model, you can adjust the user's movement in space in space based solely on this data. The brightness of the pixels outlining objects in the resulting image ranges from 0.0 to 1.0. Objects that are closest to the user take on a value close to 1.0 and appear as light, white in the final image. Objects that are farther away from the user take on a value close to 0.0 and are displayed as dark, black objects.

Spatial Orientation.
With the existing configured image processing flow for depth estimation, the original image is used to calculate the user's movement options to avoid obstacles. Processing large data sets is a complex and resource-intensive operation. At the same time, the system assumes an intensive flow of image processing, and a potential increase in frequency, and at the same time, one of the requirements is to provide the user with a positive user experience. Therefore, processing by a simple brute force method, through a direct walk and the sum of all values, is not a desirable option due to its efficiency, the complexity of such an algorithm will be linear $O(n)$, because the sum of all values of the image array requires a direct walk. The algorithm implemented in this system works as a recursive sum of all values of a balanced binary tree. Visually, getting one value for the sum can be displayed in Fig. 4a. With this approach, the complexity of the algorithm will be logarithmic $O(log\ n)$. To confirm this, we implemented and tested the algorithm under ideal conditions without loading the processor with third-party operations. The algorithm was run for 202 repetitions on randomly generated data sets of different dimensions [64, 128, 256, 512, 1024, 2048] to determine the processing time according to the image size. The results of the study are given in Table 1, where the values are indicated in milliseconds and on the corresponding graph in Fig. 4b.

Table 1. Results of the algorithm performance.

Dim	count	mean	std	min	25%	50%	75%	max
64	202.0	0.806931	1.692051	0.0	0.0	0.0	1.0	9.0
128	202.0	1.490099	3.454379	0.0	0.0	1.0	1.0	27.0
256	202.0	4.054455	5.970242	1.0	2.0	2.0	4.0	62.0
512	202.0	11.95049	13.399247	6.0	7.0	9.0	14.0	157.0
1024	202.0	37.4900	25.837464	26.0	29.0	2.0	37.0	367.0
2048	202.0	127.831	35.029361	100.0	107.0	121.0	139.0	473.0

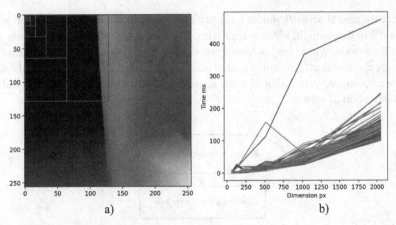

Fig. 4. The principle of the algorithm for recursive passing deep into the array to determine the image depth a) and the performance of the algorithm in terms of image processing time for different sizes b).

Figure 5 shows the block diagram of the algorithm, which defines the output condition and the conditions for changing the parameters for the recursion.

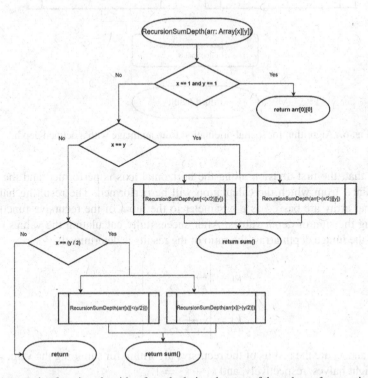

Fig. 5. A recursive function algorithm for calculating the sum of the values of a quantized source image with a certain depth.

Since the neural network model for depth estimation produces an array of 256 pixels wide and 256 pixels high, we can approximately focus on the average execution time for this dimension, which ranges from 1 ms to 62 ms and is equal to 4.054455 ms.

Figure 6 shows the algorithm of spatial orientation in the context of the overall system with the existing pre-processing of a one-dimensional array into a two-dimensional one and quantization of values.

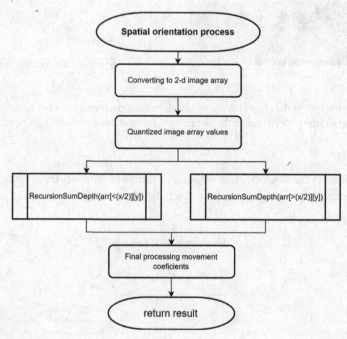

Fig. 6. Algorithm for spatial orientation from an image with a defined depth.

After that, the first division along the horizontal axis is performed and the center is determined from which the calculation will be performed. The resulting halves of the original array are passed as a parameter to the input of the recursive function for calculating the sum of depth values. After successfully calculating the values of both halves of the image depth array, the ratio of the results is determined.

$$k_1 = \left| \frac{x_1}{x_1 + x_2} - 1 \right| \tag{1}$$

$$k_2 = \left| \frac{x_2}{x_1 + x_2} - 1 \right| \tag{2}$$

where x_1 and x_2 are the results of the recursive algorithm for summing the values of the left and right halves, respectively, and $k_1 + k_2 = 1$.

The more obstacles there are on one side in relation to the other, the higher the coefficient.

4 Implementation and Results

Testing of the implemented prototype of the system was carried out on a Google Pixel 6 mobile device, which has the following characteristics that are important for this experiment and verification of the system's performance (Android operating system, 1st generation Tensor processor, 50-megapixel camera). To display the result of the spatial orientation function, we configured components whose brightness depends on the coefficients obtained at the output of image depth processing.

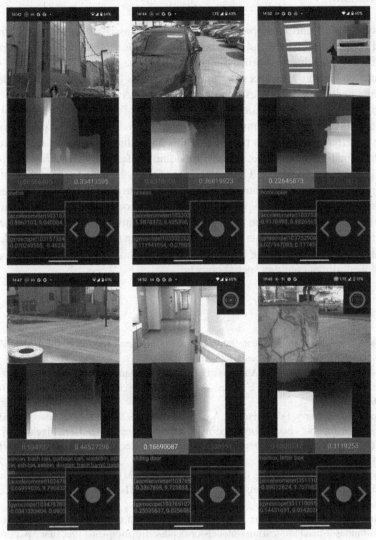

Fig. 7. Testing results of the proposed system.

In the tested cases (Fig. 7), we can see that objects that are closer to the camera reflect more light and appear brighter (image depth factor is close to 1), while distant objects reflect less light and appear darker (image depth factor is close to 0). By assigning brightness values depending on the distance, the proposed system creates a depth map that reflects the three-dimensional structure of the environment with object detection. Also, by analyzing the obtained image depth coefficients (from 0 to 1) for the left and right parts, it provides notifications about avoiding obstacles for visually impaired people.

5 Conclusion

A prototype of a smartphone-based computer vision assistance system for visually impaired people was created and tested. A multi-module architecture was designed to enable efficient asynchronous processing of big data. The approach of the spatial orientation function through the processing of camera images by neural network models for object classification and depth estimation was chosen. A spatial orientation algorithm based on a recursive function for calculating the sum of image array values is implemented, and its effectiveness is investigated according to the criterion of image processing time of different sizes. It is proved that this algorithm provides image processing for depth estimation in real-time, thereby providing the fastest possible information for visually impaired people to avoid obstacles. In the future, the main focus of the work will be to improve the spatial orientation algorithm in order to train the system to determine the distance to objects. It is also planned to take into account additional factors that can increase the accuracy and ensure processing of all variants, such as taking into account accelerometer and gyroscope data to strengthen or weaken the signal, processing the case of complete surroundings or the absence of obstacles, taking into account the vertical axis to move through complex spatial objects.

References

1. Blindness and vision impairment. https://www.who.int/news-room/fact-sheets/detail/blindness-and-visual-impairment. Accessed 25 Apr 2023
2. Khan, S., Nazir, S., Khan, H.U.: Analysis of navigation assistants for blind and visually impaired people: a systematic review. IEEE Access. **9**, 26712–26734 (2021). https://doi.org/10.1109/access.2021.3052415
3. Mahendran, J.K., Barry, D.T., Nivedha, A.K., Bhandarkar, S.M.: Computer vision-based assistance system for the visually impaired using mobile edge artificial intelligence. In: 2021 IEEE/CVF Conference on Computer Vision and Pattern Recognition Workshops (CVPRW). IEEE (2021)
4. Wang, H.-M., Lin, H.-Y., Chang, C.-C.: Object detection and depth estimation approach based on deep convolutional neural networks. Sensors (Basel). **21**, 4755 (2021). https://doi.org/10.3390/s21144755
5. Cochard, D.: Midas: A machine learning model for depth estimation. https://medium.com/axinc-ai/midas-a-machine-learning-model-for-depth-estimation-e96119cc1a3c. Accessed 25 Apr 2023

Hybrid Learning Model for Satellite Forest Image Segmentation

Clopas Kwenda$^{(\boxtimes)}$, Mandlenkosi Victor Gwetu ,
and Jean Vincent Fonou-Dombeu

School of Mathematics, Statistics and Computer Science,
University of KwaZulu-Natal, Pietermaritzburg, South Africa
221072651@stu.ukzn.ac.za, {gwetum,fonoudombeuj}@ukzn.ac.za

Abstract. Image segmentation is an essential image processing technique as the quality of individual object detection significantly affects subsequent global image classification accuracy. The segmentation process can be performed by a varying number of different algorithms, but to date, these different algorithms are not yet able to guarantee a level of performance similar to or superior to human capability. This study adopts a supervised approach toward satellite forest image segmentation. The proposed model used a feature vector obtained through transfer learning from ResNet50; these features were then passed to a Random Forest for segmentation. The satellite images used for training and testing were obtained from the Land Cover Classification Truck in Deep-Globe Challenge. Metrics such as precision, recall, F1-Score, accuracy, Root Mean Square Error (RMSE), and Mean Average Error (MAE) were used to assess the performance of the model. The model achieved a testing accuracy of 94%, RMSE value of 0.2499, and MAE value of 5.92. For detecting forest areas the proposed model obtained a precision of 0.94, recall of 0.96, and F1-Score of 0.95. For non-forest areas, the proposed model achieved a precision of 0.93, recall of 0.89, and F1-Score of 0.91.

Keywords: Segmentation · Supervised approach · ResNet50 · Random Forest · Remote Sensing Image

1 Introduction

Image segmentation is a process whereby an image is partitioned into separate regions, which ideally relate to different real-world objects [1]. Such a process is of paramount importance for subsequent computational image content analysis and understanding. Hence, image segmentation quality significantly affects subsequent image classification accuracy. The segmentation process can be performed by a varying number of different algorithms, but to date, a satisfactory level of high performance by these different algorithms has not yet been realized. This can be attributed to different standards of what constitutes a good segmentation, the sheer complexity of the segmentation context as well as a possible mismatch between the applied segmentation technique and its domain use

L. Rutkowski et al. (Eds.): ICAISC 2023, LNAI 14126, pp. 37–47, 2023.
https://doi.org/10.1007/978-3-031-42508-0_4

case. Given the complexity and application dependence of the image segmentation task, this study advocates for the design of a segmentation technique that leverages algorithm variance. Segmentation quality is assessed by measuring the discrepancy between the delineated image region (DIR) and the actual image region (AIR) of the scene image.

Unsupervised methods (empirical goodness methods) and Supervised methods (empirical discrepancy methods) [2] are the dominant evaluation algorithms used in remote sensing images. Supervised methods evaluate a segmented image object with a reference to a gold standard image (i.e a manually segmented image). The quality of the segmented image is determined by the similarity between gold standard image and the segmented image. The main advantage of this approach is that there is a direct comparison between the manually generated image and the segmented image. Unsupervised methods depend solely on the segmented image, i.e. it does not require to be compared with manually segmented reference image [1]. The main advantage of Unsupervised evaluation assessment methods is that they do not require to be assessed against a truth value (i.e. manually segmented reference image). Therefore they are most suited for general-purpose segmentation applications. However, Cheng [3] pointed out that, whenever a sound ground truth is established, supervised methods are desirable for segmentation assessment evaluation. It is against this backdrop that this study has adopted a supervised approach toward satellite forest image segmentation. The proposed model used a feature vector obtained through transfer learning from ResNet50; these features were then passed to a Random Forest for segmentation. The satellite images used for training and testing were obtained from the Land Cover Classification Truck in DeepGlobe Challenge. Metrics such as precision, recall, F1-Score, accuracy, Root Mean Square Error (RMSE), and Mean Average Error (MAE) were used to assess the performance of the model. The model achieved a testing accuracy of 94%, RMSE value of 0.2499, and MAE value of 5.92. For detecting forest areas the proposed model obtained a precision of 0.94, recall of 0.96, and F1-Score of 0.95. For non-forest areas, the proposed model achieved a precision of 0.93, recall of 0.89, and F1-Score of 0.91.

The rest of the paper is structured as follows. Section 2 discusses related work. The materials and methods used in the study are presented in Sect. 3. Section 4 describes and discusses the results of the study. The paper is concluded in Sect. 5.

2   Related Work

A study [4] investigated the use of auto-encoders to estimate forest biomass on Landsat8 and LiDAR data sets. The auto-encoders outperformed the traditional machine learning algorithms such as the k-nearest neighbor, support vector regression, and multiple step-wise linear regression by 1% to 7% in terms of relative RMSE. The main limitation of their study was that there was no mechanism or method for selecting optimal predictor variables, and separate estimates for different forest types, hence the study obtained lower RMSE values. InceptionV3 and GoogleNet architectures were successfully implemented to estimate forest-above biomass from LiDAR data with RMSE of 26% and bias of 0.7% respectively [5]. The study demonstrated that the use of deep learning methods such as CNN for interpreting LiDAR datasets is an improvement upon traditional methods for area-based predictions of forest attributes. However such improvements brought about some drawbacks. The CNN deep learning model requires large amounts of training data, effort, and time to perform the modeling process. As a result, it is upon's modeler's judgment to decide whether the improvements in the model's performance are worth the effort required to train the model. The proposed model in this study can successfully produce good results on limited data set as it is only the RF section that performs the key segmentation process and it performs best on the limited dataset.

In another study [6], the authors came up with a multi-task recurrent CNN that integrated data from several sources, including aerial and satellite image time series, and climate data for classifying different forest cover types and forest proprieties such as above-ground biomass, canopy cover, basal area and quadratic mean diameter. The multi-task method outclassed support vector machines and random forests. Since the model was purely based on CNN, the model required a large amount of training data, and as result, the model failed to make predictions of hardwood forests of the Eastern US due to a lack of images for specific forest types. The model proposed in this study can produce good results on limited datasets.

A study [7] implemented a deep convolutional encoder-decoder Segnet model to distinguish between crops, weeds, and background. A line detection algorithm was used to determine the row of the crops, then the distance of both the crops and weeds from the detected line was fed into a random forest algorithm to label the plant as either weed or crop. The major limitation of this study was the weak features adopted for crop detection which resulted in the misidentification of crops and weeds. To address this issue, a hybrid model based on CNN was used, which excels at producing features required for image segmentation and classification [8].

A U-net deep CNN was used [9] for orchard tree segmentation using aerial images. The aim was to detect and localize a canopy of orchard trees under various conditions. The study en-counted a lot of false positives based on the segmentation results. This could be attributed to high compression of training images which resulted in the loss of vital information. The proposed model includes an image pre-processing phase in which all input images are resized to 512×512, which is large enough for the CNN model to capture all vital features [10].

A model based on semantic segmentation and lidar odometry for the tree diameter estimation was proposed [11]. Virtual reality tool was used to label 3D scans that were in turn used to train a semantic segmentation network. The resulting masks were used to compute a trellis graph that uniquely identifies each instance and extracts relevant features for the SLAM module. The model was able to automatically generate tree diameter estimations. The study encountered the challenge of quantifying the performance of the traditional SLAM algorithm as it was difficult to obtain ground truth measurements of trajectories in the natural environment. To address this issue, ground truth measurements of easily obtained landmark shapes can be used to benchmark various algorithms. The proposed model made use of easily accessible image labels from [12].

3   Materials and Methods

This section presents the ResNet50 architecture used in this study for feature extraction, the RF method employed for the segmentation of images, the metrics for evaluating segmentation results, and describes various operations such as image processing and feature extraction, fine-tuning, sorting of features by importance and performance test of the model.

3.1   Random Forest

Random forest (RF) is regarded as an ensemble classification method that uses a set of classifiers instead of one classifier to classify a new set of data points by considering their vote predictions. Bagging and Boosting algorithms are also under the category of ensemble classification techniques. Boosting uses the concept of iterative retraining to update the weights of incorrectly classified samples. However, it is sensitive to noise, very slow, and can over-train [13]. The Bagging algorithm draws many bootstrap samples from training data and for each bootstrap, a tree is constructed. The idea is that the successive trees are constructed independently from earlier trees and a simple majority vote is taken for prediction [14]. RF is an advanced version of Bagging which is simply described as the collection of tree-structured classifiers [15]. RF splits each node by considering the absolute best split from a randomly chosen subset of predictors at that particular node. A new training data set referred to as the bootstrap is created from the original data set. The random feature selection is then used to grow a tree. RF is initialized by setting two parameters that are of paramount importance, that is, the number of trees to grow, referred to as N, and the number of variables m to split at each node. Then the N bootstrap is obtained by taking two-thirds of the training data, whilst the remaining one-third of the training data that is referred to as out-of-bag (OOB) data is reserved for testing. An unpruned tree from each bootstrap is constructed with a constraint that, each node is based on what is considered the best split (GINI Index) from randomly chosen subset predictor variables. The GINI index also referred to as GINI impurity measures class homogeneity and is expressed as follows.

$$G = \sum_{m=1}^{J} c_m (1 - c_m) \tag{1}$$

where J is the number of classes and c_m corresponds to a set of items labelled with classes m $\in$ 1, 2, ..., J.

3.2   ResNet50

The ResNet50 model was formulated to provide solutions to difficulties in the training process of deep CNN and to reduce saturation and degradation problems. ResNet50 architecture has been developed to overcome the degradation problem by using residual learning. It is an extremely deep type of CNN with 48 convolutional layers, one Maxpooling layer, and one Average pooling layer. An input instance and an output instance are summed up such that the original mapping function

$$H(x) = F(x) - x \tag{2}$$

is redefined as:

$$H(x) = F(x) + x \tag{3}$$

The refinement of the mapping function greatly approximates the desired functions while also making learning simple. This reformulation was initiated to mitigate the degradation problem. The redefined mapping function in Eq. 3 is implemented by having feed-forward neural networks with short connections. The short or skip connections are direct connections that skip some of the layers of the model. The shortcut connections carry out identity mapping operations, and the results are added to the outputs of the stacked layers. If the additional layers can be built as identity mappings, the training error of a deeper model should be not greater than that of its shallower counterpart.

3.3   Metrics for Segmentation Evaluation

The authors in [16] revealed that the segmentation of remote sensing images hugely suffers from over-segmentation and under-segmentation problems and there is no standard way of assessing remote sensing segmentation quality. Metrics that are commonly used for evaluation involve accuracy, precision, recall, F1-Score, support, confusion matrix, Root Mean Square Error (RMSE), and Mean Absolute Error (MAE) [17].

3.4   Image Preprocessing and Features Extraction

Image pre-processing tasks enhance the quality of image datasets prior to the image segmentation and classification tasks. Generally, this pre-processing task includes image scaling, rotation, and image translation. For this study, all images were resized to 512×512 pixels. Due to their architecture, deep learning models generally require that all images in a dataset should be of the same size. CNNs are commonly used for feature extraction. The ResNet50 model which was optimized using transfer learning produced a feature vector with 64 features from the pre-processed original image. Figure 1 shows the distribution of features obtained.

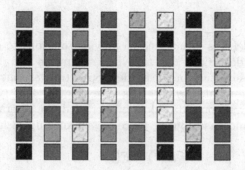

Fig. 1. ResNet50 feature vector

3.5   Fine Tuning

Fine-tuning involves making some modifications to a function or a model in order to improve its effectiveness. The first three layers of ResNet50, up to batch normalization, were considered for feature generation. The layers are shown in Table 1. The batch normalization layer was chosen for tapping the output because the size of images would not have been significantly reduced. The number of estimators in the RF was set to 100. Training image masks were resized to 256 × 256 to correspond to the output shape of the batch normalization layer.

Table 1. Three ResNet50 layers considered for feature generation

Layer(type)	Output Shape	Parameter
input_1(input layer)	[(None,512,512,3)]	0
conv1_pad(ZeroPadding2D)	(None,518,518,3)	0
conv1_conv(con2D)	(None,256,256,64)	9472
conv1_bn(BathNormalisation)	(None,256,256,64)	256

3.6   Sorting Features by Importance

The stage that was of paramount importance was to identify the features that are more critical than others. Feature importance was used to fish out significant features required for forest image segmentation. The Gini index provides the basis for determining feature importance values. Feature importance in RF is expressed as the decrease in node impurity weighted by the probability likelihood of reaching that node. The probability of reaching a node is determined by the number of samples that vote for the node, divided by the number of samples. The higher the value obtained, the higher the importance of the feature. The study adopted the Scikit-learn Python package for the calculation of the gini indexes. All features with values above 0.00, were considered for the image segmentation process.

3.7   Performance Tests

In order to determine the performance of the proposed model, several tests were conducted. The dataset was split into 80% for training purposes and 20% for testing purposes. Other experiments were performed by replacing ResNet50 with other popular pre-trained models such as InceptionV3, VGG16, and Exception.

4   Experimental Results and Discussions

The dataset, the platform used to carry out this study as well as the experimental results achieved are presented and discussed in this section.

4.1   Platform and Dataset

The experiment was carried out on the Google Colab platform which offers free TPU and GPU resources on the cloud. The GPU acceleration of NVIDIA Tesla was used due to the high computational nature of the experiment. A standard, publicly accessible dataset was obtained from Land Cover Classification Truck in DeepGlobe Challenge [12]. Figure 2 shows an original image and its corresponding labeled-mask from the dataset, as used in the study.

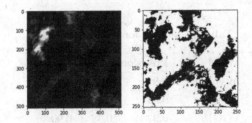

Fig. 2. Extracted RGB-patches and their corresponding masks.

4.2   Results and Discussions

In the experiment of the proposed model, the original image was resized to 512 × 512. Under transfer learning, pre-trained weights of ResNet50 were obtained. ResNet50 architecture produced 64 features when applied to aerial satellite input images. The elements of the 64 feature vectors were taken in as independent variables by the RF classifier to segment forest region areas from non-forest region areas. Several experiments were done by changing the number of classifiers in the RF. The model was then compared against VGG16, Inception, and Xception. Metrics used to evaluate the proposed model were confusion matrix, precision, recall, F1-Score, MAE, and RMSE. The confusion matrix is a two-dimensional table that reflects the performance of a classification algorithm. It is important

Table 2. Metrics for forest areas

Model	Precision	Recall	F1-Score
InceptionV3	0.93	0.94	0.94
Xception	0.93	0.94	0.94
VGG16	0.94	0.97	0.95
Resnet50	**0.94**	**0.96**	**0.95**

for visualizing and summarizing the performance of a classification algorithm. The confusion matrix obtained is presented in Fig. 3. Comparing the segmentation results for each model in Table 2 and Table 3, all the models could effectively segment forest region areas from non-forest region areas, though there are marginal differences in terms of accuracy as presented in Table 4. Both RMSE and MAE are regularly employed for model evaluation studies. [18] argued that RMSE is not a good metric to measure the performance of a model as it gives a misleading average error, hence MAE would be a better metric for such purpose. However, [17] presented that RMSE is not ambiguous in its meaning and hence it is more appropriate to use than MAE when a model's error follows a normal distribution. Also, RMSE satisfies the triangle inequality required for a distance function metric. Because of the argument by [17] the study gives more preference to the RMSE metric.

Table 3. Metrics for non-forest areas

Model	Precision	Recall	F1-Score
InceptionV3	0.89	0.88	0.88
Xception	0.89	0.88	0.88
VGG16	0.93	0.88	0.90
Resnet50	**0.93**	**0.89**	**0.91**

Table 4. Metrics for determining accuracy

Model	Accuracy	RMSE	MAE
InceptionV3	0.9184	0.2857	9.72
Xception	0.9163	0.2893	10.16
VGG16	0.9332	0.2579	5.75
ResNet50	**0.9375**	**0.2499**	**5.92**

The Precision, Recall, and F1-Score values for forest areas (Table 2) are higher than those of non-forest areas (Table 3). InceptionV3 and Xception values follow each other, hence it can be concluded that these models have got the same computational power for the segmentation task in the context of remote sensing-related images. The hybrid model used by this study achieved a high F1-score (Table 3) as compared to the research done by [19] which achieved an F1-score value of 0.34. Their study was centered on Unet deep learning model for segmenting forest images. The confusion matrix results in Fig. 3 show on the main diagonal that 55 297 pixels were classified correctly while only 3686 pixels were misclassified. In terms of accuracy, Table 4 shows that the hybrid model with ResNet50 produced the best results in performing the segmentation task as it produced an accuracy of 94% and an optimal RMSE value of 0.25. The hybrid model with VGG16 produced closely related results to ResNet50 as it obtained an accuracy of 93% and RMSE of 0.26. For this study VGG16 and ResNet50 had more refined segmentation results, hence they are better at segmenting forest region areas from non-forest region areas. The proposed model achieved an accuracy of 94%, RMSE of 0.2499, and MAE of 5.92 (Table 4). The final segmentation is shown in Fig. 4, where the first, second, and third images are the source, ground truth, and algorithm prediction images, respectively.

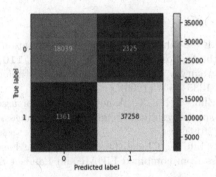

Fig. 3. Confusion Matrix

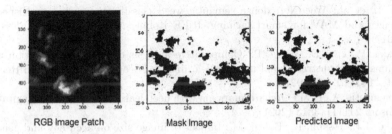

RGB Image Patch   Mask Image   Predicted Image

Fig. 4. Forest Image segmentation.

5   Conclusion

In this paper, a hybrid of CNN (ResNet50) and a traditional learning method (Random Forest) was constructed to identify forest areas and non-forest areas. The CNN was employed to produce features which in turn were used by a Random Forest to segment aerial satellite images. The model performance was assessed against other transfer learning models. The proposed model achieved an overall accuracy of 94%. In conclusion, there is no absolute algorithm that is guaranteed to be good in segmentation as it depends on the specific application. The supervised evaluation approach is suitable only if the golden standard truth image is established. The main advantage of this approach is that it produces accurate and reliable results. The fact that unsupervised evaluation approaches do not require standard images and are a low-level data-driven evaluation method, is a factor in the difficulty of obtaining high accuracy and lack of flexibility to accommodate versatility on image features. Future research should consider a model that incorporates ensembling deep learning approaches for feature generation, with an aim of increasing classification accuracy.

References

1. Zhang, H., Fritts, J.E., Goldman, S.A.: Image segmentation evaluation: a survey of unsupervised methods. Comput. Vis. Image Underst. **110**(2), 260–280 (2008)
2. Zhang, Y.J., et al.: A survey on evaluation methods for image segmentation. Pattern Recogn. **29**(8), 1335–1346 (1996)
3. Cheng, J., Bo, Y., Zhu, Y., Ji, X.: A novel method for assessing the segmentation quality of high-spatial resolution remote-sensing images. Int. J. Remote Sens. **35**(10), 3816–3839 (2014)
4. Zhang, L., Shao, Z., Liu, J., Cheng, Q.: Deep learning based retrieval of forest aboveground biomass from combined LiDAR and Landsat 8 data. Remote Sens. **11**(12), 1459 (2019)
5. Ayrey, E., Hayes, D.J.: The use of three-dimensional convolutional neural networks to interpret LiDAR for forest inventory. Remote Sens. **10**(4), 649 (2018)
6. Chang, T., Rasmussen, B.P., Dickson, B.G., Zachmann, L.J.: Chimera: a multi-task recurrent convolutional neural network for forest classification and structural estimation. Remote Sens. **11**(7), 768 (2019)
7. Sa, I., et al.: WeedNet: dense semantic weed classification using multispectral images and MAV for smart farming. IEEE Robot. Autom. Lett. **3**(1), 588–595 (2017)
8. Wang, P., Fan, E., Wang, P.: Comparative analysis of image classification algorithms based on traditional machine learning and deep learning. Pattern Recogn. Lett. **141**, 61–67 (2021)
9. Anagnostis, A., et al.: Orchard mapping with deep learning semantic segmentation. Sensors **21**(11), 3813 (2021)
10. Luke, J.J., Joseph, R., Balaji, M.: Impact of image size on accuracy and generalization of convolutional neural networks. Int. J. Res. Anal. Rev. **6**, 70–80 (2019)
11. Chen, S.W., et al.: SLOAM: semantic LiDAR odometry and mapping for forest inventory. IEEE Robot. Autom. Lett. **5**(2), 612–619 (2020)
12. Quadeer, S.: Forest aerial images for segmentation

13. Halmy, M.W.A., Gessler, P.E.: The application of ensemble techniques for land-cover classification in arid lands. Int. J. Remote Sens. **36**(22), 5613–5636 (2015)
14. Liaw, A., Wiener, M., et al.: Classification and regression by randomForest. R. News **2**(3), 18–22 (2002)
15. Breiman, L.: Random forests. Mach. Learn. **45**(1), 5–32 (2001)
16. Wang, Z., Wang, E., Zhu, Y.: Image segmentation evaluation: a survey of methods. Artif. Intell. Rev. **53**(8), 5637–5674 (2020)
17. Chai, T., Draxler, R.R.: Root mean square error (RMSE) or mean absolute error (MAE)? - arguments against avoiding RMSE in the literature. Geosci. Model Dev. **7**(3), 1247–1250 (2014)
18. Willmott, C.J., Matsuura, K., Robeson, S.M.: Ambiguities inherent in sums-of-squares-based error statistics. Atmos. Environ. **43**(3), 749–752 (2009)
19. Khryashchev, V., Pavlov, V., Ostrovskaya, A., Larionov, R.: Forest areas segmentation on aerial images by deep learning. In: 2019 IEEE East-West Design & Test Symposium (EWDTS), pp. 1–5. IEEE (2019)

Adaptive Pruning for Multi-Head Self-Attention

Walid Messaoud[1]([✉]), Rim Trabelsi[2], Adnane Cabani[3], and Fatma Abdelkefi[1]

[1] Supcom Lab-MEDIATRON, Carthage University, Ariana, Tunisia
walid.messaoud@supcom.tn
[2] Hatem Bettaher IResCoMath Research Unit, National Engineering School
of Gabes, University of Gabes, Gabes, Tunisia
[3] UNIROUEN, ESIGELEC, IRSEEM, Normandie University, Rouen, France

Abstract. This paper provides an adaptive pruning approach to compress Multi-Head Self Attention (MHSA) models. The main aim is to suppress redundant attention heads, requiring high computational complexity, without substantially affecting performance. Through head pruning, we propose more flexible and efficient models for the object detection tasks. Specifically, we propose to enhance the architectures of the two state-of-the-art MHSA-based models: Bottleneck Transformers (BoT-Net) and Attention Augmented Convolutional Networks (AACN). Our approach relies on the alternation between the escalation and the ablation of heads. We selected the less productive heads. We suggest to exploit two and four heads, rather than four and eight heads for Bot-Net and AACN models, respectively. Our experiments on ImageNet and Pascal VOC datasets prove that our light-weighted architectures are more efficient compared with the original heavy-weighted ones. We reach close performances and achieve faster convergence during training, which allows easier transfer and deployment.

Keywords: object detection · Multi-head attention mechanism · head's pruning

1 Introduction

Deep learning object detection task is used in several real-world applications including health surveillance, automated vehicles, video monitoring, anomaly detection, and object tracking. In recent years, imaging technology has advanced significantly. Cameras are more compact, affordable, and high-quality than ever. Meanwhile, computing power has sharply expanded and greatly improved. Computing platforms have shifted toward sophistication through multi-core processing, graphics processing units (GPU), and tensor processing units (TPU). Therefore, object detection is witnessing a revolutionary improvement and two distinct historical eras. The traditional object detection period is based on conventional computer vision and machine learning tools such as Histogram of Oriented Gradients (HOG) detector [1], Support Vector Machine [2], and Deformable Part-based

Model (DPM) [3], etc. Subsequently, deep learning achieves significant innovation within the used processes and methods. Object detection models may be classified into two families: one-stage and two-stage models. On the one hand, YOLOv2 (2016) [4], YOLOv4 (2020) [7], Single Shot multi-box Detector (SSD) (2016) [5] and RetinaNet (2017) [6] are examples of efficient one-stage algorithms. On the other hand, RCNN and SPPNet [8], Fast RCNN and Faster RCNN [9], Mask R-CNN [10] and Transformer [11] prove the performance of two-stage algorithms. Currently, the transformer becomes one of the crucial neural architectures used in Natural Language Processing (NLP) [11] and different computer vision tasks such as object detection. Transformer is the cornerstone of question answering models, machine translation and parsing tasks [12]. Bidirectional Encoder Representations from Transformers (BERT) [13], Generative Pre-trained Transformer (GPT-2) [15], GPT-3 [16], Robustly-optimized BERT approach (RoBERTa) [17], and Enhanced Representation through kNowledge IntEgration (ERNIE2.0) [18] are the most relevant natural language processing models using transformers. Likewise, in computer vision, Detection Transformer (DETR) [19], Bottleneck Transformers (BoTNet) [20], and Attention Augmented Convolutional Networks (AACN) [21] reached significant results in computer vision tasks. They exploited MHSA (Multi-Head Self Attention) to enhance the performance of object detection tasks. The attention mechanism could be an effective component allowing neural models to focus on specific pieces of data or image.

Many recent studies have focused on MHSA, Cordonnier et al. [22] outlined the importance of attention mechanism and proved that MHSA with sufficient number of heads can outperform any convolutional layer. Bian et al. [23] outline the redundancy found among heads functions. They illustrated that numerous attention heads may affect the convergence time. Therefore, it is necessary to decrease the model's size to reach swiftness and velocity. In fact, computer science deployment is crucial within the model life-cycle. After the training process, the deployment is the next stage to bring the model to life. There are many deciding factors that intervene during this phase. The model accuracy is an important metric. However, the size, number of parameters, and convergence time are additionally pivotal aspect. Therefore, it is necessary to enhance the model's simplicity to ensure the starting of its life cycle. Recent works proved that an expansive number of heads in a MHSA can be pruned away without affecting the effectiveness. The study of Voita et al. [25] assessed the improvement made by each attention head to the model effectiveness and examined their tasks. They pruned the less effective heads employing a method supported stochastic gates. They used the Layer-Wise Relevance Propagation (LWRP) presented by Ding et al. [24] to select the foremost important and efficient heads. Subsequently, they eliminated a significant number of heads on the English-Russian WMT dataset without major effects in model performance. Also, within the machine translation and natural language processing, Li et al. [12] proposed other method via stochastic gradient descent to learn the importance of variables and prune the less effective BERT heads self-attentions. The increasing interest in enhancing simplicity and model execution rapidity have heightened the need for pruning the heads of MHSA. Michel et al. [26] presented comprehensive study named

"Are Sixteen Heads Really Better than One?" to examine and to analyze the effectiveness of WMT [11] and BERT [13] models. They concluded that several heads can be eliminated without critical downgrading in their efficiency.

Beyond the NLP tasks, several object detection models took advantage of MHSA to enhance their effectiveness. They intended to create a new and more efficient alternatives to CNNs. This motivates us to line up another adaptive pruning method for MHSA models, specifically, AACN and BoTNet, the state-of-the-art models used for object detection tasks. Our ultimate objective is to explore the importance and evaluate the role of every head using the aforementioned LWRP method. We alternate between the pruning and the addition of heads for our adaptive approach to upgrade the simplicity and rapidity without losing the detection's accuracy. The selection of less effective heads is based on the Layer-Wise Relevance Propagation (LWRP) method presented by Ding *et al.* [24].

The main contributions of this paper include:

- A new adaptive approach for pruning MHSA models' heads in a safe process in order to prune away heads without significantly harming the performance of the networks using LWRP method.
- We propose modified architectures for the BoTNet and AACN MHSA models as a use case for our adaptive approach
- We carried out extensive experiments to prove the efficiency of our proposal compared with the baseline MHSA models using ImageNet and Pascal VOC datasets.

2 Adaptive Heads Pruning

Modern transformer models are heavily reliant on multi-head attention. However, consistent with current studies, there are several redundant heads and replicated patterns. Pruning the heads or the ablation of the heads is the course of action used to reduce the model parameters and to ensure efficiency combined with simplicity. Each head of MHSA has a specific task. To ablate the heads, it is mandatory to spot the foremost effective heads and find out a compromise between model accuracy and simplicity to reach better efficiency. We chose to prune the model's heads to eliminate the redundancy among its architecture. We exploit the aforementioned LWRP method to select the less productive heads.

Given a sequence of m d-dimensional vectors $y = y_1, y_2, ...y_m \in \mathbb{R}^d$, and a query vector $q \in \mathbb{R}^d$, the attention layer parametrized by $W_k, W_q, W_v, W_0 \in \mathbb{R}^{d*d}$

$$Att_{W_k,W_q,W_v,W_0}(Y,q) = W_0 \sum_{i=1}^{m} \alpha_i W_v y_i \qquad (1)$$

where $\alpha_i = softmax\left(\frac{q^T W_q^T W_k y_i}{\sqrt{d}}\right)$

In self-attention, every y_i is used as the query q to compute a new sequence of representations, whereas in sequence-to-sequence models q is typically a decoder state while y corresponds to the encoder output. The aforementioned Eq. (1)

define the various parameters of single head attention. Concerning the multi-head attention (MHA), M_h independently parameterized attention layers are used synchronously as shown in Eq. (2).

$$MHAtt\,(Y,q) = \sum_{h=1}^{N_h} Att_{W_k^h, W_q^h, W_v^h, W_0^h}\,(Y,q) \tag{2}$$

where $W_k^h, W_q^h, W_v^h \in \mathbb{R}^{d_h * d}$ and $W_0^h \in \mathbb{R}^{d * d_h}$ [14] $Att_h(y)$ as a shorthand for the output of head h on input y. Our proposal is to prune heads as follow.

$$MHAtt\,(Y,q) = \sum_{h=1}^{N_h} \beta_h Att_{W_k^h, W_q^h, W_v^h, W_0^h}\,(Y,q) \tag{3}$$

where β_h pruning variables. Its value may be 0 or 1 depending on preserving or pruning the head [26]. Equation (3) is that the same as Eq. (2) when all β_h are equal to 1. We fix $\beta_h = 0$ to prune the less productive heads after selection using LWRP method as can be seen in Fig. 1.

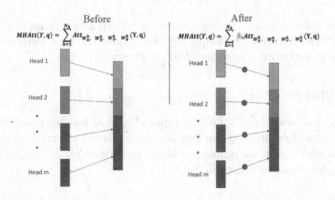

Fig. 1. Pruning the heads process. β_h value may be 0 or 1, So that β_h present a gate used to allow or deny the head exploitation.

To reach the aforementioned objective, we chose two state-of-the-art object detection models (BoTNet and AACN) based on Multi-Head Self-Attention. Both of them are implemented in many computer vision tasks. They demonstrated preciseness, exactness, and veracity in object detection projects. Furthermore, they outperformed many state-of-the-art models such as RCNN and Faster RCNN. We went through a series of experiments during which we pruned one or more attention heads from the model architecture. We evaluated and assessed the accuracy and performance contrasts. Such pruning leads to models that are discernibly smaller and faster. Moreover, we increased the number of heads to seek the correct answer to Michel et al. study "Are Sixteen Heads Really Better than One?" [26]. All aforementioned experiments are conducted using ImageNet and Pascal VOC datasets [28]. The assessment and comparison between different models employed three metrics: training loss, validation loss, and accuracy. In this paper, we use the LWRP method to select the less effective heads before changing the number of model's heads. Subsequently, we assessed the modified model metrics and appraised their performance and efficiency. This research aims to gauge the importance of various heads using LWRP method based on ImageNet and Pascal VOC dataset and choose the best number of heads that compromises between accuracy and simplicity.

ImageNet dataset is composed of 3.2 million annotated images divided into 5247 categories. More than 600 pictures were aggregated for each synset [27]. PASCAL Visual Object Classes (VOC) upholds 20 object categories divided into three subsets: 1,464 images for training, 1,449 images for validation, and a private test set [27]. Throughout our experiments, we optimized AACN, and BoTNet using AdamW, and Adam, respectively. AACN and BoTNet learning rate was set to 0.0001. The threshold for interpreting probabilities to class labels is 0.5 for the three models.

3 Experimental Results

The research aims to gauge the importance of various heads using the ImageNet and Pascal VOC datasets. Subsequently, we choose the best number of heads that compromises between accuracy and simplicity.

3.1 Modified BoTNet

ImageNet. The reference BoTNet composed of four heads preserves the best accuracy results after pruning the less productive heads selected by the LWRP method. The increase in the number of heads did not result on the improvement of model performance as shown in Table 1.

Table 1. BoTNet's metrics variation using the ImageNet datase

Number of heads	Accuracy	Training Loss	Validation Loss
2 Heads (ours)	0.8947	0.0029	0.5934
4 Heads [20]	**0.8999**	0.0032	0.6089
8 Heads	0.8991	**0.002**	0.5800
16 Heads	0.8904	0.0095	**0.5611**

The accuracy of the BoTNet-50 model reached 89.4% with only two heads. The reference BotNet accuracy with four heads attained 89.9%. Therefore, the pruning of less effective heads from four to two did not affect significantly the accuracy. However, the values of training loss are better with only two heads (0.00295) than with four heads (0.003267). Likewise, the validation loss value is more prominent with only two heads (0.59349) than the reference model with four heads (0.6089). Subsequently, we assessed the impact of the increment in the number of heads from four to eight. The accuracy declined slightly by 0.08% from 89.99% within the reference model to 89.91% with the addition of 100% of heads. The training loss and validation loss reached better values compared with the reference model. Furthermore, to answer the question of Mickel et al. "Are Sixteen Heads Really Better than One?" [26], we surged the number of heads during our experiment to sixteen. However, the accuracy is dropped by 0.945% compared with the reference model combined with the escalation of complexity and less convergence rapidity. Therefore, based on this observation, we further propose a simpler model where we cannily prune attention heads and preserve the model performance using the LWRP method to select the less effective heads. We introduce a modified BoT-Net model based only on two heads. Our ultimate objective is to consolidate the model's simplicity, enhance its rapidity and reduce its size.

PascalVOC. Likewise, based on the Pascal VOC dataset, The experiments results depicted in Table 2 prove that removing 50% of heads did not affect the accuracy. BoTNet maintains comparable metrics values even with only two heads.

Table 2. BoTNet's metrics variation using the Pascal VOC dataset.

Number of heads	Accuracy	Training Loss	Validation Loss
2 heads (ours)	**0.3300**	**0.7782**	**3.0182**
4 heads [20]	0.3151	0.8154	3.0266
8 heads	0.3300	0.8660	3.0957

Pruning 50% of less effective heads preserves the accuracy with better training and validation loss results. Moreover, the proposed model with only two heads is characterized by more simplicity, less time for training, and easier deployment. Therefore, We observe that the exploitation of the LWRP method to select the less effective heads permits us to prune 50% of BoTNet's heads without causing any discernible negative impact on model accuracy and performance. Finally, Modified BoTNet with only two heads is the compromise between accuracy and size.

3.2 Modified AACN

We removed the less effective heads of AACN multi-head self-attention using ImageNet and Pascal VOC dataset to evaluate the effects.

ImageNet Dataset. Based on 8 heads, AACN reaches the best value of accuracy. Furthermore, the pruning of 50% of heads did not affect significantly the model performance. In fact, during our experiments, we decreased the number of heads from eight to four. The accuracy was reduced only by 0.5%. This perception stimulates the interrogation: is more than four heads indeed required?

Table 3. AACN's metrics variation using the ImageNet dataset

Number of heads	Accuracy	Training Loss	Validation Loss
2 heads	0.8594	0.0220	0.8925
4 heads (ours)	0.8662	**0.0028**	**0.6840**
8 heads [21]	**0.8715**	0.0082	0.7016

The ablation of 50% of model heads did not affect its performance. In contrast, using only 25% of heads, altered significantly the AACN accuracy. Therefore, we introduced Modified AACN based on the concatenation of convolutional neural network and MHSA with only four heads. Our model furnishes more simplicity and rapidity with less number of parameter, and preserves the model's accuracy. Moreover, the proposed Modified AACN with only four heads guarantees better training loss and validation loss values as depicted in Table 3. To sum up, Modified AACN using only four heads offers similar accuracy results compared to the reference model with better training loss and validation loss findings. Furthermore, the pruning of 50% of the model heads preserves the accuracy and enhances the rapidity of execution, simplicity, and reduces the model's size for easier deployment.

Pascal VOC Dataset. Same experiments were performed based on Pascal VOC dataset as illustrated in Table 4.

Table 4. AACN's metrics variation using the Pascal VOC dataset

Number of heads	Accuracy	Training Loss	Validation Loss
2 heads	0.3027	0.9026	2.7221
4 heads (ours)	**0.3275**	**0.7681**	**2.6631**
8 heads [21]	0.3215	0.8082	2.7020

Pruning of four less effective heads selected using the LWRP method did not affect significantly the accuracy based on the Pascal VOC dataset. Moreover, the training and validation loss value is better than the original model. Furthermore, we reached less training and convergence time. As hinted before, the attention mechanism is currently the cornerstone of different natural language processing. To guarantee the deployment of models based on Multi-Head self-attention, it is paramount to boost simplicity, reduce the number of parameters, and cut down the size. In this paper, we manage the pruning of MHSA heads of two promising models that reached auspicious results in different computer tasks. Previous sections proved that simplicity and rapidity combined with efficiency can be achieved by the ablation of 50% of both models' heads by the exploitation of the LWRP method to select the less effective heads. The suggested models Modified BoTNet and Modified AACN reached a similar accuracy compared with the mentioned reference models and guarantee more simplicity and rapidity during the execution. Moreover, our experiments highlighted the fact that the increase in the number of heads in Multi-Head Self Attention did not mean the enhancement of model performance. This paper aims to introduce simpler and faster models based on the ablation of heads without affecting the accuracy metric based on the LWRP method. Moreover, both modified models achieved better training and validation loss than the reference models. The mentioned results can be enhanced using AACN 101 and BoTNet 101 based on ResNet 101. However, such study deserves dedicated experiments to improve the model's efficiency, and preserve simplicity and rapidity.

4   Conclusions

Throughout this paper, we introduce modified BoTNet based on the insertion of MHSA with only 2 heads in ResNet 50. The illustrated modification preserved the model performance and guarantee more simplicity and rapidity. Moreover, Modified AACN with only 4 heads instead of 8 reached auspicious results and maintained the model efficiency. The selection of pruned heads is based on the LWRP method to highlight the less effective heads and preserve the model's accuracy. Furthermore, the experiments proved that, on the one hand, the augmentation of the number of heads did not mean the escalating of accuracy. On the other hand, the pruning of heads can preserve performance combined with optimized model size. The conducting of the pruning of heads in multi-head self-attention aims to reduce the model parameters to find a compromise between accuracy and performance to guarantee the model deployment and to insure the kickoff of the model life cycle. Therefore, both proposed models can relieve the deployment impediment and offer a better scope of application and exploitation in the real life.

References

1. Dalal, N., Triggs, B.: Histograms of oriented gradients for human detection. In: 2005 IEEE Computer Society Conference on Computer Vision and Pattern Recognition, CVPR 2005 (2005)
2. Wang, X., Han, T.X., Yan, S.: An HOG-LBP human detector with partial occlusion handling. In: 2009 IEEE 12th International Conference on Computer Vision, pp. 32–39 (2009)
3. Wang, X., Yang, M., Zhu, S., Lin, Y.: Regionlets for generic object detection. In: Proceedings of the IEEE International Conference on Computer Vision, pp. 17–24 (2013)

4. Redmon, J., Divvala, S., Girshick, R., Farhadi, A.: You only look once: Unified, real-time object detection. In: Proceedings of the IEEE Conference on Computer Vision and Pattern Recognition, pp. 779–788 (2016)

5. Liu, W., et al.: SSD: single shot multibox detector. In: Leibe, B., Matas, J., Sebe, N., Welling, M. (eds.) ECCV 2016. LNCS, vol. 9905, pp. 21–37. Springer, Cham (2016). https://doi.org/10.1007/978-3-319-46448-0_2

6. Lin, T.-Y., Goyal, P., Girshick, R., He, K., Dollár, P.: Focal loss for dense object detection. In: Proceedings of the IEEE International Conference on Computer Vision, pp. 2980–2988 (2017)

7. Bochkovskiy, A., Wang, C.-Y., Liao, H.-Y.M.: Yolov4: Optimal speed and accuracy of object detection. arXiv preprint arXiv:2004.10934 (2020)

8. Girshick, R.: Fast R-CNN. In: Proceedings of the IEEE International Conference on Computer Vision, pp. 1440–1448 (2015)

9. Ren, S., He, K., Girshick, R., Sun, J.: Faster R-CNN: towards real-time object detection with region proposal networks. In: Advances in Neural Information Processing Systems, vol. 28 (2015)

10. He, K., Gkioxari, G., Dollár, P., Girshick, R.: Mask R-CNN. In: Proceedings of the IEEE International Conference on Computer Vision, pp. 2961–2969 (2017)

11. Vaswani, A., et al.: Attention is all you need. In: Advances in Neural Information Processing Systems, vol. 30 (2017)

12. Li, J., Cotterell, R., Sachan, M.: Differentiable subset pruning of transformer heads. Trans. Assoc. Comput. Linguist. **9**, 1442–1459 (2021)

13. Devlin, J., Chang, M.-W., Lee, K., Toutanova, K.: BERT: pre-training of deep bidirectional transformers for language understanding. arXiv preprint arXiv:1810.04805 (2018)

14. Luong, M.-T., Pham, H., Manning, C.D.: Effective approaches to attention-based neural machine translation. arXiv preprint arXiv:1508.04025 (2015)

15. Radford, A., et al.: Language models are unsupervised multitask learners, vol. 1, p. 9. OpenAI blog (2019)

16. Brown, T., et al.: Language models are few-shot learners. In: Advances in Neural Information Processing Systems, vol. 33, pp. 1877–1901 (2020)

17. Liu, Y., et al.: RoBERTa: a robustly optimized BERT pretraining approach. arXiv preprint arXiv:1907.11692 (2019)

18. Sun, Y., et al.: ERNIE 2.0: a continual pre-training framework for language understanding. In: Proceedings of the AAAI Conference on Artificial Intelligence, vol. 34, no. 5, pp. 8968–8975 (2020)

19. Carion, N., Massa, F., Synnaeve, G., Usunier, N., Kirillov, A., Zagoruyko, S.: End-to-end object detection with transformers. In: Vedaldi, A., Bischof, H., Brox, T., Frahm, J.-M. (eds.) ECCV 2020. LNCS, vol. 12346, pp. 213–229. Springer, Cham (2020). https://doi.org/10.1007/978-3-030-58452-8_13

20. Srinivas, A., Lin, T.-Y., Parmar, N., Shlens, J., Abbeel, P., Vaswani, A.: Bottleneck transformers for visual recognition. In: Proceedings of the IEEE/CVF Conference on Computer Vision and Pattern Recognition, pp. 16519–16529 (2021)

21. Bello, I., Zoph, B., Vaswani, A., Shlens, J., Le, Q.V.: Attention augmented convolutional networks. In: Proceedings of the IEEE/CVF International Conference on Computer Vision, pp. 3286–3295 (2019)

22. Cordonnier, J.-B., Loukas, A., Jaggi, M.: On the relationship between self-attention and convolutional layers. arXiv preprint arXiv:1911.03584 (2019)

23. Bian, Y., Huang, J., Cai, X., Yuan, J., Church, K.: On attention redundancy: a comprehensive study. In: Proceedings of the 2021 Conference of the North Amer-

ican Chapter of the Association for Computational Linguistics: Human Language Technologies, pp. 930–945 (2021)

24. Ding, Y., Liu, Y., Luan, H., Sun, M.: Visualizing and understanding neural machine translation. In: Proceedings of the 55th Annual Meeting of the Association for Computational Linguistics, vol. 1, pp. 1150–1159 (2017)

25. Voita, E., Talbot, D., Moiseev, F., Sennrich, R., Titov, I.: Analyzing multi-head self-attention: specialized heads do the heavy lifting, the rest can be pruned. arXiv preprint arXiv:1905.09418 (2019)

26. Michel, P., Levy, O., Neubig, G.: Are sixteen heads really better than one? In: Advances in Neural Information Processing Systems, vol. 32 (2019)

27. Deng, J., Dong, W., Socher, R., Li, L.-J., Li, K., Fei-Fei, L.: ImageNet: a large-scale hierarchical image database. In: 2009 IEEE Conference on Computer Vision and Pattern Recognition, pp. 248–255. IEEE (2009)

28. Everingham, M., Winn, J.: The PASCAL visual object classes challenge 2012 (VOC2012) development kit. Pattern Analysis, Statistical Modelling and Computational Learning, Technical report, vol. 2007, pp. 1–45 (2012)

Fast Visual Imperfection Detection when Real Negative Examples are Unavailable

Patryk Najgebauer[1]([⊠])[iD], Rafał Scherer[1][iD], Rafał Grycuk[1][iD],
Jakub Walczak[2][iD], Adam Wojciechowski[2][iD], and Ewa Łada-Tondyra[3][iD]

[1] Department of Intelligent Computer Systems, Częstochowa University
of Technology, al. Armii Krajowej 36, 42-200 Częstochowa, Poland
{patryk.najgebauer,rafal.scherer,rafal.grycuk}@pcz.pl
[2] Institute of Information Technology, Lodz University of Technology, Łódź, Poland
{jakub.walczak,adam.wojciechowski}@p.lodz.pl
[3] Faculty of Electrical Engineering, Częstochowa University of Technology,
al. Armii Krajowej 36, 42-200 Częstochowa, Poland
e.lada-tondyra@pcz.pl

Abstract. We present a method of detecting defects and impurities in materials on an example of knitted fabrics. We describe problems related to the real-time imaging detection system. Furthermore, we propose a new fast, small fully convolutional networks with a special configuration for taking into account even small impurities. We also present a method of pattern learning having only small datasets without many defects. That can be connected with difficulties in physically preparing material samples for a traditional, full-fledged training set. The experiments demonstrated high accuracy and real-time speed of the proposed method.

Keywords: Fully convolutional networks · Image recognition · Knitted fabric · Defects detection

1 Introduction

Textile production is one of the oldest industries. Currently, significant technical development allows for the production of huge quantities of fabrics in a fully automated process that is no longer able to be fully supervised by a human. A lack of quality control of manufactured fabric can lead to significant material losses in downstream production processes. The fabric inspection process usually uses machines that rewind fabric under illumination. The technician visually inspects the fabric for any defects during rewinding. Two types of illumination are mostly used to reveal defects. Normal top light is used to inspect the top surface of the material, but bottom illumination could be more important as it shines through the fabric. Most deformations are visible under the light as lighter or darker areas. Any gaps allow more light to pass through the fabric. The existing methods can be divided into methods based on machine learning and earlier-developed traditional methods. Traditional methods are usually

L. Rutkowski et al. (Eds.): ICAISC 2023, LNAI 14126, pp. 58–68, 2023.
https://doi.org/10.1007/978-3-031-42508-0_6

much faster and do not require a long training process. Most of them are based on comparing fabric patterns and detecting anomalies. Examples are structural approach methods [7,10]. There are also model-based method that uses simple hand-crafted feature extractors and vector distance-based feature comparison by or PCA [2,9] or SVDD [3].

More modern methods based on machine learning are more robust to fabric natural deformation but have significantly higher computational complexity. There are many commercial applications, and in the literature, we can find some applications that use general purpose models such as VGG-16 [13], YOLO, Fast-RCNN [4,5], that bring very good results and high accuracy of segmented fabric defects. Yet, such methods have also higher computationally complexity. The other problem is the training dataset that needs to contain a much higher number of image samples. In traditional methods, we design an algorithm that bases on a manually extracted pattern. In the case of machine learning, in general, we create samples with labelled defects. In the real use case it is problematic to physically create imperfections in the fabric. Some solution is to use synthetic defects that could be used with the fabric without defects [6].

In the paper we use a novel deep learning model acting as a one-class classifier. A one-class classifier [1,12] is a machine learning algorithm that learns to recognize and classify instances of a single class. In other words, it is a type of unsupervised learning algorithm that aims to learn a decision boundary that separates instances of the target class from all other instances. One-class classifiers are commonly used in anomaly detection, where the goal is to identify instances that deviate from normal behaviour. They are also used in novelty detection, where the goal is to identify instances that are significantly different from the training data. We train our model to recognize flawless material and all possible imperfections.

Our model is a sort of a fully convolutional networks [8] (FCN). FCNs are deep learning architectures designed for image segmentation tasks. Unlike traditional convolutional neural networks (CNNs) that are used for image classification, FCNs can handle images of arbitrary size and produce dense pixel-wise predictions. FCNs achieve this by replacing the fully connected layers at the end of a typical CNN with convolutional layers, which can preserve the spatial information of the input image. Additionally, they incorporate upsampling layers to increase the resolution of the output prediction maps to match the size of the input image. One of the most popular FCN architectures is the U-Net [11], which consists of an encoder-decoder structure with skip connections that connect the corresponding layers of the encoder and decoder. The skip connections help to combine high-resolution information from the encoder with low-resolution information from the decoder, improving the quality of the segmentation results. FCNs have been applied successfully in various image segmentation tasks, including biomedical image analysis, scene parsing, and object segmentation.

The remainder of the paper is organised as follows. In Sect. 2 we describe the problem of detecting material imperfection in images. The proposed system is described in Sect. 3 and Sect. 4. Section 5 concludes the paper.

2   Problem Description

The method described in the paper is applicable to any imperfection detection, yet in this section we describe some problems related to our example application. The method of visual inspection of knitted fabrics using artificial neural networks is characterized by several problems that should be taken into account. Knitted fabrics have a fairly uniform texture where defects are poorly visible; for this reason, a human during the inspection must also use visual augmentations through, e.g., appropriate lighting. For this reason, many of the typical camera imaging system imperfections have a very significant effect on the visual quality system.

2.1   Camera Sharpness Range

The first problem is the width of the fabric, which can be up to 2.5 m. This wide area cannot be covered by a single camera due to the viewing angles and the resolution of the sensor. Thus, many cameras can be used in a line to capture enough details of the fabric to detect even minor defects. For practical reasons, the cameras should be placed as close as possible to the surface, which allows the use of lenses with smaller focal lengths, which leads to image deformation. The next problem with this is the range of the sharp image, called the depth of field (DOF). The system searches for defects in the entire fabric area, so the entire image area is important. The fabric is scrolled on a flat surface; however, the focus plane of the camera is often spherical depending on the lens and the focal length. Because of this, the image is not sharp over the entire surface. This is a problem that had a significant impact on the model training and the prediction process.

2.2   Fabric Back-Lighting

The next problem to consider is the backlighting of the knitted fabric (Fig. 1). This aspect is closely related to the cameras. Knitted fabrics are relatively thick material; in our case, the knitted fabrics were 3 to 10 millimetres thick. This is related to the amount of light that the fabric transmits and is different for different basis weight of materials. The woven pattern creates a spatial structure and changing the camera angle has some impact on the image pattern. In a single video frame, we have a different angle in the centre and a different angle on the borders of the image.

Fig. 1. A test bench using a camera and monitor as a knitted backlight.

2.3 Dataset Problem

Another problem, as we already mentioned, is datasets. The usual approach would be to create a diverse set of defects. However, in the case of knitted defects, this is quite troublesome due to the large variety of combinations of defects that we may encounter. They arise in the event of a machine failure, soiling, or damage in transport. The only known constant element is the knit pattern. Some defects, such as dirt or damage, can be prepared, however, their type may be random and require the destruction of the fabric. The preparation of other types of defects is quite troublesome and requires interference in the production process.

2.4 Defects Type

Defects, in our case, can be divided into several groups (Fig. 2). First one is small local defects such as stains, fabric pull, and fabric tear. These may be defects resulting from the machine's malfunction, but also usually from soiling or destruction of the fabric during transport. Second one is horizontal or vertical defects extending over the entire width of the fabric, such as lack of weft, damage to the needle, or wrong yarn. These errors usually arise as a result of worker errors or machine damage. And at last, the group that we also consider and that is related to the fabric pattern deformation during the production process, e.g. shifting the pattern.

2.5 Method Performance

The assumption is that the system is to operate in real-time mode, i.e. while rewinding the knitted fabric. The scrolling time will be limited by the prediction speed of the model as well as the image acquisition time. The speed of image acquisition is significantly influenced by the light intensity and the exposure of the camera. Scrolling too fast will result in video blurring and loss of detail. As

Fig. 2. Examples of defects. The first column shows an eyelet and dirt, the second column, vertical defects of a damaged needle, the third column horizontal defect of missing thread and wrong yarn, and the last column, pattern mismatch defect, respectively.

we use a deep learning model, the most important factor regarding the prediction speed is the size of the model, i.e., the number of parameters, and the number of model layers. For this reason, the use of general-purpose models that usually have more than several hundred thousand parameters and more can slow down the process significantly. The image will be captured from several cameras, so the model will have to process several video frames in a single batch.

2.6   Knitted Fabric Samples

As mentioned earlier, our research has a more practical purpose of developing our knitwear defect detection system, and it is a part of the cooperation with a knitwear producer. Of course, the proposed method is directly applicable to other types of materials. We desired to use real samples of fabric provided by the manufacturer for which the system is created. This was four mattress knitwear with different thicknesses and different patterns (Fig. 3). Some of the knitted fabrics required tensioning due to their deformation. This is not a problem because the inspection and rewinding machine provides a knitted tension.

3   Method Description

In the presented method, we aim at recognizing any defects of knitted fabric, but for practical reasons, we do not need an exact annotation, such as a mask, bounding box or a precise outline of the defect as in the literature. Thus, we decided to mark only areas with defects, which reduces the computational complexity of the model. Besides, a human ultimately decides how to solve the problem of the found defect, so location accuracy is not particularly important (Fig. 4).

Fig. 3. Fabric samples provided from a knitwear producer.

Fig. 4. Samples of video frames for each fabric captured from the camera with backlight. Each fabric is equally bright; the differences in brightness are due to different basis weight of the knitted fabrics.

Moreover, because we wanted also to validate the pattern of the fabric and not only to detect defects, we decided to create separately trained models for each type of fabric. The model is the same, but we load different files with trained parameter definitions for each fabric type. We assume that model training and dataset preparation will be made on the same inspection machine, so the model will learn also the specific configuration of cameras, and backlighting like a device calibration. Therefore, before inspecting each new type of fabric on the inspection machine, we need to train a new model. The training process will be conducted on the inspection machine.

We used the PyTorch framework in Python to implement the model and the training process, which alleviates to modify the training scripts. A properly trained model is exported to a PyTorch JIT (Just-In-Time) script that can be later imported into a more efficient inspection application in C++ language. JIT is a tool in the PyTorch library that allows users to dynamically compile and optimize PyTorch code at runtime. Such code can be executed more efficiently by the CPU or GPU. This can further result in significant performance improvements, especially for deep learning models that involve complex computations on large datasets.

3.1 Fully Convolutional Network

We decide to use a fully convolutional model because of a few reasons. First, we use a different shape of the image in training and inspection modes. During the inspection, we use entire raw frames of video, but during the training mode, we use cropped frames to avoid black borders of rotated images after augmentation.

Second, we can change camera models with higher resolution or divide frames in the case of using multiple areas of different backlight, and then we do not need to make any changes to the model. We empirically checked many models. In the case of our fabric samples, the best results of defect detection were obtained by the model presented in Fig. 5, where parameters f1 and f2 are equal to 32. This model has about 50 thousand trainable parameters, and we can train the model it in less than two hours witch using NVIDIA RTX2080 GPU. The model has four max pooling layers what, in result, divide the image into predicable areas (Fig. 7) so we do not use any upsampling layers that increase the size of the model. We made an important modification to the general model. We bypassed the output from the second max pooling layer to the last layer to improve the detection of tiny defects. The rationale behind this idea is transferring higher frequencies to the last layers not letting the details to be lost during downsampling.

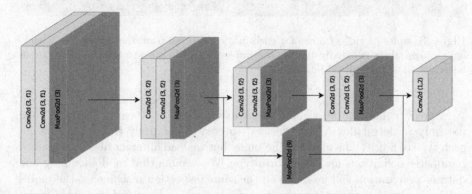

Fig. 5. Scheme of the model that obtained the best tradeoff between the prediction results to the number of parameters. Parameters f1 and f2 are modifiable but the default is 32 which determines the number of convolutional filters.

3.2   Learning

In our approach, during the training process, we only need a dataset of correct fabric video frames. We also do not use any specific synthetic defects applied to the image. We use two types of random noise; the first is standard noise for image augmentation, and the second is the noise for defects simulation. Defects noise is scaled to the size of irregular spots, horizontal and vertical lines (Fig. 6). By default, the width of scaled defects is in the range between 3 to 15 pixels and can be changed. This random noise can be quickly generated and added to input data on GPU during training. On the output of the model, we have a tensor of classified blocks of the frame to two classes correct fabric (blue blocks) and defects (green blocks). Because defects blocks occur much less frequently we apply a weight to classes into the cross-entropy loss function. We apply 0.2 weight for the correct fabric class and 0.8 for the defect class.

Fig. 6. An example of synthetic defects generated from resized noise and original images.

4   Results

Each model was trained for 200 epochs of 50 image frames per batch. Models for each trained fabric, detect all the defects of any type such as stains (Fig. 8), tears (Fig. 7), damaged needles (Fig. 9), and missing threads (Fig. 10) that were made by a knitwear manufacturer. The model can also detect other unpredictable elements such as leftovers of a metal wire or a piece of paper (Fig. 12). The method obtains the worst results in the case of defects of mistaken yarn where the weave of the fabric is not broken but is hardly visible. In this case, only a few pixels are properly marked (Fig. 11). Moreover, we have some errors in false positive defect detection. This type of detection could be a resulting form of small datasets for fabric that tend to deform. Such applications are hard to be quantitatively evaluated as the defects are highly subjective.

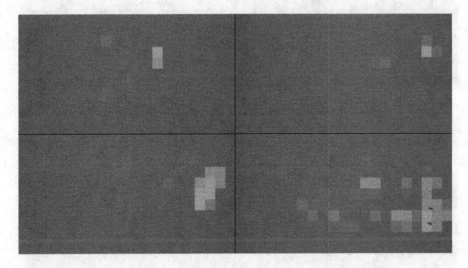

Fig. 7. Prediction examples of tears defects. The red block is manually marked areas as defects, blue is predicted valid area, green is predicted defect areas, and yellow is the intersection between marked defects and predicted defects. (Color figure online)

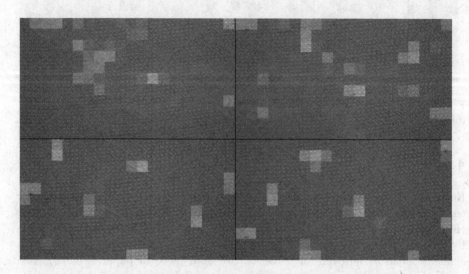

Fig. 8. Prediction examples of stains defects.

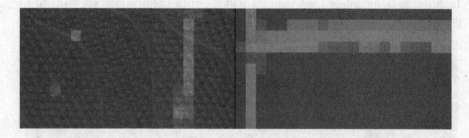

Fig. 9. Prediction examples of damaged needle defects.

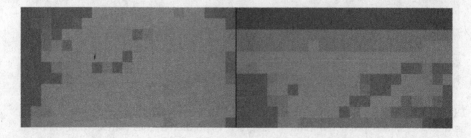

Fig. 10. Prediction examples of missing thread defects.

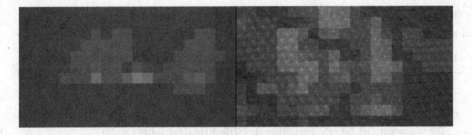

Fig. 11. Prediction examples of damaged needle defects.

Fig. 12. Prediction examples of unpredicted defects like wire fragments or paper fragments.

5 Conclusions

In the article, we present a conception of an inspection system with multiple fast and compact models trained for each type of fabric. This conception can reduce the size of models and reduce uncorrected prediction, because some defects from one fabric may look like the correct pattern of another fabric. The smaller model means that it can be trained quickly on the inspection rig, by a machine technician.

Separate models offer the possibility of adding some modification to the camera or light configuration and testing it for a single fabric type. In this conception to prepare the system for a new material type, we need a fragment without defects of the knit (any defects will be learned as part of the correct pattern) and a small sample with some defects to validate the model. This approach, using various types of random noise as a defect generator, can significantly reduce the amount of work involved in preparing physical samples of knitted fabrics for training purposes.

References

1. Bishop, C.M.: Pattern Recognition and Machine Learning. Springer, Cham (2006)
2. Bissi, L., Baruffa, G., Placidi, P., Ricci, E., Scorzoni, A., Valigi, P.: Automated defect detection in uniform and structured fabrics using Gabor filters and PCA. J. Vis. Commun. Image Represent. **24**(7), 838–845 (2013)

3. Bu, H.G., Wang, J., Huang, X.B.: Fabric defect detection based on multiple fractal features and support vector data description. Eng. Appl. Artif. Intell. **22**(2), 224–235 (2009)

4. Das, S., Wahi, A., Sundaramurthy, S., Thulasiram, N., Keerthika, S.: Classification of knitted fabric defect detection using artificial neural networks. In: 2019 International Conference on Advances in Computing and Communication Engineering (ICACCE), pp. 1–5. IEEE (2019)

5. Guosheng, X., Yang, X., Zhiqi, Y., Yize, S.: An intelligent defect detection system for warp-knitted fabric. Text. Res. J. **92**(9–10), 1394–1404 (2022)

6. Han, Y.J., Yu, H.J.: Fabric defect detection system using stacked convolutional denoising auto-encoders trained with synthetic defect data. Appl. Sci. **10**(7), 2511 (2020)

7. Jia, L., Liang, J.: Fabric defect inspection based on isotropic lattice segmentation. J. Franklin Inst. **354**(13), 5694–5738 (2017)

8. Long, J., Shelhamer, E., Darrell, T.: Fully convolutional networks for semantic segmentation. In: Proceedings of the IEEE Conference on Computer Vision and Pattern recognition, pp. 3431–3440 (2015)

9. Ngan, H.Y., Pang, G.K., Yung, N.H.: Ellipsoidal decision regions for motif-based patterned fabric defect detection. Pattern Recogn. **43**(6), 2132–2144 (2010)

10. Ngan, H.Y., Pang, G.K., Yung, S.P., Ng, M.K.: Wavelet based methods on patterned fabric defect detection. Pattern Recogn. **38**(4), 559–576 (2005)

11. Ronneberger, O., Fischer, P., Brox, T.: U-Net: convolutional networks for biomedical image segmentation. In: Navab, N., Hornegger, J., Wells, W.M., Frangi, A.F. (eds.) MICCAI 2015. LNCS, vol. 9351, pp. 234–241. Springer, Cham (2015). https://doi.org/10.1007/978-3-319-24574-4_28

12. Ruff, L., et al.: Deep one-class classification. In: International Conference on Machine Learning, pp. 4393–4402. PMLR (2018)

13. Simonyan, K., Zisserman, A.: Very deep convolutional networks for large-scale image recognition. In: International Conference on Learning Representations (2015)

Vision-Based Mobile Robots Control
Along a Given Trajectory

Jan Rodziewicz-Bielewicz[✉][iD] and Marcin Korzeń[iD]

West Pomeranian University of Technology in Szczecin,
ul. Żołnierska 49, 71-210 Szczecin, Poland
{jrodziewicz,mkorzen}@wi.zut.edu.pl
http://www.wi.zut.edu.pl

Abstract. The paper presents the application of a computer vision approach to tracking the mobile robot's state. As an exemplary environment,
we use a feedback control system for the trajectory planning and control.
The system in the feedback loop use images taken from a centrally placed
camera and, based on this, calculates the robots states, i.e. position and
angle of rotation. The solution is adopted for indoor experiments. The
experimental part shows the application of trajectory planning for multiple robots to cover a given area. The robot state is calculated using
the YOLO model. We show that current machine learning techniques
are fast and accurate for such applications and do not require image
preprocessing or camera calibration.

Keywords: Mobile robotics · Computer vision · Vision-based control ·
Visual servoing · iRobot · YOLO · Trajectory planing

1 Introduction and Motivation

The vision-based robot control or visual servoing [2] is a type of feedback control
that uses visual information in the feedback loop to control a mobile robot. Such
an approach is less popular than robot-placed sensors as feedback, but it also
has many possible applications.

In a vision-based control, we register the operational area by the fixed camera, and next, we measure the system's state using computer vision techniques
for captured images. From the machine learning point of view, it is the task
of detecting the robot's position and orientation. In the paper, we use robot
detection by marking them with characteristic symbols and trying to detect the
robot and its marker. This approach is far from being new, a similar approach
can be found e.g. in [3,9]. In some solutions of vision-based robot controlling
necessary is camera calibration [13]. However, it is more convenient to control a
robot without any information about camera parameters [10,19].

In recent years, Convolutional Neural Networks have had a significant impact
on the development of computer vision. This resulted in the development of
object detectors, based on deep learning – like Single Shot MultiBox Detector

L. Rutkowski et al. (Eds.): ICAISC 2023, LNAI 14126, pp. 69–77, 2023.
https://doi.org/10.1007/978-3-031-42508-0_7

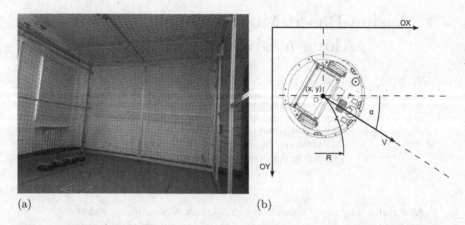

(a)   (b)

Fig. 1. (a) The view of research laboratory. (b) The robot's state (x, y, α) and control signals: V, R

[11] or R-CNN [5]. Another popular deep learning model, fast and accurate for real-time object detection, is YOLO [17] and is still under-developed by different groups. We use the Ultralytics version of YOLO, named YOLOv5, which is wider described in [7]. Machine vision methods are widely used in robotics. For example in [12,20] authors used the YOLO model for moving target detection.

In the paper, we present the application YOLOv5 algorithm to track the mobile robot state (position and orientation) using the global fixed camera without knowledge about camera parameters and any preprocessing of images. We use the measurement (output of detector) to feedback control system for the robot trajectory planning and control.

The next part of the paper is organized as follows: first, we provide technical details about the experimental environment; next, we describe the visual feedback loop with the machine learning part and next, the control and planning trajectory part; finally, we describe the experimental results.

2   Experimental Environment

Operating Area and Robot Communication. The view of the research laboratory is presented in Fig. 1a. The operational area is a rectangle of 5m × 4m.

The controlled objects are four mobile robots, iRobot 650. Robots have two driven wheels that we can control in three ways: (1) an independent PWM control signal for two motors, (2) independent controlling velocity for each wheel, (3) control a given velocity and radius of turn. Controlling robots is possible using commands complies with iRobot® Create® 2 Open Interface (OI) [6]. We have used the third possibility: steering with velocity and radius (see Fig. 1b).

Our goal is a remote control, but this iRobot robot cannot communicate wirelessly. Thus we connected iRobot with a board based on the ESP8266 module, which we use as the communication hub. The board receives commands from the controller and forwards them to iRobot using Roomba's External Serial Port Mini-DIN. The commands from the controller are sent using WiFI via the MQTT Server implemented using the Paho MQTT Python library. The board receives commands with the usage of packages PubSubClient [14] and ESP8266WiFi [4].

Vision-Based Feedback. We present the control loop scheme in Fig. 2. The main part of the feedback loop is the camera that observes the whole operational area (Fig. 1a). We use a wide-angle camera that poses in-built a fisheye effect correction. The images are recorded using OpenCV [1] library, in a resolution of 1280×720 pixels with a frame rate of 30 FPS.

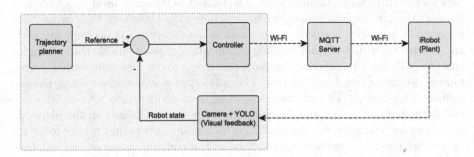

Fig. 2. A block diagram of the control system.

The captured RGB image is the input to YOLO - a popular real-time object detection deep learning model. Currently, YOLO is not one model but a group of models with a similar structure and way of prediction. In our experiments, we use Ultralytics implementation [8]. We did not use any preprocessing steps. For learning purposes, we collected the data from cameras placed in different places. Cameras observed the robots' operating space at various angles. In the experimental part, we used a centrally placed camera.

In our experiments, robots were marked by: cross (robot 1), circle (robot 2), triangle (robot 3), and star (robot 4) (Fig. 3). The model's goal was detection

Fig. 3. Four robots used in experiments marked by: cross (robot 1), circle (robot 2), triangle (robot 3), stat (robot 4). One can see ESP8266 module with power bank, and serial connection to the robot.

four robots and four symbols. This results in eight classes for detection. Bounding boxes of the robot and symbol are used to estimate the robot's central position (x, y) and angle of rotation *alpha* (Fig. 1). In case of a model mistake during control (e.g. no detection of some robots in a given image of more than one detection per class on one image), we ignored incorrect results and used previously stored prediction. In such a case robot hold on to the control signal from the previous step.

We performed the machine learning part in Python environment with libraries: NumPy, SciPy, Pandas, PyTorch [15].

Planning and Path-Following Control. We tested the quality of visual feedback in the trajectory planning task. The iRobot is typically used as a vacuum cleaner. Thus in the experiment, we have planned the trajectory that covers the rectangular area with a given covering radius. To generate a trajectory, we used an iterative algorithm of simultaneous densification of points inside the rectangle and the path until to produce the path covering a given rectangle with a given radius, details can be found in [16]. The trajectory was smoothed using Bézier splines (with SciPy). The planned trajectory was divided into four equal subpaths, the part for each robot. In each time step, moving points on the planned trajectory are the reference points for corresponding robots and robots follows-up on the moving reference points. Solving the control equation was not the paper's aim, and for control purposes, we used simple heuristic rules and the advantages of feedback control. More mathematical details can be found e.g. in [18]. Let's note the difference between the reference and the robot stare as e:

$$e(t) = \begin{bmatrix} e_x \\ e_y \\ e_\alpha \end{bmatrix} = \begin{bmatrix} x_{ref}(t) - x(t) \\ y_{ref}(t) - y(t) \\ \text{mod}_{2\pi}\left(\alpha_{ref}(t) - \alpha(t)\right) \end{bmatrix} \tag{1}$$

where $\text{mod}_{2\pi}$ is a symmetrical modulo function with values in the interval $(-\pi, \pi]$, $\alpha_{ref}(t)$ ia an angle between the vector $[x_{ref}(t) - x(t), y_{ref}(t) - y(t)]$ and the X axis. A controller produces the control signal using the following heuristic rules for the velocity V and radius R:

$$V = \min(k_1\sqrt{e_x{}^2 + e_y{}^2}, 300) \quad [\text{mm/sec}] \tag{2}$$

$$R = \text{sign}(e_\alpha) * \frac{2000}{k_2|e_\alpha|^{k_3} + 1} \quad [\text{mm}] \tag{3}$$

A positive radius means that robot turn to the left, and a negative value turns the robot to the right, k_1, k_2, and k_3 are some coefficients that were fitted experimentally. Acceptable maximal values for controll signals are: ± 500 [mm/sec] V, and ± 2000 [mm] and for R.

3   Experiments

We trained and compared four YOLO models with various neural network sizes: YOLOv5n6, YOLOv5s6, YOLOv5m6, YOLOv5l6. The learning dataset consists of

Table 1. Comparison of YOLO models.

Model	Precision	Recall	Percentage of fully correctly recognized images	Prediction time per image
YOLOv5n6	0.980	0.936	0.684	17.69 ms
YOLOv5s6	0.938	0.946	0.599	15.53 ms
YOLOv5m6	0.977	0.951	0.773	28.03 ms
YOLOv5l6	0.985	0.966	0.815	42.22 ms

about 100 000 with an input image of 1280×720 pixels, taken from different views and cameras. We labelled manually only a small part of the data (about 1,5 %). Most of the data was labelled using a pre-trained YOLO model with a small amount of hand-made corrections. On the validation subset, such a model worked perfectly with an accuracy of about 100%. During experiments, we used a server with Nvidia A100 40 GB GPU for learning, and for prediction, we used a local machine with Intel i7-10700 CPU and Nvidia GeForce RTX 3090 24 GB GPU. The learning procedure was set on 100 iterations with the SGD algorithm, and the batch size was automatically fitted to the model size (about 17–89 samples).

Table 2. Detailed model quality on testing set of used model YOLOv5n6.

Class	Precision	Recall	mAP@.5	mAP@.5:.95
cross	0.997	0.991	0.995	0.854
cross_center	0.901	1	0.99	0.936
circle	0.991	0.851	0.883	0.755
circle_center	0.957	0.931	0.983	0.904
triangle	0.992	0.88	0.912	0.762
triangle_center	0.99	0.897	0.973	0.861
star	0.996	1	0.995	0.87
star_center	0.957	1	0.995	0.956
all	**0.973**	**0.944**	**0.966**	**0.862**

We tested YOLO models on an independent testing dataset containing 1000 images with challenging lighting conditions. The results are presented in Table 1. As we can see, even in such challenging conditions, the procedure worked quite well. Some of false detections we present in Fig. 4. Based on this results, we decided to use the smallest and fastest model i.e. YOLO5n6. Detailed results per classes for the selected model we present in Table 2. We stress that in typical conditions, the model behaves much better.

Fig. 4. Examples of incorrect detections for YOLO model: on the left, a doubled detection of the fourth robot (star symbol), on the center the false positive - cable loop is marked as a triangle symbol and on the right, the false negative – a missing triangle.

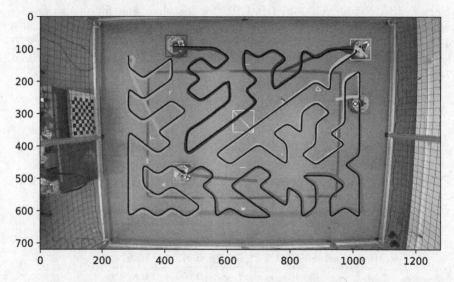

Fig. 5. The planned (black line) trajectory and actual (colored lines) trajectories obtained by robots. Robots are placed in the final position.

Planning and Control. The selected model we used in a feedback loop to steer robots along the test trajectory. Figure 5 presents the reference trajectory and result trajectories for each robot. A detailed comparison of planned and realized trajectories is shown in Fig. 6. During this experiment, YOLO did not perform any false detection. covering algorithm. In Fig. 7b, we give, for comparison, the covering by the in-build algorithm in iRobot. The experiment time for our algorithm was about 60 s, and the time for the default method the time was set as 100 s.

The processing time was about 29.8 msec per iteration - similar to the set speed of the camera (30FPS). The delay in following the trajectory was about 0.5 sec. The accuracy was 10.7 pixels per X axis and 9.5 pixels per Y axis, much less than the diameter of the robot on the screen (about 60 pixels).

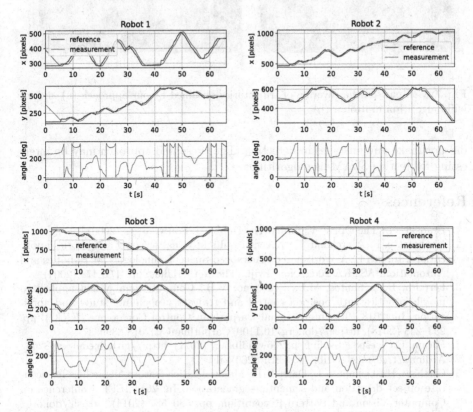

Fig. 6. System state (positions x, y and angle of rotation) for all robots during the experiment, reference: black line, measurement: red line. (Color figure online)

4 Summary

The experiments show that the presented computer vision approach is sufficiently fast and accurate. In experiments, we have used a wide-angle central placed camera that poses in-build fisheye effect correction, but the YOLO model behaves very robustly for images without correction. The model was also robust on the angle of view of the camera. Still, in those cases, correction between the robot's position in the image and the position in physical space is more important.

In our approach, we used pure output from the YOLO model. Smoothing measurements by the Kalman filter may increase tracking accuracy, but as experiments have shown, it was not required. In our test trajectory, YOLO detector

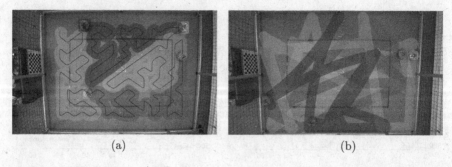

(a)   (b)

Fig. 7. Comparison the covering of trajectories obtained by our approach (a) and in-build algorithm in iRobot (b)

did not make any mistakes in detection. The presented approach may be interesting for testing SLAM-like algorithms.

References

1. Bradski, G.: The OpenCV library. Dr. Dobb's J. Softw. Tools (2000)
2. Chaumette, F., Marchand, E.: Recent results in visual servoing for robotics applications. In: 8th ESA Workshop on Advanced Space Technologies for Robotics and Automation, ASTRA 2004, Noordwijk, The Netherlands, pp. 471–478 (2004)
3. Ferreira, F.C., Santos, M.F., Schettino, V.B.: Computational vision applied to mobile robotics with position control and trajectory planning: study and application. In: 2018 19th International Carpathian Control Conference (ICCC), pp. 253–258 (2018). https://doi.org/10.1109/CarpathianCC.2018.8399637
4. Forum, E.C.: esp8266wifi: Esp8266wifi library (2021). http://github.com/esp8266/Arduino/tree/master/libraries/ESP8266WiFi
5. Girshick, R., Donahue, J., Darrell, T., Malik, J.: Rich feature hierarchies for accurate object detection and semantic segmentation. In: 2014 IEEE Conference on Computer Vision and Pattern Recognition, pp. 580–587 (2014). https://doi.org/10.1109/CVPR.2014.81
6. iRobot Corp: iRobot® Create® 2 Open Interface (OI) Specification based on the iRobot® Roomba® 600. Technical report, iRobot Corp (2018). www.edu.irobot.com/learning-library/create-2-oi-spec
7. Jia, W., et al.: Real-time automatic helmet detection of motorcyclists in urban traffic using improved yolov5 detector. IET Image Processing **15**(14), 3623–3637 (2021). https://doi.org/10.1049/ipr2.12295, www.ietresearch.onlinelibrary.wiley.com/doi/abs/10.1049/ipr2.12295
8. Jocher, G.: ultralytics/yolov5 (2022). http://github.com/ultralytics/yolov5. Accessed 9 Aug 2022
9. Liang, X., Wang, H., Chen, W., Guo, D., Liu, T.: Adaptive image-based trajectory tracking control of wheeled mobile robots with an uncalibrated fixed camera. IEEE Trans. Control Syst. Technol. **23**(6), 2266–2282 (2015). https://doi.org/10.1109/TCST.2015.2411627
10. Liang, X., Wang, H., Liu, Y.H., Chen, W., Jing, Z.: Image-based position control of mobile robots with a completely unknown fixed camera. IEEE Trans. Autom. Control **63**(9), 3016–3023 (2018). https://doi.org/10.1109/TAC.2018.2793458

11. Liu, W., et al.: SSD: single shot MultiBox detector. In: Leibe, B., Matas, J., Sebe, N., Welling, M. (eds.) ECCV 2016. LNCS, vol. 9905, pp. 21–37. Springer, Cham (2016). https://doi.org/10.1007/978-3-319-46448-0_2

12. Ma, Y., Zhu, W., Zhou, Y.: Automatic grasping control of mobile robot based on monocular vision. Int. J. Adv. Manufact, Technol. **121**(3), 1785–1798 (2022). https://doi.org/10.1007/s00170-022-09438-z

13. Nurlaili, R., Sulistijono, I.A., Risnumawan, A.: Mobile robot position control using computer vision. In: 2019 International Electronics Symposium (IES), pp. 382–386 (2019). https://doi.org/10.1109/ELECSYM.2019.8901619

14. O'Leary, N.: PubSubClient: this library provides a client for doing simple publish/subscribe messaging with a server that supports MQTT (2020). http://github.com/knolleary/pubsubclient

15. Paszke, A., et al.: PyTorch: an imperative style, high-performance deep learning library. In: Wallach, H., Larochelle, H., Beygelzimer, A., d' Alché-Buc, F., Fox, E., Garnett, R. (eds.) Advances in Neural Information Processing Systems, vol. 32, pp. 8024–8035. Curran Associates, Inc. (2019). https://www.papers.neurips.cc/paper/9015-pytorch-an-imperative-style-high-performance-deep-learning-library.pdf

16. Pluciński, M., Korzeń, M.: Application of the Peano curve for the robot trajectory generating. In: Pejaś, J., Saeed, K. (eds.) Advances in Information Processing and Protection, pp. 25–34. Springer, US, Boston, MA (2007). https://doi.org/10.1007/978-0-387-73137-7_3

17. Redmon, J., Divvala, S.K., Girshick, R.B., Farhadi, A.: You only look once: unified, real-time object detection. In: 2016 IEEE Conference on Computer Vision and Pattern Recognition (CVPR), pp. 779–788 (2015)

18. Sarjoughian, H.S., et al.: Model-based development of multi-iRobot simulation and control (2013)

19. Wang, H., Liu, Y.H., Chen, W.: Uncalibrated visual tracking control without visual velocity. IEEE Trans. Control Syst. Technol. **18**(6), 1359–1370 (2010). https://doi.org/10.1109/TCST.2010.2041457

20. Zhong, J., Sun, W., Cai, Q., Zhang, Z., Dong, Z., Gao, M.: Deep learning based strategy for eye-to-hand robotic tracking and grabbing. In: Yang, H., Pasupa, K., Leung, A.C.S., Kwok, J.T., Chan, J.H., King, I. (eds.) Neural Information Processing. Lecture Notes in Computer Science(), pp. 787–798. Springer International Publishing, Cham (2020). https://doi.org/10.1007/978-3-030-63833-7_66

Text Guided Facial Image Synthesis Using StyleGAN and Variational Autoencoder Trained CLIP

Anagha Srinivasa[✉], Anjali Praveen, Anusha Mavathur, Apurva Pothumarthi, Arti Arya, and Pooja Agarwal

PES University, Bangalore 560100, Karnataka, India
anagha190601@gmail.com, anjalipraveen2110@gmail.com,
anushamavathur@gmail.com, apurva.pothumarthi@gmail.com,
{artiarya,poojaagarwal}@pes.edu
http://www.pes.edu

Abstract. The average user may have little to no artistic skills but can describe what they envision in words. The user-provided text can be instantly transformed into a realistic image with the aid of generative neural architectures. This study intends to propose a novel approach to generate a facial image based on a user-given textual description. Prior works focus less on the manipulation aspects, hence the approach also emphasizes on manipulating and modifying the image generated, based on additional textual descriptions as required to further refine the expected face. It consists of a multi-level Vector-Quantized Variational Auto Encoder (VQVAE) that provides the image encodings, the Contrastive Language-Image Pre-Training (CLIP) module to interpret the texts and compute how close the final image encodings and the text are with each other within a common space, and a StyleGAN2 to decode and generate the required image output. The combination of such components within the architecture is unseen in previous studies and yields promising results, capturing the context of the text and generating realistic good quality images of human faces.

Keywords: Facial synthesis · Image manipulation · Vector Quantized Variational Autoencoders (VQVAE) · Contrastive Language Image Pre-training (CLIP) · StyleGAN2

1 Introduction

Synthetic image generation is one of the most significant applications of machine learning that has evolved over time. The use of different generative adversarial networks (GANs), diffusion models and several other neural architectures has made this task possible. Applications in this field include not just creating visuals that have never existed but also creating incredibly realistic images that exactly match a given written description.

L. Rutkowski et al. (Eds.): ICAISC 2023, LNAI 14126, pp. 78–90, 2023.
https://doi.org/10.1007/978-3-031-42508-0_8

Artists who work in the criminal department are specialized in creating portraits of people's faces. But this can frequently be accompanied by bias. It is beneficial to utilize an automated approach that synthesizes realistic faces as opposed to merely a human-made illustration. The proposed approach helps in generating the face of a missing person or a criminal, according to the text-based description provided, by any witness or victim. Additionally, the various images that are generated by using the architecture, accumulates data to be a source for future research or work, where the images are annotated along with their respective textual descriptions that match.

The suggested work attempts to address the identified research gaps with a novel architecture consisting of a Vector Quantized Variational Autoencoder (VQVAE) [1], a Contrastive Language Image Pre-training (CLIP) [2] module and a StyleGAN [3]. The autoregressive VQVAE helps in learning a low level representation of the image data as discrete latent vectors. The latent space is discretized instead of being continuous as opposed to vanilla autoencoders. A three level VQVAE is applied for the purpose of acquiring the best reconstructions of the images. The StyleGAN is known for its hyper-realistic generation of images and hence acts as the decoder of the model to get the desired results. Consequently, a functional generative model architecture is developed leveraging the combined capabilities of these components.

The remaining portion of the work is articulated and structured as follows: The preceding research in this field is discussed and highlighted in Sect. 2. The multimodal CelebA-HQ dataset is used for training our model which is described in Sect. 3. The remaining sections discuss the methodology in reference to the high level design flow, and contain the results of the study. The research is summarized and the future scope of the work is discussed in the concluding section.

2 Related Work

Text-to-image generation has taken shape since the mid 2010s s as an effect of the advancement in neural networks. The language and generative models are combined to achieve the same. A variety of adversarial networks that are generative in nature have been proposed in earlier works which have been able to produce photo-realistic images and also reach the quality of human-illustrated art.

For text encoding purposes, prior attempts employed skip-thought vectors, however Siamese-BERT (SBERT) proved to produce high-quality semantic vectors [11]. Their approach begins with the creation of a dataset of facial images and textual descriptions using SBERT and a custom algorithm for producing N captions for each image. A comparative study of DCGAN, DFGAN and SAGAN is done based on these captions. The discriminator assesses if a particular image-text combination corresponds in addition to verifying the validity of created images.

A fully trained GAN [13] generates realistic and natural images by training the text encoder as well as the image decoder simultaneously for accurate results utilizing a conditional GAN-based architecture comprising of one generator and two discriminators. The unique aspect of the study is that it combines locally created images with several publicly accessible data sets to create a face generating data set. However, the user input was restricted to pre-defined tags making it specific to only a certain type of input. Speaking of other variations of GANs, Semantic-Spatial Aware GAN [15] aims at applying batch normalization to the whole image based on the semantics of the text with respect to locality within the image rather than uniform and concurrent training of the text and image encoder.

Some implementations such as the TediGAN [7] and StyleCLIP [8] focus on architectures intended towards generating and manipulating facial images. While both approach the problem differently, the utilization of a StyleGAN within the architectures is justified primarily for its capability of generating photorealistic images at high resolutions [3] and disentangled attributes within the latent representation. The disentanglement of the attributes allows the manipulation of an image's encodings as desired while retaining as much of the other properties as possible, which is crucial to this problem.

Two prior works depict a combination of two models in their architecture: a Conditional Variational Autoencoder(CVAE) and a Generative Adversarial Network(GAN). One such work made use of a feature-preserving dense UNet-based generator architecture called AUDeNet [9]. The attributes are given as input to the CVAE which generates a sketch. This sketch is further enhanced by the GAN where the generator sub-network takes advantage of UNet and DenseNet architectures. The other talks about using these models along with a context-aware technique [14] to reliably convert text-to-images, maintaining the distinction between the foreground and background and producing high-quality images. The CVAE component captures the basic layout and colour composition and the GAN component substantially enhances the CVAE output, recovering lost features and fixing errors for realistic image production.

Another emerging solution over the recent years comes with the advent of diffusion models [16] which train while diffusing the image slowly into noise and reconstructing the original image from the same. The interest lies upon its training stability and avoidance of vanishing gradients that are prominent in traditional GANs. Despite the potential to surpass GANs in terms of usage, it faces time and computation bottlenecks which is unlike the latest GANs that are based on more thorough research.

The famous DALL-E [10] by Ramesh, Aditya, et al. proposes a two-stage design which consists of training a VQVAE [4] and subsequently, their autoregressive transformer that predicts tokens one after the other. On the MS-COCO images in particular, the zero-shot method generates reasonably good-quality images, negating the requirement for labels during training. However it is computationally expensive due to the billion parameters and long training time. The model also struggles to overcome strong priors and spatial relationships are not so easily comprehended. VQGAN [5] is another interesting work which also uses a VQVAE [4], in combination with a cycle GAN that produces relatively sharper images as compared to DALL-E too. It blends the expressive potential of transformers with the effectiveness of convolutional techniques. Since they no longer employ mean squared error and instead use perceptual and adversarial losses, they improve the reconstruction loss compared to that computed in the study of VQVAE. The authors are also successful in conditioning the transformer on different modalities. A simple GAN is used in their approach. The proposed methodology in our work however uses the more recent StyleGAN2 as a decoder to the architecture, which also assists in the manipulation aspect.

VQVAE-2 [1] is an improved version of the original VQVAE, which gives much better reconstructions and imagery by using a hierarchical structure of latents and priors with two levels of codebook vectors that capture the different levels of granularity in the image. They prove to be good encoders for images, as far as discrete vector representations of images are concerned.

CLIP [2] is a multimodal model that connects images to text in a non-generative manner by concurrently training the image and text encoders. It can determine the most suitable text extract for a given image using natural language processing, without directly optimising for the objective. This demonstrates that CLIP has zero shot functionality similar to Generative Pre trained (GPT) transformers. Other state-of-the-art models like DALL-E and VQGAN utilize CLIP as a main bridge between text and images while models like the CLIP-Gen [12] use it to gather the image embeddings of the given text description along with encoding received from a VQGAN codebook.

Inception Score (IS) and Frechet Inception Distance (FID) are the two standard evaluation measures used to assess the image resolution and quality. However, they fail to evaluate the correctness of the text-to-image conversion and hence would not be the appropriate metric of evaluation. Semantic Object Accuracy [6] is one such metric implemented which determines whether the text-to-image conversion is accurate. As the COCO dataset, an object-based dataset, was used to develop this metric, there is a scope of exploring the same on facial datasets.

Some of the gaps identified in the existing works in developing an automated face generation module are as follows: (1) distortions and splotchy patterns are observed in the final image generated; (2) synthesized images occasionally do not meet the text criteria keyed in by the user; and (3) it is challenging to achieve good accuracy in altering some portions of the existing facial image generated while keeping all the other elements intact and maintaining the integrity of the image.

3   Data

Multi-modal CelebA-HQ dataset [7] is used to train the architecture. The 30,000 face images of high resolution and their respective descriptive texts are utilized in this research study. This specific dataset is selected to meet the requirement of having a diversified dataset with as little bias as possible, and to satisfy the criterion of having images labeled with their respective textual descriptions to train on, for the tasks that involve using texts to generate and manipulate the generated facial image. The images in the dataset also have sketches and excellent high quality segmentation masks for the facial images. This allows for a future expansion of the application of this study to generate sketch drawings of faces as well.

4   Proposed Methodology

The two primary phases of the study's proposed architecture are the training and testing phases. Algorithm 1 and 2 indicate a high level understanding of the sequence of the steps that are taken to implement the two phases of our model.

4.1   Training Phase

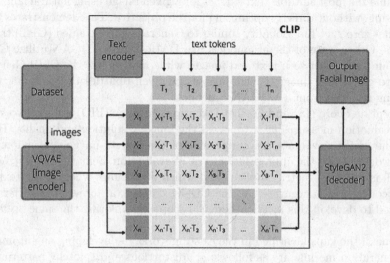

Fig. 1. Training Phase.

Figure 1 is a descriptive representation of the training phase of the architecture design.

VQVAE: The Vector quantized Variational Autoencoder [1] is the image encoder. During training, the images from the image-only CelebA dataset were passed to the three levelled VQVAE. The VQVAE takes in the image and transforms it into a discrete vector representation. This is done as follows: The encoder of the VQVAE encodes the image into latent vectors, which are however continuous. A codebook is used which is mainly responsible for the quantization of these continuous vectors into discrete variables. The codebook has a list of vectors each having a corresponding index. L2 Norm distance is used when comparing the encoded continuous vector outputs with the codebook vectors. The quantized closest vector grid is what finally represents the image. In the case of a single level simple VQVAE, gradient descent is generally used to learn these

---

Algorithm 1. Training Phase

Input: CelebA dataset of 30k images

Output: A trained CLIP to identify text-image similarity, the trained VQVAE being the CLIP's image encoder

1: **Dataset split into train and test sets passed to the VQVAE.**
   torchvision.datasets.ImageFolder used in *getdataset()*

2: **Training of the VQVAE begins.**
   Rloss and Lloss are the reconstruction and latent losses:

3: **for** $i, (tensor,) \in enumerate(tqdm(trnload))$ **do**

4:     $loss, Rloss, Lloss, \leftarrow train(torchTensor)$

5: **end for**

For validation, the above loop remains same except *eval()* is called instead of *train()*, and *tstload* that is obtained from *getdataset()* is used.

6: **Testing of the trained VQVAE**
   $Reconstructions \leftarrow VQVAE(RandomImgSample)$

7: **Latent data generation**
   For every image it is stored in a *.ptfile*

8: **CLIP is trained using the image latent data generated in previous step.**

9: **A config file containing the hyperparameters is defined for training purposes.** Models included like the text encoder and the encoding size are declared and set respectively.

10: **CLIP class comprises of 2 functions:**
   $\_init\_()$: initialises all the attributes of the model like TextEncoder, ImageEncoder, ProjectionHead.
   $forward()$: text is encoded into fixed size vectors of size 768.

11: **Projection of image and text embeddings in the same dimensional space for comparison.**
   ▷ *projection_dim* is set to 256.

12: **The result of the matrix multiplication between batches of text and image embeddings are normalized.**
   $NormalisedProbabilities \leftarrow logSoftmax(logits)$

13: **Loss is calculated based on cross entropy.**
   It based on how close the product is with respect to identity matrix I
   $loss \leftarrow (-targets * normalisedOutput).sum(1)$

---

codebook vectors, similar to the encoder and decoder of the VAE. However in this three leveled VQVAE, the gradient from the previous decoder layer is transmitted directly to the subsequent encoder layer, bypassing the codebook. The codebook is updated by the exponential moving average of the outputs of the encoder.

The trained VQVAE is also made to generate reconstructions and this is done by sampling a random set of images from the test dataset and reconstructing them from their VAE generated codes. The latent data of the train and test sets is generated and stored in a separate directory for further use by the CLIP module. CLIP subsequently loads and inputs the latent codes and combines the same with the text embeddings.

VQVAEs employ discrete latent spaces as opposed to the continuous distribution that standard VAEs operate on. VQVAEs seem to be an excellent option for the encoding of the pictures since they are stable in terms of training and assessment.

CLIP: The CLIP [2] which stands for Contrastive Language Image Pre Training is a model recently proposed by OpenAI to jointly learn and represent images and text. Every single image in the dataset is associated with a text file that contains multiple textual descriptions of the image. A Comma Seperated Value (CSV) file is created with the image number, text description ID and the respective textual description. As mentioned previously, since each text file contains the description of the face phrased in different ways in separate sentences, all those lines are split and added to the CSV file. This file is useful for generating an intermediate dataset which is used to combine the latent data of the VQVAE and the textual description. This model inputs the image encodings created in the previous stage along with the respective description of the image. The text encoder in the CLIP model is DistilBERT [17] from Hugging Face. The DistilBERT tokenizer is used to tokenize the phrases and sentences. The token ids and attention masks are then input into the DistilBERT model. A 768 element vector serves as the output representation. This offers us with a text encoding of the phrase that best matches the provided image.

One of the layered embedding (64X64) of the three levelled VQVAE is chosen and fed to the CLIP in order to combine the same with the corresponding text embedding. Both the image encoding of size 4096 and the text encoding of size 768 is projected onto a vector space of length 256 since they need to be compared for computing the loss. The importance of this loss calculation lies in the fact that the texts and images that match must be pulled closer together while those that do not must be pushed apart. Dot product calculation allows us to measure if two vectors are similar and this is the intuition behind bringing together the image and text embeddings. Since there is also a batch size associated in the loop and groups of vectors (matrices) need to be compared rather than two single vectors, the transpose of one matrix is taken and multiplied with the other. The softmax of the resultant product should ideally be an identity matrix, and loss calculation of the obtained product using simple cross entropy is done with respect to the same.

4.2 Testing Phase

StyleGAN2, a generative adversarial network presented by the NVIDIA researchers uses the transfer learning technique to create realistic images. The model expands upon the group's earlier StyleGAN project. This performs a significant role in our testing phase to generate the image output based on the user's text. Figure 2 is a descriptive representation of the testing phase of our architecture design.

Algorithm 2. Testing Phase

Input: Textual description of a desired facial image
Output: A facial image corresponding to the description

1: **Input is broken into a list of sentences and passed into generate_image.**

2: **Initial latent code is generated with a random vector using StyleGAN's mappers.**
   $rand\_z \leftarrow random(get\_dimensions(StyleGAN2model))$
   $initial\_latent\_code = model.mapping(rand\_z)$

3: **For each pass, Loss of current image and expected image from CLIP is calculated for all sentences.**
   $initial\_latent\_code \leftarrow initial\_latent\_code * (1 - loss) + new\_latent\_code * (loss)$

4: **After iterations the latent code is decoded and returned along with the newly generated image**

5: **To manipulate, new description is taken and broken into a list of sentences.**

6: **The sentence list and previously generated latent code are passed into manipulate_image.**

7: **Steps 3 to 6 repeat as needed.**

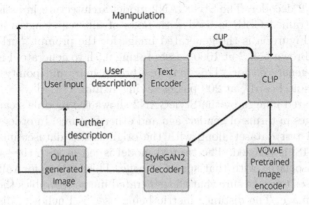

Fig. 2. Testing Phase.

The user contributes by providing a textual description of a desired facial image. A random vector is first generated in the dimensions that the StyleGAN2 was previously trained on. This vector is converted into a latent code using the StyleGAN's mapper module. Based on the number of iterations provided and the number of sentences within the text the latent code goes through multiple passes. In each pass, the similarity between each sentence and their respective closest image is taken from CLIP to calculate the total loss. At the end of the pass this loss is used to update the latent code. After all the iterations the decoder produces the resulting final image. A further written description can be provided if the user wants to make more changes to the image and the image previously generated is used for further modification.

5   Results and Discussion

The VQVAE is trained on the CelebA-HQ images and the number of epochs for which it was run was 12, with a training time of 6 h and 6 min. The trained VQVAE is then applied to a random sample of images from the test set and Fig. 4c shows the reconstructed result. As seen from the results, the VQVAE is three leveled which helps in capturing different levels of granularity of the image and the reconstructions are very close to the original images. The intermediate reconstructions improved with respect to colour and sharpness of the images from the first epoch till the 12th epoch and Fig. 4a and Fig. 4b represent the same. The training loss throughout the 12 epochs that the VQVAE is trained on is shown in Fig. 3 along with the validation loss which is computed over our validation set once the ongoing training epoch completes. The training loss reduces from 0.194 to 0.012 while the reduction in validation loss is from 0.055 to 0.004 which then remains constant, indicating the goodness of the model in generating the reconstruction outputs. The CLIP model is trained for a total of 4 epochs until the training loss, initially at 2.24 substantially reduces to 0.27 and remains constant as shown in Fig. 5. The best model is stored for later use by the StyleGAN2 decoder. The StyleGAN2 model architecture in assistance with our VQVAE trained CLIP is used with texts of different lengths and number of iterations. Figure 6a is the generated image for the prompt "girl with green eyes. She has brown hair." at 1000 passes taking 0.5 h to generate. Figure 6b was subsequently generated for "This man has brown hair, and pointy nose. He is young. He has no beard." at 200 passes taking 10 min.

The generated images by the StyleGAN2 shows the module's capabilities of handling images in terms of gender, age and other features. In order to compare the generated test dataset along with the original test dataset images, Deep-Face library [18] is utilized. The trained model is fed in with the same textual description associated with that specific image. This is done for validation and testing purposes to make sure that the generated image resembles the respective test dataset image. The distance metric being used is Euclidean distance with L2 normalization and the set threshold for this combination is 0.75.

100 images are sampled from the test set and one out of the many descriptions for each image is given as the input to our model to generated a facial image that

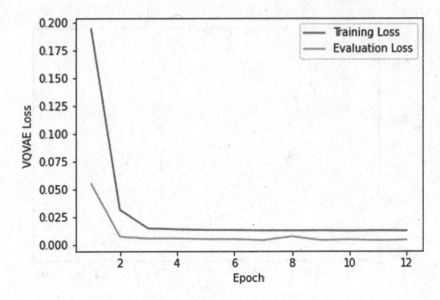

Fig. 3. VQVAE Training and Evaluation Loss

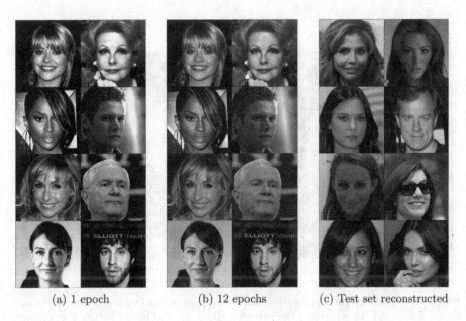

(a) 1 epoch   (b) 12 epochs   (c) Test set reconstructed

Fig. 4. (a) and (b) represent intermediate reconstructions obtained from VQVAE during training and (c) is the reconstruction obtained from the trained model of VQVAE on a random sample of images from the test set.

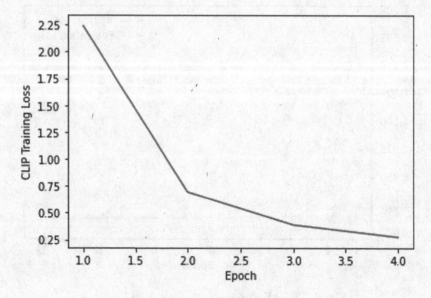

Fig. 5. CLIP Training Loss

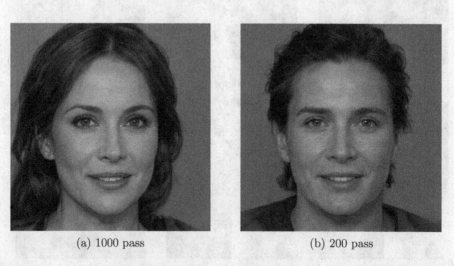

(a) 1000 pass   (b) 200 pass

Fig. 6. (a) represents the generated image for the prompt "girl with green eyes. She has brown hair." and (b) represents the subsequently generated image for the text prompt "This man has brown hair, and pointy nose. He is young. He has no beard." (Color figure online)

Table 1. DeepFace results for the generated images.

DeepFace Results			
Generated Image No.	Comparison Result with Original Image	Distance(L2 Norm)	Threshold
1	True	0.73	0.75
2	True	0.66	0.75
3	True	0.61	0.75
4	True	0.71	0.75
5	True	0.58	0.75
6	True	0.59	0.75
7	False	0.78	0.75

matches the text. Out of 100 images that are generated by the StyleGAN2, 65% are classified True. The results for the first seven images have been summarised in Table 1.

6 Conclusion

The purpose of this research is to bring about a novel approach that can generate realistic portraits of human faces from interpretations of the textual input given by any user. The model may use the text input to produce an image that matches it adequately, but there are times when it may produce an image that does not meet our expectations. The neural architecture proposed in this work, enables further textual command manipulation of the generated image and accomplishes this, without compromising the image's integrity. No other related works have achieved the same, utilizing an architecture consisting of a combination of a multi-level VQVAE, CLIP and a StyleGAN2, to the best of our knowledge.

Future directions of this work include incorporating additional features like producing black and white sketch based drawings of people as it could benefit the art community and utilizing vocal language inputs to produce realistic photos. As the architecture uses a StyleGAN2 that is already pre-trained on the CelebA HQ dataset, more studies can be conducted on the effects of training and utilizing a StyleGAN3 model.

References

1. Razavi, A., Van den Oord, A., Vinyals, O.: Generating diverse high-fidelity images with VQ-VAE-2. In: Advances in Neural Information Processing Systems, vol. 32 (2019)
2. Radford, A., et al.: Learning transferable visual models from natural language supervision. In: International Conference on Machine Learning. PMLR (2021)
3. Karras, T., et al.: Analyzing and improving the image quality of StyleGAN. In: Proceedings of the IEEE/CVF Conference on Computer Vision and Pattern Recognition (2020)
4. Van Den Oord, A., Vinyals, O.: Neural discrete representation learning. In: Advances in Neural Information Processing Systems, vol. 30 (2017)

5. Esser, P., Rombach, R., Ommer, B.: Taming transformers for high-resolution image synthesis. In; Proceedings of the IEEE/CVF Conference on Computer Vision and Pattern Recognition (2021)
6. Hinz, T., Heinrich, S., Wermter, S.: Semantic object accuracy for generative text-to-image synthesis. In: IEEE Transactions on Pattern Analysis and Machine Intelligence (2020)
7. Xia, W., et al.: TediGAN: text-guided diverse face image generation and manipulation. In: Proceedings of the IEEE/CVF Conference on Computer Vision and Pattern Recognition (2021)
8. Patashnik, O., et al.: StyleCLIP: text-driven manipulation of StyleGAN imagery. In: Proceedings of the IEEE/CVF International Conference on Computer Vision (2021)
9. Di, X., Patel, V.M.: Face synthesis from visual attributes via sketch using conditional VAEs and GANs. arXiv preprint: arXiv:1801.00077 (2017)
10. Ramesh, A., et al.: Zero-shot text-to-image generation. In: International Conference on Machine Learning. PMLR (2021)
11. Deorukhkar, K., Kadamala, K., Menezes, E.: FGTD: face generation from textual description. In: Ranganathan, G., Fernando, X., Shi, F. (eds.) Inventive Communication and Computational Technologies. Lecture Notes in Networks and Systems, vol. 311. Springer, Singapore (2022). https://doi.org/10.1007/978-981-16-5529-6_43
12. Wang, Z., et al.: CLIP-GEN: language-free training of a text-to-image generator with CLIP. arXiv preprint: arXiv:2203.00386 (2022)
13. Khan, M.Z., et al.: A realistic image generation of face from text description using the fully trained generative adversarial networks. IEEE Access 9, 1250–1260 (2020)
14. Zhang, C., Peng, Y.: Stacking VAE and GAN for context-aware text-to-image generation. In: 2018 IEEE Fourth International Conference on Multimedia Big Data (BigMM). IEEE (2018)
15. Liao, W., et al.: Text to image generation with semantic-spatial aware GAN. In: Proceedings of the IEEE/CVF Conference on Computer Vision and Pattern Recognition (2022)
16. Nichol, A., et al.: GLIDE: towards photorealistic image generation and editing with text-guided diffusion models. arXiv preprint: arXiv:2112.10741 (2021)
17. Sanh, V., et al.: DistilBERT, a distilled version of BERT: smaller, faster, cheaper and lighter. arXiv preprint: arXiv:1910.01108 (2019)
18. Serengil, S.I., Ozpinar, A.: LightFace: a hybrid deep face recognition framework. In: 2020 Innovations in Intelligent Systems and Applications Conference (ASYU), pp. 1–5 (2020). https://doi.org/10.1109/ASYU50717.2020.9259802

Application of Object Detection Models for the Detection of Kitchen Furniture - A Comparison

Benjamin Stecker$^{(\boxtimes)}$ and Hans Brandt-Pook

Bielefeld University of Applied Sciences, Interaktion 1, 33619 Bielefeld, Germany
{benjamin.stecker,hans.brandt-pook}@fh-bielefeld.de

Abstract. Object detection is being applied in an increasing number of areas. In this paper, the authors investigate the application of object detection in a use case for the kitchen industry. The main goal of the use case is to extract information from kitchen scenes that can be used for kitchen planning. The use case is located in a medium-sized company that has little experience with the application of deep learning models. Therefore, this paper proposes a methodology that ensures fast and reliable testing of different object detection models to identify a suitable model for the given use case. In the first step, a dataset with kitchen images is built. Further, augmentation methods are applied to the dataset, to increase the amount and variety of the data. For object detection, there is a variety of models that are freely available, and the question of which model is best for the use case cannot be answered easily. A selection of models (Faster R-CNN, SSD, and EfficentDet) from the TensorFlow Object Detection API will therefore be tested on the image dataset created. The achieved mean average precision (mAP) of the trained models will be used as a metric to determine the best model for the use case. The purpose of this work is to provide an approximate solution, that proves that object detection and the methodology work for the use case.

Keywords: Object detection · Deep learning · Faster R-CNN · SSD · EfficientDet · Computer vision

1 Introduction

Object detection is a fundamental and challenging problem in computer vision and has received increasing attention in recent years. It deals with the recognition and localization of objects from images. The goal is to obtain information about where in an image objects are located by using computer-aided models [13]. According to Deloitte, the relevance of deep learning and computer vision technologies is yet considered very low by medium-sized enterprises in Germany [10]. From this it can be concluded, that the use of deep learning methods such as object detection is not yet state of the art in small and medium-sized enterprises

L. Rutkowski et al. (Eds.): ICAISC 2023, LNAI 14126, pp. 91–101, 2023.
https://doi.org/10.1007/978-3-031-42508-0_9

in Germany. One of the struggles for these enterprises is the question of how to use these technologies in their field. Even if a company knows which deep learning method it wants to implement (e.g. object detection), there are a variety of models to choose from (e.g. YOLO, Faster R-CNN, SSD, EfficientDet). And a good performance on a standard benchmark dataset like MS Coco doesn't give any indication on how these models will perform in a new domain. This means that companies must first build up know-how on the use of these technologies [1]. Therefore, in this work, the authors propose a methodology for applying and comparing different object detection models to see how they perform in a new domain, in this case, kitchen scenes. As a condition, the methodology must be easily adaptable for small and medium-sized enterprises. CRISP-DM (Cross Industry Standard Process for Data Mining) is a common industry standard, which is why the methodology in this work is strongly oriented toward the phases of that process model (business understanding, data understanding, data preparation, modeling, evaluation, and deployment) [12]. The deployment step is left out in this context. For the application and testing of the methodology, a use case from a medium-sized German company is used as a background. The construction of a suitable dataset for the use case is presented and experiments with different models are performed on it. In the evaluation, the results of the experiments are compared and discussed.

The company's use case is based on the question of how objects and areas relevant to kitchen planning, such as furniture, appliances, windows or doors, can be extracted from an image using object detection. Therefore, a suitable object detection model must be selected from the vast selection of model types. The question of which model is best suited for detecting relevant objects in a kitchen is difficult to answer. There is a multitude of object detection models and the selection of the appropriate model depends on the concrete task. The goal is to find an approximate solution that, on the one hand, proves that object detection is applicable in the domain and, on the other hand, specifies a methodology applicable to small and medium enterprises. For a quickly implementable solution, a standard framework for Machine Learning should be used. TensorFlow was chosen because its object detection API (TFOD API) provides a selection of several object detection models in different architectures that can be compared in experiments for the use case. The TFOD API is an open-source framework based on TensorFlow for the creation, training, and deployment of object detection models. For this purpose, a selection of pre-trained object detection models is provided, including MS COCO-trained Faster R-CNN, EfficientDet, and SSD models [8].

2   Object Detection

Image classification is a necessary step and therefore the basis for object detection. From a fixed set of categories, a label is assigned to an input image. This label normally corresponds to the most salient object in the image. Classification works best when the object is centered and dominant in the image. However, for images that contain multiple objects scattered with different scales, a simple label is not sufficient to describe the contextual meaning of the images. Object detection, on the other hand, provides much more information. Thus, multiple labels can be generated for different objects with their corresponding region. This information can contribute to the understanding of an image [3]. Deep learning methods have led to significant improvements in object detection. Among these, methods based on Convolutional Neural Networks (CNNs/ConvNets) are among the most commonly used. These can in turn be divided into two classes: Two-stage methods and One-stage methods, which are presented in the following [4].

Two-Stage Methods. In two-stage methods, object detection is considered as a multi-stage process. In the first step, suggestions for the position of possible objects are extracted from an input image. Subsequently, these suggestions are classified into specific object categories by a trained classifier. These methods have the following advantages:

1. the number of suggestions given to the classifier is reduced, which accelerates the speed of recognition.
2. based on suggestions of possible objects, the classifier can focus on the classification task during the training phase, with little influence of the background, which improves the accuracy of recognition.

Among these methods, the series of Region-Based-CNN (R-CNN) is strongly represented (e.g., R-CNN, Fast R-CNN, Faster R-CNN, Mask R-CNN) [4].

One-Stage Methods. In contrast to this multi-stage process, one-stage methods aim to predict the object category and the object location simultaneously. Thus, compared to two-stage methods, they are significantly faster in object detection, with comparable detection accuracy. Representative methods for this are: Single Shot MultiBox Detector (SSD), RetinaNet, and You Only Look Once (YOLO) [4].

2.1   Faster R-CNN

The individual steps of Faster R-CNN can be seen in Fig. 1. The first step is a shared CNN network. The Region Proposal Network (RPN) takes the shared feature maps as input, from which it generates region suggestions with scores. The scores provide information about how confident the network is that objects are included in the image. Further, in RPN, a small network slides over the input feature map. Here, each sliding window generates a low-dimension vector. This is given two fully connected layers, a bounding box regression layer (reg layer) and a bounding box classification layer (cls layer). For increasing non-linearity, ReLUs (rectified linear activation functions) are applied to the output of the CNN layer. For each sliding window, n-region proposals are generated. As a result, the reg layer outputs 4n outputs for bounding box coordinates and the cls layer outputs 2n values. The 2n values indicate the probability of each region being an object or no object. Values called anchors are assigned to the n-region proposals, each of which contains a box. An anchor represents the center of a sliding window, with its specific values [3]. For training the RPN, binary class labels are assigned to each anchor, stating whether it is an object (positive class label) or not (non-positive class label). For each anchor, the overlap with the bounding box of each contained object is calculated. This overlap is divided by the non-overlap, which is called the intersection-over-union (IoU). For the anchor with the highest IoU, as well as for anchors with an IoU above 0.7, positive class labels are generated. For anchors with an IoU below 0.3, non-positive class labels are generated. During training, the positive as well as the non-positive anchors contribute to the loss functions [7].

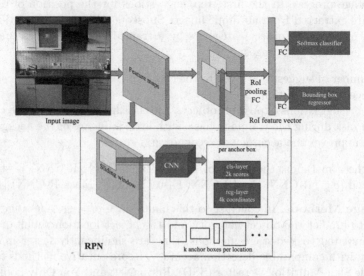

Fig. 1. Faster R-CNN

2.2   SSD

The Single Shot MultiBox Detector (SSD) was introduced by Liu et al. in 2016. The goal was to develop a one-stage detector that is suitable for real-time applications and has comparable accuracy to region-proposal detectors [6]. The SSD architecture (Fig. 2) has three characteristic features. The first characteristic is the use of multiscale feature maps. Figure NUMBER shows that the output layers, after a truncated base network, gradually decrease in size. Here, the layers are chosen to output at different scales and perform detection. This allows prediction at different scales. Shallower layers with more details give better results for smaller objects, while the deeper layers, with information about the background of the image, are suitable for larger objects. The second characteristic is: SSD's network is fully convolutional. This is different from YOLO, which uses fully connected layers at the end. The third characteristic is the predefined bounding boxes and aspect ratios. SSD divides the input image into grid cells. In the feature maps, each cell associates a set of default bounding boxes and aspect ratios. SSD then computes a confidence score and bounding box offsets for the default bounding boxes. During prediction, recognition, for objects of different sizes, is performed on the feature maps with different scales [3].

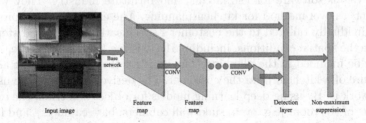

Fig. 2. SSD

2.3   EfficientDet

The goal of EfficientDet was to develop an object detection model with an architecture in the form of a scalable framework that can be easily applied to different object detection use cases. For this purpose, EfficientDet uses EfficientNet, which is also developed by the Google Brain team, as a ConvNet model and backbone. The architecture of the model (Fig. 3), largely follows the one-stage methods paradigm. A bi-directional feature pyramid network (BiFPN) serves as a feature network in the architecture, which accepts 3–7 (P3, P4, P5, P6, P7) features from the backbone and repeatedly applies a bi-directional top-down and bottom-up feature fusion. The fused features are fed into a class network and a box network, in which the object class and bounding box are predicted, respectively. The weights of the class and box networks are shared at all feature levels [11].

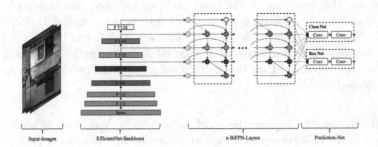

Fig. 3. EfficientDet

3   Methodology

3.1   Business Understanding

The basis of the project of this paper is a use case of a medium-sized company, which develops software for the kitchen and furniture industry. They want to implement a novel method for kitchen planning. The entire planning process is to be individually tailored to the customer's specifications. A crucial step is to recognize the spatial conditions, including the existing kitchen furniture, so that they can be included in the planning. The basis for the planning is the analysis of a picture of a kitchen, from the customer. The derived goal from the use case for this work is: By using deep learning models for object detection, the existing furnishing of the room (e.g. oven, sink, wall cabinets, base cabinets), and further relevant room information (e.g. windows, doors) shall be recognized.

3.2   Data Understanding and Data Preparation

As previously mentioned, the goal is to recognize objects in kitchen scenes with object detection. For training the models, a data basis is needed and an understanding of the required data must exist. Due to the high variance in colors, materials, and shapes that kitchens exhibit, the analysis of kitchen scenes with object detection models is very complex. The focus is on a selection of objects rather than all objects existing in kitchens to ensure a fast approximate solution that serves as a proof of concept. These objects are oven, sink, extractor hood, and dishwasher. The selection of the oven, sink, and dishwasher objects was made because these objects contain relevant information for kitchen planning (e.g. power and water outlets). When looking at various kitchen images, it was observed that extractor hoods exist in different geometries, materials, and color tones, which can be a challenge for object detection models. Therefore, the extractor hood is a suitable object to determine the limitations of the models. In summary, the detection of the oven, sink, dishwasher, and extractor hood objects from images of kitchens using object detection are stated as deep learning goals. The goals are considered to be achieved if they can be detected with a mean Average Precision (map) of at least 80 %, according to the primary MS COCO metric. Since real-time detection is not a requirement, detection speed is not considered in this work.

Dataset. In order to achieve the goals defined above, a dataset is needed that contains images of kitchens in which at least one of the objects to be recognized can be seen. Before manually building a dataset, it is necessary to check whether public datasets exist that depict kitchen scenes in this way. Platforms like Google, kaggle, and paperswithcode, among others, offer comprehensive searches for datasets. No suitable dataset could be found on one of the mentioned platforms. Because of this, it was decided to build up a new dataset. For this purpose, the first step was to collect data. For the collection of the image data, various sources on the Internet were searched for images of kitchens. Particular care was taken to ensure that the images matched the use case as closely as possible. The search results should contain images of kitchens as they would be found in a potential customer's home, instead of images that do not reflect reality. The selection of images in an environment that is as real as possible should help the models to learn the entire context and to be able to generalize. After collecting the images, they must be annotated. For this purpose, the objects to be recognized are provided with bounding boxes and corresponding labels. For this purpose, an annotation pipeline was set up based on the model of Shao et al. which defines the steps to be followed and guidelines for the annotation. Shao et al. divide the annotation pipeline into three steps: filtering, super-category tagging, and bounding boxes annotation. This is to reduce the workload for the people performing the annotations and to ensure quality. To further ensure the quality of the annotations, inspectors, and reviewers are used. For the purpose of this paper, this is considered redundant [9]. Similarly, super-category tagging, where the entire image is tagged for a super-category, is not necessary because the number of objects in this project is limited to a small number (4) and the scene will always be a kitchen scene. For this project, the steps described below, which are also shown in Fig. 4, were followed in annotating the images.

Annotation Pipeline

Filtering: Even though the data has already been checked in the previous step, it cannot be ruled out that there are images in the dataset that are not suitable for the training. Therefore, during annotation, each image is checked again to see if it should be transferred to the final dataset or not.

Bounding Box Annotation: For the four object categories, all objects in the image that correspond to one of these categories are annotated with a bounding box. Care should be taken to ensure that the bounding box encloses the entire object, but does not extend beyond it and terminates at the corners of the object. In this way, the ground truth of the respective object is defined. In case the object to be annotated is partially hidden by another object, the size of the bounding box has to be chosen such that it corresponds to the estimated actual size of the object to be annotated.

Revision: In the third step, all annotations are gone through again and checked whether objects have been forgotten and whether the ground truth of the annotated objects is correct.

Data Augmentation. The larger the amount of training data, the better a machine learning model can generalize [2]. However, the amount of data is limited, and obtaining more data is very time-consuming. Therefore, data augmentation can help to artificially increase the dataset. The images needed for object detection are highly dimensional and contain many factors that can be used to map variations of them. Therefore, data augmentation is a particularly good

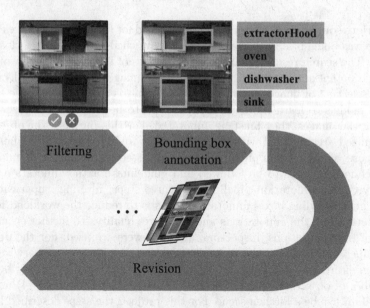

Fig. 4. Annotation pipeline

tool in object detection. For example, moving images by a few pixels can help the model to generalize better [2]. When selecting augmentation methods, care should be taken so that they do not deviate too much from the later use case. For example, it makes no sense to rotate the images of kitchens by 180°, as it is assumed that kitchens will not be photographed at such an angle in the use case. The following augmentations were each applied to 25 % of the dataset:

- Exposure: Between –25 % and +25 %; Were chosen as augmentations to allow the model to better respond to changes in lighting and camera settings [5].

- Hue: Between –25° and +25°; Randomly changing colors makes the model less sensitive [5].

- Rotation: Between –10° and +10°; Rotations of images are considered an effective geometric manipulation for extending image datasets [2]. In reality, cameras are often not held straight. By applying this augmentation, it is expected that the model will learn to deal with it when the camera is not perfectly aligned.

The result is a dataset with 1,006 images and 2,217 annotations (2.2 per image). Of these, 859 are for the object oven, 820 for sink, 377 for extractor hood, and 161 for dishwasher. The lowest resolution included in the dataset is 667 × 500 pixels and the highest is 3,000 × 1,997 pixels. The average resolution of all images included in the dataset is approximately 838 × 838 pixels. For training, the dataset was split into a trainingset (90%) and a testset (10%).

3.3   Modeling and Evaluation

A Jupyter Notebook was created in Google Colab for training the models. The computations were performed with GPUs provided by Colab. For each model, several experiments were conducted with different architectures and settings. The following table shows the best results achieved in the experiments with the respective models. The best result obtained with Faster R-CNN was achieved with a "Faster R-CNN ResNet101 V1 640 × 640" model. This was trained in 15,000 training steps, with a batch size of 4. EfficientDet achieved the best results with "EfficientDet D1 640 × 640". Here, 15,000 training steps, with a batch size of 8, were set for training. For SSD, the best result was achieved with "SSD MobileNet v1 FPN 640 × 640". Which was also trained at 15,000 training steps and a batch size of 6.

Table 1. SSD, Faster R-CNN, and EfficientDet in comparison.

IoU	MaxDets	Area	Average Precision		
			SSD	F R-CNN	EffDet D1
0.5:0.95	100	All	0.846	0.848	0.765
0.5	100	All	0.993	0.987	0.970
0.75	100	All	0.960	0.968	0.917
0.5:0.95	100	Small	−1.000	−1.000	−1.000
0.5:0.95	10	Medium	0.818	0.884	0.646
0.5:0.95	1	Large	0.852	0.850	0.786

As shown in Table 1, Faster R-CNN gave slightly better results than SSD. Both models could exceed the above-mentioned target of at least 80%. EfficientDet could not reach 80%, although it is the newest of the three tested models and performs best of them in benchmarks on MS COCO. Thus, it can be seen that conducting experiments to identify the appropriate model is beneficial. Faster R-CNN would be a good choice for a solution to the use case in this application. However, to make a final decision for the model, further experiments with more objects have to be performed.

4   Conclusion

In this paper, different models for object detection were implemented and compared. For the methodology, the steps of the standard procedure model CRISP-DM were used except for the deployment. For the experiments carried out, an image dataset was set up containing images of kitchen scenes. In the dataset, a selection of objects was annotated that are relevant for the planning of kitchens and thus for the use case. In order to create a higher data variety, augmentations were applied to the dataset. The models chosen for the experiments were SSD,

Faster R-CNN, and EfficientDet. Faster R-CNN and SSD are two algorithms that are already established. Whereas EfficientDet is the latest released and considered the best object detector in benchmarks with state-of-the-art results in 2020. The results from the experiments showed that Faster R-CNN achieved the best detection accuracies, followed by SSD. The detection accuracy of EfficientDet was the lowest, with larger distances to the other models. This proved that looking at benchmarks alone is no guarantee that an algorithm is also well suited for adaptation to a different task. In order to make a concrete statement about which object detection algorithm is the best for the use case, the use case must be further specified and other aspects considered. Nevertheless, the results provide information that object detection can be used as a tool for the use case and which algorithms can generally be considered for this purpose. As such, they represent valuable information for the company. The methodology used provides a lean process that is easy to apply and customize, making it suitable to be used in small and medium enterprises.

References

1. Dahm, M.H., Constantine, B.: Machine Learning für den Mittelstand. In: Dahm, M.H., Thode, S. (eds.) Digitale Transformation in der Unternehmenspraxis, pp. 327–344. Springer, Wiesbaden (2020). https://doi.org/10.1007/978-3-658-28557-9_16
2. Goodfellow, I., Bengio, Y., Courville, A.: Deep learning. Das umfassende Handbuch: Grundlagen, aktuelle Verfahren und Algorithmen, neue Forschungsansaetze. mitp Professional. MITP, Frechen, 1 edn, February 2018. ISBN 978-3-95845-700-3
3. Hassaballah, M., Awad, A.I.: Deep Learning in Computer Vision: Principles and Applications. Digital Imaging and Computer Vision. CRC Press, Boca Raton (2020). ISBN 978-1-138-54442-0
4. Jiang, X., Hadid, A., Pang, Y., Granger, E., Feng, X.: Deep Learning in Object Detection and Recognition. Springer, Singapore (2019)
5. Kang, L.-W., Wang, I.-S., Chou K.-L., Chen, S.-Y., Chang, C.-Y.: Image-based real-time fire detection using deep learning with data augmentation for vision-based surveillance applications. In: 2019 16th IEEE International Conference on Advanced Video and Signal Based Surveillance (AVSS), pp. 1–4, Taipei, Taiwan, September 2019, IEEE. ISBN 978-1-72810-990-9. https://doi.org/10.1109/AVSS.2019.8909899
6. Liu, W., et al.: SSD: single shot multibox detector. arXiv:1512.02325 [cs], 9905:21–37 (2016). https://doi.org/10.1007/978-3-319-46448-02
7. Ren, S., He, K., Girshick, R., Sun, J.: Faster R-CNN: towards real-time object detection with region proposal networks. arXiv:1506.01497 [cs], January 2016
8. Sai, B.N.K., Sasikala, T.: Object detection and count of objects in image using tensor flow object detection API. In: 2019 International Conference on Smart Systems and Inventive Technology (ICSSIT), pp. 542–546 (2019). https://doi.org/10.1109/ICSSIT46314.2019.8987942
9. Shao, S., et al.: Objects365: a large-scale, high-quality dataset for object detection. In: 2019 IEEE/CVF International Conference on Computer Vision (ICCV), pages 8429–8438, Seoul, Korea (South), October 2019. IEEE. ISBN 978-1-72814-803-8. https://doi.org/10.1109/ICCV.2019.00852

10. Statista, KI: Relevante Technologien in Mittelstandsunternehmen. www.de. statista.com/statistik/daten/studie/1297723/umfrage/relevante-technologien-kuenstlicher-intelligenz-in-mittelstandsunternehmen/. Accessed 18 Nov 2022

11. Tan, M., Pang, R., Le, Q.V.: EfficientDet: scalable and efficient object detection. arXiv:1911.09070 [cs, eess], July 2020

12. Wirth, R., Hipp, J.: CRISP-DM: towards a standard process model for data mining. In: Proceedings of the 4th International Conference on the Practical Applications of Knowledge Discovery and Data Mining, vol. 1, pp. 29–39, April 2000

13. Zou, Z., Shi, Z., Guo, Y., Ye, J.: object detection in 20 years: a survey. arXiv:1905.05055 [cs], May 2019

Support Learning Vovinam Exercises Based on Computer Vision

Pham Son Tung, Thai Thanh Do, Pham Hong Giang, and Phan Duy Hung[✉]

FPT University, Hanoi, Vietnam
{tungpshe140670,dotthe140695,giangphhe140700}@fpt.edu.vn,
hungpd2@fe.edu.vn

Abstract. Computer vision has many applications which has attracted many researchers, especially with the problems of recognizing actions, postures, movements. This study offers a method to support students to perform correct postures during martial arts practice. We have collected and labeled data the movements of a traditional Vietnamese martial art called Vovinam. The deep learning architecture is based on the ST-GCN model with an additional processing stage for the input. On our dataset, adding the input processing stage to the recognition model has yielded much better results than applying the original model. The final accuracy is 99.23%, showing that the model has the potential to be applied in practice.

Keywords: Computer Vision · ST-GCN · Martial Art · Vovinam

1 Introduction

People have long been undertaking physical activity to maintain and improve health. This is considered as an indispensable part of life. In multiple forms of physical activities that people use today, Martial arts is one of the most effective and popular ways. In Vietnam, the national traditional martial art form of the country - Vovinam, originated in 1938 [1]. On the 80th founding day anniversary, Vietnam Vovinam Federation confirmed there were more than 2.5 million practicing the martial art in 70 countries and territories. The strong growth of the art form can be seen through the establishment of the world federation, as well as continental federations in Asia, Europe and Africa. From the research of Dung et al. [2], the writer claims that the strengths and technique will increase parallel to practice time. Since the instructor could not always supervise and guide the trainee, it requires the learner to spend most of the time practicing by themselves in order to master the required skills. Along with a tremendous amount of time on self-training, learners could also utilize the application of computer vision as a useful tool to support self-training. This can later create an immensely positive effect in the training process. The support of self-training can help improve the self-assessment technique and as a result, the apprentice can achieve better results. Controlling the techniques could also ensure that trainees do not encounter any unwanted injuries or train in inappropriate ways.

L. Rutkowski et al. (Eds.): ICAISC 2023, LNAI 14126, pp. 102–111, 2023.
https://doi.org/10.1007/978-3-031-42508-0_10

The application of action recognition has been widely researched in recent years. Especially, the rise of new research on human body skeleton dynamics contributes an important part for recognizing human actions. A variety of applications were found by learning attributes from the skeleton to recognize human actions in temporal data. In the field of evaluating the effectiveness and performance of human action recognition, some of the studies can be mentioned such as: tracking body movements by Malaguti et al. [3], Classification of activities by Atvar et al. [4], Detection of fallen persons by Solbach et al. [5], Cheating Detection System by Samir et al. [6], Fighting Detection by Pan et al. [7]. To collect data on physical activities, studies using RGBD cameras [8], Accelerometers [9], Kinect [10]. Existing methods often manually extract features from human motion data and then use basic machine learning algorithms such as SVM, k-nearest, iso-forest.

Related to the research on the system of training, grading or support in learning martial arts can include some recent studies. In [11], Pang et al. review martial arts applications of computer vision. These applications, which expand the reach of martial arts and provide more scientific instruction and technical analysis, include action recognition, stance estimation, intelligence judgment, etc. According to an analysis of the previous research, the investigation in this paper serves as inspiration for subsequent research. Based on convolutional neural networks (CNN), Cai et al. studies the human behavior detection algorithm and its interactive key technology in the martial art field [12]. The detection impact is enhanced by the important frame extraction, joint point optimization, and improved bottom-up technique. At the same time, a new neural network is created that consists of a style generating network and a separable multi branch network. In order to create the style AI image, Generative Adversarial Networks (GAN) first precisely identify the human skeleton and judge the behavior. This study lays the groundwork for future research in the area of AI art. For grading movements of Vietnamese martial arts, Tuong Thanh et al. in [13] proposes the implementation of data analysis of the depth of scoring Kinect users' camera movements in grading Vietnamese traditional martial arts movements. It is an evaluation of traditional Vietnamese martial arts, aiding in the growth and preservation of ethnic elites.

To support martial arts training, this article focuses on the issue of evaluating whether Vovinam movements are correct or not to help users raise the movement level as well as adjust the right movements according to the martial arts exercise being practiced. In this effort, we approached the evaluation of temporal movements using STGCN [14], a model of dynamic skeletons known as Spatial-Temporal Graph Convolutional Networks, which automatically learns not only spatial but also temporal patterns from the data. Our goal is to develop an end-to-end action recognition model that leverages the STGCN model with several input modifications and some recent computer vision techniques to deal with the complex moves of vovinam martial arts. With the new dataset we have built and shared with the community, we would further introduce our work in the following sections. This study suggests an advanced pipeline, which were considerately chosen by the authors. Each of the blocks has been precisely examined by the writers to generate the final process graph. Following the pipeline, we have performed auto-generator data from video to keypoints sequence and processed them appropriately for material arts movements. Later on, the data would be put into the ST-GCN model to deal with the problem of classification of martial arts poses.

2 Methodology

We propose the pipeline (Fig. 1) to classify martial art action as follows:

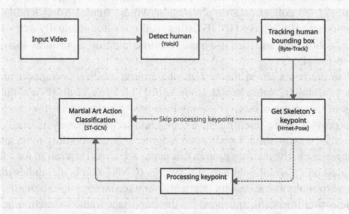

Fig. 1. Block diagram for classifying martial art action

In the initial phase of the pipeline for this study, we employ **Yolox** [15]. With the input from each frame of the video to determine the bounding-boxes for each person in the frames. We chose YoloX for this model because it improved object detection by emphasizing anchor-free detectors [16] and had superior detector performance than the Yolo-series [17, 18]. It is also recommended that Yolox be used with the byte-track method [19], which will be introduced in the next part of the model, for better performance. We use a pretrained model for the Yolox method according to [15].

In the next phase of the pipeline, after determining the bounding-boxes for each person in the frames, **Byte-track** [19] will be used to match the bounding-boxes of each person in the frames. Most previous approaches obtain identities by identifying association detection boxes with scores greater than a threshold, then discarding the rest of the objects with low detection scores, resulting in significant actual object loss and fractured trajectories. To deal with that problem, we chose Byte-track which has the advantage of tracking by associating virtually every detection box rather than only the high-scoring ones.

After matching the bounding-boxes for each person in the frames, **HRNet** [20] is used to define keypoints. The HRNet method uses input as input bounding-boxes and outputs a sequence of keypoints positions for each frame of each person. HighResolution Net (HRNet) technique is interested in the human pose estimation issue in this section, with an emphasis on creating accurate high-resolution representations, which may keep high-resolution representations throughout the process.

In the next phase, before we input them into the **ST-GCN** model, we propose two different processing keypoints techniques to enhance the input:

- Technique 1: In the training process, we keep the number of frames constant for each action. If the video has an extra frame, it will be cut; or else if the video is missing some part, it will be processed to fill in the missing frames by interpolation as follows: Put all the action's frames in a list with a predetermined number of frames for each action. With the first and last frames appended to the top and bottom of the list, the remaining frames of the action will be evenly placed in the positions in the list and retain the original order between frames. Finally, we go through the list in order to find the empty frames and fill them with the value of the previous frame.
- Technique 2: We use data augmentation techniques such as shifting to increase the diversity and volume of the data, allowing the model to perform better in learning.

After processing the above technique, we process the keypoints sequences of each processed frame into the ST-GCN model to train and predict the martial art movements.

A novel strategy for automatically capturing the patterns encoded in the joint's spatial configuration as well as their temporal dynamics is deep neural networks. However, as previously stated, rather than 2D or 3D grids, the skeletons take the shape of graphs, making it challenging to apply proven models such as convolutional networks. The use of GCNs to represent dynamic graphs spanning large-scale datasets, like as human skeletal sequences, has not yet been examined. By extending graph neural networks to a spatial-temporal graph model known as Spatial Temporal Graph Convolutional Networks for Skeleton-Based Action Recognition (**ST-GCN**).

In Fig. 2, blue dots denote the body joints. The intra-body edges between body joints are defined based on the natural connections in human bodies. The inter-frame edges connect the same joints between consecutive frames. Joint coordinates are used as inputs to the ST-GCN. Edges are classified into two types: spatial edges that adhere to the inherent joint connectedness and temporal edges linking the same joints across successive time steps. On top of it, Information may be merged in not just the spatial but also the temporal dimensions due to the construction of many layers of spatial temporal graph convolution.

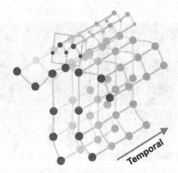

Fig. 2. The spatial temporal graph of a skeleton sequence [14] (Color figure online)

The data is typically a sequence of frames, with each frame including a set of joint coordinates. Given a sequence of body joint coordinates in 2D or 3D, The joints served as the graph's nodes, while the inherent connectivities between human body structures and time served as the network's edges. As a result, The vector of joint coordinates in the graph nodes is the input of the ST-GCN. This can be compared to image-based CNNs, where the input consists of pixel intensity vectors analyzed on a 2D picture grid. On the input data, to create higher-level feature mappings on the graph, the method applies numerous layers of spatial-temporal graph convolution operations. The basic SoftMax classifier will then assign it to the appropriate action category. Backpropagation is used to train the entire model from beginning to end.

3   Experiments and Results

3.1   Data Collection

We gathered data by recording martial arts exercises of university students. We have selected the 9 most basic movements of the practice. This is a core subject in the program so recording is quite easy. The data is then labeled with martial arts moves. The data results are listed in Table 1.

Table 1. Data statistic

Type	Value
Number people	10
Number class	9
Total number action	778

The classes include standing still, defense and 7 basic martial arts movements of Vovinam. The following is an illustration of two actions (Fig. 3, Fig. 4).

Fig. 3. Scooping movement (đấm múc)

Fig. 4. Double punch movement (song đấm)

3.2 Experiments

We tested the problem on GPU-3090, Cuda 11.3, Ubuntu 22.04, Python 3.7. We divided the data into the train and test set in an 80/20 ratio. Each class we take the length of the sequence is 100 frames.

For evaluating system's performance, this work uses Top-1 accuracy. The configuration for the ST-GCN is described in Table 2.

Table 2. The parameter of ST-GCN model

Parameter	Value
base_lr	0.1
batch_size	32
num epoch	100
optimizer	SGD
weight_decay	0.0001

3.3 Result and Analysis

We have tested two cases as suggested in the pipeline and the results are listed in Table 3 as well as detailed in Fig. 5 and Fig. 6.

Table 3. Result of two cases with and without processing keypoints

Model	Top1-Accuracy	Mean loss
Without processing keypoints	94.62%	0.065
With processing keypoints	99.23%	0.047

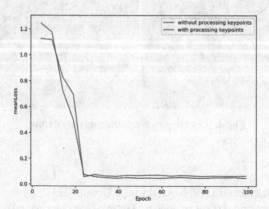

Fig. 5. The meanLoss.

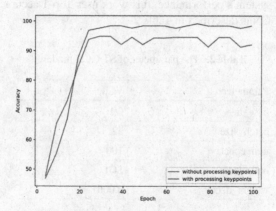

Fig. 6. The accuracy

The above results show that the proposed keypoints processing has significantly improved the accuracy from 94.62 to 99.23%. The improved results are relatively stable after the 25th epoch, which also proves that the efficiency of the keypoints processing is stable. Figure 7 are a few examples of Vovinam movement recognition:

Double punch movement (song đấm)

Straight punch movement (đấm thẳng)

Straight punch movement (đấm thẳng)

Hook punch movement (đấm móc)

Fig. 7. Some examples of Vovinam movement recognition

4   Conclusion and Future Works

This study proposed a pipeline for identifying martial arts movements in Vovinam, a Vietnamese martial art. Each phase's appropriate approaches are thoroughly considered and selected from the most recent methods. The data was gathered and labeled, including nine classes separated into three categories: standing still, defense, and basic martial arts movement. A new processing phase for keypoints is added to enhance input for the ST-GCN model. Based on the collected dataset, we fine-tuned the loss function and parameters accordingly to achieve more accurate results as well as increase performance. Outstanding results when handling keypoints with 99.23% accuracy.

The model can be further developed on a complete database of all lessons, movements. The development of the application into a mobile application product in order to provide the easiest support for learners is also worth paying attention to. The work is also a good reference for image pattern recognition problems [21–25].

References

1. Vietnam's vovinam takes on the world. https://vietnamnet.vn/en/vietnams-vovinam-takes-on-the-world-E217255.html. Accessed 10 Oct 2022
2. Dung, V.V., Vy, B.T.K, My, P.T.: The role of Vovinam in the life of Vietnamese people. In: European Journal of Physical Education and Sport Science, ISSN: 2501–1235 (2016)

3. Malaguti, A., Carraro, M., Guidolin, M., Tagliapietra, L., Menegatti, E., Ghidoni, S.: Real-time tracking-by-detection of human motion in RGB-D camera networks. In: Proceedings of the IEEE International Conference on Systems, Man and Cybernetics (SMC), pp. 3198–3204 (2019). https://doi.org/10.1109/SMC.2019.8914539

4. Atvar, A., Cinbiş, N.İ.: Classification of human poses and orientations with deep learning. In: Proceedings of the 26th Signal Processing and Communications Applications Conference (SIU), pp. 1–4 (2018). https://doi.org/10.1109/SIU.2018.8404498

5. Solbach, M.D., Tsotsos, J.K.: Vision-based fallen person detection for the elderly. In: Proceedings of the IEEE International Conference on Computer Vision Workshops (ICCVW), pp. 1433–1442 (2017). https://doi.org/10.1109/ICCVW.2017.170

6. Samir, M.A., Maged, Y., Atia, A.: Exam cheating detection system with multiple-human pose estimation. In: Proceedings of the IEEE International Conference on Computing (ICOCO), pp. 236–240 (2021). https://doi.org/10.1109/ICOCO53166.2021.9673534

7. Pan, H., et al.: Fighting detection based on pedestrian pose estimation. In: Proceedings of the 11th International Congress on Image and Signal Processing, BioMedical Engineering and Informatics (CISP-BMEI), pp. 1–5 (2018). https://doi.org/10.1109/CISP-BMEI.2018.8633057

8. Das, S., et al.: Quantitative measurement of motor symptoms in Parkinson's disease: a study with full-body motion capture data. In: Proceedings of the Ánnual International Conference of the IEEE Engineering in Medicine and Biology Society, pp. 6789–6792 (2011)

9. Um, T.T., Babakeshizadeh, V., Kulic, D.: Exercise motion classification from large-scale wearable sensor data using convolutional neural networks. In: Proceedings of the IEEE/RSJ International Conference on Intelligent Robots and Systems (IROS), pp. 2385–2390 (2017)

10. Lee, M.H., Siewiorek, D.P., Smailagic, A., Bernardino, A., Badia, S.B.I.: Learning to assess the quality of stroke rehabilitation exercises. In: Proceedings of the 24th Proceedings of the 24th International Conference on Intelligent User Interfaces, pp. 218–228 (2019)

11. Pang, Y., Wang, Q., Zhang, C., Wang, M., Wang, Y.: Analysis of computer vision applied in martial arts. In: Proceedings of the 2nd International Conference on Consumer Electronics and Computer Engineering (ICCECE), pp. 191–196 (2022)

12. Cai, Z., Yang, Y., Lin, L.: Human action recognition and art interaction based on convolutional neural network. In: Proceedings of the Chinese Automation Congress (CAC), pp. 6112–6116 (2020)

13. Thanh, N.T., Tuyen, N.D., Dung, L., Cong, P.T.: Implementation of technical data analysis of skeleton extracted from camera kinect in grading movements of vietnamese martial arts. In: Proceedings of the International Conference on Advanced Technologies for Communications (ATC), pp. 241–244 (2017)

14. Yan, S., Xiong, Y., Lin, D.: Spatial Temporal Graph Convolutional Networks for Skeleton-Based Action Recognition. In CoRR abs/1801.07455 (2018)

15. Ge, Z., Liu, S., Wang, F., Li, Z., Sun, J.: YOLOX: Exceeding YOLO Series in 2021. In CoRR abs/2107.08430 (2021)

16. Xiaosong, Z., Fang, W., Chang, L., Rongrong, J., Qixiang, Y.: Freeanchor: learning to match anchors for visual object detection. In: Advances in Neural Information Processing Systems (NeurIPS) (2019)

17. Joseph, R., Ali, F.: Yolo9000: Better, faster, stronger. In: Conference on Computer Vision and Pattern Recognition (CVPR) (2017)

18. Joseph, R., Ali, F.: YOLOv3: An incremental improvement. In arXiv preprint arXiv:1804.02767 (2018)

19. Zhang, Y., et al.: ByteTrack: Multi-Object Tracking by Associating Every Detection Box. In book: Computer Vision – ECCV 2022, pp. 1–21 (2022)

20. Sun, K., Xiao, B., Liu, D., Wang, J.: Deep high-resolution representation learning for human pose estimation. In: Proceedings of the IEEE/CVF Conference on Computer Vision and Pattern Recognition (CVPR), pp. 5686–696 (2019). https://doi.org/10.1109/CVPR.2019.00584

21. Hung, P.D., Kien, N.N.: SSD-mobilenet implementation for classifying fish species. In: Vasant, P., Zelinka, I., Weber, GW. (eds.) Intelligent Computing and Optimization. ICO 2019. Advances in Intelligent Systems and Computing, vol. 1072. Springer, Cham (2020). https://doi.org/10.1007/978-3-030-33585-4_40

22. Hung, P.D., Su, N.T., Diep, V.T.: Surface classification of damaged concrete using deep convolutional neural network. Pattern Recognit. Image Anal. **29**, 676–687 (2019)

23. Hung, P.D., Su, N.T.: Unsafe construction behavior classification using deep convolutional neural network. Pattern Recognit. Image Anal. **31**, 271–284 (2021)

24. Duy, L.D., Hung, P.D.: Adaptive graph attention network in person re-identification. Pattern Recognit. Image Anal. **32**, 384–392 (2022)

25. Su, N.T., Hung, P.D., Vinh, B.T., Diep, V.T.: Rice leaf disease classification using deep learning and target for mobile devices. In: Al-Emran, M., Al-Sharafi, M.A., Al-Kabi, M.N., Shaalan, K. (eds.) Proceedings of International Conference on Emerging Technologies and Intelligent Systems. ICETIS 2021. Lecture Notes in Networks and Systems, vol. 299. Springer, Cham (2022). https://doi.org/10.1007/978-3-030-82616-1_13

Semantic Segmentation Neural Network in Automatic Weapon Detection

Michał Wieczorek[✉][ID], Jakub Siłka[ID], Martyna Kobielnik[ID], and Marcin Woźniak[ID]

Faculty of Applied Mathematics, Silesian University of Technology, Gliwice, Poland
michal wieczorek@hotmail.com, {martyna.kobielnik,marcin.wozniak}@polsl.pl

Abstract. The goal of this paper is to introduce a semantic segmentation neural network designed for the detection of firearms. The proposed network applies a fully convolutional architecture, incorporating features such as skip connections and batch normalization to enhance its performance. The network was trained using a vast dataset of annotated images and its performance was evaluated using a separate dataset. The results show that the proposed network is highly effective, achieving top-notch results in the detection of firearms. The network's high accuracy 99.1% and ability to perform pixel-wise classification make it a valuable solution for real-world gun detection applications.

Keywords: Neural Network · Deep Learning · Security · Gun Detection · Semantic Segmentation Neural Network

1 Introduction

Gun violence is a pressing issue in many parts of the world [3], with severe consequences for public safety and security. One of the key challenges in addressing this problem is the ability to detect firearms quickly and accurately in various settings, such as public spaces or videos captured by surveillance cameras. Traditional methods of gun detection, such as manual inspection or motion detection, have limitations in terms of speed and accuracy, particularly in crowded or cluttered environments. Recent advances in computer vision and deep learning have led to the development of more sophisticated methods for gun detection, such as semantic segmentation neural networks. These networks are capable of performing pixel-wise classification of an image, enabling accurate identification of objects within an image. In this article, we present a semantic segmentation neural network that has been specifically designed for gun detection and has achieved an accuracy of 99.1%. The proposed network utilizes a fully convolutional architecture, which is well suited for image segmentation tasks. The architecture incorporates features such as skip connections and batch normalization, which have been shown to improve performance in other semantic segmentation tasks. The network was trained on a large dataset of annotated images and evaluated on a

L. Rutkowski et al. (Eds.): ICAISC 2023, LNAI 14126, pp. 112–120, 2023.
https://doi.org/10.1007/978-3-031-42508-0_11

held-out test set. The results demonstrate the effectiveness of the proposed app-roach in achieving state-of-the-art performance in gun detection. This research is important for many aspects such as security, public safety, and surveillance. The ability to detect firearms quickly and accurately in various settings can be used to help prevent gun violence and protect public safety. Due to a high demand for automatic gun detection systems, many different approaches have been used over time. For example, in [10] a surveillance camera combined with a simple convolutional neural network resulted in a system capable of detecting various guns with the precision of 0.7006. Other papers focused on retraining existing CNN models, such as Fast R-CNN on top of CCTV cameras' videos [5] to cre-ate rectangular masking over detected rifles. The high accuracy of the proposed network and its ability to perform pixel-wise classification make it a promising solution for real-world gun detection applications. When dealing with semantic segmentation networks, the dataset plays an important role. It must contain pixel-perfect masks of desired objects for all images collected. In the past, such a dataset had to be manually prepared by a team of people spending hundreds of hours on hand-masking all features, which often led to a small amount of images in the final set due to time and money limits. Moreover, the control over the dataset is very limited or even impossible as we are basing all images on real-world data. To overcome those issues, in this paper, we decided to create an artificial dataset with automatic mask creation. This way, there is full con-trol over the number of images, ideal masking, short preparation times, variable lighting conditions per scene, and much more. Additionally, the randomness is added for better results using mathematical functions. In this paper, we describe the method and architecture of the proposed model in detail, analyze the results of the evaluation, and discuss the potential applications of this technology. We also discuss some of the limitations of the applied approach and areas for future development, including the need for larger and more diverse training datasets. The ability to handle real-world scenarios, such as occlusion and varying lighting conditions, is also discussed.

2 Dataset

Dataset was created in Blender with a novel procedural generator powered by the Geometry Nodes engine for the purpose of this research. First, a need to generate weapons in the 3D environment arose. It was achieved by creating a grid with random points distributed according to a Poisson model. It enabled control over the minimal distance between points. The seed was selected for better control over the variation between frames. At each generated point, a randomly chosen type of weapon was placed with random attributes (size, rota-tion, brightness). The created images were placed on top of some real images, for the better imitation of the real-life conditions. To achieve that, a grid has been created on which points were distributed using Poisson model for better control, such as minimal distance between particles. The random seed value has been animated to achieve controlled variation between frames. Later on each point a random weapon model has been instanced with randomly selected size, rotation and material. Such collection has been later put on top of real images to add more busy backgrounds for better accuracy. To reduce the inaccuracies in mask creation for each configuration a variable lighting has been created to remove network's bias to specific directional lighting. The final dataset contains 5000 generated images with appropriate masks. The generator's node tree can be seen in Fig. 1.

The motivation to use custom data is the lack of good-quality datasets containing enough number of instances. Experiments have shown that the use of synthetic data removes the need for data augmentation in post-processing. Moreover, the image quality could be customized for better reproduction of real-life conditions and the gathering of the data together with mask creation was much less time consuming. Such approach was made due to few contributing factors such as lack of available datasets with needed quality and quantity, need for more control over the data, etc. In performed experiments synthetic data has proven to be highly effective and removed the need of data augmentation in post processing as all the needed images has been generated from the start. What's more the image quality could be fully customized and the preparation times were much shorter than gathering real-world data and manual creation of appropriate masks.

During the training phase, the final dataset has been additionally augmented using classical approaches such as

- horizontal/vertical flip,
- hue shift,
- random image rotation,
- noise addition.

In this way, even more randomness was easily added.

3   Network Architecture

The network consists of 66 layers. In most of them, the bottleneck effect is evident. To enhance the signal strength in the encoder part, a combination of batch normalization and residual layers has been used. The decoder part uses a more classical approach of concatenating encoder layers data into its input for better understanding and less output noise.

As an activation function, Rectified-Linear-Unit (ReLU) [9] has been used, as it showed promising quality with less computational complexity. The output layer is, however, handled by the sigmoid function due to its binary requirement.

Training has been optimized by Adam algorithm with initial learning rate of 0.0002 and custom weighted loss function based on binary cross entropy.

Adam [6] is based on an idea similar to RMSProp. The algorithm can be described as follows:

$$l_t = \beta_1 l_{t-1} + (1 - \beta_1)g_t, \tag{1}$$

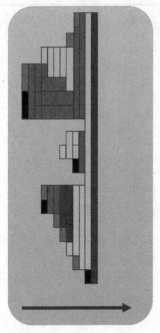

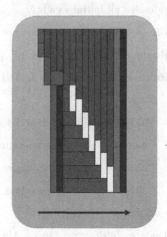

(b) Scheme of shader generator

(a) Scheme of weapons generator

Fig. 1. The diagram above shows how to create a database. The Black and Pink cells define the inputs and their sources, the Blue cells are scalar operations and the Purple cells are vector operations. The orange cells appear in the shader generator as the database background. Yellow, on the other hand, means an operation on the image. Finally, the green cell shows the shader type change. The arrows in the diagrams indicate the direction of data transfer. Which eventually get to the output cells marked in maroon. (Color figure online)

$$s_t = \beta_2 s_{t-1} + (1 - \beta_2) g_t^2, \tag{2}$$

where hyper-parameters $\beta_1 = 0.9$, $\beta_2 = 0.998$ and g is gradient value of applied loss function. Next, we calculate the correlations of mean and variation

$$\hat{l}_t = \frac{l_t}{1 - \beta_1^t} \tag{3}$$

$$\hat{s}_t = \frac{s_t}{1 - \beta_2^t}. \tag{4}$$

which are used to update the weights

$$w_{t+1} = w_t - \frac{\eta}{\sqrt{\hat{s}_t} + \epsilon} \hat{l}_t, \tag{5}$$

where η is the learning rate and ϵ is a small constant value. The training process is presented in Alg. 1 and the used custom loss function is described in Alg. 2, while construction of the model is presented in Fig. 2.

Algorithm 1. Adam training process

Input: $\epsilon = 0.001$, $\beta_1 = 0.9$, $\beta_2 = 0.998$, $\eta = 0.0025$

1: Randomize all initial weights,

2: **while** *global error value* $\varepsilon < error\_value$ **do**

3:     Re-shuffle training data as TS,

4:     **for** each batch inside TS as MBP **do**

5:         Step $++$,

6:         Calculate gradient vector for MBP,

7:         Calculate values of momentum eq. 1 and oscillations eq. 2

8:         Calculate correction values eq. 3 and eq. 4

9:         Calculate new weights values eq. 5

10:    **end for**

11:    Update *global error* ε using Alg. 2.

12: **end while**

Output: trained model

Algorithm 2. Loss function

Input: $floatER = 0.001$, $YTrue$, $YPred$

1: $LossWeight = 8$,

2: $LossOnes = LossWeight * YTrue * log(YPred + floatER)$,

3: $LossZeros = (1 - YTrue) * log(1 - YPred + floatER)$,

4: $Loss = -LossOnes - LossZeros$,

5: $ReduceMean(Loss)$.

Output: output error value

---

4   Results

After 500 iterations of training, our network reached 99.1% accuracy in the validation data. The masks generated on randomly selected images from the Internet can be seen in Fig. 3. The Table 2 shows more metrics based on the confusion matrix in Table 1. For the sake of comparison, the accuracy calculation were performed for results simplified to binary classification, by adding all mask values. If the number of "gun" pixels reached a preset threshold, the image was classified as containing the gun. This technique allows users to set their own threshold regarding their own preference, but a 50/50 ratio or a slight bias toward gun detection is recommended in most cases. Regardless of the high

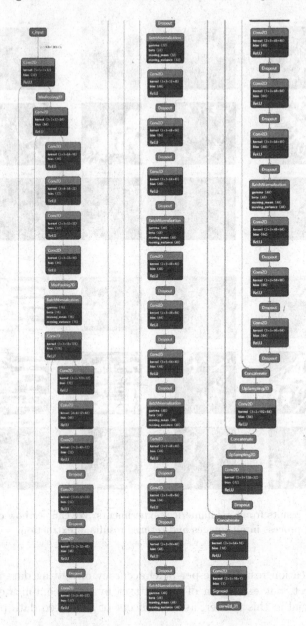

Fig. 2. The above diagram shows the architecture of our model, it allows to accurate and unambiguous differentiation of the objects of our interest from the background. The diagram was created by using the Netron application used to visualize neural network architectures.

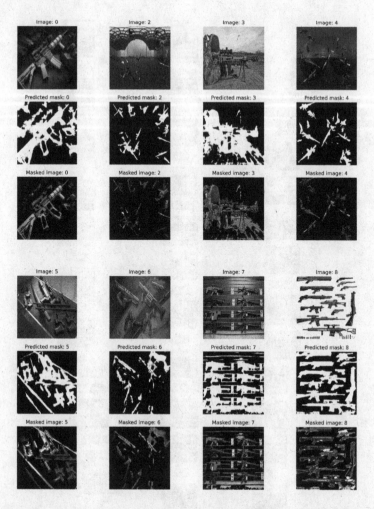

Fig. 3. Sample results from our numerical experiments. We can see how our proposed neural network process input images and returns results of extraction.

binary classification results, the per-pixel accuracy on testing data is, however, still not perfect, but expansion of the dataset by more complicated scenarios can be beneficial in this matter, as the concept of generated data proved to be effective.

Table 1. Confusion matrix for validation data.

	Gun	No Gun
Gun	147	2
No Gun	0	74

Table 2. Metrics for validation data.

	Type	Year	Accuracy	Precision	F1
Our Network	SCNN	2022	99.1%	98.66%	0.9932
F. Gelana et al. [2]	CNN	2018	97.78%	–	–
J. Harsh et al. [4]	Faster R-CNN	2020	94%	–	–
G. Verma et al. [8]	CNN	2017	93.1%	–	–
R. Olmos et al. [7]	VGG-16 +ImageNet	2018	87.93%	95.66%	91.81%
R. Debnath et al. [1]	TM-ISBS	2020	82%	83.5%	0.8477

5   Conclusions

This paper presented a semantic segmentation neural network for gun detection that achieved an accuracy of 99.1%. The proposed network utilized a fully convolutional architecture and incorporated features such as skip connections and batch normalization for improved performance. The network was trained on a large dataset of annotated images and evaluated on a held-out test set, demonstrating its effectiveness in detecting firearms in various settings. This approach has the potential to be used in various applications such as security, public safety, and surveillance. The ability to detect firearms quickly and accurately can help prevent gun violence and protect public safety. Additionally, the network's ability to perform pixel-wise classification makes it a promising solution for real-world gun detection applications. However, it is important to note that there are still some limitations in this approach and there is a need for future development. For example, larger and more diverse training datasets are needed. In addition, the ability to handle real-world scenarios, such as occlusion and varying lighting conditions, could be improved. Additionally, it is important to note that even though the network has high accuracy in detection, the final decision of identifying an object as a gun or not should be made by an expert such as human or legal authority to avoid false alarm or identifying other object as a gun. Overall, this research demonstrates the potential of semantic segmentation neural networks for gun detection and highlights the importance of continuing research in this area. With further improvements in algorithms, training datasets, and testing scenarios, it is expected that the proposed method will have a significant impact on gun detection and its related areas.

Acknowledgments. Authors would like to acknowledge contribution of the project "Q-learning techniques in modeling the behavior of artificial intelligence" under no.

MEiN/2022/DIR/2966, as part of the "The Best of the Best 4.0" program, co-financed by the Ministry of Science and Higher Education, Poland.

References

1. Debnath, R., Bhowmik, M.K.: Automatic visual gun detection carried by a moving person. In: 2020 IEEE 15th International Conference on Industrial and Information Systems (ICIIS), pp. 208–213. IEEE (2020)
2. Gelana, F., Yadav, A.: Firearm detection from surveillance cameras using image processing and machine learning techniques. In: Tiwari, S., Trivedi, M.C., Mishra, K.K., Misra, A.K., Kumar, K.K. (eds.) Smart Innovations in Communication and Computational Sciences. AISC, vol. 851, pp. 25–34. Springer, Singapore (2019). https://doi.org/10.1007/978-981-13-2414-7_3
3. Hemenway, D., Nelson, E.: The scope of the problem: gun violence in the USA. Curr. Trauma Rep. **6**(1), 29–35 (2020)
4. Jain, H., Vikram, A., Kashyap, A., Jain, A., et al.: Weapon detection using artificial intelligence and deep learning for security applications. In: 2020 International Conference on Electronics and Sustainable Communication Systems (ICESC), pp. 193–198. IEEE (2020)
5. Kakadiya, R., Lemos, R., Mangalan, S., Pillai, M., Nikam, S.: Ai based automatic robbery/theft detection using smart surveillance in banks. In: 2019 3rd International conference on Electronics, Communication and Aerospace Technology (ICECA), pp. 201–204 (2019). https://doi.org/10.1109/ICECA.2019.8822186
6. Kingma, D.P., Ba, J.: Adam: a method for stochastic optimization. arXiv preprint arXiv:1412.6980 (2014)
7. Olmos, R., Tabik, S., Lamas, A., Pérez-Hernández, F., Herrera, F.: A binocular image fusion approach for minimizing false positives in handgun detection with deep learning. Inf. Fusion **49**, 271–280 (2019)
8. Verma, G.K., Dhillon, A.: A handheld gun detection using faster R-CNN deep learning. In: Proceedings of the 7th International Conference on Computer and Communication Technology, pp. 84–88 (2017)
9. Xu, B., Wang, N., Chen, T., Li, M.: Empirical evaluation of rectified activations in convolutional network. arXiv preprint arXiv:1505.00853 (2015)
10. Xu, S., Hung, K.: Development of an AI-based system for automatic detection and recognition of weapons in surveillance videos. In: 2020 IEEE 10th Symposium on Computer Applications & Industrial Electronics (ISCAIE), pp. 48–52 (2020). https://doi.org/10.1109/ISCAIE47305.2020.9108816

Various Problems of Artificial Intelligence

An Application of Fuzzy Techniques to Predict the Polymorphism of Selected Microsatellite Sequences

Adam Kiersztyn[1]([✉]) [iD], Krystyna Kiersztyn[2] [iD], Grzegorz Panasiewicz[3] [iD], and Martyna Bieniek-Kobuszewska[4,5] [iD]

[1] Department of Computer Science, Lublin University of Technology, Lublin, Poland
a.kiersztyn@pollub.pl, adam.kiersztyn.pl@gmail.com
[2] Department of Mathematical Modelling, The John Paul II Catholic University of Lublin, Lublin, Poland
[3] Department of Animal Anatomy and Physiology, University of Warmia and Mazury in Olsztyn, Olsztyn, Poland
panasg@uwm.edu.pl
[4] Department and Clinic of Dermatology, Sexually Transmitted Diseases and Clinical Immunology, Medical Department, Collegium Medicum, University of Warmia and Mazury in Olsztyn, Olsztyn, Poland
martyna.bieniek@uwm.edu.pl
[5] The Voivodship Sanitary and Epidemiological Station in Olsztyn, Olsztyn, Poland

Abstract. The complexity of genetic issues is unquestionable and it is therefore advisable to provide new techniques to support the analysis of genetic data. The paper presents an innovative use of data analysis methods based on the use of fuzzy techniques for genetic research. The proposed approach is based on the use of degrees of membership to fuzzy classes describing the degree of heterozygosity. A number of numerical experiments have shown that the proposed method is highly effective. Numerical experiments also checked the impact of the choice of explanatory variables on the effectiveness of forecasting. The proposed application of fuzzy techniques is completely unknown to specialists in the field of genetics.

Keywords: Fuzzy sets · classification · prediction · heterozygosity · microsatellite markers · genetics · loci

1 Introduction

Microsatellite markers (STR - *short tandem repeat*) have now become commonly used markers in genetic studies of populations [2,24]. This is related to the fact that STR markers are characterised by stable inheritance and high polymorphism, expressed in the occurrence of several to a dozen or so allelic variants in

The work was co-financed by the Lublin University of Technology Scientific Fund: FD-20/IT-3/002.

a given locus [8,27]. This class of genetic markers enables the determination and assessment, among other features, of the diversity of domestic and wild animal populations as well as verification of pedigrees of breeding and purebred animals. In addition, the accuracy and effectiveness of STR marker analyses have made them a recognised and popular tool in forensic and paternity testing [1,26].

The innovative method of predicting the level of markers proposed in the paper is based on the use of fuzzy classification. In order to standardise the considerations, three classes describing the level of heterozygosity were introduced. Thanks to the use of fuzzy classification, considerations are transferred to a higher level of abstraction, similarly to the construction of information granules [15,16,18]. Based on the degrees of membership to the classes of heterozygosity within the selected markers, the degrees of membership for the remaining markers are predicted. Skilful use of known data analysis techniques opens up a completely new field of application in genetics.

The work is organised as follows. Sections 2 and 3 provide a description of the analyzed data in biological and analytical terms, respectively. In the next Sect. 4, the use of fuzzy sets to determine the level of uncertainty is presented. After that, Sect. 5 provides the results of numerical experiments. Finally, Sect. 6 contains conclusions and future work directions.

2 Description of Data in Biological Terms

The research material (hair bulbs and skin tissue) was obtained from 254 red deer (Cervus elaphus L. 1758) from the Słowiński National Park (54°42′12″N 17°18′25″E) and forest areas directly adjacent to the National Park. Hair bulbs were obtained from deer from the Słowiński National Park (consent of the Local Ethical Committee for Experiments on Animals of the University of Warmia and Mazury in Olsztyn No. 72/2015 of July 29, 2015). Skin tissues were collected from legally hunted deer (hunted in accordance with the Hunting Law of October 13, 1995; Journal of Laws No. 147, item 713, as amended) in the areas adjacent to the Park.

Genomic DNA (gDNA) was isolated from hair follicles and skin tissues using a commercial Sherlock AX kit according to the manufacturer's procedure (A&A Biotechnology, Poland). The obtained gDNA templates were used for PCR amplification of ten microsatellite markers: CSSM43, CSSM66 [3], BM1818, BM888 [7], OarFCB193 [9], RT13 [28], TGLA94 [12], NVHRT21, NVHRT48 and NVHRT73 [23]. The composition of the reaction mixtures, amplification thermal conditions, electrophoretic separation in the ABI3130 genetic analyser (Applied Biosystems, USA) were described earlier [6]. The obtained genotypes of individual individuals were evaluated using the GeneMapper® software (Applied Biosystems, USA). The obtained data (lengths of DNA fragments, measured by the number of base pairs) were used for further analysis, as previously described [6].

3   Analytical Description of the Data

Information from empirical research on a group of 254 individuals (red deer) from the Słowiński National Park and forest areas directly adjacent to the National Park was used for the analysis. The data included deer genotypes determined by polymorphism within 10 microsatellite loci. Due to the purpose of the study, differences in the levels of individual alleles were determined. Allele distributions for individual microsatellite loci differ from each other. Basic statistics for individual distributions are presented in Table 1.

Table 1. Basic characteristics of alleles (microsatellite markers) difference distributions

No.	STR markers	Min	Quartile 1 (Q_1)	Median (Me)	Quartile 3 (Q_3)	Average	STD	Max	Quartile deviation (QD)
1	OarFCB193	0	0	6	13	7.64	7.38	26	6.5
2	NVHRT21	0	0	2	8	3.73	4.55	20	4
3	BM1818	0	0	4	6	4.90	13.71	200	3
4	RT13	0	0	4	11	7.50	9.65	36	5.5
5	BM888	0	0	3.5	10	5.48	6.30	26	5
6	NVHRT48	0	2	7	18	9.91	8.72	31	8
7	TGLA94	0	0	0	0	1.40	3.22	14	0
8	CSSM43	0	2	4	12	6.79	6.25	28	5
9	CSSM66	0	0	4	10	5.46	4.94	14	5
10	NVHRT73	0	0	0	4	2.59	4.06	16	2

When analysing the results presented in Table 1, it is worth noting that the individual distributions differ significantly. Values of individual quartiles show differences in values for individual STR markers. The median value for most distributions is positive, so in more than half of the observations we note differences between alleles. The mean and standard deviation values clearly highlight the differences. The least stable are the results observed for the BM1818 marker. This is probably due to the presence of an outlier. It should be noted that for the BM1818 marker, the maximum value of the difference is as much as 200, which is related to the relatively large range of alleles that make up this STR marker.

4   Application of Fuzzy Sets to Determine the Level of Uncertainty

The effect of significant differences between the distributions of individual primers was levelled by the use of fuzzy sets. From a practical point of view, it is not the numerical value of the difference between individual alleles that matters, but the level of this difference compared to other observations. Due to the significant differences between individual STR markers, the determined value of the difference may be significant in one case, and marginal for another primer.

In connection with the above, 3 conventional classes of differences between alleles within individual markers were introduced. It is possible to enter a different number of classes, but 3 is the most reasonable value. On the one hand, it is intuitive and easy to interpret, on the other hand, it allows the introduction of classes that differ from each other. In most cases, using granular computations [14–18] and statistical semantics [20], a fuzzy generalised three-sigma rule is used. The proposed approach introduces transformations based on the values of individual quartiles. In addition, it was proposed to use the trapezoidal membership function due to its high intuitiveness. Nevertheless, there are no objections to the use of other classes of membership functions. Membership functions with the following formulas were used

$$\mu(x, \text{equal}) = \begin{cases} 1 & x \leq Me \\ \frac{Me + QD - x}{QD} & Me < x \leq Me + QD \\ 0 & x > Me + QD \end{cases} \tag{1}$$

$$\mu(x, \text{slightly different}) = \begin{cases} 1 & Me + QD < x \leq Me + 2QD \\ \frac{x - Me}{QD} & Me < x \leq Me + QD \\ \frac{Me + 3QD - x}{QD} & Me + 2QD < x \leq Me + 3QD \\ 0 & x \notin (Me, Me + 3QD] \end{cases} \tag{2}$$

$$\mu(x, \text{different}) = \begin{cases} 1 & x > Me + 3QD \\ \frac{x - Me - 2QD}{QD} & Me + 2QD < x \leq Me + 3QD \\ 0 & x \leq Me + 2QD \end{cases} \tag{3}$$

It should be emphasised once again that the statistics of individual distributions are used in the above transformations. Therefore, the patterns of the membership function differ from each other. As a result of the transformation, we obtain degrees of membership to unified classes. Through the skilful use of fuzzy sets, the considerations have been moved to a slightly higher level of abstraction. By breaking away from the analysis of numerical values, it is possible to compare completely different entities with each other.

After determining the value of the membership function for individual deer, it is possible to indicate to which class, within a single marker, a given individual belongs. In other words, we indicate the descriptor with the highest value of the membership function as the winning class.

The distributions of individual winning descriptors differ significantly between markers (see Table 2). In the case of Markers STR 7 and 9, there are no cases classified as "different" at all. This proves a high level of homozygosity within these markers. However, in the case of the STR marker number 10, we observe the greatest variation. Therefore, this microsatellite marker seems to be the most interesting object of analysis. The purpose of numerical experiments is to compare the effectiveness of standard classification tools.

Table 2. The distribution of the winning descriptors for individual markers

No.	STR markers	Equal	Slightly different	Different
1	OarFCB193	143	74	7
2	NVHRT21	147	76	1
3	BM1818	161	61	2
4	RT13	149	67	8
5	BM888	144	78	2
6	NVHRT48	137	83	4
7	TGLA94	172	52	0
8	CSSM43	132	91	1
9	CSSM66	139	85	0
10	NVHRT73	142	69	13

5   Results of Numerical Experiments

The numerical experiments used classical classification tools. The research used algorithms implemented on the KNIME Analytic Platform [5]. Among the tools used were Naive Bayes (NB) [22] Fuzzy Rule (FR) [4], SOTA [13], Decision Trees (DT) [25], Gradient Boosted Tree (GBT) [11], Random Forest (RF) [21], and Tree Ensemble (TE) [10]. In order to facilitate the considerations, and in particular to enable repeating the analyses by people with less experience, the default settings of each of the considered methods were left.

The analyses were carried out in a comprehensive way, changing not only the size of the training and testing sets, but also changing the data used in the analysis. The complete analysis approach uses a very extensive set of variables. Namely, the following variables were available for each STR marker:

- allele difference value;
- the value of the membership function for the "equal" descriptor;
- the value of the membership function for the "slighty different" descriptor;
- the value of the membership function for the "different" descriptor;
- winning descriptor.

The predicted variable was the winning descriptor for the marker NVHRT7. If a full set of variables is used, the effectiveness of individual methods for different sizes of training sets is presented in the table. In order to reduce the impact of random division of elements on the training and test sets, all experiments were repeated 10 times and the results were averaged. The values of the efficiency measure are presented in Table 3.

As the most important conclusion from the analysis of the results presented in Table 3, it should be noted that the SOTA classifier is not suitable for this type of issues. This is very valuable information, because people with less experience in data analysis will be able to consciously resign from its use. Interestingly,

Table 3. Effectiveness level for different classifiers and different sizes of the training set

Method Size of training set (%)	50	60	70	80	90
NB	93.75	100	100	100	100
FR	90.32	96.51	98.50	100	100
SOTA	61.61	75.33	78.53	70.35	47.83
DT	100	100	100	100	100
GBT	100	100	100	100	100
RF	100	100	100	100	100
TE	99.10	100	100	100	100

as the number of elements in the training set increases, the efficiency of this classifier decreases. This effect is caused by the tendency of this classifier to overlearn. In addition, the selection of elements for the training set has a very large impact on the efficiency [19].

For the other classifiers we have a very high efficiency. Already at the level of 50% of elements in the training set, a stable efficiency of 100% is achieved by some classifiers. It is worth verifying these values and conducting a more complete analysis of the results. For each of the methods used, the KNIME environment allows model analysis. However, for illustrative purposes, a classifier based on decision trees was selected for further analysis, because in its case the model can be presented graphically. Such a clear presentation of the model facilitates its analysis by people with less experience in data analysis.

For 20% of the elements in the training set, the classifier achieves 100% efficiency. In this case, the decision model has the form shown in Fig. 1.

An in-depth analysis of the model presented in Fig. 1 leads to a very interesting conclusion. Namely, the decision tree learned how the winning descriptor is determined. Based on the values of the function of membership to the three classes under consideration, the winning descriptor is determined. Full access to all variables significantly simplifies the considerations and the classification problem becomes almost trivial. Therefore, it is advisable to reduce the number of variables used. If the information on the degree of membership to individual classes was removed from the analysis, the efficiency results are presented in Table 4.

In the case that all information about the STR marker No. 10 is removed, none of the considered algorithms is able to perform classification with acceptable efficiency. Efficiency oscillating around 50% proves a rather random classification. However, it is enough to add even fragmentary information (e.g. the value of a variable describing the degree of membership to the "slighty different" class and most of the algorithms achieve very high efficiency. In this case, the decision tree (cf. Figure 2) achieves an efficiency of 95%, and the model itself is much more complicated).

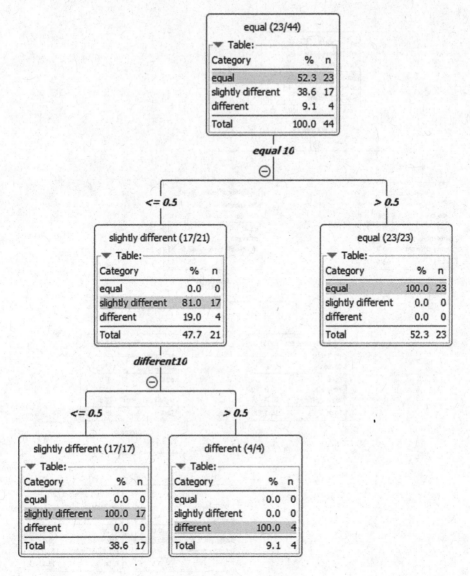

Fig. 1. Decision tree model

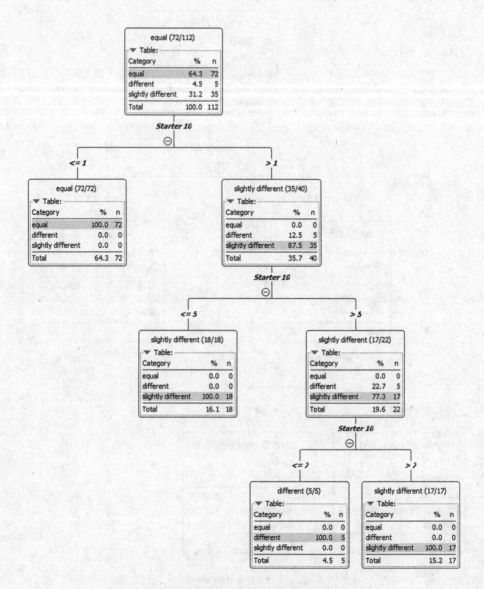

Fig. 2. Extended decision tree model

Table 4. Effectiveness level for different classifiers and various sizes of the training set. Reduced number of explanatory variables

Method Size of training set (%)	50	60	70	80	90
NB	30	17.78	26.47	44.44	52.17
FR	85.56	87.67	89.15	90.24	100
SOTA	72.32	63.33	57.35	66.66	69.56
DT	94.64	100	100	100	100
GBT	100	100	100	100	100
RF	89.28	97.77	94.20	97.78	95.65
TE	88.39	96.67	94.20	97.78	95.65

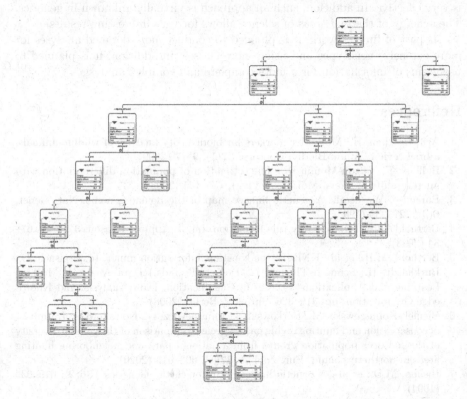

Fig. 3. A decision tree model for bounded explanatory variables

The decision tree model presented in Fig. 3 is very extensive. Nevertheless, based on residual information, it was possible to carry out an effective classification.

6   Conclusions and Future Work

It happens that sometimes the biological material entering the laboratory is of poor quality, and the genomic DNA isolated from such material is partially degraded. This makes it difficult to amplify all the microsatellite sequences selected for analysis. The lack of a full microsatellite genotype of individual individuals hinders population studies and assignment to the right group. The use of fuzzy techniques to predict the polymorphism of selected microsatellite sequences may in the future become a helpful tool in various types of population studies based on STR markers.

To sum up, it can be concluded that forecasting using various techniques of data analysis based on the membership degrees to fuzzy classes of heterozygosity is very effective. In addition, such an approach is virtually unknown in genetics. The synergy of the two areas of science allows for very interesting results.

As part of further work, it is planned to conduct more detailed analyses for more extensive genotypes and using more classes. In addition, it is planned to use grains of information for a more complete and complex analysis.

References

1. Arif, I., Khan, H.: Molecular markers for biodiversity analysis of wildlife animals: a brief review. Anim. Biodiv. Conserv. **32**(1), 9–17 (2009)
2. Balloux, F., Lugon-Moulin, N.: The estimation of population differentiation with microsatellite markers. Mol. Ecol. **11**(2), 155–165 (2002)
3. Barendse, W., et al.: A genetic linkage map of the bovine genome. Nat. Genet. **6**(3), 227–235 (1994)
4. Berthold, M.R.: Mixed fuzzy rule formation. Int. J. Approx. Reason. **32**(2–3), 67–84 (2003)
5. Berthold, M.R., et al.: KNIME: the konstanz information miner. In: Preisach, C., Burkhardt, H., Schmidt-Thieme, L., Decker, R. (eds.) Data Analysis, Machine Learning and Applications. Studies in Classification, Data Analysis, and Knowledge Organization, pp. 319–326. Springer, Berlin (2008)
6. Bieniek-Kobuszewska, M., Borkowski, J., Panasiewicz, G., Nowakowski, J.: Impact of conservation and hunting on big game species: comparison of the genetic diversity of the red deer population groups from a national park and neighboring hunting areas in northern poland. Eur. Zool. J. **87**(1), 603–615 (2020)
7. Bishop, M.D., et al.: A genetic linkage map for cattle. Genetics **136**(2), 619–639 (1994)
8. Bowling, A., Eggleston-Stott, M., Byrns, G., Clark, R., Dileanis, S., Wictum, E.: Validation of microsatellite markers for routine horse parentage testing. Anim. Genet. **28**(4), 247–252 (1997)
9. Buchanan, F., Crawford, A.: Ovine microsatellites at the OarFCB11, OarFCB128, OarFCB193, OarFCB266 and OarFCB304 loci. Anim. Genet. **24**(2), 145–145 (1993)
10. Coppersmith, D., Hong, S.J., Hosking, J.R.: Partitioning nominal attributes in decision trees. Data Min. Knowl. Discov. **3**(2), 197–217 (1999)
11. Friedman, J.H.: Stochastic gradient boosting. Comput. Stat. Data Anal. **38**(4), 367–378 (2002)

12. Georges, M., Massey, J.: Polymorphic dna markers in bovidae, patent wo 92/13102 (1992)
13. Herrero, J., Valencia, A., Dopazo, J.: A hierarchical unsupervised growing neural network for clustering gene expression patterns. Bioinformatics **17**(2), 126–136 (2001)
14. Kiersztyn, A., Karczmarek, P., Kiersztyn, K., Łopucki, R., Grzegórski, S., Pedrycz, W.: The concept of granular representation of the information potential of variables. In: 2021 IEEE International Conference on Fuzzy Systems (FUZZ-IEEE), pp. 1–6. IEEE (2021)
15. Kiersztyn, A., Karczmarek, P., Kiersztyn, K., Pedrycz, W.: The concept of detecting and classifying anomalies in large data sets on a basis of information granules. In: 2020 IEEE International Conference on Fuzzy Systems (FUZZ-IEEE), pp. 1–7. IEEE (2020)
16. Kiersztyn, A., Karczmarek, P., Kiersztyn, K., Pedrycz, W.: Detection and classification of anomalies in large data sets on the basis of information granules. IEEE Trans. Fuzzy Syst. **30**(8), 2850–2860 (2021)
17. Kiersztyn, A., et al.: The use of information granules to detect anomalies in spatial behavior of animals. Ecol. Indic. **136**, 108583 (2022)
18. Kiersztyn, A., et al.: Data imputation in related time series using fuzzy set-based techniques. In: 2020 IEEE International Conference on Fuzzy Systems (FUZZ-IEEE), pp. 1–8. IEEE (2020)
19. Kiersztyn, A., et al.: A comprehensive analysis of the impact of selecting the training set elements on the correctness of classification for highly variable ecological data. In: 2021 IEEE International Conference on Fuzzy Systems (FUZZ-IEEE), pp. 1–6. IEEE (2021)
20. Kiersztyn, K.: Intuitively adaptable outlier detector. Stat. Anal. Data Min. **15**(4), 463–479 (2022)
21. Pal, M.: Random forest classifier for remote sensing classification. Int. J. Remote Sens. **26**(1), 217–222 (2005)
22. Rish, I.: An empirical study of the naive bayes classifier. In: IJCAI 2001 Workshop on Empirical Methods in Artificial Intelligence, pp. 41–46 (2001)
23. Røed, K., Midthjell, L.: Microsatellites in reindeer, rangifer tarandus, and their use in other cervids. Mol. Ecol. **7**(12), 1773–1776 (1998)
24. Sánchez-Fernández, B., Soriguer, R., Rico, C.: Cross-species tests of 45 microsatellite loci isolated from different species of ungulates in the iberian red deer (cervus elaphus hispanicus) to generate a multiplex panel. Mol. Ecol. Resour. **8**(6), 1378–1381 (2008)
25. Shafer, J.C., Agrawal, R., Mehta, M.: A scalable parallel classifier for data mining. In: Proceedings of 22th International Conference on Very Large Data Bases, vol. 96, pp. 544–555 (1996)
26. Szabolcsi, Z., et al.: Genetic identification of red deer using autosomal STR markers. Forensic Sci. Int. Genet. Suppl. Ser. **1**(1), 623–624 (2008)
27. Tautz, D.: Hypervariability of simple sequences as a general source for polymorphic DNA markers. Nucleic Acids Res. **17**(16), 6463–6471 (1989)
28. Wilson, G., Strobeck, C., Wu, L., Coffin, J.: Characterization of microsatellite loci in caribou rangifer tarandus, and their use in other artiodactyls. Mol. Ecol. **6**(7), 697–699 (1997)

Monte Carlo Tree Search
with Metaheuristics

Jacek Mańdziuk[(✉)] [iD] and Patryk Walczak

Warsaw University of Technology, Warsaw, Poland
mandziuk@mini.pw.edu.pl, patryk.walczak.stud@pw.edu.pl

Abstract. Monte Carlo Tree Search/Upper Confidence bounds applied
to Trees (MCTS/UCT) is a popular and powerful search technique applicable to many domains, most frequently to searching game trees. Even
though the algorithm has been widely researched, there is still room
for its improvement, especially when combined with metaheuristics or
machine learning methods. In this paper, we revise and experimentally
evaluate the idea of enhancing MCTS/UCT with game-specific heuristics
that guide the playout (simulation) phase. MCTS/UCT with the proposed guiding mechanism is tested on two popular board games: Othello
and Hex. The enhanced method clearly defeats the well-known Alpha-
beta pruning algorithm in both games, and for the more complex game
(Othello) is highly competitive to the vanilla MCTS/UCT formulation.

Keywords: Monte Carlo Tree Search · Upper Confidence bounds
applied to Trees · Two-player games · Metaheuristics

1 Introduction

Since its introduction, the Monte Carlo Tree Search/Upper Confidence bounds
applied to Trees (MCTS/UCT) algorithm [9] has been widely used in games
and other combinatorial domains [14]. In recent years, it has been part of the
superhuman Go playing program [12] that defeated the Go world champion.
It has also been applied to Security Games [7,8], chemical synthesis [11], or
operation research [16], among others. In each of the above-mentioned cases, the
baseline MCTS/UCT formulation has been significantly extended and tuned,
usually by adding domain-knowledge.

Monte Carlo Tree Search. MCTS is an iterative algorithm that searches the
state space and builds statistical evidence about the decisions available in particular states. In non-trivial problems, the state space (e.g. a game tree) is too large
to be fully searched. Hence, in practical applications, MCTS is allotted some
computational budget (a number of iterations) available for making a decision.
Once this budget is fulfilled, MCTS returns the calculated best action/decision
according to Eq. 1:

$$a^* = \arg \max_{a \in A(s)} Q(s, a) \tag{1}$$

© The Author(s), under exclusive license to Springer Nature Switzerland AG 2023
L. Rutkowski et al. (Eds.): ICAISC 2023, LNAI 14126, pp. 134–144, 2023.
https://doi.org/10.1007/978-3-031-42508-0_13

where $A(s)$ is a set of actions available in state s, in which decision is to be made, and $Q(s,a)$ denotes the empirical average result of playing action a in state s. Naturally, the higher the number of iterations, the more confident the statistics, and the higher the chances that a finally recommended action is indeed the optimal one.

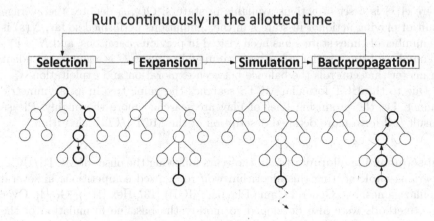

Fig. 1. Monte Carlo Tree Search phases.

Building a game tree starts with a single node (the root) representing the current position. Next, multiple iterations are performed, each of them consisting of four phases, depicted in Fig. 1.

1. **Selection** - In the first phase, the algorithm searches the portion of the tree that has already been represented in memory. Selection always starts from the root node and, at each level, selects the next node according to the *selection policy*. *Selection* terminates when a leaf node is reached.
2. **Expansion** - Unless the *selection* process reached a terminal state, the *expansion* phase takes place, which adds a new child node to the currently represented tree. The new node is a child of the node finally reached in the *selection* phase.
3. **Simulation** - In this phase, a **fully random** simulation of the game/problem is performed from the newly-added node, which reaches a terminal state of the game and calculates the players' scores/payoffs.
4. **Backpropagation** - This phase propagates back the payoff of the player represented in the root node along the path from the newly-added leaf node in the tree (the *expansion* node) to the root, and updates the nodes' statistics ($Q(s,a), N(s,a), N(a)$, described below).

Upper Confidence Bounds Applied to Trees. UCT [9] is typically used as the basic *selection policy* in MCTS. The algorithm attempts to balance the exploration (of yet not well tested actions) and the exploitation (of the best actions found so far). In a given node, UCT advises to first check each possible action once and then follow Eq. 2:

$$a^* = \arg \max_{a \in A(s)} \left\{ Q(s,a) + C\sqrt{\frac{ln\,(N(s))}{N(s,a)}} \right\} \tag{2}$$

where $A(s)$ is a set of actions available in state s, $Q(s,a)$ denotes the average result of playing action a in state s in the simulations performed so far, $N(s)$ is the number of times state s has been visited in previous iterations, and $N(s,a)$ - the number of times action a has been sampled in state s. C is a game-dependent parameter that controls the balance between exploration and exploitation.

Due to the UCT formula, MCTS searches the game tree in an asymmetric manner, i.e. the promising lines of play are searched more thoroughly. Please consult [14] for a more detailed description of the MCTS/UCT algorithm.

Subsequent Developments. In the years following the onset of MCTS/UCT, programs implementing this algorithm won recognized competitions in several popular games, e.g. General Game Playing (GGP) [13], Hex [1], or Go [4]. Over time, methods were also developed to modify the baseline formulation of the algorithm, e.g. RAVE [6] or MAST [3]. There have also been ideas related to combining the MCTS/UCT algorithm with neural networks [2], or its parallel implementation [14].

Contribution. In large search spaces (e.g. for games with high branching factor) MCTS/UCT may prove inefficient (assuming reasonable time limits) as it requires many simulations to assess the relevance of each move. For this reason, instead of using random simulations (*playouts*) one may consider using more focused, game-dependent, guided playouts that could lead to more meaningful information about the payoff structure than random playouts.

One particular approach is the *strategy switching mechanism* (SSM) [15] proposed in the context of GGP [13], which consists in utilizing a bunch of general or domain-specific heuristics that guide the MCTS/UCT *simulation* phase.

The main contribution of this paper is fourfold.

- We simplify the SSM method (and name it *strategy switching* (SS)), by excluding the possibility of making random moves, with certain probability, in the playout phase (see Sect. 2 for a detailed explanation).
- We thoroughly examine the efficacy of MCTS/UCT/SS approach in two popular board games of very different characteristics: Hex and Othello.
- Based on the conducted experiments, we analyse the strengths and weaknesses of MCTS/UCT/SS in particular setups.
- We compare MCTS/UCT/SS with the well-known Alpha-beta pruning algorithm, the vanilla MCTS/UCT, and several other enhancements to MCTS/UCT.

2   MCTS/UCT with *Strategy Switching*

The proposed extension of the MCTS/UCT algorithm utilizes a set of provided heuristics to modify the *simulation (playout)* phase of MCTS according to Algorithm 1.

Algorithm 1: *Simulation* phase of MCTS/UCT algorithm with SS

---

1 *policy* = strategy switching algorithm chooses the strategy;
2 **while** *node* is not a leaf **do**
3 ⌊ *node* = a child of *node* chosen according to *policy*;

A critical component of SS is proper selection of a playout strategy (*policy*) in the current simulation. We follow a solution proposed in [15] in the context of GGP [13]. Namely, a selection is performed according to the UCB1 formula (Eq. 3), i.e. using the same exploration-exploitation balancing mechanism as the one used in MCTS/UCT in the *Selection* phase:

$$s^* = \arg\max_{s \in S} \left\{ Q(s,n) + b\sqrt{\frac{ln(n)}{T(s,n)}} \right\} \tag{3}$$

In Eq. 3, s^* is the strategy selected in the current simulation, n is the number of completed simulations, $Q(s,n)$ and $T(s,n)$ are the average score of strategy s in n simulations and the number of simulations that have used s in n performed simulations, respectively. b is the exploration-exploitation balancing factor.

For each strategy, a value in the parenthesis $\{\}$ is calculated based on the balance between the average score $Q(s,n)$ obtained in the previous simulations and the exploration factor (the part multiplied by b). A strategy with the maximum value is selected.

Please observe that in a broader perspective, SS implements a general idea of heterogeneous optimization, where particular components of the method (e.g. populations in a multi-population approach [17] or evolutionary operators in a multi-operator settings [18]) are dynamically selected from a certain pool, to maintain a proper exploration-exploitation balance in the optimization search.

3   Experiments

3.1   Tested Games and Heuristics

Hex. Hex [10] owes its name to the hexagonal tiles that form a rhombus-shaped board. Its rules are very simple. Players take turns placing their pieces on the empty fields of the board, trying to create a path connecting parallel sides of the board. The player who first manages to chain their edges of the board wins. Hex can have multiple board sizes. One can find small 7×7 boards, but also definitely larger ones with sides consisting of as many as 19 tiles. The most popular size is 11×11, and this is the one used in this work.

The following four general heuristics have been used in the experiments, to guide the move selection process in the playout phase: (1) random; (2) player's mobility (i.e. the number of possible moves/actions available to the player); (3) the difference between the player's and the opponent's mobilities; (4) simple game state evaluation function.

Othello. Othello (also known as Reversi) is a two-player game played on an 8×8 square board. The goal of the game is to possess on the board as many player's pieces as possible. Players take turns placing their pieces, and the game ends when one of the following conditions occurs: (a) all squares are filled with pieces; (b) none of the players can make a valid move; (c) one of the players lost all their pieces.

Initially, four pieces are placed on the board, two of each colour (black and white). The player with black pieces starts the game by placing their piece on a square that causes the "surrounding" of some number of white pieces. In effect, the surrounded pieces are captured, i.e. flipped to become black pieces. Next, the player with white pieces takes their turn and places their piece in a way that surrounds some number of black pieces. The surrounded pieces are captures and turned into white pieces. And so on.

Due to the above rule of changing the ownership of surrounded pieces, the difference between black and white pieces changes rapidly, which makes proper assessment of the game situation a non-trivial task.

In MCTS/UCT/SS, four general heuristics, the same as in Hex, have been tested: (1) random; (2) player's mobility; (3) the difference between the player's and the opponent's mobilities; (4) simple game state evaluation (a difference in the numbers of players' pieces). Furthermore, an additional Othello-specific heuristic, such as (5) weighted piece counter (WPC), has been considered. WPC assigns a certain weight w_i to the ith board square, $i = 1, \ldots, 64$, and computes a linear combination: $WPC = \sum_{i=1}^{64} w_i \cdot x_i$, where $x_i = 1, 0, -1$ if square i is occupied by the player's piece, is empty, is occupied by the opponent's piece, respectively.

3.2   Benchmark Approaches

Alpha-beta Pruning. The main method MCTS/UCT/SS has been compared with is the Alpha-beta algorithm, well-known in the game domain. In brief, the method improves the Minimax algorithm by means of adding two parameters: α and β, which store respectively the minimum and maximum value of the part of the tree that has already been checked. The values of α and β allow verifying the validity of further search. The method requires an evaluation function to work properly. In Hex it is the well-known Dijkstra shortest path algorithm, whereas in Othello it is a difference between the number of pieces of the player and the opponent.

Rapid Action Value Estimation (RAVE). RAVE algorithm [5,6] optimizes the MCTS/UCT selection phase by offering an alternative way to calculate the node score that determines the selection of the child node. In short, in MCTS/UCT/RAVE, besides the $Q(s, a)$ value (cf. Eq. 2) an additional measure $Q_{RAVE}(s, a)$ is maintained for all state-action pairs (s, a). Suppose the current simulation is composed of actions $a_1 a_2 \ldots a_n$ and states $s_1 s_2 \ldots s_{n+1}$, i.e. action a_i is played in state $s_i, i = 1, \ldots, n$. For each action a_i, if it is valid in any of the states $s_j, j = 1, \ldots n + 1, j \neq i$ (but was not played in that state in this simulation), the value $Q_{RAVE}(s_j, a_i)$ is updated based on the simulation score, in the same manner as $Q(s_i, a_i)$. The underlying assumption is the following: since action a_i has been played in state s_i and the simulation led to win/loss of a game, the impact of a_i is generally positive/negative also in other states of the simulated path. Using Q_{RAVE} statistics speeds up the MCTS/UCT state-action estimations. $Q(s, a)$ in Eq. 2 is redefined as follows:

$$Q(s, a) := \beta(s, a) \times Q_{RAVE}(s, a) + (1 - \beta(s, a)) \times Q(s, a); \quad \beta(s, a) = \sqrt{\frac{k}{3N(s, a) + k}} \quad (4)$$

where k is a parameter that defines the number of simulations with action a played in state s at which $Q_{RAVE}(s, a)$ and $Q(s, a)$ are given equal weight, i.e. $\beta(s, a) = 1/2$.

3.3   Experimental Setup

In the experiments, two versions of the SS algorithm have been tested. The first one had access to all heuristics considered for a given game (Hex and Othello, respectively). The other one was limited to the top 3 most effective heuristics devised in some number of preliminary tests, devoted to the methods' tuning. The former will be denoted as **MCTS/UCT/SS(all)**, the latter as **MCTS/UCT/SS(top3)**. The following selection of methods was used in comparative tests to assess both MCTS/UCT/SS versions:

1. **MCTS/UCT** – vanilla approach;
2. **MCTS/UCT/E** – the playout phase is guided by the evaluation function used in Alpha-beta - the bigger its value, the higher the assessment of a given node;
3. **MCTS/UCT/Mp** – the playout phase is guided by the player's mobility - the more actions are available, the higher the assessment of a given node;
4. **MCTS/UCT/Md** – the playout phase is guided by the difference between player's and opponent's mobilities - the bigger the difference, the higher the assessment of a given node;
5.**MCTS/UCT/RAVE** – in the selection phase, UCT is replaced by UCT/RAVE (cf. Eq. 4);
6.-7. **Alpha-beta(10), Alpha-beta(12)** – Alpha-beta pruning algorithm with depth 10 and 12, respectively and simple evaluation function (see Sect. 3.2);

In the last three tested methods there is no tree search involved, and the move is chosen directly based on:

8. **E** – the evaluation function used in Alpha-beta;
9. **R** – uniform distribution;
10. **WPC** – the WPC evaluation – only in Othello;

Tests were carried out with the following parameters: Hex game board size - 11×11, $k = 1000$ in RAVE (Eq. 4), $b = 4$ in the switching mechanism (Eq. 3), 10 000 simulations per move in MCTS/UCT algorithms. Parameter values were selected based on a limited number of preliminary tests and reflected a tradeoff between the quality of obtained results and computational time requirements. The methods have been compared based on a round-robin tournament in which every pair of methods was pitted 100 times, with different seeds and with sides swapped after each game.

4   Results

Table 1. Hex results. The top 3 heuristics used in the MCTS/UCT/SS(top3) setting were player's mobility, the difference between the player's and the opponent's mobilities and simple game state evaluation. In rows 7 and 9 the evaluation function is Dijkstra's algorithm (the same as in the Alpha-beta algorithm).

No	Algorithm	Win	Loss	Avg. Time (h)
1	MCTS/UCT	88,42%	11,58%	4,85
2	MCTS/UCT/SS(all)	72,73%	27,27%	17,52
3	MCTS/UCT/SS(top3)	64,72%	35,28%	21,95
4	MCTS/UCT/Mp	64,67%	35,33%	18,10
5	Alpha-beta(12)	64,61%	35,39%	6,64
6	Alpha-beta(10)	64,61%	35,39%	6,95
7	MCTS/UCT/E	52,42%	47,58%	12,89
8	MCTS/UCT/Md	52,17%	47,83%	31,66
9	E	37,08%	62,92%	6,69
10	R	21,50%	78,50%	7,50
11	MCTS/UCT/RAVE	12,00%	88,00%	9,89

Hex. Table 1 presents the results of by the algorithms in Hex. It can be seen that vanilla MCTS/UCT algorithm dominates not only in the win/loss scores, but also in the average computation time. Second and third on the podium is MCTS/UCT/SS algorithm, with all 4 and top 3 heuristics to choose from, respectively (without random choice in the latter case). Note, however, that the differences between positions 3 to 6 are practically negligible.

Most probably, the reason for vanilla MCTS/UCT leadership is the relative simplicity of Hex. In simpler games, standard MCTS/UCT proved very effective and the selection of additional heuristics to guide the playout simulations is, in some sense, a waste of time. Nevertheless, leaving aside MCTS/UCT,

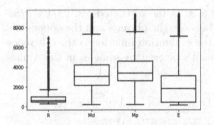 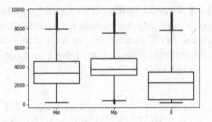

(a) All 4 strategies are available   (b) Only top 3 strategies are available

Fig. 2. Statistics of the MCTS/UCT/SS strategy selection in Hex

the MCTS/UCT/SS approach outperformed all the remaining competitors, including other MCTS/UCT implementations, as well as all non-MCTS/UCT approaches. A possible reason for the poor MCTS/UTC/RAVE performance is the aforementioned simplicity of Hex, which makes the more sophisticated versions of MCTS/UCT actually overcomplex.

Figure 2 shows statistics of strategy selection by the switching mechanism in case all strategies are available for selection (Fig. 2a) and when the algorithm chooses among the 3 most effective strategies only (Fig. 2b). The favourite strategy of SS having four policies to choose from was the player's mobility. In case MCTS/UCT/SS could only choose among the top 3 policies (excluding the random one), all quartiles, together with the mean, clearly show that the player's mobility strategy was again the most frequently used in the simulations, which is in line with the results presented in Table 1. This strategy was followed by the difference between player's and opponent's mobilities strategy, and then by the evaluation function based strategy.

Othello. The game of Othello is much more complex than Hex in terms of both the rules and tactical complexity. In this game MCTS/UCT/SS(top3) turned out to be the strongest approach, followed by MCTS/UCT/Md and MCTS/UCT/WPC (see Table 2). Both runner-up approaches utilized the well known Othello strategies, widely considered in the game literature. Due to very "unstable" pieces configurations in Othello, the strategies that refer to the numbers of pieces possessed by the players are generally weaker than the mobility-based strategies. In this respect, the second place of MCTS/UCT/Md is not surprising. Likewise, WPC in known to be the strong evaluation measure, as it considers critical aspects of the game, e.g. highly weights placing pieces on the corner squares, and penalizes placing them next to the corners. The fourth and the fifth were MCTS/UCT/SS(all) and the MCTS/UCT with the strategy based on the player's mobility, respectively.

Apparently, in a more complex game like Othello, the SS idea proved useful and showed its superiority over all other methods. The MCTS/UCT algorithm with the switching mechanism was first and fourth in the overall ranking.

Table 2. Othello results. The top 3 heuristics used in the restricted MCTS/UCT/SS approach were player's mobility, the difference between the player's and the opponent's mobilities, WPC evaluation. In rows 2 and 10 the evaluation function is the difference between the numbers of the player's and opponent's pieces (the same as in the Alpha-beta algorithm).

No	Algorithm	Win	Draw	Loss	Avg. Time (s)
1	MCTS/UCT/SS(top3)	81,58%	1,75%	16,67%	1127,28
2	MCTS/UCT/E	79,67%	2,00%	18,33%	2061,46
3	MCTS/UCT/WPC	77,25%	2,25%	20,50%	504,98
4	MCTS/UCT/SS(all)	71,00%	1,17%	27,83%	1203,60
5	MCTS/UCT/Mp	69,67%	1,92%	28,42%	1316,78
6	MCTS/UCT	55,67%	1,92%	42,42%	524,69
7	MCTS/UCT/RAVE	42,33%	1,33%	56,33%	506,90
8	Alpha-beta(12)	19,67%	0,25%	80,08%	374,12
9	Alpha-beta(10)	19,67%	0,25%	80,08%	381,77
10	E	17,00%	0,25%	82,75%	390,81
11	R	9,58 %	1,08%	89,33%	421,08

Detailed summaries of the average number of SS choices are shown in Fig. 3, respectively in case all strategies are available for selection (Fig. 3a) and when only top 3 strategies are considered (Fig. 3b).

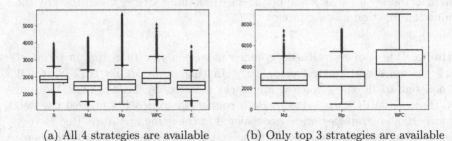

(a) All 4 strategies are available   (b) Only top 3 strategies are available

Fig. 3. Statistics of the MCTS/UCT/SS strategy selection in Othello

In both cases, the analysis of statistics of the switching mechanism, clearly points to the WPC heuristics as the most popular, hence the most advantageous among all. In the case of 5 possible choices, i.e. MCTS/UCT/SS(all), the advantage of WPC is not as striking as in the top 3 case.

5   Conclusions and Future Work

In this paper, we revise and experimentally evaluate the strategy switching mechanism combined with the popular MCTS/UCT search algorithm. The major findings from the presented research can be summarized as follows.

- In simple games, such as Hex, enhancing MCTS/UCT with SS does not seem to have much reason. Since MCTS/UCT is sufficiently strong method for this game, making the approach more complex, actually deteriorates the results.
- In more complex problems, e.g. the game of Othello, MCTS/UCT/SS shows its advantages, as the switching mechanism guides the MCTS playouts in a focused manner, hence saving time and resources.
- The choice of switching strategies is crucial for the SS efficacy. This issue was clearly observed in Hex which, despite being a game simple enough to be effectively approached with the vanilla MCTS/UCT, also did not seem to have the best choice of the supporting strategies. Apparently, heuristics based on mobility are not so strong and relevant in this game as in Othello, where along with WPC they constitute the core set of the effective strategies.
- The more effective of the two MCTS/UCT/SS setups is the one based on top 3 (generally top n) heuristics, as opposed to using all of them. This observation supports the intuition that selection among a smaller set of stronger strategies is generally more effective (easier) than the selection from a larger set, which also contains relatively weaker strategies.
- MCTS/UCT supported with a proper set of heuristic strategies outperforms the well-known Alpha-beta pruning algorithm, with the evaluation function relying on basic material assessment.
- MCTS/UCT with a lightweight evaluation function (either assigned directly or via the SS mechanism) is clearly a more powerful approach than a direct application of the same heuristics to move selection.

Our future research plans include verification of the MCTS/UCT/SS approach in more complex games, such as Hive and in other problem domains, e.g. project scheduling. We also plan to compare the SSM approach proposed in [15] with our simplified SS version and discuss the similarities and differences between these two implementations.

Acknowledgements.. This research was carried out with the support of the Laboratory of Bioinformatics and Computational Genomics and the HPC Center of the Faculty of Mathematics and Information Science, Warsaw University of Technology under computational grant number A-22-03.

References

1. Arneson, B., Hayward, R., Henderson, P.: Mohex wins hex tournament. In: ICGA, vol. 32, pp. 114–116, September 2013. https://doi.org/10.3233/ICG-2009-32218
2. Barratt, J., Pan, C.: Playing go without game tree search using convolutional neural networks. ArXiv abs/1907.04658 (2019)

3. Björnsson, Y., Finnsson, H.: Cadiaplayer: a simulation-based general game player. Comput. Intell. AI Games IEEE Trans. **1**, 4–15 (2009). https://doi.org/10.1109/TCIAIG.2009.2018702

4. Enzenberger, M., Müller, M., Arneson, B., Segal, R.: Fuego-an open-source framework for board games and go engine based on monte carlo tree search. IEEE Trans. Comput. Intell. AI Games **2**(4), 259–270 (2010). https://doi.org/10.1109/TCIAIG.2010.2083662

5. Gelly, S., Silver, D.: Combining online and offline knowledge in UCT. In: Proceedings of the 24th International Conference on Machine Learning, pp. 273–280 (2007). https://doi.org/10.1145/1273496.1273531

6. Gelly, S., Silver, D.: Monte-carlo tree search and rapid action value estimation in computer go. Artif. Intell. **175**(11), 1856–1875 (2011). https://doi.org/10.1016/j.artint.2011.03.007

7. Karwowski, J., Mańdziuk, J.: A new approach to security games. In: Rutkowski, L., Korytkowski, M., Scherer, R., Tadeusiewicz, R., Zadeh, L.A., Zurada, J.M. (eds.) ICAISC 2015, Part II. LNCS (LNAI), vol. 9120, pp. 402–411. Springer, Cham (2015). https://doi.org/10.1007/978-3-319-19369-4_36

8. Karwowski, J., Mańdziuk, J.: A monte carlo tree search approach to finding efficient patrolling schemes on graphs. Eur. J. Oper. Res. **277**(1), 255–268 (2019)

9. Kocsis, L., Szepesvári, C.: Bandit based monte-carlo planning. In: Fürnkranz, J., Scheffer, T., Spiliopoulou, M. (eds.) ECML 2006. LNCS (LNAI), vol. 4212, pp. 282–293. Springer, Heidelberg (2006). https://doi.org/10.1007/11871842_29

10. Maarup, T.: Everything you always wanted to know about hexbut were afraid to Ask. Ph.D. thesis (2005). www.maarup.net/thomas/hex/hex3.pdf

11. Segler, M.H., Preuss, M., Waller, M.P.: Planning chemical syntheses with deep neural networks and symbolic AI. Nature **555**(7698), 604–610 (2018)

12. Silver, D., et al.: Mastering the game of Go without human knowledge. Nature **550**(7676), 354–359 (2017)

13. Świechowski, M., Park, H.S., Mańdziuk, J., Kim, K.J.: Recent advances in general game playing. The Scientific World Journal 2015, Article ID: 986262 (2015)

14. Świechowski, M., Godlewski, K., Sawicki, B., Mańdziuk, J.: Monte carlo tree search: a review of recent modifications and applications. Artif. Intell. Rev. **56**, 2497–2562 (2023). https://doi.org/10.1007/s10462-022-10228-y

15. Świechowski, M., Mańdziuk, J.: Self-adaptation of playing strategies in general game playing. IEEE Trans. Comput. Intell. AI Games **6**(4), 367–381 (2014). https://doi.org/10.1109/TCIAIG.2013.2275163

16. Walędzik, K., Mańdziuk, J.: Applying hybrid monte carlo tree search methods to risk-aware project scheduling problem. Inf. Sci. **460–461**, 450–468 (2018)

17. Łapa, K., Cpałka, K., Kisiel-Dorohinicki, M., Paszkowski, J., Dębski, M., Le, V.H.: Multi-population-based algorithm with an exchange of training plans based on population evaluation. J. Artif. Intell. Soft Comput. Rese. **12**(4), 239–253 (2022). https://doi.org/10.2478/jaiscr-2022-0016

18. Łapa, K., Cpałka, K., Laskowski, Ł, Cader, A., Zeng, Z.: Evolutionary algorithm with a configurable search mechanism. J. Artif. Intell. Soft Comput. Res. **10**(3), 151–171 (2020). https://doi.org/10.2478/jaiscr-2020-0011

Phishing Attack Detection: An Improved Performance Through Ensemble Learning

Benjamin McConnell, Daniel Del Monaco, Mahdieh Zabihimayvan[✉],
Fatemeh Abdollahzadeh, and Samir Hamada

Department of Computer Science, Central Connecticut State University, New Britain, CT, USA
{b.mcconnell,ddelmonaco}@my.ccsu.edu, {zabihimayvan,abdollah,
hamadas}@ccsu.edu

Abstract. Phishing is a cybercrime that deceives online users and steals their confidential information by impersonating a legitimate website or URL. Several machine learning-based strategies have been proposed to detect phishing websites. These techniques utilize a set of features extracted from website samples, the structure and syntax of URLs, the content of the pages, and querying external resources. In this work, we use a dataset of 11,430 samples with 87 extracted features that are designed to be used as a benchmark for machine learning-based phishing detection systems. Our classification is based on an ensemble learning technique, which is further optimized using grid search. The experiments provide a detailed description of tuning the model's hyperparameters and its optimization. We evaluate the model using well-known evaluation metrics of accuracy, precision, recall, F1-score, and area under the ROC curve. The findings indicate that our optimized ensemble model classifies legitimate and phishing URLs with an accuracy of 95.36%, a precision of 96.29%, a recall of 94.24%, an F1 score of 95.26%, and the area under the ROC curve of 0.9876.

Keywords: Phishing attack · ensemble learning · classification · grid search

1 Introduction

Phishing is a type of social engineering attack that coheres online users to perform adverse actions on behalf of a cybercriminal [1]. The goal of phishing attacks is to deceive users to steal their personal or confidential information. To this end, phishers intend to mimic emails, web pages, or URLs to have high similarity in terms of content or appearance to legitimate emails, web pages, or URLs. The attacker usually accompanies a web page with a login form that requests users to enter their personal information [2]. To design the phishing web page or email, the attacker utilizes social engineering practices to persuade victims to follow specific instructions with the purpose of updating or validating their information, winning a big prize, or receiving a significant discount to a service.

According to the most up-to-date trend reports by the Anti Phishing Working Group [3], during the third quarter of 2022, over 1,270,883 total phishing attacks have been

L. Rutkowski et al. (Eds.): ICAISC 2023, LNAI 14126, pp. 145–157, 2023.
https://doi.org/10.1007/978-3-031-42508-0_14

documented and financial institutions were the main target of attacks (23.2% of all phishing attacks). A range of technical strategies have been proposed to detect phishing emails and websites. The strategies can broadly be categorized into three classes: (i) list-based; (ii) heuristic; and (iii) and machine learning (ML)-based approaches [4]. The first class simply references different lists of legitimate and phishing URLs. While these lists are frequently updated, there is an inevitable time gap between the emergence of a phishing website, its observation, reporting, and finally, addition to a suspicious URL list. This makes list-based strategies vulnerable to emerging and zero-day phishing attacks [5]. Heuristic approaches can automatically recognize a phishing web page based on a suite of features extracted from them [6].

One method, for example, focuses on the similarity of the suspicious web page with the legitimate one based on visual features such as image, logo, and textual content of the page [7]. However, there is no guarantee that a phishing site and a legitimate web page or email have features in common, which can cause poor detection accuracy in practice. Furthermore, heuristic techniques can be bypassed by a knowledgeable attacker that ensures their phishing website does not contain the detected features. ML methods [8] are also dependent on the set of features extracted for each web page and further require ground truth phishing and legitimate websites for training. The quality and variety of websites in this training set has a strong effect on the final detection accuracy [9], and it can be expensive to obtain a training set that is suitably sized and diverse. Despite these challenges, ML approaches for phishing detection have been an active area of research. Several studies have been conducted on different data sets using various classification algorithms [10–12].

In this work, we implement a classifier that works based on an ensemble learning technique to detect phishing attacks on a benchmark data set of 87 features extracted from 11,430 URLs. We utilize gradient-boosting ensemble learning as the classifier to distinguish legitimate and phishing URLs. We optimize our model using a grid search method to tune the model's hyperparameters and improve its performance. We evaluate the model using well-known evaluation metrics of accuracy, precision, recall, F1-score, and the area under the ROC curve. Our findings indicate that the optimized model can classify the URL samples into two classes legitimate and phishing with an accuracy of 95.36%, a precision of 96.29%, a recall of 94.24%, the F1 score of 95.26%, and an area under the ROC curve of 0.9876.

The rest of this paper is organized as follows: Section II discusses the related work on phishing detection. Section III presents the description of the data used in this work. Sections IV and V tune the model's hyperparameter and evaluate the classification method, respectively. Finally, Section VI provides the main conclusions and future work.

2   Related Work

ML-based approaches to detect phishing websites are an active research area that employs a wide range of supervised classification techniques to segregate phishing classes. Feng et al. propose a novel neural network for phishing detection [10]. They improve the generalization ability of the network by designing the risk minimization principle. The performance of the proposed network is evaluated over a UCI repository

1 containing 11,055 samples labeled as phishing/legitimate. The dataset also specifies 30 features for each website categorized as Address bar-based, Abnormal- based, HTML/JavaScript-based, and Domain-based features. Rao and Pais propose a novel algorithm to detect phishing websites using both machine learning techniques and image checking. They also extract features from URLs, website content, and third-party services [9]. It is worth mentioning that although using the features from third-party services can increase the detection time, it increases the detection accuracy in practice [12]. They evaluate the performance of the proposed algorithm over 1407 legitimate and 2119 phishing websites collected from Phish Tank 2 and Alexa database 3, respectively.

Mohammad et al. propose a novel self-structuring neural network for detecting phishing websites [4]. They specify 17 features, some extracted from third-party service, for 600 legitimate and 800 phishing websites collected from Phish Tank and Miller smiles 4 archives. Their experiments indicate the high generalizability and ability of the neural network in phishing detection. In another work, they propose a feed-forward neural network trained by backpropagation to classify websites [11]. 18 features are specified for 859 legitimate and 969 phishing websites, respectively. Jain and Gupta propose a machine learning-based technique using only client-side features to detect phishing websites [13]. They extract 19 features from the URL and source code of the web pages and evaluate their method over 2,141 phishing web pages from PhishTank1 and Openfish2 and 1,918 legitimate pages from Alexa database3, some online payment, and banking websites.

3 Data Description

The experiments are based on a dataset of 11,430 URLs with 87 extracted features [14]. The dataset is designed to be used as a benchmark for machine learning-based phishing detection systems. Features are from three different classes: 56 are extracted from the structure and syntax of URLs, 24 are extracted from the content of their correspondent pages, and 7 are extracted by querying external services. The dataset is balanced, it contains exactly 50% phishing and 50% legitimate URLs.

The plot of the correlation matrix measures the correlation between every possible pair of features. This can be helpful in determining if there are columns that are essentially capturing the same information. Figure 1 indicates the correlation matrix of the data set used in this research.

The axes are both the entire feature sets, and their intersections show the resulting correlation between each pair of features. A lighter shade shows a strong positive correlation which can signify that the features essentially are having the same effect on the model and may be redundant. The solid white columns, belonging to five features in the data, indicate columns with only zero values. Such features are removed from the data since they do nothing to improve the model and only increase the computation time. The diagonal is the only area expected to be white as it represents the correlation between a feature and itself, which will always yield one.

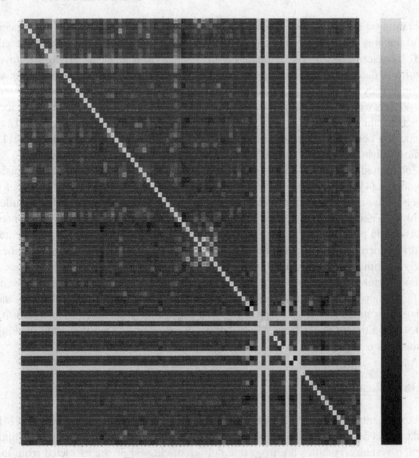

Fig. 1. Correlation Matrix of Features

4 Tuning Hyperparameters

Now, we tune a set of hyperparameters before evaluating our classification model. Hyperparameters are model specific characteristics that can be changed to improve the model performance [15]. The set comprises of both categorical and numerical hyperparameters. The categorical parameters tuned in this work are used by gradient boosting method that we use to create the trees. The numerical hyperparameters are the parameters related to the trees generated in each step of the classification.

4.1 Tuning Numerical Parameters

First, we focus on numerical hyperparameters, create lists of values for a given parameter, and evaluate the model's performance at each individual value. The classifier has predetermined default values and choices for the set of hyperparameters, which are used to determine our baseline for tuning. The goal is to train the model on the training data and then evaluate its performance on the test using accuracy as the metric. The output of each iteration is captured and used to create a validation curve, which plots the accuracies on both training and testing data across the given value range for each hyperparameter.

Maximum Depth

The Max depth hyperparameter controls the number of nodes each decision tree is allowed to grow up to [16]. A higher max depth has the potential to make the model too complex and overfit. This would result in increased accuracy on the training data while decreasing performance on unknown test data. Setting the depth too low will make the model too simplistic and potentially not capture enough patterns to make accurate predictions altogether. Figure 2 indicates the validation curve of max depth for the values between 0 and 7.

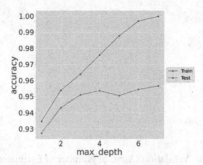

Fig. 2. Validation Curve of Maximum Depth.

Based on both the validation curve in Fig. 2 and the accuracies listed in Table 1, a maximum depth of 4 results in the highest performance on the test without straying farther from the training performance. A depth of 5 will decrease the performance of the model on unseen data. Further increasing the depth beyond 5 increases the test performance but the model is overfitting on the training data as evidenced by the increasing difference between the two sets' performances.

Table 1. Validation of maximum depth on Train and Test Data

Value	Accuracy on Train Data	Accuracy on Test Data
1.0	0.9346	0.9274
2.0	0.9540	0.9431
3.0	0.9639	0.9510
4.0	0.9758	0.9536
5.0	0.9876	0.9506
6.0	0.9969	0.9545
7.0	0.9999	0.9567

Number of Estimators

This parameter indicates the total number of trees that the classifier comprises of [16]. The trees are collectively used in voting to determine the result of the given classification. Increasing the number of trees allows a more diverse set of decision trees and a stronger prediction likelihood. There is the potential to overfit if increased too much as there will be more repetition of individual trees and potential for inaccuracies in the data set to have a larger effect on the model. Limiting the number of trees can again lead to not capturing enough information as there is the chance some features are not utilized. Having a low tree count and a relatively low tree depth can cause the model to underfit.

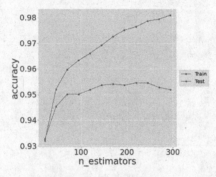

Fig. 3. Validation Curve of Number of Estimators

The validation curve in Fig. 3 and the accuracies listed in Table 2 indicate a significant increase in performance on test data when increasing the value for values less than 100. The increase in performance gradually reaches a point of minimal change and this is generally where the model will not gain any significant performance but continue to become exponentially more complex. We set the number of estimators to 160.

Table 2. Validation of number of estimators on Train and Test Data

Value	Accuracy on Train Data	Accuracy on Test Data
20.0	0.9320	0.9326
45.0	0.9520	0.9453
70.0	0.9596	0.9501
95.0	0.9633	0.9501
120.0	0.9660	0.9519
145.0	0.9692	0.9536
170.0	0.9726	0.9541
195.0	0.9751	0.9536

(*continued*)

Table 2. (*continued*)

Value	Accuracy on Train Data	Accuracy on Test Data
220.0	0.9764	0.9545
245.0	0.9786	0.9545
270.0	0.9793	0.9528
295.0	0.9809	0.9519

Learning Rate

As mentioned earlier, gradient boosting uses previous trees to better make successive trees in each step [16]. The trees are created sequentially and depend on the previous trees. The learning rate, or shrinkage, is a means of controlling the amount of effect that the previous tree has on the successive trees. A lower learning rate will slow down the correction process and requires more trees to generate. This has the potential to underfit as the model is not making as many corrections on successive trees. A higher learning rate will increase the effect that the previous tree corrections have on resulting trees. This will allow the model to converge faster but tends to overfit. It is effectively decreasing the total trees required to converge and overfit too closely on the resulting smaller tree total. Figure 4 and Table 3 present the validation curve and accuracies on both train and test data for the learning rate between 0 and 0.3.

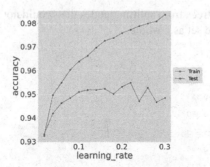

Fig. 4. Validation Curve of Learning rate

The plot of Fig. 4 and the accuracy values in Table 3 indicate that the performance on the test set stagnates for values higher than 0.12, and eventually displays unpredictable behavior as the model begins to overfit. We set the learning rate to 0.12 in the experiments.

Minimum number of samples per node

Minimum number of samples per node determines the minimum number of data samples that must be present to warrant a split within a node [16]. During the creation of trees nodes, random feature sets are assigned to individual trees and are then randomly split into further nodes within the tree with their own subset of random features taken from the

Table 3. Validation of learning rate on Train and Test Data

Value	Accuracy on Train data	Accuracy on Test data
0.02	0.9324	0.9331
0.04	0.9497	0.9418
0.06	0.9549	0.9462
0.08	0.9603	0.9484
0.10	0.9639	0.9510
0.12	0.9662	0.9519
0.14	0.9697	0.9519
0.16	0.9726	0.9523
0.18	0.9738	0.9501
0.20	0.9758	0.9532
0.22	0.9773	0.9549
0.24	0.9788	0.9471
0.26	0.9800	0.9528
0.28	0.9809	0.9466
0.30	0.9837	0.9484

tree. This value prevents trees from splitting nodes that would not have enough samples to be representative of the set as a whole.

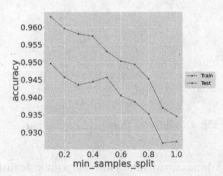

Fig. 5. Validation Curve of minimum number of samples per node

Both the validation curve in Fig. 5 and the data presented in Table 4 reveal that by increasing the parameter value accuracy decreases on both train and test sets. Therefore, we set the minimum number of samples per node to 0.1 as the model simply performed poorly on all higher values.

Table 4. Validation of minimum number of samples per node on Train and Test Data

Value	Accuracy on Train Data	Accuracy on Test Data
0.10	0.9630	0.9497
0.20	0.9596	0.9458
0.30	0.9581	0.9436
0.40	0.9575	0.9444
0.50	0.9531	0.9458
0.60	0.9503	0.9405
0.70	0.9494	0.9388
0.80	0.9453	0.9353
0.90	0.9370	0.9269
1.00	0.9346	0.9274

Maximum Features

This hyperparameter determines the highest percentage of features that can be considered when looking for the best split [16]. The trees are generated using randomly assigned feature sets and are then split into further subsets on that original random set of features. This hyperparameter specifies the largest possible proportion of the original tree feature set that can be applied when making a split. Correlated features as well as features with varying importance could have effect on the value of this parameter. This parameter can potentially give less important features a larger effect on the model performance which will in turn decrease accuracy.

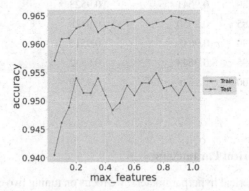

Fig. 6. Validation Curve of maximum number of features

According to the validation curve in Fig. 6 and the accuracies presented in Table 5, the maximum feature is set to 0.2, which means a maximum of 20% of the features are considered for a given node split per tree. Increasing the value of the parameter past this point (0.2) displays an erratic pattern in the accuracies. Also, the performance on the test data do not increase when considering a higher proportion of features for each split. This value allows the splits to be diverse enough to capture enough patternicity on the data but do not increase the complexity to the point of overfitting.

Table 5. Validation of maximum features on Train and Test Data

Value	Accuracy on Train Data	Accuracy on Test Data
0.05	0.9571	0.9405
0.10	0.9610	0.9462
0.15	0.9611	0.9488
0.20	0.9628	0.9541
0.25	0.9634	0.9514
0.30	0.9648	0.9514
0.35	0.9622	0.9541
0.40	0.9631	0.9510
0.45	0.9635	0.9484
0.50	0.9629	0.9497
0.55	0.9639	0.9528
0.60	0.9641	0.9510
0.65	0.9648	0.9532
0.70	0.9634	0.9532
0.75	0.9638	0.9549
0.80	0.9641	0.9523
0.85	0.9650	0.9528
0.90	0.9648	0.9510
0.95	0.9643	0.9532
1.00	0.9639	0.9510

4.2 Tuning Categorical Parameters

After tuning the numerical hyperparameters, we focus on tuning two categorical parameters, criterion and loss, used in the gradient boosting [16]. To try out different values and then select the value that results in the best score, we utilize grid search. The function used to tune the hyperparameters takes a dictionary of parameter names as well as their corresponding values that we intend to cross validate. The grid search technically cross validates using every potential parameter combination passed through it and returns the parameter combination that yielded the highest performance. Table 6 lists the dictionary of categorical values for each boosting parameter.

Table 6. Tuning Categorical parameters of the model

Parameter Name	Categorical Values
criterion	friedman_mse squared_error
loss	log_loss deviance exponential

In gradient boosting, the optimizations are made on successive trees, building upon the errors of the trees generated in previous steps. The trees are made to minimize a specific loss function which represents the error of the previous tree. This loss function is what gives way to the naming of the classifier as the loss is reduced over each tree with a gradient trend. There are two categorical values for this parameter, deviance, and exponential. The other parameter to be grid searched is the criterion. This parameter is responsible for the evaluation of the splits of the individual decision trees. Its value is dependent on the data set details and needs to be cross validated to determine which will yield the highest performance.

5   Model Evaluation

After tuning the hyperparameters, we create our model and evaluate its performance in terms of accuracy, precision, recall, and F1 score. The evaluation indicates an accuracy of 95.36%, the precision of 96.29%, the recall of 94.24%, and the F1 score of 95.26%. Table 7 indicate the confusion matrix of the model.

Table 7. Confusion matrix of the model

	Actual True	Actual False
Predicted True	1116	41
Predicted False	65	1064

Figure 7 presents the ROC curve of the gradient boosting classifier and the area under the curve is 0.9876.

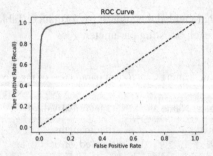

Fig. 7. ROC curve of the Gradient Boosting model

6 Conclusion

In this work, we classify 11,430 URLs using a gradient boosting ensemble learning. We utilize grid search method to tune the model's hyperparameters and improve the classification performance. The model is evaluated using evaluation metrics of accuracy, precision, recall, F1-score, and the area under the ROC curve. Our findings indicate that the optimized model can classify the URL samples in two classes of legitimate and phishing with an accuracy of 95.36%, the precision of 96.29%, the recall of 94.24%, the F1 score of 95.26%, and area under the ROC curve of 0.9876.

As a future work, we intend to compare the model's performance with other classification techniques such as K-nearest neighbors, AdaBoost, and random forest. We also plan to design and implement a deep neural network, which classifies the samples in a parallel mode to decrease the execution time. Exploring other benchmark data sets and evaluating the classification performance on new benchmarks could be another direction for our future study.

References

1. Basnet, R., Mukkamala, S., Sung, A.H.: Detection of phishing attacks: a machine learning approach. In: Prasad, B. (ed.) Soft Computing Applications in Industry, pp. 373–383. Springer Berlin Heidelberg, Berlin, Heidelberg (2008). https://doi.org/10.1007/978-3-540-77465-5_19
2. Abu-Nimeh, S., Nappa, D., Wang, X., Nair, S.: A comparison of machine learning techniques for phishing detection. In: Proceedings of the Anti-Phishing Working Groups 2nd Annual eCrime Researchers Summit. ACM, pp. 60–69 (2007)
3. APWG. Phishing activity trends report, 3rd quarter of 2022 (2023). https://www.apwg.org/resources/apwg-reports/
4. Mohammad, R.M., Thabtah, F., McCluskey, L.: Predicting phishing websites based on self-structuring neural network. Neural Comput. Appl. **25**(2), 443–458 (2014)
5. Jain, A.K., Gupta, B.B.: A novel approach to protect against phishing attacks at client side using auto-updated white-list. EURASIP J. Inf. Secur. **2016**(1), 9 (2016)
6. Tan, C.L., Chiew, K.L., Wong, K., et al.: PhishWHO: phishing webpage detection via identity keywords extraction and target domain name finder. Decis. Support Syst. **88**, 18–27 (2016)
7. Chiew, K.L., Chang, E.H., Tiong, W.K., et al.: Utilisation of website logo for phishing detection. Comput. Secur. **54**, 16–26 (2015)

8. Qabajeh, I., Thabtah, F., Chiclana, F.: A recent review of conventional vs. automated cybersecurity anti-phishing techniques. Comput. Sci. Rev. **29**, 44–55 (2018)
9. Rao, R.S., Pais, A.R.: Detection of phishing websites using an efficient feature-based machine learning framework. Neural Comput. Appl. 1–23 (2018)
10. Feng, F., Zhou, Q., Shen, Z., Yang, X., Han, L., Wang, J.: The application of a novel neural network in the detection of phishing websites. J. Ambient Intell. Human. Comput. (2018). https://doi.org/10.1007/s12652-018-0786-3
11. Mohammad, R., McCluskey, T., Thabtah, F.A.: Predicting Phishing Websites Using Neural Network Trained with Back-Propagation. World Congress in Computer Science, Computer Engineering, and Applied Computing (2013)
12. Sahingoz, O.K., Buber, E., Demir, O., Diri, B.: Machine learning based phishing detection from URLs. Expert Syst. Appl. **117**, 345–357 (2019)
13. Jain, A.K., Gupta, B.B.: Towards detection of phishing websites on client-side using machine learning based approach. Telecommun. Syst. **68**(4), 687–700 (2018)
14. Abdelhamid, N., Ayesh, A., Thabtah, F.: Phishing detection based associative classification data mining. Expert Syst. Appl. **41**(13), 5948–5959 (2014)
15. Nematzadeh, S., Kiani, F., Torkamanian-Afshar, M., Aydin, N.: Tuning hyperparameters of machine learning algorithms and deep neural networks using metaheuristics: a bioinformatics study on biomedical and biological cases. Comput. Biol. Chem. **97**, 107619 (2022)
16. Dong, X., et al.: A survey on ensemble learning. Front. Comput. Sci. **14**, 241–258 (2020)

Removing Ambiguity in Natural Language for Generating Self-Join Queries

Pradnya Sawant[✉][iD] and Kavita Sonawane[iD]

St. Francis Institute of Technology, Mumbai, India
{pradnyarane,kavitasonawane}@sfit.ac.in

Abstract. Databases systems are used almost everywhere in modern life and a prior knowledge of query languages like SQL is required to interact with these systems. Generally, relational databases are very useful for storing a significant amount of the world's data. But the user must know a query language to access this data efficiently. Nowadays, Natural Language Processing is used in almost every field of human-to-machine interaction. Mapping natural language into the form of structured query Language (SQL) has many benefits. An interface that uses natural language processing allows the user to interact with the relational database as if the communication is happening between human beings. There are different models available for mapping the natural language to SQL addressing various types of SQL queries. But some of the SQL queries like self join where the table needs to join with itself for generating the results, can not be handled by these existing state-of-the-art models as they require some common sense knowledge. And because of these ambiguities in natural language, converting natural language to SQL becomes a complex task. In this paper, a novel approach using word sense disambiguation, for understanding the context of the natural language question addressing self-join queries is being proposed. This proposed approach can be integrated with existing text to SQL models to understand the natural language questions which require common sense knowledge.

Keywords: Word Sense Disambiguation · Self-Join · Synset · Glosses

1 Introduction

In this advancing world, there is a need for humans to interact with computers to provide support in different fields like education, medicine, business, etc. The retrieval of such essential information from the database is a complex task. Database Management System (DBMS) software helps us to provide the storage and manipulation of this data. To extract information from the database, some prior knowledge is required by the user. Non-technical users face difficulty in retrieving the data from the database. To find the solution and to ease human-computer interaction, Natural Language Processing(NLP) techniques are being

© The Author(s), under exclusive license to Springer Nature Switzerland AG 2023
L. Rutkowski et al. (Eds.): ICAISC 2023, LNAI 14126, pp. 158–169, 2023.
https://doi.org/10.1007/978-3-031-42508-0_15

used. Hence natural language interfaces (NLIs) are developed to help the users in retrieving relevant information from the database. Several recent NLP to SQL systems address various SQL queries and achieve promising results. The SQL queries like self join where some common sense knowledge is required are not answered by these models because of the ambiguity in the natural language. In a real-world scenario, the practical use of these systems has not been sufficiently demonstrated yet. In this paper, we present an approach for finding the similarity value between the ambiguous word in the natural language and corresponding column headers in table schema using word sense disambiguation(WSD) where Wordnet, a database that has a set of lemmas along with a set of senses [22] is being used. Every sense of a word has a GLOSS (a dictionary-style definition), and a synset (a list of synonyms). These definitions of synsets are used to find the similarity value.

2   Related Work

There have been different approaches and architectures available in the field of Natural Language Interface to the database (NLIDB) [16–19]. Also, various methodologies are being suggested to evaluate the performance of these approaches [13]. The majority of the above-said systems are use-case specific i.e. they are dependent on the database domain. In recent years, many efforts have been made by researchers to find a perfect solution to the problem of converting Natural Language into SQL. Nowadays, recent deep learning techniques leverage the encoder-decoder models with a semantic analysis approach.

Following are the different models used for mapping Natural language questions to structured queries.

In **Seq2SQL** [1,14,15] Seq2SQL proposed a deep neural network model using reinforcement learning for converting natural language to SQL. Also, WikiSQL, a dataset of natural language questions and SQL queries is being introduced. Seq2SQL suffers from an "order-matter" problem, in which for the SQL WHERE clause if the order of the two conditions is changed, it changes the query results.

SQLNET [3] SQLNET is a sketch-based approach where a sequence-to-set model and column attention mechanism is being used. The model can solve the order problem in the conditions of the SQL WHERE clause. But this model does not work with SQL OR condition.

Bi-Attention [4] This model uses the bidirectional attention mechanisms along with character-level embedding(out of vocabulary words) and convolutional neural networks (CNNs) [5,6]. The model does not work with queries in which retrieval of more than one column is required. Also, complex SQL clauses like GROUP-BY, ORDER-BY, and JOIN conditions are not supported.

TypeSQL [7] extends on the sketch-based approach [3] used by SQLNet [4] by adding a type system. TypeSQL does not support complex SQL join conditions.

SyntaxSQLNet [8] solves complex, cross-domain natural language to SQL tasks to some extent. The Spider, cross-domain dataset was used for the same

[20]. The model uses a tree-based approach for generating nested SQL queries on unseen databases. It also uses table-aware column attention encoders and path history. Still, this model failed to generate queries having join conditions because it predicts the column names first, and then it chooses tables.

F-SemtoSql [9] This fuzzy semantic to SQL (F-SemtoSql) approach is used for converting NLP to SQL query on unseen and cross-domain databases. To avoid the order problem in the traditional model, an attention mechanism and a fuzzy decision mechanism are used to improve the model decision. It also proposes a new "randomly masked" used in Bidirectional Encoder Representations from Transformers (BERT) [10] training method. Still, this model failed to generate self-join queries where some common sense knowledge is required.

BERT neglects dependency between the masked positions hence new approaches like Roberta (Robustly optimized BERT approach) [11] and XLNet (Generalized Autoregressive Model) [12] is being used. Table 1 shows the summary of the comparison of existing approaches for converting natural language to SQL.

Table 1. Summary of comparison of existing approaches for NLP to SQL queries.

Model	Dataset	Methodology	Merits	Gaps	Remarks
SEQ2SQL	WikiSQL	Reinforcement Learning	Works with Basic SQL queries having where clause and aggregate functions	Suffers from Order matter problem	Works only on a single table
SEQ2NET	WikiSQL	Sketch based query synthesis	Does not suffer from Order matter problem	Does not support complex queries	Works only with single table
Bi-Attention Model	WikiSQL	Sketch based query synthesis, CNN based character level embedding	Does not suffer from Order matter problem	Model does not support complex queries	Works only with single table
TypeSQL	WikiSQL	Sketch-based query synthesis and type system	Works faster for SELECT queries.	Does not support complex and join queries	Works only with a single table
Syntax-SQLNet	Spider	Tree based SQL generator, Path History	Handles complex and cross-domain queries on unseen databases	Does not work well with queries having join conditions	Works with multiple tables but not for all join conditions
F-SemtoSql	Spider	Sketch based generator, Random masked mechanism, Fuzzy decision mechanism	Handles complex, nested, and cross-domain queries on unseen databases	Does not work for self-join queries	Works with multiple tables but not for all types of queries

3 Proposed Architecture

The following section focuses on the proposed system architecture along with the algorithm and proposed solution.

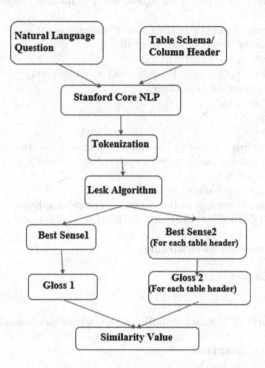

Fig. 1. Proposed Architecture.

3.1 Proposed Architecture

The proposed architecture depicted in Fig. 1 uses the concept of Word Sense Disambiguation(WSD) which is used for determining the sense of each word used in the given context [23]. The supervised algorithms fail on the words which are not seen during the training phase. These words can be unknown, ambiguous words, or out-of-vocabulary (OOV) words. To understand the context of these words during the testing phase, Lesk Algorithm [26] and Wordnet [22] are being used. Lesk algorithm is used to find the overlap between the dictionary definition of an ambiguous word with the words present in its neighborhood. Word net is used to find these dictionary definitions. Wordnet is a database that has a set of lemmas along with a set of senses. Every sense of a word has a GLOSS (a dictionary-style definition) and a synset (a list of synonyms). The existing algorithms used for finding similarity values between any two words only use the synset of the words and corresponding glosses(definitions) [24].

Algorithm 1: Semantic Similarity Algorithm

Input: Natural language question, column headers in table schema
Output: Similarity value, Column-header
Begin
bestsense1 = frequent-sense for an ambiguous word in natural language question
maximum-overlap $\leftarrow$ 0
inputcontext1 $\leftarrow$ words present in the natural language question
for each sense in senses of ambiguous word **do**
definition1 $\leftarrow$ words in the gloss(definition)
overlap $\leftarrow$ COMPUTE-OVERLAP (definition1,inputcontext1)
    if overlap $\leftarrow$ maximum-overlap **then**
maximum-overlap $\leftarrow$ overlap
bestsense1 $\leftarrow$ sense

inputcontext2 $\leftarrow$ words present in the natural language question after replacing an ambiguous word in natural language with each column-header[i] // i $\leftarrow$ 1 to n where n = no.of column headers
for each sense in senses of each table header[i] **do**
definition2[i] $\leftarrow$ words present in the gloss of every column-header[i]
overlap[i] $\leftarrow$ COMPUTE-OVERLAP (definition2[i],inputcontext2) // for every column-header[i]
    if overlap[i] $\leftarrow$ maximum-overlap **then**
maximum-overlap[i] $\leftarrow$ overlap
bestsense2[i] $\leftarrow$ sense

similarity[i] $\leftarrow$ 0;
similarity[i]=similarity(bestsense1.definition1, bestsense2[i].definition2) // for every column-header[i]
if similarity[i]>=threshold **then**
return(similarity, column-header)
end

To understand the context of the natural language(NL)question better, the proposed algorithm is a modified version of the Lesk algorithm where the Lesk algorithm is firstly used for finding the correct sense/synset of the ambiguous word (out of vocabulary) for the given input natural language question. At the same time, the sense of corresponding table headers is found for the natural language question using the Lesk algorithm. Then the semantic similarity is found between the definitions(gloss) of the best senses of the ambiguous word and the glosses of the table headers in the context of a given natural language question.

Depending on the experimentation, the threshold of similarity value is chosen as 0.5 to find which table headers are matching with the ambiguous or OOV word in the natural language question.

3.2 Proposed Solution

Some of the natural language questions require common sense knowledge which is outside the scope of the given database [20]. Consider the following example.
  Input:
NL question: "Find employee id for the employees who report to Kavita".
Table Schema: Employee(id, name, manager, age, salary)
Output(SQL Query):
SELECT id FROM employee WHERE manager = (SELECT id FROM employee WHERE name = 'Kavita')
Such SQL queries need common sense knowledge. For example, in this case, to interpret "X reports to Y" there is a need to join the same employee table itself. The existing datasets available for converting NLP to SQL do not address self-join queries. Hence the current state-of-the-art methods fail to address such NLP questions. T proposed system can handle such self-join queries which require some common sense knowledge e.g. interpreting the word "reports" means "who is a manager to whom" where "manager" can be one of the table headers. The similarity value between this ambiguous word "report" and the corresponding table headers can be found using the proposed semantic similarity algorithm.

4 Results and Discussion

There are various senses/ synsets present for English words in Wordnet. As shown in Fig. 2 there are different senses of the word "report" present in the Wordnet. Following are the step-by-step results of the proposed algorithm for finding the correct sense of the ambiguous/ OOV word in the given natural language question.

```
Synset('report.n.01') a written document describing the findings of some individual or group
Synset('report.n.02') the act of informing by verbal report
Synset('report.n.03') a short account of the news
Synset('report.n.04') a sharp explosive sound (especially the sound of a gun firing)
Synset('report_card.n.01') a written evaluation of a student's scholarship and deportment
Synset('composition.n.08') an essay (especially one written as an assignment)
Synset('reputation.n.03') the general estimation that the public has for a person
Synset('report.v.01') to give an account or representation of in words
Synset('report.v.02') announce as the result of an investigation or experience or finding
Synset('report.v.03') announce one's presence
Synset('report.v.04') make known to the authorities
Synset('report.v.05') be responsible for reporting the details of, as in journalism
Synset('report.v.06') complain about; make a charge against
```

Fig. 2. Synsets for word "report" from Wordnet.

4.1   Find the Best Sense for Ambiguous Word

The example which we have considered for self-join is "Find employee id for the employees who report to Kavita". The word tokenization is done first on the input sentence. Then we find the best sense of the ambiguous/OOV word "report" using the Lesk algorithm. The input sentence and the ambiguous word are given as input to the Lesk algorithm. It is clear from the Lesk algorithm that the ambiguous word "report" is used as the verb in the given natural language question. Also we can find the definition of the corresponding sense of the word "report" using Wordnet. So the definition(gloss) of word "report" in given natural language context is "make known to authorities". Figure 3 shows the best sense and gloss for the word "report" in the given context of a natural language question.

```
Sense= Synset('report.v.04')
Definition1 <- make known to the authorities
```

Fig. 3. Best sense and gloss for word "report" using Lesk and Wordnet.

4.2   Find the Best Sense and Gloss for Every Column Header

Replace the ambiguous word in the given natural language question with each column header one at a time and repeat the above procedure for each column header. The output of this step will be definitions of the best sense for each column header in the context of the input sentence. We have considered the table employee with column headers(id, name, manager, age, salary). Table 2 shows the best sense for every table header in the context of a given natural language question.

Table 2. Column header and corresponding gloss using Lesk and Wordnet.

Column Header	Synset using Lesk	Gloss/Definition
id	null	null.
name	Synset('name.v.02')	give the name or identifying characteristics of.
manager	Synset('director.n.01')	someone who controls resources and expenditures.
age	Synset('age.v.01')	begin to seem older; get older.
salary	Synset('wage.n.01')	something that remunerates.

4.3   Find Similarity Value

The similarity value between the gloss of ambiguous words and the glosses of each table header is found using cosine similarity as follows.

$$similarity(A, B) = \frac{A.B}{\|A\|\|\mathbf{B}\|} \tag{1}$$

where the attribute vectors A and B are the glosses of the best senses of the words.

SpaCy's large English model, en_core_web_lg is used to get the best word embedding. Word tokenization is done before calculating the similarity value. The similarities are found with stopwords and without stopwords as given in Table 3. Table 3 shows the similarity value between "report" and other column headers present in the table schema of the employee table using the proposed algorithm. Following are the results of similarities. The threshold value is selected as 0.5 depending on experimentation done on different glosses.

Table 3. Semantic similarity value between the glosses.

Word	Respective Glosses	Similarity with Stopwords	Similarity without Stopwords
(report,manager)	make known to the authorities, someone who controls resources and expenditures	0.73	0.5
(report, name)	make known to the authorities, give the name or identifying characteristics of	0.75	0.6
(report, age)	make known to the authorities, begin to seem older; get older	0.72	0.34
(report, salary)	make known to the authorities, something that remunerates	0.6	0.0

As shown in Table 3 it is observed that the similarity value between the glosses without using stop word removal is high even if the context of the glosses is different. But with stopword removal the similarity is marginal but it is making sense for the context of two glosses. Also the similarity of the word "report" is high for both manager and name, as both employee and manager can have id and name. In that case, as we need to map the word "report" with the "manager" column, we can consider the data type of columns or table contents. It is better understood that if the datatype of a manager column is similar to the datatype of the id column, it can be considered as a self-join query as the manager column is the id of the corresponding manager to every employee.

Table 4. Semantic similarity between the glosses.

words	Respective Glosses	Similarity with stopwords	Similarity without stopwords
(report, mentor)	make known to the authorities, serve as a teacher or trusted counselor.	0.62	0.5
(report, supervisor)	make known to the authorities, one who supervises or has charge and direction of	0.68	0.499
(report, administrator)	make known to the authorities, someone who manages a government agency or department	0.70	0.56
(report, boss)	make known to the authorities, a leader in a political party who controls votes and dictates appointments	0.68	0.52
(report, controller)	make known to the authorities, a person who directs and restrains	0.69	0.49

The proposed algorithm is evaluated on SyntaxSQL Model which was the first model that works with the cross-domain dataset SPIDER [8]. As self-join queries were not supported by the SyntaxSQL model, as cross-domain dataset SPIDER does not contain such queries. We augmented the SPIDER dataset with tables that support self-join queries and these tables contain the table headers like mentor, supervisor, administrator, boss, and controller depending on the use case. The model is again trained for this augmented dataset. During the testing phase, the words which require common sense knowledge like the word "report" is used to check the performance of the proposed algorithm. Table 4 shows the similarity value of the ambiguous word "report" with other table headers. From this experimentation it is found that the similarity value is always higher than the

Table 5. Similarity value between the glosses of semantically similar table headers.

words	Respective Glosses	Similarity with stopwords	Similarity without stopwords
(administrator, boss)	someone who manages a government agency or department, a leader in a political party who controls votes and dictates appointments	0.82	0.67
(supervisor, boss)	one who supervises or has charge and direction of, a leader in a political party who controls votes and dictates appointments	0.76	0.62
(supervisor, administrator)	one who supervises or has charge and direction of, someone who manages a government agency or department	0.79	0.70
(manager, controller)	someone who controls resources and expenditures, a person who directs and restrains	0.86	0.67
(manager, supervisor)	someone who controls resources and expenditures, one who supervises or has charge and direction of	0.80	0.70
(manager, administrator)	someone who controls resources and expenditures, someone who manages a government agency or department	0.81	0.71

threshold 0.5 as the word "report" has higher similarity with the table headers mentor, supervisor, administrator, boss, and controller.

The proposed algorithm is also used to check the similarity values for the glosses of the table headers which can be semantically similar to guarantee that the gloss of the ambiguous word "report" is highly mapping with the glosses of other table headers like a mentor, supervisor, etc. as shown in Table 5. The similarity value for all of the glosses of semantically similar table headers is found to be greater than the threshold of 0.5. The proposed algorithm performs fairly well for understanding the context of common sense words that are out of the scope of the database.

5   Conclusion and Future Scope

The proposed work is the first attempt to cover self-join queries in the task of converting natural language to SQL queries. The proposed algorithm can be incorporated into the existing models for understanding the context of the words which require common sense knowledge. Also, it is using the benefits from the Lesk algorithm and glosses of the synsets which again improves the similarity value between the ambiguous words in natural language and the actual table headers present in the database schema.

References

1. Zhong, V., Xiong, C., Socher, R.: Seq2sql: Generating structured queries from natural language using reinforcement learning. arXiv:1709.00103 (2017)
2. Vaswani, A., et al.: Attention is all you need. In: 31st Conference on Neural Information Processing Systems (NIPS 2017), Long Beach, CA, USA (2017). arXiv:1706.03762
3. Xu, X., Liu, C., Song, D.: SQLNET: generating structured queries from natural language without reinforcement learning. arXiv:1711.04436 (2017)
4. Huilin, G., Tong, G., Fan, W., Chao, M.: Bidirectional attention for SQL generation. In: IEEE 4th International Conference on Cloud Computing and Big Data Analytics (2019)
5. Pennington, J., Socher, R., Manning, C.: Glove: global vectors for word representation. In: Proceedings of the 2014 Conference on Empirical Methods in Natural Language Processing (EMNLP), pp. 1532–1543 (2014)
6. Kim, Y.: Convolutional neural networks for sentence classification. In: Proceedings of the 2014 Conference on Empirical Methods in Natural Language Processing (EMNLP) (2014)
7. Yu, T., Li, Z., Zhang, Z., Zhang, R., Radev, D.: TypeSQL: knowledge-based type-aware neural text-to-sql generation. In: 16th Annual Conference of the North American Chapter of the Association for Computational Linguistics, New Orleans (2018)
8. Yu, T., et al.: SyntaxSQLNet: syntax tree networks for complex and cross-domain text-to-SQL task. In: Proceedings of the Conference Empirical Methods Natural Language Processing, pp. 1653–1663 (2018)
9. Li, Q., Li, L., Li, Q., Zhong, J.: A comprehensive exploration on spider with fuzzy decision text-to-SQL model. IEEE Trans. Industr. Inf. **16**(4), 2542–2550 (2020)
10. Devlin, J., Chang, M.-W., Lee, K., Toutanova, K.: Bert: pre-training of deep bidirectional transformers for language understanding. arXiv:1810.04805 (2018)
11. Ahkouk, K., Machkour, M., Ennaji, M.: Data agnostic RoBERTa-based natural language to SQL query generation. In: IEEE 6th International Conference for Convergence in Technology (I2CT) (2021)
12. Li, H., Choi, J., Lee, S., Ho Ahn, J.: Comparing BERT and XLNet from the perspective of computational characteristics. In: IEEE International Conference on Electronics, Information, and Communication (ICEIC) (2020)

13. Kummerfeld, J., Zhang, L., Ramanathan, K., Radev, D.: Improving text-to-SQL evaluation methodology. In: Proceedings of the 56th Annual Meeting of the Association for Computational Linguistics (Long Papers), pp. 351–360 (2018)

14. Dong, L., Lapata, M.: Language to logical form with neural attention. arXiv:1601.01280 (2016)

15. Zaremba, W., Sutskever, I., Vinyals, O.: Recurrent neural network regularization. arXiv:1409.2329 (2015)

16. Pal, D., Sharma, H., Chaudhuri, K.: Comparative study of existing approaches on the task of natural language to database language. In: IEEE International Conference of Computer Science and Renewable Energies (ICCSRE) (2019)

17. Kumar, R., Dua, M.: Translating controlled natural language query into SQL query using pattern matching technique. In: International Conference for Convergence of Technology (2014)

18. Bais, H., Machkour, M., Koutti, L.: Querying database using a universal natural language interface based on machine learning. In: International Conference on Information Technology for Organizations Development (IT4OD) (2016)

19. Majhadi, K., Machkour, M.: The history and recent advances of natural language interfaces for databases querying. In: The 3rd International Conference of Computer Science and Renewable Energies, Volume 229, (2021)

20. Yu, T., et al.: Spider: A large-scale human-labeled dataset for complex and cross-domain semantic parsing and text-to-SQL task. In: Proceedings of the 2018 Conference on Empirical Methods in Natural Language Processing, pp. 3911–3921 (2018)

21. Yu, T.: Learning to map natural language to executable programs over databases, Ph. D. thesis, Yale University, Stamford (2021)

22. Brunner, U., Stockinged, K.: ValueNet: a neural text-to-SQL architecture incorporating values. In: IEEE Proceedings of the VLDB Endowment, ISSN 2150–8097 (2017)

23. Miller, G.A.: Wordnet: a lexical database for English. Commun. ACM **38**(11), 39–41 (1995)

24. Pedersen, T., Banerjee, S., Patwardhan, S.: Maximizing semantic relatedness to perform word sense disambiguation. University of Minnesota supercomputing institute research report UMSI, vol. 25, p. 2005 (2005)

25. Ezzikouri, H., Madani, Y., Erritali, M., Oukessou, M.: A new approach for calculating semantic similarity between words using wordnet and set theory. Elsevier proc. Comput. Sci. **151**, 1261–1265 (2019). https://doi.org/10.1016/j.procs.2019.04.182

26. Wikipedia. www.en.wikipedia.org/wiki/Leskalgorithm. Accessed 13 April 2023

Predicting Churn Rate in Companies

Magdalena Scherer[✉][iD]

Faculty of Management, Czestochowa University of Technology, Czestochowa, Poland
magdalena.scherer@pcz.pl

Abstract. Customer retention is a critical concern for companies, and as part of a Customer Relationship Management (CRM) approach. The article presents a method of predicting churn rate based on neuro-fuzzy systems. Such approach allows to achieve interpretability comparing to e.g. neural networks. We demonstrate the usefulness of the approach on a bank customer dataset.

1 Introduction

Churn prediction, also known as customer churn or customer attrition prediction, is a process of using data analysis and predictive modeling techniques to identify and predict customers who are most likely to stop using a product or service. Churn refers to the phenomenon where customers discontinue their relationship with a business, which can have negative implications for a company's revenue and growth. Churn prediction is sometimes as important as advertisement analysis [6,7].

Churn prediction involves analyzing historical data on customer behavior, such as purchase history, engagement metrics, customer demographics, and interactions with the company's products or services. This data is used to build predictive models that can identify patterns and indicators of customer churn. The goal of churn prediction is to proactively identify customers who are at risk of churning and take appropriate actions to retain them. By identifying these customers in advance, companies can implement targeted retention strategies, such as personalized offers, incentives, or proactive customer support, to reduce the likelihood of churn. Churn prediction models typically use machine learning algorithms, such as logistic regression, decision trees, random forests, or neural networks, to analyze the data and generate predictions. These models can consider various features and factors that influence churn, including customer behavior, satisfaction, tenure, product usage, and external factors like competitive offerings or market trends. The output of churn prediction models is a probability or score indicating the likelihood of a customer churning. Companies can use these predictions to prioritize their retention efforts and allocate resources effectively to retain customers who are most at risk. Churn prediction is widely used in industries such as telecommunications, banking, e-commerce, subscription services, and software-as-a-service (SaaS) companies. It helps businesses to proactively manage customer retention, improve customer satisfaction,

L. Rutkowski et al. (Eds.): ICAISC 2023, LNAI 14126, pp. 170–175, 2023.
https://doi.org/10.1007/978-3-031-42508-0_16

and ultimately reduce customer churn, leading to increased revenue and long-term business growth.

In the paper we use neuro-fuzzy systems [11] to predict churn rate. While neural networks are often considered "black boxes" due to their complex internal structure, neuro-fuzzy systems generate human-readable rules that can be easily understood and modified. Similar concept but for handling missing data are rough set-based systems [8].

The rest of the paper is organized as follows. In Sect. 2 we describe shortly other approaches. Neuro-fuzzy systems are described in Sect. 3. Section 4 presents the results of experiments on the bank customer dataset and Sect. 5 concludes the paper.

2   Related Work

In [10] the authors analyzed the performance of different algorithms for predicting customer churn in order to maximize financial benefits for companies. They evaluated four algorithms by examining Receiver Operating Characteristics (ROC) curves and Area Under Curve (AUC) metrics. The results showed that the Stochastic Gradient Booster model performed exceptionally well with an AUC of 0.84, while the K-Nearest Neighbor model had a relatively lower AUC of 0.781. The researchers also found that using Grid Search CV for hyperparameter optimization increased computation time, and that Randomized Search CV did not guarantee the selection of optimal hyperparameters even when considering a larger hyperparameter space. Grid Search Cross-Validation, is a technique used in machine learning to find the best combination of hyperparameters for a model.

In [1] the authors explore the use of Adaptive Neuro Fuzzy Inference System (ANFIS) as a neuro-fuzzy classifier for customer churn prediction. The authors used a publicly available dataset called "Telecom Customer Churn Dataset" from the UCI Machine Learning Repository. The proportion of churners was oversampled in the training set to give the predictive model a better ability of discerning discriminating patterns. The proportion of churner and non-churner in the training data set is 50%-50%. The test set was not oversampled to provide a more realistic test set, and the churn rate remained 14.3%. The paper compares the ANFIS model with two state-of-the-art crisp classifiers, C4.5 and RIPPER, and introduces generating fuzzy inference system using fuzzy C-means clustering. The paper also describes the data preprocessing, evaluation metrics, and model building used in the experiments. The results show that ANFIS models have acceptable performance in terms of accuracy, specificity, and sensitivity, and are also more comprehensible than traditional rule-based classifiers.

The authors of [12] aimed at predicting whether the student will churn in the future. The research focuses on higher education institutes with the engineering field in Indonesia The researchers and uses 100 datasets of informatics engineering students from 2014 to 2020. The authors used the Fuzzy C-Means algorithm to group students and predict churn.

In [2] a fuzzy based prediction and retention model for identifying potential churners and devising effective retention strategies in the telecom industry is proposed. The dataset used in the paper is provided by a telecom company operating in South Asia. It consists of 1,000,000 instances of customers with 722 attributes taken from a CDR dataset containing variables like data, voice and SMS usage detail. It covers 3 months usage information of Jan, Feb and Mar 2016 along with complaints data of same months.

The authors of [9] study fuzzy logic-based methods and improve the forecast of customer churn through the use of a fuzzy neural network. The object of research was the process of predicting the churn of customers of telecommunications companies based on fuzzy logic and neural networks. The research is based on the application of an approach that is implemented through the combined use of fuzzy logic and neural networks. The main assumption of the study is the hypothesis that the use of a fuzzy neural network formed on the basis of fuzzy logic algorithms can improve the prediction of customer churn relative to available solutions. The authors also used the Sugeno algorithm for integrated methods of fuzzy logic and neural networks. The paper does not provide specific information about the datasets used in the study. However, it mentions that the object of research was the process of predicting the churn of customers of telecommunications companies based on fuzzy logic and neural networks. The authors proposed a model for predicting customer churn based on the combined use of fuzzy logic and neural networks.

In [14] machine learning techniques are used to predict bank churn and provide insights into the factors that contribute to it. The authors also aim to construct balanced data to train and explain their models, and to analyze the performance results of their experiment.

3   Mamdani-Type Neuro-Fuzzy Systems

In this section we describe Mamdani neuro-fuzzy systems [11]. We consider multi-input-single-output fuzzy system mapping $\mathbf{X} \to Y$, where $\mathbf{X} \subset R^n$ and $Y \subset R$. Theoretically, the system is composed of a fuzzifier, a fuzzy rule base, a fuzzy inference engine and a defuzzifier. The fuzzifier performs a mapping from the observed crisp input space $\mathbf{X} \subset R^n$ to a fuzzy set defined in X. The most commonly used fuzzifier is the singleton fuzzifier which maps $\bar{\mathbf{x}} = [\bar{x}_1, \ldots, \bar{x}_n] \in X$ into a fuzzy set $A' \subseteq X$ characterized by the membership function

$$\mu_{A'}(x) = \begin{cases} 1 \text{ if } x = \bar{x} \\ 0 \text{ if } x \neq \bar{x} \end{cases} \tag{1}$$

Equation (1) means that, in fact, we get rid of the fuzzifier. The knowledge of the system is stored in the fuzzy rule base which consists of a collection of N fuzzy IF-THEN rules in the form

$$R^{(k)} : \text{IF } x_1 \text{ is } A_1^k \text{ AND } x_2 \text{ is } A_2^k \ldots \text{AND } x_n \text{ is } A_n^k \text{ THEN } y \text{ is } B^k \tag{2}$$

where $\mathbf{x} = [x_1, \ldots, x_n] \in \mathbf{X}$, $y \in Y$, $A^k = A_1^k \times A_2^k \times \ldots \times A_n^k$, $A_1^k, A_2^k, \ldots, A_n^k$ are fuzzy sets characterized by membership functions $\mu_{A_i^k}(x_i)$, $i = 1, \ldots, n$, $k = 1, \ldots, N$, whereas B^k are fuzzy sets characterized by membership functions $\mu_{B^k}(y)$, $k = 1, \ldots, N$. The firing strength of the k-th rule, $k = 1, \ldots, N$, is defined by

$$\tau_k(\bar{\mathbf{x}}) = \overset{n}{\underset{i=1}{T}}\left\{\mu_{A_i^k}(\bar{x}_i)\right\} = \mu_{A^k}(\bar{\mathbf{x}}).\tag{3}$$

The defuzzification is realized by the following formula

$$\bar{y} = \frac{\sum_{r=1}^N \bar{y}^r \cdot \mu_{\bar{B}^r}(\bar{y}^r)}{\sum_{r=1}^N \mu_{\bar{B}^r}(\bar{y}^r)}.\tag{4}$$

The membership functions of fuzzy sets $\bar{B}^r$, $r = 1, 2, \ldots, N$, are defined using the following formula:

$$\mu_{\bar{B}^r}(y) = \sup_{\mathbf{x} \in \mathbf{X}}\left\{\mu_{A^r}(\mathbf{x}) \overset{T}{*} \mu_{A^r \to B^r}(\mathbf{x}, y)\right\}.\tag{5}$$

With singleton type fuzzification, the formula takes the form

$$\mu_{\bar{B}^r}(y) = \mu_{A^r \to B^r}(\bar{\mathbf{x}}, y) = T\left(\mu_{A^r}(\bar{\mathbf{x}}), \mu_{B^r}(y)\right).\tag{6}$$

Since $\mu_{A^r}(\bar{\mathbf{x}}) = \overset{n}{\underset{i=1}{T}}\left(\mu_{A_i^r}(\bar{x}_i)\right)$, we have

$$\mu_{\bar{B}^r}(y) = \mu_{A^r \to B^r}(\bar{\mathbf{x}}, y) = T\left[\overset{n}{\underset{i=1}{T}}\left(\mu_{A_i^r}(\bar{x}_i)\right), \mu_{B^r}(y)\right],\tag{7}$$

where T is any t-norm. Because $\mu_{B^r}(\bar{y}^r) = 1$ and $T(a, 1) = a$, we obtain the following formula

$$\mu_{\bar{B}^r}(\bar{y}^r) = \overset{n}{\underset{i=1}{T}}\left(\mu_{A_i^r}(\bar{x}_i)\right).\tag{8}$$

Finally we obtain

$$\bar{y} = \frac{\sum_{r=1}^N \bar{y}^r \cdot T_{i=1}^n\left(\mu_{A_i^r}(\bar{x}_i)\right)}{\sum_{r=1}^N T_{i=1}^n\left(\mu_{A_i^r}(\bar{x}_i)\right)}.\tag{9}$$

Input linguistic variables are described by means of Gaussian membership functions, that is

$$\mu_{A_i^r}(x_i) = \exp\left[-\left(\frac{x_i - \bar{x}_i^r}{\sigma_i^r}\right)^2\right],\tag{10}$$

If we apply the Larsen (product) rule of inference, we obtain the following formula for the output of the single Mamdani neuro-fuzzy system

$$\bar{y} = \frac{\sum_{r=1}^N \bar{y}^r \left(\prod_{i=1}^n \exp\left[-\left((\bar{x}_i - \bar{x}_i^r)/\sigma_i^r\right)^2\right]\right)}{\sum_{r=1}^N \left(\prod_{i=1}^n \exp\left[-\left((\bar{x}_i - \bar{x}_i^r)/\sigma_i^r\right)^2\right]\right)}.\tag{11}$$

The neuro-fuzzy systems can be trained by gradient methods [3–5] or e.g. by evolutionary algorithms [13, 15, 16].

4 Training the Fuzzy Model

To demonstrate usefulness of the method we used the Bank Customer Churn Prediction dataset from kaggle.com. It is presented partially in Table 1 after meaningless columns removed. Then we one-hot encoded countries. We created a system with two fuzzy sets for every input. The after gradient training we obtained precision 0.85 and F1-score 0.89.

Table 1. Example rows of the Bank Customer Churn Prediction dataset

Row number	CreditScore	Geography	Gender	Age	Tenure	Balance	NumOf Products	HasCr Card	IsActive Member	Estimated Salary	Exited
0	619	France	Female	42	2	0.00	1	1	1	101348.88	1
1	608	Spain	Female	41	1	83807.86	1	0	1	112542.58	0
2	502	France	Female	42	8	159660.80	3	1	0	113931.57	1
3	699	France	Female	39	1	0.00	2	0	0	93826.63	0
4	850	Spain	Female	43	2	125510.82	1	1	1	79084.10	0
...	...	...	...	...	...	...	...	...	...	...	...
9995	771	France	Male	39	5	0.00	2	1	0	96270.64	0
9996	516	France	Male	35	10	57369.61	1	1	1	101699.77	0
9997	709	France	Female	36	7	0.00	1	0	1	42085.58	1
9998	772	Germany	Male	42	3	75075.31	2	1	0	92888.52	1
9999	792	France	Female	28	4	130142.79	1	1	0	38190.78	0

5 Conclusions

We proposed a method to predict churn by neuro-fuzzy systems. One of the main benefits of neuro-fuzzy systems is their ability to provide interpretable rules. Neural networks are known for their ability to learn from data, and neuro-fuzzy systems inherit this capability. By combining the learning ability of neural networks with the interpretability of fuzzy logic, neuro-fuzzy systems can adapt to new data and improve their performance over time.

References

1. Abbasimehr, H., Setak, M., Tarokh, M.: A neuro-fuzzy classifier for customer churn prediction. Int. J. Comput. Appl. **19**(8), 35–41 (2011)
2. Azeem, M., Usman, M.: A fuzzy based churn prediction and retention model for prepaid customers in telecom industry. Int. J. comput. intell. syst. **11**(1), 66–78 (2018)
3. Bilski, J., Kowalczyk, B., Kisiel-Dorohinicki, M., Siwocha, A., Zurada, J.: Towards a very fast feedforward multilayer neural networks training algorithm. J. Artif. Intell. Soft Comput. Res. **12**(3), 181–195 (2022). https://doi.org/10.2478/jaiscr-2022-0012
4. Bilski, J., Rutkowski, L., Smolag, J., Tao, D.: A novel method for speed training acceleration of recurrent neural networks. Inf. Sci. **553**, 266–279 (2021) https://doi.org/10.1016/j.ins.2020.10.025, www.sciencedirect.com/science/article/pii/S0020025520310161

5. Bilski, J., Smolag, J., Kowalczyk, B., Grzanek, K., Izonin, I.: Fast computational approach to the Levenberg-Marquardt algorithm for training feedforward neural networks. J. Artif. Intell. Soft Comput. Res. **12**(2), 45–61 (2023). https://doi.org/ 10.2478/jaiscr-2023-0006

6. Gabryel, M., Lada, D., Filutowicz, Z., Patora-Wysocka, Z., Kisiel-Dorohinicki, M., Chen, G.Y.: Detecting anomalies in advertising web traffic with the use of the variational autoencoder. J. Artif. Intell. Soft Comput. Res. **12**(4), 255–256 (2022)

7. Gabryel, M., Scherer, M.M., Sułkowski, Ł, Damaševičius, R.: Decision making support system for managing advertisers by ad fraud detection. J. Artif. Intell. Soft Comput. Res. **11**, 331–339 (2021)

8. Nowicki, R.K., Seliga, R., Zelasko, D., Hayashi, Y.: Performance analysis of rough set-based hybrid classification systems in the case of missing values. J. Artif. Intell. Soft Comput. Res. **11**(4), 307–318 (2021). https://doi.org/10.2478/jaiscr-2021-0018

9. Papa, A., Shemet, Y., Yarovyi, A.: Analysis of fuzzy logic methods for forecasting customer churn. Technol. Audit Prod. Reserves **1**(2), 57 (2021)

10. Prabadevi, B., Shalini, R., Kavitha, B.: Customer churning analysis using machine learning algorithms. Int. J. Intell. Netw. **4**, 145–154 (2023) https:// doi.org/10.1016/j.ijin.2023.05.005, www.sciencedirect.com/science/article/pii/ S2666603023000143

11. Scherer, R.: Multiple Fuzzy Classification Systems. Springer Publishing Company, Incorporated (2014)

12. Supangat, S., Bin Saringat, M., Kusnanto, G., Andrianto, A.: Churn prediction on higher education data with fuzzy logic algorithm. SISFORMA **8**(1), 22–29 (2021)

13. Szczypta, J., Przybył, A., Cpałka, K.: Some aspects of evolutionary designing optimal controllers. In: Rutkowski, L., Korytkowski, M., Scherer, R., Tadeusiewicz, R., Zadeh, L.A., Zurada, J.M. (eds.) ICAISC 2013. LNCS (LNAI), vol. 7895, pp. 91–100. Springer, Heidelberg (2013). https://doi.org/10.1007/978-3-642-38610-7_9

14. Tekouabou, S.C., Gherghina, S.C., Toulni, H., Mata, P.N., Martins, J.M.: Towards explainable machine learning for bank churn prediction using data balancing and ensemble-based methods. Mathematics **10**(14), 2379 (2022)

15. Zalasiński, M., Cpałka, K., Hayashi, Y.: New fast algorithm for the dynamic signature verification using global features values. In: Rutkowski, L., Korytkowski, M., Scherer, R., Tadeusiewicz, R., Zadeh, L.A., Zurada, J.M. (eds.) ICAISC 2015. LNCS (LNAI), vol. 9120, pp. 175–188. Springer, Cham (2015). https://doi.org/10. 1007/978-3-319-19369-4_17

16. Zalasiński, M., Cpałka, K., Rakus-Andersson, E.: An Idea of the dynamic signature verification based on a hybrid approach. In: Rutkowski, L., Korytkowski, M., Scherer, R., Tadeusiewicz, R., Zadeh, L.A., Zurada, J.M. (eds.) ICAISC 2016. LNCS (LNAI), vol. 9693, pp. 232–246. Springer, Cham (2016). https://doi.org/10. 1007/978-3-319-39384-1_21

Training Set Preparation for Deep Model Learning Inpatients with Ischemic Brain Lesions and Gender Identity Disorder

Ana Starcevic[1] , Boris Vucinic[1], and Ilona Karpiel[2]([✉])

[1] Laboratory for Multimodal Neuroimaging, Institute of Anatomy, Medical Faculty, University of Belgrade, 11000 Belgrade, Serbia
[2] Łukasiewicz Research Network – Krakow Institute of Technology, The Centre for Biomedical Engineering, Zakopianska Str. 73, 30-418 Krakow, Poland
Ilona.karpiel@kit.lukasiewicz.gov.pl

Abstract. Increasing number of stress related cerebrovascular insults becomes alerting younger involved as well. Cerebrovascular diseases are the most common cause of functional disabilities, stroke being first, of which 87% are ischemic strokes in the USA. The cause of ischemia likely lies in cerebral small vessel disease, which includes lacunar infarcts, microbleeds, white matter lesions (WML) and enlarged perivascular spaces. The pathophysiology of ischemic WML is unclear, despite the development of radiological markers. The gold standard in the evaluation of WML is a volumetric analysis using magnetic resonance imaging (MRI).

The aim of this study was training set preparation and volumetric analysis of multiple or solitary WML due to ischemic changes in patients with depressions and comparing it with a control group without white matter lesions and ischemic changes.

We included 20 participants, 10 with WML and 10 controls as part of the process of applying deep machine learning and preparing a training set for the automated detection of WML. Participants under went 1.5 T 3D-T1v, MPRAGE and 3D FLAIR MRI. Images were aligned with MNI space to normalize their intensity. Manual segmentation was then performed as the gold standard for segmentation in MNI space with ITK-SNAP using T1v and FLAIR images.

A summary estimation of all volumes of the image sections was performed. The total volume of all brain lesions was measured without division into hemispheres and their localization. The total volume of the brain was measured and correlated with the same parameters of subjects without noticeable ischemic changes in the brain.

We have shown that ischemic lesions of the cerebrum white matter affect reduced total brain volume. The studies will aid in coming up with better treatment guidelines for preventive health care and management of cerebrovascular diseases to address the specific needs of individuals with gender identity disorders or transgenders.

Keywords: white matter lesions · WML · transsexual · imaging · lesion detection · volumetric analysis · training · MRI

L. Rutkowski et al. (Eds.): ICAISC 2023, LNAI 14126, pp. 176–191, 2023.
https://doi.org/10.1007/978-3-031-42508-0_17

Abbreviations

TBV   total brain volume
WML   white matter lesions
MRI   magnetic resonance imaging
CSVD   Cerebral small vessel disease
CMB   cerebral microbleeds
DICOM digital imaging and communications in medicine
NIfTI   Neuroimaging Informatics Technology Initiative
WMH   white matter hyperintensities
PD   proton density

1 Introduction

Term gender identity disorder is defined as one in which an individual exibits persistant discomfort or dysphoria in his or hers own body and inappropriatness in biological gender role. There are other terms used transsexual, trasgendered or transvestite as genderrole and sexual idehe search for the origin of gender identity and sexual orientation is part of the debate on the impact of nature and culture on human life [1]. This topic is highly controversial, due to its cultural, social, and political implications, and it is widely debated within the scientific community. Despite the efforts of scientists in conducting objective research, research on social problems are influenced by the cultural environment, and often reflect the dominant theories of their time [2]. There is an eternal question asking to what extent are gender and sexual orientation biologically determined and/or socially constructed by personal experiences and cultural expectations? Many neuroanatomical, neurophysiological, and neurometabolic features in transgender individuals resemble those of their experienced gender despite the majority resembling those from their birth sex [3].

It is always difficult to interpret findings with noninvasive neuroimaging. Given the gross nature of these measures, it is possible that more differences too subtle to measure with available tools yet contributing to gender identity and sexual orientation could be found. Conflicting results contributed to the difficulty of identifying specific brain features which consistently differ between cisgender and transgender or between heterosexual and homosexual groups. The small number of studies, the small-to-moderate sample size of each study, and the heterogeneity of the investigations made it impossible to meta-analyze all the data extracted. Further studies are necessary to increase the understanding of the neurological substrates of human sexuality. Due to conflicting results, it was, however, not possible to identify specific brain features which consistently differ between cisgender and transgender nor between heterosexual and homosexual groups. Very small brain changes, to date undetectable using the current neuroimaging tools, may affect behavior [4]. Individuals with gender identity disorder are always under stress which triggers neuroinflammatory mechanism and therefore impact vascular substrates causing events in the brain.

Cerebrovascular diseases are the most common diseases that cause functional disability [5]. According to data from the World Health Organization, over 15 million people suffer a stroke annually, of which 5 million die, while 5 million become permanently disabled [6]. In the United States, the most common form is ischemic stroke with a share of about 87% [7]. In Serbia, the incidence of strokes among diseases is decreasing - from 3.6% in 2013 to 1.3% in 2019, with a 1.5% share in men and 1% in women in 2019 [8]. According to clinical manifestations, characteristics of lesions and existing vascular diseases, ischemic strokes can be divided into lacunar, embolic and thrombotic cerebral infarctions.

Cerebral small vessel disease (CSVD), which includes all pathological processes of the small blood vessels of the brain, is associated with cognitive decline [9]. Visible consequences of CSVD on the brain parenchyma include lacunar infarcts, cerebral microbleeds (CMB), white matter lesions (WML) and enlarged perivascular spaces [10]. Previous studies have shown that numerous factors are associated with CSVD, the most common of which are hypertension [11] and age [12]. It has been shown that salt intake can also be a factor in pathogenesis, due to the effect on endothelial cells [13]. Despite the progress of radiological markers, it is not possible to directly study pathological changes in small blood vessels in detail. With the aging of the population and the development of more precise methods for neuroimaging, the frequency of WML is gradually increasing. Histopathological features of WML are pale myelin, demyelination, apoptosis of oligodendrocytes and vacuolization. Although attracting increasing attention, the pathogenesis of WML remains unclear [14]. High levels of microglial activity are associated with greater WML volume [15], suggesting that the innate immune system may contribute to inflammatory neurodegeneration. It has been suggested that WMLs may be due to atherosclerosis [16] and consequent brain hypoperfusion or ischemia, while some researchers have linked them to hypertension [17]. The spatial pattern of WML occurrence may provide insight into the pathophysiology of CSVD. WMLs have a tendency to appear in the periventricular and deep white matter, the region of the central border zone of the brain (IBZ, eng. Internal border zone) [18]. The white matter is the most vulnerable region in terms of damage from hypoxia, i.e. hypoperfusion, due to the "watershed" effect, which implies reduced blood flow in the border areas of the supply area of large cerebral arteries [19]. Categorization of WML is primarily done through two radiographic approaches - visual scaling and volumetric analysis. The scales most commonly used today for visual assessment were developed by van Swieten et al. [20] and Fazekas et al. [21]. An alternative approach to assessing WML is volumetric analysis using MRI. Compared to the qualitative visual assessment of WML, volumetrics provide greater accuracy and precision [22, 23]. In T2W (eng. T2-weighted) and FLAIR (eng. Fluid-attenuated inversion recovery) MRI, WMLs appear as hyperintensity signals in the white matter of the brain [24]. FLAIR MRI is preferred for the analysis of WML [25], because the strong signal originating from cerebrospinal fluid in T2 is suppressed, which allows better visualization of brain white matter disease in FLAIR [26]. Because of this, the increase in water content due to ischemia or demyelination is much better observed in FLAIR than in T1 or T2 [27]. The need for objective, consistent and efficient analysis of WML has put automatic methods for segmentation in the focus of research.

Automatic segmentation methods proposed in the literature include clustering and thresholding [28]. Jack et al. [29] proposed a thresholding method for segmentation of WML from FLAIR MRI based on multiple (step-wise) regression. Statistical data were used to find thresholds for separating cerebrospinal fluid, healthy brain tissue (gray and white matter) and WML. Admiraal-Behloul et al. [30] proposed a two-level segmentation scheme that combines data from proton density (PD), T2W and FLAIR images. Using deep learning algorithms, such as convolutional neural networks [31, 32], as well as machine learning algorithms, it is possible to further improve and automate the analysis process, sensitivity and prognostic accuracy of volumetric analysis [33]. However, such an approach to research is conditioned by the availability of tools that can often be too complicated to use and impractical in everyday clinical practice.

The aim of this work is the volumetric analysis of white matter lesions and its relationship with the volume of the cerebrum in transsexual individuals with chronic ischemic brain changes, and the comparison of the total brain volume in individuals with chronic ischemic brain changes with the total brain volume of a healthy control group. This pilot analysis is part of a preparatory training set for deep machine learning of an experimental paradigm on a large number of recordings.

2 Materials and Methods

2.1 Subjects

Our research included 20 transsexual individuals, namely 10 subjects with ischemic changes in the cerebrum and 10 control subjects. Respondents were selected by simple randomization - using tables of random numbers. They were not divided and categoraized into MtF and FtM (male to female and female to male) in this preparation of training set. The aim was just to evaluate and distinguish morphometric parameters between two different groups and make separation between brains with WMH and brains without WMH in transsexual individuals in order to further process dana and expand analysis with more variables included. The recordings were made in transsexual patients with chronic ischemic changes due to hypertension and atherosclerotic changes in the branch of the common carotid artery (arteria carotis communis) in order to evaluate the volumetric discrepancies of the white matter of the cerebrum due to ischemic changes.

2.2 MRI, Image Acquisition

For the purposes of our pilot analysis, T1-sequence MRI images were used in order to visualize lesions that exist in certain segments of the cerebrum. The database consists of DICOM MRI images (digital imaging and communications in medicine) format. These data are part of the process of applying deep machine learning, preparation of the so-called training set for the synthesis of the paradigm of automated detection of lesions of the white matter of the cerebrum [34], i.e. masking of lesions based on which the machine/computer needs to discern what the lesion is. The subjects underwent 1.5T 3D-T1v (eng. T1 relaxation value), MPRAGE (eng. Magnetization-prepared 180 degrees radio-frequency pulses and rapid gradient-echo sampling) and 3D FLAIR MRI. All images are aligned to MNI (Montreal Neurological Institute) space, in order to normalize their intensity. The MNI space defines the boundaries around the brain expressed in millimeters, from the set origin, and is routinely used as a tool of the software in which the analysis is done. After that, manual segmentation was performed as the gold standard segmentation in MNI space for all subjects and the control group with ITK-SNAP using T1v and FLAIR images [35] (Appendix I-IV). As mentioned before, our data consisted of MRI sequences of 24 subjects and the manual segmentation of their existing WMH by an expert neuroradiologist and neuroscientist. The pilot study was performed on 20 subjects, 10 with gender identity disorder and 10 who had no known mental disorder. T1-weighted sequences were acquired in a transverse direction (z), and the resulting image shape of the MRI sequence was (x, y, z) (512, 512, 256). The voxels on the 3DT1 were isotropic, with a size of 1 mm in each direction and a width of 1.0 mm. The FLAIR is a neuroimaging informatics technology initiative (NifTI) image corresponding to the fluid-attenuated inversion recovery MRI sequence. The manual segmentation was realized on the images as is, where the WMH were visually appreciable. As a consequence of the fact that the coordinates of the WMH are in the space of the images, the algorithms must run in this image space to be able to evaluate the results. The FLAIR sequences were taken in the coronal direction ($\hat{y}$). The resulting image shape of the sequences is ($\hat{x}$, $\hat{y}$, $\hat{z}$) − → (512, 22, 512). The pixels in the $\hat{x}$ and $\hat{z}$ directions correspond to 0.4297 mm each, and the ones in the $\hat{y}$ direction correspond to 6 mm each. Each voxel of the 3D image has a size of $0.4297 \times 6.0 \times 0.4297$ mm^3. The FLAIR image space is relevant, as is where the manual delimitation is performed and where the algorithms output their results for the WMH segmentation.

2.3 Prepared and Preprocessing Data

Because our segmentation methods are designed to work in the FLAIR image space, the plain 3DT1 serves little purpose. To be able to correlate each voxel in the FLAIR image to one or more of the 3DT1 images, we must align both images. This is a common issue in neuroimaging and has received a lot of attention. There are numerous possible transformations, some simple and some more complex. The transformation parameters, as well as the final T1 image aligned in FLAIR space, are provided in a text file. The registration of both images could be considered a preprocessing step. If we've done so, it's because some of the methods rely on it, but most simply take the original 3DT1 image and do the registration with their own procedure. Although bias field correction is just one of the small and general steps before training a model to segment WMH, our analyzed data is already considered preprocessed. Despite the correction, most methods in the challenge perform further preprocessing on the data to achieve better performance results. They must decide whether to use the original data or the bias field corrected data. Sometimes both samples might be used. An SPM12 [36] was used to correct the bias field. Our initial data set included manual WMH segmentation for each subject. The precise data was made up of the central coordinates of each WMH, the subject to which it belonged, and a label indicating its approximate size. The labels were not classified into different categories using Fazekas' scale [37]. An expert neuroradiologist and expert neuroscientist reviewed all of the annotations twice. As a gold standard, we consider this data our manual standard, as it is the only reliable source we have available for the localization of WMH in our data as a preparation training data set. Before generating the evaluation masks and to give some insight into our data, we computed some statistics of our manual segmentations. These are displayed and discussed below.

First, by checking the number and distribution of WMH present in each subject, we realized that all our subjects had at least 2 WMH, independently of suffering certain cognitive issues. Acknowledging if a subject suffers from some cognitive or other mental disorders can't be directly extracted from the WMH distribution, only presumably. Deeply analyzing patterns in the distributions, sizes, and other characteristics of WMH in brains suffering from dementia or other mental disorders is the key point for which automatic detection of WMH is important. As a counterpart to our manual segmentation of WMH, we have the masks output by the segmentation methods. Binary masks classify those voxels on which the probability of pertaining to a WMH is above a certain threshold. The general idea behind segmentation masks is to overlay them on the original image to visualize the segmented regions. As explained, this is exactly the kind of masks outputted by the algorithms, but it is not what we have as a manual standard. We could have coarse-grained the result masks into unique coordinates and compared them with our manual standard, but we favored the opposite approach. Doing so opens the possibility of using the usual evaluation coefficients and is the typical way to proceed. Consequently, we created two different masks from the manual segmentation of WMH. First, we used the data defining the centers of the WMH to create binary masks. We created these masks by simply generating NifTI binary images in which all the voxels categorized as WMH centers were assigned a 1, while the rest of the voxels were assigned a 0. These masks are sufficiently direct to compute, but they do not represent all the information given by the annotations of the expert neuroradiologist and neuroscientist. An important consideration is to understand that WMH are not spherical in general. If we do use Gaussian filters resulting in spherical shapes to define the probability volume of our hyperintensities, it is because we do not have any data giving the exact shape of the WMH. Using these isotropic shapes introduces a systematic error in the posterior evaluation, but, as we are no experts on the topic, we thought this path to be better than segmenting it by ourselves.

2.4 Statistical Analysis

Statistical analysis was performed using the EZR software package (version 1.61, Y. Kanda). A t-test for two independent samples with a 95% confidence interval was used to test the significance of the difference in the brain volume of patients with WML and the brain volume of controls. Spearman's rank correlation test was used to test the association between WML volume and brain volume. Data were considered significant when the p-value was less than 0.05.

3 Results

The mean age of patients with WML was 56.56 ± 8.47 years, while the mean age of controls was 52.89 ± 10.8 years. The mean brain volume in patients with WML was 1207.89 ± 62.18 cm^3, while the mean brain volume in controls was 1367.89 ± 115.86 cm^3 (Appendix IV, Appendix V). The average volume of WML was 197 ± 154.18 mm^3. The smallest volume of WML was 28.92 mm^3, and the largest volume was 552.8 mm^3. A t-test for two independent samples showed that there was a significant difference in the brain volume of WML patients and controls (p-value $= 0.00216$, $p < 0.05$). It can be concluded that brain volume was significantly lower in patients with lesions than in controls. Spearman's rank correlation coefficient showed that there is a weak negative correlation between WML volume and brain volume ($\rho = -0.167$), that is, patients with a larger brain volume had a smaller lesion volume (Appendix VI).

4 Discussion

Transgender healthcare issues have slowly emerged in recent years, but more research on the epidemiology and clinical profile of cerebrovascular diseases in this special population is needed. These studies will help us develop better treatment guidelines for preventive health care and cerebrovascular disease management to address the specific needs of MTF transgenders. There are limited studies in the existing literature that have reported on cerebrovascular diseases in the transgender population. Even fewer studies have described the clinical characteristics and outcomes of stroke in this particular population subset. Detection of lesions using MRI is an irreplaceable component of both diagnosis and monitoring of various diseases. In this study, we confirmed that the use of volumetric analysis in MRI is a sufficiently sensitive tool for the evaluation of white matter lesions, because it is structural neuroimaging and the validation of this method by manual segmentation, which was performed, represents the gold standard in the delineation/drawing of structures whose volume is measured [38], and that other parameters, such as total brain volume, may play a role in predicting the occurrence of WML, and can easily be implemented in future WML detection algorithms, although our results cannot be generalized due to the sample size. The use of automated segmentation and artificial intelligence in MRI has great potential in the fields of central nervous system disease monitoring and diagnosis guidance [39], which further improves the quality of non-invasive diagnosis and patient monitoring.

As WMLs only partially contribute to the explanation of clinical disease progression and cognitive outcomes, cortical lesions are a growing focus of research [40]. Therefore, the characterization of particularly silent cortical infarcts, in addition to WML, may be crucial for the identification of patients at risk and adequate prevention [41]. It should be borne in mind that our sample is small and consists of pre-selected patients with existing brain lesions, as well as being part of the training set at the same time. A further limitation of our study is its retrospective nature. Therefore, future prospective studies should include a larger number patients and controls, as well as potentially detailed biochemical analyzes and histopathological findings, to provide greater insight into the importance of WMLs and their contribution to brain disease development.

In addition to the application in the presented research group white matter lesions are common in older adults and may be associated with the aging processes of the brain, but they can also indicate various neurological disorders, such as Alzheimer's disease (AD) [42, 43], Parkinson's disease, stroke, multiple sclerosis, or hypertension. In older adults, WMLs can affect brain function and be associated with a decline in memory, concentration, and other cognitive functions. In younger individuals, the presence of WMLs may be related to neurological or genetic diseases. Both WMLs and WMHs have an indirect or direct association with neurodegenerative and dementia-related diseases, such as Alzheimer's disease cognitive impairments or depression [44]. They are continuously subjected to research in order to better understand and find a relationship between WMH volumes and cross-sectional cognitive measures because has been inconsistent. A truly reliable and fully automated method for quantitative assessment of WMH on magnetic resonance imaging has not yet been identified [28]. In [45] presented developed and evaluated "DeepWML", a deep learning method for fully automated white WML segmentation of multicenter FLAIR images and successfully applied to a wide spectrum of MRI data in the three white matter disease types. It's worth mentioning that in the work [46] an algorithm for automatic segmentation has been proposed, which may help in the assessment of the burden of WMLs on MRI images.

The need for continuous development of new algorithms for WML analysis arises from the need to improve the accuracy of diagnosing and monitoring neurological diseases associated with changes in the white matter of the brain. New algorithms can also enable faster and more effective analysis of large MRI datasets and help physicians make decisions about patient care and treatment.

5   Conclusion

We have shown that ischemic lesions of the cerebrum white matter affect reduced total brain volume. The results we obtained are a confirmation of what we want to learn and prepare the machine/computer to do - to learn to discern what is a lesion and what is not, based on masking it and marking its automatic technical specifications. In the future, we want to process a larger sample, in the context of the application of artificial intelligence and deep learning paradigms in research and their role in predicting the occurrence of WML and investigating compromised microstructural integrity in CSVD using multimodal neuroimaging, as well as the microvascular contribution to changes in the brain. Limitations of this pilot study include small sample size but also the paucity of the relevant previous studies on impact of cerebrovascular conditions on individuals with gender identity disorder. An association between hormonal therapy use and stroke cannot be made based on this study. The relationship between cross-sex hormone treatment and cardiovascular risk profile in any kind of transgenders is complex. The studies like this ours will aid us as a society in coming up with better treatment guidelines for preventive health care and management of cerebrovascular diseases to address the specific needs of individuals with gender identity disorders or transgenders.

Acknowledgment. This research was funded by the National Centre for Research and Development and prepared within the framework of the scientific project "A new Model of medical care with use of modern methods of non-invasive clinical assessment and Telemedicine in patients with heart failure" (STRATEGMED3/305274/8/NCBR/2017).

Conflict of Interest. None declared.

Appendix (I–VI)

See Figs. 1, 2, 3, 4, 5 and 6

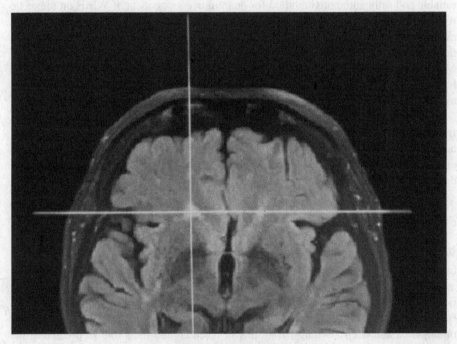

Fig. 1. Targeted lesion

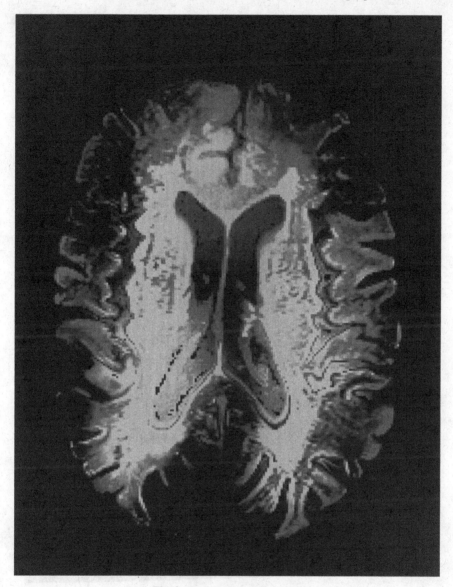

Fig. 2. Lesion probability mask

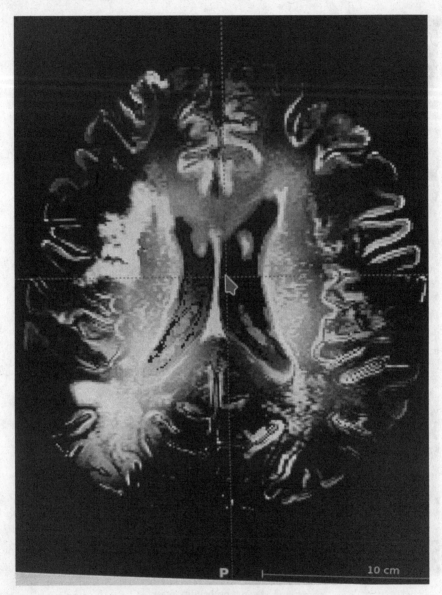

Fig. 3. Lesion probability mask

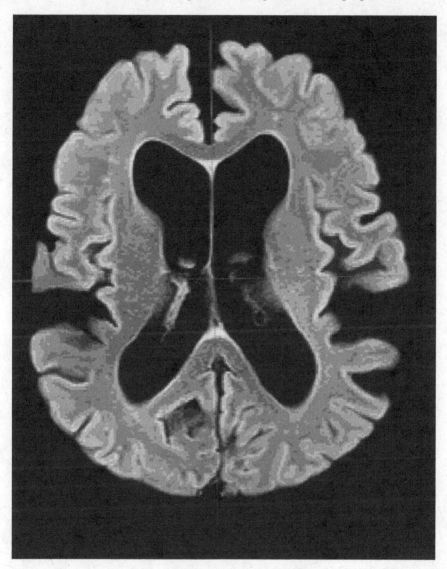

Fig. 4. Masked lesion

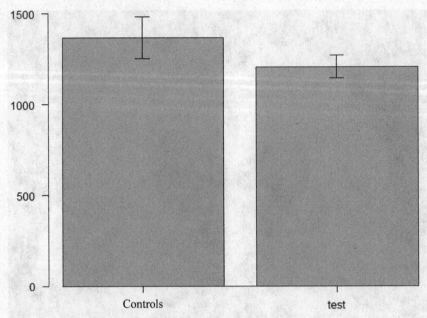

Fig. 5. Total volume WMH and controls (± SD).

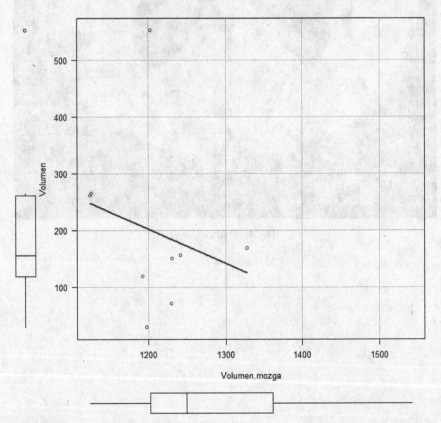

Fig. 6. Volumetric differences between brains

References

1. Gender, Nature, and Nurture - 2nd Edition – Richard, A. Lippa – Routle. https://www.routle dge.com/Gender-Nature-and-Nurture/Lippa/p/book/9780805853452. Accessed 23 Mar 2023
2. Luders, E., et al.: Regional gray matter variation in male-to-female transsexualism. Neuroimage **46**, 904–907 (2009). https://doi.org/10.1016/j.neuroimage.2009.03.048
3. Majid, D.S.A., et al.: Neural systems for own-body processing align with gender identity rather than birth-assigned sex. Cereb. Cortex. **30**, 2897–2909 (2020). https://doi.org/10.1093/cercor/bhz282
4. Mohammadi, M.R., Khaleghi, A.: Transsexualism: a different viewpoint to brain changes. Clin. Psychopharmacol. Neurosci. **16**, 136–143 (2018). https://doi.org/10.9758/cpn.2018.16.2.136
5. Cuadrado-Godia, E., et al.: Cerebral small vessel disease: a review focusing on pathophysiology, biomarkers, and machine learning strategies. J. Stroke. **20**, 302–320 (2018). https://doi.org/10.5853/jos.2017.02922
6. World Health Organization. Stroke, Cerebrovascular accident (2014). https://www.emro.who.int/health-topics/stroke-cerebrovascular-accident/index.html. Accessed 14 Feb 2023
7. Centers for Disease Control and Prevention. Stroke facts (2014). https://www.cdc.gov/stroke/facts.html. Accessed 14 Feb 2023
8. Istraživanje zdravlja stanovništva Srbije (2019). https://www.batut.org.rs/download/publik acije/ZdravljeStanovnistva2019.pdf. Accessed 14 Feb 2023
9. Kühne, M., et al.: For the swiss-AF investigators: silent brain infarcts impact on cognitive function in atrial fibrillation. Eur. Heart J. **43**, 2127–2135 (2022). https://doi.org/10.1093/eur heartj/ehac020
10. Swieten, J.C.V., Hout, J.H.W.V.D., Ketel, B.A.V., Hijdra, A., Wokke, J.H.J., Gijn, J.V.: Periventricular lesions in the white matter on magnetic resonance imaging in the elderly: a morphometric correlation with arteriolosclerosis and dilated perivascular spaces. Brain **114**, 761–774 (1991). https://doi.org/10.1093/brain/114.2.761
11. van Swieten, J.C., et al.: Hypertension in the elderly is associated with white matter lesions and cognitive decline. Ann. Neurol. **30**, 825–830 (1991). https://doi.org/10.1002/ana.410300612
12. Meyer, J.S., Kawamura, J., Terayama, Y.: White matter lesion in the elderly. J. Neurol. Sci. **110**, 1–7 (1992)https://doi.org/10.1016/0022-510X(92)90002-3
13. Dickinson, K.M., Clifton, P.M., Keogh, J.B.: Endothelial function is impaired after a high-salt meal in healthy subjects. Am. J. Clin. Nutr. **93**, 500–505 (2011). https://doi.org/10.3945/ajcn.110.006155
14. Lin, J., Wang, D., Lan, L., Fan, Y.: Multiple factors involved in the pathogenesis of white matter lesions. BioMed Res. Int. **2017**, 1–9 (2017). https://doi.org/10.1155/2017/9372050
15. Bright, F., et al.: Neuroinflammation in frontotemporal dementia. Nat. Rev. Neurol. **15**, 540–555 (2019). https://doi.org/10.1038/s41582-019-0231-z
16. Bots, M.L., et al.: Cerebral white matter lesions and atherosclerosis in the Rotterdam study. The Lancet. **341**, 1232–1237 (1993). https://doi.org/10.1016/0140-6736(93)91144-B
17. Liao, D., et al.: Presence and severity of cerebral white matter lesions and hypertension, its treatment, and its control: the ARIC study. Stroke **27**, 2262–2270 (1996). https://doi.org/10.1161/01.STR.27.12.2262
18. Rostrup, E., et al.: The spatial distribution of age-related white matter changes as a function of vascular risk factors—results from the LADIS study. Neuroimage **60**, 1597–1607 (2012). https://doi.org/10.1016/j.neuroimage.2012.01.106
19. Momjian-Mayor, I., Baron, J.-C.: The pathophysiology of watershed infarction in internal carotid artery disease: review of cerebral perfusion studies. Stroke **36**, 567–577 (2005). https://doi.org/10.1161/01.STR.0000155727.82242.e1

20. van Swieten, J.C., Hijdra, A., Koudstaal, P.J., van Gijn, J.: Grading white matter lesions on CT and MRI: a simple scale. J. Neurol. Neurosurg. Psychiatry. **53**, 1080–1083 (1990). https://doi.org/10.1136/jnnp.53.12.1080

21. Fazekas, F., et al.: CT and MRI rating of white matter lesions. Cerebrovasc. Dis. **13**, 31–36 (2002). https://doi.org/10.1159/000049147

22. Gouw, A.A., et al.: Reliability and sensitivity of visual scales versus volumetry for evaluating white matter hyperintensity progression. Cerebrovasc. Dis. **25**, 247–253 (2008). https://doi.org/10.1159/000113863

23. van Straaten, E.C.W., et al.: Impact of white matter hyperintensities scoring method on correlations with clinical data: the LADIS study. Stroke **37**, 836–840 (2006). https://doi.org/10.1161/01.STR.0000202585.26325.74

24. Marek, M., Horyniecki, M., Frączek, M., Kluczewska, E.: Leukoaraiosis – new concepts and modern imaging. Pol. J. Radiol. **83**, 76–81 (2018). https://doi.org/10.5114/pjr.2018.74344

25. Azizyan, A., Sanossian, N., Mogensen, M.A., Liebeskind, D.S.: Fluid-attenuated inversion recovery vascular hyperintensities: an important imaging marker for cerebrovascular disease. Am. J. Neuroradiol. **32**, 1771–1775 (2011). https://doi.org/10.3174/ajnr.A2265

26. Lao, Z., et al.: Computer-assisted segmentation of white matter lesions in 3D MR images using support vector machine. Acad. Radiol. **15**, 300–313 (2008). https://doi.org/10.1016/j.acra.2007.10.012

27. Gorelick, P.B., et al.: Vascular contributions to cognitive impairment and dementia: a statement for healthcare professionals from the American heart association/American stroke association. Stroke **42**, 2672–2713 (2011). https://doi.org/10.1161/STR.0b013e3182299496

28. Caligiuri, M.E., Perrotta, P., Augimeri, A., Rocca, F., Quattrone, A., Cherubini, A.: Automatic detection of white matter hyperintensities in healthy aging and pathology using magnetic resonance imaging: a review. Neuroinformatics **13**, 261–276 (2015). https://doi.org/10.1007/s12021-015-9260-y

29. Jack, C.R., et al.: FLAIR histogram segmentation for measurement of leukoaraiosis volume. J. Magn. Reson. Imaging. **14**, 668–676 (2001). https://doi.org/10.1002/jmri.10011

30. Admiraal-Behloul, F., et al.: Fully automatic segmentation of white matter hyperintensities in MR images of the elderly. Neuroimage **28**, 607–617 (2005). https://doi.org/10.1016/j.neuroimage.2005.06.061

31. Amador, K., Wilms, M., Winder, A., Fiehler, J., Forkert, N.D.: Predicting treatment-specific lesion outcomes in acute ischemic stroke from 4D CT perfusion imaging using spatio-temporal convolutional neural networks. Med. Image Anal. **82**, 102610 (2022). https://doi.org/10.1016/j.media.2022.102610

32. Chen, L., Bentley, P., Rueckert, D.: Fully automatic acute ischemic lesion segmentation in DWI using convolutional neural networks. NeuroImage Clin. **15**, 633–643 (2017). https://doi.org/10.1016/j.nicl.2017.06.016

33. Rachmadi, M.F., Valdés-Hernández, M.D.C., Makin, S., Wardlaw, J., Komura, T.: Automatic spatial estimation of white matter hyperintensities evolution in brain MRI using disease evolution predictor deep neural networks. Med. Image Anal. **63**, 101712 (2020). https://doi.org/10.1016/j.media.2020.101712

34. Clèrigues, A., Valverde, S., Bernal, J., Freixenet, J., Oliver, A., Lladó, X.: Acute and sub-acute stroke lesion segmentation from multimodal MRI. Comput. Methods Programs Biomed. **194**, 105521 (2020). https://doi.org/10.1016/j.cmpb.2020.105521

35. Yushkevich, P.A., et al.: User-guided 3D active contour segmentation of anatomical structures: significantly improved efficiency and reliability. Neuroimage **31**, 1116–1128 (2006). https://doi.org/10.1016/j.neuroimage.2006.01.015

36. SPM12. https://www.fil.ion.ucl.ac.uk/spm/software/spm12/. Accessed 01 Feb 2023

37. El-Feky, M., Gaillard, F.: Fazekas scale for white matter lesions. In: Radiopaedia.org (2014). https://doi.org/10.53347/rID-28447

38. Lo, B.P., Donnelly, M.R., Barisano, G., Liew, S.-L.: A standardized protocol for manually segmenting stroke lesions on high-resolution T1-weighted MR images. Front. Neuroimaging. **1**, 1098604 (2023). https://doi.org/10.3389/fnimg.2022.1098604

39. Gryska, E., Schneiderman, J., Björkman-Burtscher, I., Heckemann, R.A.: Automatic brain lesion segmentation on standard magnetic resonance images: a scoping review. BMJ Open **11**, e042660 (2021). https://doi.org/10.1136/bmjopen-2020-042660

40. Jiménez de la Peña, M.M., Gómez Vicente, L., García Cobos, R., Martínez de Vega, V.: Correlación neurorradiológica de las afasias. Mapa cortico-subcortical del lenguaje. Radiología. 60, 250–261 (2018)https://doi.org/10.1016/j.rx.2017.12.008

41. Schaller-Paule, M.A., Fritz, D., Schaefer, J.H., Hattingen, E., Foerch, C., Seiler, A.: Distribution pattern analysis of cortical brain infarcts on diffusion-weighted magnetic resonance imaging: a hypothesis-generating approach to the burden of silent embolic stroke. J. Am. Heart Assoc. **11**, e026438 (2022). https://doi.org/10.1161/JAHA.122.026438

42. Tubi, M.A., et al.: White matter hyperintensities and their relationship to cognition: effects of segmentation algorithm. Neuroimage **206**, 116327 (2020). https://doi.org/10.1016/j.neuroimage.2019.116327

43. Barber, R., et al.: White matter lesions on magnetic resonance imaging in dementia with lewy bodies, Alzheimer's disease, vascular dementia, and normal aging. J. Neurol. Neurosurg. Psychiatry. **67**, 66–72 (1999). https://doi.org/10.1136/jnnp.67.1.66

44. Wang, L., Leonards, C.O., Sterzer, P., Ebinger, M.: White matter lesions and depression: a systematic review and meta-analysis. J. Psychiatr. Res. **56**, 56–64 (2014). https://doi.org/10.1016/j.jpsychires.2014.05.005

45. Zhang, Y., et al.: A deep learning algorithm for white matter hyperintensity lesion detection and segmentation. Neuroradiology **64**, 727–734 (2022). https://doi.org/10.1007/s00234-021-02820-w

46. Scherer, M., et al.: Development and validation of an automatic segmentation algorithm for quantification of intracerebral hemorrhage. Stroke **47**, 2776–2782 (2016). https://doi.org/10.1161/STROKEAHA.116.013779

From Simulated to Real Environments:
Q-Learning for MAZE-Navigation
of a TurtleBot

Tobias Weiss[ID], Simon Reichhuber[✉][ID], and Sven Tomforde[ID]

Christian-Albrechts-Universität, Christian-Albrechts-Platz 4, 24118 Kiel, Germany
{stu115020,sir,st}@informatik.uni-kiel.de
https://www.ins.informatik.uni-kiel.de/en

Abstract. MAZE environments are popular test environments for reinforcement learning techniques as they are characterised by a sequence of discrete decisions of a learner, i.e. a multi-step learning problem where the reward is just available after reaching a goal. Further, MAZE scenarios can easily be altered to change the complexity of the learning problem. However, this is usually done in simulations and is seldom based on real hardware. In this paper, we investigate how far the simulation-based results can be transferred to an example platform, the ROBOTIS TurtleBot3 system. We explain the concept of setting up a discrete environment that is perceivable by the robot, investigate the behaviour of a Q-learner in simulations and describe how far the simulation-based behaviour can be reproduced with the robot.

Keywords: TurtleBot3 · Maze · Q-learning · Reinforcement Learning · Simulation · Reality Gap · Organic Computing

1 Introduction

The steadily growing interest in intelligent systems has led to several advances in the field of machine learning applied to technical systems. However, these contributions focus mainly on virtual agents, i.e. they research different learning methods only in simulations. The ability of a robot to navigate in grid-like environments has also been widely studied in simulation [2,4], but the feasibility of these methods in the real world has hardly been explored. With modern, small and inexpensive robots such as the ROBOTIS TurtleBot3 platform, it is now possible to test those learning methods in a dedicated laboratory environment. Thus, a comparison can be made between the simulation results and implementation in the real world with real hardware.

The purpose of this paper is therefore to reconstruct a reinforcement learner implementing the standard Q-learning technique within a grid-based MAZE to find the shortest path as close to the simulation as possible. In particular, this means comparing the simulation results with those obtained in the real world. Additionally, the question arises of where the momentary limits in the real world

© The Author(s), under exclusive license to Springer Nature Switzerland AG 2023
L. Rutkowski et al. (Eds.): ICAISC 2023, LNAI 14126, pp. 192–203, 2023.
https://doi.org/10.1007/978-3-031-42508-0_18

are and what complexity a MAZE instance may have in order to be solved by the robot.

The remainder of this paper is organised as follows: Sect. 2 provides a brief overview of Reinforcement Learning (RL) and introduces the robot platform used for our experiments. In the following Sect. 3, we schematically explain our simulation, provide information about our laboratory setup and introduce the implementation of our robotic system. Section 4 provides the key finding of our work when presenting the results of our experiments in the simulation and with the robot. This is then discussed and interpreted in Sect. 4.3. Finally, Sect. 5 summarises the paper and gives an outlook on future works.

2   Background

Reinforcement Learning is increasingly popular method for controlling robots in real-world applications. Altuntas et al. proposed a system that navigates a robot from a starting point to a goal both in simulations and the real world using Q-Learning and Sarsa [5]. The system was tested both with and without obstacles.

In [3], Ruan et al. propose an autonomous system to navigate mobile robots in unknown environments using deep reinforcement learning techniques. They tested their system in a simulated environment using only depth images as input and successfully navigated the robot to its destination while avoiding obstacles after the learning process.

Zuo et al. proposed a system based on the Q-Learning algorithm to let a robot escape a MAZE instance [6]. The paper introduces a new concept of states called health and sub-health states for obstacle avoidance. However, none of the contributions looked into a possible transfer gap between simulation and reality.

2.1   The TurtleBot Platform

A TurtleBot3 Waffle Pi from ROBOTIS serves as the agent. The 1.8 kg robot is operated with a Raspberry Pi 3 Model B+ micro-controller and measures $281 \times 306 \times 141$ mm. The outer radius of the robot is 22 cm. At the front axle, there are two movable wheels, which are powered by servo motors. The rear axle has two freely movable balls without a drive. The TurtleBot is delivered with an 1800 mAh battery, which promises up to two hours of operation. It is equipped with the 360 LiDAR sensor LDS-01, a Raspberry Pi Camera Module v2, a gyroscope, an accelerometer, and a magnetometer. The main controller of the TurtleBot, which is used for the integration of the ROS framework [1], is OpenCR1.0 and comes with an ARM Cortex-M7 processor. The sensor technology of the controller consists of an ICM-20648, a 6-axis motion tracking device, equipped with a 3-axis gyroscope, 3-axis accelerometer and a digital motion processor. For our experiments, we kept the standard configuration of the robot and just used a larger battery with 3000 mAh.

3 Approach

3.1 Simulation of Agent Behaviour in MAZE Environments

The simulations we have designed are based on Python 3.8. In our simulation, we tested two different approaches with two different agent classes. First, we tested the learning behaviour of an agent which was designed to operate strictly in a static, unchanging MAZE environment. In the second approach, a different agent has to be able to learn in a dynamic environment that potentially changes its layout after each action. The agent's goal is to find the shortest path from the starting point to a goal.

We use Q-learning as the learning algorithm. Since we studied two different agent behaviours, the environment was modelled differently depending on the use case. In the first approach, the agent is aware of its position in the grid by storing the current indices of the array used to model the environment in the form of two variables. This allows storing the data (i.e. colour codes) of previously seen cells and is especially crucial for real-world experiments regarding approaches for saving energy as described in Sect. 3.3. The Q-Table is initialised as a three-dimensional array of the size of the MAZE instance and the possible actions. The MAZE instance itself is also implemented by an array. The second agent is designed to operate in dynamic environments, i.e. the agent cannot store data and the data structure of the Q-Table is a dictionary implemented using a string consisting of the encoding of the colours of the Moore Neighbourhood and the possible actions. Here, the agent does not know its position in the grid.

We simulated three different MAZE instances which are shown in Fig. 1a and tested each of them with exploration rates of 0.1, 0.5 and 0.9 five times for both approaches. In terms of rewards, if the agent reaches the goal it receives a reward of 100, a step towards a walkable cell results in −1 and if the agent tries to walk into a wall, the action is rewarded with −100.

(a) Maze instances for comparing simulation and real-world results.

(b) Setup of a maze instance in the laboratory.

Fig. 1. Maze instances in simulation and real environments.

In order to be able to make statements about a comparison between simulation and reality, we first looked for suitable parameters with which the agent needed the fewest episodes to learn the shortest path on average. For this, we simulated the third MAZE instance 10000 times. The particular focus here was on the decay value, as this is crucial for instances of lower complexity, as was the case in these experiments, in order to quickly use what was learned at a high exploration rate. Therefore, we chose a decay of 0.6 and a discount of 0.9. Depending on the setup, we used a learning rate of 0.1 with the static approach (A1) testing instances (1) and (2). For the dynamic approach (A2), we set the learning rate to 0.3 for instance (3).

3.2   MAZE- World in Real Environments

To build a MAZE instance, paper of the size 50 cm × 70 cm in the colours green, red and blue were used. The pieces of paper were put into 50 cm × 50 cm blocks, taped and laid out symmetrically in a grid structure. Between the edges of the cells, 50 cm × 1 cm red paper strips were taped. Also, blue strips of the same size represent the path that the robot is supposed to follow when moving to another cell and is placed in the middle of a cell. The green cells represent the walkable part of the MAZE instance, red symbolises walls and blue is the colour of a target. Only ceiling lights and daylight are used for lighting. Depending on the weather, more or less daylight was added with the help of blinds (adding noise to the scenario). Figure 1b shows the setup of a real-world MAZE instance in our laboratory.

3.3   Q-Learning and Navigation with the TurtleBot

The first approach A1 uses the static properties of the MAZE. The action space is defined by the von Neumann neighbourhood, where the order is north, east, south and west. The possible values gathered by analysing the cell (i.e. $v = \{red, green, blue\}$) depend on the colour of the cell. Figure 2 shows the processes of the robot. The data of the neighbourhood is analysed in the above order. The robot does this by first aligning itself to the north, analysing the colour and then rotating three times by 90° and repeating the procedure after each of these rotations. The rotation is done with the help of odometry data and is based on a translation from quaternion values to Euler values. In addition, the robot is aware of its position in terms of rows and columns and stores the registered colour codes in a data structure to access them again later. This saves the need

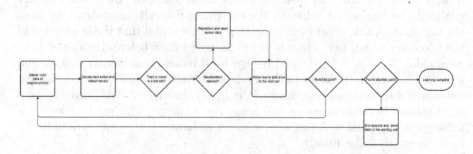

Fig. 2. Flowchart describing the processes of robot operating.

for another rotation routine when the robot travels to a cell on which it has already stood once.

The success of this approach depends on the accuracy of the rotation. It was found that the sensors do not have one hundred percent accuracy. With a rotation of 360° in total, there is a deviation of up to 3° with our robot model. Since a high degree of inaccuracy sooner or later led to the detection of a wrong cell or to driving over red cells, a method was designed that made the robot align with the red lines between the green and blue cells and resets its original sensor values. The blue lines also provided guidance as the robot moved along to compensate for any unevenness in the ground or inaccuracies in the physical layout of the cells. The robot adjusted its route based on the difference between the mid of the image and the blue line. When the robot enters a new cell, it always travels straight ahead until it detects the next red line or the next red cell at the bottom of the image.

In general, the robot is allowed to try to drive against the wall. In that case, the physical command is not executed, but a reward for the action is received. The robot updates its Q-table after each action according to the formula:

$$Q_{t+1}(s_t, a_t) = (1 - \alpha) \times Q_t(s_t, a_t) + \alpha \times [r_t + \gamma \times \max_a Q(s_{t+1}, a)] \qquad (1)$$

The second approach A2 differs from A1 in that the instances are theoretically changeable at run-time. This means that the robot can neither remember its position nor get back to already collected colour data. Consequently, the robot must re-examine its entire environment after each action. In this approach, we extend the sensor view to the Moore neighbourhood. Consequently, the robot had to rotate 45° seven times to analyse all cells, which in turn resulted in an increased importance of rotational accuracy. Due to this, the robot had to re-align itself very often, which consequently led to further rotations.

Under these conditions, it was clear that the stress on the battery per physical action in this approach would be significantly higher than was the case for A1. Consequently, we tested another variant of the dynamic approach, that assumes that the near environment, i.e. the Moore neighbourhood, of the robot in the MAZE instance does not change. This reduces the required rotation from at least 315° to at least 135°. The robot first analyses the new cell in front of it, rotates 45° to the left, and then 90° to the right. Thus, the three new cells are analysed and the colour values of the remaining five cells are taken over from the last state. A side effect of this rotation process is also that the inaccuracy of the odometry values per action is less pronounced than before. Because of this, we decided that the robot should realign itself based on an action counter and when it takes a step to the north since this is the statically most frequent physical movement due to the arrangement of the MAZE instances. This proved to be a good balance between accuracy and power consumption. This methodology was subsequently applied to A1 as well, in order to have a better comparison in the experiments to find a limit.

4   Evaluation

4.1   MAZE Simulation

For the comparison between simulation and reality, we tested three different MAZE instances with three different exploration rates (0.1, 0.5, 0.9) for two of the three implemented approaches A1 and A2. Figure 1a shows the three instances that were tested. Each instance was simulated five times for each exploration rate for both approaches. Table 1 shows both the average episodes required to learn the shortest path and the standard deviation across all tests.

Table 1. Average values and standard deviation of the simulation results.

Maze	ϵ	Avg_{A1}	σ_{A1}	Avg_{A2}	σ_{A2}
1	0.1	3	0	2.2	1.1
1	0.5	3.4	0.55	3.2	0.45
1	0.9	3	0.71	3.2	0.45
2	0.1	4	0	2.8	1.64
2	0.5	4.6	0.89	4.4	0.55
2	0.9	3.8	0.45	3.8	0.44
3	0.1	7.6	0.55	3.4	0.89
3	0.5	7.6	0.55	4	0.71
3	0.9	6	2.12	4.6	1.52

Comparing the results, some key points stand out. First, it is evident that an increase in complexity means an increase in the average number of episodes required to learn the shortest path for approach A1. However, this is not the case for approach A2. This was to be expected since we increased the learning rate to 0.3 while testing the third instance for the experiments with approach A2 and a direct comparison of the results was not possible. For this reason, we tested the same simulation with a learning rate of 0.1 and we observed an increasing average value, although not as large as for A1. Thus, the dynamic approach initially appears to produce better results. In Section IV-B, we tested more instances for the purpose of finding a limit and simulated these to identify optimal parameters. These more complex instances can be seen in Fig. 4. Figure 3 shows the rewards across episodes for instances (3), (5), and (6), where the blue line represents A1 and the orange line represents A2. This diagram shows that the learning process for instances (3) and (5) is still very similar, but for more complex instances like the sixth, the learning curve of A2 decreases drastically. For this instance, this approach has managed to learn the shortest way only three out of ten times with a set time hard limit of 1000 episodes (Table 2).

Furthermore, it is noticeable that for approach A1 better results are achieved with higher exploration rates, while the opposite seems to be the case for the second approach.

Table 2. Average values and standard deviation of the simulation results with learning rate 0.3.

Maze	ϵ	Avg_{A2}	σ_{A2}
3	0.1	3.2	0.45
3	0.5	4.2	0.84
3	0.9	5.6	0.55

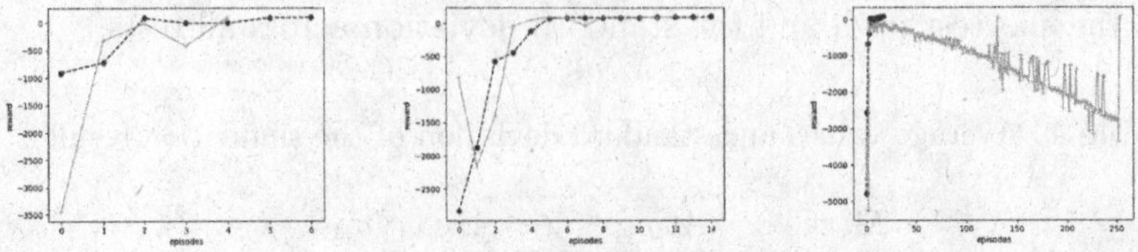

(a) Learning curve for instance (3).

(b) Learning curve for instance (5).

(c) Learning curve for instance (6).

Fig. 3. Rewards per episode in comparison of A1 and A2.

4.2 Robot-Based Experiments

After the simulation, initial results on the feasibility of the instances were available. Subsequently, the experiments were run with the same parameters by the TurtleBot in the real world. The results are summarised in Table 3, again for the average used episodes for learning the shortest path and the corresponding values of the standard deviation.

Table 3. Average values and standard deviation of the real-world results.

Maze	ϵ	Avg_{A1}	σ_{A1}	Avg_{A2}	σ_{A2}
1	0.1	3	0	3.2	0.45
1	0.5	3.4	0.89	3	1.22
1	0.9	3.2	1.1	3.8	0.84
2	0.1	4.2	0.45	4	0
2	0.5	3.4	0.55	4.4	0.55
2	0.9	4.2	1.1	4.4	0.55
3	0.1	7.8	0.45	3	0
3	0.5	7.2	1.48	3.6	0.89
3	0.9	5.2	0.84	4.4	1.14

A comparison between A1 and A2 for the real-world tests shows that the complexity increase of the instances achieves a higher value for A1, but not for

A2. Thus, for these instances, A2 performs better than A1. A comparison of the exploration rates shows that A1 benefits from a higher exploration rate for the third instance, but for the other two instances there is no clear difference between the exploration rates. A2 seems to benefit from lower exploration rates.

Finding the Limit. Unlike in the simulation, there are restrictions for the robot in the real world, such as the accuracy of sensors or the battery capacity and thus the operation time of the robot. To find these limits, we iteratively increased the complexity of our instances for approaches A1, A2 and A2.1 by adding or moving cells. We defined the limit for an approach as found as soon as the robot was not able to solve the MAZE instance within three attempts despite using optimal parameters. In this context, the best parameters do not mean the least number of episodes needed, but the least number of steps the robot has to make to find the shortest path, which is not necessarily the same. The choice of parameters depended on the results of the simulation and is described below.

Since our three different implementations would yield different results, the three approaches were also run accordingly with different parameters and are not directly comparable.

First, we counted the actual physically executable steps of the robot, i.e. how often the robot can rotate and move to the next cell. The implementation for the static approach varies more than the other two implementations because the robot scans the cells only once and otherwise only rotates to the next cell. This results in a higher variation of the actual executable actions, because the number of scans depends on the number of green cells, unlike the dynamic approach, where the robot scans the environment completely or halfway after each action. Basically, the number of executable actions of the robot can be expressed approximately by:

$$S = S_{max} - E * S_{shortest\_path} \tag{2}$$

where E is the number of episodes needed to find the shortest path, $S_{shortest\_path}$ is the number of steps from the starting point to a goal on the shortest path, and S_{max} is a constant describing the average number of maximum possible steps without considering actions after reaching a goal.

S_{max} depends on our implementation with the values:

$$S_{max} = \begin{cases} 370 & \text{for approach A1} \\ 100 & \text{for approach A2} \\ 170 & \text{for approach A2.1} \end{cases} \tag{3}$$

To find the optimal parameters, 1000 simulations were performed over different parameters, testing the learning rates and exploration rates from 0.05 to 0.95 and the decay from 0.5 to 0.95 in steps of 0.05. The parameters were chosen for which the robot had to execute on average the fewest actions to learn the shortest path. If results were nearly identical ($+/- 1$), parameters were chosen so that the learning rate took the lower value and the exploration rate and decay value took the higher value. The discount value of 0.9 remained unaffected.

Figure 4 displays the unsolvable MAZE instances for their respective approaches A1, A2 and A2.1 and Fig. 5 illustrates a distribution of robot actions simulated over 1000 executions, which shows how large the probability was that the instance could be solved by our robot. The chosen parameters can be seen in Table 4. Also listed in the table is which cell would need to be removed for the MAZE instance to be solved. The first value describes the column and the second value describes the row. The start cell is located at position 1/3.

A strongly increased learning rate and a low exploration rate are noticeable, although it must be said that minimising robot actions does not directly lead to a minimisation of the number of episodes needed to learn the shortest path. Therefore, the attempts to find a limit are not comparable to the previous attempts. Such a low exploration rate is not advantageous in dynamic environments anyway, since changes can hardly be reacted to, and makes sense only in this explicit use case.

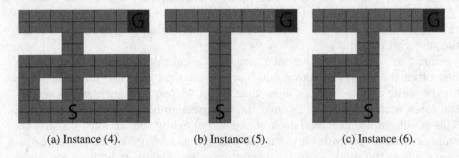

(a) Instance (4).   (b) Instance (5).   (c) Instance (6).

Fig. 4. Unsolvable MAZE instances.

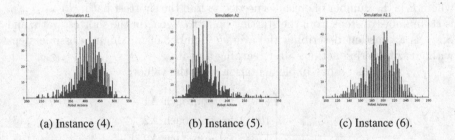

(a) Instance (4).   (b) Instance (5).   (c) Instance (6).

Fig. 5. Number of robot actions over 1000 simulations.

4.3   Discussion

First, we check whether we can transfer the simulation to the real world. This is the case if the results of the robot are very similar to those of the simulation.

Table 4. Q-Learning parameters for finding limits.

Approach	LR	ϵ	Decay	Cell
1	0.95	0.05	0.65	3/6
2	0.8	0.55	0.7	5/5
2.1	0.9	0.25	0.55	1/2

After replicating the environment of the simulation in the real world, it was possible to compare the results and draw conclusions about the transferability of simulated MAZE instances to the real-world. The simulation results showed that approach A1 requires more episodes to learn the shortest path as the complexity of the instances increases. Combining the results of the exploration rates of instances (2) and (3), we see that instance (3) in the simulation requires an increase of a rounded 42% over instance (2) to learn the shortest path to the goal. The identical value of 42% can also be seen in the experiments with the robot.

Both the simulation and the real tests with approach A1 show increased performance with an exploration rate of 0.9 for instance (3). This is also true for the exploration rate of 0.1 with approach A2 for the third instance. While the simulation results suggest that low exploration rates are more beneficial, these results could not be confirmed with the TurtleBot. However, the simulation results also show an increased standard deviation.

The fundamental difference in the average number of episodes needed to find the shortest path between A1 and A2 for all instances can be observed in both the simulation and the real world. Approach A2 performs better for instance (3) in the simulation as well as in the real world. There are slight differences for instances (1) and (2). In the simulation, approach A2 learns the shortest path faster on average than approach A1, in the real world the opposite is the case. However, the differences are so small that we classify them as insignificant. A comparison of instances (1) and (2) with instance (3) was not possible due to the changed learning rate, because the robot could not solve them in the time limited by the battery capacity. Therefore, a comparison with the simulation is not possible in this respect.

A decisive factor in the real implementation is the error proneness of the robot. There are different sources of errors, which can be summarised as follows: errors in image processing, errors in the network, errors during robot navigation, and errors in the robot's hardware and battery exhaust.

Table 5 shows the error rate broken down into individual categories. The tests for finding the limit are not included.

The more complex the instance was, the higher the error rate became. The error data combined gives a probability of 72% to fulfil its goal to find the shortest path. Based on our observations the error rate increase with the increasing complexity of the instances, which follows directly from the higher operation time. In general, the error rate is still quite high and further improvement is

Table 5. List of errors and error rates.

Reason for the error	Total errors	Error rate
Image-processing	2	5.7%
Navigation	13	37.1%
Network	5	14.3%
Robot Hardware	6	17.1%
Battery Capacity	9	25.7%

needed, especially in the navigation system, to enable more reliable operation of the robot. This is part of further research.

5   Conclusion

Two different approaches for learning the shortest path from a starting point to a destination were developed and tested in the simulation. Afterwards, these instances were tested in the real world with the help of different assistive devices and a TurtleBot3 in order to compare the results with those of the simulation and to draw conclusions regarding the transferability of simulation environments to real applications. Finally, a limitation of the current system with the robot was presented.

The results of the simulation showed that the approach for solving a static MAZE instance A1 has a worse performance for low complexity instances than the approach for solving dynamic instances A2. However, as the complexity of the instances increased, A1 proved to be the superior approach.

When comparing the simulation and real-world results, it was found that the real-world system was successfully mimicking the simulation. The average episodes needed to find the shortest path of the TurtleBot and the simulation were comparable. The limitations of the robot were shown, on the one hand errors in the environment of the robot e.g. badly aligned guidelines or disturbances in the WiFi, on the other hand, due to limited battery capacity. To make this limitation visible, instances for the respective approaches A1, A2 and A2.1 were presented.

The overall error rate of 28% proved to be high, but acceptable and made it clear that the system needs to be optimised.

5.1   Future Works

The strongest limitation of the TurtleBot is still the battery capacity or the battery consumption. We would like to implement a method that adjusts the parameters of the learner, in particular exploration rate and decay, to the current battery state of the robot, in order to prevent the robot from failing due to battery capacity despite sufficient learning success. Optimisation in the robot system to reduce the required energy as well as changes in the system to scan the environment more efficiently remain research topics for the future work. In particular, more instances should be tested to confirm the results of this paper or to gain further insights. At the same time, it is important to improve the system in terms of reliability and to test further solutions for navigation.

References

1. Kay, J.: Proposal for implementation of real-time systems in ROS 2. ROS.org (2016)
2. Osmanković, D., Konjicija, S.: Implementation of q-learning algorithm for solving maze problem. In: 2011 proceedings of the 34th international convention MIPRO, pp. 1619–1622. IEEE (2011)
3. Ruan, X., Ren, D., Zhu, X., Huang, J.: Mobile robot navigation based on deep reinforcement learning. In: 2019 Chinese Control and Decision Conference (CCDC), pp. 6174–6178 (2019). https://doi.org/10.1109/CCDC.2019.8832393
4. Tijsma, A.D., Drugan, M.M., Wiering, M.A.: Comparing exploration strategies for q-learning in random stochastic mazes. In: 2016 IEEE Symposium Series on Computational Intelligence (SSCI), pp. 1–8. IEEE (2016)
5. Zhu, K., Zhang, T.: Deep reinforcement learning based mobile robot navigation: a review. Tsinghua Sci. Technol. **26**(5), 674–691 (2021). https://doi.org/10.26599/TST.2021.9010012
6. Zuo, B., Chen, J., Wang, L., Wang, Y.: A reinforcement learning based robotic navigation system. In: 2014 IEEE International Conference on Systems, Man, and Cybernetics (SMC), pp. 3452–3457 (2014). https://doi.org/10.1109/SMC.2014.6974463

Bioinformatics, Biometrics and Medical Applications

3D Reconstructions of Brain from MRI Scans Using Neural Radiance Fields

Khadija Iddrisu[1]($\boxtimes$), Sylwia Malec[2], and Alessandro Crimi[2]

[1] African Institute for Mathematical Sciences, Cape Town, South Africa
khadija@aims.edu.gh
[2] Sano Centre for Computational Medicine, Kraków, Poland
a.crimi@sano.science

Abstract. The advent of 3D Magnetic Resonance Imaging (MRI) has revolutionized medical imaging and diagnostic capabilities, allowing for more precise diagnosis, treatment planning, and improved patient outcomes. 3D MRI imaging enables the creation of detailed 3D reconstructions of anatomical structures that can be used for visualization, analysis, and surgical planning. However, these reconstructions often require many scan acquisitions, demanding a long session to use the machine and requiring the patient to remain still, with consequent possible motion artifacts. The development of neural radiance fields (NeRF) technology has shown promising results in generating highly accurate 3D reconstructions of MRI images with less user input. Our approach is based on neural radiance fields to reconstruct 3D projections from 2D slices of MRI scans. We do this by using 3D convolutional neural networks to address challenges posed by variable slice thickness; incorporating multiple MRI modalities to ensure robustness and extracting the shape and volumetric depth of both surface and internal anatomical structures with slice interpolation. This approach provides more comprehensive and robust 3D reconstructions of both surface and internal anatomical structures and has significant potential for clinical applications, allowing medical professionals to better visualize and analyze anatomical structures with less available data, potentially reducing times and motion-related issues.

Keywords: 3D reconstruction · MRI scans · Neural radiance fields · Structure from motion

1 Introduction

Magnetic resonance imaging (MRI) is a powerful medical imaging technology that allows non-invasive examination of the internal structures and functions of the body. In recent years, 3D projections of MRI scans have become an increasingly popular tool for medical diagnosis and treatment planning, as they offer a detailed and accurate representation of the complex internal anatomy of the body [7]. However, long MRI acquisition sequences are particularly subject to motion-related artifacts due to breathing and cardiac pulsation [2]. This can lead

L. Rutkowski et al. (Eds.): ICAISC 2023, LNAI 14126, pp. 207–218, 2023.
https://doi.org/10.1007/978-3-031-42508-0_19

to inaccuracies in 3D reconstruction, which can have significant consequences in a clinical setting where precise measurements are important for treatment planning and monitoring. This paper will explore the challenges of creating 3D projections from MRI scans and discuss the various methods and techniques used to address these challenges. Several theories have been proposed for 3D image reconstructions of MRI and computed tomography (CT) scans, some focusing on data mining and machine learning [4] while others focus on deep learning approaches [13].

Neural Radiance Fields (NeRF) is a recently developed method for synthesizing novel views of a scene from a set of 2D images taken from different viewpoints. This method uses a neural network to represent the radiance (i.e., the color and intensity of light) at each point in a 3D space within a scene, allowing the generation of photorealistic 3D visualizations [9]. The main idea behind NeRF is to learn a continuous 5D function that maps the spatial coordinates and viewing direction of a scene point to its corresponding radiance value. This function is learned from a set of training images that are captured from different viewpoints, allowing the network to infer the radiance at each point from different perspectives. NeRF has shown promising results in generating photorealistic 3D visualizations from real-world data and has demonstrated improved performance over traditional methods such as multi-view stereo and voxel-based approaches. Despite its promising results, NeRF has some limitations, including the requirement for a dense set of input views covering the entire scene from many viewpoints, which can be challenging to acquire in the medical domain, where privacy regulations can hinder data collection. In addition, in the context of MRI scans, NeRF faces further challenges due to the high dimensionality of MRI data, low contrast or missing information in the images, and computational costs in processing these data. Several variations have been made to adopt NeRF to several applications while trying to solve its limitations. D-NeRF [10] extends NeRF to a dynamic domain, which aids in the reconstruction and rendering of novel images of objects in motion compared to static scenes in NeRF. [12] proposed modifications on NeRF to eliminate the need for known camera parameters, such as poses and intrinsics, while PixelNeRF [15] presents a learning framework architecture to train NeRF via a fully convolutional network on just a few input images to predict a continuous neural scene representation. There is growing interest in the use of NeRF based technologies in medical imaging, more specifically surgery scene monitoring [8] and endoscopy [6]. MedNeRF [1] is an adaptation of the generative radiance fields (GRAF) model [11] for rendering CT projections given a few or even a single-view X-ray in the medical domain. The approach not only synthesizes realistic images but also captures the data manifold and provides a continuous representation of how the attenuation and volumetric depth of anatomical structures vary with the viewpoint without 3D supervision. A new discriminator architecture provides a stronger and more comprehensive signal to GRAF when dealing with CT scans. This framework relies on an innovative architecture that builds from neural radiance fields and learns a continuous representation of CT scans by decoupling the volumetric depth and shape of the surface and intrinsic structures of the body from 2D CT scans.

In this paper, we introduce a novel method to reconstruct 3D projections inspired by MedNeRF due to its ability to model complex scenes with high fidelity, which we could call extended-MedNeRF. Although 3D reconstruction with NeRF seems promising, MRI scans present several challenges due to the multiple 2D slices and variable slice thicknesses typical of MRI data. To address these challenges, we will incorporate slice-level information by modifying the neural network architecture to take into account the unique characteristics of MRI slices. This will involve using a 3D convolutional neural network (CNN) to extract features from each MRI slice or modifying the graph neural network used in MedNeRF to incorporate information from adjacent slices. Secondly, we will address variable slice thicknesses by using slice interpolation to resample the slices to a common thickness before building the 3D model. Additionally, we will incorporate information from multiple MRI modalities into the MedNeRF framework to improve the accuracy and robustness of the resulting 3D models. Finally, we will train the model on the BraTS Challenge dataset which is a large dataset of MRI scans to ensure it can be generalized to a wide range of applications. However, reconstructions are meant to be used for visualization purposes or for healthy control subjects, our extended-MedNeRF cannot be meant to be a prediction of all clinical cases such as glioma, meningioma, or other types of lesions.

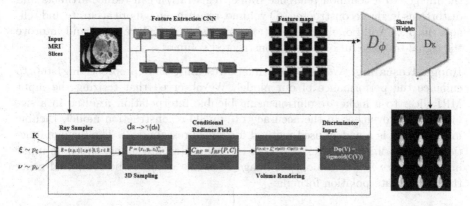

Fig. 1. The overall architecture after preprocessing. The steps include the proposed 3D CNN, generating a feature map that highlights regions in the input image that are most important for the classification decision, and the subsequent generative radiance fields.

2   Methods

The proposed approach comprises several parts, which are described in the following sub-sections as well as depicted in Fig. 1:

1. Preprocessing
2. Feature extraction from input slices using a CNN architecture to provide a better input to extended-MedNeRF
3. Use of our extended-MedNeRF to generate 3D reconstruction

2.1   MRI Preprocessing

Generating quality results of our method on MRI slices does not come without challenges. Some of these challenges associated with the use of MRI data include low contrast and poor resolution, and we present preprocessing techniques to improve data quality. Specifically, we used image registration to correct patient movement during scans and re-scale images to improve resolution. We also propose a conditional radiance field approach, which conditions the NeRF model on additional latent codes to disentangle shape and appearance information, allowing for separate manipulation of these attributes during inference. Our experimental results demonstrate the effectiveness of our proposed approach in producing high-quality 3D reconstructions of MRI data, highlighting the potential for clinical applications in medical imaging. **Image Registration:** Aligning multiple MRI scans of the same patient can improve the quality of the data by reducing motion artifacts and allowing for better visualization of small details. Image registration improved the performance of the model by correcting for any spatial misalignments or inconsistencies in the input MRI images. By aligning the images to a common reference frame, registration can reduce artifacts and distortions in the reconstructed 3D volume, resulting in a more accurate and reliable output. Additionally, registration can also help reduce noise and improve the signal-to-noise ratio in the reconstructed volume.

Image Rescaling: We employed image rescaling as a preprocessing step to enhance the performance of our model. We observed that resizing the input MRI slices to a higher resolution using bicubic interpolation resulted in a significant improvement in the accuracy of our 3D reconstruction model. Bicubic interpolation is a widely used method for image rescaling [3]. The bicubic function is a two-dimensional extension of the cubic Hermite spline. Given an input image I of size $m * n$, the output image I' of size $p * q$ can be computed using the bicubic interpolation formula:

$$I'(x,y) = \sum_{i=-1}^{2} \sum_{j=-1}^{2} h_{i+2,j+2} I(x+i, y+j) \tag{1}$$

$h_{i+2,j+2}$ are the bicubic coefficients, computed from the four nearest neighbour pixels to the interpolated location (x,y). The bicubic interpolation method produces smoother and more accurate results than the bilinear interpolation method, but requires more computation. This is because higher resolution images provide more detailed information about the underlying anatomy and structures, leading to more precise reconstruction of the 3D volume.

Contrast Enhancement: Techniques such as contrast enhancement were applied to the input images before feeding them into the network. This was done using a histogram equalization technique [14], which extends the histogram of the image to cover the entire dynamic range of the pixel values. Let $p_r(r_k)$ denote the probability mass function of the input image intensities, where r_k represents the kth intensity level. The corresponding cumulative distribution function (CDF) is given by $C(r_k) = \sum_{j=0}^{k} p_r(r_k)$.

The histogram equalization transformation function $T(r_k)$ is defined as:

$$T(r_k) = \left\lfloor \left(L - 1\right) C(r_k) + \frac{1}{2} \right\rfloor \tag{2}$$

This results in a more evenly distributed pixel intensity across the image, which can help reveal subtle details that could have been hidden in the original image. By applying contrast enhancement to the input images, we were able to improve the visual quality of the reconstructed 3D projections and increase the accuracy of our model in identifying anatomical structures in the images. This is particularly important in medical imaging applications where accurate diagnosis and treatment planning depend on the ability to accurately identify and localize subtle changes in images.

2.2   Feature Extraction with 3D CNN

MRI data typically consists of multiple images, each representing a different slice of the 3D volume. Depending on the specific format of the MRI data, we need to do a lot of pre-processing. To adapt the baseline model on MRI slices, we used a 3D CNN for feature extraction. The 3D CNN can extract features from the MRI slices and output a 3D feature representation for each slice. To use this 3D feature representation as input to the NeRF model, we generated different views of the MRI slices from different angles. We then pass the MRI slices through the 3D CNN to extract the 3D feature representation. Next is to flatten the 3D feature representation for each MRI slice into a 1D vector, concatenate the flattened feature vectors which will result in a matrix where each row corresponds to a different slice and each column corresponds to a different feature. Our architecture consists of a 3D convolutional neural network that extracts features from the MRI slices followed by a 2D convolutional neural network to the output of the 3D CNN to generate a 2D feature representation for each MRI slice. The model comprises multiple blocks that combine a convolutional layer with an average pooling layer to reduce the size of the input feature maps while maintaining some of the original resolutions. We also perform feature recalibration by the addition of a Squeeze-and-Excitation (SE) block. The SE block is a lightweight and effective module that learns to recalibrate feature maps by adaptively weighting them based on their channel-wise importance. It consists of two operations: a squeeze operation that aggregates the spatial dimensions of each feature map into a global descriptor and an excitation operation that generates a set of channel-wise weighting coefficients. These coefficients are then multiplied with the original feature maps to obtain the recalibrated features. The features tensor generated from the CNN architecture is a 2D feature representation for each MRI slice, and can be visualized as a stack of 2D images. Each 2D image corresponds to one MRI slice and contains the learned features for that slice. We then feed the concatenated feature matrix as input to our model. The goal is to enable the model to learn to generate a 3D reconstruction of the MRI volume based on the concatenated feature matrix and the different views of the MRI slices.

2.3   Slice Interpolation

Slice interpolation is a commonly used technique in medical imaging to improve the resolution and quality of MRI images. It involves estimating the value of a pixel at a higher resolution based on the values of adjacent pixels using mathematical algorithms. This technique is particularly useful when the MRI slices have low resolution or when additional slices are needed to better visualize the structure or pathology of interest [5]. In our study, we employed slice interpolation not only as a preprocessing step but also as a means of generating intermediate slices between two adjacent slices in an MRI volume. This was necessary because the method we used to generate slices was completely random and we wanted to ensure that all parts of the volume were adequately sampled. We first preprocessed the MRI data by rescaling it to a common resolution, converting it to a standard file format, and applying any necessary corrections or adjustments. We then trained our model on the preprocessed MRI data to generate a 3D volume of radiance fields. However, to improve the quality of the generated images, we applied slice interpolation to generate additional slices between existing MRI slices. There are several interpolation algorithms and techniques that can be used, including linear interpolation, cubic interpolation, and Fourier interpolation. To balance the trade-off between computational resources, time, and image quality, we chose to use the cubic interpolation method, which allows us to estimate the value of a pixel at a higher resolution using a cubic polynomial based on the values of adjacent pixels. Given a set of n data points $(x0, y0), (x1, y1), \cdot, (xn - 1, yn - 1)$, the goal of cubic interpolation is to find a function f(x) that passes through each data point and approximates the underlying curve. The cubic interpolation function takes the form:

$$f(x) = a3(x - xk)^3 + a2(x - xk)^2 + a1(x - xk) + a0 \tag{3}$$

xk is the x-coordinate of the k-th data point, ak is the coefficient of the k-th term in the cubic polynomial To find the coefficients a0, a1, a2, and a3, we need to solve a system of equations that ensures that the interpolation function passes through each data point and has a continuous first and second derivative. The resulting system of equations takes the form of a tridiagonal matrix, which can be solved efficiently using standard numerical methods. Cubic interpolation is a popular choice for slice interpolation because it provides a good balance between accuracy and computational efficiency. By estimating the value of a pixel at a higher resolution using a cubic polynomial based on the values of adjacent pixels, we can generate high-quality MRI images that better represent the underlying structure and pathology of interest. In summary, slice interpolation is a useful technique for improving the resolution and quality of MRI images, and the choice of interpolation method should be carefully considered based on the specific application and data. Using slice interpolation, we were able to generate high-quality MRI images that better represent the underlying structure and pathology of interest.

2.4   3D Reconstruction via Extended-MedNeRF

NeRF is a machine learning technique that can be used for the 3D reconstruction of MRI scans. As depicted in Fig. 2, NeRF uses a neural network to learn a function that maps a 3D point in space to a color and opacity, which can be used to reconstruct the 3D geometry and appearance of organs or tissues in the body from a collection of 2D MRI images. The neural network is trained on a set of images that capture the same scene from different viewpoints, and can then be used to render new views of the scene from any viewpoint. Compared to traditional methods, NeRF has the potential to produce more accurate and detailed 3D reconstructions, particularly when dealing with complex shapes or structures.

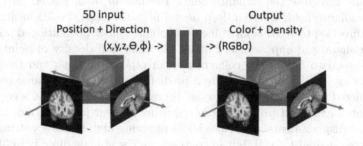

Fig. 2. An overview of NeRF Architecture with 2D Slices of MRI scans

Adapting NeRF to MRI scans presents challenges due to differences in imaging systems, and overlapping anatomical structures in MRI data make it difficult to define edges. To address these challenges, we propose a method that adopts a generative radiance field approach. This approach employs GRAF as a backbone architecture to generate reconstructions from slices of MRI data that have undergone slice interpolation and feature extraction via NeRF.

   GRAF is a generative model that uses a continuous representation of 3D space to generate high-quality images of scenes from any viewpoint. One of the key contributions of GRAF is its hierarchical sampling approach, which enables it to generate high-resolution images efficiently. The model also incorporates a novel attention mechanism that allows it to focus on relevant parts of the scene when generating images. The potential application of GRAF to MRI is exciting, as it could enable the generation of high-quality medical images from any viewpoint. The GRAF architecture is made up of a generator $G\theta$ and a discriminator $D\Phi$. Given a set of images, $G\theta$ predicts a patch P_{pred}, while $D\Phi$ compares the predicted patch with a ground-truth patch P_{real} extracted from a real image. The $K*K$ patch $P(\mathbf{u}, s)$ constituting the ray sampler of the Generator is denoted by 2D coordinates which depict the locations of pixels of the patch in the domain Ω

$$P(\mathbf{u}, s) = \left\{ (sx + u, sy + v \Big| x, y \in \left\{ -\frac{K}{2}, \cdot, \frac{K}{2} - 1 \right\} \right\} \qquad (4)$$

The 3D rays corresponding to the patch are determined by the patch's image coordinates, the camera pose ε, and intrinsics $\mathbf{K}$. The pixel/ray index is denoted by "r", the normalized 3D rays by "dr", and the number of rays by "R". The 3D rays corresponding to the patch are determined by the patch's image coordinates, the camera pose, and intrinsics. The pixel/ray index is denoted by "r", the normalized 3D rays by "dr", and the number of rays by "R". During training, the number of rays is R = K2, where K is a constant. During inference (the process of generating the final image), the number of rays is R = WH, where W and H are the width and height of the final image.

A 3D point sampling technique with stratified sampling is then applied to numerically integrate the radiance fields. Patches are then passed into a conditional radiance field, where a deep neural network maps the 3D location and viewing direction to RGB color value and volume density, conditioned on latent codes for shape and appearance. Finally, the color and density of points along a ray are used to obtain the color of the corresponding pixel, and the results of all rays are combined to generate a predicted patch in the volume renderer. The predicted patches are passed to the discriminator $D\Phi$, where it is compared with a patch extracted from a real image using bilinear interpolation, allowing continuous displacements and scales while retaining high-frequency details.

Our goal is similar to [1], but in contrast, we disentangle directly in 3D MRI instead of DRR-generated CT scans. To adapt GRAF to our task of using MRI data instead of CT scans, we needed to modify the method to obtain the radiation attenuation response from MRI data. This involves sampling MRI scans to extract information on the 3D shape and appearance of anatomical structures. The density and pixel values are then computed at each sampled point using a multi-layer perceptron. The final pixel response is then obtained using a compositing operation, and the generator can predict an image patch based on the sampled MRI scans. Due to the small size of the medical datasets, the GRAF discriminator $D(\omega)$ cannot provide enough refined features to the generator $G\theta$, resulting in inaccurate volumetric estimation. Furthermore, limited training data may lead to the generator or discriminator falling into ill-posed settings, resulting in a suboptimal data distribution estimation. Classic data augmentation techniques may also mislead the generator to learn infrequent or non-existent augmented data distributions.

2.5   Dataset

The study employs the publicly available International Brain Tumor Segmentation (BraTS) Challenge 2021 dataset, which encompasses multi-institutional routine clinically acquired multi-parametric MRI (mpMRI) scans of glioma[1]. The dataset comprises scans with pathologically confirmed diagnoses, along with the available MGMT promoter methylation status for glioblastoma cases with these pertinent data. Notably, the dataset has undergone augmentation since BraTS'20, with the inclusion of numerous additional routine clinically acquired mpMRI scans. To train our models, we utilized 40 slices for each of 3 patients in the 2021 dataset of the Challenge. The choice of slices was made erratically. This method was utilised to avoid bias or preconceptions about what should be included or excluded. Additionally, we performed digitally reconstructed radiograph (DRR) generation, which facilitates the removal of patient data and enables control in capture ranges and resolutions. Our training dataset consisted of 30 patients, while the remaining subjects served as the testing set.

3   Results

We make comparisons between our model's outcomes, two other benchmarks, and conduct a study on the impact of specific variables. Both qualitative and quantitative assessments are presented, and all models are trained for 100,000 iterations with a batch size of 8. To uniformly sample points on a sphere's surface, we select projection parameters (u, v) that elevate slightly horizontally between 70–85° and have umin = 0, umax = 1 for a complete 360° vertical rotation. During training, we only offer a fifth of the views (72-views each at five degrees) and allow the model to render the remaining ones.

3.1   Rendering from Single View MRI

The proposed reconstruction approach used has the ability to produce results of volumetric rendering which involves generating a complete 3D representation of a medical instance from a series of 2D MRI slices. However, with the use of a trained model, it is now possible to achieve this with just a single MRI slice. To achieve this, the model is trained using a relaxed reconstruction formulation, as described in [23], which involves fitting the generator to a single image. Then, the parameters of the generator are fine-tuned alongside the shape and appearance of latent vectors zs and za. In order to balance the trade-off between distortion and perception, a Mean Square Error (MSE) loss is added to the generation objective, as is common in GAN methods [24]. With this approach, it is now possible to generate a complete 3D volumetric rendering from a single MRI slice. In Fig. 3 the qualitative results obtained by the proposed method are reported. This features reconstructed slices given a single MRI scan and contrast transformation of slices showing the model's ability to differentiate between bones

---

[1] http://braintumorsegmentation.org.

and other tissues by enhancing the contrast between them. This is achieved by increasing the brightness of pixels that correspond to denser structures such as bone, making them stand out more clearly from the surrounding tissue.

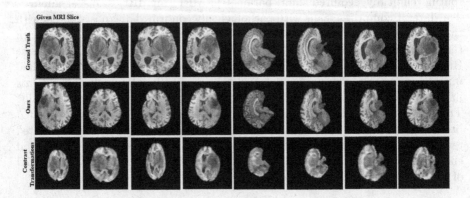

Fig. 3. Qualitative results of MRI reconstruction

3.2   PSNR and SSIM

PSNR and SSIM are metrics that are used to evaluate the quality of images or videos in the field of machine learning. PSNR (Peak Signal-to-Noise Ratio) is a measure of the amount of noise present in an image or video. It compares the original image or video to a compressed or distorted version of that image or video. PSNR is defined as the ratio between the maximum possible value of a signal and the mean squared error (MSE) of the distorted signal, expressed in decibels (dB). Higher PSNR values indicate higher image or video quality, while lower PSNR values indicate lower quality. SSIM (Structural Similarity Index) is a metric that measures the similarity between two images. It takes into account both the structural information (i.e., the organization of pixels in the image) and the luminance and contrast information of the image. SSIM values range from -1 to 1, with 1 indicating perfect similarity between the two images and -1 indicating complete dissimilarity. In the proposed experiments, the PSNR and SSIM were, respectively, 25.01 ± 1.17 and 0.879 ± 0.07.

3.3   FID and KID with Other Models

FID measures the similarity between two datasets of images, one generated by a generative model and the other real, using feature statistics calculated from a pre-trained neural network. Specifically, FID measures the distance between the feature distributions of the generated images and the real images. Lower FID scores indicate higher quality generated images that are more similar to real images. KID also measures the similarity between two datasets of images, but instead of using feature statistics, it uses kernel-based methods to compare the distributions of the images. KID measures the distance between the two distributions of feature representations from the generated images and the real images. Lower KID scores also indicate higher quality generated images that are more similar to real images. More specifically, the proposed experiments result in a FID and KID score, respectively, of 160.12 and 0.16 ± 0.003.

4 Discussions

A 3D model of a scene can be created from a collection of 2D images using the computer vision method known as structure from motion (SfM). SfM is a multi-step process that includes point-cloud reconstruction, feature recognition and matching, and camera pose estimation. Recent advances in deep learning have led to a new method, called NeRF, to create photo-realistic 3D scenes from a collection of 2D images. NeRF has produced stunning outcomes when producing high-fidelity 3D models in several fields, and its adoption by the medical imaging community is also growing. In this paper we explored the idea of reconstructing an MRI volumes from heterogeneous slices, with the ultimate goal of reducing the number of scans during an MRI session or motion artefacts related to long acquisitions at least for educational purposes. Given a data driven generation, it should be used carefully in clinical context as the reconstructed data might hide relevant specific elements in certain pathological cases, and this represents a limitation shared by many generative approaches. Nevertheless, this can lead new ways for data visualization. We called the proposed approach extended-MedNeRF. In particular, we introduced a radiation attenuation response from MRI in the generative radiance field. Moreover, we used challenging scenarios as low-sample size for training and non-uniform slicing. The reconstruction produced promising results that, even if they cannot be used for clinical evaluation, opens a new way to reduce MRI acquisitions and consequent motion corrections. Future work includes tests on brain scans from people of different ages and other MRI modalities.

Acknowledgments. This publication is partially supported by the European Union's Horizon 2020 research and innovation programme under grant agreement Sano No 857533, and partially by the International Research Agendas programme of the Foundation for Polish Science, co-financed by the European Union under the European Regional Development Fund.

References

1. Corona-Figueroa, A., et al.: Mednerf: medical neural radiance fields for reconstructing 3D-aware CT-projections from a single X-ray. In: EMBC, pp. 3843–3848. IEEE (2022)
2. Godenschweger, F., et al.: Motion correction in MRI of the brain. Phys. Med. Biol. **61**(5), R32 (2016)

3. Han, D.: Comparison of commonly used image interpolation methods. In: Conference of the 2nd International Conference on Computer Science and Electronics Engineering (ICCSEE 2013), pp. 1556–1559. Atlantis Press (2013)

4. Hua, S., Liu, Q., Yin, G., Guan, X., Jiang, N., Zhang, Y.: Research on 3D medical image surface reconstruction based on data mining and machine learning. Int. J. Intell. Syst. **37**(8), 4654–4669 (2022)

5. Lin, Q., Zhang, Q., Tongbin, L.: Slice interpolation in MRI using a decomposition-reconstruction method. In: 2017 4th International Conference on Information Science and Control Engineering (ICISCE), pp. 678–681. IEEE (2017)

6. Long, Y., Li, C., Dou, Q.: Robotic surgery remote mentoring via AR with 3D scene streaming and hand interaction. Comput. Methods Biomech. Biomed. Eng. Imaging Visual. 1–6 (2022)

7. Maken, P., Gupta, A.: 2D-to-3D: a review for computational 3D image reconstruction from x-ray images. Arch. Comput. Methods Eng. 1–30 (2022)

8. Masuda, M., Saito, H., Takatsume, Y., Kajita, H.: Novel view synthesis for surgical recording. In: Mukhopadhyay, A., Oksuz, I., Engelhardt, S., Zhu, D., Yuan, Y. (eds.) DGM4MICCAI 2022. LNCS, vol. 13609, pp. 67–76. Springer, Cham (2022). https://doi.org/10.1007/978-3-031-18576-2_7

9. Mildenhall, B., et al.: Nerf: representing scenes as neural radiance fields for view synthesis. Commun. ACM **65**, 99–106 (2021)

10. Pumarola, A., Corona, E., Pons-Moll, G., Moreno-Noguer, F.: D-NeERF: neural radiance fields for dynamic scenes. In: Proceedings of the IEEE/CVF Conference on Computer Vision and Pattern Recognition, pp. 10318–10327 (2021)

11. Schwarz, K., et al.: Graf: generative radiance fields for 3D-aware image synthesis. Adv. Neural. Inf. Process. Syst. **33**, 20154–20166 (2020)

12. Wang, Z., Wu, S., Xie, W., Chen, M., Prisacariu, V.A.: Nerf-: neural radiance fields without known camera parameters. arXiv preprint arXiv:2102.07064 (2021)

13. Yaqub, M., et al.: Deep learning-based image reconstruction for different medical imaging modalities. Comput. Math. Methods Med. (2022)

14. Yeganeh, H., Ziaei, A., Rezaie, A.: A novel approach for contrast enhancement based on histogram equalization. In: 2008 International Conference on Computer and Communication Engineering, pp. 256–260. IEEE (2008)

15. Yu, A., Ye, V., Tancik, M., Kanazawa, A.: Pixelnerf: neural radiance fields from one or few images. In: Proceedings of the IEEE/CVF Conference on Computer Vision and Pattern Recognition, pp. 4578–4587 (2021)

Exploring Target Identification for Drug Design with K-Nearest Neighbors' Algorithm

Karina Jimenes-Vargas[1,2]([✉])[iD], Yunierkis Perez-Castillo[1][iD],
Eduardo Tejera[1]([✉])[iD], and Cristian R. Munteanu[2][iD]

[1] Bio-Cheminformatics Research Group, Universidad de Las Américas,
Quito 170504, Ecuador
{karina.jimenes,yunierkis.perez,eduardo.tejera}@udla.edu.ec
[2] RNASA Group, Department of Computer Science and Information Technologies,
Computer Science Faculty, CITIC, University of A Coruña, 15071 A Coruña, Spain
{karina.jimenes,c.munteanu}@udc.es

Abstract. The identification of possible targets for a known compound by its sole molecular representation is one of the most important tasks for drug design and development. In this work, a methodology is proposed for target identification using supervised machine learning. To predict drug binding targets, classification models across targets were constructed using the k-NN algorithm by integrating multiple data types. Two different groups of descriptors are used: 1) Morgan's fingerprint and 2) general molecular properties of interest. The findings demonstrate that the k-NN classification models achieved a higher f1-score with descriptors based on molecular properties of interest with 0.7 in comparison to the Morgan fingerprint descriptors that achieved a score of 0.57 or the fusion of both with a score of 0.58.

Keywords: target identification · k-nearest neighbors · molecular compounds

1 Introduction

Target identification (TI) refers to predict targets capable to interact with a query molecule based on the similarity principle. Its states that similar compounds may have similar bio-activity profile [1]. This problem attracts close attention from industries and academies due to this is a crucial issue in drug discovery to determine research focus and strategy, which is a time-consuming task and an extremely expensive industry [2]. Additionally, applications include everything from basic mode-of-action analysis to poly-pharmacology to predicting side effects to drug repositioning [3].

In recent years, computational methods for predicting targets of small molecules have become increasingly relevant and popular. According to [4], this

L. Rutkowski et al. (Eds.): ICAISC 2023, LNAI 14126, pp. 219–227, 2023.
https://doi.org/10.1007/978-3-031-42508-0_20

is due to three factors: a) polypharmacology, b) the growing availability of chemical and biological information and c) advances algorithms and hardware-based technology. The traditional computational methods for identifying interactions mainly include ligand-based approaches and structure-based approaches [5]. The first approach is related to the main topic of this document.

The ligand-based approach predicts compound-target interactions by comparing the candidate compounds with other molecules in which we were aware of a given set of targets. These predictions are driven by the "similarity principle" which says that similar small molecules are likely to have similar target-binding profiles [6]. This approach is based on independent protein targets, is fast and depends on the available molecular bio-activity data [7]. It also typically requires libraries of chemogenomics annotated with compound-target interactions. Additionally, the prospective targets may be deduced from either the bioactive compounds in which the query shares a high degree of chemical similarity or from either the thoroughly tested machine learning(ML) models [5].

The simplest and quite efficient method is chemical similarity searching, which involves scoring reference library compounds according to how closely they resemble the targets. ML based methods, on the other hand, learn one or more predictive models that associate composite descriptors with target labels after being trained on samples with known target labels. ML methods have a superior extrapolation capabilities to discover the targets of novel compounds. This is because ML performs feature selection whereas similarity search perspectives use all available descriptors [4,5].

In contrast, the structure-based approach uses docking algorithms and molecular dynamics simulations to identify probable interactions based on the known three-dimensional 3D structures of targets. For most proteins that do not have this preliminary information, these approaches are inadequate [8]. This perspective is more expensive and time-consuming than ligand-based methods, as this technique necessarily involves searching the conformational space of the ligand or target proteins [9].

The rising amount of available bio-activity data makes the unknown chemical space to diminish; consequently, it allows to perform better prediction models. Moreover, nowadays, there are several public databases for storing information regarding compounds bio-activities like: ChEMBL [10,11], DrugBank [12] Pub-Chem [13].

This pilot study suggests a methodology for building ML models across the targets. It is designed to cover the target space, taking advantage of the large amount of chemical information and measured bioactivity data available. Furthermore, multiple data types to predict compound binding targets are integrated. Most of the existing studies only explore Morgan's fingerprinting as descriptors [14–17] but few of them explore the effectiveness of using the physicochemical molecular compounds properties of interest [18,19]. Therefore, the binary character fingerprint descriptors and continuous character properties of interest are examined separately and together due to explore their importance and their effectiveness.

Hence, in this paper, TI is studied using a binary classification ML algorithm and the mass bioactivity data stored in the CHEMBL. The rest of the work is organized as follows: Sect. 2 presents a methodology which indicates how the compound structures are transformed into descriptors and how a set of classification models are trained across the available targets. Section 3 presents the discussion of the results. Finally, the last section presents the conclusion and the future work.

2 Methods

2.1 Data Pre-processing

CHEMBL is a database maintained by the *European Bioinformatics Institute* collects data from scientific literature and contains compounds bioactivity data against targets [11]. The release 27 (434984 compounds, 2677 targets, 641042 interactions) and 28 (465230 compounds, 2851 targets, 686263 interactions) from CHEMBL were used to build our dataset of compound-target interactions.

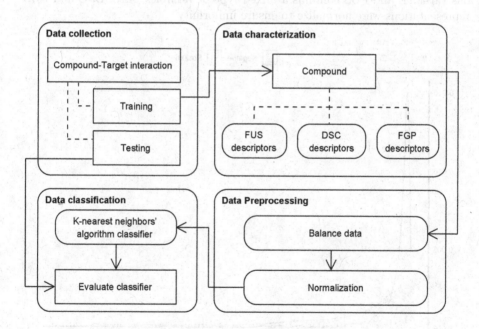

Fig. 1. Classification process for target identification

Raw data of homo-sapiens was pre-processed as follow: 1) only assays with an IC50 were used, 2) units in µM 3) Compound-target interactions classified as active ($IC50 > 10\,\mu M$) or inactive ($IC50 < 10\,\mu M$). After applying these steps approaches in release 27 and 28 a total of 350818 compounds, 1521 target and 507553 common interactions between both database versions was obtained.

Then, just the targets that have at least 10 unique positive and 10 negative compound interactions were considered for the construction of predictive models. A total of 770 target were considering with 443016 interactions with 311930 compounds.

The data for external validation was performed using all unique compound found in release 28 and not in release 27 with a set of 27118 molecules which covers a set of 939 targets and 37676 compound-target interactions. Nevertheless, just 526 targets from the 770 were validated because only those proteins have new data in the external validation set.

2.2   Classification Models

The classifiers across the targets were built as follows (Fig. 1). First, three different molecular representations computed with RDKit [20] are: a) 1024 bits of long Morgan's fingerprint up to eight bonds (FGP) and b) A set of 123 general molecular properties of interests (DSC) and c) The fusion of both FGP and DSC descriptors (FUS). FGP contains binary variables, DSC contains continuous variables and FUS contains a mixed type of variables. Also, DSC and FUS representations were normalize to ensure uniformity.

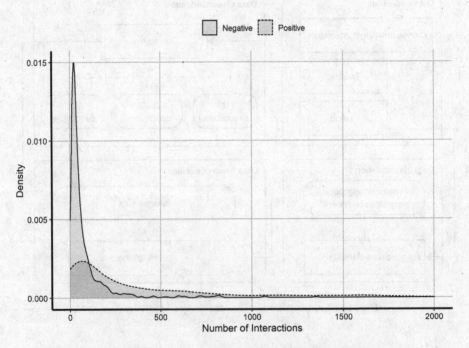

Fig. 2. Density distribution of the compound-target interactions

The problem of imbalance data was addressed with stratified sampling procedure. Most of the targets have an average of 500 positive/negative interactions with compounds, which does not represent a large amount of data as its shown in Fig. 2. TI was treated as a binary classification problem and an individual prediction model was constructed for each target using the popular K-nearest neighbors' algorithm (k-NN) with the three set of descriptors and a k value of 3 which is a number of nearest neighbors that are included in the contribution of the voting process [21].

Neighbors are usually calculated based on distances, and the distance between two points are calculated using the distance metric Minkowski. Minkowski is a generalized distance metric in a normed vector space, which can be considered as a generalization of both the Euclidean distance and the Manhattan distance [22].

The k-NN is one of the most popular distance-based algorithms and it uses proximity to make classifications and works off the assumption that similar points can be found near one another. It is easy to implement, adapts easily and has few hyperparamenters; even though, as a dataset grows, its becomes increasingly inefficient, compromising overall model performance [23].

Besides, regarding data types, the focus of k-NN classifiers has so far been on data sets with purely numerical features [24]; however, k-NN can also be applied to other data types, including categorical data [25]. Consequently, several studies [26, 27] were used to classify data described by numerical and categorical features.

The k-NN models trained with FGP and DSC descriptors were evaluated using a 5-fold cross-validation technique, a data resampling technique to prevent overfitting and assess the generalizability of predictive models [28]. Finally, the results of the external validation dataset were reported in terms of the f1-score metric, which is the harmonic mean of precision and recall.

3 Discussion

The outcome of the binary classification is reported for all the target k-NN prediction models built across targets with scikit-learn for 526 targets represented by at least 20 compound interactions and with known bioactivity. The results obtained for the three different types of descriptors are presented in Fig. 3. It indicates that the DSC density curve is left skewed due to most of the values fall near one in models trained with DSC descriptors which refers to a good performance. In contrast, FGP and FUS descriptors density curve have no skew, with a lot of variation in a wide range of f1-scores.

The f1-score achieved by the trained models with the DSC descriptors was 0.73 ± 0.2 which is better than the f1-scores achieved by the FGP and FUS descriptors with values of 0.57 ± 0.2 and 0.58 ± 0.2 respectively. It means that general molecular properties of interests of DSC descriptors allows modeling better the bioactivity of compound-targets. Indeed, employing FGP or combining it with DSC does not necessarily allow to train good models even though there are more descriptors. It can be due the k-NN could not handle this higher dimensionality [29] and the length of descriptor vector is higher for FGP (1024 length) and FUS (1147 length) than the DSC descriptors (123 length).

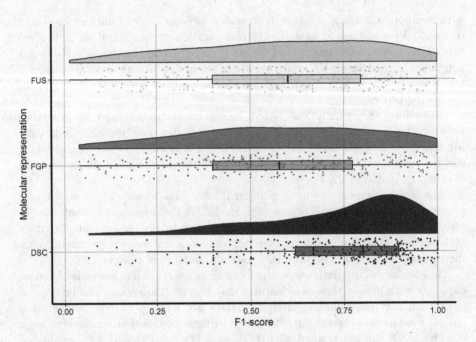

Fig. 3. F1-score distribution for models trained with K-NN algorithm and the three group of molecular compound representations FGP, DSC and FUS.

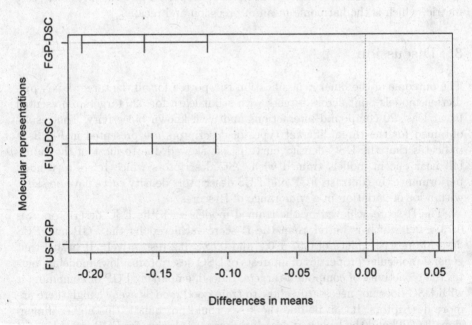

Fig. 4. Tukey's Test over F1-score of trained models.

On the other hand, the one-way ANOVA test across the f1-scores of the three groups evidence there are significant difference between three groups of descriptors (FGP, DSC, FUS) because the p-value of $2.43e - 16$ is less than the significance level of 0.05 in the analysis of variance. Also, the Tukey's Post Hoc Test pairwise comparison was performed with 95 of confidence level to see differences between groups (Fig. 4). The difference between groups of descriptors FGP-DSC and FUS-DSC are statistically significant because the intervals for the mean differences do not contain the zero as it is shown in Fig. 4.

In short, the overall results of the experiment showed that k-NN is not suitable for classification of categorical (FGP) or mixed-type (FUS) data; however, DSC are good. It is also important to mention that only bioassays archived in the CHEMBL database were considered and these models rely on available molecular bioactivity data. So, an unknown interaction cannot be predicted if the compound lies outside the measured bio-activity data [30]. TI methods like this based on the bioactivity profile rely on large amounts of bioactivity data tested experimentally [31].

4 Conclusions

The TI could be conducted using the bioassays collected in the CHEMBL database. The prediction trained models across the targets with DSC descriptors achieved a f1-score average of 0.7 in contrast to FGP and FUS that achieved a f1-score average of 0.57 and 0.58 respectively. The DSC descriptors seems to perform better than the FGP and FUS descriptors for modeling with k-NN. The DSC descriptors are enough good to be able to distinguish between active and inactive protein-compounds interactions. It means that k-NN is not suitable for classifying categorical or a mixed type data.

In future developments, other algorithms with several hyper-parameters could be explore to get better models and to achieved a higher f1-score. Also, a tool could be built to facilitate researchers use the predictions models in tasks related with biological mechanisms and drug discovery in academic institutes and pharmaceutical industries.

References

1. Czarnecki, W.M.: Weighted Tanimoto extreme learning machine with case study in drug discovery. IEEE Comput. Intell. Mag. **10**(3), 19–29 (2015)
2. Zhang, W., Lin, W., Zhang, D., Wang, S., Shi, J., Niu, Y.: Recent advances in the machine learning-based drug-target interaction prediction. Curr. Drug Metab. **20**(3), 194–202 (2019)
3. Sydow, D., et al.: Advances and challenges in computational target prediction. J. Chem. Inf. Model. **59** (2019)
4. Mathai, N., Kirchmair, J.: Similarity-based methods and machine learning approaches for target prediction in early drug discovery: performance and scope. Int. J. Mol. Sci. **21**(10), 3585 (2020)

5. Yang, S., et al.: Current advances in ligand-based target prediction. Wiley Interdisc. Rev. Comput. Mol. Sci. **11**, 1–21 (2020)
6. Schuffenhauer, A., Floersheim, P., Acklin, P., Jacoby, E.: Similarity metrics for ligands reflecting the similarity of the target proteins. J. Chem. Inf. Comput. Sci. **43**(2), 391–405 (2003)
7. Nogueira, M.S., Koch, O.: The development of target-specific machine learning models as scoring functions for docking-based target prediction. J. Chem. Inf. Model. **59**(3), 1238–1252 (2019). PMID: 30802041
8. Zhao, S., Shao, L.: Network-based relating pharmacological and genomic spaces for drug target identification. PLoS ONE **5**(7) (2010)
9. Shaikh, F., Tai, H.K., Desai, N., Siu, S.: Ligtmap: ligand and structure-based target identification and activity prediction for small molecules. J. Cheminform. (2020)
10. Bento, A.P., et al.: The ChEMBL bioactivity database: an update. Nucleic Acids Res. **42**(D1), D1083–D1090 (2013)
11. Mendez, D., et al.: ChEMBL: towards direct deposition of bioassay data. Nucleic Acids Res. **47**(D1), D930–D940 (2018)
12. Wishart, D.S., et al.: DrugBank 5.0: a major update to the DrugBank database for 2018. Nucleic Acids Res. **46**(D1), D1074–D1082 (2017)
13. Wang, Y., et al.: PubChem BioAssay: 2017 update. Nucleic Acids Res. **45**(D1), D955–D963 (2016)
14. Ding, Y., Tang, J., Guo, F.: Identification of drug-target interactions via multiple information integration. Inf. Sci. **418–419**, 546–560 (2017)
15. Peón, A., et al.: Moltarpred: a web tool for comprehensive target prediction with reliability estimation. Chem. Biol. Drug Des. **94** (2019)
16. Cockroft, N.T., Cheng, X., Fuchs, J.R.: Starfish: a stacked ensemble target fishing approach and its application to natural products. J. Chem. Inf. Model. **59**(11), 4906–4920 (2019). PMID: 31589422
17. Awale, M., Reymond, J.-L.: The polypharmacology browser ppb2: target prediction combining nearest neighbors with machine learning. J. Chem. Inf. Model. **59**, 12 (2018)
18. Cui, X., Liu, J., Zhang, J., Qiuyun, W., Li, X.: In silico prediction of drug-induced rhabdomyolysis with machine-learning models and structural alerts. J. Appl. Toxicol. **39**, 1224–1232 (2019)
19. Shi, Y., Hua, Y., Wang, B., Zhang, R., Li, X.: In silico prediction and insights into the structural basis of drug induced nephrotoxicity. Front. Pharmacol. **12**, 01 (2022)
20. Landrum, G., et al.: rdkit/rdkit: 2022_09_1b1 (q3 2022) release, October 2022
21. Prakisya, N.P.T., Liantoni, F., Hatta, P., Aristyagama, Y.H., Setiawan, A.: Utilization of k-nearest neighbor algorithm for classification of white blood cells in AML m4, m5, and m7. Open Eng. **11**, 662–668 (2021)
22. Klimo, M., Škvarek, O., Tarábek, P., Šuch, O., Hrabovsky, J.: Nearest neighbor classification in Minkowski quasi-metric space. In: 2018 World Symposium on Digital Intelligence for Systems and Machines (DISA), pp. 227–232 (2018)
23. Cover, T., Hart, P.: Nearest neighbor pattern classification. IEEE Trans. Inf. Theory **13**(1), 21–27 (1967)
24. Wettschereck, D.: A study of distance-based machine learning algorithms. Ph.D. thesis, Oregon State University, USA, AAI9507711 (1994)
25. Bramer, M.: Principles of Data Mining. Springer, London (2007). https://doi.org/10.1007/978-1-84628-766-4
26. Li-Yu, H., Huang, M.-W., Ke, S.-W., Tsai, C.-F.: The distance function effect on k-nearest neighbor classification for medical datasets. Springerplus **5**, 12 (2016)

27. Williams, J., Li, Y.: Comparative study of distance functions for nearest neighbors. Adv. Tech. Comput. Sci. Softw. Eng. 79–84 (2008)

28. Berrar, D.: Cross-validation. In: Ranganathan, S., Gribskov, M., Nakai, K., Schönbach, C. (eds.) Encyclopedia of Bioinformatics and Computational Biology, pp. 542–545. Academic Press, Oxford (2019)

29. Deegalla, S., Boström, H.: Classification of microarrays with kNN: comparison of dimensionality reduction methods. In: Yin, H., Tino, P., Corchado, E., Byrne, W., Yao, X. (eds.) IDEAL 2007. LNCS, vol. 4881, pp. 800–809. Springer, Heidelberg (2007). https://doi.org/10.1007/978-3-540-77226-2_80

30. Gfeller, D., Michielin, O., Zoete, V.: Shaping the interaction landscape of bioactive molecules. Bioinformatics **29**(23), 3073–3079 (2013)

31. Wang, L., Ma, C., Wipf, P., Liu, H., Weiwei, S., Xie, X.-Q.: Targethunter: an in silico target identification tool for predicting therapeutic potential of small organic molecules based on chemogenomic database. AAPS J. **15**(2), 395–406 (2013)

Computational Models for COVID-19 Dynamics Prediction

Andrzej Kloczkowski[1,2]([envelope]) [ORCID], Juan Luis Fernández-Martínez[3] [ORCID],
and Zulima Fernández-Muñiz[3] [ORCID]

[1] Institute for Genomic Medicine, Nationwide Children Hospital, Columbus, OH 43205, USA
Andrzej.Kloczkowski@nationwidechildrens.org
[2] Department of Pediatrics, The Ohio State University, Columbus, OH 43205, USA
[3] Department of Mathematics, University of Oviedo, 33007 Oviedo, Spain

Abstract. In a viral pandemic, predicting the number of infected per day and the total number of cases in each wave of possible variants is intended to aid decision-making in real public health practice. This paper compares the efficiency of three very simple models in predicting the behavior of COVID-19 in Spain during the first waves. The Verhulst, Gompertz and SIR models are used to predict pandemic behavior using past daily cases as observed data. The parameters of each model are identified at each wave by solving the corresponding inverse problem through a member of the PSO family and then their posterior distribution is calculated using the Metropolis-Hastings algorithm to compare the robustness of each predictive model. It can be concluded that all these models are incomplete without the corresponding parameter uncertainty analysis. In these cases, the comparison of the posterior prediction with respect to the predictive model used shows that this work can be used for real-life decision making.

Keywords: Uncertainty Analysis · Particle Swarm Optimization · Population Models · Metropolis-Hastings algorithm · Inverse Problems · COVID-19

1 Introduction

The mathematical models used in the study of a transmitted disease must be able to adjust the behavior of the disease when the available data are adequate, and be simple enough to be used in a dynamic and understandable way. In the case of COVID-19, due to its health and economic interest, a multitude of methods have appeared with the aim of predicting its behavior and making conjectures that help the health system of each country to make the most effective decisions.

In this sense, in the scientific literature one can find models that use time series [1], that use artificial intelligence [2] or that simulate the behavior of individuals to study the spread of the virus [3]. All of them also present some weakness such as having difficulty predicting changes or lacking sufficient training data. In addition, all these models are characterized by their own parameters, which are unknown, and which influence the prediction of disease transmission.

© The Author(s), under exclusive license to Springer Nature Switzerland AG 2023
L. Rutkowski et al. (Eds.): ICAISC 2023, LNAI 14126, pp. 228–238, 2023.
https://doi.org/10.1007/978-3-031-42508-0_21

On the other hand, there are models based on differential equations that have been widely used for some time for the study of viral diseases [4]. Some of these models are the ones used in this work to predict the transmission of the disease. One of these models is the SIR, which owes its name to the fact that it considers the population separated into three groups, Susceptible, Infected and Recovered, and is governed by a system of three ordinary differential equations that has no explicit solution, which does not make it difficult for valuable information about the solution can be obtained [5, 6]. The SIR model [7] considers that the population is made up of a large and closed group, without natural births or deaths, in which the rate of encounters between susceptible and infected is proportional to the size of the population. It is a short-lived outbreak with no latency period and, once recovered, each individual acquires permanent immunity. For this, the members of each group must be homogeneously distributed, with the probability of encounters per unit of time being the same for all individuals. Since it is an unrealistic model, there are some variations of it, which try to alleviate its weaknesses.

Another way to treat the outbreak (Verhults, 1838) [8] is to work only with the infected group, considering it as a population that grows up to a limit. At first, the virus spreads rapidly, but as the number of infected grows, the rate of spread slows. The Verhulst model was devised to predict the human population in an area, with the aim of making decisions for socioeconomic and demographic development [9]. But this model, with its bounds to determine the unlimited growth of the population [10], is a computationally reliable alternative to deal with population problems [11].

Finally, the Gompertz model (1825) [12] has been used mainly in the study of tumor growth [13–16]. It is a sigmoid function that describes slower growth at the extremes of a given period.

Fernández-Martínez et al. [17] presented the analysis of the Verhulst and Gompertz models for the short- and long-term prediction of the COVID-19 pandemic by solving the corresponding inverse problem through a member of the PSO family.

In this article, this comparison is extended to the SIR model, inferring the posterior distributions of the model parameters through the Metropolis-Hastings algorithm. The results obtained are used to make predictions and obtain a range of possible variation in the evolution of both the number of daily cases of infection and the total number of cases during each wave in Spain. Although none of the models accurately describe the COVID-19 pandemic, it is not necessary to predict the start or end date of the pandemic, as well as the peaks of the different waves.

2   Three Models

2.1   SIR Model

The model is governed by the following system of ordinary differential equations:

$$\frac{dS}{dt} = -\frac{r}{K}SI \quad \frac{dI}{dt} = -\frac{r}{K}SI - \gamma I \quad \frac{dR}{dt} = \gamma I$$

where $r > 0$ is the transmission rate, $\gamma > 0$ the recovery rate (being the duration of infection $D = 1/\gamma$) and r/K the transmission rate. The incidence rSI/K of the number of newly infected individuals per unit time involves individuals in the infected and susceptible classes. Also, the sum of the three previous equations is the derivative of the total population size, the result of which is zero. Therefore, the total population size $K = R(t) + S(t) + I(t)$ remains constant.

If each infected person has on average κ contacts capable of transmitting the disease per unit time, irrespective of the total population size, $\kappa S / K$ of those contacts will be with susceptible persons and, if we finally take that a fraction τ of suitable contacts result in susceptible persons, it follows that each person carrying the virus infects $\tau \kappa S / K$ people per unit of time. Therefore, defining $r = \kappa \tau$, with the parameter τ known as transmissibility, the system described above is obtained.

Taking a sufficiently large, initially susceptible population $(S(0) = K - 1, \quad I(0) = 1, \quad R(0) = 0)$, we define the effective reproductive number $R_e = (S(0)/K)r/\gamma$ and the basic reproductive number $R_0 = r/\gamma$, then $R_e = ((K - 1)/K)r/\gamma$ is approximately equal to R_0.

This R_e is the threshold value that determines whether a disease outbreak will die out quickly or instead spread and cause a pandemic. If $R_e \leq 1$, then $I(t)$ is a monotonic function that decreases towards zero as it grows, while if $R_e > 1$, then $I(t)$ starts growing, reaches a maximum, and finally decreases towards zero as t increases. This scenario of growing numbers of infected individuals will serve to describe an epidemic.

It is important to emphasize that the existence of a threshold for determining whether a disease outbreak becomes an epidemic or not, is far from obvious and goes unnoticed by many public health and infectious disease experts. The reason is that this threshold cannot be derived from data but requires mathematical modelling.

There are some strategies for $R_e \leq 1$, such as reducing the duration of infection with antivirals; adopting strategies to reduce the number of κ contacts or τ transmissibility; vaccinating the population to reduce the number of initial susceptible population. Related to the latter strategy, it is possible to avoid a pandemic by vaccinating only part of the population. This is the phenomenon known as herd immunity and the critical vaccination threshold is achieved when the fraction of susceptible people who are vaccinated is $\rho > 1 - 1/R_e$. On the other hand, the maximum number of infected can be expressed as a function of the single parameter R_0, as $I_{max} = K(1 - (1/R_0)(1 + \log R_0))$.

Finally, as an epidemic progresses, the number of susceptible people and the rate at which new infections occur decreases. Eventually, $S(t)$ decreases below $\gamma K / r$, and the rate of recovery exceeds the rate of infection. Thus, $I(t)$ begins to decline and the epidemic ends because of a lack of newly infected individuals and not for lack of the susceptible population.

2.2 Verhulst Model

Verhulst's model falls into the class of limited growth models as a modification of the model of Malthus (1766–1834) [18], which advocated exponential population growth. In this model the rate of reproduction is proportional to the existing population and the available resources, and is governed by the following first-degree differential equation, representing the number of daily cases:

$$\frac{dP}{dt} = rP\left(1 - \frac{P}{K}\right),$$

$$P(0) = P_0$$

(1)

where $P(t)$ is the population size, which applied to epidemiology is the number of infected, r is the intrinsic growth rate and K is the maximum population size that can be sustained by the environment, known as the carrying capacity.

The solution of the Verhulst's model is given by

$$P(t) = \frac{KP_0 e^{rt}}{K + P_0(e^{rt} - 1)}$$

(2)

which depends on the parameters P_0, K y r.

The maximum number of daily cases obtained is

$$max\left(\frac{dP(t)}{dt}\right) = \frac{rK}{4},$$

(3)

corresponding to $t = t_{max} = \ln A/r$, where A is a constant that must satisfy the initial condition

$$P_0 = \frac{K}{1 + A}$$

(4)

Therefore, the peak of the daily infections depends on r and K, while the time at which this peak occurs depends on P_0.

2.3 Gompertz Model

There are several forms of the so-called Gompertz equation (1938) in the literature, but in this paper, we will consider the following one

$$\frac{dP}{dt} = rP \ln\left(\frac{K}{P}\right)$$

$$P(0) = P_0$$

(5)

where $P(t)$, is the population at time t, r is an intrinsic growth constant, with $r > 0$, and $K > 0$, is the carrying capacity or maximum population size. The general solution is

$$P(t) = Ke^{-Be^{-rt}},$$

(6)

where B represents a real constant satisfying the initial equation

$$P(0) = Ke^{-B}. \tag{7}$$

Equation (9) can be expressed in terms of the same parameters as the Verhulst model:

$$P(t) = K\left(\frac{P_0}{K}\right)^{e^{-rt}} \tag{8}$$

being the maximum number of daily cases, obtained for $t_{max} = \ln B / r$:

$$max\left(\frac{dP(t)}{dt}\right) = \frac{Kr}{e}, \tag{9}$$

Identical considerations to Verhulst model can be made for the peak and the time at which the peak occurs. The number of infected is higher than in the case of Verhulst model for the same values of K and r. This result can be seen in Figs. 1 and 2 in which the Verhulst's and Gompertz's models have been simulated for an initial population $P_0 = 1$ and taking different values of K and r (the same in each model).

In the Verhulst's and Gompertz's models, the model parameters B and P_0 to K are related via a logarithmic expression. In the case of Verhulst, the logarithmic equation is

$$\ln K = \ln P_0 + B. \tag{10}$$

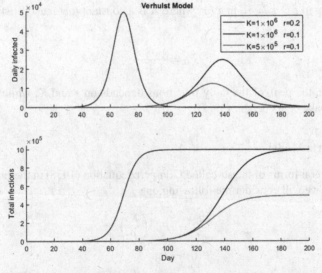

Fig. 1. Epidemic simulation with Verhulst model for $P_0 = 1$.

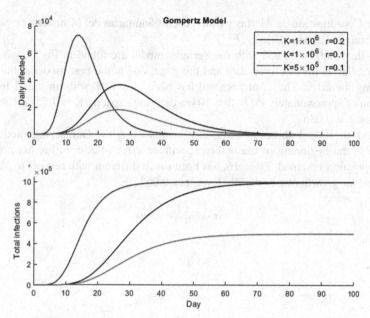

Fig. 2. Epidemic simulation with Gompertz model for $P_0 = 1$.

3   Results Comparison

For the purpose of this article, we will focus our attention on the third wave, which starts around 8th December 2020 and it is characterized by an upturn in the daily cases a few days after Christmas holidays. The data have been obtained from reports provided by the

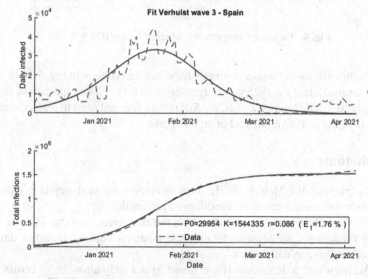

Fig. 3. Fit using Verhulst model wave 3 COVID-19 Spain.

Centro de Coordinacion de Alertas y Emergencias Sanitarias del Ministerio de Sanidad del Gobierno de España [19].

First, the results obtained with the Verhulst model are found in Fig. 3, where the red dashed line is the observed data and the green one is the best model obtained by minimizing the error. The error obtained has been of 1.76% with an initial infected population of approximately P0 $\approx$ 3 × 104, a carrying capacity K $\approx$ 1.55 × 106 and a growth rate r = 0.086.

Second, the Fig. 4 shows how the fit obtained using the Gompertz's model fails primarily at the beginning of the outbreak, with an error of 3.98%. Furthermore, the initial population obtained, P0 = 16, has been much different with respect to Verhulst results and the growth rate is slightly lower r = 0.062.

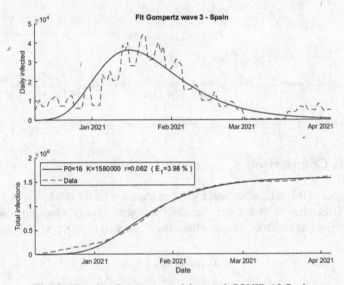

Fig. 4. Fit using Gompertz model wave 3 COVID-19 Spain.

Finally, the SIR model returns a precise fit, which can be seen in Fig. 5, with an error of 2.15%, a growth rate r = 0.255 and a recovery rate 0.161. It is important to note that, unlike Verhulst's and Gompertz's fits, the SIR model does not need to reach the carrying capacity, K $\approx$ 2.5 × 106, at the end of an outbreak.

4   Predictions

After sampling with the Metropolis Hastings algorithm, the next step is to extrapolate the pandemic curves and calculate the different percentiles.

With the aim of giving a general idea about the effectiveness of the different models at making predictions, we present one example made on January 25, a few days after the peak of the wave in daily cases.

The Verhulst and SIR models (Figs. 6 and 8) not only allow us to obtain a very precise frame of daily cases, but they fit the wave shape very good.

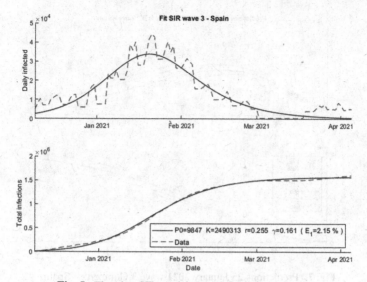

Fig. 5. Fit using SIR model wave 3 COVID-19 Spain.

In Fig. 7, the Gompertz's predictions maintain that long-term trend that fails to adjust the peak of the wave but is the most accurate when it comes to predicting the number of daily cases over April.

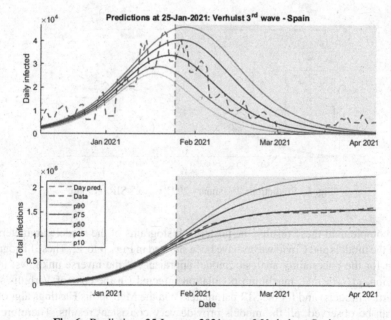

Fig. 6. Predictions 25 January 2021 wave 3 Verhults – Spain.

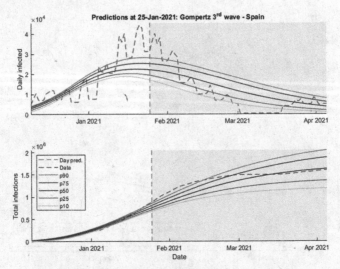

Fig. 7. Predictions 25 January 2021 wave 3 Gompertz – Spain.

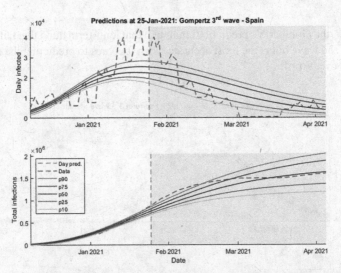

Fig. 8. Predictions 25 January 2021 wave 3 SIR – Spain.

To complement these results, the posterior histograms of the model parameters for each of the models and Covid waves have been showed in Figs. 9 to 12. These histograms account for the uncertainty analysis (model appraisal) of the inverse unknows: initial population, growth rate, maximum population infected (in the case of Verhults's and Gompertz's models) and for the SIR parameters, via the Metropolis Hastings algorithm. As it can be observed, all the models provide very consistent results. Therefore, the conclusions achieved by the posterior analysis are similar.

5 Conclusion

In this article, a comparison is made between the Verhulst's, Gompertz's and SIR models in terms of their effectiveness in predicting the effects of COVID-19 outbreaks in Spain and for the purpose of socio-health planning. The analysis of the different solutions obtained by each model shows the daily prediction of infected people and the total number of infections. The three models show similar results, but it is easier to refine the parameters of the Verhulst's model. In view of these facts, it would be more appropriate to use the Verhulst model for long-term forecasts, and the SIR model for short-term forecasts, or when precise information on the recovery rate is available. Finally, it is clear that none of the models is perfect, but precisely because of these differences in the predictions of each model, they could be used in a complementary way to inform decision-making during a pandemic.

Acknowledgment. AK acknowledges the financial support from NSF grant DBI 1661391, and NIH grants R01GM127701, and R01HG012117.

References

1. Elmousalami, H.H., Hassanien, A.E.: Day level forecasting for coronavirus disease (COVID-19) spread: Analysis, modeling and recommendations, arXiv preprint arXiv:2003.07778 (2020)
2. Hu, Z., Ge, Q., Jin, L., Xiong, M.: Artificial intelligence forecasting of covid-19 in China. arXiv preprint arXiv:2002.07112 (2020)
3. Kim, Y., Ryu, H., Lee, S.: Agent-based modeling for super-spreading events: a case study of MERS-CoV transmission dynamics in the Republic of Korea. Int. J. Environ. Res. Public Health **15**, 2369 (2018)
4. Satsuma, J., Willox, R., Ramani, A., Grammaticos, B., Carstea, A.: Extending the SIR epidemic model. Phys. A. **336**, 369–375 (2004)
5. Britton, T.: Stochastic epidemic models: a survey. Math. Biosci. **225**, 24–35 (2010)
6. Zhou, Y., Ma, Z., Brauer, F.: A discrete epidemic model for SARS transmission and control in China. Math. Comput. Model. **40**, 1491–1506 (2004)
7. Kermack, W.O., McKendrick, A.G.: A contribution to the mathematical theory of epidemics. Proc. R. Soc. London, Serie A Containing Pap. Math. Phys. Charact. **115**, 700–721 (1927)
8. Verhulst, P.F.: Notice sur la loi que la population suit dans son accroissement. Correspondance Math. Phys. **10**, 113–121 (1838)
9. Dawed, M.Y., Koya, P.R., Goshu, A.T.: Mathematical modelling of population growth: the case of logistic and von bertalanffy models. Open J. Model. Simul. **02**(04), 113–126 (2014). https://doi.org/10.4236/ojmsi.2014.24013
10. Hillen, T.: Applications and limitations of the verhulst model for populations. Math Biol. **6**, 19–20 (2003)
11. Sunday, J., James, A., Ibijola, E., Ogunrinde, R., Ogunyebi, S.A.: Computational approach to verhulst-pearl model. IOSR J. Math. **2**(6), 45–52 (2012)
12. Gompertz, B.: On the nature of the function expressive of the law of human mortality, and on a new mode of determining the value of life contingencies. Philos. Trans. R. Soc. London B: Biol. Sci. **182**, 513–585 (1825)

13. Altrock, P.M., Liu, L.L., Michor, F.: The mathematics of cancer: integrating quantitative models. Nat. Rev. Cancer. **15**(12), 730–745 (2015). https://doi.org/10.1038/nrc4029

14. Barbolosi, D., Ciccolini, J., Lacarelle, B., Barlesi, F., André, N.: Computational oncology–mathematical modelling of drug regimens for precision medicine. Nat. Rev. Clin. Oncol. **13**(4), 242–254 (2016). https://doi.org/10.1038/nrclinonc.2015.204

15. Benzekry, S., et al.: Classical mathematical models for description and prediction of experimental tumor growth. PLOS Comput. Biol. **10**(8), e1003800 (2014)

16. Winsor, C.P.: The Gompertz curve as a growth curve. Proc. Nat. Acad. Sci. **18**(1), 1–8 (1932). https://doi.org/10.1073/pnas.18.1.1

17. Fernández-Martínez, J.L., Fernández-Muñiz, Z., Cernea, A., Kloczkowski, A.: Predictive mathematical models of the short-term and long-term growth of the COVID-19 pandemic. Comput. Math. Methods Med. **2021**, 1–14 (2021). https://doi.org/10.1155/2021/5556433

18. Malthus, T.R.: An Essay on the Principle of Population, as it Affects the Future Improvement of Society. First edition with remarks on the speculations of Godwin, M, Condorcet, and other writers (1798)

19. Centro de Coordinación de Alertas y Emergencias Sanitarias. Ministerio de Sanidad. Gobierno de España. Actualización covid-19. https://www.mscbs.gob.es/profesionales/saludPublica/ccayes/alertasActual/nCov/documentos/Actualizacion_365_COVID-19.pdf. Accessed 30 Apr 2021

Electrochemical Biosensor Design Through Data-Driven Modeling Incorporating Meta-Analysis and Big Data Workflow

Martsenyuk Vasyl[1](✉) [iD], Klos-Witkowska Aleksandra[1] [iD], and Semenets Andrii[2] [iD]

[1] University of Bielsko-Biala, Willowa 2, 43-300 Bielsko-Biała, Poland
{vmartsenyuk,awitkowska}@ath.bielsko.pl
[2] Ivan Horbachevsky Ternopil National Medical University, 1 Maidan Voli, Ternopil 46001, Ukraine
semteacher@tdmu.edu.ua

Abstract. The objective of the work is to offer workflow enabling us to execute both empirical and analytical studies of enzyme kinetics. For this purpose, on the one hand, we are based on a series of experimental research involving the traditional methods and techniques used when studying biochemical reactions and designing electrochemical biosensors: conductance research, spectroscopy, and electromagnetic field study.

On the other hand, when studying enzyme kinetics analytically we employ the Michaelis-Menten approach while modelling enzyme-substrate-inhibitor interactions and extend it to multi-substrate multi-inhibitor complexes.

Enforcing traditional Big Data workflow is offered with the help of meta-analysis facilities of existing repositories of biochemical studies located on the BRENDA platform.

Keywords: Electrochemical biosensor · enzyme kinetics · Big Data workflow · parameter estimation

1 Introduction

Nowadays, the study of biochemical reactions is cutting edge of Industry 4.0 as it is an important stage of electrochemical biosensor design. Besides experimental research of physical and chemical characteristics of chemicals and their metabolites, there is need to estimate calibration curves, including biosensor response and for example substrate concentration. The opportunities of current analytical tools involving artificial intelligence is of importance here.

The data which are being used and have been generated along with the process of biochemical study correspond to the definition of Big Data, which can be formulated in a simple way with the help of 3 Vs, namely, "volume", "variety", and "velocity". In fact, the current volume of meta-data collected as a result of biochemical research is estimated by 2 Gigabytes. The data of biochemical research have complex nature and are

L. Rutkowski et al. (Eds.): ICAISC 2023, LNAI 14126, pp. 239–250, 2023.
https://doi.org/10.1007/978-3-031-42508-0_22

in the form of numbers, plots, signals, and images. Such data are updating, upgrading, and growing soon, which can be observed on BRENDA project [1].

The objective of the work is to offer workflow enabling us to execute both empirical and analytical study of enzyme kinetics. For this purpose, on one hand, we are based on a series of experimental research involving the traditional methods and techniques used when studying biochemical reactions and designing electrochemical biosensors.

On the other hand, when studying enzyme kinetics analytically we employ Michaelis-Menten approach while modeling enzyme-substrate interactions and extend it to multi-enzyme multi-substrate complexes. There is offered to enforce traditional Big Data workflow with the help of meta-analysis facilities of existing repositoria of biochemical studies. In turn, we are focusing on BRENDA platform.

Related Works. The studies which lie on the basis of electrochemical biosensors design incorporate a few traditional experimental techniques. Spectrometry allows us to determine the appearance of some substances during enzymatic interactions and to monitor the changes of different substrates under different external influences. The application of spectrometry technique for such problems study was presented in [2].

One of the most important study during biosensor design is related to effects of electromagnetic field to substances used, primarily different substrates. They were studied in the works [3].

Study of enzyme kinetics is based on the experimental data of dynamic changes of conductivity of electrolyte solution, which allows us to get the corresponding concentrations using the Kohlrausch's Law (or its generalization). The method allows us to determine optimal quantities of the initial substance concentrations through calibration curves. The description of corresponding technique can be found in [4], the recent results, when studying enzyme-substrate-inhibitor interaction.

A lot of experimental works were devoted to finding the parameters of enzyme-substrate interaction trying to get various experimental data. Michaelis-Menten constants for a lot of enzyme-substrate pairs were determined in with the help of capillary electrophoresis technique. On the other hand, a lot of attempts were directed to estimating the enzyme kinetics parameters as a numerical problem of non-linear optimization. In [5] there was presented R package renz offering us parameters of Michaelis-Menten canonical model as the solution of "non-linear least squares" problem.

2 Material and Methods

The general workflow for the electrochemical design incorporate both experimental research and modeling combined with the meta-analysis. It means the sequential implementation of experimental research (conductance research, spectroscopy, magnetic field research), meta-analysis (EC-numbers, kM constants), and modeling.

2.1 Conductance Research

Conductivity tests were carried out using a specially constructed measuring station including: conductivity meter model CC-401 with a probe, a special stand allowing to place the probe in the measured solution, measuring vessel. The measurements were performed at a constant temperature of 22 °C and a constant solution volume of 4 ml. Tests were carried out for aqueous solutions: BSA (2 mg/ml), BSA + Au (2 mg/ml + 2 mg/ml), BSA + NAA (2 mg/ml + 2 mg/ml). The choice of concentrations was based on previously performed experiments. All samples were exposed to various external factors on the first day of the experiment such as:

1. Reduced temperature (-4 °C). Exposure 2 × 5 min, 10 min, 3 × 5 min, 15 min.
2. UV radiation. Exposure 2 × 5 min, 10 min, 3 × 5 min, 15 min.
3. 125 W microwave radiation. Exposure 2 × 5 s, 10 s, 3 × 5 s, 15 s.
4. Control (without external factor).

Conductivity was measured for the test substances. For each substance 20 conductivity measurements were made with a time interval of 5 s. In addition, at 3, 4, 11, 15, 18 days of the experiment the conductivity of the samples was measured in order to follow changes in their stability. Table showing the experimental scheme for the first day. The scheme was analogous for days 3, 4, 11, 15, 18. A total of 288 sample measurements x 20 measurements per sample were collected, giving 5760 conductivity measurements.

2.2 Spectroscopy

The database considered in this compilation contains about 300 spectra from five experiments recorded under names in the database:1. Effect of 200 MHz field- fractional doses; 2. Impact of 125,180, 230 MHz; 3. Impact of 125 MHz RF and UV radiation; 4. Effect of applied UV radiation; 5. Influence of gold nanoparticles on the stability of the biosensor receptor layer component. The aim of each experiment was to investigate the effect of external factors on the stability of BSA. The studies were carried out using a dual beam UV/Vis spectrophotometer (Hallo DB-20 R) from Dynamica. Absorption spectra of aqueous solutions of BSA in the range 220–350 nm were collected. The experiments differed in the type of external agent used and the time intervals at which the conformational changes occurring in the protein with time were observed. The results of the research have been published successively in papers [3, 7–10].

2.3 Electromagnetic Field

Experiment 1 was executed with the help of solutions. Namely, aqueous solutions of BSA-Au was used.

Bovine serum albumin (BSA) in solid form (crystallized and lyophilized powder (purity 99%_SLBK3063V) and gold Au nanoparticles _MKCD3520), 10 nm in diameter. The suspension of gold nanoparticles stabilized in 0.1 mM PBS, was obtained from Sigma-Aldrich. Aqueous solutions of BSA-Au mixtures were tested with concentrations of 2 mg/ml for BSA and 0.1 mg/ml; 1 mg/ml; 10 mg/ml for Au, respectively. Dematerialized water was used as solvent.

The study was carried out on aqueous solutions, following scientific reports [10] that such a solution allows a better understanding of the physicochemical properties of the studied substances. Scans of the electromagnetic field distribution were performed for frequencies: 180, 195, 240 MHz. Tests were performed for solutions immediately after preparation, for 2-day and 20-day solutions. In order to track changes in the stability of solutions through changes in electromagnetic field distribution.

Changes in electromagnetic field distribution were studied after passing through biological substances and, for comparison, through water and reference layers.

The test substances were placed in special containers made of Plexiglas with dimensions of $25 \times 15 \times 60$ mm. The specially constructed measuring station contained 4 main components:

An electromagnetic field source, a spectrum analyzer with a near-field probe and a scanner model RSE321 equipped with a probe coupled to the scanner with the ability to perform movements in the XYZ plane and a computer. During the experiment, the near-field probe was moved to specific measuring points with a step of 2 mm, where point amplitude and frequency were measured. On this basis, scans of the electromagnetic field were created using specialized software. A photograph of the measuring station is shown in Fig, 1. The scans were performed in the YZ plane and in the XZ plane at a distance of 0–50 mm from the sample (Fig. 2.)

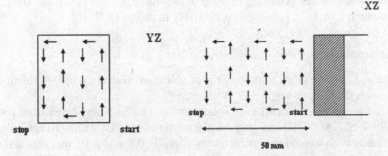

Fig. 1. Experimental measuring station for electromagnetic field investigation.

Fig. 2. Diagram of the probe movements in the YZ plane and in the XZ plane

A total of 18×6 field scans were taken of 108 scans. In each scan 312 measurements of field points were made. Ultimately, 29952 measuring points of the electromagnetic field were used in the experiment.

Experiment 2 was executed with the help of solids. Using a previously constructed measuring set-up, a similar experiment was performed with powdered samples. The following chemical reagents were used: Fe (MKBS9265V), Zn (STBD9796V), Si

(MKBQ2161V). The tests were performed at frequencies: 100 kHz 1, 5, 10, 50, 100, 150, 170, 190, 200, 230, 250 MHz.

A total of 96 spectra measurements were made in each measurement 132 electromagnetic field measurements were made. Finally, 12672 electromagnetic field measurement points were used in the experiment.

2.4 Meta-analysis

The purpose of this stage is to gather meta-data on enzyme kinetics exploring previous Research from database which can be downloaded from BRENDA platform https://www. brenda-enzymes.org/ as a text file. firstly, we convert.txt into sqlite database Brenda. Db (See code in Supplementary materials). Further we explore data for enzymes, substrates, and inhibitors. For the purpose of Exploratory Data Analysis (EDA) KNIME software was used. The data were obtained with the help of EC code of enzyme (Tables 1, 2 and 3). For this purpose the workflow has been constructed (Fig. 3)

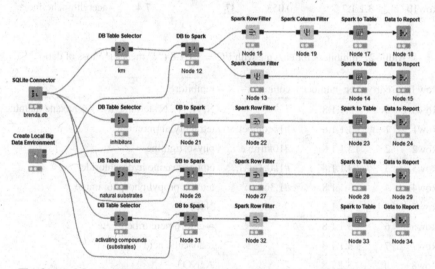

Fig. 3. Workflow in KNIME for the purpose of meta-analysis of BRENDA database

2.5 Michaelis-Menthen Modeling for Multisubstrate-Multiinhibitor Studies

The goal is to develop and analyze the models of the enzyme–substrate and enzyme–substrate–inhibitor complexes numerically and experimentally.

Enzyme Kinetics for the Case of One Substrate. Here we apply continuously distributed delays for modeling the enzyme–substrate binding. Pursuing the goal of mapping the processes of combining as well as possible, here we have chosen to use the gamma distribution of delays $\tau \geq 0$ as:

$$f(a, m, \tau_{min}, s) := \begin{cases} 0 & s \leq \tau_{min}, \\ \frac{a^{m+1}}{\Gamma(m+1)}(s - \tau\_min)^m e^{-a(s-\tau_{min})} & s > \tau_{min} \end{cases} \quad (1)$$

Table 1. Metabolites for enzyme with EC = 3.1.1.7 ("?" means the loss of data).

Row ID	ec_number	km	temperature	ph	metabolite
Row0	3.1.1.7	−999	?	?	more
Row1	3.1.1.7	0.082	?	7.4	acetylthiocholine
Row2	3.1.1.7	0.144	?	7.4	acetylthiocholine
Row3	3.1.1.7	0.181	?	7.4	acetylthiocholine
Row4	3.1.1.7	0.124	?	7.4	acetylthiocholine
Row5	3.1.1.7	0.106	?	7.4	acetylthiocholine
Row6	3.1.1.7	0.139	?	7.4	acetylthiocholine
Row7	3.1.1.7	0.14	?	7.4	acetylthiocholine
Row8	3.1.1.7	0.064	25	7.5	acetylthiocholine
Row9	3.1.1.7	0.097	25	7.5	butyrylthiocholine
Row10	3.1.1.7	0.053	37	7.4	acetylthiocholine

Table 2. Inhibitors for enzyme with EC = 3.1.1.8 ("?" means the loss of data).

Row ID	entry	ec_number	comment	inhibitor
Row0	0	3.1.1.8	?	N, N, N', N'-tetramethyl-1,6-hexane diamine
Row1	1	3.1.1.8	#1#compet...	tetrabutylammonium
Row2	2	3.1.1.8	#10#irreve...	physostigmine
Row3	3	3.1.1.8	#1#0.1mM...	ethopropazine hydrochloride
Row4	4	3.1.1.8	#1,36#iso...	tetraizopropyl phosphoramide
Row5	5	3.1.1.8	?	NaCl
Row6	6	3.1.1.8	?	p-chloromercuribenzoate
Row7	7	3.1.1.8	?	iodoacetic acid
Row8	8	3.1.1.8	?	AgNO3
Row9	9	3.1.1.8	#10#comp...	atropine
Row10	10	3.1.1.8	#10#comp...	Scopolamine

where a, m, $\tau_{min} \geq 0$ are the parameters which are determining the corresponding probability density function. Namely, m determines the shape of the density curve, whereas a stands for its rate parameter, and $\tau_{min} \geq 0$ is the minimal possible value of the delay. The distribution was considered earlier in a different context, for example, describing cell maturation times, where an efficient method of distribution parameter estimation based on experimental population data was offered. In addition, the non-symmetricity of gamma distribution fits the processes of chemical kinetics better as compared with the symmetric normal distribution. Let τ_M be the largest value of the

Table 3. Substrates for enzyme with EC = 3.1.1.8 ("?" means the loss of data).

Row ID	entry	ec_number	comment	activator
Row0	0	3.1.1.8	#1#20mM, 140% activity <14>	citrate
Row1	1	3.1.1.8	#16# nonessential activator < ...	2-trimethylsilyl-ethyl-N-n-butylcarbamate
Row2	2	3.1.1.8	#16# nonessential activation, ess...	3,3-dimethylbutyl-N-n-butylcarbamate
Row3	3	3.1.1.8	#16#i.e. TNT, a nonessential...	2,4,6-trinitrotoluene
Row4	4	3.1.1.8	#16# activating effect at acidic...	2,6-dichlorophenolindophenyl acetate
Row5	5	3.1.1.8	#16# activating effect at acidic...	indophenyl acetate
Row6	6	3.1.1.8	#26# activating effect at acidic...	indophenylacetate
Row7	7	3.1.1.8	#26# activating effect at acidic...	2,6-dichlorophenolindophenylacetate
Row8	8	3.1.1.8	#5# non-substrate activation...	homocysteine thiolactone
Row9	9	3.1.1.8	#5# substrate activation, over...	Butyrylcholine
Row10	10	3.1.1.8	#5# activation kinetics and more...	more

delay, which is probably achievable. Assuming τ is a random variable, which is gamma distributed given by f, we can estimate its confidence interval with confidence level $c \in (0, 1)$, resulting in determining the largest value of τ as:

$$\tau_M := E(\tau) + \sqrt{\frac{Var(\tau)}{1-c}} = \tau_m + \frac{m+1}{a} + \sqrt{\frac{(m+1)}{a^2(1-c)}} \tag{2}$$

Enzyme Kinetics for Enzyme–Substrate–Inhibitor Interaction

Introducing density functions f0,1, f1,1, g1,0, and g1,1 for distributed delays, corresponding to discrete delays $\tau0,1$, $\tau1,1$, $h1,0$, and $h1,1$ respectively, we come to the following model based on the system of differential equations with distributed delays:

$$\frac{dn_{P_{0,1}}}{dt} = \alpha_{0,1,d} \int_{-\tau_{M,0,1}}^{0} f_{0,1}(s)n_E(t+s)n_{s_1}(t+s)ds,$$

$$\frac{dn_{P_{1,1}}}{dt} = \alpha_{0,1,d} \int_{-\tau_{M,1,1}}^{0} f_{0,1}(s)n_E(t+s)n_{s_1}(t+s)ds,$$

$$\frac{dn_{s_{1,}}}{dt} = -(\alpha_{0,1,d} + \alpha_{1,1,d})n_{s_1}(t)n_E(t),$$

$$\frac{dn_e}{dt} = \alpha_{0,1,d} \int_{-\tau_{M,0,1}}^{U} f_{0,1}(s)n_E(t+s)n_{s_1}(t+s)ds, \qquad (3)$$

$$+\alpha_{1,1,d} \int_{-\tau_{M,1,1}}^{0} f_{1,1}(s)n_E(t+s)n_{s_1}(t+s)ds - (\alpha_{0,1,d} + \alpha_{1,1,d})n_{s_1}(t)n_E(t),$$

$$+\beta_{0,1,d} \int_{-h_{M,1,1}}^{0} g_{0,1}(s)n_{I_1}(t+s)n_E(t+s)ds,$$

$$+\beta_{1,1,d} \int_{-h_{M,1,1}}^{0} g_{1,1}(s)n_{I_1}(t+s)n_E(t+s)ds - (\beta_{0,1,d} + \beta_{1,1,d})n_{I_1}(t)n_E(t),$$

$$\frac{dn_{I_{1,}}}{dt} = -(\beta_{0,1,d} + \beta_{1,1,d})n_{I_1}(t)n_E(t),$$

Following (2), we let:

$$\tau_{M,i,j} := \tau_{m,i,j} + \frac{m_{i,j}+1}{a_{i,j}} + \sqrt{\frac{(m_{i,j}+1)}{a_{i,j}^2(1-c)}},$$

$$h_{M,i,j} := h_{m,i,j} + \frac{k_{i,j}+1}{b_{i,j}} + \sqrt{\frac{(k_{i,j}+1)}{b_{i,j}^2(1-c)}},$$

$$i, j \in \{0, 1\}, i = j \neq 0$$

where $a_{i,j}$, $m_{i,j}$, $\tau_{m,i,j}$, and $b_{i,j}$, $k_{i,j}$, $h_{m,i,j}$ are the parameters of the corresponding density functions $f_{i,j}$ and $g^{i,j}$ as in (1) and c is the confidence level.

Parameter Estimation. The idea is to use the model (3) for estimating the time series of the product with the respect to the enzyme–substrate-inhibitor reaction. In turn, these values correspond to the initial conditions of nS, nE, and nP, which are known from experimental data in advance. Estimation should include the rate constant and the gamma distribution parameters within f function in the system given by (3). In order to adjust the predicted data (product concentration nP), we need to make them compatible with the data accessible from the experiment ("expected data"), namely, specific conductance κ, which is related with the molar conductivity Λm as follows:

$$\Lambda_m = \frac{\kappa}{n_p} \qquad (4)$$

When analyzing the conductivity characteristics of the considered solution, we may conclude that it is a strong electrolyte. It follows from the pH value of BSA (4.5–4.8), that was primarily added when obtaining the CLEA. Hence, we can use Kohlrausch's law for a solution of a strong electrolyte:

$$\Lambda_m = \Lambda_m^0 - K\sqrt{n_p} \tag{5}$$

Combining (4) and (5), we introduce the denotation for the specific conductance as follows:

$$\kappa_{pred}(t) := \Lambda_{mn_{P,pred}}^0(t) - K(n_{P,pred}(t))^{3/2} \tag{6}$$

where the parameters Λ_0^m and K are estimated. Hence, the enzyme kinetics model (3) depends on six unknown parameters, namely:

$$\Pi = \{k_d, a, m, \tau_{min}, \Lambda_m^0, K\} \in R_+^6 \tag{7}$$

In principle, this set of parameters can be estimated from a given time series of enzyme– substrate interaction. Pursuing the goal to find parameter estimates as accurately as we can, we conducted the experiments with different amounts of the initial dose of the substrate, namely, $nS(0) = n 0 S, i, i = 1, 1$. Basing on our experiment design, we obtain 1 sets of n pointwise experimental data in the time series, say $\kappa exp, i(tj) i = 1, 1, j = 1,n$, with t1, t2,..., tn being the times of observations. The identification of parameters can be carried out with the following constrained optimization calculations that are expressed in the following form:

$$\left. \begin{array}{l} \textit{minimize } J(\Pi),\ \Pi \in R_+^6 \\ \textit{subject to } c_i(\textstyle\prod) \ge \theta, i = 1, 2 \end{array} \right\} \tag{8}$$

Here

$$J(\Pi) := \left(\sum_{i=1}^{l}\left(\sum_{j=1}^{n}((\kappa_{exp,i}(t_j) - \kappa_{pred,i}(t_j))^2)\right)\right)^{1/2} \tag{9}$$

is the objective function and

$$g_i(\textstyle\prod) = \textstyle\prod - \textstyle\prod_{lower} \ge \theta \tag{10}$$

$$g_2(\textstyle\prod) = \textstyle\prod_{upper} - \textstyle\prod \ge \theta$$

are inequality constraints, where $\Theta \in R 6$ is a null-vector and $\Pi lower$, $\Pi upper$ are the lower and upper bounds for the parameter values, respectively. The offered solution of the nonlinear optimization problem (8) is based on the COBYLA Algorithm 1, which linearly approximates objective function and constraints on 6-simplex $C = C(\Pi 0, \Pi 1,..., \Pi 6)$ and optimizes the simplex on each algorithm iteration. The algorithm transforms problem (8) to the problem without constraints with the help of the following objective function

$$\Phi(\Pi) := J(\Pi) + \xi[\max\{-g_i(\Pi), i = 1, 2\}]^+ \tag{11}$$

We denote its linear approximation on the simplex C as $\Phi^\wedge C(\Pi)$. An implementation of COBYLA to the problem (8) can be reformulated as the Algorithm 1. Here, stop condition covers the improvement of objective function, the changes of vertices, and allowed number of iterations.

Algorithm 1: COBYLA algorithm implementation to the problem

Input data: $X_{exp}, \Pi_{lower}, \Pi_{upper}, \Pi_{init}$

Result: Π_{opt}

1 form the initial simplex C_{init} with the vertices $\Pi_0^{init}, \Pi_1^{init}, \ldots, \Pi_6^{init}$;
2 **repeat**
3 | for the current simplex C calculate the values $\hat{\Phi}_C(\Pi_i), i = \overline{0,6}$;
4 | search the vertex Π_p determined by the equation
   | $\Phi_C(\Pi_p) = \min\{\Phi_C(\Pi_i), i = \overline{0,6}\}$;
5 | calculate new vertex as $\Pi_{new} := -\theta\Pi_p + (1+\theta)\frac{1}{6}\sum_{i=\overline{0,6}, i\neq p}\Pi_i$, where
   | reflection coefficient $\theta \in (0,1)$ being chosen as small as possible in order
   | $\Phi_C(\Pi_p)$ not were the least calculated function value so far;
6 | form modified simplex C_{new} replacing vertex Π_p with Π_{new};
7 | search Π_{opt} as a solution of the problem of linear optimization

$$\begin{array}{ll} \text{minimize} & \Phi_{C_{new}}(\Pi), \\ \text{subject to} & \Pi \in C_{new} \end{array} \Big\}$$

8 **until** *stop condition*;
9 **return** Π_{opt};

---

3 Results

Experimental Study: Enzyme–Substrate–Inhibitor Interaction. The experimental study used butyryl cholinesterase (BuChE) (EC 3.1.1.8, from Horse Serum) with a specific activity of 13 U/mg solid bovine albumin (fraction V, 98% purity), butyryl choline chloride (BuChCl) (98% purity), a-chaconine (95% purity) from potato sprouts, and glutaraldehyde (grade II, 25% aqueous solution), which were purchased from Sigma-Aldrich Chemie GmbH (Steinheim, Germany). All other reagents were of analytical grade and were used without any further treatment. Biologically active membranes were formed by cross-linking butyryl cholinesterase with BSA on the transducer surface in a saturated glutaraldehyde vapour. The mixture containing 5% (w/v) butyryl cholinesterase, 5% (w/v) BSA, and 10% (w/v) glycerol in 20 mM phosphate buffer (pH 7.2) was deposited on the sensitive surface of one transducer by the drop method, while the mixture of 10% (w/v) BSA and 10% (w/v) glycerol in 20 mM phosphate buffer (pH 7.2) was placed on the surface of a reference transducer. The sensor chip was then placed in a saturated glutaraldehyde vapor. After a 30 min exposure in glutaraldehyde, the membranes were dried at room temperature for 15 min. All measurements were performed in daylight at room temperature in an open glass vessel filled with a vigorously stirred 5 mM phosphate buffer solution, pH 7.2. The 200 mM stock solution of BuChCl in deionised H2O, and 2 mM stock solution of the a-chaconine in 5 mM acetic acid were prepared. The concentrations of substrates and inhibitors were adjusted by adding defined volumes of the stock solution of proper concentration. The differential output signal between the measuring and reference Ion-Sensitive Field Effect Transistors (ISFETs) was registered using portable device. After the response measurement (determination of enzyme inhibition), the initial enzyme activity was restored by washing out the biosensor enzymatic membrane in the working buffer solution for 10 to 15 min.

Numerical Simulation of Enzyme–Substrate–Inhibitor Model. Algorithm 1 was modified for the estimation of the parameters of the model (3). The optimal values of the parameters were used for the simulation using different initial values for the inhibitor. The visualization of the simulations results is presented in Fig. 4.

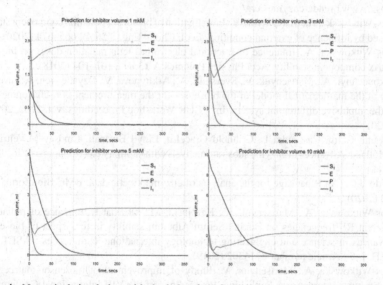

Fig. 4. Numerical simulation with the help of (3) for different initial values of inhibitors

4 Conclusions

Therefore, the work has offered workflow enabling us to execute both empirical and analytical studies of enzyme kinetics. For this purpose, on the one hand, we have used a series of experimental research involving the traditional methods and techniques used when studying biochemical reactions and designing electrochemical biosensors: conductance research, spectroscopy, and electromagnetic field study.

When studying enzyme kinetics analytically we implement the Michaelis-Menten approach while modeling enzyme-substrate-inhibitor interactions and extend it to multi-substrate multi-inhibitor complexes.

Traditional Big Data workflow was offered to be enforced with the help of meta-analysis facilities of existing repositories of biochemical studies located on the BRENDA platform.

Acknowledgments. This work was supported by the European Union's Erasmus+ Program for Education under Key Action 2: Partnerships for Cooperation Grant (The Future is in Applied Artificial Intelligence) under Project 2022-1-PL01-KA220-HED-000088359. It was fulfilled within the framework of studies of the work package 2 "Good practices in the use of Artificial Intelligence and Machine Learning".

References

1. https://www.brenda-enzymes.org/
2. Kłos-Witkowska, A., Martsenyuk, V.: Investigation of biosensor potential component stability caused by influence of external condition. Ecol. Chem. Eng. S **26**(4), 665–674 (2020)
3. Kłos-Witkowska, A.: Influence of fractional electromagnetic radiation doses on biosensor matrix component stability. Acta Physica Polonica A **133**(1), 101–104 (2018)
4. Nakonechnyi, A., Martsenyuk, V., Sverstiuk, A., Arkhypova, V., Dzyadevych, S.: Investigation of the mathematical model of the biosensor for the measurement of α-chaconine based on the impulsive differential system. In: CEUR Workshop Proceedings, vol. 2762, 209–217 (2020)
5. Srikanth Gattu, Cassandra L, Crihfield GraceLu, Lloyd Bwanali, Lindsay M.Veltri, Lisa A.Holland. Advances in enzyme substrate analysis with capillary electrophoresis 146, 93–106 (2018)
6. Aledo, J.C.: An R package for the analysis of enzyme kinetic data. BMC Bioinform. **23**(1), 182 (2020)
7. Kłos-Witkowska, A., Martsenyuk, V., Karpiński, M.: Obeidat I ,Influence of radiation at different RF frequencies on Bovine Serum Albumin stability in the aspect of biosensor'', Advances in science and engineering technology international conferences : ASET 2019, IEEE, 1–5 : Article number 8714302 (2019)
8. Kłos-Witkowska, A., Martsenyuk, V.: Study of improvement of biosensor matrix stability, Springer International Publishing, Proceedings of the VIII International Conference of students, PhD students and young scientists, pp. 153–161 (2020)
9. Kłos-Witkowska, A., Kajstura, K.: Effect of UV radiation applied fractionally or continuously on stability of biosensor receptor layer component, Acta Physica Polonica A **138**(6), 781–786 (2020)
10. Kłos-Witkowska, A., Martsenyuk, V.: Stability of biosensor receptor layer crosslinking component after addition of gold nanoparticles. Measurements, Automation, Robot. **25**(1), 49–52 (2021)
11. Michnik, A.: Michalik K, Drzazga Z, Effect of UVC radiation on conformational restructuring of human serum albumin. J. Photochem Photobiol B **90**, 170–178 (2008)

A New Method of Verification of Dynamic Signatures Changing over Time with Decomposition and Selection of Characteristic Descriptors

Mateusz Mastalerczyk[1]($\boxtimes$), Tomasz Szczepanik[2], and Marcin Zalasiński[2]

[1] AGH University of Science and Technology, Cracow, Poland
mastalerczyk@student.agh.edu.pl
[2] Department of Computational Intelligence, Czestochowa University of Technology,
Czestochowa, Poland
{tomasz.szczepanik_22,marcin.zalasinski}@pcz.pl

Abstract. Dynamic signature verification (DSV) has practical applications in banking, commerce, accounting, medicine, law, etc. DSV is important in comparison to the verification of other biometric attributes because the dynamic signature is one of the most widespread and commonly used biometric features. DSV methods are being systematically developed and improved. At the same time, expectations regarding these methods are changing. For example, they are expected to take into account changes of the individual's signature appearing over time. In this paper, we propose a new DSV method that uses partitioning supported by partitions' selection and characterized by the use of signatures created in different acquisition sessions in the training phase. This algorithm has been tested using a publically available, known xLongSignDB, dynamic signature database. In the simulations very good results were obtained.

Keywords: Biometrics · Identity verification · Dynamic signature verification · Signature decomposition · Selection of signature areas · Population-based algorithm

1 Introduction

Dynamic signature verification (DSV) (see e.g. [7,18]) has practical applications in many different fields, such as, for example, banking, commerce, accounting, medicine, law, etc. It prevents counterfeiting and unauthorized access, allows you to control access to buildings or devices, supports electronic banking systems, etc. Therefore, development of effective verification methods can help improve the quality and safety of identified application areas.

DSV is also important in comparison to other biometric features used for identity verification because: (a) the dynamic signature (DS) is one of the most widespread and widely used biometric features, (b) the acquisition of DS is easy and socially acceptable (as opposed to the acquisition of many other biometric features), (c) DS processing provides a high level of security, (d) it can be used in conjunction with other verification methods (password, PIN, facial recognition, etc.).

DSV methods are being systematically developed and improved. Some of the trends include: (a) division of signals describing the dynamics of DS into areas in order to increase the precision of an analysis [22], (b) selection of user-specific DSs areas by population-based algorithms (PBA [21]), (c) applying deep learning methods to difficult-to-extract (and different for each user) features of DSs [16], (d) using extended information describing the dynamics of DSs, e.g. hand movements, pen pressure, writing sound [2], (e) analysis of variability over time and its impact on the effectiveness of verification [4].

Expectations towards DSV methods have been changing recently. For example, they are supposed to take into account changes of the individual's signature taking place over time. The shape and dynamics of the user's signature may change over time as a result of physical changes in the human body or under the influence of his/her emotional experiences. Moreover, using neural (see e.g. [1,9,11]) classifiers in the DSV approach necessitates the use of skilled or random forgeries at the learning stage, which was not desirable before (this ensured the scalability of the approach and guaranteed its effectiveness regardless of the number of users in the database). Since machine-learning systems work best with patterns and anti-patterns, it is convenient to use skilled forgeries and signatures of other users in the training phase.

1.1 Motivation

Among the previously mentioned approaches to DSV, the approach concerning the partitioning of signatures and their analysis in partitions is interesting. It increases the precision of such analysis by: the ability to include a subset of the most characteristic fragments of signatures [17], ignoring fragments with low (or unfavorable) verification potential [22], the ability to adapt the algorithm to the specificity of signatures of individual users [19], the possibility of combination with various approaches to signature verification [10], and the possibility of creating hybrid solutions [20]. At the same time, in these works, in the training phase for a given user, we limited ourselves to using the signatures of this user only.

1.2 Contribution of the Paper

The purpose of this paper is to develop a new DSV algorithm that uses partitioning supported by descriptors selection, takes into account changes in the individual's signature appearing over time, and uses signatures of other users in the training phase. This algorithm was embedded in the signature partitioning concept that we proposed earlier but required a different approach to partition processing. Its use gives the possibility of individual interpretation of the results in the context of each user independently. The algorithm proposed in this paper has not been considered in the literature so far in the proposed form.

Algorithm 1. A new method of verification of dynamic signatures changing over time with decomposition and selection of characteristic descriptors.

1: Creation of $Nsig$ reference signatures by each user and their acquisition using digital input device (usually a graphic tablet). Each such signature is a collection of velocity signal values v (it is the derivative of pen position) and pressure z, x trajectory signal and y trajectory signal.

2: Selection of the base signature for each user from his/her reference signatures. This is the signature most similar to others in the context of the adopted distance measure.

3: Matching (normalization) of the reference signatures of each user to his/her base signature.

4: Division of signatures of each user into $Nver$ vertical sections (usually 3).

5: Division of all vertical sections of each user into $Nhor$ horizontal sections (usually 2).

6: Determination of the reference signatures' template for each user in each partition created as a combination of horizontal and vertical sections.

7: Determination of reference signatures descriptors for each user in each partition. Number of descriptors for signals $\{x, y, v, z\}$ is for one user: $Nsig \cdot Nver \cdot Nhor \cdot 4$.

8: Using a population-based algorithm (e.g. genetic as a combinatorial optimization method, see e.g. [3,6,12–14]) for each user to select a subset of his/her most characteristic descriptors in the context of other users' signature descriptors. The evaluation function of such an algorithm takes into account the value of the assumed measure of the distance between the descriptors (usually Euclidean, Manhattan, Mahalanobis, Hamming or cosine). This procedure is run for $Nsig_{Lrn} << Nsig$ randomly selected signatures for each user independently. Remaining $Nsig_{Tst} = Nsig - Nsig_{Lrn}$ signatures are treated as test ones.

9: Verification of the test signature of the user. This verification takes into account a pre-selected subset of its characteristic descriptors for each user. It involves the use of a selected one-class classifier (usually one class K-Nearest Neighbors) and the calculation of typical biometric measure Equal Error Rate (EER).

1.3 Structure of the Paper

In Sect. 2 we characterized the algorithm proposed in this article. In Sect. 3 we included sample simulation results, and in Sect. 4 we summarized the most important conclusions and plans for future research.

2 Description of the Algorithm

The purpose of the proposed algorithm is a selection of the most important descriptors of the individual's signature which can be used in the identity verification process. Proposed algorithm should be resistant to signature changes over time. The algorithm uses a classic genetic algorithm to select the most important descriptors of the dynamic signature in the context of an individual user. The steps of the algorithm are described in listing Algorithm 1.

The descriptors of the signatures used by the proposed algorithm are created on the basis of velocity and pressure signal values in the determined partitions of the signature. The details concerning determination of the descriptors are presented in Table 1.

Table 1. The formulas used to determine the descriptors of the signature.

No.	Description and formula
1.	User index: i
2.	Signature index: $j \in \{1, ..., N_{sig}\}$
3.	Pen trajectory: $a \in \{x, y\}$
4.	Dynamic signal: $s \in \{velocity, pressure, ...\}$
5.	Horizontal partition index: $p \in \{1, ..., N_{hor}\}$
6.	Vertical partition index: $r \in \{1, ..., N_{ver}\}$
7.	Discretization point index in partition (p, r): $k \in \left\{1, ..., N_{i,p,r}^{\{s,a\}}\right\}$
8.	template of the signature: $\mathbf{tc}_{i,p,r}^{\{s,a\}} = \left[tc_{i,p,r,k=1}^{\{s,a\}}, ..., tc_{i,p,r,k=N_{i,p,r}^{\{s,a\}}}^{\{s,a\}}\right]$, where $tc_{i,j,p,r,k}^{\{s,a\}} = \frac{1}{J} \sum_{j=1}^{J} a_{i,j,p,r,k}^{\{s\}}$.
9.	Descriptor of the signature: $d_{i,j,p,r}^{\{s,a\}} = \frac{1}{N_{i,p,r}^{\{s,a\}}} \sum_{k=1}^{N_{i,p,r}^{\{s,a\}}} \left| a_{i,j,p,r,k}^{\{s\}} - tc_{i,p,r,k}^{\{s,a\}} \right|$

3 Simulations

In the simulations xLongSignDB distributed by Biometrics and Data Pattern Analytics (BiDA) Lab was used to test effectiveness of descriptors' selection performed by the proposed algorithm. The database contains signatures of 29

Table 2. The accuracy of our method in comparison to other methods tested using xLongSignDB.

Method	Equal Error Rate
HMM-based method presented in [15]	0.20%
GMM-based method presented in [15]	0.07%
DTW-based method presented in [15]	0.01%
Our method presented in [5]	0.96%
Our method presented in this paper	**0.00%**

individuals (46 samples and 10 forgeries per user) created in 6 sessions (the first and the last sessions were conducted 16 months apart).

In the training phase of the simulations 4 genuine signatures of the individual from session number 1 were used to create the signature template, 20 genuine signatures and 20 signatures of other users (treated as random forgeries) from sessions number 2–6 were used in the process of descriptors' selection. In the test phase of the simulations 5 genuine signatures and 5 forgeries from session number 6 were used.

In the classification process a commonly known one-class K-Nearest Neighbors classifier was used (see e.g. [8]). The simulations were repeated 5 times and the average results are presented in Table 1 using a typical biometric measure in the form of Equal Error Rate (EER). The results were compared to other methods implemented by us earlier without using random forgeries.

The results from the simulations can be summarized as follows:

- The proposed method achieves very good results in comparison to other methods.
- The use of genuine signatures created at various intervals in the training phase increases effectiveness of the signature verification process.
- The use of skilled forgeries in the training phase increases effectiveness of the signature verification process.
- Verification of skilled forgeries is more complex process than verification of random forgeries (see results of method presented in [5]).

4   Conclusions

In this paper we considered a new method of verification of dynamic signatures changing over time with decomposition and selection of characteristic descriptors. Its construction uses partitioning in terms of velocity, pressure, and signing time. The boundaries between the partitions were determined consistently for each user (according to the same formula) and were not subject to individual selection. However, in the construction of our method, a genetic algorithm was used (as the base population-based method) to select a subset of partitions, individually for each user. The algorithm was tested for xLongSignDB dynamic signature database. Finally, EER of 0% was obtained. This confirms the correctness of the adopted assumptions and makes the method proposed in this paper competitive in comparison to other signature verification methods (Table 2).

Our plans for further research include performing an analysis of selected signature areas, using other signature classification methods, and using other partition selection methods.

Acknowledgment. The project financed under the program of the Polish Minister of Science and Higher Education under the name "Regional Initiative of Excellence" in the years 2019–2023 project number 020/RID/2018/19 the amount of financing PLN 12,000,000.

References

1. Bilski, J., Smoląg, J., Kowalczyk, B., Grzanek, K., Izonin, I.: Fast computational approach to the levenberg-marquardt algorithm for training feedforward neural networks. J. Art. Intell. Soft Comput. Res. **13**(2), 45–61 (2023)
2. Chakladar, D.D., Kumar, P., Roy, P.P., Dogra, D.P., Scheme, E., Chang, V.: A multimodal-Siamese Neural Network (mSNN) for person verification using signatures and EEG. Inf. Fusion **71**, 17–27 (2022)
3. Cpałka, K., Łapa, K., Przybył, A.: Genetic programming algorithm for designing of control systems. Inf. Technol. Control **47**(4), 668–683 (2018)
4. Cpałka, K., Zalasiński, M.: On-line signature verification using vertical signature partitioning. Expert Syst. Appl. **41**, 4170–4180 (2014)
5. Cpałka, K., Zalasiński, M., Rutkowski, L.: A new algorithm for identity verification based on the analysis of a handwritten dynamic signature. Appl. Soft Comput. **43**, 47–56 (2016)
6. Dziwiński, P., Przybył, A., Trippner, P., Paszkowski, J., Hayashi, Y.: Hardware Implementation of a Takagi-Sugeno Neuro-Fuzzy System Optimized by a Population Algorithm. J. Art. Intell. Soft Comput. Res. **11**(3), 243–266 (2021)
7. Galbally, J., Martinez-Diaz, M., Fierrez, J.: Aging in biometrics: an experimental analysis on on-line signature. PLOS ONE **8**(7), e69897 (2013)
8. Khan, S.S., Ahmad, A.: Relationship between variants of one-class nearest neighbors and creating their accurate ensembles. IEEE Trans. Knowl. Data Eng. **30**, 1796–1809 (2018)
9. Kumar, D., Sharma, D.: Feature map augmentation to improve scale invariance in convolutional neural networks. J. Art. Intell. Soft Comput. Res. **13**(1), 51–74 (2023)
10. Kumar, P., Saini, R., Kaur, B., Roy, P.P., Scheme, E.: Fusion of neuro-signals and dynamic signatures for person authentication. Sensors, **19**(21), 4641 (2019)
11. Lv, J., Pawlak, M.: Bandwidth selection for kernel generalized regression neural networks in identification of hammerstein systems. J. Art. Intell. Soft Comput. Res. **11**(3), 181–194 (2021)
12. Łapa, K.: Meta-optimization of multi-objective population-based algorithms using multi-objective performance metrics. Inf. Sci. **489**, 193–204 (2019)
13. Łapa, K., Cpałka, K., Kisiel-Drohinicki, M., Paszkowski, J., Dębski, M., Le, V.H.: Multi-population-based algorithm with an exchange of training plans based on population evaluation. J. Art. Intell. Soft Comput. Res. **12**(4), 239–252 (2022)

14. Szczypta, J., Przybył, A., Cpałka, K.: Some Aspects of Evolutionary Designing Optimal Controllers. In: Rutkowski, L., Korytkowski, M., Scherer, R., Tadeusiewicz, R., Zadeh, L.A., Zurada, J.M. (eds.) ICAISC 2013. LNCS (LNAI), vol. 7895, pp. 91–100. Springer, Heidelberg (2013). https://doi.org/10.1007/978-3-642-38610-7_9

15. Tolosana, R., Vera-Rodriguez, R., Fierrez, J., Ortega-Garcia, J.: Reducing the template aging effect in on-line signature biometrics. IET Biometrics (2019)

16. Xie, L., Wu, Z., Zhang, X., Li, Y., Wang, X.: Writer-independent online signature verification based on 2D representation of time series data using triplet supervised network. Measurement **197**, 111312 (2022)

17. Zalasiński, M., Cpałka, K.: A new method for signature verification based on selection of the most important partitions of the dynamic signature. Neurocomputing **289**, 13–22 (2018)

18. Zalasiński, M., Cpałka, K., Hayashi, Y.: New Fast Algorithm for the Dynamic Signature Verification Using Global Features Values. In: Rutkowski, L., Korytkowski, M., Scherer, R., Tadeusiewicz, R., Zadeh, L.A., Zurada, J.M. (eds.) ICAISC 2015. LNCS (LNAI), vol. 9120, pp. 175–188. Springer, Cham (2015). https://doi.org/10.1007/978-3-319-19369-4_17

19. Zalasiński, M., Cpałka, K., Hayashi, Y.: A Method for Genetic Selection of the Most Characteristic Descriptors of the Dynamic Signature. Lecture Notes in Computer Science **10245**, 747–760 (2017)

20. Zalasiński, M., Cpałka, K., Rakus-Andersson, E.: An Idea of the Dynamic Signature Verification Based on a Hybrid Approach. Lecture Notes in Computer Science **9693**, 232–246 (2016)

21. Zalasiński, M., et al.: Evolutionary algorithm for selecting dynamic signatures partitioning approach. J. Art. Intell. Soft Comput. Res. **4**, 267–279 (2022)

22. Zalasiński, M., Duda, P., Lota, S., Cpałka, K.: Dynamic Signature Verification Using Selected Regions. Lecture Notes in Computer Science **13589**, 388–397 (2023)

Impact of the Pre-processing and Balancing of EEG Data on the Performance of Graph Neural Network for Epileptic Seizure Classification

Szymon Mazurek[1]([envelope]) [iD], Rosmary Blanco[1] [iD], Joan Falcó-Roget[1] [iD],
Jan K. Argasiński[1,2] [iD], and Alessandro Crimi[1] [iD]

[1] Sano Centre for Computational Medicine, Computer Vision Group, Kraków, Poland
{s.mazurek,r.blanco,j.roget,j.argasinski,a.crimig}@sanoscience.org
[2] Jagiellonian University, Kraków, Poland

Abstract. Automated seizure detection in electroencephalography (EEG) recordings is a time consuming task, dependent on the expert performing the review. The rapid development in the field of deep learning shows promise in the creation of automated models performing EEG signal classification. However, EEG data requires careful artifact removal, as well as strategies for dealing with inherent imbalance present within samples extracted from epileptic patients. In this work, a simple graph neural network (GNN) using attention to perform classification of EEG segments is proposed. We also elaborate on the effectiveness of signal pre-processing and imbalance handling methods, showing their impact on the model's performance. The results demonstrate that the classificator's performance can be enhanced by choosing proper pre-processing and signal balancing methods. We anticipate that these approaches can be adopted by the researchers working on EEG classification with deep learning models, helping to improve the the robustness of constructed models.

Keywords: Electroencephalography. · EEG · Epilepsy · Graph neural network · Seizure detection · EEG classification

1 Introduction

Electroencephalography (EEG) is a non-invasive neuroimaging technique that measures the electrical activity of the brain. It has been widely used in the clinic for the diagnosis and management of various neurological disorders, including epilepsy. Epilepsy is a neurological disorder that is characterized by recurrent seizures, which are the result of abnormal electrical activity in the brain. It is the fourth most common neurological disorder in the world, affecting approximately 50 to 60 million people worldwide [18,23]. EEG plays a crucial role in the diagnosis of epilepsy. It is the most specific method to define the epileptogenic cortex, as it can detect abnormal brain activity that is associated with

L. Rutkowski et al. (Eds.): ICAISC 2023, LNAI 14126, pp. 258–268, 2023.
https://doi.org/10.1007/978-3-031-42508-0_24

seizures. In recent years, there have been significant advances in EEG technology which have improved the accuracy and reliability of EEG in the diagnosis and management of epilepsy. However, the process of analyzing EEG recordings is a time-consuming task that requires the evaluation of trained experts making it highly subjective.

1.1 Related Work

The rapid growth in the field of deep learning resulted in increased interest in applying it to the seizure detection task. In parallel, the availability of the data sets also increased, sparking interest in such applications even further. Comparing the results in the domain of EEG classification is difficult, as the data sets, data handling, and evaluation methods vary greatly. We, therefore, narrowed our scope to existing research on the CHB-MIT data set, the one we chose for this work. This data set alone has been greatly explored [22]. To solve the EEG classification problem, numerous deep-learning approaches can be employed. They can be divided into ones exploiting the time domain, frequency domain, and time-frequency domain. Wang et. al. use the time domain features via a 1D convolutional neural network (CNN) to perform the classification of epileptic EEG periods [25]. Yao et. al. created an attention-based LSTM architecture to analyze temporal properties of the signals [26]. Li and Chen work in the frequency domain, applying the Fast Fourier Transform (FFT) to the signal before using CNN-based architecture to perform classification [13]. There is also evidence that a combination of spectral and temporal features results in improved results [1,6].

In literature, there is a great variability in pre-processing steps that are performed prior to the EEG signal classification. Some authors use only basic methods, such as band-pass [9] or wavelet [6] filtering. Others extend the approach into more advanced decomposition and filtering methods [14]. Moreover, there are also works that do not implement any pre-processing technique, working on raw noisy data [13,25,26]. The literature shows numerous EEG artifact removal methods and their effectiveness in improving the EEG signal readability both for human experts and automated algorithms for variety of tasks [10,11], therefore this step seemed vital prior to the use of deep learning methodologies also in seizure detection. Furthermore, we noted that the problem of class imbalance is also handled differently across researchers [9,25]. We decided to explore this area, investigating how pre-processing and data imbalance handling can help to improve the performance of the classifiers in EEG seizure detection.

Aim of the Study and Contributions. In this work (i) a neural network architecture that is able to detect abnormal EEG patterns based on its spectral features is proposed. We also elaborate on (ii) artifact removal methods, the necessity of their usage, and their effects on the classifier's performance. Finally (iii) methods of handling data imbalance in EEG classification problems are explored. We highlight some possible solutions to this problem and show their effects on performance and the potential negative effects accompanying their misuse.

2   Materials and Methods

2.1   Data Set

In this work, the Children Hospital Boston (CHB-MIT) data set was used [21]. This is a collection of heterogeneous EEG recordings from 23 subjects with drug-resistant epilepsy (ages from 1.5 to 22). Subjects had not ingested anti-epileptic therapy prior to the recordings. EEG data were collected by means of 23, 24, or 26 electrodes placed according to the international 10–20 system and sampled at 256 Hz with 16-bit resolution. The data consist of total of 916 h of recordings, separated into 24 cases. Noteworthy, case 21 and 01 come from the same patient, the latter being recorded 1.5 years after the former one. The files contain 198 length-varying epileptic seizures annotated by clinical experts.

2.2   Data Pre-processing

Raw EEG signals have amplitudes of the order of μV and contain frequency components of up to 300 Hz. They are contaminated by different sources of inter-ference or artifacts related to the measuring system itself (less contact between the electrodes and the scalp), arising from the environment (power line noise or electromagnetic fields) or other biological signals captured by the electrodes but not related to brain activity (electrooculogram, electromyogram, electrocar-diogram). The artefactual activity can cause a severe decrease in signal quality. To retain the effective information contained in the signals, there is a need to increase the signal-to-noise ratio by cleaning the EEG from the artifacts. The standard pre-processing steps are filtering, re-referencing, interpolating the bad channels, and removing the artifacts via different methods (signal decomposition, wavelet filtering, template subtraction, regression, and others). These techniques are chosen accordingly to the examined data and to the subsequent analysis. To date, artifact elimination in electroencephalography is still a challenging task, and most of the pre-processing is done manually, but it is a time-consuming task, requiring also expert knowledge of the domain. Moreover, the results may be prone to errors and inconsistencies because of the non-analytical approach. Therefore, attempts to formalize and automate EEG denoising can be found in the literature [7,16,19,24]. Two of the most used blind source separation-based methods for cleaning the EEG signals are Principal Component Analysis (PCA) [20] and Independent Component Analysis (ICA) [8]. The ICA method has been shown to give better results, mostly for blinks and muscular artifact removal. However, this analysis works best when an expert visually inspects all components and discards those related to different types of artifacts. It is a time-consuming approach even if some automatic algorithms for artifact recognition are used [12]. On the contrary, the PCA method has proven to be faster and less demanding in terms of computational capability, giving good results for both dimensionality reduction and artifact elimination [16].

As a first approach, the PrepPipeline [2] and ICA decomposition associated with an automated component labeling algorithm [12] were applied, but with poor results. Then, we decided to combine the filtering process (by setting the high cut-off frequency at 30 Hz) and the PCA decomposition (by using a threshold based on a large amount of variance explained by the first two components) to eliminate the most represented eye blinks and muscular artifacts along with power line noise. Indeed, the variance of EEG signals refers to the amount of fluctuation in the electrical activity recorded from the scalp. Artifacts in EEG signals can significantly contribute to the overall variance of the data, especially if they are large in amplitude and occur frequently, such as eye blinks and muscle activity. Then, the amount of variance explained by each component after the PCA decomposition can provide useful information about the presence of artifacts in the data. Moreover, since the method preserves the orthogonality of the components, it allows for an automatic selection of those representing the artefactual activity. However, it is important to note that not all artifacts have high variance. For instance, some types of environmental noise, such as electrical interference from power lines (50 Hz), may have low amplitude and contribute relatively little to the overall variance of the signal, but they can be easily removed by filtering.

The proposed pipeline involves the following steps: first, the electrode montages are unified by choosing 18 channels appearing across all recordings (FP1-F7, F7-T7, T7-P7, P7-O1, FP1-F3, F3-C3, C3-P3, P3-O1, FZ-CZ, CZ-PZ, FP2-F4, F4-C4, C4-P4, P4-O2, FP2-F8, F8-T8, T8-P8 and P8-O2). Next, the recordings are filtered to only contain frequencies between 0.5 and 30 Hz, since we are interested in retaining the EEG frequency content related to the resting state condition. Then, the channels were average-referenced, and finally, PCA was performed for removing the large artifacts still present in the signals.

2.3   Sample Extraction and Representation

After the pre-processing, the data samples containing seizures were extracted from every recording. As a first step in the proposed EEG classification and detection system, we decided to perform classification between pre-ictal and ictal periods, hence stating the problem as binary classification. The seizure period was determined using annotations provided in the data set [21], where the beginning and end of the seizure were labeled. The pre-ictal period was chosen as 10 min maximum before the seizure onset. The signal was then divided into samples of 6 s in length. The length of the sample was chosen based on the annotated data for which an abnormal activity was considered a seizure only when its length is greater or equal to 6 s. It is worth noting that following these criteria, some of the epileptic activity present in the data was not considered seizures due to their short duration. This creates a challenge for the models trying to perform supervised epileptic activity detection, as some samples included into classes other than ictal can present patterns very similar to the ictal ones.

Data Representation. The data samples were represented as graphs. This approach allows modeling the electrodes on the scalp as the nodes of the graphs and the sampled periods as the edges of the graphs representing the relationship (weights) between the nodes. Contrary to the approaches found in literature, where usually the connectivity is established between the nodes based on their physical location and the values measuring their relationship by means of different metrics [9, 28], the graph was modeled as a fully connected one to allow the attention network to learn the relationships during training.

Data Standardization. All samples were standardized using the mean and standard deviation obtained from all negative (pre-ictal) samples. This allowed for preserving the bigger amplitudes in the ictal samples relative to pre-ictal samples, which is an important feature allowing to distinguish epileptic activity from normal one.

Final Feature Processing. As final steps, each sample time series was downsampled to 60 Hz to decrease the computational costs. Then, the features were converted from the time domain into the frequency domain using the Fast Fourier Transformation (FFT), and the power spectrum for each node was extracted.

2.4   Model Architecture and Hyperparameters

A graph neural network was implemented to extract the features from graphs and to perform graph classification. Graph Attention (GAT) v2 [3] layers were used as a backbone feature extractor. This method allows the network to learn the edge weights in form of attention scores, which removes the need to manually calculate the connectivity in the graph. After feature extraction, global mean pooling is applied before passing the features into fully connected layers. The graphical representation of the network with hyperparameters is shown in Fig. 1. The network was implemented in Python 3.10, using the Pytorch 1.13.1 [17] and Pytorch Geometric 2.2 libraries [5] for graph data processing.

2.5   Experiment Design

Data Split and Testing Method. The effectiveness of the model was tested using leave-one-out cross-validation (LOOCV) where, for every fold, a new model is trained and evaluated on all samples from a different patient each time. The leave-one-out (LOO) subject's data was also standardized, using the values computed for the data remaining for training. The data used for training was further split - 10% of the training data was subtracted from the set and used as validation data. The split was done using the stratification, which preserved the initial class samples ratio. To avoid the creation of non-representative training and validation sets, stratification was also done on the patient level - both sets contained samples for every non-LOO patient.

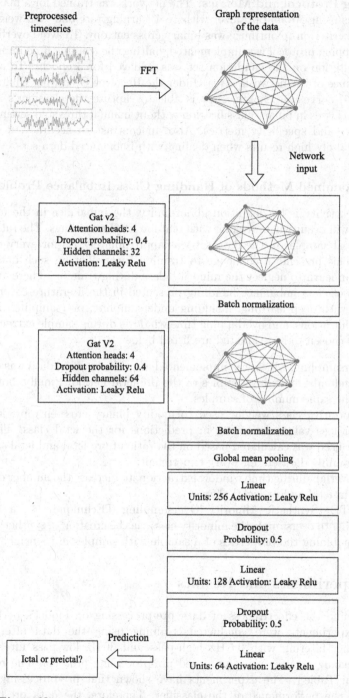

Fig. 1. Network architecture and hyperparameters of the layers.

Training Protocol and Metrics. The network was trained for a maximum of 60 epochs using Adam optimizer with 1e-4 learning rate and 1e-3 weight decay [15]. The criterion to optimize was binary cross entropy. To avoid overfitting, an early stopping protocol was implemented, halting the training if no improvement of the criterion on the validation set was achieved for 3 epochs. To assess the performance of the network, Area Under the Receiver Operating Characteristic (AUROC) curve was chosen, as it is able to capture the classifier's ability to separate classes in binary classification without manual threshold setting as with sensitivity and specificity metrics. Also, in contrast to accuracy, it does not provide falsely high results when dealing with imbalanced data sets.

2.6   Examined Methods of Handling Class Imbalance Problem

As ictal activity is by definition abnormality, the imbalance in the number of samples will occur when working with real-life EEG recordings. The ratio of ictal to pre-ictal samples in the data set was approximately 1:9 for every evaluated model. This presents a challenge to training a classifier on such data, as the model can learn to neglect the minority class during training. There are several methods of class imbalance handling presented in the literature covering EEG analysis with deep learning, including undersampling, oversampling, loss function modifications, and overlapping time windows during sample extraction. The methods chosen to be evaluated are listed below:

- Undersampling, which was implemented after the training data was extracted by randomly removing samples of the pre-ictal period. Finally, both classes had the same number of samples.
- The positive class weight, used to modify binary cross-entropy, leading to higher loss values for errors in predictions for the ictal class. The weight factor used was calculated based on the ratio of pre-ictal and ictal samples in the training datasets for every experiment.
- The overlap during time window extraction, to increase the number of samples both in ictal and pre-ictal classes.
- SMOTE (Synthetic Minority Oversampling TEchnique) [4], a technique allowing to oversample the minority class via the creation of synthetic samples by combining the properties of a sample with samples in its neighborhood.

3   Experiments and Results

To examine the effectiveness of data pre-processing on model's performance, three experiments were conducted: training using the data after no pre-processing, filtering with 0.5 Hz high-pass and 30 Hz low-pass filter followed re-referencing or after using proposed pre-processing protocol. The results are shown in Table 1. The experiments have shown that pre-processing helps to improve the performance of the classifier. Therefore, the data pre-processing with proposed pipeline was chosen for further analysis, which aims to examine the influence of the methods of handling class imbalance on the final performance of the model. The results are shown in Table 2. For every experiment testing overlapping windows, the overlap length was set to 5 s. All experiments were run using 4 AMD EPYC 7742 64-Core CPUs and 1 Nvidia A-100 GPU on the HPC cluster.

Table 1. Performance of the model using different data pre-processing methods. Bold numbers indicate the best results.

Data pre-processing	Average epochs	Average AUROC
None	46	0.7872
Filtering and re-reference	46	0.8069
Our protocol	**44**	**0.8754**

Table 2. Performance of the model using different class imbalance handling methods. Bold numbers indicate the best results.

Method	Average epochs	Average AUROC
Undersampling	21	0.8623
Window overlap (ictal samples only)	21	0.8851
Window overlap (all samples)	13	**0.8919**
Window overlap (all samples) + undersampling	20	0.8858
Positive class weight	21	0.876
Window overlap (ictal samples only) + positive class weight	19	0.8845
Window overlap (all samples) + positive class weight	**12**	**0.8919**
Window overlap (all samples) + SMOTE (training set and LOO patient)	35	0.8793
Window overlap (all samples) + SMOTE (training set)	36	0.8101
Window overlap (all samples) + SMOTE (LOO patient)	13	0.8506
Window overlap (all samples) + SMOTE (LOO patient) + positive class weight	13	0.8474

4   Discussion

The results indicate that a simple EEG data pre-processing procedure can improve the performance of the classification model used, despite the heterogeneity of the data set. This translates into the possibility of automating a procedure, which would otherwise be time-consuming and resource intensive. Compared with other studies, proposed model reaches performance without discarding any recordings [9], reaching 0.09 improvement in AUROC score compared to baseline.

From data imbalance handling methods, the usage of overlapping windows for both ictal and interictal samples resulted in the best performance with AUROC score of 0.8919, requiring 13 epochs to converge. Enhancing this approach by adding positive class weight to the loss function resulted in the same results. Undersampling only led to decreased performance compared to baseline. What came as a surprise was the performance degradation using SMOTE. It turned out that even after applying SMOTE on minority samples for LOO patient only, the performance degraded. Only applying SMOTE on both training, validation and LOO subsets led to a slight improvement in performance. However, the computational cost of using this augmentation technique significantly increased.

Limitations and Future Work. The main goal of this work was to evaluate the effects of pre-processing and data balancing on the classifier's performance. The architecture and the hyperparameters of the model did not undergo any architecture optimization protocol, hence further improvement seems possible. Also, the experiments were done using data in the frequency domain, which leads to loss of temporal information present in the signal. Finally, the structure of the input graphs could be changed from complete to sparse one based on chosen criterion for determining connectivity. In the upcoming work, we aim to also include interictal periods as an additional class for the classification problem. This would allow to expand the usefulness of the solution for patients, allowing to predict epileptic seizures by detecting the onset of pre-ictal periods. Also, such an algorithm could be used to automatically detect the ictal activity in the recordings, as this process is time consuming and requires participation of expert. We also aim to further investigate the data augmentation via SMOTE algorithm. The classic implementation of the algorithm used in this work did not take into account the time domain relationship between the signal samples. Recent work introducing T-SMOTE [27] shows promising results that could help to improve the obtained results for class oversampling.

5   Conclusion

Summarizing, data pre-processing is a crucial step when working with EEG signals that can improve the performance of the classifier substantially. We show that our pre-processing method led to observable improvement in the network's performance. It was also noted that class imbalance has to be handled with caution, as some common methods may fail to improve or even degrade the performance, increasing the computational costs of training.

Data availability

The source code used for conducting the experiments will be published upon the completion of all the work regarding this project. In case of request for implementation details, please contact the leading author.

Acknowledgments. This publication is supported by the European Union's Horizon 2020 research and innovation programme under grant agreement Sano No 857533. This publication is supported by Sano project carried out within the International Research Agendas programme of the Foundation for Polish Science, co-financed by the European Union under the European Regional Development Fund. This research was supported in part by the PLGrid infrastructure on the Athena computer cluster (https://docs. cyfronet.pl/display/~plgpawlik/Athena).

References

1. Assali, I., et al.: CNN-based classification of epileptic states for seizure prediction using combined temporal and spectral features. Biomed. Signal Process. Control **82**, 104519 (2023)
2. Bigdely-Shamlo, N., Mullen, T., Kothe, C., Su, K.M., Robbins, K.A.: The prep pipeline: standardized preprocessing for large-scale EEG analysis. Front. Neuroinformatics **9**, 16 (2015)
3. Brody, S., Alon, U., Yahav, E.: How attentive are graph attention networks? (2022)
4. Chawla, N.V., Bowyer, K.W., Hall, L.O., Kegelmeyer, W.P.: SMOTE: synthetic minority over-sampling technique. J. Art. Intell. Res. **16**, 321–357 (2002)
5. Fey, M., Lenssen, J.E.: Fast graph representation learning with pytorch geometric (2019)
6. Gao, Y., Gao, B., Chen, Q., Liu, J., Zhang, Y.: Deep convolutional neural network-based epileptic electroencephalogram (EEG) signal classification. Front. Neurol. **11**, 375 (2020)
7. Geetha, G., Geethalakshmi, S.: Artifact removal from EEG using spatially constrained independent component analysis and wavelet denoising with otsu's thresholding technique. Procedia Eng. **30** (2012), International Conference on Communication Technology and System Design (2011)
8. Hyvärinen, A., Oja, E.: Independent component analysis: algorithms and applications. Neural networks: Official J. Int. Neural Netw. Soc. **13**(4–5), 411–430 (2000)
9. Jia, M., et al.: Efficient graph convolutional networks for seizure prediction using scalp EEG. Front. Neuroscience **16**, 967116 (2022)
10. Jin, Z.: State-of-the-art EEG artifact removal evaluation. bioRxiv (2021)
11. Kingphai, K., Moshfeghi, Y.: On EEG Preprocessing Role in Deep Learning Effectiveness for Mental Workload Classification. In: Longo, L., Leva, M.C. (eds.) H-WORKLOAD 2021. CCIS, vol. 1493, pp. 81–98. Springer, Cham (2021). https://doi.org/10.1007/978-3-030-91408-0_6
12. Li, A., Feitelberg, J., Saini, A.P., Höchenberger, R., Scheltienne, M.: Mne-icalabel: Automatically annotating ICA components with ICLabel in python. J. Open Source Softw. **7**, 4484 (2022)
13. Li, M., Chen, W.: FFT-based deep feature learning method for EEG classification. Biomed. Signal Process. Control **66**, 102492 (2021)

14. Lo Giudice, M., et al.: Convolutional neural network classification of rest eeg signals among people with epilepsy, psychogenic non epileptic seizures and control subjects. Int. J. Environ. Res. Public Health **19**(23), 15733 (2022)
15. Loshchilov, I., Hutter, F.: Decoupled weight decay regularization (2019)
16. Mumtaz, W., Rasheed, S., Irfan, A.: Review of challenges associated with the EEG artifact removal methods. Biomed. Signal Process. Control **68**, 102741 (2021)
17. Paszke, A., et al.: Pytorch: an imperative style, high-performance deep learning library (2019)
18. Perucca, E., Covanis, A., Dua, T.: Commentary: epilepsy is a global problem. Epilepsia **55**(9), 1326–1328 (2014)
19. Satyender, Dhull, S.K., Singh, K.K.: EEG artifact removal using canonical correlation analysis and EMD-DFA based hybrid denoising approach. Procedia Computer Science, In: International Conference on Machine Learning and Data Engineering p. 218 (2023)
20. Shlens, J.: A tutorial on principal component analysis (2014)
21. Shoeb, A., Guttag, J.: Application of machine learning to epileptic seizure detection. In: Proceedings of the 27th International Conference on International Conference on Machine Learning. p. 975–982. ICML'10, Omnipress, Madison, WI, USA (2010)
22. Shoeibi, A., et al.: An overview of deep learning techniques for epileptic seizures detection and prediction based on neuroimaging modalities: Methods Challenges future works Comput. Bio. Med. **149** (2022
23. Thurman, D.J., et al.: ILAE Commission on Epidemiology: Standards for epidemiologic studies and surveillance of epilepsy. Epilepsia 52(s7) (2011)
24. Upadhyay, R., Padhy, P., Kankar, P.: EEG artifact removal and noise suppression by discrete orthonormal s-transform denoising. Comput. Electrical Eng. **53**, 125–142 (2016)
25. Wang, X., Wang, X., Liu, W., Chang, Z., Kärkkäinen, T., Cong, F.: One dimensional convolutional neural networks for seizure onset detection using long-term scalp and intracranial EEG. Neurocomputing **459**, 212–222 (2021)
26. Yao, X., Li, X., Ye, Q., Huang, Y., Cheng, Q., Zhang, G.Q.: A robust deep learning approach for automatic classification of seizures against non-seizures. Biomed. Signal Process. Control **64**, 102215 (2021)
27. Zhao, P., et al.: T-smote: Temporal-oriented synthetic minority oversampling technique for imbalanced time series classification. In: Proceedings of the Thirty-First International Joint Conference on Artificial Intelligence, IJCAI-22. International Joint Conferences on Artificial Intelligence Organization (2022)
28. Zhao, Y., et al.: EEG-based seizure detection using linear graph convolution network with focal loss. Comput. Methods Programs Biomed. **208**, 106277 (2021)

A New Rebinning Reconstruction Method for the Low Dose CT Scanners with Flying Focal Spot

Piotr Pluta[ID] and Robert Cierniak[✉][ID]

Department of Intelligent Computer Systems, Czestochowa University of Technology,
Czestochowa, Poland
robert.cierniak@pcz.pl
https://www.kisi.pcz.pl

Abstract. This paper presents an original approach to the image reconstruction problem for spiral CT scanners where the multi-source and/or the Flying Focal Spot (FFS) technology is implemented. The geometry of those scanners causes problems for computed tomography systems based on traditional (FDK) reconstruction methods. Therefore, we propose an original rebinning strategy, where does not occur the problem of non-equiangular X-rays. It is possible to implement this approach in all three types of CT scanners (only Multi-Source, only Flying Focal Spot, mixed Multi-Source with Flying Focal Spot). This approach is divided into two blocks (rebinning and iterative reconstruction procedure). This method is based on statistical model-based iterative reconstruction (MBIR), where the reconstruction problem is formulated as a shift-invariant system (a continuous-to-continuous data model). Our method allows for reducing the X-ray dose absorbed by patients during examinations. The most significant feature of the proposed method is the possibility of parallel implementation using the various GPU graphic card - what we have done for the NVIDIA graphic card. This fact resulted in the acceleration of the calculation and the significantly shortened time for the first reconstructed image.

Keywords: X-ray computed tomography · multi source tomography · flying focal spot · statistical method · image reconstruction from projections · rebinning method

1 Introduction

Multiple-source cone-beam scanning is a promising mode for dynamic volumetric CT/micro-CT. The first dynamic CT system is the Dynamic Spatial Reconstructor (DSR) designed in 1979. The pursuit for higher temporal resolution has primarily driven the development of computed tomography. Recently, it led to the emergence of Siemens dual-source CT scanners. Given the impact and limitation of dual-source cardiac CT, triple-source cone-beam CT seems a natural extension for future cardiac CT [12]. Developed in the early2000 s, the progress in longitudinal spatial resolution from 4-slice to 64-slice CT has enhanced the spiral scanner to make use of a flying focal spot (FFS) [6,8,11]. The FFS feature doubles the sampling density in the channel direction and in the longitudinal direction [8]. This so-called double z-sampling technique can further enhance longitudinal resolution and image quality in clinical routine [7]. Realized in cooperation with multidetector row CT (MDCT) scanners, this new technique aims at increasing the density of simultaneously acquired views in the longitudinal direction and the sampling density of the integral lines in the reconstruction planes. It also allowed by view-by-view deflections of the focal spot in the rotational α-direction (αFFS), and in the longitudinal z-direction (zFFS). Due to its geometric scheme, the FFS implementation does not allow to use of popular traditional methods to reconstruct an image from projection. Therefore, manufacturers decided to primarily modify the adaptive multiple plane reconstruction (AMPR) method for this purpose (see for details [4,7]).

2   Geometry of the Scanner

This section presents the geometry of individual projection systems for individual computer tomographs. It is worth noting that both construction schemes of presented construction can exist in one as a mixed version.

2.1   Geometry of Multi-Source System

The Multi-Source technique utilizes the specific design of a CT, where it is implemented in two or more X-ray tubes, using a matrix with the same number

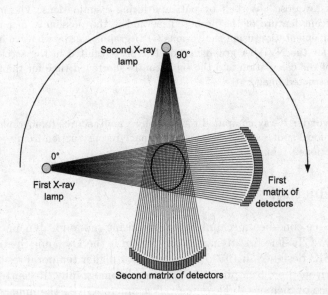

Fig. 1. Schema of dual-source CT scanners.

of detectors. The two-source system resulted in an increase in the acceleration of data acquisition and, depending on the arrangement of the second matrix, in an increase in resolution. The second X-ray tube has offset from the first by 90°. The detector array of the second X-ray tube has also offset 90° relative to the first one. In such a system, two interconnected measurement systems were obtained, remaining in a rigid relationship with each other. These geometrical conditions are shown in Fig. 1.

Given the impact and limitation of dual-source cardiac CT, triple-source cone-beam CT seems a natural extension for future cardiac CT [12]. Triple-source resulted in an increase in speed and also an increase in resolution. Those three X-ray tubes were physically offset from the first by 60° and 120°. The detector array of the second X-ray tube was also offset 60° and the third X-ray tube was also offset 120° relative to the first. In such a system, three coupled measurement systems were obtained, remaining in a rigid relationship with each other. These geometrical conditions e are shown in Fig. 2.

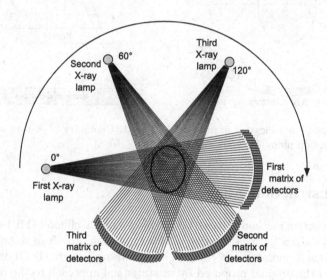

Fig. 2. Schema of triple source CT scanners.

2.2 Geometry of Flying Focal Spot System

The Flying Focal Spot technique uses a specific design of the X-ray tube in which it is possible to deflect the electron beam (using an electric field) before it hits the anode of the X-ray tube. This mechanism allows the view to be tilted after observing the focus for X-rays emitted from this anode. In order to obtain FFS, it is possible to create more lines of straight rays in the reconstruction process, both as a result of the reconstructed image and along the z axis around which the projection system rotates. These geometrical conditions are presented in 3 and 4. A simulation study showing reconstructions of mathematical phantoms further provided that the quality of the reconstructed images can be improved using the FFS. The aliasing artifacts that manifest as streaks emerging from high-contrast objects, and windmill artifacts are reduced by almost an order of magnitude with the FFS compared to a simulation without FFS [5,8].

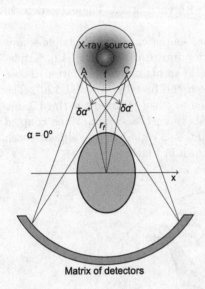
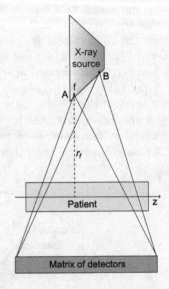

Fig. 3. Scheme of densification of rays in the reconstruction plane (αFFS).

Fig. 4. Geometry of X-rays along the z axis (zFFS).

3   Reconstruction Algorithm

The reconstruction method is based on the maximum-likelihood (ML) estimation (see e.g. [10]). Usually, the objective of this kind of approach to the reconstruction problem is formulated according to a discrete-to-discrete (D-D) data model. According to the original proposed by us statistical approach to the reconstruction problem, it is possible to present a practical model-based iterative reconstruction procedure, as follows:

$$\mu_{\min} = \arg\min_{\mu} \left(\sum_{i=1}^{I} \sum_{j=1}^{J} \left(\sum_{\bar{i}} \sum_{\bar{j}} \mu^* \left(x_{\bar{i}}, y_{\bar{j}} \right) \cdot h_{\Delta i, \Delta j} - \tilde{\mu} \left(x_i, y_j \right) \right)^2 \right), \quad (1)$$

and $\tilde{\mu}(i,j)$ is an image obtained by way of a back-projection operation, in the following way:

$$\tilde{\mu} \left(x_i, y_j \right) = \Delta_{\alpha} \sum_{\theta} \dot{p} \left(s_{ij}, \alpha_{\psi} \right), \quad (2)$$

where $\dot{p}\,(s_{ij}, \alpha_\psi)$ are measurements performed using parallel beams, and:

$$h_{\Delta i, \Delta j} = \Delta_\alpha \sum_{\psi=0}^{\Psi-1} int\,(\Delta i \cos \psi \Delta_\alpha + \Delta j \sin \psi \Delta_\alpha), \qquad (3)$$

and $int\,(\Delta s)$ is an interpolation function (we used the linear interpolation function).

Our reconstruction procedure comprises two blocks. In the first part, we prepare and perform rebinning of all cone beam X-ray raw data from CT scanners. After the rebinning, we determine a set of parallel projections, which can be used directly for back-projection operation and statistical iterative method.

3.1   Rebinning Method

In the rebinning process, we will describe each new virtual parallel X-ray by only elementary parameters, namely the following specific points: Focus, Semi-Isocenter, Detector [9]. Each of these parameters has coordinates in 3D space that result from CT geometry. As a consequence of this description, we have to implement a special procedure that can translate from spiral cone beam X-ray to our parallel X-ray. This redefining can be described as follows [9]:

$$xray(F_x^A, F_y^A, F_z^A, F_x^B, F_y^B, F_z^B, Q_x, Q_y, Q_z, D_x, D_y, D_z, p, s_m, \alpha_\psi), \qquad (4)$$

We will describe and compare all virtual and physical X-rays based on these elementary parameters during the rebinning process. This advantage allows us to be independent of any X-ray changes in 3D space. Thanks to this, the algorithm is resistant to future changes in CT scanners.

One of the most difficult things is to determine the position of the actual focal coordinates:

$$f_x = -(r_f + \Delta r_f^T) \cdot \sin(\alpha + \Delta \alpha^T); \qquad (5)$$

$$f_y = (r_f + \Delta r_f^T) \cdot \cos(\alpha + \Delta \alpha^T); \qquad (6)$$

$$f_z = z_0 + \Delta z^T; \qquad (7)$$

where T is the focus $(A, B, C, \dots)$, α is the angle of rotation of the projection system, r_f is the radius of the main focus, z_0 is the current position of the table with the patient relative to the starting point, $\Delta \alpha^T$ is the shift of the focus T relative to the main focus within the angle of rotation α, Δr_f^T is the change in the length of the radius of the focus T relative to the main focus, Δz is the shift of the focus T in the z axis relative to the main focus.

Having the values of the coordinates of the real focus and the virtual focus, and assuming that the number of real projections (focus) that can participate in this stage has been limited at the beginning (the same number of focus as when searching for the a plane coefficient), you can proceed to their comparison.

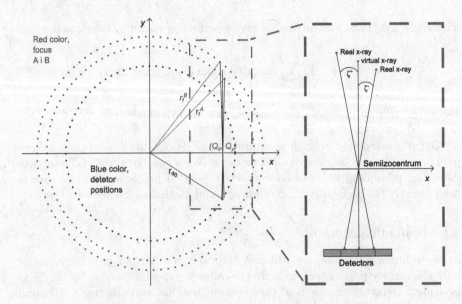

Fig. 5. Schema of virtual and real x-ray positions.

First, we need to determine the values of the ζ angle between the real focus and the virtual focus. To do this, apply the formula for the angle between two lines in a 2D coordinate system. Both segments have one common point, i.e. $SemiIsocenter$, the location of which is necessary for the correct calculation of the ζ angle:

$$\zeta = \arccos\left(\frac{\hat{w}_x \cdot \hat{v}_x + \hat{w}_y \cdot \hat{v}_y}{\sqrt{\hat{w}_x^2 + \hat{w}_y^2} \cdot \sqrt{\hat{v}_x^2 + \hat{v}_y^2}}\right), \tag{8}$$

where

$$\hat{v}_x = f_x^T - Q_x;$$
$$\hat{v}_y = f_y^T - Q_y;$$
$$\hat{w}_x = F_x^T - Q_x;$$
$$\hat{w}_y = F_y^T - Q_y. \tag{9}$$

The positions of virtual foci and real foci with the same radius value $(r_f + \Delta r_f)$ are considered here.

In addition, we should check whether the ζ angle is positive or negative because the arccos function always returns a positive angle value. Hence, it is checked whether the real focus (T) is "before" or "behind" the virtual focus (F) with respect to the direction of rotation of the projection system. For this purpose, the following value is calculated:

$$\xi = \hat{w}_x \cdot \hat{v}_y - \hat{v}_x \cdot \hat{w}_y. \tag{10}$$

If ξ is less than zero, the focus is on one side, and if it is greater than zero, the focus is on the other side of the virtual radius.

After all these operations, we perform standard interpolation and standard back-projection to prepare data for the iterative procedure. They are described below.

3.2   Iterative Procedure

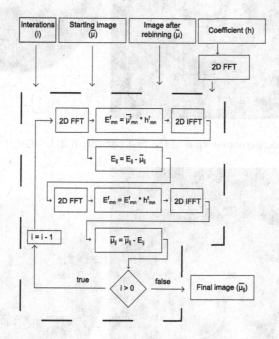

Fig. 6. Schema of the iterative procedure.

The iterative reconstruction procedure is illustrated schematically in a diagram in Fig. 6. The important note in this diagram is the part responsible for preparing the convolution kernel matrix (h) that has been excluded from the iterative procedure area to increase the speed of calculations. That means it can be determined before starting the iterative reconstruction procedure. This diagram shows the exclusion of the part responsible for preparing the starting image ($\bar{\mu}$) and image after rebinning ($\tilde{\mu}$) outside the area of the iterative method, which was described in the previous subsection as well. The result of transferring the most demanding calculations into the frequency domain makes it possible to reduce the computational complexity from K^4 to $8log_2 4K^2$ where K is the dimension of the reconstruction image.

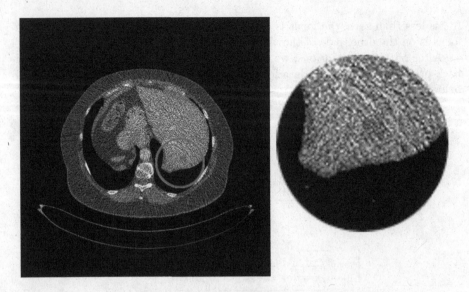

Fig. 7. Reconstruction view of the first patient. Z 211; FDK; Dose 1/4.

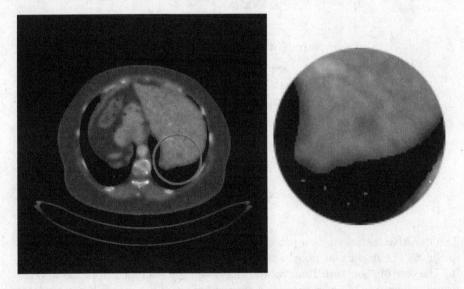

Fig. 8. Reconstruction view of the first patient. Z 211; Rebinning & 5000 Iterations; Dose 1/4.

4   Results

This section is devoted to the presentation of the results of our research based on data obtained by participants in the Low-Dose Grand Challenge. The physical data has been prepared artificially to simulate a quarter-dose of the X-ray

Table 1. Comparison of the computation times for the realizations of the rebinning and iterative reconstruction procedure on GPU.

Iterations	GTX960M	GTX1080Ti	TitanV	RTX2080	RTX3080
2 500	31 846 ms	3 799 ms	1 831 ms	2 914 ms	1 545 ms
5 000	62 301 ms	7 573 ms	3 562 ms	5 446 ms	2 867 ms
10 000	123 007 ms	14 886 ms	7 105 ms	10 673 ms	5 617 ms

radiation. Figure 7 was reconstructed using the traditional method (FDK), while 8 was reconstructed using an iterative-statistical method with rebinning, both with a high level of noise. We also presented the table 1 with the calculation time of this approach. This method is open for parallelization, which can be done using multiple cores/threads, with particular consideration for GPU implementation.

5 Conclusion

An original complete statistical iterative reconstruction method with an original rebinning method has been presented. The proposed here algorithm can be applied in scanners with multi-source and with flying focal spot, or in mixed version multi-source with FFS. Experiments conducted by us have proved that our reconstruction approach is fast, mainly thanks to applying an FFT algorithm during the most demanding calculations in the iterative reconstruction procedure, and thanks to very efficient parallel programming techniques on GPU. Our research will be developed to integrate computational intelligence methods (e.g. [1,2]) into the approach presented here.

References

1. Bilski, J., Kowalczyk, B., Kisiel-Dorohinicki, M., Siwocha, A., Żurada, J.: Towards a very fast feedforward multilayer neural networks training algorithm. J. Art. Intell. Soft Comput. Res. **12**(3), 181–195 (2022). https://doi.org/10.2478/jaiscr-2022-0012
2. Bilski, J., Smoląg, J., Kowalczyk, B., Grzanek, K., Izonin, I.: Fast computational approach to the levenberg-marquardt algorithm for training feedforward neural networks. J. Art. Intell. Soft Comput. Res. **12**(2), 45–61 (2023). https://doi.org/10.2478/jaiscr-2023-0006
3. Cierniak, R., Pluta, P.: Statistical iterative reconstruction algorithm based on a continuous-to-continuous model formulated for spiral cone-beam CT. Lecture Notes in Computer Science pp. 613–620 (2020). https://doi.org/10.1007/978-3-030-50420-5-46
4. Cierniak, R., Pluta, P., Kaźmierczak, A.: A practical statistical approach to the reconstruction problem using a single slice rebinning method. J. Art. Intell. Soft Comput. Res. **10**(2), 137–149 (2020). https://doi.org/10.2478/jaiscr-2020-0010

5. Cierniak, R.: A new statistical reconstruction method for the computed tomography using an x-ray tube with flying focal spot. J. Art. Intell. Soft Comput. Res. **11**(4), 271–286 (2021). https://doi.org/10.2478/jaiscr-2021-0016

6. Flohr, T.G., Stierstorfer, K., Ulzheimer, S., Bruder, H., Primak, A.N., McCollough, C.H.: Image reconstruction and image quality evaluation for a 64-slice CT scanner with z-flying focal spot. Med. Phys. **32**(8), 2536–2547 (2005). https://doi.org/10.1118/1.1949787

7. Flohr, T., Stierstorfer, K., Bruder, H., Simon, J., Polacin, A., Schaller, S.: Image reconstruction and image quality evaluation for a 16-slice CT scanner. Med. Phys. **30**(5), 832–845 (2003). https://doi.org/10.1118/1.1562168

8. Kachelriess, M., Knaup, M., Penssel, C., Kalender, W.: Flying focal spot (FFS) in cone-beam CT. IEEE Trans. Nucl. Sci. **53**(3), 1238–1247 (2006). https://doi.org/10.1109/TNS.2006.874076

9. Pluta, P.: A new approach to statistical iterative reconstruction algorithm for a CT scanner with flying focal spot using a rebinning method. Lecture Notes in Computer Science pp. 286–299 (2023). https://doi.org/10.1007/978-3-031-23480-4-24

10. Sauer, K., Bouman, C.: A local update strategy for iterative reconstruction from projections. IEEE Trans. Signal Process. **41**(2), 534–548 (1993). https://doi.org/10.1109/78.193196

11. Schardt, P., et al.: New x-ray tube performance in computed tomography by introducing the rotating envelope tube technology. Med. Phys. **31**(9), 2699–2706 (2004). https://doi.org/10.1118/1.1783552

12. Zhao, J., Lu, Y., Zhuang, T., Wang, G.: Overview of multisource CT systems and methods. Society of Photo-optical Instrumentation Engineers (2010). https://doi.org/10.1117/12.860307

Data Mining and Pattern Classification

Advancing Singular Value Decomposition Techniques for Enhanced Data Mining in Recommender Systems

Mykola Beshley[1,2(✉)] 🆔, Olena Hordiichuk-Bublivska[1] 🆔, Halyna Beshley[1,2] 🆔, and Iryna Ivanochko[1,2] 🆔

[1] Department of Telecommunication, Lviv Polytechnic National University, Lviv 79013, Ukraine
{mykola.i.beshlei,halyna.v.beshlei,iryna.v.ivanochko}@lpnu.ua
[2] Department of Information Systems, Faculty of Management, Comenius University in Bratislava, 82005 Bratislava, Slovakia

Abstract. The development of effective algorithms for processing large volumes of information is a very urgent problem for modern information systems. The work examines the problems of content analysis and data mining by recommender systems. Features of automatic systems management using machine learning algorithms are presented. The importance of using recommender systems for more accurate prediction of goods or services of interest to users, determination of interrelationships between various production factors, etc. have been determined. The operation of the FunkSVD algorithm, which allows accurate and fast processing of sparse data sets of a large volume, has been studied. A modification of FunkSVD is proposed to use fewer data about users and items when forming recommendations. The simulation of the proposed algorithm was carried out and it was determined that it works faster than the usual one, while maintaining fairly high accuracy, so it can be used in the processing of large data. It is also proposed to increase the privacy and accuracy of FunkSVD recommendations in distributed systems by using the Fed SVD algorithm. The results of the experiments showed the high accuracy of the proposed algorithm but at the expense of a certain increase in the duration of calculations. According to the conducted research, it was concluded that both modifications can be used in systems with different requirements for data mining and distributed architecture.

Keywords: Big Data · Recommender Systems · Data Mining · Funk SVD · Fed SVD

1 Introduction

Thanks to data mining on the information systems state, essential problems are solved. Identifying clear and hidden patterns in large data sets solves problems in various industries. A decrease in demand for a particular product type means the need to modernize the production line or change the marketing strategy. Surveying users about the level

L. Rutkowski et al. (Eds.): ICAISC 2023, LNAI 14126, pp. 281–290, 2023.
https://doi.org/10.1007/978-3-031-42508-0_26

of service quality allows businesses to identify service weaknesses and correct them as soon as possible. Analyzing data on industrial production results reduces the risks of production costs, which does not find feedback from users. Comparing performance indicators over different periods allows us to find optimal work strategies depending on the influence of various external and internal factors. The distribution of the load on different parts of the production system and selecting the necessary software and hardware straight affect production efficiency [1, 2]. Such indicators mean the need to attract new or discard existing technologies. Since a person cannot process the entire amount of data about the work of a large-scale enterprise on his own, algorithms that determine the most important information and discard the redundant ones come to the rescue. Also, software algorithms search for the necessary data and store and analyze it. Recommender systems are used to work with user and product data. Singular Value Decomposition (SVD) is a powerful mathematical technique that can be used to analyze and extract information from large datasets. It works by breaking down a matrix into its constituent parts, allowing patterns and relationships within the data to be identified. The paper investigates the Funk SVD algorithm, which allows efficient processing of information to provide recommendations to users about the most likely interesting products [3]. Algorithm modifications are also proposed for systems with different workloads and more efficient users data processing in distributed systems [4].

2 Peculiarities of Data Analysis Methods

Excess data in modern information systems is a real problem for the efficiency of user service providing. Data mining is a collection of methods for finding patterns in large data sets and presenting an understandable result. For this, the methods of mathematical analysis, statistics, artificial intelligence, and machine learning (ML) are most often used. ML is a powerful tool for solving a wide range of tasks. In various fields, ML contributes to the acceleration and automation of big data processing, object recognition, intelligent management, etc. Unlike traditional computer programs that work according to a predetermined algorithm, ML methods solve the optimal problem by themselves, receiving a set of data and a predicted result. ML allows us to solve tasks that a person cannot cope with alone. For example, voice recognition and identification. Since ML algorithms receive a huge amount of data as input, they can quickly determine the main characteristics of a human voice and identify its owner. Also, ML helps to establish the characteristics of users of information systems and provides them with personalized offers. The most frequently solved problems with the help of ML are also:

- Identification of suspicious activity related to the user's bank account or credit card.
- Recognition of patterns (images, words).
- Content generation.
- Predicting the behavior of certain people groups.

The improvement of ML algorithms and artificial intelligence has already dramatically changed the everyday life of many people. At the same time, the problem of the correctness of calculation results and privacy of users data is still relevant. Therefore, new methods and tools for solving problems in a specific field are constantly being developed. ML is divided into types:

- Supervised learning. In this case, the algorithm receives both input data and special labels about what the result should be.
- Unsupervised learning works without indicating the required result of program execution.
- Reinforcement learning involves providing hints (rewards) in case of performing certain actions.

An example of unsupervised learning is recommender systems that help predict future user preferences and select the most interesting products for them, as shown in Fig. 1.

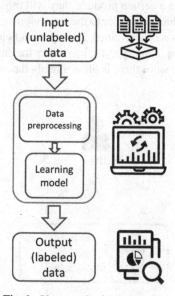

Fig. 1. Unsupervised ML algorithm.

The growth of data volumes in information systems requires the use of more effective methods of their processing. The concept of Big Data was introduced to define large volumes of information collected from various sources and types. Ordering and structuring them allows us to speed up the calculation process [5].

In order to automate and speed up computational processes, we should apply methods of working with big data that allow presenting different sets of information in a form that is convenient for perception. Recommender systems (RS) are used to determine the relationship between users and products. By applying user behavior analysis, it is possible to find the most interesting services for them. Thus, the time for necessary goods is reduced, and the industrial system can adjust production capacity based on the analysis of their popularity [6, 7].

For example, modern commercial and industrial information systems are quite complex and include control over all stages of production, as well as over the sale of products, it is important to track user interaction with items. If a certain product or service is not popular, it must be modified or replaced with a more effective one. If, in small information systems, it was possible to control user behavior manually, then in modern large-scale industrial structures, it is necessary to involve methods of mathematical data analysis [8–10]. Recommender systems are an example of an ML algorithm that uses large amounts of data obtained from various sources to determine the relationships between different categories of users and products. With the help of RS, it is much easier and more qualitative to determine the statistical features of the object's interaction in the system, the most and least popular products. Commercial systems collect such data as information about the purchase of a product by a certain user, preferences in social networks, distribution, use of special applications, etc. In this way, correspondences between product characteristics and their popularity among different groups of users are formed. If the customers like a certain product, they will most likely be interested in it in the future. The products that are similar to those previously added are offered as well as similarities between users are determined. If the person belongs to a certain category (for example, age, occupation, country, etc.), it is easier for the recommendation system to choose products for them, since there is often already data on the behavior of similar users (Fig. 2).

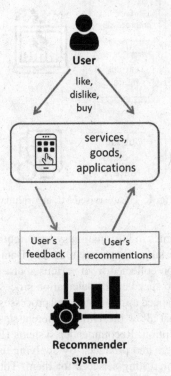

Fig. 2. Recommender systems.

The following methods of forming recommendations are distinguished:

- Content filtering is based on selecting elements similar to those previously liked by the user.

- Context filtering uses contextual information and additional interaction parameters to create a model for predicting subsequent preferences.
- Collaborative filtering uses the similarity between users and the history of their preferences to form recommendations.

Following the tasks set, the type of information system, the number of users, and the amount of data, we can choose the most appropriate way of forming recommendations [3, 11, 12].

3 Improving Singular Value Decomposition Methods for Data Mining

FunkSVD is a popular algorithm used for collaborative filtering in data mining. Collaborative filtering is a technique used in recommender systems to predict user preferences by analyzing data from multiple users. This algorithm decomposes the data matrix into the product of submatrices U and I.

$$R(u, i) = U \times I^T, \tag{1}$$

At the same time, recommendations for a specific user u regarding the product i defined as the product of the corresponding rows and columns of the matrices U and I:

$$r_{user\_item} = \sum_{k=u,i} (u_k \times i_k^T), \tag{2}$$

The relationship between the user and the product can generally be described as:

$$\alpha_{user\_item} = \alpha_{user} + \alpha_{item} + \beta, \tag{3}$$

where α_{user} is the user's bias relative to the overall average score, α_{item} is the item's bias, β is the bias correction.

It is possible to adjust the values of the matrices responsible for the characteristics of users and products, according to the calculated error $r_{user\_item\_err}$, the correction factor φ and the learning speed factor τ:

$$u_u = u_u + (2 \times i_i \times r_{user\_item\_err} - \varphi \times u_u) \times \tau, \tag{4}$$

$$i_i = i_i + (2 \times u_u \times r_{user\_item\_err} - \varphi \times i_i) \times \tau, \tag{5}$$

The recommendation calculation error r'_{user_item} is defined as:

$$r_{user\_item\_err} = r_{user\_item} - r'_{user\_item} \tag{6}$$

Therefore, it is possible to calculate an improved recommendation, taking into account the coefficient of the average rating of the product by all users ϵ:

$$r'_{user\_item} = \alpha_{user} + \alpha_{item} + U_u \times I_i^T + \epsilon, \tag{7}$$

In our previous investigations we proposed an improved algorithm in which not all user data is used to provide recommendations, but only part of it, where $n < u$ [13]. In this paper, we also propose to change the amount of items data: $m < i$:

$$r_{user\_item\_mod} = \sum_{l=n} u_l \times \sum_{k=m} i_k^T, \tag{8}$$

We also calculate the recommendation error:

$$r_{user\_item\_err\_mod} = r_{user\_item\_mod} - r'_{user\_item\_mod} \tag{9}$$

$$u_u = u_u + (2 \times (\sum_{k=m} i_k^T) \times r_{user\_item\_err\_mod} - \varphi \times u_u) \times \tau, \tag{10}$$

$$i_i = i_i + (2 \times (\sum_{l=n} u_l) \times r_{user\_item\_err\_mod} - \varphi \times i_i) \times \tau. \tag{11}$$

The accuracy of the algorithms is defined as the square root of the average deviation of the calculated recommendations from the real ones.

In one of the previous studies [13], we also used the Fed SVD algorithm to work with distributed systems based on the SVD method. We proposed to use for improving the privacy of Funk SVD in distributed systems. For improving the efficiency of calculations and protecting data from external influences during transmission over the communication channel, the data matrix is processed by the user:

$$R_1 = R \times J \times H^T, \tag{12}$$

where H and J are the masking data generated by the client. After transferring the data to the central computing device, Fank SVD is performed, the results are returned to the user and he can remove the mask to display them correctly (Fig. 3).

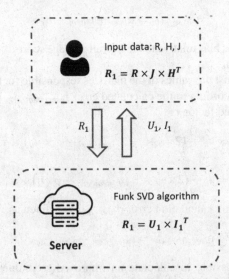

Fig. 3. Federated Funk SVD algorithm.

This approach allows low-power user devices to transmit data for calculation to the server, while maintaining their privacy.

4   An Experimental Study of the Modified Funk SVD Algorithms

As mentioned in the previous sections, recommender systems are examples of ML for solving problems of faster analysis of user preferences, the behavior of interconnected processes, and quick management of them. For comparing the effectiveness of the proposed algorithm, simulations were conducted using the Pandas and SVD libraries in the Python programming language. We investigated the performance of the Funk SVD algorithm, as it is often used to work with sparse data. Improvement of the algorithm according to Eq. 8 means that we do not use data on all users and items, but only a part. Thus, we reduce the load on the recommender system. The scheme of the modified Funk SVD algorithm is shown in Fig. 4.

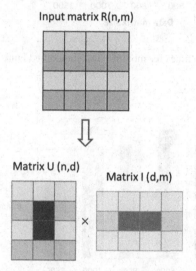

Fig. 4. Modified Funk SVD algorithm.

From Fig. 4 we can see that the selected cells in the matrices are smaller in size than the entire row and column. Accordingly, fewer computing resources are spent on multiplication. Comparison of the calculations duration for two algorithms is shown in Fig. 5.

Since the proposed modification of the Funk SVD algorithm contains fewer data to process, the result can be obtained faster. This approach allows more efficient processing of user requests and recommendations formation. A comparison of the accuracy of the providing recommendations for the two algorithms is shown in Fig. 6.

From Fig. 5 and Fig. 6, we can conclude that the modified FunkSVD works faster than the usual one but maintains relatively high calculation accuracy.

For solving the problem of data processing in real information systems, their distributed architecture should be taken into account. A large number of end devices are not powerful enough to compute Funk SVD. Then you can use the services of a remote server, but you should protect private data.

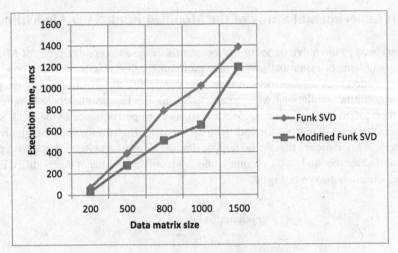

Fig. 5. Calculation times for modified and unmodified Funk SVD algorithms.

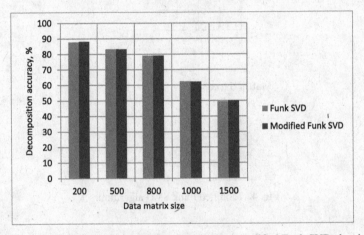

Fig. 6. Recommendation accuracy for modified and unmodified Funk SVD algorithms.

In this paper, we propose to combine Funk SVD and Fed SVD (Eq. 12) to increase the accuracy and privacy of calculations. Comparison of the duration of calculations for two algorithms is shown in Fig. 7.

Because the Fed SVD algorithm requires additional operations on user data, its use slows down the computation. However, the use of additional information increases the accuracy of further processing. A comparison of the accuracy of providing recommendations for two algorithms is shown in Fig. 8.

From Fig. 7 and Fig. 8, it is clear that the second modification of Funk SVD allows for increasing the accuracy of providing recommendations compared to the standard algorithm by adding more marked information. Instead, the duration of data processing

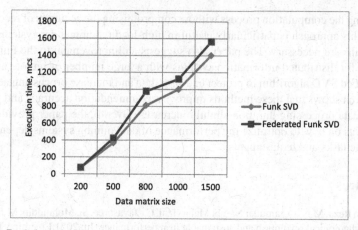

Fig. 7. Calculation times for distributed and non-distributed Funk SVD algorithms.

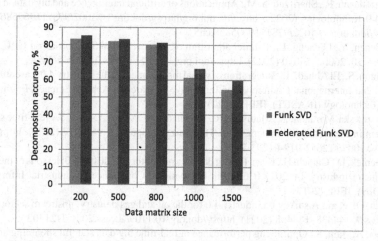

Fig. 8. Recommendation accuracy for distributed and non-distributed Funk SVD algorithms.

naturally increases. Thus, if the first modification offered fast calculation of recommendations under high load, the second one is better to use in systems where high accuracy is a priority. It is also a way to protect private data during transmission to the server for calculations. The process of data mining for large volumes of data is simplified. In further work, we will continue investigating the proposed modifications to obtain optimal performance indicators of various systems.

5 Conclusion

The paper discusses the challenges of big data mining in information systems, particularly in the context of recommender systems. It proposes a modified version of the Funk SVD algorithm that can provide recommendations using fewer data about users, thereby accelerating the computation process without compromising the accuracy of recommendations. This approach is particularly useful in high-load recommender systems where quick results are necessary. The paper also suggests an improvement to the Funk SVD algorithm for distributed information systems with a large number of remote users, by using the Fed SVD algorithm to protect end-user data and increase processing accuracy. The research shows that these methods improve recommendation accuracy and privacy, although data processing duration slightly increases. Overall, the paper provides valuable insights on how to optimize the performance of data mining systems depending on the specific tasks and requirements.

References

1. Hassan Reza, M.N., Agamudai Nambi Malarvizhi, C., Jayashree, S., Mohiuddin, M.: Industry 4.0-technological revolution and sustainable firm performance. In: 2021 Emerging Trends in Industry 4.0 (ETI 4.0). IEEE (2021)
2. Rezazadegan, R., Sharifzadeh, M.: Applications of artificial intelligence and big data in industry 4.0 technologies (2022). http://dx.doi.org/https://doi.org/10.1002/9781119695868.ch5. https://doi.org/10.1002/9781119695868.ch5
3. Xiaochen, Y., Qicheng, L.: Parallel algorithm of improved FunkSVD based on GPU. IEEE Access 10, 26002–26010 (2022). https://doi.org/10.1109/access.2022.3156969
4. El Manti, S., El Abbadi, L.: Integration of visual management in the industry 4.0: case study. In: 2022 2nd International Conference on Innovative Research in Applied Science, Engineering and Technology (IRASET). IEEE (2022)
5. Poniszewska-Maranda, A., Matusiak, R., Kryvinska, N., Yasar, A.-U.-H.: A real-time service system in the cloud. J. Ambient Intell. Humaniz. Comput. 11, 961–977 (2020). https://doi.org/10.1007/s12652-019-01203-7
6. Cemernek, D., Gursch, H., Kern, R.: Big data as a promoter of industry 4.0: lessons of the semiconductor industry. In: 2017 IEEE 15th International Conference on Industrial Informatics (INDIN). IEEE (2017)
7. Elijah, O., et al.: A survey on industry 4.0 for the oil and gas industry: upstream sector. IEEE Access 9, 144438–144468 (2021). https://doi.org/10.1109/access.2021.3121302
8. Gupta, A., Jain, S.: Optimizing performance of real-time big data stateful streaming applications on cloud. In: 2022 IEEE International Conference on Big Data and Smart Computing (BigComp). IEEE (2022)
9. Aggour, K.S., et al.: Federated multimodal big data storage & analytics platform for additive manufacturing. In: 2019 IEEE International Conference on Big Data (Big Data). IEEE (2019)
10. Hashemipour, S.N., et al.: Big data compression in smart grids via optimal singular value decomposition. In: 2020 IEEE Industry Applications Society Annual Meeting. IEEE (2020)
11. Nti, I.K., Quarcoo, J.A., Aning, J., Fosu, G.K.: A mini-review of ML in big data analytics: applications, challenges, and prospects. Big Data Min. Anal. 5, 81–97 (2022). https://doi.org/10.26599/bdma.2021.9020028
12. Hordiichuk-Bublivska, O., Beshley, H., Kyryk, M., Pyrih, Y., Urikova, O., Beshley, M.: A modified federated singular value decomposition method for big data and ML optimization in IIoT systems. In: Klymash, M., Luntovskyy, A., Beshley, M., Melnyk, I., Schill, A. (eds.) Emerging Networking in the Digital Transformation Age, TCSET 2022. LNEE, vol. 965, pp. 246–267. Springer, Cham (2023). https://doi.org/10.1007/978-3-031-24963-1_14
13. Beshley, M., Hordiichuk-Bublivska, O., Beshley, H., Ivanochko, I.: Data optimization for industrial IoT-based recommendation systems. Electronics (Basel) 12, 33 (2022). https://doi.org/10.3390/electronics12010033

An Experimental Analysis on Mapping Strategies for Cepstral Coefficients Multi-projection in Voice Spoofing Detection Problem

Rodrigo Colnago Contreras[1](✉) [iD], Monique Simplicio Viana[2] [iD],
and Rodrigo Capobianco Guido[1] [iD]

[1] Institute of Biosciences, Letters and Exact Sciences, São Paulo State University,
São José do Rio Preto, SP 15054-000, Brazil
rodrigo.contreras@unesp.br, guido@ieee.org
[2] Department of Computing, Federal University of São Carlos,
São Carlos, SP 13565-905, Brazil
monique.viana@ufscar.br

Abstract. With the cheapening of certain electronic devices, the use of biometric user authentication systems is becoming increasingly common. In particular, the use of microphones for user recognition is a reality for many people in the most common tasks, such as accessing their own cell phone or even their own bank account at an ATM. However, recent works demonstrate that the practice of frauds such as the improper presentation of a recording of an authentic user to the recognition system can pose a threat to the security of these systems. As a countermeasure to such practices, liveness detection techniques have emerged with the intention of ensuring that the signal presented to the system comes from the human vocal tract or from a recording. Techniques based on the analysis of spectrograms, which consist of a matrix representation of the relationship between the frequency of the signal and its temporal duration, are widely used in this topic. However, little study has been carried out on the use of mapping operators on such representations in order to make feature vectors belonging to $\mathbb{R}^n$ and, consequently, facilitate its definition and use in most binary classifiers. In this work, we perform an experimental analysis on different mapping operators applied in the construction of handcrafted features on spectrograms calculated by various techniques. In addition, we also analyze the effect of fusing and projecting such features. Finally, we were able to observe that, with the use of the proposed material, which consists of a tool of simple definition and low complexity, we obtained competitive results to those presented by the baselines of the theme.

Keywords: Liveness Detection · Spoofing Detection · Voice Authentication System · Spectrograms · Pattern Recognition

1 Introduction

The automation of tasks that require a considerable level of security has been occurring frequently in recent years [28]. As an example, we can note activities involving

L. Rutkowski et al. (Eds.): ICAISC 2023, LNAI 14126, pp. 291–306, 2023.
https://doi.org/10.1007/978-3-031-42508-0_27

financial transactions [12]. For this type of operation, the use of user recognition and authentication systems has become essential [40]. Among such systems, those based on user biometrics [31] are the ones that offer the highest level of security and, in many cases, ease, since authentication is based on some physiological and/or behavioral characteristic inherent to the user, which eliminates the use of access keys and memorizing passwords. In this sense, the Voice Authentication Systems (VAS) [4] stand out, which are used in well-known applications such as Amazon Alexa [26], Google Home [24], Apple Siri [3], among others [20]. The popularization of these systems is due to the following reasons: the collection of biometrics can be done without any contact with the electronic device [34], which guarantees ease and asepsis, which is an important attribute in pandemic scenarios; wide availability of literature [10] and computational libraries [22]; high user representation capacity due to the uniqueness of the human vocal apparatus [21]; low cost of collection devices [27], since simple microphones can efficiently represent the characteristics of the human voice [35]; etc.

As a counterpart to the benefits of using VASs, its vulnerability [17] to attacks like *spoofing* [9] stands out. In particular, it was demonstrated that the presentation of the voice recording of legitimate users in the recognition system can ensure the access of an improper agent [41]. This type of fraud is known as replay attack (RA) [11] and poses a real threat to VASs. To mitigate this deficiency, countermeasures based on the processing and analysis of voice signals have been proposed in recent works [43]. As an example, we can cite techniques based on the discrimination of features made from spectrograms, such as the Mel-frequency Cepstral Coefficients (MFCC) [7,33,42], this being one of the most popular categories of methods employed to solve this problem. In fact, different variations of Cepstral Coefficients (CCs) have been considered in this matter. For example, the Constant Q Cepstral Coefficients (CQCC) [36] together with the Linear Frequency Cepstral Coefficients (LFCC) [32] became the reference techniques, or baselines, from the ASVspoof competitions [37].

In general, features based on CCs are given in a matrix form [1,29] and are used for training a Gaussian Mixture Model (GMM), more specifically the universal background model (GMM-UBM) [23]. For the proper functioning of these models, an array of features $C \in \mathbb{R}^{n_{ceps} \times n_{frames}}$ is required as input, with n_{ceps} being the number of CCs and n_{frames} being the number of temporal windows considered, for each sample analyzed in the training stage, which may correspond to a high computational cost in terms of processing and, mainly, in memory level. As an example, for the case of the benchmark ASVspoof 2019 [39], 22800 samples are made available for training and another 22296 for development, which could correspond to the cost of storage in memory of up to $O(45096 \cdot n_{ceps} \cdot n_{frames})$ to configure a GMM-UBM.

An alternative to this complication is the use of mapping and projection functions on the matrix C that represent it from embeddings in $\mathbb{R}^{n_{ceps}}$ and, consequently, reduce the memory cost of these techniques and make it possible to consider other classifiers, such as Support Vector Machines (SVMs). This type of strategy was successfully used to detect spoofings in fingerprint images [5,6], however, there are few works carried out in this sense for the detection of voice spoofings. Therefore, in this work, we experimented with several projection measures to represent the features extracted by a set of spectrograms on a benchmark of voice spoofing. Furthermore, we consider a feature fusion and reduction procedure to train an SVM-based classification model. As a result, we emphasize that we obtained metrics associated with the average classification error with values smaller than those obtained by the baselines of the problem from methods that demand less computational resources and that fall within the area of soft computing. Therefore, in this work, our contributions are related to two main fronts:

- A new multi-projection framework for voice spoofing detection method that is efficient and uses reduced computational resources; and
- An extensive computational experimentation of mapping projection techniques applied over a set of spectrogram-based features.

The remainder of the manuscript is divided as follows: in Sect. 2, a recap of the main CC extraction techniques is presented; in Sect. 3, we present details of the proposed material; experiments are presented and discussed in Sect. 4; finally, the work is concluded in Sect. 5 with some final considerations on the developments.

2 Cepstral Coefficients Fundamentals

Techniques based on the representation of the voice signal to define a classification model must make use of a feature extraction step. This process consists of making a model that highlights patterns from characteristics inherent to the signal and that are considered important for the addressed problem. On the one hand, features extracted directly from the raw version of the sound signal such as energy [13], entropy [16], zero crossing rate [14], Teager energy operator [15], among others, are the most used in several audio processing and analysis problems. On the other hand, it may be more appropriate in problems that demand a higher level of detail in the signal representation, such as the voice spoofing detection problem, the use of a feature category that is capable of representing harmonic and sidebands characteristics in the signal and in its spectral domain. As an example, we can highlight the techniques that are based on the extraction of CCs from the signal, such as the MFCC, the CQCC, the LFCC, among others. Specifically, the features obtained by these techniques are based on a process in which the signal is modified by a pre-emphasis step to compensate for the suppression of high frequencies, followed by steps of framing and windowing of the signal so that its representation in the domain of frequencies is driven by some specialized transformation, such as the Fast Fourier Transform (FFT), and finally, the CCs are calculated using some filter bank scale. In Fig. 1, we have a scheme that summarizes and generalizes the process of calculating CCs from sound signals.

Therefore, for each sound signal $x \in \mathbb{R}^n$, we can extract n_{ceps} CCs over n_{frames} frames of time using the technique Φ. Mathematically, these CCs can be represented by the matrix $\mathbf{C}_x^{\Phi} \in \mathbb{R}^{n_{\text{ceps}} \times n_{\text{frames}}}$ given in Eq. (1).

$$\mathbf{C}_x^{\Phi} = \begin{bmatrix} - & \vec{c}_1 & - \\ - & \vec{c}_2 & - \\ & \vdots & \\ - & \vec{c}_{n_{\text{ceps}}} & - \end{bmatrix} \in \mathbb{R}^{n_{\text{ceps}} \times n_{\text{frames}}}, \tag{1}$$

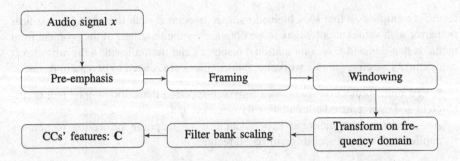

Fig. 1. General process for making features based on CCs from an audio signal x.

in which $\vec{c}_i \in \mathbb{R}^{n_{ceps}}, \forall i$, the CCs of x according to the Φ technique. More details on the mathematical foundation and the implementation of this category of methods can be found in the works of Prabakaran and Shyamala [29] and Alim et al. [2].

3   Proposed Multi-projection Framework Based on Sets of Cepstral Coefficients for Voice Liveness Detection

In this section, we present the components that form the proposed method for replay attack detection in VAS. For this, we present in detail the formulation of all stages of the proposed method, highlighting its mathematical formulation and the algorithms that determine its operation. Specifically, we intend to highlight the following innovations of the proposed work:

- A new multi-projection framework for the extraction and classification of features in voice signals to conduct the discrimination of these samples into two distinct categories: the set of legitimate user sound and the set of replayed sounds;
- Experimental analysis of various configurations of the proposed generalization. Thus, it is also a contribution of our work the computational evaluation of the representation performance of several features based on CCs created by different types of mappings in face of the voice spoofing detection problem.

3.1   Multi-projection

The mapping of given patterns in their matrix form across various functions has already been explored for fingerprint liveness detection problems. For example, using five different mappings on the well-known Dense Scale-Invariant Feature Transform (Dense-SIFT) [25] descriptor, Contreras et al. [5] propose a vector representation of statistical measures of the referred pattern descriptor which is originally given in matrix form. Contreras et al. [6] generalized this concept in order to make it functional for any texture matrix descriptor using a set of mapping functions. In this work, we will introduce this concept for the case of patterns described by CCs, which are also defined in the form of a matrix. For this, we consider the set $\mathcal{M}$ of mapping functions given in Eq. (2):

$$\mathcal{M} = \{m_1, m_2, ..., m_{n_{\mathcal{M}}}\}, \tag{2}$$

in which, $m_i : \mathbb{R}^{n_{\text{ceps}} \times n_{\text{frames}}} \to \mathbb{R}^{n_{\text{ceps}}}, \forall i \in \{1, 2, ..., n_{\mathcal{M}}\}$.

Thus, we consider a matrix $\mathbf{C}_x^{\Phi}$ of CCs features obtained with a technique Φ from the signal x, as presented in Eq. (1). Then, the representation of this features of x through the proposed multi-projection strategy is given by the vector $\vec{v}_x$:

$$\vec{v}_x = \left(m_1\left(\mathbf{C}_x^{\Phi}\right), m_2\left(\mathbf{C}_x^{\Phi}\right), ..., m_{n_{\mathcal{M}}}\left(\mathbf{C}_x^{\Phi}\right)\right) \in \mathbb{R}^{n_{\text{ceps}} \cdot n_{\mathcal{M}}}. \tag{3}$$

It is worth noting that, using the proposed routine, we reduced the number of coordinates of the cepstral feature, which originally has $n_{\text{ceps}} \cdot n_{\text{frames}}$ coordinates, to $n_{\text{ceps}} \cdot n_{\mathcal{M}}$ coordinates, and this reduction is normally efficient, since it is common that the number of frames considered in the representation of CCs is very high and, consequently, much larger than $n_{\mathcal{M}}$, which is the number of mapping functions that we will consider. This economy tends to be even greater when we consider that it is common to use features of a dynamic order such as Δ and $\Delta\Delta$ together with features considered static in CCs. By way of comparison, this value is equal to five in the works by Contreras et al. [5] and Contreras et al. [6].

3.2 Cepstral Coefficient Features Extraction

For extracting features from the signal, we will also consider a strategy similar to that of Contreras et al. [6], which makes use of merging several pattern descriptors to represent a fingerprint image with greater information richness. In fact, the intention of this strategy is based on the fact that each pattern descriptor has an advantage in representing a specific type of characteristic inherent to the signal. We propose the generalization of this concept to the voice spoofing detection problem since each technique based on the extraction of CCs has an advantage in representing a type of sound pattern. Therefore, let's consider a set $\mathcal{P}$ formed by techniques for calculating CCs, as highlighted in Eq. (4):

$$\mathcal{P} = \{\Phi_1, \Phi_2, ..., \Phi_{n_{\mathcal{P}}}\}, \tag{4}$$

in which $\Phi_i : \mathbb{R}^n \to \mathbb{R}^{n_{\text{ceps}} \times n_{\text{frames},i}}$ is a technique that extracts n_{ceps} CCs from the signal $x \in \mathbb{R}^n$ considering $n_{\text{frames},i}$ time frames.

Furthermore, we propose to analyze the patterns inherent to the source generating the voice signal in order to highlight the characteristics of the human vocal apparatus from artificial sources. For this, we will represent the signal produced through its energy by the Teager operator [15]. Thus, from each signal x, we will calculate its transformation by the Teager energy operator (TEO) by the function $\text{TEO}(\cdot)$ and we will extract the respective CCs by the techniques of $\mathcal{P}$. Finally, both made-up feature vectors must be concatenated to represent the voice signal in the classifier, as represented in the Algorithm 1 given below.

Algorithm 1. Proposed feature vector construction.

	x	A given voice signal.
Input:	$\mathcal{M}$	The set with $n_{\mathcal{M}}$ mapping functions to be extracted from the CCs.
	$\mathcal{P}$	The set with $n_{\mathcal{P}}$ CC extraction technique.

1: $\hat{x} := \text{TEO}(x)$ ▷ Calculate the Teager energy of the signal x.

2: **for** $\phi_i \in \mathcal{P}$ **do**

3:     $C_x^{\Phi_i} := \Phi_i(x)$ ▷ Calculate the CCs of the original signal x using Φ_i.

4:     $C_{\hat{x}}^{\Phi_i} := \Phi_i(\hat{x})$ ▷ Calculate the CCs of the Teager energy of the signal x using Φ_i.

5:     $\vec{v}_{\text{original},i} := \left(m_1(C_x^{\Phi_i}), m_2(C_x^{\Phi_i}), ..., m_{n_{\mathcal{M}}}(C_x^{\Phi_i})\right)$ ▷ Calculate the multi-projection of the CCs of the original signal.

6:     $\vec{v}_{\text{TEO},i} := \left(m_1(C_{\hat{x}}^{\Phi_i}), m_2(C_{\hat{x}}^{\Phi_i}), ..., m_{n_{\mathcal{M}}}(C_{\hat{x}}^{\Phi_i})\right)$ ▷ Calculate the multi-projection of the CCs of the Teager energy of the signal.

7: **end for**

8: $\vec{v}_x := [\vec{v}_{\text{original},1}, \vec{v}_{\text{TEO},1}, \vec{v}_{\text{original},2}, \vec{v}_{\text{TEO},2}, ..., \vec{v}_{\text{original},n_{\mathcal{P}}}, \vec{v}_{\text{TEO},n_{\mathcal{P}}}]$ ▷ Concatenate the vectors.

Output: $\vec{v}_x$ | The multi-projected CCs feature vector extracted from x.

3.3 Classification Model

To define a classification model, we propose a strategy based on SVM with a Gaussian kernel (SVM-RBF). In detail, the feature vectors must have their dimension reduced, since they are the result of the Algorithm 1 and, consequently, have the number of coordinates equal to $2 \cdot n_{\text{ceps}} \cdot n_{\mathcal{M}} \cdot n_{\mathcal{P}}$. To carry out the dimensionality reduction process, we propose the use of the Singular Value Decomposition (SVD) method. In this case, the number of coordinates that minimize the average classification error is conducted by a grid search routine. In addition, the calculated feature vectors must be normalized. Experimentally, and because it is widely considered in sound signal analysis problems, the z-score technique, or standard scale [19], was supposed to present the best results. Finally, the metric used to measure the model's effectiveness is the point where the false acceptance rate is equal to the false rejection rate, known as the Equal Error Rate (EER). The lower this rate, the better the model.

3.4 Proposed Algorithm and Considered Instances

In summary, we can represent the proposed framework in four main steps: extracting the Teager energy from the signal; definition of CCs by specialized technique set; multi-feature projection; and classification. The interaction scheme between these steps is defined in the flowchart of Fig. 2.

According to the reasoning of the proposed material, it is clear that this is a generalization. Therefore, it is necessary to define the techniques that compose the sets $\mathcal{M}$ and $\mathcal{P}$. In this case, we will consider several configurations for these sets. Specifically, as mapping functions the metrics of sum, mean, standard deviation, skewness, kurtosis and entropy will be considered; while, for CC extraction techniques, the following methods will be considered: CQCC, MFCC, inverse MFCC (iMFCC), LFCC, Gammatone Frequency Cepstral Coefficients (GFCC) [38], Bark Frequency Cepstral Coefficients (BFCC) [18], Linear Predictive Cepstral Coefficients (LPCC) [30], and

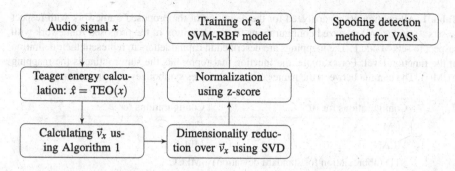

Fig. 2. General process for making features based on CCs from an audio signal x.

Normalized Gammachirp Cepstral Coefficients (NGCC) [44], all of which are defined for $n_{\text{ceps}} = 20$ statics CCs, 20 first-order dynamics (Δ) and 20 second-order dynamics ($\Delta\Delta$), and being normalized by mean and variance, which configures the Cepstral mean and variance normalization (CMVN) strategy. In detail, all adopted configurations for sets $\mathcal{M}$ and $\mathcal{P}$ are shown in Table 1.

4   Experiments and Results

In this section of experiments, we attest to the functioning of several configurations of the proposed material and compare our results with the baselines of the area. All our developments were implemented in Python with the help of well-known libraries like scikit-learn[1], spafe[2] and librosa[3]. The used computer is an i5-4460 with 3.2 GHz and 8 GB of RAM memory with an NVIDIA GTX-1050 ti, which is a modest configuration to address the problem in question. In addition, our evaluations were conducted on the database ASVSpoof 2017 version 2.0 [8], which is one of the most used databases on the theme. Table 2 presents a summary of the information in this benchmark, which is sectioned into three subsets: one with samples that must be used for training the model (Training); one with samples that must be used to adjust methodologies (Development); and one with samples for testing and evaluating the developed material (Evaluation).

In all the configurations of our experiments, we considered the use and non-use of approximation of the source of the voice signal. In other words, our analyzes were obtained from two distinct and disjoint hypotheses: $\hat{x}$ and all its features are disregarded, making the feature vector only with the concatenations of the projections of the pure original signal's CCs, which defines the hypothesis H_1; considering $\hat{x} = \text{TEO}(x)$ and their respective features, as described in the Algorithm 1, which defines the hypothesis H_2. In addition, we will compare our results with the reference values presented by the baselines of the ASVSpoof 2017 competition. In this case, these are the following: $B01$, in which the features are made from 19 CCs extracted by the CQCC technique together with plus 19 first-order dynamic features and 19 second-order dynamic features, which

---

[1] https://scikit-learn.org/stable/.

[2] https://superkogito.github.io/spafe/index.html.

[3] https://librosa.org/.

Table 1. All configurations analyzed for the definition of the proposed framework with respect to sets $\mathcal{M}$ and $\mathcal{P}$. All analyzed configurations for the definition of the proposed framework with respect to sets M and P. The mappings are described in capital letters to represent their definition at the function level. For example, the function that represents the sum routine is the mapping SUM($\cdot$). The comma between the names of the techniques symbolizes concatenation.

Configurations for $\mathcal{M}$	Configurations for $\mathcal{P}$
SUM	CQCC
MEAN	MFCC
STD (abbreviation for standard deviation)	iMFCC
SKEW (abbreviation for skewness)	BFCC
ENTROPY	LFCC
KURTOSIS	LPCC
SUM, MEAN	GFCC
SUM, SKEW	NGCC
SUM, STD	CQCC, MFCC
SUM, KURTOSIS	CQCC, LFCC
MEAN, SKEW	CQCC, LPCC
MEAN, ENTROPY	CQCC, GFCC
MEAN, STD	CQCC, NGCC
MEAN, KURTOSIS	CQCC, MFCC, LFCC
SKEW, ENTROPY	CQCC, MFCC, BFCC
SKEW, STD	CQCC, MFCC, GFCC
SKEW, KURTOSIS	CQCC, MFCC, NGCC
KURTOSIS, ENTROPY	CQCC, MFCC, BFCC, LFCC
KURTOSIS, STD	CQCC, MFCC, BFCC, GFCC
ENTROPY, STD	CQCC, MFCC, BFCC, NGCC
MEAN, STD, SKEW	
MEAN, STD, KURTOSIS	
MEAN, STD, ENTROPY	
MEAN, STD, SKEW, KURTOSIS	
MEAN, STD, SKEW, ENTROPY	

Table 2. Details on the benchmark ASVSpoof 2017 version 2.0 used for the evaluations of the proposed material.

Subset	Speakers	Sessions	Replay Config	Utterances	
				Real	Spoofing
Training	10	6	3	1507	1507
Development	8	10	10	760	950
Evaluation	24	161	57	1298	12008
Total	42	177	61	3565	14465

are used for training a GMM classifier from samples of the training and development set; $B02$, which consists of the same feature manufacturing technique as $B01$ with the exception that only samples from the benchmark training set are used for the definition of the GMM classifier.

For the first situation, we will analyze, for each configuration of $\mathcal{M}$, that is, for each considered multi-projection, which is the best configuration for the set $\mathcal{P}$ of CCs extraction techniques in relation to the EER metric. In Tables 3 and 4, we present the results considering, respectively, only the voice signal, according to H_1, and the voice signal with its version obtained by the Teager's energy operator, according to H_2.

Table 3. EER metric obtained for all evaluated multi-projection configurations. The configuration of $\mathcal{P}$ responsible for achieving the best EER value according to the respective configuration of $\mathcal{M}$ is presented in the central column. In this case, only the pure speech signal is analyzed, corresponding to the hypothesis H_1. EER values in bold symbolize lower values than those presented by both baselines B01 and B02.

Configuration for $\mathcal{M}$	Respective best configuration for $\mathcal{P}$	EER (%)
SUM	CQCC, MFCC, BFCC, NGCC	25.32
MEAN	CQCC, MFCC, BFCC, GFCC	27.29
STD	CQCC, MFCC, BFCC, NGCC	**21.37**
SKEW	CQCC, MFCC, BFCC	25.03
ENTROPY	CQCC, MFCC, BFCC, GFCC	36.84
KURTOSIS	CQCC, MFCC, BFCC, NGCC	28.53
SUM, MEAN	CQCC, MFCC, BFCC, NGCC	25.9
SUM, SKEW	CQCC, MFCC, BFCC, NGCC	**20.74**
SUM, STD	CQCC, MFCC, BFCC, NGCC	**16.21**
SUM, KURTOSIS	CQCC, MFCC, BFCC, NGCC	24.26
MEAN, SKEW	CQCC, MFCC, BFCC, NGCC	**22.58**
MEAN, ENTROPY	iMFCC	29.98
MEAN, STD	CQCC, MFCC, BFCC, NGCC	**17.04**
MEAN, KURTOSIS	CQCC, MFCC, BFCC, NGCC	25.08
SKEW, ENTROPY	CQCC, MFCC, BFCC, LFCC	24.22
SKEW, STD	CQCC, MFCC, BFCC, NGCC	**22.48**
SKEW, KURTOSIS	iMFCC	24.07
KURTOSIS, ENTROPY	CQCC, MFCC, BFCC, NGCC	28.65
KURTOSIS, STD	CQCC, MFCC, BFCC, NGCC	**22.93**
ENTROPY, STD	CQCC, MFCC, BFCC, NGCC	24.32
MEAN, STD, SKEW	CQCC, MFCC, BFCC, NGCC	**18.56**
MEAN, STD, KURTOSIS	CQCC, MFCC, BFCC, NGCC	**18.42**
MEAN, STD, ENTROPY	CQCC, MFCC, BFCC, NGCC	**18.46**
MEAN, STD, SKEW, KURTOSIS	CQCC, MFCC, BFCC, NGCC	**20.37**
MEAN, STD, SKEW, ENTROPY	CQCC, MFCC, BFCC, NGCC	**18.39**

Observing Table 3, we notice that there is a predominance regarding the configuration of $\mathcal{P}$ to H_1 since the set of four techniques CQCC, MFCC, BFCC, and NGCC obtained the best value of EER in 19 of the 25 configurations considered for $\mathcal{M}$. Furthermore, only this configuration was able to present EER values smaller than the values obtained by $B01$ and $B02$ over H_1. In fact, it is worth mentioning that this fact occurred for half of the configurations of $\mathcal{M}$, presenting 16.21% as the best EER value for the case where $\mathcal{M}$ is composed only by the sum and the standard deviation.

Table 4. EER metric obtained for all evaluated multi-projection configurations. The configuration of P responsible for achieving the best EER value according to the respective configuration of M is presented in the central column. In this case, the pure voice signal and its version by Teager's energy operator are analyzed, corresponding to hypothesis H_2. EER values in bold symbolize lower values than those presented by both baselines B01 and B02.

Configuration for $\mathcal{M}$	Respective best confiuration for $\mathcal{P}$	EER (%)
SUM	CQCC, MFCC, LFCC	27.32
MEAN	iMFCC	28.13
STD	CQCC, MFCC, BFCC, NGCC	**18.18**
SKEW	CQCC, MFCC, BFCC, LFCC	**22.43**
ENTROPY	CQCC, MFCC, BFCC, GFCC	34.56
KURTOSIS	CQCC, NGCC	27.62
SUM, MEAN	CQCC, MFCC, BFCC, LFCC	28.37
SUM, SKEW	CQCC, MFCC, BFCC, LFCC	**22.3**
SUM, STD	CQCC, MFCC, BFCC, LFCC	**18.13**
SUM, KURTOSIS	CQCC, MFCC, BFCC, NGCC	26.06
MEAN, SKEW	CQCC, MFCC, BFCC, LFCC	**21.4**
MEAN, ENTROPY	iMFCC	28.59
MEAN, STD	CQCC, MFCC, BFCC, NGCC	**16.77**
MEAN, KURTOSIS	CQCC, MFCC, BFCC, LFCC	25.69
SKEW, ENTROPY	CQCC, MFCC, BFCC, LFCC	**22.19**
SKEW, STD	CQCC, MFCC, LFCC	**19.74**
SKEW, KURTOSIS	iMFCC	24.09
KURTOSIS, ENTROPY	CQCC, MFCC, BFCC, LFCC	27.68
KURTOSIS, STD	CQCC, MFCC, BFCC	23.47
ENTROPY, STD	CQCC, MFCC, BFCC, LFCC	**20.93**
MEAN, STD, SKEW	CQCC, MFCC, LFCC	**15.02**
MEAN, STD, KURTOSIS	CQCC, MFCC, LFCC	**20.19**
MEAN, STD, ENTROPY	CQCC, MFCC, BFCC, LFCC	**18.6**
MEAN, STD, SKEW, KURTOSIS	CQCC, MFCC, LFCC	**22.22**
MEAN, STD, SKEW, ENTROPY	CQCC, MFCC, LFCC	**19.03**

Given what is exposed in Table 4, we observe that the use of Teager's energy operator on the voice signal as presented in the Algorithm 1, which configures H_2, was able to aid the method to obtain better results than those presented under the conditions of H_1. Specifically, it is possible to note that the best EER value obtained, which is 15.02%, occurs when we consider mean, standard deviation, and skewness projections for $\mathcal{M}$, and as $\mathcal{P}$ the CQCC, MFCC, and LFCC techniques. We can also note that, according to H_2, some configurations of $\mathcal{P}$ with less than four techniques were able to outperform the baselines. Specifically, when $\mathcal{P}$ is formed by the CQCC, MFCC, and LFCC techniques, four multi-projection configurations can make the proposed framework present EER lower than 23%. This indicates that, with the use of the features obtained with Teager's energy operator on the pure signal, the number of techniques needed to compose $\mathcal{M}$ and $\mathcal{P}$ can be reduced without impairing the representation capacity of the method. In detail, Fig. 3 shows histograms that indicate for how many configurations of $\mathcal{M}$ a given configuration of $\mathcal{P}$ achieved the best result in terms of EER for H_1, in (a), and for H_2, in (b).

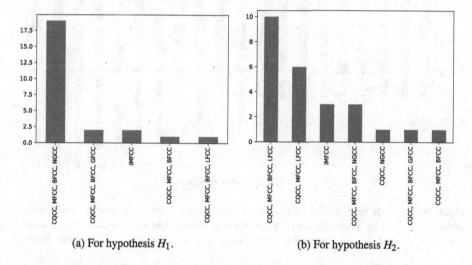

(a) For hypothesis H_1.   (b) For hypothesis H_2.

Fig. 3. Number of times each configuration of $\mathcal{P}$ reached the best EER value in each configuration of $\mathcal{M}$ according to the constraints of hypothesis H_1, in (a), and H_2, in (b). As an example, $\mathcal{P}$ defined by the CQCC, MFCC, BFCC, and NGCC techniques reached the best EER value in 19 of the 25 multi-projection configurations considered when only the pure signal was used to make the feature vector (H_1).

Let's analyze in more detail the effect of the multi-projection setting that was able to obtain the best result. In this case, it is the joint use of mean, standard deviation, and skewness projections. For this, in Fig. 4, a bar chart is presented with the EER measures for each CC extraction technique and with respect to hypotheses H_1, represented by the blue bars, and H_2, represented by the orange bars, for the configuration in question for $\mathcal{M}$. With this representation, we can see that there is a tendency that, as the number of techniques in $\mathcal{P}$ increases, the EER value tends to be lower than the baseline values. However, there are configurations for $\mathcal{P}$, such as the one formed by the CQCC and NGCC techniques, or even by the CQCC and MFCC techniques, which make the proposed framework outperform the baselines. Furthermore, we point out that the best EER value on the analyzed multi-projection is obtained on H_2 with the use of three techniques: CQCC, MFCC, and LFCC.

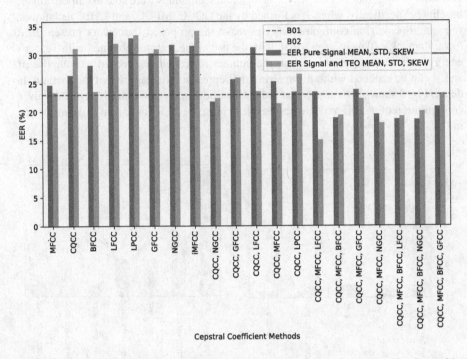

Fig. 4. Bar chart of EER metrics displayed for each configuration of $\mathcal{P}$ setting for the multi-projection defined by mean, standard deviation, and skewness. The values that concern the constraints of H_1 and H_2 are represented, respectively, in blue and orange. (Color figure online)

Similarly, we will analyze the different multi-projection configurations in $\mathcal{M}$ for the set of techniques in $\mathcal{P}$ responsible for helping the framework to present the best EER value in this work. For this, in Fig. 5, a bar chart is presented with the EER values for each configuration of $\mathcal{M}$, considering that $\mathcal{P}$ is formed by the CQCC, MFCC and LFCC techniques and considering the constraints of H_2. In this case, we also noticed that there is a tendency for the bars below the line representing the EER of $B01$ to be associated with configurations of $\mathcal{M}$ composed of more mapping functions. However, it should be noted that just using standard deviation mapping on such a $\mathcal{P}$ configuration is already capable of providing the framework with an EER value lower than those presented by the baselines.

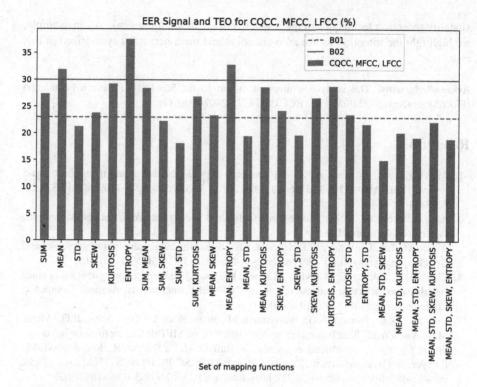

Fig. 5. Bar chart of EER metrics presented for each configuration of M for P defined by the techniques CQCC, MFCC, and LFCC.

5   Conclusion

In this work, a new approach based on multi-projection and fusion of CC for the creation of vector features of sound signals was proposed. Even keeping in mind that the proposal was initially experimental, the material proved to be effective when compared with the baselines for detecting spoofings in VASs. In addition, all developments were conducted on soft computing principles, since the vectorization of the used features allowed the use of classifiers that demand less computational resources without compromising performance.

The proposed framework is mainly parameterized by two sets: $\mathcal{P}$ consisting of CCs extraction techniques; and $\mathcal{M}$ composed of mapping techniques. The presented material is, to the best of our knowledge, a first experimental approach with respect to the projection and fusion of CCs features in the treated theme. In addition, the proposed material was evaluated against a large number of configurations, which could prove its robustness and versatility in the problem in question.

In future work, we intend to employ the concept of multi-filtering by Contreras et al. [6] in our framework in order to enrich the representation capacity of the constructed features, since certain filtering can act in a specific way on legitimate signals and on fake signals. Furthermore, we intend to evaluate the functioning of other dimensionality reduction techniques in the respective stage of the framework. As an example, we highlight the intention to use auto-encoders and meta-heuristics specialized in this task.

Acknowledgments. This study was financed in part by the São Paulo Research Foundation (FAPESP), processes #22/05186-4 (RCC) and #21/12407-4 (RCG).

References

1. Abdul, Z.K., Al-Talabani, A.K.: Mel frequency cepstral coefficient and its applications: a review. IEEE Access **10**, 122136–122158 (2022). https://doi.org/10.1109/ACCESS.2022. 3223444
2. Alim, S.A., Rashid, N.K.A.: Some Commonly Used Speech Feature Extraction Algorithms. IntechOpen, London (2018)
3. Assefi, M., Liu, G., Wittie, M.P., Izurieta, C.: An experimental evaluation of apple Siri and Google speech recognition. In: Proceedings of the 2015 ISCA SEDE 118 (2015)
4. Chandra, E., Sunitha, C.: A review on speech and speaker authentication system using voice signal feature selection and extraction. In: 2009 IEEE International Advance Computing Conference, pp. 1341–1346. IEEE (2009)
5. Contreras, R.C., Nonato, L.G., Boaventura, M., Boaventura, I.A.G., Coelho, B.G., Viana, M.S.: A new multi-filter framework with statistical dense SIFT descriptor for spoofing detection in fingerprint authentication systems. In: Rutkowski, L., Scherer, R., Korytkowski, M., Pedrycz, W., Tadeusiewicz, R., Zurada, J.M. (eds.) ICAISC 2021. LNCS (LNAI), vol. 12855, pp. 442–455. Springer, Cham (2021). https://doi.org/10.1007/978-3-030-87897-9_39
6. Contreras, R.C., et al.: A new multi-filter framework for texture image representation improvement using set of pattern descriptors to fingerprint liveness detection. IEEE Access **10**, 117681–117706 (2022). https://doi.org/10.1109/ACCESS.2022.3218335
7. De Leon, P.L., Pucher, M., Yamagishi, J., Hernaez, I., Saratxaga, I.: Evaluation of speaker verification security and detection of HMM-based synthetic speech. IEEE Trans. Audio Speech Lang. Process. **20**(8), 2280–2290 (2012)
8. Delgado, H., et al.: ASVspoof 2017 version 2.0: meta-data analysis and baseline enhancements. In: Odyssey 2018-The Speaker and Language Recognition Workshop (2018)
9. Ergünay, S.K., Khoury, E., Lazaridis, A., Marcel, S.: On the vulnerability of speaker verification to realistic voice spoofing. In: 2015 IEEE 7th International Conference on Biometrics Theory, Applications and Systems (BTAS), pp. 1–6. IEEE (2015)
10. Folorunso, C., Asaolu, O., Popoola, O.: A review of voice-base person identification: state-of-the-art. Covenant J. Eng. Technol. (2019)
11. Font, R., Espín, J.M., Cano, M.J.: Experimental analysis of features for replay attack detection-results on the ASVspoof 2017 challenge. In: Interspeech, pp. 7–11 (2017)
12. Gao, W., Su, C.: Analysis on block chain financial transaction under artificial neural network of deep learning. J. Comput. Appl. Math. **380**, 112991 (2020)
13. Guido, R.C.: A tutorial on signal energy and its applications. Neurocomputing **179**, 264–282 (2016)
14. Guido, R.C.: ZCR-aided neurocomputing: a study with applications. Knowl.-Based Syst. **105**, 248–269 (2016)
15. Guido, R.C.: Enhancing teager energy operator based on a novel and appealing concept: signal mass. J. Franklin Inst. **356**(4), 1341–1354 (2018)
16. Guido, R.C.: A tutorial-review on entropy-based handcrafted feature extraction for information fusion. Inf. Fusion **41**, 161–175 (2018)

17. Hautamäki, R.G., Kinnunen, T., Hautamäki, V., Leino, T., Laukkanen, A.M.: I-vectors meet imitators: on vulnerability of speaker verification systems against voice mimicry. In: Interspeech, pp. 930–934 (2013)
18. Herrera, A., Del Rio, F.: Frequency bark cepstral coefficients extraction for speech analysis by synthesis. J. Acoust. Soc. Am. **128**(4), 2290–2290 (2010)
19. Jain, A., Nandakumar, K., Ross, A.: Score normalization in multimodal biometric systems. Pattern Recogn. **38**(12), 2270–2285 (2005)
20. Kepuska, V., Bohouta, G.: Next-generation of virtual personal assistants (Microsoft Cortana, Apple Siri, Amazon Alexa and Google Home). In: 2018 IEEE 8th Annual Computing and communication Workshop and Conference (CCWC), pp. 99–103. IEEE (2018)
21. Kersta, L.G.: Voiceprint identification. J. Acoust. Soc. Am. **34**(5), 725–725 (1962)
22. Khoury, E., El Shafey, L., Marcel, S.: SPEAR: an open source toolbox for speaker recognition based on bob. In: 2014 IEEE International Conference on Acoustics, Speech and Signal Processing (ICASSP), pp. 1655–1659. IEEE (2014)
23. Kumar, C., Ur Rehman, F., Kumar, S., Mehmood, A., Shabir, G.: Analysis of MFCC and BFCC in a speaker identification system. In: 2018 International Conference on Computing, Mathematics and Engineering Technologies (iCoMET), pp. 1–5. IEEE (2018)
24. Li, B., et al.: Acoustic modeling for google home. In: Interspeech, pp. 399–403 (2017)
25. Liu, C., Yuen, J., Torralba, A.: Sift flow: dense correspondence across scenes and its applications. IEEE Trans. Pattern Anal. Mach. Intell. **33**(5), 978–994 (2010)
26. Lopatovska, I., et al.: Talk to me: exploring user interactions with the Amazon Alexa. J. Librariansh. Inf. Sci. **51**(4), 984–997 (2019)
27. Memon, Q., AlKassim, Z., AlHassan, E., Omer, M., Alsiddig, M.: Audio-visual biometric authentication for secured access into personal devices. In: Proceedings of the 6th International Conference on Bioinformatics and Biomedical Science, pp. 85–89 (2017)
28. Mohammad, S.M., Surya, L.: Security automation in information technology. Int. J. Creat. Res. Thoughts (IJCRT) **6** (2018)
29. Prabakaran, D., Shyamala, R.: A review on performance of voice feature extraction techniques. In: 2019 3rd International Conference on Computing and Communications Technologies (ICCCT), pp. 221–231. IEEE (2019)
30. Rao, K.S., Reddy, V.R., Maity, S.: Language Identification Using Spectral and Prosodic Features. SECE, Springer, Cham (2015). https://doi.org/10.1007/978-3-319-17163-0
31. Rui, Z., Yan, Z.: A survey on biometric authentication: toward secure and privacy-preserving identification. IEEE access **7**, 5994–6009 (2018)
32. Sahidullah, M., Kinnunen, T., Hanilçi, C.: A comparison of features for synthetic speech detection (2015)
33. Sanchez, J., Saratxaga, I., Hernaez, I., Navas, E., Erro, D., Raitio, T.: Toward a universal synthetic speech spoofing detection using phase information. IEEE Trans. Inf. Forensics Secur. **10**(4), 810–820 (2015)
34. Senk, C., Dotzler, F.: Biometric authentication as a service for enterprise identity management deployment: a data protection perspective. In: 2011 Sixth International Conference on Availability, Reliability and Security, pp. 43–50. IEEE (2011)
35. Tait, B.L.: Applied phon curve algorithm for improved voice recognition and authentication. In: Georgiadis, C.K., Jahankhani, H., Pimenidis, E., Bashroush, R., Al-Nemrat, A. (eds.) e-Democracy/ICGS3 -2011. LNICST, vol. 99, pp. 23–30. Springer, Heidelberg (2012). https://doi.org/10.1007/978-3-642-33448-1_4
36. Todisco, M., Delgado, H., Evans, N.: Constant Q cepstral coefficients: a spoofing countermeasure for automatic speaker verification. Comput. Speech Lang. **45**, 516–535 (2017)
37. Todisco, M., et al.: ASVspoof 2019: future horizons in spoofed and fake audio detection. arXiv preprint arXiv:1904.05441 (2019)

38. Valero, X., Alias, F.: Gammatone cepstral coefficients: biologically inspired features for non-speech audio classification. IEEE Trans. Multimedia **14**(6), 1684–1689 (2012)
39. Wang, X., et al.: ASVspoof 2019: a large-scale public database of synthesized, converted and replayed speech. Comput. Speech Lang. **64**, 101114 (2020)
40. Wang, X., Yan, Z., Zhang, R., Zhang, P.: Attacks and defenses in user authentication systems: a survey. J. Netw. Comput. Appl. **188**, 103080 (2021)
41. Wang, Z.F., Wei, G., He, Q.H.: Channel pattern noise based playback attack detection algorithm for speaker recognition. In: 2011 International Conference on Machine Learning and Cybernetics. vol. 4, pp. 1708–1713. IEEE (2011)
42. Wu, Z., Chng, E.S., Li, H.: Detecting converted speech and natural speech for anti-spoofing attack in speaker recognition. In: Thirteenth Annual Conference of the International Speech Communication Association (2012)
43. Yan, C., Ji, X., Wang, K., Jiang, Q., Jin, Z., Xu, W.: A survey on voice assistant security: attacks and countermeasures. ACM Comput. Surv. **55**(4), 1–36 (2022)
44. Zouhir, Y., Ouni, K.: Feature extraction method for improving speech recognition in noisy environments. J. Comput. Sci. **12**(2), 56–61 (2016)

Mining Correlated High-Utility Itemsets Using the Cosine Measure

Huynh Anh Duy, Huynh Anh Khoa, and Phan Duy Hung[(✉)]

FPT University, Hanoi, Vietnam
{duyhahe153764,khoahahe153759}@fpt.edu.vn, hungpd2@fe.edu.vn

Abstract. High utility itemset mining (HUIM) is a problem posed to find itemsets in transaction database with high utility. However, using only utility as selection criterion makes most of the found itemsets have a very low correlation between their items, therefore it cannot be effectively applied in practice. Fast correlation high-utility itemset miner (FCHM) is an efficiency algorithm that applies correlation to HUIM problem to discover correlated high-utility itemsets (CHIs). The correlation measures used in FCHM include bond and all-confidence. This paper proposes a new version of FCHM algorithm by using cosine measure to calculate correlation between items which is FCHM$_{cosine}$. Experimental results on three benchmark real-life datasets show that the proposed algorithm not only significantly reduces weakly correlated itemsets but also improves running time and memory consumption.

Keyword: High-utility itemset mining · correlated high-utility itemsets · correlation · cosine measure

1 Introduction

HUIM [1–4] is a problem that evolved from the basics problem of Frequent itemset mining (FIM) [5]. For HUIM, each item will be assigned a value that represents their subjective measure, which can simply be understood as the utility or profit that item brings. Instead of looking for frequently occurring itemsets like in FIM, HUIM will look for itemsets that offer high utility. This approach is clearly more valuable when applied to practical problems where profit is a top priority.

HUIM is widely applied in real-world problems, however, it is also a more complex problem than FIM because of performance issues. The anti-monotonic property is considered to be the core factor to effectively solve FIM algorithms, but this property cannot be applied to the HUIM problem. This makes solving HUIM become very computationally expensive. Many algorithms have been proposed to improve this problem such as: Two-Phase [4], IHUP [6], UP-Growth [7], UP-Growth+ [3], HUI-Miner [2], FHM [1]. Among them, FHM is considered as one of the most efficient algorithms.

Besides performance constraints, the quality of the itemsets found is also an important issue with HUIM problems. Using utility as the only criteria of selection makes the result contains many itemsets that have high utility, but the correlation between items in these

L. Rutkowski et al. (Eds.): ICAISC 2023, LNAI 14126, pp. 307–319, 2023.
https://doi.org/10.1007/978-3-031-42508-0_28

itemsets is very low. The use of these itemsets in real life problem such as business will not bring the expected effect for users, even loss. Therefore, the CHIM problem was proposed to solve this problem. FCHM [8] is an improved version of FHM and also one of the most efficient algorithms in the CHIM area.

This work proposes a new version of FCHM algorithm named $FCHM_{cosine}$. The $FCHM_{cosine}$ algorithm uses a null-invariant measure which is the cosine measure to evaluate the correlation between items. Besides, some pruning strategies in previous version of FCHM algorithm are also applied to improve performance. Experimental results on three bench mark real-life datasets show that the proposed algorithm eliminates a large amount of weakly correlated itemsets compared to FHM algorithm and in some cases improve performance compared to other versions of FCHM algorithm including $FCHM_{bond}$ and $FCHM_{all-confidence}$.

2 Related Works

In recent years CHIM is an area that has received a lot of attention with many algorithms and prune strategies are proposed. Some of these works are described below:

Paper [8] proposes the FCHM algorithm. This algorithm is an upgrade of the FHM algorithm by combining the correlation factor to find itemsets that satisfy both high utility and high correlation. The author used the bond measure and took advantage of its anti-monotonicity property to significantly reduce the computational cost. Experimental result shows that $FCHM_{bond}$ can discover more than five orders of magnitude less patterns compare to FHM due to eliminate weakly correlated itemsets, $FCHM_{bond}$ is also two orders of magnitude faster than FHM.

Another version of FCHM algorithm is presented in paper [9]. Here the author uses all-confidence measure for FCHM algorithm, thereby present $FCHM_{all-confidence}$. The all-confidence measure is used because this measure also has the same anti-monotonicity property as the bond measure. Besides, several prune methods corresponding to each measure are applied. Experimental results show that both versions of FCHM reduce running time by considering only high correlation itemsets. However, the $FCHM_{bond}$ version is said to consume more memory because of using disjunctive bit vectors.

Paper [10] is the first paper that use a null-invariant measure to find high utility itemsets. The author developed an algorithm named CoHUIM based on a project-based approach to reduce search space and memory usage. The measure used is Kulczynsky measure (Kulc). Although this measure does not have an anti-monotonicity property, the author has introduced another property that can also help prune candidates effectively which is the sorted downward closure property. Experimental results show that the algorithm returns a smaller number of itemsets but carries more valuable information to the user. Runtime and memory of this algorithm are also within acceptable thresholds.

In [11], the author proposes CoUPM algorithm to find itemsets that satisfy both utility threshold and correlation threshold using Kulc measure. The author has taken advantage of the downward closure property of Kulc measure to increase the performance of the algorithm. In addition, CoUPM also introduces revised utility list, which helps the algorithm does not need to go through the entire database several times. Experiments on many real-world datasets show that CoUPM works well in terms of both effectiveness and efficiency.

The author in [12] proposed a single phase algorithm named CoHUI-Miner to find correlated high utility patterns. This algorithm uses the database projection mechanism to reduce the database size. Beside that a new concept is introduced called the prefix utility of projected transactions. This new concept helps to effectively eliminate patterns which do not meet the minimum threshold during the mining process. Experiments on many datasets of different types show that the proposed algorithm has better performance than the CoHUIM algorithm [10].

From all above study, it can be seen that the common point of CHIM algorithms is that the measure must satisfy some properties that support the process of pruning candidates. Besides, it is also necessary to apply suitable strategies for each different measure to improve the performance of the algorithm. Therefore, finding other measures that satisfy the above conditions will help expand the limit of usable measures, thereby facilitating the improvement of both effectiveness and efficiency of the CHIM algorithms in general.

3   Method

3.1   Preliminaries

Definition 1. Transaction database

Let $I = \{i_1, i_2, ..., i_m\}$ be the set of items, a set of items T satisfy $T \subseteq I$ is called a transaction. A transaction database D is the set containing all transactions in the dataset. Each item will have two utility properties including internal utility, denoted as $q(i)$ and external utility, denoted as $p(i)$. Internal utility shows the quantity of that item in a transaction and external utility shows the unit profit of that item. Table 1 presents a sample of transaction database, Table 2 presents the external utility of items.

Table 1. An example of transaction database

TID	Transaction	Quantity
T_1	{a,b,d}	{2,3,1}
T_2	{a,c,e,f}	{4,2,7,3}
T_3	{b,f}	{2,6}
T_4	{c,d,g}	{1,3,4}
T_5	{a,c,e,g,h}	{2,5,2,1,1}

Table 2. Unit profit of items

Item	a	b	c	d	e	f	g	h
Profit	7	2	2	6	2	1	7	5

Definition 2. Utility value of an item and utility value of an itemset

- The utility of item i in transaction T_k is denoted and calculated as

$$u(i, T_k) = p(i) \times q(i, T_k)$$

    where $q(i, T_k)$ is the internal utility of item i in transaction T_k
- The utility of itemset X in transaction T_k is denoted and calculated as

$$u(X, T_k) = \sum_{i \in X} u(i, T_k)$$

- The utility of itemset X in transaction database D is denoted and calculated as

$$u(X) = \sum_{T_k \in D} u(X, T_k)$$

Definition 3. High utility itemset mining problem
The HUIM problem is the field of finding all high utility itemsets (HUIs) that satisfy a user-defined utility threshold. (*minUtil*).

Definition 4. Support
Support value of itemset X in transaction database D is defined as

$$support(X) = |\{T_k | T_k \in D \land X \subseteq T_k\}|$$

Definition 5. Correlated high utility itemset
An itemset is considered to be correlated high utility itemset if and only if it satisfies the following two conditions:

- Is an HUIs
- *Correlation measure $\geq$ Minimum correlation threshold (minCore)*

Definition 6. Correlated high utility itemset mining (CHIM)
The CHIM problem is the field of using appropriate correlation measure to find all CHIs that satisfy a user-defined utility threshold and correlation threshold.

3.2 FCHM Algorithm

FCHM is an efficiency CHIM algorithm first proposed in 2016 [8]. In general, the FCHM algorithm uses TWU (Transaction-Weighted Utilization) [1] and some structures such as EUCS (Estimated Utility Co-Occurrence Structure) [1], utility-list [1] to prune search space and improved performance in terms of utility. In terms of correlation, FCHM algorithm has two versions corresponding to two different measures used including bond and all-confidence [9]. The prune search space is made efficiently by taking advantage of the anti-monotonicity property of these two measures. Besides, for each measure, the author also uses other appropriate prune strategies to improve algorithm performance.

3.3 Proposed Approach

Cosine measure is a measure used to calculate correlation between items. The formula of cosine measure is defined as in [13] and [14].

- In the case we have two items A_1 and A_2, the cosine measure of these two items is calculated as:

$$cosine(A_1, A_2) = \frac{P(A_1 \cup A_2)}{\sqrt{P(A_1) \times P(A_2)}} = \frac{sup(A_1 \cup A_2)}{\sqrt{sup(A_1) \times sup(A_2)}}$$

- In the case we have more than two items, the cosine measure is extended as:

$$cosine(A_1, A_2, \ldots, A_n) = \frac{P(A_1 \cup A_2 \cup \cdots \cup A_n)}{\sqrt{P(A_1) \times P(A_2) \times \cdots \times P(A_n)}}$$
$$= \frac{sup(A_1 \cup A_2 \cup \cdots \cup A_n)}{\sqrt{sup(A_1) \times sup(A_2) \times \cdots \times sup(A_n)}}$$

This paper proposes another version of the FCHM algorithm named FCHM$_{cosine}$, which uses the cosine measure as the correlation measure for the FCHM algorithm. The two main reasons the cosine measure is preferred in this work are:

- Cosine measure is a null-invariant measure [14, 15].
- Cosine measure has the anti-monotonicity property (1)

Proof for Statement (1):
From definition, we have

$$cosine(A_1, A_2, \ldots, A_n) = \frac{sup(A_1 \cup A_2 \cup \ldots A_n)}{\sqrt{sup(A_1) \times sup(A_2) \times \ldots \times sup(A_n)}} (*)$$

$$cosine(A_1, A_2, \ldots, A_n, A_{n+1})$$
$$= \frac{sup(A_1 \cup A_2 \cup \ldots \cup A_n \cup A_{n+1})}{\sqrt{sup(A_1) \times sup(A_2) \times \ldots \times sup(A_n) \times sup(A_{n+1})}} (**)$$

Since $sup(A_1 \cup A_2 \cup \cdots \cup A_n) \geq sup(A_1 \cup A_2 \cup \cdots \cup A_n \cup A_{n+1})$ and $\sqrt{sup(A_1) \times sup(A_2) \times \cdots \times sup(A_n)} \leq \sqrt{sup(A_1) \times sup(A_2) \times \cdots \times sup(A_n) \times sup(A_{n+1})}$ then we can conclude that $(*) \geq (**)$. (2).

Denote *minimum cosine threshold* as α, from (2) we have:

$$cosine(A_1, A_2, \ldots, A_n) < \alpha \Rightarrow cosine(A_1, A_2, \ldots, A_n, A_{n+1}) < \alpha$$

This means if the itemset does not satisfy *minimum cosine α*, it is no need to traverse its superset.

From the definition, the calculation of the *cosine(X)* value of an itemset X is depend on the product of support value of all 1-items in itemset X and the support value of itemset X. To optimize performance, this product is calculated during the construction of the utility lists in FCHM algorithm. Specifically in the Construct procedure [8, 9], when the utility-list of itemset Pxy is constructed from utility-list of Px and utility-list of Py, this product can be calculated as $product(Pxy) = product(Px) \times product(Py)$ if prefix P is null, else $product(Pxy) = \frac{product(Px) \times product(Py)}{product(P)}$. Since support value of itemset X can be derived easily from utility list, the $cosine(X)$ can be obtained efficiently.

These two following strategies from previous version of FCHM are also applied to further improve the performance of the $FCHM_{cosine}$ algorithm: Directly Outputting Single items (DOS) and Pruning Supersets of Non correlated itemsets (PSN) [8, 9].

4   Experiments and Analyze

The algorithms and all experiments are carried out in the environment with the following configuration: Intel(R) Core™ I3, 2.40 GHz, memory capacity: 4 GB, operating system: Microsoft Windows 10, programming language: Java. The experiments used three evaluation criteria including effectiveness, runtime and memory consumption. The $FCHM_{cosine}$ algorithm is in turn compared with the traditional HUIM algorithm which is FHM and some CHIM algorithms including $FCHM_{bond}$ and $FCHM_{all-confidence}$. Several experiments are performed under various parameter. Specifically, parameters are set up by fixing $minUtil$ varying $minCor$ and fixing $minCor$ varying $minUtil$. Three benchmark datasets are used: foodmart, mushroom, retail. Each dataset represents a particular type of data, making the experiment more general. These datasets are downloaded from the SPMF open-source data mining library [16]. Table 3 shows the information of these datasets.

Table 3. Dataset's characteristic

Dataset	No. of distinct items	No. of transactions	Average transaction length	Type
Foodmart	21,556	1,559	4.4	sparse with short transactions
Mushroom	88,162	16,470	23	dense
Retail	88,162	16,470	10.3	sparse with many items

4.1   Effectiveness Analysis

Table 4 compares the number of patterns between $FCHM_{cosine}$ algorithm and FHM algorithm. $FCHM_{cosine}$ with *minimum correlation* α is denoted as C_α. The various *minimum utility* value for each dataset is represented by the parameters from a_1 to a_5. In addition, the comparison between patterns count of the $FCHM_{cosine}$, $FCHM_{bond}$ and $FCHM_{all-confidence}$ is also performed in Fig. 1 and Fig. 2.

Table 4. Compare patterns count with FHM

Dataset	Algorithm	Number of patterns				
		a_1	a_2	a_3	a_4	a_5
foodmart	**FHM**	233,231	231,904	219,012	154,670	59,351
	$C_{0.01}$	101,629	100,303	87,966	36,252	3,274
	$C_{0.02}$	81,511	80,222	68,745	25,409	2,530
	$C_{0.03}$	48,912	47,687	3,7667	10,546	2,063
	$C_{0.04}$	41,674	40,457	30,759	7,262	1,847
	$C_{0.1}$	9,659	9,453	7,804	3,486	1,676
mushroom	**FHM**	1,045,780	585,013	273,448	179,215	92,656
	$C_{0.005}$	1740	1379	921	711	435
	$C_{0.008}$	501	406	303	253	178
	$C_{0.01}$	207	140	85	59	37
	$C_{0.1}$	161	109	63	40	20
	$C_{0.4}$	160	109	63	40	20
retail	**FHM**	14,045	13,017	12,103	11,234	10,479
	$C_{0.1}$	1910	1820	-1741	1651	1575
	$C_{0.12}$	1852	1765	1687	1598	1523
	$C_{0.14}$	1812	1728	1650	1562	1488
	$C_{0.16}$	1779	1696	1619	1533	1461
	$C_{0.4}$	1,490	1,482	1,470	1,455	1,445

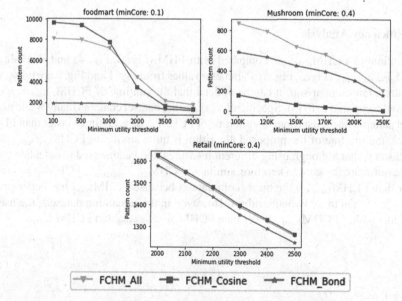

Fig. 1. Compare pattern count with other versions (varying *minUtil*, fixing *minCore*)

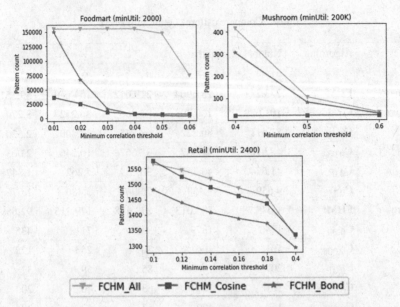

Fig. 2. Compare pattern count with other versions (varying *minCore*, fixing *minUtil*)

From Table 4, it can be seen that the proposed algorithm helps to reduce a large number of weakly correlated patterns compared to the traditional HUIM algorithm FHM. Besides, Fig. 1 and Fig. 2 show that the number of patterns generated by the proposed algorithm is generally quite similar to the previous two versions of the FCHM algorithm. Except for the mushroom dataset, $FCHM_{cosine}$ returns significantly less patterns at small *minUtil* and *minCore*. This shows that the constraint set by the proposed algorithm can be considered tighter than previous versions in some cases.

4.2 Efficiency Analysis

The runtime of $FCHM_{cosine}$ is compared with FHM (Fig. 3, Fig. 4) and $FCHM_{bond}$, $FCHM_{all-confidence}$ (Fig. 5, Fig. 6). Parameter values from Fig. 1 and Fig. 2 are preserved to ensure a fair comparison. It can be noticed that the runtime of $FCHM_{cosine}$ is much improved compared to FHM. Specifically, in case the dataset contains many weakly correlated patterns like mushroom, the runtime of $FCHM_{cosine}$ is 20 times faster than FHM. Besides, the runtime of the proposed algorithm is quite similar to $FCHM_{all-confidence}$. The reason is that although using different measures, the factors used to calculate these two measures are the same. Therefore, similar to $FCHM_{all-confidence}$, $FCHM_{cosine}$ is also slower than $FCHM_{bond}$ in the mushroom dataset because $FCHM_{bond}$ has better prune search space than these two algorithms. However, in the remaining datasets, the use of bit vectors makes $FCHM_{bond}$ slower than $FCHM_{all-confidence}$ and $FCHM_{cosine}$.

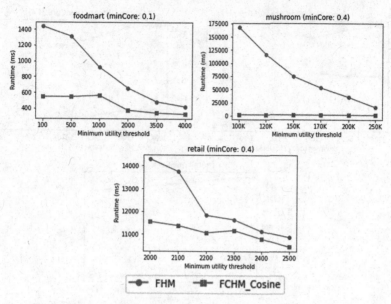

Fig. 3. Compare runtime with FHM (varying *minUtil*, fixing *minCore*)

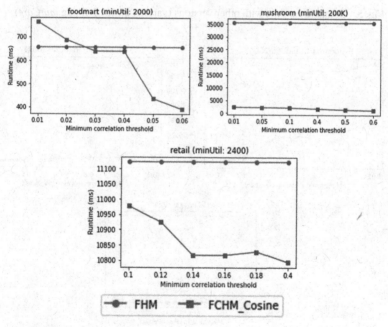

Fig. 4. Compare runtime with FHM (varying *minCore*, fixing *minUtil*)

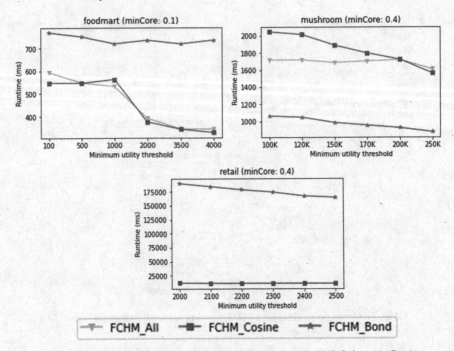

Fig. 5. Compare runtime with other versions (varying *minUtil*, fixing *minCore*)

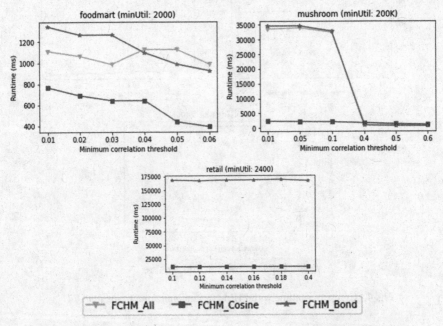

Fig. 6. Compare runtime with other versions (varying *minCore*, fixing *minUtil*)

4.3 Memory Analysis

This section performs a memory evaluation between the compared algorithms above. Parameter values continue to be preserved. The results are shown in Fig. 7 and Fig. 8.

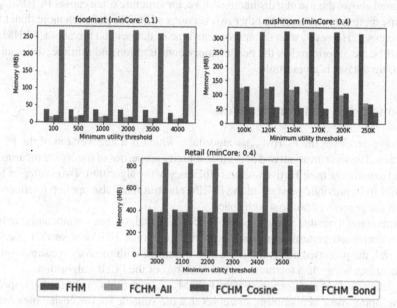

Fig. 7. Compare memory with FHM and other versions (varying *minUtil*, fixing *minCore*)

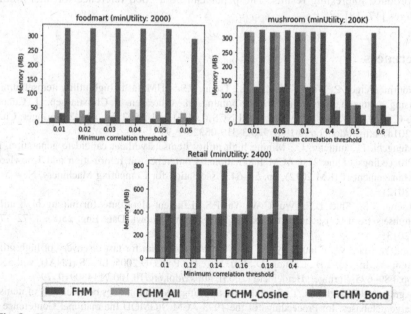

Fig. 8. Compare memory with FHM and other versions (varying *minCore*, fixing *minUtil*)

In general, FCHM$_{all-confidence}$ and FCHM$_{cosine}$ have lower memory consumption than FHM algorithms because they can avoid a huge number of weakly correlated patterns and their measures can also be efficiently calculated. Specifically, the FCHM$_{cosine}$ algorithm is always in the top two algorithms with the lowest memory consumption. Besides, as mentioned above, the use of a disjunctive bit vector structure often causes FCHM$_{bond}$ to consume more memory than the other two versions of FCHM and even more than FHM in some cases. However, with the appropriate type of dataset and threshold, FCHM$_{bond}$ can still be the algorithm has the best memory consumption and runtime, the result on mushroom dataset is an example.

5 Conclusion and Perspectives

This paper proposes the FCHM$_{cosine}$ algorithm, which is a new version of the FCHM algorithm. The null-invariant and anti-monotonicity properties of the cosine measure are utilized to optimize the effectiveness and efficiency of the algorithm. Two strategies DOS and PSN from previous versions of the FCHM algorithm are also applied to effectively support the process of prune search space.

Experimental results show that the FCHM$_{cosine}$ algorithm significantly reduces weakly correlated patterns compared with the traditional HUIM algorithm. Besides, in general, the proposed algorithm has a stable runtime with memory consumption and in some cases better than the previous two versions of the FCHM algorithm.

In future study, the performance of the FCHM$_{cosine}$ algorithm can be further improved by developing some new pruning strategies that are suitable for the cosine measure. In addition, the study of some other measures, especially the null-invariant measures, may also produce interesting results. The paper can be a good reference for data mining problems [17, 18].

References

1. Fournier-Viger, P., Wu, C.-W., Zida, S., Tseng, V.S.: FHM: faster high-utility itemset mining using estimated utility co-occurrence pruning. In: Andreasen, T., Christiansen, H., Cubero, J.-C., Raś, Z.W. (eds.) ISMIS 2014. LNCS (LNAI), vol. 8502, pp. 83–92. Springer, Cham (2014). https://doi.org/10.1007/978-3-319-08326-1_9

2. Mengchi, L., Junfeng, Q.: Mining high utility itemsets without candidate generation. In: Proceedings of the 21st ACM International Conference on Information and Knowledge Management (CIKM 2012), pp. 55–64. Association for Computing Machinery, New York (2012)

3. Tseng, V.S., Shie, B.E., Wu, C.W., Yu, P.S.: Efficient algorithms for mining high utility itemsets from transactional databases. IEEE Trans. Knowl. Data Eng. 25(8), 1772–1786 (2013)

4. Liu, Y., Liao, W., Choudhary, A.: A two-phase algorithm for fast discovery of high utility itemsets. In: Ho, T.B., Cheung, D., Liu, H. (eds.) PAKDD 2005. LNCS (LNAI), vol. 3518, pp. 689–695. Springer, Heidelberg (2005). https://doi.org/10.1007/11430919_79

5. Agrawal, R., Imielinski, T., Swami, A.N.: Mining association rules between sets of items in large databases. In: Proceedings of the 1993 ACM SIGMOD International Conference on Management of Data (ICDM 1993), pp. 207–216 (1993)

6. Ahmed, C.F., Tanbeer, S.K., Jeong, B.-S., Lee, Y.-K.: Efficient tree structures for high utility pattern mining in incremental databases. IEEE Trans. Knowl. Data Eng. **21**(12), 1708–1721 (2009)
7. Tseng, V.S., Wu, C.-W., Shie, B.-E., Yu, P.S.: UP-Growth: an efficient algorithm for high utility itemset mining. In: Proceedings of the 16th ACM SIGKDD International Conference on Knowledge Discovery and Data Mining (KDD 2010), pp. 253–262. Association for Computing Machinery, New York (2010)
8. Fournier-Viger, P., Lin, J.C.-W., Dinh, T., Le, H.B.: Mining correlated high-utility itemsets using the bond measure. In: Martínez-Álvarez, F., Troncoso, A., Quintián, H., Corchado, E. (eds.) HAIS 2016. LNCS (LNAI), vol. 9648, pp. 53–65. Springer, Cham (2016). https://doi.org/10.1007/978-3-319-32034-2_5
9. Philippe, F.-V., Lin, J.C.W., Dinh, T., Le, H.B.: Mining correlated high-utility itemsets using various measures. Logic J. IGPL **28**(1), 19–32 (2020)
10. Gan, W., Lin, J.C.W., Philippe, F.-V., Chao, H.C., Fujita, H.: Extracting non-redundant correlated purchase behaviors by utility measure. Knowl.- Based Syst. **143**, 30–41 (2018)
11. Gan, W., Lin, J.C.W., Chao, H.C., Fujita, H., Yu, P.S.: Correlated utility-based pattern mining. Inf. Sci. **504**, 470–486 (2019). ISSN 0020-0255
12. Vo, B., et al.: Mining correlated high utility itemsets in one phase. IEEE Access **8**, 90465–90477 (2020)
13. Bagui, S., Just, J., Bagui, S.C., Hemashinha, R.: Using a cosine-type measure to derive strong association mining rules. Int. J. Knowl. Eng. Data Min. **1**(1), 69–83 (2010)
14. Han, J., Kamber, M., Pei, J.: Data Mining Concepts and Techniques, 3rd edn., The Morgan Kaufmann Series in Data Management Systems (2011)
15. Tianyi, W., Yuguo, C., Jiawei, H.: Association mining in large databases: a re-examination of its measures. In: Proceedings of the International Conference on Principles and Practice of Knowledge Discovery in Databases (PKDD 2007) (2007)
16. Philippe, F.-V., Gomariz, A., Gueniche, T., Soltani, A., Wu, C., Tseng, V.S.: SPMF: a Java open-source pattern mining library. J. Mach. Learn. Res. **15**, 3389–3393 (2014)
17. Ngoc Tram, N., Duy Hung, P.: Analysing hot Facebook users posts' sentiment using deep learning. In: Hassanien, A.E., Bhattacharyya, S., Chakrabati, S., Bhattacharya, A., Dutta, S. (eds.) Emerging Technologies in Data Mining and Information Security. AISC, vol. 1300, pp. 561–569. Springer, Singapore (2021). https://doi.org/10.1007/978-981-33-4367-2_53
18. Phan, D.H., Do, Q.D.: Analysing effects of customer clustering for customer's account balance forecasting. In: Nguyen, N.T., Hoang, B.H., Huynh, C.P., Hwang, D., Trawiński, B., Vossen, G. (eds.) ICCCI 2020. LNCS (LNAI), vol. 12496, pp. 255–266. Springer, Cham (2020). https://doi.org/10.1007/978-3-030-63007-2_20

Bayesian Inference in Infinite Multivariate McDonald's Beta Mixture Model

Darya Forouzanfar[1]([⊠]) [iD], Narges Manouchehri[1,2] [iD], and Nizar Bouguila[1] [iD]

[1] Concordia University, Concordia Institute for Information Systems Engineering, Montreal, Canada
d_forouz@encs.concordia.ca, nizar.bouguila@concordia.ca
[2] Algorithmic Dynamics Lab, Unit of Computational Medicine, Karolinska Institute, 17177 Stockholm, Sweden
narges.manouchehri@ieee.org

Abstract. This paper presents a nonparametric Bayesian technique to overcome the challenge of selecting the appropriate number of mixture components for clustering. Our approach extends the finite McDonald's Beta mixture model (FMcDBMM) to an infinite one, allowing us to effectively capture the underlying data distribution with an unknown number of mixture components. Specifically, we use a Dirichlet process prior that enables us to infer the number of mixture components and cluster assignments simultaneously. Additionally, our Bayesian learning approach leverages MCMC techniques for posterior estimation, making our proposed framework powerful and flexible for modelling and analyzing complex data. To demonstrate the effectiveness of our approach, we evaluated the proposed framework on two challenging real-world applications and compared its performance to Gaussian mixture model (GMM) and FMcDBMM. The results show the merits of our model.

Keywords: Multivariate McDonald's Beta distribution · Infinite mixture model · Nonparametric Bayesian inference · Dirichlet process

1 Introduction

Data mining and machine learning techniques have made a significant impact on various scientific and industrial fields [13]. The development of more sophisticated and efficient algorithms to uncover hidden patterns, make predictions, and facilitate decision-making becomes increasingly important. Among the myriad of machine learning techniques, clustering plays a crucial role in partitioning data points into distinct groups based on their similarities [14]. Gaussian Mixture Models (GMMs) have been a popular choice for clustering tasks due to their ability to model complex data distributions [21]. However, GMMs have several limitations, one of which is the requirement to specify the number of clusters a priori, which is often unknown in real-world scenarios [18]. Traditional

L. Rutkowski et al. (Eds.): ICAISC 2023, LNAI 14126, pp. 320–330, 2023.
https://doi.org/10.1007/978-3-031-42508-0_29

model parameter estimation techniques, such as maximum likelihood (ML) and Expectation-Maximization (EM), provide limited flexibility in estimating model complexity, including the number of clusters [5]. These deterministic methods can lead to overfitting and local optima issues, which may result in lower performance in clustering tasks [5].

In the context of medical applications, clustering and mixture models have been employed to identify patterns in patient data, which can aid in the early diagnosis and treatment of various conditions, Specifically diseases such as cancer [10,22]. Additionally, clustering techniques have been applied to human activity recognition, where the objective is to classify different types of activities based on sensor data [26]. Accurate human activity recognition is essential for a wide range of applications, including healthcare, sports, and security [20]. In this paper, we present an infinite multivariate McDonald's Beta mixture model (IMcDBMM), a novel approach that extends the finite mixture model using a mixture of Dirichlet processes [1]. Our model overcomes the limitations of GMM by incorporating a Bayesian learning framework that employs Markov Chain Monte Carlo (MCMC) using its two sampling methods, Gibbs sampling and Metropolis-Hastings algorithm (M-H), to learn this model and estimate the parameters [2]. A key advantage of our approach is the automatic estimation of model's complexity, which includes the number of clusters, allowing for more accurate and meaningful results in real-world applications [9]. The mixture of Dirichlet processes, an essential component of our model, provides the foundation for adaptively estimating the number of clusters present in the data without prior knowledge [11]. This flexibility enables the model to better represent the underlying structure of the data and improve the performance of clustering tasks [6].

Our proposed infinite mixture model is applied to two specific domains: medical diagnostics, with a focus on lung cancer diagnosis, and human activity recognition by the use of scale-invariant feature transform and Bag of Visual Words to extract features from the images [16,17]. By leveraging the strengths of Bayesian learning and the flexibility of infinite mixture models, our approach addresses the limitations of traditional GMM, particularly in terms of model selection, and demonstrates its potential to enhance the performance of clustering tasks in these critical applications. In summary, this paper introduces an infinite mixture model that combines the strengths of Bayesian learning with the mixture of Dirichlet processes for automatic model complexity estimation in clustering tasks. The application of our approach to medical diagnostics, specifically lung cancer diagnosis and human activity recognition, underscores its versatility and efficacy in real-world scenarios, making it a valuable contribution to the field of data mining and machine learning.

The paper is organized as follows: Sect. 2 presents the model specifications, the finite mixture model structure and the integration of the feature selection into the mixture model. Afterward, Sect. 3 explains the Bayesian learning framework and the extension of the finite model to the infinite case. In Sect. 4, we discuss the experimental results from two real-world applications: Lung Cancer Analysis and Human Activity Recognition and compare the results with other methods. Finally, the paper concludes in Sect. 5.

2   Model Specification

2.1   McDonald's Beta Distribution

Let us consider a D-dimensional data point $\vec{X}_n$, represented by $(x_{n1}, \ldots, x_{nd})$, that follows the McDonald's Beta distribution (McBD), which is characterized by four shape parameters [4]: $\vec{a}_j = (a_{j1}, \ldots, a_{jD})$, $\vec{b}_j = (b_{j1}, \ldots, b_{jD})$, $\vec{p}_j = (p_{j1}, \ldots, p_{jD})$, $\vec{q}_j = (q_{j1}, \ldots, q_{jD})$. It is worth noting that the values of $a_{jd} > 0$, $b_{jd} > 0$, $p_{jd} > 0$ for $d = 1, \ldots, D$ are all greater than zero. Additionally, $0 \leq x_{nd} \leq q_{jd}$, $q_{jd} > 0$, where $q_{jd} > 0$ is greater than zero for $d = 1, \ldots, D$. For the purpose of this study, we have made the assumption that q equals 1 in order to constrain the support of the data between zero and one. Consequently, the joint density function of the observation with this assumption is defined as:

$$p(\vec{X}_n \mid \vec{a}_j, \vec{b}_j, \vec{p}_j, \vec{q}_j) = \prod_{d=1}^{D} \frac{p_{jd} x_{nd}^{a_{jd} p_{jd} - 1} (1 - x_{nd}^{p_{jd}})^{b_{jd} - 1}}{B(a_{jd}, b_{jd})} \tag{1}$$

where $B(a_{jd}, b_{jd}) = \int_0^1 t^{a_{jd} - 1}(1 - t)^{b_{jd} - 1} dt = \frac{\Gamma(a_{jd})\Gamma(b_{jd})}{\Gamma(a_{jd} + b_{jd})}$. By setting the values of both q and p in McBD to 1, we can observe that the resulting distribution takes the form of a Beta distribution.

2.2   Finite McDonald's Beta Mixture Model

As our next step, we will present the FMcDBMM with M components and N independent and identically distributed observations with D dimensions:

$$p(\mathcal{X} \mid \Theta) = \prod_{n=1}^{N} \left[\sum_{j=1}^{M} w_j p(\vec{X}_n \mid \vec{\theta}_j) \right]$$

$$= \prod_{n=1}^{N} \left[\sum_{j=1}^{M} w_j \prod_{d=1}^{D} \frac{p_{jd} x_{nd}^{a_{jd} p_{jd} - 1} (1 - x_{nd}^{p_{jd}})^{b_{jd} - 1}}{B(a_{jd}, b_{jd})} \right] \tag{2}$$

where w_j and $\vec{\theta}_j = (\vec{a}_j, \vec{b}_j, \vec{p}_j)$ are the weight and parameters for component j. Θ, consists of $\vec{w} = (w_1, \ldots, w_M)$ and $\vec{\theta} = (\vec{\theta}_1, \ldots, \vec{\theta}_M)$ is the complete set of mixture parameters. Note that $\sum_{j=1}^{M} w_j = 1$ and $w_j >= 0$ for $j = 1, \ldots, M$.

2.3   Feature Selection

In this section, we will focus on incorporating feature selection into the finite McDonald's Beta mixture model using the complete set of observations $\mathcal{X}$. Thus, weights are assigned to features based on their significance in the model. Saliency weights improve model accuracy, prevent overfitting, and simplify interpretation. Equations are initially based on a single observation but are expanded for all observations. Observations are represented as a D-dimensional vector $\vec{X}_n$, with dimensions denoted as x_{nd}. Binary parameters $\mathcal{B} = \{\beta_{jd}\}$ indicate the relevance of each feature d to the jth component. If the distribution of a feature doesn't rely on component labels, it's irrelevant and represented by $q(. \mid \vec{\vartheta}_d)$ [15]. We assume McBD as the common density in this study resulting in the following:

$$p(\vec{X}_n \mid \vec{w}, \vec{\theta}, \vec{\vartheta}, \mathcal{B}) = \sum_{j=1}^{M} w_j \prod_{d=1}^{D} [p((x_{nd} \mid \theta_{jd})]^{\beta_{jd}} [q(x_{nd} \mid \vec{\vartheta}_d)]^{1-\beta_{jd}}] \tag{3}$$

Equation (3) defines $\vec{\vartheta}_d$ as the parameter of the common density of the dth feature, where $\vec{\vartheta}_d = (\hat{a}_d, \hat{b}_d, \hat{p}_d)$. To describe β_{jd}, we introduce $\mathcal{P} = \{\rho_{jd}\}$, which is known as the component-based feature saliency. The value of ρ_{jd}, which indicates the degree to which component j^{th} is related to the dth feature, is defined as $p(\beta_{jd} = 1)$. It is also possible to infer that $p(\beta_{id} = 0) = 1 - \rho_{jd}$. Thus:

$$p(\beta_{jd} \mid \rho_{jd}) = \rho_{jd}^{\beta_{jd}} (1 - \rho_{jd})^{1-\beta_{jd}} \tag{4}$$

Therefore, the mixture model can be derived based on (3) and (4) as follow:

$$p(\vec{X}_n \mid \Lambda) = \sum_{j=1}^{M} w_j \prod_{d=1}^{D} (\rho_{jd} p(x_{nd} \mid \theta_{jd}) + (1 - \rho_{jd}) q(x_{nd} \mid \vec{\vartheta}_d)) \tag{5}$$

where $\Lambda = \{\{w_j\}, \{\theta_{jd}\}, \{\rho_{jd}\}, \{\vec{\vartheta}_d\}\}$. Next, we define a membership vector $\vec{Z}_n = (Z_{n1}, \ldots, Z_{nM})$ of dimension M for each observation $\vec{X}_n$, where $Z_{n,j} = 1$ indicates that $\vec{X}_n$ belongs to component j, and $Z_{n,j} = 0$, otherwise. Thus, we can consider a set of membership vectors for $\mathcal{X}$ defined by $\mathcal{Z} = (Z_1, \ldots, Z_N)$ and have a complete form of data as $(\mathcal{X}, \mathcal{Z})$ which follows $p(\mathcal{X}, \mathcal{Z} \mid \Lambda)$. The density of the complete form of data can be defined as follows:

$$p(\mathcal{X}, \mathcal{Z} \mid \Lambda) = \prod_{n=1}^{N} \prod_{j=1}^{M} [w_j \prod_{d=1}^{D} (\rho_{jd} p(x_{nd} \mid \theta_{jd}) + (1 - \rho_{jd}) q(x_{nd} \mid \vec{\vartheta}_d))]^{Z_{n,j}} \tag{6}$$

By considering the latent multinomial variable $\hat{Z}_{nj}$ for each $\vec{X}_n$, such that $\vec{Z}_n \sim \mathcal{M}(1; \hat{Z}_{n1}, \ldots, \hat{Z}_{nM})$, we have:

$$\hat{Z}_{nj} = \frac{p\left(\vec{X}_n \mid \vec{\alpha}_j\right) w_j}{\sum_{j=1}^{M} p\left(\vec{X}_n \mid \vec{\alpha}_j\right) w_j} \tag{7}$$

3 Model Learning

3.1 Bayesian Learning Framework

During the learning phase of mixture models, estimating model's parameters is a complicated task. While there are several deterministic and stochastic approaches available, we put forth a Bayesian framework, as it enables the integration of prior knowledge and assumptions about the model's parameters along with their related uncertainties into the estimation process. Our suggested framework employs the M-H algorithm and Gibbs sampling to learn the model through posterior inference. The first step in Bayesian inference is to define the prior and posterior. As a result, we will determine the posterior by applying Bayes' theorem. Given the complete data $(\mathcal{X}, \mathcal{Z})$, the joint distribution of $p(\mathcal{X}, \mathcal{Z} \mid \Lambda)$ and the prior density function $p(\Lambda)$, we will define the posterior distribution as:

$$p(\Lambda \mid \mathcal{X}, \mathcal{Z}) \propto p(\mathcal{X}, \mathcal{Z} \mid \Lambda)p(\Lambda) \tag{8}$$

Considering that $0 < \rho_{jd} < 1$, we assume a Beta distribution as a prior:

$$p(\rho_{jd}) = \frac{\Gamma(\xi_{jd} + \zeta_{jd})}{\Gamma(\xi_{jd})\Gamma(\zeta_{jd})}\rho_{jd}^{\xi_{jd}-1}(1 - \rho_{jd})^{\zeta_{jd}-1} \tag{9}$$

Therefore, based on (9), the posterior is defined as follows:

$$p(\mathcal{P} \mid \mathcal{X}, \mathcal{Z}, \mathcal{B}) = \prod_{j=1}^{M} \prod_{d=1}^{D} \text{Beta}(n_{jd}^* + \xi_{jd}, n_j - n_{jd}^* + \zeta_{jd}) \tag{10}$$

where $n_{jd}^* = \sum_{n=1}^{N} z_{nj}\phi_{n,jd}$ and $\phi_{n,jd} \in \{0, 1\}$ meets the following conditions:

$$\phi_{n,jd} = \{\begin{matrix} 1 & h \geq 1 \\ 0 & \text{else} \end{matrix}, \quad h = \frac{\rho_{jd}p(x_{nd} \mid a_{jd}, b_{jd}, p_{jd})}{(1 - \rho_{jd})q(x_{nd} \mid \hat{a}_d, \hat{b}_d, \hat{p}_d)}. \tag{11}$$

Additionally, considering the positive constraints applied to all parameters, the Gamma distribution serves as a suitable choice for the prior distribution of each parameter. Therefore, to optimize the implementation and based on previous steps, we will condition the likelihood on $\mathcal{B}$ and $\mathcal{Z}$, resulting in the following:

$$p(\mathcal{X} \mid \mathcal{Z}, \vec{\theta}, \vec{\vartheta}, \mathcal{B}) = \prod_{n=1}^{N} \prod_{d=1}^{D} [p((x_{nd} \mid \theta_{jd})]^{\beta_{jd}}[q(x_{nd} \mid \vec{\vartheta}_d)]^{1-\beta_{jd}}] \tag{12}$$

By utilizing the priors and likelihood defined earlier, we calculate the posteriors:

$$p(\vec{\theta}_j \mid \mathcal{Z}, \mathcal{X}, \vec{\theta}, \vec{\vartheta}, \mathcal{B}) \propto p(\vec{\theta}_j) \prod_{z_{n,j}=1} p(X_n \mid \mathcal{Z}, \vec{\theta}_j, \vec{\vartheta}, \mathcal{B})$$

$$\propto p(\vec{\theta}_j) \prod_{z_{n,j}=1} \prod_{d=1}^{D} [p((x_{nd} \mid \vec{\theta}_{jd})]^{\beta_{jd}}[q(x_{nd} \mid \vec{\vartheta}_d)]^{1-\beta_{jd}}]]$$

$$\propto \prod_{d=1}^{D} [(\frac{v_{jd}^{u_{jd}}}{\Gamma(u_{jd})}a_{jd}^{u_{jd}-1}e^{-v_{jd}a_{jd}}) \times (\frac{s_{jd}^{r_{jd}}}{\Gamma(r_{jd})}b_{jd}^{r_{jd}-1}e^{-s_{jd}b_{jd}})$$

$$\times (\frac{g_{jd}^{f_{jd}}}{\Gamma(f_{jd})}p_{jd}^{f_{jd}-1}e^{-g_{jd}p_{jd}}) \times \prod_{z_{n,j}=1} \prod_{d=1}^{D} [\frac{p_{jd}x_{nd}^{a_{jd}p_{jd}-1}(1 - x_{nd}^{p_{jd}})^{b_{jd}-1}}{B(a_{jd}, b_{jd})}]^{\beta_{jd}}$$

$$\times [\frac{\hat{p}_{jd}x_{nd}^{\hat{a}_{jd}\hat{p}_{jd}-1}(1 - x_{nd}^{\hat{p}_{jd}})^{\hat{b}_{jd}-1}}{B(\hat{a}_{jd}, \hat{b}_{jd})}]^{1-\beta_{jd}}] \tag{13}$$

$$p(\vec{\vartheta} \mid \mathcal{Z}, \mathcal{X}, \vec{\theta}, \vec{\vartheta}, \mathcal{B}) \propto p(\vec{\vartheta}) \prod_{z_{n,j}=1} p(X_n \mid \mathcal{Z}, \vec{\theta}_j, \vec{\vartheta}, \mathcal{B}) \tag{14}$$

$p(\vec{\vartheta} \mid \mathcal{Z}, \mathcal{X}, \vec{\theta}, \vec{\vartheta}, \mathcal{B})$ will be computed in the same way as $p(\vec{\theta}_j \mid \mathcal{Z}, \mathcal{X}, \vec{\theta}, \vec{\vartheta}, \mathcal{B})$.

3.2 Extension to Infinite Finite Mixture Model

Determining the number of components M to accurately represent data is essential but difficult. As the need to set M beforehand is a major drawback, researchers have suggested nonparametric Bayesian techniques, which can automatically figure out the number of clusters and expand them indefinitely based on a specific choice of prior for mixing weights [6]. Unlike finite mixture models, where each vector $\vec{X}_n$ is derived from one of M undefined McB, we present that a Dirichlet process of McBDs can be used to model our data. In the following, we will demonstrate the fundamentals of the Dirichlet process mixture model and its ability to create or eliminate components. consider a symmetric Dirichlet with a concentration parameter $\frac{\tau}{M}$ as the prior for mixing weights:

$$p(\vec{w} \mid \tau) = \frac{\Gamma(\tau)}{\prod_{j=1}^{M} \Gamma(\frac{\tau}{M})} \prod_{j=1}^{M} w_j^{\frac{\tau}{M}-1} \tag{15}$$

where $\vec{w}$ is the vector of mixing weights defined by $(w_1, \ldots, w_M) : \sum_{j=1}^{M-1} w_j < 1$. In addition, for Z_n as the latent variable to show which cluster does X_n belongs to, such that $w_j = p(Z_n = j), j = 1, \ldots, M$ we have the following:

$$p(\mathcal{Z} \mid \vec{w}) = \prod_{j=1}^{M} w_j^{n_j} \tag{16}$$

where $n_j = \sum_{n=1}^{N} \mathbb{I}_{Z_{n,j}=1}$. Since the Dirichlet distribution is a conjugate prior for the multinomial distribution, we can calculate the prior distribution for $\mathcal{Z}$ by integrating out the mixing proportions vector $\vec{w}$ as follows:

$$p(\mathcal{Z} \mid \tau) = \int_{\vec{w}} p(\mathcal{Z} \mid \vec{w}) p(\vec{w} \mid \tau) d\vec{w} = \frac{\Gamma(\tau)}{\Gamma(N+\tau)} \prod_{j=1}^{M} \frac{\Gamma(\frac{\tau}{M}+n_j)}{\Gamma(\frac{\tau}{M})} \tag{17}$$

Therefore using (15) to (17), we obtain:

$$p(\vec{w} \mid \mathcal{Z}, \tau) = \frac{\Gamma(\tau+N)}{\prod_{j=1}^{M} \Gamma(\frac{\tau}{M}+n_j)} \prod_{j=1}^{M} w_j^{n_j+\frac{\tau}{M}-1} \propto \mathcal{D}(n_1 + \frac{\tau}{M}, \ldots, n_M + \frac{\tau}{M}) \tag{18}$$

where $\mathcal{D}$ is a Dirichlet distribution with parameters $(n_1 + \frac{\tau}{M}, \ldots, n_M + \frac{\tau}{M})$. According to [19], the conditional prior for a single indicator is defined as below:

$$p(Z_{n,j} = 1 \mid \tau, \mathcal{Z}_{-n}) = \frac{n_{-n,j} + \frac{\tau}{M}}{N - 1 + \tau} \tag{19}$$

where $\mathcal{Z}_{-n}$ is $\mathcal{Z}$ excluding Z_n and $n_{-n,j}$ is the number of observations excluding $\vec{X}_n$ which belongs to cluster j. To tackle the model's complexity challenges, we will suppose $M \to \infty$ and by applying that on (19), we have the following [19]:

$$p(Z_{n,j} = 1 \mid n; \mathcal{Z}_{-n}) = \begin{cases} \frac{n_{-n,j}}{N-1+\tau} & \text{if } n_{-n,j} > 0 \quad (j \in \mathcal{R}) \\ \frac{\tau}{N-1+\tau} & \text{if } n_{-n,j} = 0 \quad (j \in \mathcal{U}) \end{cases} \tag{20}$$

Note that $\mathcal{R}$ and $\mathcal{U}$ indicate the sets of represented and unrepresented components. It is worth noting that the conditional prior distribution for the members of R is dependent on the number of observations assigned to the component, whereas, for the members of U, it only depends on the parameters τ and N [25]. Therefore having (20) as the priors, we present the conditional posteriors [8]:

$$p(Z_{n,j} = 1 \mid \vec{\theta}_j, \vec{\vartheta}, \beta_j, \tau; \mathcal{Z}_{-n}) = \begin{cases} \frac{n_{-n,j}}{N-1+\tau} p(\vec{X}_n \mid \vec{\theta}_j, \vec{\vartheta}, \beta_j) & \text{if } j \in \mathcal{R} \\ \int \frac{\tau p(\vec{X}_n \mid \vec{\theta}_j, \vec{\vartheta}, \beta_j) p(\vec{\theta}_j, \vec{\vartheta})}{N-1+\tau} d\vec{a}_j db_j d\vec{p}_j d\vec{\vartheta} & \text{if } j \in \mathcal{U} \end{cases} \tag{21}$$

Equation (21) represents a Dirichlet process mixture model [12]. Each observation is assigned to a cluster based on a set of mixing proportions, with the number of clusters determined automatically from the data. One of the key advantages of this model is its ability to adapt to the data and generate new clusters as needed, avoiding overfitting and allowing for a flexible representation of the data. If an observation is assigned to an unrepresented cluster, a new cluster is generated to accommodate it, while a represented cluster may become unrepresented if all its observations are assigned to other clusters during the sampling process.

3.3   Algorithm Overview

To estimate the parameters of our mixture model as our final step, we have used the M-H algorithm and Gibbs sampler technique [24], which are widely used in Bayesian inference to sample from complex posterior distributions and avoid direct sampling. For the choice of the proposal distribution, we have used a random walk M-H with the following proposal distribution:$\tilde{\theta}_{jd} \sim \mathcal{LN}(\log(\theta_{jd}^{(t-1)}), \sigma^2)$, where $\mathcal{LN}(\log(\theta_{jd}^{(t-1)}), \sigma^2)$ is the log-normal distribution with mean and variance of $\log(\theta_{jd}^{(t-1)})$ and σ^2 where $d = 1, \ldots, D$.

To summarize the algorithm, first, we initialize the algorithm by assigning all observations to the same cluster. We then generate the vector $\vec{Z}_n$ and update the number of represented clusters based on the generated vector. Since the integral in equation (21) is not analytically tractable, we employ the technique proposed in [23] to approximate it and enable sampling from the vector $\vec{Z}_n$.

Fig. 1. Sample of each type of lung cancer images.

Algorithm 1. Nonparametric Bayesian learning of IMcBMM

1. Initialization
2. **Repeat**
3. Generate $\vec{Z}_n$ from (21) and then update n_j.
4. Update the number of represented components.
5. Update the mixing weights for the represented components by $w_R = \frac{n_j}{N+\tau}$.
6. Update the mixing weights for the unrepresented components by $w_U = \frac{\tau}{N+\tau}$.
7. Generate the model parameters from (13) using M-H algorithm.
8. **until** Convergence

---

4   Experimental Results

We evaluate our proposed model on two real-world applications: lung cancer analysis and human activity recognition. We compared its performance with the widely-used GMM and FMcDBMM using accuracy, precision, recall, and F1-score metrics to assess its effectiveness.

4.1   Lung Cancer Analysis

We conducted our first experiment on a dataset of lung cancer images [7], which contains 2500 images classified into three categories: benign, adenocarcinoma, and squamous cell carcinoma. Examples of cell image samples are shown in fig.1. We compared the performance of our proposed model with GMM using the mentioned metrics. The results in Table 1 indicate that our model achieved better accuracy of 90.84% than GMM and FMcDBMM. In addition, we analyzed the feature saliencies of eight random features, as shown in Table 2. The analysis indicated that the eighth feature was the most relevant among the other seven features across all components.

Table 1. Results on Lung Cancer Dataset.

Method	Accuracy	Precision	Recall	F1-score
IMcDBMM	90.84	91.02	90.88	90.94
FMcDBMM	87.95	88.1	87.96	88.02
GMM	83.33	79.88	80.43	81.59

Table 2. Feature Relevancy Across All Components for Lung Cancer dataset.

Feature	F1	F2	F3	F4	F5	F6	F7	F8
Relevancy	0.109292	0.114260	0.107499	0.096567	0.089167	0.074779	0.108384	0.116302

4.2 Human Activity Recognition (HAR)

As our second experiment, we used a publicly available dataset of 2220 samples [3] collected from 30 participants aged between 19 and 48 performing four activities (laying, sitting, standing, and walking) while wearing a waist-mounted Samsung Galaxy S II smartphone with two embedded sensors. We employed features such as triaxial acceleration, the estimated body acceleration, and triaxial angular velocity to analyze the data. Our proposed model achieved promising performance compared to GMM and FMcDBMM, as shown in Table 3. Additionally, we analyzed the feature saliency among components for eight sample features, as illustrated in Table 4.

Table 3. Results on HAR Dataset.

Method	Accuracy	Precision	Recall	F1-score
IMcDBMM	93.14	91.32	91.27	91.29
FMcDBMM	89.27	89.18	89.34	89.25
GMM	86.71	86.39	86.41	86.39

Table 4. Feature Relevancy Across All Components for HAR dataset.

Feature	F1	F2	F3	F4	F5	F6	F7	F8
Relevancy	0.527548	0.432727	0.435073	0.894909	0.879438	0.900135	0.934092	0.870970

5 Conclusion

We proposed a nonparametric Bayesian framework for a multivariate McDonald's Beta mixture model. The aim of this work was to determine the optimal number of components by extending the finite model to the infinite case using the Dirichlet process. In our proposed framework, we employed a fully Bayesian learning approach that utilized MCMC techniques. Furthermore, we evaluated the effectiveness of the model through two real-world applications: Lung Cancer analysis and Human Activity Recognition, and the experimental results demonstrated that our proposed framework outperformed both GMM and FMcDBMM.

Acknowledgement. The accomplished research was enabled by support from the Natural Sciences and Engineering Research Council of Canada (NSERC).

References

1. Amirkhani, M., Manouchehri, N., Bouguila, N.: A nonparametric bayesian framework for multivariate beta mixture models. In: 2021 IEEE 22nd International Conference on Information Reuse and Integration for Data Science (IRI), pp. 83–90 (2021)
2. Andrieu, C., De Freitas, N., Doucet, A., Jordan, M.I.: An introduction to mcmc for machine learning. Mach. Learn. $50(1/2)$, 5–43 (2003)
3. Anguita, D., Ghio, A., Oneto, L., Parra, X., Reyes-Ortiz, J.L.: A public domain dataset for human activity recognition using smartphones. In: 21st European Symposium on Artificial Neural Networks, Computational Intelligence and Machine Learning, ESANN. Bruges, Belgium, 24–26 April 2013 https://www.kaggle.com/datasets/uciml/human-activity-recognition-with-smartphones
4. Aryal, G., Nadarajah, S.: Information matrix for beta distributions. Serdica Math. J. $30(4)$, 513–526 (2004)
5. Bishop, C.M.: Pattern Recognition and Machine Learning. Springer, 1 edn. (2006)
6. Blei, D.M., Jordan, M.I.: Variational inference for dirichlet process mixtures. Bayesian Anal. $1(1)$, 121–143 (2006)
7. Borkowski, A.A., Bui, M.M., Thomas, L.B., Wilson, C.P., DeLand, L.A., Mastorides, S.M.: Lung and colon cancer histopathological image dataset (lc25000). arXiv preprint arXiv:1912.12142 (2019) https://www.kaggle.com/datasets/andrewmvd/lung-and-colon-cancer-histopathological-images
8. Bouguila, N., Ziou, D.: A dirichlet process mixture of generalized dirichlet distributions for proportional data modeling. IEEE Trans. Neural Netw. $21(1)$, 107–122 (2010)
9. Bouguila, N., Ziou, D.: A countably infinite mixture model for clustering and feature selection. Knowl. Inf. Syst. $33(2)$, 351–370 (2011)
10. Esteva, A., Kuprel, B., Novoa, R.A., Ko, J., Swetter, S.M., Blau, H.M., Thrun, S.: Dermatologist-level classification of skin cancer with deep neural networks. Nature $542(7639)$, 115–118 (2017)
11. Gelfand, A.E., Kottas, A.: A computational approach for full nonparametric bayesian inference under dirichlet process mixture models. J. Comput. Graph. Stat. $11(2)$, 289–305 (2002)
12. Hjort, N.L., Holmes, C., Müller, P., Walker, S.G. (eds.): Bayesian Nonparametrics. Cambridge University Press, Cambridge, April 2010
13. Jordan, M.I., Mitchell, T.M.: Machine learning: trends, perspectives, and prospects. Science $349(6245)$, 255–260 (2015)
14. Kelleher, J.D.E.A.: Fundamentals of Machine Learning for Predictive Data Analytics: Algorithms, Worked Examples, and Case Studies. 2 edn. MIT Press, Cambridge (2019)
15. Ketabchi, K., Manouchehri, N., Bouguila, N.: Fully bayesian libby-novick beta mixture model with feature selection. In: 2022 IEEE International Conference on Industrial Technology (ICIT), IEEE, August 2022
16. Lowe, D.G.: Distinctive image features from scale-invariant keypoints. Int. J. Comput. Vis. $60(2)$, 91–110 (2004)
17. Lowe, D.: Object recognition from local scale-invariant features. In: Proceedings of the Seventh IEEE International Conference on Computer Vision, IEEE (1999)
18. Murphy, K.P.: Machine Learning: A Probabilistic Perspective. MIT Press, Cambridge 1 edn. (2012)

19. Neal, R.M.: Markov chain sampling methods for dirichlet process mixture models. J. Comput. Graph. Stat. **9**(2), 249–265 (2000)
20. Ordóñez, F., Roggen, D.: Deep convolutional and LSTM recurrent neural networks for multimodal wearable activity recognition. Sensors **16**(1), 115 (2016)
21. Pedregosa, F.E.A.: Scikit-learn: machine learning in python. J. Mach. Learn. Res. **12**, 2825–2830 (2021)
22. Rajkomar, A., et al.: Scalable and accurate deep learning with electronic health records. npj Dig. Med. **1**(1) (2018)
23. Rasmussen, C.E.: The infinite gaussian mixture model. In: Advances in Neural Information Processing Systems, pp. 554–560 (2000)
24. Robert, C., Casella, G.: Monte Carlo Statistical Methods. Springe, New York (2013). https://doi.org/10.1007/978-1-4757-4145-2
25. Xu, G., Zhou, W.: Bayesian inference for mixture models with an unknown number of components using reversible jump mcmc. Comput. Stat. Data Anal. **132**, 1–15 (2019)
26. Yang, J.E.A.: Deep convolutional neural networks on multichannel time series for human activity recognition. In: Proceedings of the 24th International Joint Conference on Artificial Intelligence, pp. 3995–4001 (2015)

Cannabis Use Estimators Within Canadian Population Using Social Media Based on Deep Learning Tools

Doaa Ibrahim[✉], Diana Inkpen, and Hussein Al Osman

Ottawa University, Ottawa, ON K1N 6N5, Canada
{dibra041,diana.inkpen,hussein.alosman}@uottawa.ca

Abstract. Cannabis has become the most used drug worldwide with the highest risks and associated criminal problems in many countries. Therefore, identifying users at risk of cannabis use is an important and essential task. This will help doctors and people with authority to react fast and on time. We used two datasets (8,725 users in total) to build a strong model for predicting users at-risk in a sample of Twitter users that is representative of the Canadian population. Using a Bidirectional GRU classifier, we achieved high accuracy and F1-score (84.74% and 87.56%, respectively). This model was applied on the population dataset to predict the patterns of cannabis users all over Canada. The geographic patterns of cannabis users highly match the cannabis users statistics reported by Statistics Canada (with a small overall difference of 1.4%). To the best of our knowledge, this is the first study to demonstrate that the number of cannabis users in a country can be accurately estimated by analyzing a representative sample of Twitter users from various regions of the country.

Keywords: CNN · LSTM · BERT · BioBERT · attention · cannabis · marijuana · weed · substance use · classification · risk behavior · natural language processing · social media · transfer learning · deep learning

1 Introduction

Cannabis is the most used drug in the world. About 4% of the global population aged 15-64 (209 million people) used cannabis in 2020. Also, cannabis use increased by 8% in 2020 from 3.8% in 2010 worldwide.[1]. Although cannabis use is illegal in most countries, in the last few years there is an increase in the number of countries that legalized it[2]. There are concerns in the World Health Organization (WHO) regarding countries that have legalized cannabis including Canada. WHO requested those countries to analyze the impact of cannabis legalization. The WHO report in 2021 found that about 90% of Canadians who

---

[1] UNODC World Drug Report 2022 https://www.unodc.org/unodc/data-and-analysis/world-drug-report-2022.html.

© The Author(s), under exclusive license to Springer Nature Switzerland AG 2023
L. Rutkowski et al. (Eds.): ICAISC 2023, LNAI 14126, pp. 331–342, 2023.
https://doi.org/10.1007/978-3-031-42508-0_30

use cannabis could be considered addicted since the legalization in 2017 [5]. Most countries that legalized cannabis use provide recommendations to limit cannabis use. In Canada, the Lower-Risk Cannabis Use Guidelines contain recommendations to reduce consumption risk. Unsurprisingly, the first recommendation is "The most effective way to avoid the risks of cannabis use is to abstain from use" [4]. Consuming a small amount of cannabis over a prolonged period of time will produce adverse health outcomes. Another recommendation is to delay the start of cannabis consumption until at least after adolescence to limit the probability of adverse effects [4]. Researchers have confirmed the association between consuming cannabis and different psychological and behavioral problems [22].

Our objective is to use social media posts to build an effective automated model for cannabis use population estimation in Canada that matches the governmental surveys.

Our contributions can be summarized as follow:

- Employing social media text to estimate cannabis use within the Canadian population, using national surveys as a reference. To the best of our knowledge, this marks the first time such an analysis has been conducted for an entire nation using a representative sample.
- Evaluating the generalizability of traditional and deep learning (DL) algorithms at the user-level, despite the limitations of our unstructured datasets in comparison to the larger datasets often used to train DL architectures. By carefully tuning hyperparameters and employing the most effective generalization techniques, we were able to develop a robust predictive model using our data.

Recognizing that cannabis use detection is a sub-field of substance use detection, our population estimation approach could potentially be applied to estimate the prevalence of other substance use based on social media text.

2   Related Work on Cannabis Use Detection

Identifying the cannabis use level and the necessary treatments is a complex task. Recently, researchers tries to detect cannabis use risk through social media using different traditional and DL techniques [6–8].

Hassanpour *et al* [6] in their study on Instagram posts tried to build a DL model to predict different substance use such as cannabis. The study analyzed data collected from surveys and compared it to data collected from Instagram posts. Comparing the surveys of 2,287 persons and their substance use behavior were used to label different collocated posts as high or low risk for each substance use. An average number of 183.5 Instagram posts per user were collected for those users. Due to memory requirements, a sample dataset of 20 images, captions, and comments for each user was created. The data set was divided into 80%, 10%, and 10% for training, validation, and testing, respectively. The data sets were used to build different models to predict substance use risks for alcohol, tobacco, prescription drugs, and illicit drugs. A binary substance use outcome using the binary cross-entropy function was detected. The unseen test set consisted of 228 selected users. They used a logistic regression model with semi-automatically extracted features from the texts and images of the dataset as a baseline model. They found that their deep learning model outperformed the logistic regression model (which was considered a baseline model) only for alcohol use risk detection. The model did not achieve statistically significant improvements over the baseline to predict any drug use risk (including cannabis). For feature extractions, they used CNNs for images and long short-term memory (LSTM) for text classification [6].

Although, Jenhani et al. [9] found that using n-grams is not effective in detecting drug use other researchers found that it could be useful [2]. The use of n-gram was effective in detecting some outcomes such as the drug side effects or routes of intervention condition while the use of unigrams was effective in classifying drugs, medical conditions, and measuring units [9]. Usually, using unigrams or n-grams was found to be useful in the annotation process. For example, the effectiveness of the automated annotator used by Jenhani et al. based on the Stanford Named Entity Recognition (NER) was inversely proportional to the value of n in the n-grams [9].

As mentioned above, using DL classifiers for any individual substance use detection (such as cannabis use detection) is still limited compared to the use of traditional classifiers. [9,14,17,19].

3   Data

The data used for building the predictive models in this study is composed of two datasets: Health-Cann and SubUse-Cann datasets. The two datasets were joined as training data to build several predictive models at the user-level. The best model will be applied for predictions on the unlabeled population dataset.

The following is a detailed description of each dataset:

The Health-Cann dataset consists of 9,724 tweets labeled as positive or negative drug use risk [7]. It consists of two batches of the data used by Hu et al. [7] (Note: We asked for permission to use the data but it is not collected by our team). We annotated the substance use tweets automatically by comparing different cannabis keywords to label them as positive cannabis use tweets (tweets that indicate usage of cannabis) or negative cannabis tweets (tweets that indicate no sign of any kind of cannabis use). To check the automatic annotation, all the positive examples in the data were re-annotated by two professional annotators following the same schema that was used in the annotation of the original data after updating it to be suitable for cannabis use. The original schema by Hu et al. was to annotate all drugs, including cannabis. The negative examples (which indicate no drug use) of the original data were used without re-annotating as they are negative examples of cannabis use too. The annotated data (Health-Cann dataset) consists of 9,724 tweets (for 8,629 users).

The SubUse-1.0 dataset was collected by our research team in 2018. The dataset was originally collected to cover seven categories (substance use, aggression, anxiety, depression, distress, sexuality, and violence). The team employed a supervised approach that uses a CNN to identify some active users on Twitter. From the active users, the team kept users who have at least 200 posts. We collected the posts by searching and using a well-prepared list of more than 300 short phrases and words that are related to each category. We specified different Twitter hashtags that were expected to have a high correlation with each category. These hashtags were used to search for Twitter posts that had the candidate hashtags and for the users that can be classified into the selected categories. If the collecting team believed that the user might be classified in at least one of our categories, all of the user's tweets were downloaded using the Twitter API. The total number of tweets collected was 17,099 for 96 users.

The SubUse-Cann dataset is part of the SubUse-1.0 dataset which has only the binary cannabis use labels. It has 6.9% positive cannabis use tweets and 93.1% negative cannabis use tweets.

The two datasets Health-Cann and the SubUse-Cann were joined at the user-level to produce the HealthSub-Cann dataset used in this research. 20% of the dataset (with the same class ratio) was set aside as an unseen dataset (called the HealthSub-Test).

We trained and evaluated the models using 80% of the dataset HealthSub-Cann dataset. K-fold cross-validation was used first to validate the models. Then, as a second validation, the models were tested on the unseen HealthSub-Test dataset to assess the generalization capacity of the proposed models.

The Population Data. The population dataset is collected by Advanced Symbolics Inc. (ASI), a market research company based in Ottawa, Canada[2]. The data is statistically representative of Canada's population. The company has collected millions of tweets. The researchers used the Conditional Independence Coupler (CIC) sampling algorithm that is based on Coupling from the Past (CFTP) with enhancing the stopping condition by measuring how far is the chosen node from the starting node on a smaller subset of the online network [21]. The company research team checked a sample representative property by comparing 5,000 Toronto Twitter user profiles during 2011 with the census patterns of the same year [20]. Eventually, the CIC algorithm is mathematically proven to generate a representative sample of the population. The ASI 2015 population dataset (P) contains a sample of Canadian users who tweeted during 2015. Canada's provinces and territories are presented in the P data. The geographical distribution of users in P was checked by comparing it to the 2016 Canadian census. The distribution differences of people between the 2016 Canadian census and the Twitter users in P for each area is shown in Table 1. All the differences are less than 5%, except for Quebec. Because it is a French-speaking province with only 13.7% anglophones[3], this result was expected as the tweets were collected in the English language. We decided to keep the Quebec province in our analysis with the collected English tweets (collected from the English-speaking

---

[2] https://advancedsymbolics.com/.

[3] https://www.canada.ca/en/canadian-heritage/services/official-languages-bilingualism/publications/statistics.html.

area in Quebec). But, we will not rely on the prediction results of Quebec in our analysis, as it is not well represented in the P dataset. The P dataset contains 141,432 users in total (with 5,828,888 tweets). The following is the description of the most important fields in the P dataset:

Location Information. If the user enabled the location property (in his/her device) then the coordination points of the user's location can be detected from the user's mobile GPS and stored with each tweet information. The K-means algorithm is used to predict the user's location using the GPS coordination points and to fill the geotag field in each tweet. In general, if the tweet is missing the geotag information, then Microsoft's Bing Maps is used to look for the address specified in the user's profile. If the previous two options are not available, then the location field is left empty.

User Creation Time and Date. This field contains the UTC date and time when the user account was created on Twitter.

Tweet Time and Date. This field contains the UTC date and time when the tweet was posted.

Tweet text A short text posted by the user. It has a limit of 140 characters. In 2017, Twitter doubled the character count to 280, but this has no effect in our case. We are using the data collected until the end of 2015.

Table 1. Geographical population difference between the P dataset and the 2016 Canadian census.

Abbreviation	Province/Territory	P	Census	Differences
NL	Newfoundland and Labrador	2,553	519,716	−0.33%
PE	Prince Edward Island	1,308	142,907	−0.52%
NS	Nova Scotia	6,895	923,598	−2.25%
NB	New Brunswick	2,805	747,101	0.14%
QC	Quebec	12,972	8,164,361	14.05%
ON	Ontario	57,312	13,448,494	−2.26%
MB	Manitoba	5,169	1,278,365	−0.02%
SK	Saskatchewan	4,704	1,098,352	−0.20%
AB	Alberta	18,721	4,067,175	−1.67%
BC	British Columbia	25,547	4,648,055	−4.84%
YT	Yukon	210	35,874	−0.05%
NT	Northwest Territories	194	41,786	−0.02%
NU	Nunavut	94	35,944	0.04%

4   Methodology

To detect the risk of cannabis use in our datasets, several text classification models have been used. We compared the performance of several traditional and DL models, to select the best one. We use the binary labels of {1,0} to differentiate between positive and negative posts of cannabis use. First, we used traditional classifiers to distinguish the positive and negative tweets of cannabis use. Second, we employed DL classifiers to build the best possible models. Several pre-trained word embeddings are implemented and made available by many researchers in the field. The GloVe word embeddings have proven to be effective for various text processing applications [7,13]. GloVe counts accumulating word co-occurrences to produce a matrix. Then, the matrix is factorized to obtain lower-dimensional representations [16]. One of the commonly used GloVe word embeddings has been trained on a corpus of 6 billion tokens (Wikipedia 2014 + Gigaword 5) with a vocabulary of the top 400,000 most frequent words. It can convert the words into vectors of 50, 100, 200, or 300 dimensions [16]. We used the GloVe word embeddings as input for the DL methods and TF-IDF vectors for the traditional methods.

For regularization, different dropout rates from 0.1 to 0.5 were applied. Also, the L2 regularization value of 0.0001 was applied in the loss function. It randomly drops neurons off the network using dropout to avoid overfitting [18]. Our performance measure focuses on minimizing the loss error for the validation set. For the DL classifiers, mini-batch gradient descent is applied to improve the network loss function through backpropagation. The Adam optimizer [11] was used with a batch size of 50 to improve the loss function.

5   Models

5.1   Traditional Classifiers

The following traditional classifiers were used: Multinomial Naive Bayes (NBA), Random Forest (RF) and Support Vector Machines (SVM). TF-IDF values for the words used as the main features with the traditional classifiers. TF-IDF represents the significance of a term within a document based on its frequency in the document and is inversely proportional to the frequency of the same term in a collection of documents (the whole corpus). Using TF-IDF all Words of the document (the document represents one entry of a group users' tweets in our case) are transformed into importance numbers. This process is called text vectorization process.

5.2   Deep Learning Classifiers

CNN-Based Models. We built two CNN-based models: CNN-GMax and CNN-DualChannel. After the optimization of the hyperparameters, we built the models on top of the GloVe word embeddings. For the CNN-GMax model, one convolutional layer was used followed by a global max pooling function which is proven by researchers to have good results using the entire record representation length [15]. Then, the model contains a fully connected dense layer that has 50 hidden units and uses a Rectified Linear Unit (ReLU) activation function. Finally, a fully connected layer with one hidden unit (that uses a sigmoid activation function) is applied. For the CNN-DualChannel model, we apply two convolutional blocks each of which has 4 features and filters of lengths 3 and 5, respectively. Then, a max-pooling layer is applied to the feature map of the convolutional layer to extract more abstract information. Max-pooling extracts the word features without considering the sequence order of the words [10].

RNN-Based Models. RNN models are widely used in NLP as they have the advantage of remembering values over a certain time duration. RNN models maintain the sequence order. These models can suffer from exploding or vanishing the calculated weights for long sequences. This disadvantage can be mostly resolved using LSTM models. LSTMs are RNN models that overcome this disadvantage using gating mechanisms. The Gated Recurrent Unit (GRU) is similar to the LSTM model but it has a different architecture. Instead of the input, output and forget gates of the LSTM, the GRU consists of two gates: the reset gate and the update gate. The reset gate decides how to combine the current input with the previous memory, and the update gate determines how much of the previous memory needs to be kept. If we keep the reset gate active (by assigning 1 to its value) and we decided to dis-activate the update gate (by assigning 0 to its value) we will get a simple RNN model. After optimization, a bidirectional GRU (BiGRU) layer with 100 units (with activated return sequence) followed by another BiGRU layer with 50 units followed by a small dense layer of 50 units was chosen. We used a BiGRU instead of a unidirectional GRU which consists of two GRUs. One GRU processes the sequence forward from left to right, while the other processes the sequence backward from right to left. The advantage of this GRU consists in giving more word-representative weights. For each word, its weight takes into consideration the context of the neighbors on both sides [1].

Transfer Learning Models. Since we have a relatively small training dataset, transfer learning models were tried to enrich the training models. We selected two of the most popular models (BERT and BioBERT) for our classification problem. The models were fine-tuned on our data. We used the models that are prepared by Hugging Face team[4].

BERT base uncased model It is a transformer model pretrained on the English language using masked language modeling (MLM). BERT is a self-supervised model which was pretrained on the raw texts without any human labeling. This helps the model to be trained on a big amount of publicly available data. Eventually, the model learns an inner representation of the English language. The

---

[4] https://huggingface.co/models?library=transformers.

BERT model was pretrained on BookCorpus (11,038 unpublished books) and English Wikipedia (excluding lists, tables, and headers) [3]. For the BERT base uncased model used in this, the English texts were lowercased and tokenized to have 30,000 tokens[5]. The uncased model is more suitable for our classification problem as we reprocessed our datasets to be lowercased too.

BioBERT Uncased Model. It is a biomedical language representation model designed for biomedical text mining tasks such as biomedical text classification. The pretrained BioBERT was trained on big raw biomedical data. It was trained on PubMed abstracts (PubMed of size 4.5B words) and PubMed Central full-text articles (PMC of size 13.5B words)[6]. The model was initialized with the pre-trained BERT weights provided by Devlin *et al.* [3] then was trained on the biomedical data mentioned above [12].

6 Experiments and Results

6.1 Classification Result

As mentioned in the methodology section, we used the HealthSub-Cann training set for the training of the models. In the first group of experiments, we used k-fold cross-validation to test the model while in the second group, we tested the models on the HealthSub-Test dataset. The experiments used Python (v.3.9) and the TensorFlow (v.2.4.1) platform to build the models. For the BERT models, PyTorch (v.1.13.1) platform was used instead of the TensorFlow platform.

The tokenized words are the main features used to create the classification models.

Using cross-validation on the HealthSub-Cann dataset, it is clear that the RNN-based model performed the best as shown in Table 2. The BiGRU using the regularization methods mentioned above besides the spatial layer regularization performed the best. It reached the highest F1-score of 87.81%. Among the traditional methods as expected RF obtained the highest F1-score of 87.42%. The SVM model performed well too (it reached 87.16% F1-score).

Using the HealthSub-Test dataset, as in the first group of experiments above, the RNN-based model performed the best again. Table 3 shows the results. The BiGRU reached the highest F1-score of 87.56%. Again, the RF obtained the highest F1-score of 85.57% among the three traditional classifiers.

6.2 Population-Level Prediction

After predicting the at-risk cannabis users, the result will be evaluated and justified by comparing the ratio of at-risk users in each province in Canada with the Canadian official surveys. The 2015 Canadian Tobacco, Alcohol, and Drugs

---

[5] https://huggingface.co/bert-base-uncased.
[6] https://huggingface.co/monologg/biobert_v1.1_pubmed/tree/main.

Table 2. The results of the models using k-fold cross-validation.

Model	Accuracy	Precision	Recall	F1-score
NB	81.25	74.08	95.38	83.15
RF	83.59	81.28	94.39	87.42
SVM	82.81	81.12	94.18	87.16
CNN-GMax	82.70	81.77	84.10	83.08
CNN-DualChannel	82.04	83.41	83.50	83.52
BiGRU	83.96	83.99	91.09	87.81
BERT	79.93	72.85	92.37	81.54
BioBERT	83.60	76.47	91.60	83.81

Table 3. The results of the models on the HealthSub-Test dataset.

Model	Accuracy	Precision	Recall	F1-score
NB	77.25	73.72	85.36	79.28
RF	83.22	81.95	88.37	85.57
SVM	82.48	81.60	86.64	84.77
CNN-GMax	83.11	82.06	83.08	83.37
CNN-DualChannel	83.45	82.92	83.49	83.74
BiGRU	84.74	84.61	88.68	87.56
BERT	81.27	75.21	87.28	81.13
BioBERT	80.28	74.78	86.58	80.59

Survey (CTADS) by Statistics Canada[7] will be used to justify our prediction result of the P dataset. This evaluation method will be used to show that each province in the P dataset is following the same ratio as in the 2015 Canadian survey. For cannabis, 12.3% of the Canadian population reporting cannabis consumption in 2015[8]. According to the 2015 survey, cannabis was the most used drug by Canadians.

Table 4 shows the prediction results for each province in Canada using the best predictive model BiGRU mentioned in the previous section. As shown in the table the predicted values were matched very well with the actual values of CTADS-15. As expected, BC has the highest difference of 4.77%. BC has a relatively high representation in the P dataset, as shown in Table 1. In general, 4.77% is an acceptable ratio as it is within the 5% difference threshold. For Quebec, even though there is a prediction in our experiments, we cannot draw conclusions from it. As mentioned above, Quebec posts had a low representation

---

[7] https://www.canada.ca/en/health-canada/services/canadian-tobacco-alcohol-drugs-survey.html.

[8] https://www.canada.ca/en/health-canada/services/canadian-tobacco-alcohol-drugs-survey/2015-summary.html.

in the P dataset, as shown in Table 1. The overall ratio of cannabis use predicted, which is 10.9%, could increase if we have more users from Quebec.

In conclusion, cannabis use in Canada (represented by its 10 provinces) was highly estimated. The predicted ratio was found to be about 10.9% which is close to the actual ratio of 12.3% that was measured by Statistics Canada's survey.

Table 4. BiGRU model estimated cannabis use percentages versus reported cannabis use percentages based on CTADS-2015 per province.

Provinces	Predicted%	Actual%	Differences%
NL	10.9	9.9	−1.02
PE	11.9	8.2	−3.69
NS	10.8	14.4	3.56
NB	11	9	−1.95
QC	10.8	9.8	−0.97
ON	10.4	12.8	2.45
MB	9.8	11.3	1.49
SK	11.1	10.2	−0.88
AB	10.4	11.1	0.65
BC	12.5	17.3	4.77
Canada	10.9	12.3	1.37

6.3 Comparison and Discussion

In this paper, we applied traditional machine learning algorithms first to predict cannabis use at the user-level. Then, we compared the results with DL algorithms. Eventually, we applied the best-performing model (BiGRU + GloVe) on the population-representative P dataset. The results showed a strong positive correlation between the predicted cannabis use and the available statistics for 2015 at the province level. The actual ratio of cannabis use in Canada was 12.3% in 2015. Our model predicted 10.9% on the sample population. Table 4 shows the prediction among the Canadian provinces.

7 Conclusion and Future Work

In order to build an optimal model for population-level prediction we experimented with the datasets on the user-level with different traditional and DL classifiers. We chose the best generalizable model (that achieves the best F1-score) to apply to the population dataset and the results were compared with Canadian statistics on cannabis use. We have successfully developed an automated model that accurately predicts cannabis usage among the Canadian population, which matches official records. To the best of our knowledge, this is the first time such a model has been created. The methodology we have developed could potentially be applied to other countries, or even on a global scale. This approach could prove to be more economically feasible than conducting population surveys, particularly in areas of the world with limited resources.

Acknowledgment. This research was funded by the Natural Sciences and Engineering Research Council of Canada (NSERC), the Ontario Centres of Excellence (OCE), and SafeToNet.

References

1. Bahdanau, D., Cho, K., Bengio, Y.: Neural machine translation by jointly learning to align and translate. arXiv preprint arXiv:1409.0473 (2014)
2. Çöltekin, Ç., Rama, T.: Drug-use identification from tweets with word and character n-grams. In: Proceedings of the 2018 EMNLP Workshop SMM4H: The 3rd Social Media Mining for Health Applications Workshop & Shared Task, pp. 52–53 (2018)
3. Devlin, J., Chang, M.W., Lee, K., Toutanova, K.: Bert: pre-training of deep bidirectional transformers for language understanding. arXiv preprint arXiv:1810.04805 (2018)
4. Fischer, B., et al.: Lower-risk cannabis use guidelines: a comprehensive update of evidence and recommendations. Am. J. Public Health **107**(8), e1–e12 (2017)
5. Hansford, B.: "unodc world drug report 2022 highlights trends on cannabis post-legalization, environmental impacts of illicit drugs, and drug use among women and youth" https://www.unodc.org/unodc/press/releases/2022/June/unodc-world-drug-report-2022-highlights-trends-on-cannabis-post-legalization-environmental-impacts-of-illicit-drugs-and-drug-use-among-women-and-youth.html
6. Hassanpour, S., Tomita, N., DeLise, T., Crosier, B., Marsch, L.A.: Identifying substance use risk based on deep neural networks and instagram social media data. Neuropsychopharmacology **44**(3), 487–494 (2019)
7. Hu, H., et al.: An ensemble deep learning model for drug abuse detection in sparse twitter-sphere. In: MedInfo, pp. 163–167 (2019)
8. Ibrahim, D., Inkpen, D., Osman, H.A.: Identifying cannabis use risk through social media based on deep learning methods. In: Rutkowski, L., Scherer, R., Korytkowski, M., Pedrycz, W., Tadeusiewicz, R., Zurada, J.M. (eds.) Artificial Intelligence and Soft Computing. ICAISC 2022, Part II, LNCS, vol. 13589, pp. 102–113. Springer, Cham (2023). https://doi.org/10.1007/978-3-031-23480-4_9
9. Jenhani, F., Gouider, M.S., Said, L.B.: Lexicon-based system for drug abuse entity extraction from twitter. In: BDAS, pp. 692–703 (2016)
10. Kalchbrenner, N., Grefenstette, E., Blunsom, P.: A convolutional neural network for modelling sentences. arXiv preprint arXiv:1404.2188 (2014)
11. Kingma, D.P., Ba, J.: Adam: a method for stochastic optimization. arXiv preprint arXiv:1412.6980 (2014)
12. Lee, J., et al.: Biobert: a pre-trained biomedical language representation model for biomedical text mining. Bioinformatics **36**(4), 1234–1240 (2020)
13. Mahata, D., Friedrichs, J., Shah, R.R., et al.: # phramacovigilance-exploring deep learning techniques for identifying mentions of medication intake from twitter. arXiv preprint arXiv:1805.06375 (2018)

14. Menon, A., Farmer, F., Whalen, T., Hua, B., Najib, K., Gerber, M.: Automatic identification of alcohol-related promotions on twitter and prediction of promotion spread. In: 2014 Systems and Information Engineering Design Symposium (SIEDS), pp. 233–238. IEEE (2014)

15. Orabi, A.H., Buddhitha, P., Orabi, M.H., Inkpen, D.: Deep learning for depression detection of twitter users. In: Proceedings of the Fifth Workshop on Computational Linguistics and Clinical Psychology: From Keyboard to Clinic, pp. 88–97 (2018)

16. Pennington, J., Socher, R., Manning, C.: Glove: global vectors for word representation. In: Proceedings of the 2014 Conference on Empirical Methods in Natural Language Processing (EMNLP), pp. 1532–1543. Association for Computational Linguistics, Doha, Qatar, October 2014. https://doi.org/10.3115/v1/D14-1162https://www.aclweb.org/anthology/D14-1162

17. Raja, B.S., Ali, A., Ahmed, M., Khan, A., Malik, A.P.: Semantics enabled role based sentiment analysis for drug abuse on social media: A framework. In: 2016 IEEE Symposium on Computer Applications & Industrial Electronics (ISCAIE), pp. 206–211. IEEE (2016)

18. Srivastava, N., Hinton, G., Krizhevsky, A., Sutskever, I., Salakhutdinov, R.: Dropout: a simple way to prevent neural networks from overfitting. J. Mach. Learn. Res. **15**(1), 1929–1958 (2014)

19. Vázquez, A.L., et al.: Innovative identification of substance use predictors: machine learning in a national sample of Mexican children. Preven. Sci. **21**(2), 171–181 (2020)

20. White, K.: Forecasting Canadian elections using Twitter. In: Khoury, R., Drummond, C. (eds.) AI 2016. LNCS (LNAI), vol. 9673, pp. 186–191. Springer, Cham (2016). https://doi.org/10.1007/978-3-319-34111-8_24

21. White, K., Li, G., Japkowicz, N.: Sampling online social networks using coupling from the past. In: 2012 IEEE 12th International Conference on Data Mining Workshops, pp. 266–272. IEEE (2012)

22. Yadav, S., Lokala, U., Daniulaityte, R., Thirunarayan, K., Lamy, F., Sheth, A.: "When they say weed causes depression, but it's your fav antidepressant": Knowledge-aware attention framework for relationship extraction. PloS ONE **16**(3), e0248299 (2021)

On the Bayesian Interpretation of Penalized Statistical Estimators

Jan Kalina[1,2（✉）] [ID] and Barbora Peštová[1]

[1] The Czech Academy of Sciences, Institute of Computer Science,
Pod Vodárenskou věží 2, 182 00 Prague 8, Czech Republic
{kalina,pestova}@cs.cas.cz
[2] The Czech Academy of Sciences, Institute of Information Theory and Automation,
Pod Vodárenskou věží 4, 182 00 Prague 8, Czech Republic

Abstract. The aim of this work is to search for intuitive interpretations of penalized statistical estimators. Penalized estimates of the parameters of three models obtained by Bayesian reasoning are explained here to correspond to the intuition. First, the paper considers Bayesian estimates of the mean and covariance matrix for the multivariate normal distribution. Second, a connection of a robust regularized version of Mahalanobis distance with Bayesian estimation is discussed. Third, regularization networks, which represent a common nonparametric tool for regression modeling, are presented as Bayesian methods as well. On the whole, selected important multivariate and/or regression models are considered and novel interpretations are formulated.

Keywords: Bayesian estimation · regularization · penalization · robustness · regression

1 Introduction

Bayesian statistical analysis plays an important role in the analysis of data in economics, biomedicine, engineering, chemistry, etc. It allows to incorporate a prior knowledge about the distribution of the parameters and the estimation is most often performed by evaluating the mean of the posterior distribution, which is obtained from the Bayes formula. Historically, the Bayes theorem for evaluating the posterior distribution first appeared in a posthumously published paper by the English theologian Rev. Thomas Bayes (1702–1761). From the beginnings, the philosophy of the Bayesian statistical data analysis was to naturally combine the results of given data with available prior information [17]. Currently, we experience a boom of Bayesian methods for the analysis of high-dimensional data [23].

Bayesian estimation allows to incorporate subjective opinion (degree of belief), to eliminate the vagueness of loosely defined concepts, or to capture unreliability (messiness) of data [2]. The prior knowledge increases the information

The research was supported by the project 21-05325S ("Modern nonparametric methods in econometrics") of the Czech Science Foundation.

L. Rutkowski et al. (Eds.): ICAISC 2023, LNAI 14126, pp. 343–352, 2023.
https://doi.org/10.1007/978-3-031-42508-0_31

available about the parameters of interest and reduces thus entropy within the considered probabilistic model. Bayesian thinking is applicable for models with uncertain parameters, if the parameters of the model are obtained with a low-precision arithmetics or are subject to measurement errors [1]. Other applications include Bayesian optimization based on the idea of surrogate modeling, Bayesian versions of quantile regression [15,16] or Bayesian classification. The Bayesian information criterion represents a popular model choice criterion for econometric models. Also in machine learning (computational intelligence), Bayesian methods have an increasing popularity (e.g. in hierarchical models [17]) with possible applications in the analysis of economic (possibly high-dimensional) data. If focusing on economic data, numerous examples of Bayesian methods were recalled in the monograph on Bayesian econometrics [4]. Other recent research includes e.g. Bayesian analysis of economic time series [25] or Bayesian methods for predicing the prices and algorithmic trading [5].

Bayesian tools may exploit non-informative priors or empirical Bayes approaches, i.e. to avoid the necessity of specifying the priors. Still, Bayesian estimation methods even for the simplest statistical models have sometimes been understood as too complicated or inaccessible. The reluctance to using Bayesian methods stems in our opinion from a lack of understanding the Bayesian methods as intuitive and natural estimation tools. Based on the classical result of Stein [28] for the location model for a multivariate normal distribution, the arithmetic mean is dominated by a shrinkage estimator obtained in a simple form as a combination of the mean with zero. In an analogous manner, shrinkage estimators obtained by shrinking standard estimates towards zero (in fact towards any arbitrary vector) in a variety of models have been shown to possess appeling properties (cf. [10]). Such estimators may often be derived in a Bayesian setup. Stein's theoretical result launched the popularity of regularization (in fact much more in machine learning than in statistics) and opened the door to the study of penalized estimators (i.e. combinations of classical methods with some prior knowledge).

The paper aims to formulate some interesting connections and interpretations related to Bayesian point estimation. The properties shown here represent carefully elaborated ideas that are straightforward but hard to find in the literature. The paper also aims to advocate the Bayesian point of view for several particular estimation tasks, where the estimates have the form of penalized methods. Starting with the simplest model, Sect. 2 is devoted to the estimation of the mean of the multivariate normal distribution. Section 3 considers the covariance matrix of normal data and the corresponding Mahalanobis distance, which is formulated here in an original form as a robustified (i.e. modified to be resistant against outliers [20]) and at the same time regularized version. Section 4 discusses regularization networks for a regression task in a nonparametric setup. Section 5 concludes the paper.

2   Estimating the Normal Mean

In this section, we discuss an interesting connection related to the Bayesian estimator of the expectation of p-variate normal distribution with a known covariance matrix. Let us consider $\mathbf{X}_1, \ldots, \mathbf{X}_n$ as a random sample of p-variate data, where $\mathbf{X}_i$ comes from the normal distribution $N_p(\boldsymbol{\mu}, \boldsymbol{\Sigma})$ for $i = 1, \ldots, n$. Let us assume to have available estimates $\mathbf{t}_1, \ldots, \mathbf{t}_R$ of the parameter $\boldsymbol{\mu}$, which come from some available (previously performed) study. Arithmetic means will be denoted in the usual way as

$$\bar{\mathbf{X}} = \frac{1}{n} \sum_{i=1}^{n} \mathbf{X}_i \quad \text{and} \quad \bar{\mathbf{t}} = \frac{1}{R} \sum_{r=1}^{R} \mathbf{t}_r. \tag{1}$$

The available prior knowledge about the vector parameter $\boldsymbol{\mu}$ will be modeled here by means of the normal distribution

$$\boldsymbol{\mu} \sim N_p(\bar{\mathbf{t}}, \boldsymbol{\eta}). \tag{2}$$

In this Bayesian setup, the mean of the posterior distribution of the vector $\boldsymbol{\mu}$ was expressed already in [8] in the form

$$\hat{\boldsymbol{\mu}} = (n\boldsymbol{\Sigma}^{-1} + \boldsymbol{\eta}^{-1})^{-1}(n\boldsymbol{\Sigma}^{-1}\bar{\mathbf{X}} + \boldsymbol{\eta}^{-1}\bar{\mathbf{t}}). \tag{3}$$

Further, we assume a specific assumption $\boldsymbol{\Sigma} = \sigma^2\boldsymbol{\mathcal{I}}$ to hold with a known $\sigma > 0$. We also assume that the precision (uncertainty) of the measurement of all the coordinates of the vector $\boldsymbol{\mu}$ is the same. The prior knowledge about the vector parameter $\boldsymbol{\mu}$ is modeled here by the normal distribution

$$\boldsymbol{\mu} \sim N_p(\bar{\mathbf{t}}, \operatorname{diag}(\gamma^2, \ldots, \gamma^2)), \tag{4}$$

where diag denotes a diagonal matrix. Then, the expectation (3) of the posterior distribution of the expectation $\boldsymbol{\mu}$ corresponds to

$$\hat{\boldsymbol{\mu}} = \frac{n\gamma^2\bar{\mathbf{X}} + \sigma^2\bar{\mathbf{t}}}{n\gamma^2 + \sigma^2}, \tag{5}$$

which represents a penalized estimator alternatively expressed as

$$\hat{\boldsymbol{\mu}} = (1 - \delta)\bar{\mathbf{X}} + \delta\bar{\mathbf{t}}, \quad \text{where} \quad \delta = \frac{\gamma^{-2}}{n\sigma^{-2} + \gamma^{-2}} = \frac{\sigma^2}{n\gamma^2 + \sigma^2}. \tag{6}$$

Under more particular assumptions, let us now assume a fixed value of the ratio denoted here as

$$\rho = \frac{\sigma^2}{n\gamma^2}. \tag{7}$$

This assumption may be realistic in many applications in the analysis of measurements (metrology), because σ^2/n represents the variance of each coordinate of $\bar{\mathbf{X}}$. Using a fixed (7) is realistic under the assumption of a non-contaminated (homoscedastic) model. Naturally, the variability of the current measurements may be the same as that of the previous measurements, but still the setup (7) allows an even more realistic situation that the previously performed measurements have a lower precision (larger variability). Now, we can plug in the expression

$$\gamma^{-2} = \frac{n\rho}{\sigma^2} \tag{8}$$

to the multivariate Bayesian estimator (5). Using straightforward calculations then leads to the expression

$$\delta = \frac{R}{R+1} \quad \text{and} \quad \hat{\mu} = \frac{1}{R+1}\bar{\mathbf{X}} + \frac{R}{R+1}\bar{\mathbf{t}}. \tag{9}$$

This represents a shrinkage estimator [28] of the vector μ in a specific form, namely as a shrunken version of $\bar{\mathbf{X}}$ towards the average $\bar{\mathbf{t}}$. The intensity of the shrinkage is determined by the value of the coefficient (7) [7].

3 Robust Regularized Mahalanobis Distance

Let us discuss the robust regularized Mahalanobis distance; as a novel result, the distance is presented in this section as a Bayesian estimator of the population Mahalanobis distance. The novel version of the Mahalanobis distance may be useful for classification, clustering, outlier detection [6], or texture analysis in images; see also the discussion in [19] on applications to economic data. Let us assume to have a p-variate random vector $\mathbf{X}_1, \ldots, \mathbf{X}_n$ coming from the normal distribution $N_p(\mu, \Sigma)$ with a known μ and unknown matrix $\Sigma \in \mathrm{PD}(p)$, where $\mathrm{PD}(p)$ denotes the set of all positive definite matrices of size $p \times p$. Because the classical estimates of Σ are vulnerable (non-robust) to the presence of outliers in the data, various robust estimates have been proposed [18].

As a particularly appealing joint estimator of both μ and Σ, let us consider the recently proposed minimum weighted covariance determinant (MWCD) estimator [26]. The estimator is based on implicit weights assigned to individual observations; the user chooses only their magnitudes and the weights as such are then assigned to individual observations only after a permutation that is optimized within the computation of the estimator. The MWCD estimator is known to be robust to the presence of outliers in the data. It is in fact highly robust in terms of the breakdown point. At the same time, the influence function and asymptotic covariance matrix were evaluated for the MWCD estimator of μ [26]. It is also important that the MWCD estimator remains highly efficient for non-contaminated data (i.e. without outliers). The MWCD estimator has appealing properties like other statistical methods based on ranks of observations [27].

We use the notation $\tilde{\mathbf{X}}_{MWCD}$ and $\mathbf{S}_{MWCD}$ to denote the MWCD-estimates of μ and Σ, respectively. We also introduce the notation

$$\mathbf{U} = n\mathbf{S}_{MWCD}. \tag{10}$$

In the following, we assume μ to be known in order to study a Bayesian alternative of $\mathbf{S}_{MWCD}$. Assuming the data without outliers, we consider the matrix $\mathbf{U}$ to follow the Wishart distribution $W_p(\mathbf{\Sigma}, n)$ so that it holds $E\,\mathbf{U}/n = \mathbf{\Sigma}$. As in [8], let us model the uncertainty about $\mathbf{\Sigma}$ (in fact about $\mathbf{\Sigma}^{-1}$) by the Wishart distribution

$$\mathbf{\Sigma}^{-1} \sim W_p(\nu + p - 1, \mathbf{\Omega}^{-1}) \quad \text{for a certain } \nu > 0 \text{ and a certain } \mathbf{\Omega} \in \text{PD}(p). \tag{11}$$

Now, $\mathbf{\Sigma}$ has the inverse Wishart distribution $W_p^{-1}(\nu + p - 1, \mathbf{\Omega})$ and it holds that

$$E\mathbf{\Sigma}^{-1} = (\nu + p - 1)\mathbf{\Omega}^{-1} \quad \text{so that} \quad E\mathbf{\Sigma} = \mathbf{\Omega}/(\nu - 2). \tag{12}$$

The posterior expectation $\mathbf{\Sigma}$ is then equal to

$$\hat{\mathbf{\Sigma}} = \frac{\mathbf{U} + \mathbf{\Omega}}{n + \nu - 2}. \tag{13}$$

The Bayesian risk of empirical Bayesian estimates of $\mathbf{\Sigma}$, which are based on estimating hyperparameters from the data, were studied for the given setup in the paper [11].

Specifically, let us interpret the Bayesian estimator obtained in (13). We use a different context than in Sect. 2, where a shrinkage coefficient was assumed to be fixed. Let us now consider available data from some previous study. The obtained estimates of $\mathbf{\Sigma}$ available from the previous study will be denoted as $\mathbf{U}_1/n, \ldots, \mathbf{U}_R/n$. In other words, the matrices $\mathbf{U}_1, \ldots, \mathbf{U}_R$ represent prior counterparts of $\mathbf{U}$. We assume that each of the previous studies used n measurements, which were performed with the same variability (precision) as the current measurements. It is natural to select $\mathbf{\Omega}$ and ν so that

$$\frac{1}{R} \sum_{r=1}^{R} \frac{\mathbf{U}_r}{n} = \frac{\mathbf{\Omega}}{\nu - 2}, \tag{14}$$

i.e. to take $\mathbf{\Omega} = \sum_{r=1}^{R} \mathbf{U}_r$ a $\nu = Rn + 2$. The estimats (13) is then obtained as an intuitive combination of the result of the measurements with the set of previous measurements. Such combination has the form of a penalized estimator

$$\hat{\mathbf{\Sigma}} = \frac{1}{n(R+1)} \left(\mathbf{U} + \sum_{r=1}^{R} \mathbf{U}_r \right). \tag{15}$$

Further, a robust regularized Mahalanobis distance based on the MWCD estimate of $\mathbf{\Sigma}$ will be defined. We consider a new observation $\mathbf{Z} \in \mathbb{R}^p$ and the task is to estimate the population Mahalanobis distance of $\mathbf{Z}$ from given data $\mathbf{X}_1, \ldots, \mathbf{X}_n$. The population version is unknown in the realistic scenario if we assume the expectation μ of $\mathbf{X}_1, \ldots, \mathbf{X}_n$ and their covariance matrix $\mathbf{\Sigma}$ to be unknown. We may express the square of the distance as

$$d^2(\mathbf{Z}; \mathbf{X}_1, \ldots, \mathbf{X}_n) = (\mathbf{Z} - \bar{\mathbf{X}}_{MWCD})^T \mathbf{S}_{MWCD}^{-1} (\mathbf{Z} - \bar{\mathbf{X}}_{MWCD}). \tag{16}$$

A joint estimation of the mean and the covariance matrix in the Bayesian setup is more complicated; it is possible to consider shrinkage versions also for $\bar{\mathbf{X}}_{MWCD}$. Replacing the means by shrinkage version in the Mahalanobis distance seems common in the context of regularized LDA in biostatistics [10].

Numerical linear algebra may be exploited for an efficient computation of $\mathbf{S}_{MWCD} + \lambda \mathcal{I}_p$ for a given λ for (16); we formulate here Algorithm 1 for this purpose with an automatically performed regularization. The notation $\mathbb{1}_A$ is used to denote the indicator of an event A. The eigenvalues used in Algorithm 1 can be easily shown to be equal to the eigenvalues of $\mathbf{S}_{MWCD} + \lambda \mathcal{I}_p$. In addition, the algorithm uses an asymptotically optimal value of λ, which was derived already in [21] for estimating $\boldsymbol{\Sigma}$ by the classical (non-robust) but regularized form of the empirical covariance matrix.

For the context of outlier detection, we suggest to perform the commonly accepted approach to assume the regularized Mahalanobis distances to approximately follow a χ^2-distribution [3]. If we assume $\boldsymbol{\mu}$ to be known, then the squared Mahalanobis distance (16) is replaced by

$$d^2(\mathbf{Z}; \mathbf{X}_1, \ldots, \mathbf{X}_n) = (\mathbf{Z} - \boldsymbol{\mu})^T \left(\mathbf{S}_{MWCD} + \lambda \mathcal{I}_p\right)^{-1} (\mathbf{Z} - \boldsymbol{\mu}), \qquad (17)$$

where the Tikhonov regularization is applied on $\mathbf{S}_{MWCD}$. The squared distance (17) can be interpreted a Bayesian version of the MWCD-based Mahalanobis distance.

4   Regularization Networks

In this section, we explain that the connection of regularization networks [9] to Bayesian estimation is very intuitive. Regularization networks represent a class of nonlinear regression (supervised learning) tools in machine learning [24]; it deserves to be stressed that they are different from regularized neural networks [13], where the latter can be described simply as regularized versions of any models of neural networks.

Let us have the total number n observations with values of a continuous response $\mathbf{Y} = (Y_1, \ldots, Y_n)^T$ and corresponding n vectors of regressors (predictors) $\mathbf{X}_1, \ldots, \mathbf{X}_n$ that are p-variate. The aim is to estimate the regression function

$$f(\mathbf{x}) = \mathsf{E}(Y|\mathbf{X} = \mathbf{x}), \quad \mathbf{x} \in \mathbb{R}^p, \qquad (24)$$

based on given data. We only assume that f exists but its shape is unknown. One possibility is to estimate f as a solution of the optimization task

$$\min_{f \in H_K} \left\{ \sum_{i=1}^{n} (Y_i - f(\mathbf{X}_i))^2 + \lambda \|f\|_{H_K} \right\}, \qquad (25)$$

with a regularization parameter $\lambda > 0$, where f is searched for in a reproducing kernel Hilbert space (RKHS), i.e. a space with with reproducible kernel,

---

Algorithm 1. Robust regularized Mahalanobis distance

Input: Data $\mathbf{X}_1, \ldots, \mathbf{X}_n$, where $\mathbf{X}_i \in \mathbb{R}^p$ for $i = 1, \ldots, n$

Input: A new observation $\mathbf{Z} \in \mathbb{R}^p$

Output: Robust regularized Mahalanobis distance of $\mathbf{Z}$ from $\mathbf{X}_1, \ldots, \mathbf{X}_n$ based on the MWCD estimation

1: $\bar{\mathbf{X}}_{MWCD} :=$ MWCD-estimate of the expectation of $\mathbf{X}_1, \ldots, \mathbf{X}_n$

2: $\mathbf{S}_{MWCD} = \left(S_{ij}^{MWCD}\right)_{i,j=1}^p :=$ MWCD-estimate of the covariance matrix of $\mathbf{X}_1, \ldots, \mathbf{X}_n$

3: Compute the eigendecomposition of $\mathbf{S}_{MWCD}$ as

$$\mathbf{S}_{MWCD} = \mathbf{Q}\mathbf{D}\mathbf{Q}^T, \tag{18}$$

where

$$\mathbf{D} = diag\{\theta_1, \ldots, \theta_p\} \quad \text{and} \quad \mathbf{Q}^T = \mathbf{Q}^{-1}. \tag{19}$$

4: For

$$\hat{\lambda} = \frac{\sum_{i=1}^p \sum_{j=1}^p \widehat{\text{var}}(S_{ij}^{MWCD})}{\sum_{i=1}^p \sum_{j=1}^p (S_{ij}^{MWCD} - \mathbb{1}_{[i=j]})^2}$$

$$= \frac{\sum_{i=1}^p \sum_{j=1}^p \widehat{\text{var}}(S_{ij}^{MWCD})}{2\sum_{i=2}^p \sum_{j=1}^{i-1} \left(S_{ij}^{MWCD}\right)^2 + \sum_{i=1}^p (S_{ii}^{MWCD} - 1)^2}, \tag{20}$$

compute

$$\mathbf{D}^* := \text{diag}\{(1 - \hat{\lambda})\theta_1 + \hat{\lambda}, \ldots, (1 - \hat{\lambda})\theta_p + \hat{\lambda}\}. \tag{21}$$

5:

$$(\mathbf{D}^*)^{-1} := \text{diag}\left\{\left((1 - \hat{\lambda})\theta_1 + \hat{\lambda}\right)^{-1}, \ldots, \left((1 - \hat{\lambda})\theta_p + \hat{\lambda}\right)^{-1}\right\} \tag{22}$$

6:

$$d(\mathbf{Z}; \mathbf{X}_1, \ldots, X_n) := \sqrt{(\mathbf{Z} - \bar{\mathbf{X}}_{MWCD})^T \mathbf{Q} \, (\mathbf{D}^*)^{-1} \mathbf{Q}^T (\mathbf{Z} - \bar{\mathbf{X}}_{MWCD})} \tag{23}$$

---

which corresponds to the Hilbert space of real functions on $\mathbb{R}^p$ [12]. Typically, K is now chosen as the Gaussian kernel

$$K(\mathbf{X}, \mathbf{y}) = \exp\left\{-\frac{\|\mathbf{X} - \mathbf{y}\|^2}{2\sigma^2}\right\}, \quad \mathbf{X}, \mathbf{y} \in \mathbb{R}^p, \tag{26}$$

with a fixed $\sigma > 0$, which can be estimated from the data. The task (25) may be expressed as

$$\min_{\alpha} \left\{\|\mathbf{Y} - \mathbf{K}\alpha\|^2 + \lambda\alpha^T\mathbf{K}\alpha\right\}, \tag{27}$$

where $\alpha = (\alpha_1, \ldots, \alpha_n)^T$ is a vector of parameters and $\mathbf{K}$ is a symmetric matrix with $K_{ij} = K(\mathbf{X}_i, \mathbf{X}_j)$ for $i, j = 1, \ldots, n$. Derivatives may be used to find out that minimum is achieved for the vector

$$\hat{\alpha} = \left(\mathbf{K}^T\mathbf{K} + \lambda\mathbf{K}\right)^{-1}\mathbf{K}^T\mathbf{Y}$$
$$= [(\mathbf{K} + \lambda\boldsymbol{\mathcal{I}})\mathbf{K}]^{-1}\mathbf{K}^T\mathbf{Y}$$
$$= (\mathbf{K} + \lambda\boldsymbol{\mathcal{I}})^{-1}\mathbf{Y}, \tag{28}$$

which corresponds to the ridge regression estimator for the linear regression model $\mathbf{Y} = \mathbf{K}\boldsymbol{\alpha} + \mathbf{e}$; therefore, the estimator (28) is commonly denoted as the generalized ridge estimator. At the same time, we can say that $\mathbf{K}$ is considered in a penalized version in (28). The fitted value for a new observation $\mathbf{Z} \in \mathbb{R}^p$ is then obtained according to

$$\hat{f}(\mathbf{Z}) = \sum_{i=1}^{n} \hat{\alpha}_i K(\mathbf{Z}, \mathbf{X}_i). \tag{29}$$

Bayesian Interpretation. The estimator (28) of the regression parameters may be obtained according to a Bayesian approach in the following way. We assume the random errors to follow $e \sim N(0, \sigma^2\boldsymbol{\mathcal{I}})$. The prior distribution will be chosen as

$$\boldsymbol{\alpha} \sim N\left(\mathbf{0}, c\mathbf{K}^{-1}\right) \quad \text{with some } c > 0. \tag{30}$$

The expectation equal to 0 is chosen here to simplify the results; if this is not realistic, the data can be transformed correspondingly. In a special situation with $c = \sigma^2/\lambda$, the mean of the posterior distribution is equal to (28).

The choice of the covariance matrix of $\boldsymbol{\alpha}$ to be directly proportional to $\mathbf{K}^{-1}$ corresponds to intuition. The covariance matrix of the parameter namely corresponds to a measure of accuracy of the prior measurements. If two particular measurements (say X_1 and X_2) are very close to each other, their element of $\mathbf{K}$ denoted as K_{12} is extraordinarily large, the corresponding element of the covariance matrix is small, i.e. we can say that the information obtained thanks to the close relationship between X_1 and X_2 is accurate. On the other hand, for two measurement very distant from each other, the corresponding element of the covariance matrix of the prior distribution is large, i.e. an individual distant (possibly outlying) measurement may be very inaccurate. To summarize, the regularization network considers the information in close (closely related) measurements to be more accurate compared to the information in outlying measurements.

5   Conclusion

The importance of Bayesian statistical estimation is without any doubt increasing hand in hand together with the increasing need to combine data from various sources. Also the availability of prior knowledge (experience) about parameters contributes to the increasing popularity of tools of Bayesian estimation. This work reveals and interprets that the Bayesian synthesis of prior and newly available information is intuitive, interpretable, mathematically elegant, and in some important models also straightforward to compute. The interpretations formulated in the paper support the idea that existing methods have a clear interpretation and represent meaningful tools also under the Bayesian way of reasoning.

Bayesian estimation has a potential to be used in many other tasks than in those discussed in this paper. Topics omitted here include other regression methods including regularized multilayer perceptrons, which may be derived in a Bayesian setup in a natural way, Bayesian optimization, or Bayesian approaches to computational intelligence in a broader sense. Further, the Bayesian Model Averaging (BMA) allows to perform an effective model choice for basically any statistical model [14]. In recent years, intensive discussions have been focused on the choice of the prior distribution; the readers may effectively exploit weakly informative priors or non-informative (Jeffreys) priors in a variety of practical tasks.

The authors of this work believe that the future belongs to applying Bayesian principles to robust estimation (i.e. resistant to outliers) in both statistics and machine learning. The connections between Bayesian thinking and robustness, which are illustrated in Sect. 3, seem to have been discussed only rarely, such as in the paper [22] in the econometric context. We also plan to investigate Bayesian approaches to (possibly robust) regularized linear discriminant analysis for high-dimensional data [10], exploiting the ideas of Sect. 3 on the robust regularized Mahalanobis distance. Another idea is to rethink regularization approaches to multilayer perceptrons or radial basis function networks from the point of view of Bayesian statistics.

Acknowledgements. The authors would like to thank Jiří Grim and Lubomír Soukup (both ÚTIA AV ČR) for discussion about Bayesian estimation.

References

1. Beaumont, M.A.: Approximate Bayesian computation. Annu. Rev. Stat. Appl. **6**, 379–403 (2019)
2. Bryant, J., Zhang, J.L.: Bayesian Demographic Estimation and Forecasting. CRC Press, Boca Raton (2019)
3. Cerioli, A., Riani, M., Atkinson, A.C., Corbellini, A.: The power of monitoring: how to make the most of a contaminated multivariate sample. Stat. Methods Appl. **27**, 559–587 (2018)
4. Chan, J., Koop, G., Poirier, D.J., Tobias, J.L.: Bayesian Econometric Methods, 2nd edn. Cambridge University Press, Cambridge (2020)
5. Cohen, G.: Algorithmic strategies for precious metals price forecasting. Mathematics **2022**, 1134 (2022)
6. Dashdondov, K., Kim, M.H.: Mahalanobis distance based multivariate outlier detection to improve performance of hypertension prediction. Neural Process. Lett. **55**, 265–277 (2023)
7. Efron, B., Morris, C.: Stein's estimation rule and its competitors–an empirical Bayes approach. J. Am. Stat. Assoc. **68**, 117–130 (1973)
8. Evans, I.G.: Bayesian estimation of parameters of a multivariate normal distribution. J. Roy. Stat. Soc. B **27**, 279–283 (1965)

9. Evgeniou, T., Pontil, M., Poggio, T.: Regularization networks and support vector machines. Adv. Comput. Math. **13**, 1–50 (2000)
10. Guo, Y., Hastie, T., Tibshirani, R.: Regularized discriminant analysis and its application in microarrays. Biostatistics **8**, 86–100 (2007)
11. Haff, L.R.: Empirical Bayes estimation of the multivariate normal covariance matrix. Ann. Stat. **8**, 586–597 (1980)
12. Hastie, T., Tibshirani, R., Wainwright, M.: Statistical Learning with Sparsity. The Lasso and Generalizations. CRC Press, Boca Raton (2015)
13. Haykin, S.O.: Neural Networks and Learning Machines: A Comprehensive Foundation, 2nd edn. Prentice Hall, Upper Saddle River (2009)
14. Hinne, M., Gronau, Q.F., van den Bergh, D., Wagenmakers, E.J.: A conceptual introduction to Bayesian model averaging. Adv. Methods Pract. Psychol. Sci. **3**, 200–215 (2020)
15. Hlubinka, D., Šiman, M.: On generalized elliptical quantiles in the nonlinear quantile regression setup. TEST **24**, 249–264 (2015)
16. Hlubinka, D., Šiman, M.: On parametric elliptical regression quantiles. REVSTAT Stat. J. **18**, 257–280 (2020)
17. Johnson, A.A., Ott, M.Q., Dogucu, M.: Bayes Rules! An Introduction to Applied Bayesian Modeling. Chapman & Hall/CRC, Boca Raton (2022)
18. Jurečková, J., Picek, J., Schindler, M.: Robust Statistical Methods with R, 2nd edn. CRC Press, Boca Raton (2019)
19. Kalina, J.: On robust information extraction from high-dimensional data. Serb. J. Manag. **9**, 131–144 (2014)
20. Kalina, J., Tichavský, J.: On robust estimation of error variance in (highly) robust regression. Meas. Sci. Rev. **20**, 6–14 (2020)
21. Ledoit, O., Wolf, M.: A well-conditioned estimator for large-dimensional covariance matrices. J. Multivar. Anal. **88**, 365–411 (2004)
22. Pacifico, A.: Robust open Bayesian analysis: overfitting, model uncertainty, and endogeneity issues in multiple regression models. Economet. Rev. **40**, 148–176 (2021)
23. Pfarrhofer, M., Piribauer, P.: Flexible shrinkage in high-dimensional Bayesian spatial autoregressive models. Spat. Stat. **29**, 109–128 (2019)
24. Pillonetto, G.: System identification using kernel-based regularization: new insights on stability and consistency issues. Automatica **93**, 321–332 (2018)
25. Qiu, J., Jammalamadaka, S.R., Ning, N.: Multivariate time series analysis from a Bayesian machine learning perspective. Ann. Math. Artif. Intell. **88**, 1061–1082 (2020)
26. Roelant, E., Van Aelst, S., Willems, G.: The minimum weighted covariance determinant estimator. Metrika **70**, 177–204 (2009)
27. Saleh, A.K.M.E., Picek, J., Kalina, J.: R-estimation of the parameters of a multiple regression model with measurement errors. Metrika **75**, 311–328 (2012)
28. Stein, C.: Inadmissibility of the usual estimator for the mean of a multivariate normal distribution. In: Proceedings of the Third Berkeley Symposium on Mathematical Statistics and Probability, University of California Press, Berkeley, vol. 1, pp. 197–206 (1956)

Synthetic Data for Feature Selection

Firuz Kamalov[1]([envelope]) [iD], Hana Sulieman[2][iD], and Aswani Kumar Cherukuri[3][iD]

[1] Department of Electrical Engineering, Canadian University Dubai, Dubai, UAE
firuz@cud.ac.ae
[2] Department of Mathematics and Statistics, American University of Sharjah, Sharjah, UAE
hsulieman@aus.edu
[3] School of IT and Engineering, Vellore Institute of Technology, Vellore, India
cherukuri@acm.org

Abstract. Feature selection is an important and active field of research in machine learning and data science. Our goal in this paper is to propose a collection of synthetic datasets that can be used as a common reference point for feature selection algorithms. Synthetic datasets allow for precise evaluation of selected features and control of the data parameters for comprehensive assessment. The proposed datasets are based on applications from electronics in order to mimic real life scenarios. To illustrate the utility of the proposed data we employ one of the datasets to test several popular feature selection algorithms. The datasets are made publicly available on GitHub and can be used by researchers to evaluate feature selection algorithms.

Keywords: feature selection · synthetic data · electronics

1 Introduction

Feature selection is a well investigated subject with a large amount of literature devoted to its study. In an effort to improve on the existing results, researchers are continuously introducing new feature selection methods [9]. The existence of such a large corpus of feature selection methods creates a challenge to compare and contrast different methods. Part of the challenge lies in the lack of agreement among researchers regarding benchmark datasets to be used for evaluating feature selection algorithms. Each team of researchers uses its own judgment and preference to decide on the data to be used for evaluating their proposed method. Given that feature selection methods are often tested on different datasets, it is hard to compare and analyze the reported results.

In this paper, we attempt to standardize the evaluation process by introducing a collection of synthetic datasets that are designed specifically for the purpose of feature selection. Synthetic data offers several advantages over real-life data [7]. Unlike real-life data, the relevant features of synthetic data are known a

Supported by the American University of Sharjah research grant: FRG22-E-S84.

L. Rutkowski et al. (Eds.): ICAISC 2023, LNAI 14126, pp. 353–365, 2023.
https://doi.org/10.1007/978-3-031-42508-0_32

priori. Thus, it is possible to directly evaluate a feature selection method with the exact knowledge of the correct features. In addition, synthetic data allows us to control the parameters of data and analyze the performance of feature selection methods under various conditions. By varying the number of irrelevant and correlated features we can investigate the precision of feature selection methods. Synthetic data also allows us to control the amount of random noise and study the corresponding effectiveness of the selection algorithms. Finally, by controlling the degrees of freedom of the target value function, we can measure the response of selection algorithms to nonlinear problems.

The proposed synthetic datasets are inspired by ideas from electrical engineering. In particular, we employ digital logic, electric circuits, and light-emitting diodes to design the synthetic datasets. Digital logic is applied in electronics and computer architecture as well as in robotics and other fields. Therefore, using digital logic allows us to construct realistic datasets for feature selection. Logic operations allow the construction of both linear and nonlinear target variables. In addition, redundant and correlated variables as well as noise can easily be implemented within synthetic data using digital logic. Similarly, electric circuits play a fundamental role in electrical engineering. Given the analog nature of electric circuits, we can generate continuous-valued data to simulate regression tasks.

While synthetic datasets have been used for feature selection in the past, their adoption as standard benchmark datasets has been limited [2,4,12]. This is partly due to the lack of datasets that are specifically designed for feature selection and not just general machine learning tasks. In addition, there does not exist a simple way for accessing these datasets. To overcome, these drawbacks the proposed synthetic data is purpose-built for feature selection. Furthermore, for convenience, the code for generating the proposed data is shared on GitHub. Thus, we hope to bring the evaluation process into a common framework to advance the research on feature selection algorithms.

Our paper is structured as follows. In Sect. 2, we provide a brief overview of the existing literature. In Sect. 3, we describe the details of the proposed synthetic datasets. In Sect. 4, we use one of the proposed datasets to evaluate the performance of feature selection methods. Section 5 concludes the paper.

2   Literature

Most of the existing synthetic data used in feature selection was originally designed for general machine learning tasks such as classification and regression. In particular, synthetic datasets based on Boolean features and operations have been utilized in the past, albeit in a limited capacity. The most well-known Boolean dataset is the XOR data which consists of two relevant features together with several irrelevant features [12]. The target variable is determined by the formula $Y = X_1 \oplus X_2$. Another commonly used Boolean data is based on the parity function. It consists of n relevant features and the target variable is given by the rule $Y = 1$ if the number of $X_i = 1$ is odd and $Y = 0$ otherwise [1]. In [6], the authors proposed the CorrAL dataset which consists of six Boolean features and the target variable is given by the formula $(x_1 \wedge x_2) \vee (x_3 \wedge x_4)$. Feature X_5 is irrelevant and feature X_6 is correlated with Y by 75%. An extension of the CorrAL dataset with 100 features was proposed in [12]. In [16], the authors use six binary features to describe the task of a robot which is used as a basis for a synthetic dataset [2]. In [20], the authors mimicked microarray data to create synthetic data with similar characteristics.

A synthetic dataset with continuous features and a binary target variable was proposed in [18], where the authors divided 100 features into 10 groups of highly correlated variables. Then the points where randomly assigned into two clusters using the Gaussian distribution. Another dataset with continuous features and a binary class value was given in [14], where the target variable was decided as a linear function of equal weights of the relevant features. In [13], the authors used a similar approach but using a nonlinear neural network to generate the class labels. Perhaps the most well-known continuous-valued synthetic data are the Friedman datasets [3,5,8]. The datasets consists of several relevant and irrelevant continuous-valued features. The target value is computed based on polynomial, rational, and trigonometric operations. The Friedman datasets were originally designed for testing regression models. Researchers have subsequently also used it in feature selection.

Synthetic data has also been employed in nontraditional feature selection tasks such as unsupervised feature selection [15], dynamic feature selection [11], and imbalanced feature selection [9]. We note that not all synthetic data is well suited for feature selection [17, 19].

3   Synthetic Data

In this section, we describe the proposed synthetic data for feature selection. The datasets are presented in order from simple to complex. The summary of the proposed datasets is provided in Table 1. Every dataset consists of a total of 100 features and a target variable. The target value is completely determined by the relevant features.

In our approach, we chose to include the same number of redundant features as the relevant ones. The redundant features are created either as a negation of the corresponding relevant feature in the case of binary features or as a linear function of the corresponding relevant feature in the case of continuous features. In addition, each dataset includes 2 correlated features. The correlated features are created by randomly changing the value of the target variable in 30% of the instances. Thus, the correlated features are correlated with the target variable 70% of the time. Note that the correlated features have no causal relation with the target variable and are not desirable. The remaining features are randomly generated to be irrelevant.

The proposed datasets cover a range of possibilities for the target variable including binary, multi-class, and continuous values. The number of observations is chosen to be small relative to the number of features. However, it can be adjusted as necessary. The details of each proposed dataset are presented in the subsequent sections.

Table 1. Summary of the proposed datasets.

Name	Relevant	Redundant	Correlated	Irrelevant	Samples	Target
ORAND	3	3	2	92	50	binary
ANDOR	4	4	2	90	50	binary
ADDER	3	3	2	92	50	4-class
LED-16	16	16	2	66	180	36-class
PRC	5	5	2	88	500	continuous

The irrelevant variables are created using a random number generator. To maintain consistency a fixed random seed is used in generating the irrelevant variables. All the datasets were created using Python programming language. The datasets and the corresponding code are publicly available on GitHub.

3.1 ORAND

The proposed dataset is based on a two-layer circuit as shown in Fig. 1. The first layer consists of an OR gate, while the second layer consists of an AND gate.

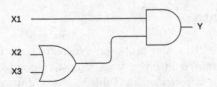

Fig. 1. The ORAND circuit diagram.

The ORAND dataset contains three relevant features X_1, X_2, and X_3. The target variable Y is calculated via the following formula:

$$Y = X_1 \land (X_2 \lor X_3). \tag{1}$$

In addition to the three relevant variables, we add three redundant (correlated) variables - one for each of X_1, X_2, and X_3. We also add 2 features that randomly match the target variable in 70% of the instances. In the end, we include $N_I = 92$ irrelevant features which are randomly generated according to the Bernoulli process. We obtain a synthetic dataset consisting of 3 relevant, 3 redundant, 2 correlated, and 92 irrelevant features. There are a total 2^{100} possible feature value combinations of which we select $n = 50$ samples. As it is often the case with high dimensional data, the number of features is high relative to the number of observations. While the default number of samples is 50, it can be changed as necessary. In fact, both the number of observations and the number of irrelevant features can be varied to analyze the performance of a feature selection algorithm under different conditions. However, it is strongly advised to employ the proposed datasets under the default settings, at least once, to obtain a benchmark reference result.

3.2   ANDOR

The proposed dataset is based on a two-layer circuit as shown in Fig. 2. The first layer consists of two AND gates, while the second layer consists of a single OR gate.

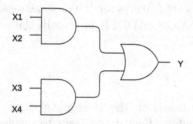

Fig. 2. The ANDOR circuit diagram.

The ANDOR dataset contains four relevant features X_1, X_2, X_3, and X_4. The target variable Y is calculated via the following formula:

$$Y = (X_1 \wedge X_2) \vee (X_3 \wedge X_4). \tag{2}$$

The expression in Eq. 2 can be viewed as the sum of products. In addition to the four relevant variables, we add four redundant (correlated) variables - one for each of X_1, X_2, X_3, and X_4. We also add 2 features that randomly match with the target variable 70% of the time. Finally, we include $N_I = 90$ irrelevant features which are randomly generated according to the Bernoulli process. We use the features to randomly generate $n = 50$ samples. We obtain a synthetic dataset consisting of 4 relevant, 4 redundant, 2 correlated, and 90 irrelevant features and 50 samples. As with the ORAND dataset, the number of irrelevant features N_I and the number of samples n can be changed to evaluate a feature selection algorithm under different scenarios.

The ANDOR dataset can be expanded by increasing the number of relevant variables up to m in the following manner:

$$Y = (X_1 \wedge X_2) \vee (X_3 \wedge X_4) \cdots \vee (X_{n-1} \wedge X_m). \tag{3}$$

Additional redundant and irrelevant features can be included in similar fashion as above.

3.3 ADDER

The ADDER dataset is based on the eponymous adder circuit. It is a multi-class target dataset. The full adder takes three inputs X_1, X_2, and X_3 and produces two outputs Y_1 and Y_2. The outputs are calculated according to the following formulae:

$$Y_1 = X_1 \oplus X_2 \oplus X_3$$
$$Y_2 = (X_1 \wedge X_2) \vee (X_3 \wedge (X_1 \oplus X_2)) \tag{4}$$

By combining the values of Y_1 and Y_2 into a single target variable $Y = (Y_1, Y_2)$, we obtain a 4-class target variable: $Y = \{(0,0), (0,1), (1,0), (1,1)\}$. As usual, we add redundant features - one for each of X_1, X_2, and X_3 - 2 correlated features, and $N_I = 92$ irrelevant features. We randomly generate $n = 50$ samples based on the full set of features. The final dataset consists of 3 relevant, 3 redundant, 2 correlated, and 92 irrelevant features and 50 observations. As mentioned above, unlike ORAND and ANDOR, ADDER is a multi-class dataset with a 4-class target variable.

3.4 LED-16

The LED-16 dataset is based on the 16-segment display configuration shown in Fig. 3. The 16-segment configuration allows to display all 26 letters of the English alphabet as well as all the digits 0-9. Each segment represents a binary feature: on/off. The target variable is the alpha-numeric value displayed by the segments. Thus, the target variable can take 36 different values. We add 16 redundant features - one for each relevant feature (segment). We also include 2 correlated and 66 irrelevant features with randomly generated binary values.

Fig. 3. The 16-segment LED display.

The dataset contains 180 observations - 5 samples for each target value. In particular, for each target value, the values of the relevant and redundant features are determined by the display configuration, while the values of remaining features are randomly generated. In summary, the LED-16 dataset consists of 16 relevant, 16 redundant, 2 correlated, and 66 irrelevant features and 180 observations. It is a multi-class dataset with a 36-class target variable.

As shown in Fig. 4, some LED segments are used more frequently than others. For example, the segment F is utilized in the majority of configurations, while the segment H is used in only a few times. While both segments are relevant, they have different levels of significance. The LED-16 dataset allows to evaluate feature selection algorithms on the basis of their sensitivity to different level of feature relevance. A robust selection algorithm should identify both strongly and weakly relevant features.

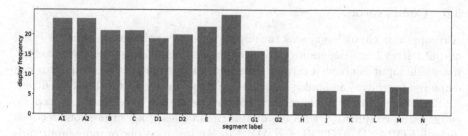

Fig. 4. Frequency distribution of the LED-16 segments over 36 alphanumeric characters.

3.5 PRC

The proposed dataset is based on the parallel resistor circuit. Given a set of resistors $\{R_1, R_2, ..., R_N\}$ that are connected in parallel, the total resistance R_T is given by the following equation:

$$\frac{1}{R_T} = \sum_{i=1}^{N} \frac{1}{R_i}. \tag{5}$$

For the proposed PRC dataset, we use 5 parallel connected resistors (relevant features). The relevant features $\{X_i\}_{i=1}^{5}$ are generated according to the Gaussian distribution with mean $\mu_i = 10$ and standard deviation $\sigma_i = i, i = 1, 2, ..., 5$. The target variable $Y = R_T$ is calculated according to Eq. 5. Since the parallel resistors as well as the total resistance are continuous valued variables, the PRC dataset implies a regression task.

We generate 5 redundant, 2 correlated, and 88 irrelevant features to include in the dataset. The redundant variables are created as linear transformations of the relevant variables. The correlated variables are created by adding a small amount of noise perturbation to the target variable. Half of the irrelevant variables are generated according to the same Gaussian distribution as the relevant variables. In particular, for each $i = 1, 2, ..., 5$, we generated nine random features according to the Gaussian distribution $\mathcal{N}(\mu_i = 10, \sigma_i = i)$. The remaining half of the irrelevant features are randomly generated according to the uniform distribution $\mathcal{U}(0, 1)$.

Since the target variable Y is continuous valued, we generate more observations for the PCR dataset than for the classification data described in the previous sections. In particular, we generate 500 samples using the full feature set, where the target variable is calculated via Eq. 5 based on the features $\{X_i\}_{i=1}^5$.

To promote the adoption of common benchmarking, the proposed datasets are made publicly available on GitHub. Alternatively, a dedicated software package to generate these datasets is also available in [10].

3.6 Comparator

A comparator circuit compares two inputs - usually voltages or currents - and outputs either 1 or 0 depending on which input is greater. It is often used to check if a single input is above a certain threshold. In this manner, a comparator can employed to convert an analog (continuous) signal into a digital (binary) output.

Since a comparator converts a continuous signal into binary, it can be employed in conjunction with the digital circuits described in previous sections including ORAND, ANDOR, and ADDER. For instance, one or more input variables in the ORAND circuit can be continuous-valued by using a comparator as a preprocessing gate. Thus, datasets with binary features can be extended to include continuous features, which increases the number of available synthetic datasets for feature selection.

4 Feature Selection Based on Synthetic Data

To illustrate the application of the proposed synthetic data we evaluate the performance of standard feature selection algorithms on the ANDOR dataset. Since the relevant features in synthetic data are known, we can directly analyze the effectiveness of the algorithms. Synthetic data also gives an option to control the number of samples and the level of noise in the data which enables researchers better understand the performance of the algorithms under different scenarios.

4.1 Methodology

We use the ANDOR dataset described in Sect. 3.2 to evaluate the feature selection algorithms. The dataset consists of 4 relevant, 4 redundant, 2 correlated, and 90 irrelevant features and a binary target class. The redundant variables are the negations of the relevant variables. The correlated variables are correlated with the target variable at 70%. To observe the effect of the sample size we consider the datasets with 50 and 20 samples.

To account for random variations, we generate the ANDOR dataset using 10 different random seeds. The feature selection algorithms are applied to each of the 10 datasets. The results are averaged and presented for analysis.

4.2   Models

We consider univariate algorithms, recursive feature elimination (RFE), and model-based algorithms for feature selection. In the univariate approach, we employ χ^2 to measure the relationship between a feature and the target variable. In the RFE approach, we use the support vector classifier (SVC) with linear kernel. The SVC model is iteratively fit to the data and at each stage the variable with the lowest coefficient is discarded. In the model-based approach, we use SVC with the L_1-penalty (lasso) and the extra-trees classifier. The lasso model automatically discards the irrelevant features as part of the fitting process. The extra-trees classifier is used to calculate the reduction in impurity of each feature during the fitting process.

4.3   Results

Four feature selection algorithms - univariate (χ^2), RFE, lasso, and extreme trees - are tested based on the ANDOR dataset. The results show that the feature selection methods perform relatively well in distinguishing between the relevant and the irrelevant features. However, the selection algorithms struggle to separate the relevant features from the redundant and correlated features. Furthermore, a decrease in the sample size leads to a lower distinction between the relevant and irrelevant features.

The results of the univariate approach for feature selection are presented in Fig. 5. The average χ^2-scores between the features and the target variable over 10 runs are provided. Since the correlated and irrelevant features are randomly generated, there exists variation in the results between the runs. To show the variations between the runs the standard deviation of χ^2-scores are represented by the red line segments.

As shown in Fig. 5a, in case when the sample size is $n = 50$, the algorithm assigns significantly higher χ^2-scores to the relevant features than the irrelevant features. On the other hand, it also assigns high scores to the redundant and correlated features. Thus, while the algorithm is able to distinguish the relevant features from the irrelevant features, it fails to distinguish the relevant features from the redundant and correlated features. As shown in Fig. 5b, in case when the sample size is $n = 20$, the difference in scores between the relevant and irrelevant features is considerably lower than in the case $n = 50$. Given the large variation of the irrelevant features, it is highly likely that at least some of the irrelevant features may obtain a higher χ^2-score than the relevant features. The features X_2 and X_3 are particularly susceptible to being overlooked.

The results of the RFE approach are presented in Table 2. The tables present RFE feature rankings for the relevant (X_1 to X_4) and redundant (X_5 to X_8) features. The left and right tables correspond to the data of size $n = 50$ and $n = 20$, respectively. The rows in the tables correspond to the datasets generated using different random seeds. The last row $\tilde{r}$ provides the median rankings of the features across 10 runs. The results show that the RFE approach is less effective than the univariate approach. There is a significant variation in the

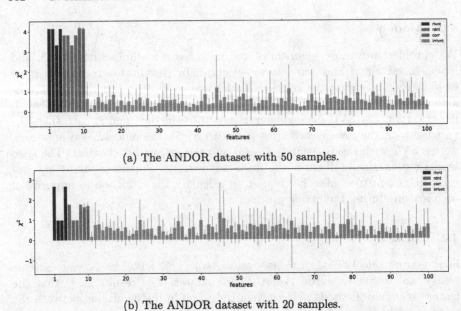

(a) The ANDOR dataset with 50 samples.

(b) The ANDOR dataset with 20 samples.

Fig. 5. The mean χ^2-scores between the features and the target variable. The red line segments show the standard deviations of the scores. (Color figure online)

Table 2. The rankings of the relevant (X_1 to X_4) and redundant (X_5 to X_8) features for each of the 10 versions of the ANDOR dataset using the RFE algorithm.

	(a)The ANDOR dataset with 50 samples.								(b) The ANDOR dataset with 20 samples.							
v	X_1	X_2	X_3	X_4	X_5	X_6	X_7	X_8	X_1	X_2	X_3	X_4	X_5	X_6	X_7	X_8
1	15	14	4	13	3	2	18	1	5	8	20	6	34	13	39	7
2	12	5	23	10	9	8	11	3	29	17	8	5	13	9	16	14
3	12	16	5	6	3	1	2	9	12	7	50	17	4	22	53	8
4	22	13	5	3	6	17	11	14	5	33	39	12	14	29	46	3
5	2	7	9	6	8	4	3	5	16	35	32	9	22	13	26	11
6	13	4	7	6	5	14	2	1	36	11	17	5	28	4	21	6
7	14	5	4	15	3	11	12	2	18	22	37	11	10	35	33	5
8	11	12	9	6	5	2	4	3	14	6	17	12	18	28	4	10
9	6	13	12	4	14	7	10	8	13	43	7	42	9	37	23	30
10	7	11	13	14	3	8	10	6	23	19	27	11	6	20	31	3
$\tilde{r}$	12	12	8	6	5	8	10	4	15	18	24	11	14	21	29	8

rankings between different versions of the dataset which suggests that RFE is not a stable method. To summarize the results we consider the median rankings. In case $n = 50$, 6 features achieved median ranking in the top 10, but only one feature X_8 is in top 4. Thus, if we were to select the top 4 features - since that is the number of relevant variables - only one feature would be correctly selected. In case the $n = 20$, the algorithm performs poorly with only one feature in top 10 and none in the top 4. It is unsurprising that the algorithm is less effective when using a small sample size.

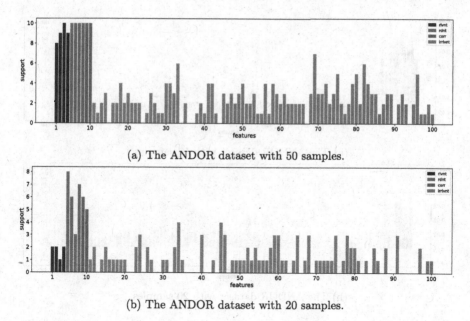

(a) The ANDOR dataset with 50 samples.

(b) The ANDOR dataset with 20 samples.

Fig. 6. The number of times each feature was chosen in the lasso model for 10 versions of the dataset.

The results of the lasso-based approach in case the $n = 50$ are presented in Fig. 6a. The y-axis represents the number of times a feature was selected in the lasso model. As shown in the figure, the lasso approach performed well in this case. The relevant features achieve significantly higher scores than the irrelevant features. However, the redundant and correlated features also achieve high scores. Thus, while the lasso approach is effective at distinguishing between the relevant and irrelevant features, it fails to differentiate the relevant features from the redundant and correlated features. The results in the case $n = 20$ are expectedly less robust. As shown in Fig. 6b, the scores for the relevant features are significantly lower than those for the correlated features. In addition, several irrelevant features have higher scores than the relevant features. On the other hand, three of the redundant features have high scores which can be an acceptable substitute for the relevant features.

The results of the approach based on extra-trees are presented in Fig. 7. The y-axis indicates the average decrease in impurity corresponding to a feature. As shown in Fig. 7a, in the case of $n = 50$, the algorithm performs better than the previous approaches by assigning higher level of importance to relevant features than the irrelevant and correlated features. We also note that the irrelevant features have low variance. So they are less likely to be selected by chance. However, the algorithm does not distinguish well between the relevant and redundant variables. As expected, the algorithm performs worse in the case $n = 20$. While the importance of the relevant variables X_1 and X_4 remains significantly above the

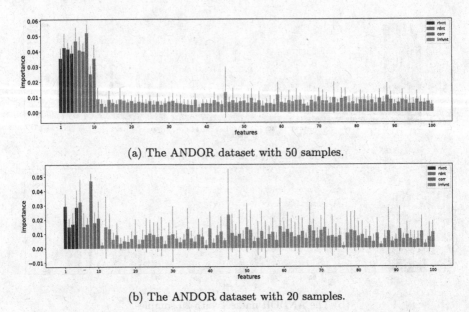

(a) The ANDOR dataset with 50 samples.

(b) The ANDOR dataset with 20 samples.

Fig. 7. The average decrease in impurity using the extra-tree classifier.

irrelevant variables, the gap between the relevant variables X_2 and X_3 and the rest of the features decreased considerably. In addition, the variance of the irrelevant variables increased which increases the likelihood of an irrelevant variable achieving a high level importance purely by chance.

5   Conclusion

Our aim in this paper was to promote common benchmarking of feature selection algorithms. To this end, we proposed a set of synthetic data that can be used as a universal reference point. The proposed synthetic datasets are motivated by ideas from electrical engineering. By mimicking real-life scenarios our goal was to produce data that can provide sensible evaluation of feature selection algorithms. Synthetic data has several advantages including the knowledge of the relevant features and the ability to vary the parameters of the data. As a result, synthetic data allows for a comprehensive evaluation of feature selection algorithms.

We encourage researchers to test their algorithms on the proposed datasets. For convenience, the code for generating the data is publicly which can be used to modify the parameters of the data as needed. However, we strongly advise to use the data under the default settings at least once.

In the future, more synthetic datasets inspired by different sources can be added to the proposed collection. In particular, synthetic data mimicking the gene data in medical research would be desirable. Data for regression tasks with continuous features would also enrich the existing collection.

References

1. Belanche, L.A., González, F.F.: Review and evaluation of feature selection algorithms in synthetic problems. arXiv preprint arXiv:1101.2320 (2011)
2. Bolon-Canedo, V., Sánchez-Marono, N., Alonso-Betanzos, A.: A review of feature selection methods on synthetic data. Knowl. Inf. Syst. **34**(3), 483–519 (2013)
3. Breiman, L.: Bagging predictors. Mach. Learn. **24**(2), 123–140 (1996)
4. Chen, J., Song, L., Wainwright, M., Jordan, M.: Learning to explain: an information-theoretic perspective on model interpretation. In: International Conference on Machine Learning, pp. 883–892. PMLR (2018)
5. Friedman, J.H.: Multivariate adaptive regression splines. Ann. Stat. **19**(1), 1–67 (1991)
6. John, G.H., Kohavi, R., Pfleger, K.: Irrelevant features and the subset selection problem. In: Machine Learning Proceedings 1994, pp. 121–129. Morgan Kaufmann (1994)
7. Jordon, J., Wilson, A., van der Schaar, M.: Synthetic data: opening the data floodgates to enable faster, more directed development of machine learning methods. arXiv preprint arXiv:2012.04580 (2020)
8. Kamalov, F.: Orthogonal variance decomposition based feature selection. Expert Syst. Appl. **182**, 115191 (2021)
9. Kamalov, F., Thabtah, F., Leung, H.H.: Feature selection in imbalanced data. Ann. Data Sci. 1–15 (2022)
10. Kamalov, F., Elnaffar, S., Sulieman, H., Cherukuri, A.K.: XyGen: synthetic data generator for feature selection. Softw. Impacts **15**, 100485 (2023)
11. Kaya, S.K., Navarro-Arribas, G., Torra, V.: Dynamic features spaces and machine learning: open problems and synthetic data sets. In: Huynh, V.-N., Entani, T., Jeenanunta, C., Inuiguchi, M., Yenradee, P. (eds.) IUKM 2020. LNCS (LNAI), vol. 12482, pp. 125–136. Springer, Cham (2020). https://doi.org/10.1007/978-3-030-62509-2_11
12. Kim, G., Kim, Y., Lim, H., Kim, H.: An MLP-based feature subset selection for HIV-1 protease cleavage site analysis. Artif. Intell. Med. **48**(2–3), 83–89 (2010)
13. Liu, B., Wei, Y., Zhang, Y., Yang, Q.: Deep neural networks for high dimension, low sample size data. In: IJCAI, pp. 2287–2293 (2017)
14. Loscalzo, S., Yu, L., Ding, C.: Consensus group stable feature selection. In: Proceedings of the 15th ACM SIGKDD International Conference on Knowledge Discovery and Data Mining, pp. 567–576 (2009)
15. Panday, D., de Amorim, R.C., Lane, P.: Feature weighting as a tool for unsupervised feature selection. Inf. Process. Lett. **129**, 44–52 (2018)
16. Thrun, S.B., et al.: The monk's problems: a performance comparison of different learning algorithms (1991)
17. Varol, G., et al.: Learning from synthetic humans. In: Proceedings of the IEEE Conference on Computer Vision and Pattern Recognition, pp. 109–117 (2017)
18. Wang, D., Nie, F., Huang, H.: Feature selection via global redundancy minimization. IEEE Trans. Knowl. Data Eng. **27**(10), 2743–2755 (2015)
19. Ward, C.M., Harguess, J., Hilton, C.: Ship classification from overhead imagery using synthetic data and domain adaptation. In: OCEANS 2018 MTS/IEEE Charleston, pp. 1–5. IEEE (2018)
20. Zhu, Z., Ong, Y.S., Zurada, J.M.: Identification of full and partial class relevant genes. IEEE/ACM Trans. Comput. Biol. Bioinf. **7**(2), 263–277 (2008)

ML Support for Conformity Checks in CMDB-Like Databases

Szymon Niewiadomski[✉][iD] and Grzegorz Mzyk[iD]

Wroclaw University of Science and Technology, Wrocław, Poland
{szymon.niewiadomski,grzegorz.mzyk}@pwr.edu.pl
http://staff.iiar.pwr.wroc.pl/grzegorz.mzyk/

Abstract. During data input into databases like CMDB (Configuration Management Databases) we usually have a conformity check. The conventional approach is to create hundreds of rules to check data quality. This article shows several ideas on how to use ML algorithms to support the quality management of CMDB. We focus on naming conventions commonly used in CI (Configuration Items) - attributes like hostnames, serial numbers, and application names. Such attributes should be consistent with some dictionary data (operating system names, vendors) and existing relationships (location, applications). We review several strategies for feature extraction including tokenization and analyze the usability of CNB, RVAE, or NN to this particular problem. We also show the results of experiments on a public dataset (USA car database) to demonstrate the efficiency and inspire other researchers to work on similar topics. Algorithms used in the experiment are published as Jupiter Lab files.

Keywords: Data management · Machine learning · Feature extraction · Error detection · Kernel methods

1 Introduction

This article is related to the ongoing deployment of the configuration management process in the [anonymized] company from the energy sector. Configuration Management Database (CMDB) is an inventory of IT equipment and systems. CMDB is confidential and therefore for experiments we choose public inventory of US cars. CMDB is an essential input for other Service Management processes in many areas: security, operations, and transition. Moreover, CMDB data related to infrastructure feeds the automatic provisioning of IT Services [3]. It is an internal part of public or private cloud solutions (sometimes not visible to customers). Mature IT organizations merge infrastructure information with business-related data, i.e. confidentiality, criticality, ownership, and stage in the lifecycle of the IT Systems.

This work is supported by the Polish Minister of Education and Science as part of an implementation doctorate, grant No. DWD/5/0286/2021.

1.1 CMDB Structure

CMDB contains information about CIs (Configuration Items) and their connections. CIs are aggregated in CI classes. Each CI class is defined by a set of fields that describe objects in the class. As a result for each class, we have a table in the database with rows of CIs. Besides CIs we have one dedicated table with relationships defined by two CIs, IDs, and the name of the relationship. The name is different depending on the direction. Example:

EXCHANGE - *runs on* → HOSTNAME1

HOSTNAME1 - *hosts* → EXCHANGE

Consequently, this special CMDB table with relationships changes the nature of CMDB into a digraph.

1.2 CMDB Quality Management

When talking about CMDB quality insurance we consider three areas [5,10]:

- *Completeness* - to ensure that at the correct stage of the lifecycle information is gathered. Without it, next statutes in the lifecycle cannot be reached. (Example: you cannot set the server to "production" if the responsible administrator group is not defined).
- *Accuracy testing* - checking data against reality - especially scans and technical repositories we can trust.
- *Conformity* - data must follow some rules - for example, IP must follow some regular expression.

The conformity check is very difficult in practice. One company from the insurance sector was able to define 700 conformity checks. A team of eleven people dedicated to the configuration management process were working on the subject for three years, and in the end, one million values were tested by these conformity rules nearly online. And here comes an idea to use algorithms [2] and machine learning [7] for conformity checking. It can enable smaller teams to reach quality and allocate people to more interesting tasks.

2 Problem Definition

To work effectively on the data quality, we need to understand why the problem happens and make some categorizations of it. In this section, we also propose a strategy for how to support data clearing with AI algorithms.

2.1 Quality Error Categories

The most common types of errors in CMDB are:

- *Duplicates* - it means that many entries in CMDB point to one real object in CMDB. It occurs in the early stages of the database, where many sources are merged. These types of errors are easy to fix and usually after a few months after implementation problem is marginal. Methods for the scientific approach are listed in [6].

- *Lack of unique names* - this is one of the most serious problems in CMDB. It means that two real objects use the same name and are registered in inventory with the same. It can lead to a situation where a change can be executed on an incorrect object.
- *Erratum (Typos)* - One of the most common problem with manually collected data. Not only in CMDB but also during standard stocktaking reconciliation processes. In 2011, a pharmaceutical company was driving a crosscheck between CMDB and a manually generated inventory list of devices in the Data Center. The first matching result was only 80%. After changing 0 to O, G to 6, I to 1, Z to 2, and S to 5 the result was 98%. The standard way of handling the problem is to eliminate manual data entry - like barcodes. Nevertheless, there are some well-documented AI algorithms presented in the next section which can help a lot.
- *Misuse of the field* - sometimes people do not know exactly what should be documented in the field. A typical example is a field called "CPU Core Count". This field can mean a Core per CPU, physical core, or logical Core (with hyperthreading). Also, sometimes people input values in the wrong field by mistake - for example, part number into the Serial Number field.
- *Unfinished runbooks* - this kind of error is specific to the automatic provisioning of IT services. Usually, we have many work orders in sequence and dependencies between them. It can be quite complex for example runbook to provide an MS SQL server on the cluster can have 140 steps. The error occurs if there is a problem in the work order and you need to roll back the whole build.
- *Incorrect lifecycle* - One of the most important field in CMDB is the status of the CI (examples: "planned", "production-ready", "production", "post-production", "archive") incorrect status cause operational, legal, or security problems. CI in status "production-ready" should be subject to licensing and security measures should be applied. This error category is caused by a poor change management process which is disconnected from the configuration management process.

2.2   Output of the Algorithms

Algorithms which support the Configuration Management team should be active during data input, during initial validation of the data, and during the periodical review of the CMDB content [9]. The expected result of the algorithm is:

- an ordered list of N CIs, candidates for manual check with a probability of the error. It is expected that algorithm selection will contain more CIs with errors than random picks,
- warnings during manual data entry,
- warnings during the automated data loads (for example in REST API interface),
- automatic correction of the data in case of p level of probability that the value is correct,

– autofill of the data in the data input form based on discovered correlations.

The list of CIs will be processed by the Configuration Management team to investigate if the algorithm suggestion is valid. In case the error is confirmed, and the correction is implemented, the case is documented as a sample for supervised learning algorithms. Of course, there must be a step in the process to confirm that CIs is checked and valid to exclude them from the next algorithm cycle.

3 Proposed Strategies

3.1 Data Preprocessing and Feature Extraction

We have a mix of data tapes in CMDB.

- *Categorical data* - this type usually can be handled by a one-hot encoding method. This is the best approach for lists that do not have orders, like Manufacturers, Models/Types, and departments. On the other hand, we should convert it to numbers taking into consideration natural order.
- *Strings* - cells that contain unstructured string values can be transformed into a set of numerical data. We recommend using the following set of numbers created based on character counts: letters, digits, spaces, non-Ascii, length, uppercase, and lowercase. For example, it helps to detect characters that are not visible or unwanted spaces at the beginning of the text. We used this method also in the experiment shown below.
- *Names, Hostnames* - these strings usually consist of a naming convention, and therefore recommended approach is to use tokenization with n-grams [1] (for example 2 characters). It allows looking for a correlation between tokens and other cells. This method is described later in this article.
- *Numerical data* - CPU count, RAM size, CPU speed, Filesystem size - these are examples of numeric values. For this information, we can apply numerical methods like kernel and kNN.

3.2 Understanding of the Naming Convention (Tokenization with n-grams)

Let's assume that we have a server with the hostname DEFRDC01WINTS. The goal is to discover that this hostname can be understood as:

$$DE_{Country}FR_{city}DC01_{DataCenter}WIN_{OsClass}SCC_{Application}TS_{Environment}$$

so we need to divide a string into short tokens and check correlations with other cells within the CI class or with other related objects [15]. In one organization we can have many naming conventions - not only for servers but for applications, network devices, and storage objects [11]. To identify the naming convention for tokens we can use the complement naive Bayes (CNB) method which works well with sparse data and takes into consideration unbalanced nature of CI classes. [12,13]. CNBs are efficient in classification documents based on the words it contains [13]. In our case, we will use it to find a correlation between substrings (n-grams) and other DB fields in CMDB. CNB is fast, so it is reasonable to repeat it and find related fields in class description (Algorithm 1). Logical extension is to use digraph edges (relationships) to look for correlations in connected tables.

Algorithm 1: Finding correlation using CNB

input : Names, CMDB table, threshold
output: CNB fit score between Names and other attributes listed in CMDB table

$x \leftarrow vectorize(Names)$;
for *column in table* **do**
  fit CNB (column,x);
  if *score > threshold* **then**
    | column correlates with naming
  end
  ;
end

3.3   Using RVAE to Discover Outliers

The main idea is to create a pair of transformations - Coder and Encoder in such a way, that only correct objects pass the process and outliers are identified. For CMDB these outliers can be a candidate for manual verification. A very good algorithm is a Robust Variational Autoencoder [4]. CMDB data is usually unbalanced (for example different number of hardware per manufacturer) therefore taking variance into consideration is important of Mixed-Type Data.

3.4   Using NN to Find CIs Which Perform Similar Role but Are Documented Differently by Mistake

Let us consider a two-column dataset (not necessarily numeric)

$$\{(x_k, y_k)\}_{k=1}^N \tag{1}$$

where $x_k \in X$ are independent/explanatory variables (regressors), $y_k \in Y$ are dependent variables, and N denotes number of data records. Let us also introduce the vectors of numeric features

$$F(x_k) = (f_1(x_k), ..., f_n(x_k))^T \tag{2}$$

$$G(y_k) = (g_1(y_k), ..., g_m(y_k))^T \tag{3}$$

where

$$f_i(x_k) \in \mathcal{R}, \; g_j(y_k) \in \mathcal{R}, \quad i = 1, 2, ..., n, \quad j = 1, 2, ..., m, \quad k = 1, 2, ..., N \tag{4}$$

and n, m denote number of considered features of x_k and y_k, respectively. We introduce the following distance metrics

$$D_x\left(x_{k_1}, x_{k_2}\right) = \|F\left(x_{k_1}\right) - F\left(x_{k_2}\right)\| \triangleq w_0 + \sum_{i=1}^{n} w_i d_x(f_i\left(x_{k_1}\right), f_i\left(x_{k_2}\right)), \quad (5)$$

$$D_y\left(y_{k_1}, y_{k_2}\right) = \|G\left(y_{k_1}\right) - G\left(y_{k_2}\right)\| \triangleq \sum_{j=1}^{m} v_j d_y(g_j\left(y_{k_1}\right), g_j\left(y_{k_2}\right)), \quad (6)$$

where w_i and v_j denote the weights determining sensitivity of D_x and D_y on particular features. Symbols $d_x()$ and $d_y()$ represent measure of distance in the feature spaces (2) and (3), respectively, e.g., square or absolute function. When a feature determines the object is belonging to a given class and assumes countable values, the indication function can also be used.

Example 1. Let x be the string variable representing the name of a device, and let y be its serial number. As examples of the extracted features $f_i\left(x\right)$, $g_j\left(y\right)$ the following can be given: total number of symbols, number of numeric symbols, number of spaces, and index of substring found in a given/external dictionary.

The aim of the research is to develop a method that will detect cases in which the distance $D_y\left(y_{k_1}, y_{k_2}\right)$ in the set Y will be large for a relatively close to each other elements (x_{k_1}, x_{k_2}) in X. Obviously, this step is preliminary as not all detected cases will be manually classified as errors. In order to optimize the operation of this stage, after the final decision is made, it is important to tune the weights

$$w = (w_0, w_1, w_2, ..., w_n)^T \text{ and } v = (v_1, v_2, ..., v_n)^T \quad (7)$$

in such a way as to maximize the effectiveness of automatic detection.

Below, we show three ideas on how to accomplish the above task. We start with the so-called complete search, which is the most computationally expensive. Next, we propose two faster methods, based on the nearest neighbor approach and kernel selection technique.

Analysis of All Pairs. For each pairs $\{(x_{k_1}, x_{k_2})\}_{k_1,k_2=1,k_1\neq k_2}^{N}$ compute

$$\varkappa_{k_1,k_2} = \frac{D_y\left(y_{k_1}, y_{k_2}\right)}{D_x\left(x_{k_1}, x_{k_2}\right)} \quad (8)$$

The pairs (k_1, k_2) with the highest $\varkappa$-value are recognized as uncertain and sent for manual verification. Since the number of unique pairs is of order $N^2/2$ the algorithm can be relatively time-consuming, particularly for huge numbers of data.

Nearest Neighbor Based Approach. As an alternative to the method presented above, we can propose to limit ourselves to the analysis of the so-called nearest neighbor in the sense of the metric D_x. For each $k = 1, 2, ..., N$ the nearest neighbor k', i.e.

$$k' = k'(k) = \arg \min_{k2} D_x \left(x_k, x_{k_2} \right),\qquad(9)$$

is found and the index

$$\chi_k = \frac{D_y \left(y_k, y_{k'} \right)}{D_x \left(x_k, x_{k'} \right)}\qquad(10)$$

is computed. Records with the highest χ-value are recognized as uncertain and sent for manual verification. Compared to (8), the problem (9) is less time-consuming as the number of required operations here is of the order $N^2/4$ and the algorithm can be run on bigger data sets.

Kernel Regression Model. Another possible proposal is the use of the kernel method. For any variable x, mean local value of $G(y)$ with the use of kernel smoothing technique

$$\widehat{R}(x) = \frac{\sum_{k=1}^{N} G(y_k) K \left(\frac{D_x(x_k,x)}{h} \right)}{\sum_{k=1}^{N} K \left(\frac{D_x(x_k,x)}{h} \right)},\qquad(11)$$

is estimated with the use of the local smoothing technique, where $K()$ is a kernel function, and h – bandwidth parameter (see e.g. [14]). Then, for a given x_k, the true $G(y_k)$ and the local mean $\widehat{R}(x = x_k)$ are compared, i.e., the following index is computed

$$\gamma_k = \left\| G(y_k) - \widehat{R}(x_k) \right\|.\qquad(12)$$

Analogously, records with the highest γ-value are recognized as uncertain and directed down to manual verification. The kernel method seems particularly promising for programming online verification algorithms, in order to test newly incoming data and assess the degree of their uncertainty. The learned regression model $\widehat{R}(x)$ can be used for rapid one-operation verification.

4   Experiment - Analysis of VIN (Vehicle Identification Number) vs. Brand in US Car Dataset

Data used for the experiment are taken from Kaggle.
https://www.kaggle.com/datasets/doaaalsenani/usa-cers-dataset
The dataset contains 1000 records representing US Cars. Experiment was done in Jupyter Lab using Python scikit-learn [12].

During the experiment, two columns were analyzed – VIN and BRAND.

4.1   All Pairs Experiment

In the first experiment, we manually manipulated 10 VINs in the dataset creating errors. The goal of the experiment was to analyze all possible pairs of records and sort them based on distance. The farthest objects can mean outliers (errors). The same error can be detected in many pairs but the goal is to identify how many errors we will be able to discover before we will hit a pair with both correct values. This is an unsupervised method that puts candidates in order - from the most probable error to less significant candidates. The brand is a discrete value, so we used the indicator for our "y" which enable distance measurement only for objects from different classes.

$$I_y = \begin{cases} 1 \text{ for the same brand} \\ 0 \text{ for brands in different classes} \end{cases} \tag{13}$$

Distance for our features was calculated according to Eq. (5), where

$$w^T = [0.0001, 1, 1, 1, 1, 1, 1, 1]$$

and our F function is to count of letters, digits, spaces, non-Ascii, length, upper characters. So the distance was a sum of differences in length, count of spaces, uppercase letters, etc. Then we calculated $D_x I_y$ for 1000*999 possible pairs, sorted them, and analyzed the result. The first 1127 pairs referred to at least one of the records with error.: The algorithm discovered eight errors out of ten before the first false positive was suggested. The result is shown in Table 1.

Table 1. Occurrences of errors in first 1127 pairs

ID	table row	occurrences in first 1127 pairs
Error 1	8	15
Error 2	32	295
Error 3	67	75
Error 4	229	228
Error 5	296	14
Error 6	320	233
Error 7	363	171
Error 8	781	101

4.2   Discovering Structure of Vehicle Identification Number to Classify Cars Using Tokenization and CNB

Again in this experiment, we were analyzing the US Cars dataset - VIN and brand. We suspected that there is a structure in VIN, but it was unknown.

The first step was tokenization. We created a set of substrings from VINs and represented it as a sparse matrix. For this step, we had to define 2 critical parameters which are significant for the final result: n-gram range (substring size) and Maximum Features (Tokens) - the limit of the most frequent substrings. These parameters can work differently depending on a dataset, however, to illustrate the general behavior of the algorithm we have shown the result in Table 2.

Table 2. Classification accuracy based on string size (n-gram range) and a number of extracted substrings in sparse matrix

Tokens	1-4	1-6	2-5	2-7	3-6	3-8
50	0.88	0.88	0.85	0.84	0.54	0.54
100	0.89	0.89	0.88	0.88	0.72	0.72
200	0.90	0.90	0.90	0.90	0.85	0.83
400	0.93	0.93	0.93	0.93	0.89	0.89
800	0.93	0.93	0.93	0.93	0.92	0.91
1600	0.95	0.95	0.94	0.94	0.94	0.94
3200	0.96	0.96	0.96	0.96	0.96	0.95
6400	0.97	0.97	0.97	0.97	0.97	0.97

After the feature extraction from VIN, we trained the model using the Complement Naive Bayes algorithm. After that, we received a model which can classify the brand of the car based on any string with 97% of probability. The example of the result for a few strings is shown in Table 3

Table 3. Example of classification results for few strings

input string	aud	bmw	bui	cad	che	dod	for	gmc	hon	hyu	jee	kia	lex	mer.	nis
1f	0	0	0	0	0	0	94	0	0	0	0	0	0	0	0
test	2	2	2	2	29	1	45	2	2	2	2	2	2	2	1
jn1by1ar	0	0	0	0	0	0	0	0	0	0	0	0	0	0	100
t	6	6	6	6	6	6	12	6	6	6	6	6	6	6	6
zakopane	4	4	8	4	16	25	1	4	4	4	4	4	4	4	9
weather	0	0	0	0	0	0	100	0	0	0	0	0	0	0	0

As you can see trained model can identify a brand based on VIN or even its part (the first row in the table is the beginning of the Ford VIN) very effectively, however it is not bulletproof (the last row shows a mistake in classification). The solution can be used as a validation of the data during input. Code of both experiments and data used for analysis can be found at:
https://www.cmdbscience.org/machine-learning.

5   Conclusions

The proposed algorithms can be implemented as low-priority processes working on the database during low-load hours. Their operation may result in a morning report indicating conflicts and inconsistencies in data that may indicate errors. The final decision on taking the appropriate action will be the result of manual verification of the generated report. The decisions made will also be used to optimize the weights in the classification learning algorithm and in the long term for reinforcement learning [8]. We hope that the effectiveness of detecting undesirable situations will increase over time, which will improve the level of system security and relieve the staff from manual verification. The software will also take care of the disciplines regarding the accuracy of entering new data into the database.

References

1. Babur, Ö., Cleophas, L.: Using n-grams for the automated clustering of structural models. In: Steffen, B., Baier, C., van den Brand, M., Eder, J., Hinchey, M., Margaria, T. (eds.) SOFSEM 2017. LNCS, vol. 10139, pp. 510–524. Springer, Cham (2017). https://doi.org/10.1007/978-3-319-51963-0_40
2. Chiang, F., Miller, R.J.: Discovering data quality rules. Proc. VLDB Endow. 1(1), 1166–1177 (2008)
3. Drogseth, D., Sturm, R., Twing, D.: CMDB Systems: Making Change Work in the Age of Cloud and Agile. Morgan Kaufmann, Burlington (2015)
4. Eduardo, S., Nazábal, A., Williams, C.K., Sutton, C.: Robust variational autoencoders for outlier detection and repair of mixed-type data. In: International Conference on Artificial Intelligence and Statistics, pp. 4056–4066. PMLR (2020)
5. Eppler, M.J.: Information quality problems and current approaches. Managing Inf. Qual. 15–49 (2003)
6. Fan, W., Ma, S., Tang, N., Yu, W.: Interaction between record matching and data repairing. J. Data Inf. Qual. (JDIQ) 4(4), 1–38 (2014)
7. Ilyas, I.F., Rekatsinas, T.: Machine learning and data cleaning: which serves the other? ACM J. Data Inf. Qual. (JDIQ) 14(3), 1–11 (2022)
8. Li, J., Zhang, X., Zhao, L.: Robust federated learning based on metrics learning and unsupervised clustering for malicious data detection. In: Proceedings of the 2022 ACM Southeast Conference, pp. 238–242 (2022)
9. Liu, Z., Zhou, Z., Rekatsinas, T.: Picket: guarding against corrupted data in tabular data during learning and inference. VLDB J. 31(5), 927–955 (2022)
10. Madnick, S.E., Wang, R.Y., Lee, Y.W., Zhu, H.: Overview and framework for data and information quality research. J. Data Inf. Qual. (JDIQ) 1(1), 1–22 (2009)
11. Nadeau, D., Turney, P.D., Matwin, S.: Unsupervised named-entity recognition: generating gazetteers and resolving ambiguity. In: Lamontagne, L., Marchand, M. (eds.) AI 2006. LNCS (LNAI), vol. 4013, pp. 266–277. Springer, Heidelberg (2006). https://doi.org/10.1007/11766247_23
12. Pedregosa, F., et al.: Scikit-learn: machine learning in python. J. Mach. Learn. Res. 12, 2825–2830 (2011)
13. Rennie, J.D., Shih, L., Teevan, J., Karger, D.R.: Tackling the poor assumptions of Naive Bayes text classifiers. In: Proceedings of the 20th International Conference on Machine Learning (ICML 2003), pp. 616–623 (2003)

14. Wand, M., Jones, H.: Kernel Smoothing. Chapman and Hall, London (1995)
15. Whitelaw, C., Patrick, J.: Evaluating corpora for named entity recognition using character-level features. In: Gedeon, T.T.D., Fung, L.C.C. (eds.) AI 2003. LNCS (LNAI), vol. 2903, pp. 910–921. Springer, Heidelberg (2003). https://doi.org/10. 1007/978-3-540-24581-0_78

An Improvement of Graph Neural Network for Multi-behavior Recommendation

Nguyen Bao Phuoc, Duong Thuy Trang, and Phan Duy Hung[✉]

FPT University, Hanoi, Vietnam
{phuocnbhe153036,trangdthe150573}@fpt.edu.vn, hungpd2@fe.edu.vn

Abstract. One of the most extensively adapted paradigms for building a recommender system is embedding users and items into a low-dimensional latent space based on their interactions. While traditional Collaborative Filtering is designed for only one type of user-item action, real-world scenarios observe multiple activities of a user such as browsing and favorites, which can serve as an effective enhancement to the method. In addition, early efforts towards multi-behavior recommendation have two main limitations: first, they fail to calculate the influence strength of users' behaviors on target behavior; second, they also ignore that behavior semantics. Therefore, taking advantage of Graph Neural Network, this work further improves the graph-based recommender system by adding residual blocks and a behavior-learnable weight for each user. The effectiveness of our model is confirmed by empirical results of a real-world e-commerce dataset. Our model outperforms the baseline in both Recall@k and NDGC@k statistics.

Keywords: Recommender system · Collaborative filtering · Graph neural network · multi-Behavior

1 Introduction

Recommendation algorithms are at the core of many online platforms for its crucial role in user engagement and reduction of information overload [1]. Specifically, Collaborative Filtering (CF) techniques [2] have attracted a great deal of effort from researchers (e.g., matrix factorization methods [3, 4]). However, traditional CF not only suffer from serious cold-start or data sparsity issues but also achieve poor recommendation quality for new users because it relies on single-typed, historical data. Recently, websites are able to collect some other types of behavior, such as click and browse. Therefore, recommender systems are expected to make use of auxiliary interactions to help predict users' intention on the target behavior.

Multi-behavior Recommendation System. Multi-behavior recommendation system is proposed to enhance the representation capability of recommender systems. Its mechanism utilizes multiple user-item feedback (e.g., click, add to favorite, purchase, etc.). Previous research can be divided into two categories: multi-task approach and auxiliary user-item interactions. While the multi-task approach considers multiple types of behaviors as multiple tasks with shared parameters for joint learning [5, 6], the latter

L. Rutkowski et al. (Eds.): ICAISC 2023, LNAI 14126, pp. 377–387, 2023.
https://doi.org/10.1007/978-3-031-42508-0_34

focuses on effectiveness of sampling and regards auxiliary user-item interactions as 'weak signals' [7, 8]. Notably, Jin et al. proposed a multi-behavior graph convolutional network-based model (MB-GCN) [9] to automatically learn the strength of each behavior without any prior knowledge on preference strength. In detail, MB-GCN includes three important components: Item-to-user Propagation, User-to-item Propagation and Item-to-item Propagation. First, with Item-to-user Propagation and User-to-item Propagation, each behavior is assigned with a learnable weight that distinguishes its influence on target behavior and helps determine user-based score at the final layer. Second, with Item-to-item Propagation, the relevance of items reflected in behaviors is extracted so that cold-start problems that previous methods suffer from can be reduced. However, what is ignored by this work is the influence of individual preferences on user-item relationship and item-item relationship.

Graph-Based Recommendation System. In recent years, graph neural networks (GNNs) are gaining attention as a cutting-edge technology for recommender systems [9, 10]. GNNs constructs the input data in the form of graphs, where users and items are represented as nodes (e.g., bi-partite in Fig. 1). Therefore, the main purpose of the recommender system - predicting the interaction between user-items, becomes the link prediction between the nodes in the corresponding user-item graph. Particularly, Graph Convolutional Network (GCN) is one of the indispensable parts of the graph learning task [11, 12]. The main idea of GCN is to extract information of a node based on its neighbors by using convolutional operation; hence it can simultaneously capture node attributes and graph structure. GCN is a powerful approach in extracting relationships between data and is widely used in recommender systems [9, 10].

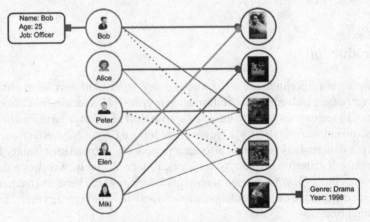

Fig. 1. Input data as a bi-partite graph

Inspired by previous research, this work proposes an improvement for MB-GCN [9] by introducing residual connection and learnable aggregate weight for user-item score and item-item score such that influence of individual preferences on user-item relationship and item-item relationship can be more accurately estimated.

2 Data Preparation

2.1 Dataset Selection

We reviewed some well-known public datasets that are relevant to our topic of concern to choose the most suitable one for training and evaluation, including Tmall[1], Taobao[2], E-commerce dataset of REES46 marketing platform[3] and MovieLens20M[4]. After considering desired characteristics such as amount of user data, variety of behavior, number of events per user, we decided to use Taobao - a famous real-world e-commerce dataset, provided by Alibaba Groups.

In detail, the authors selected about one million users who had implicit feedback including purchases ('buy'), adding an item to cart ('cart'), adding an item to favorite ('fav') and viewing product pages ('pv') during November 25th to December 3rd, 2017. Similar to real-world scenarios, the distribution of each behavior is very skewed (Table 1). Although its size is considerably large, we can select useful attributes in processing steps, as describe in part 2.2.

Table 1. Distribution of dataset

Dataset	# Users	# Items	# Categories	pv (%)	fav (%)	cart (%)	buy (%)
Original	987994	4162024	9439	89.6%	2.9%	5.5%	2.0%
Transformed	4473	18386	1772	72.7%	2.1%	7.7%	17.5%

2.2 Pre-processing Data

Pre-processing data is a crucial step because we only want efficient data for our limited computing environment. There are two steps within our handling of raw data: data cleaning and data transformation.

- **Data cleaning:** Change the timestamp format from epoch to date & time; Delete redundant columns; Delete NaN values
- **Data transformation:** Filter data of ten days in each month with the highest number of events, then select twenty thousand products that are bought by most of users and filter data of twenty thousand most frequent users. Finally, choose users that have at least five interactions under target behavior. To be most objective, we have tried to filter the data so that the distribution is as close to the original data as possible.

---

[1] https://tianchi.aliyun.com/dataset/dataDetail?dataId=649&t=1664535575440.

[2] https://tianchi.aliyun.com/dataset/53.

[3] https://www.kaggle.com/datasets/mkechinov/ecommerce-behavior-data-from-multi-category-store.

[4] https://grouplens.org/datasets/movielens/20m/.

Results: In original dataset and reduced dataset, page views account for 89.6% and 72.7% of total interactions, respectively. By contrast, a mere 2.2% goes to purchase in original dataset, and this number increases to 17.5% in transformed dataset (Table 1). This is a reflection of reality as people tend to browse through many different products before making final decision (buy an item). Pre-processing code can be accessed via Google Colab[5].

2.3 Exploratory Data Analysis

Trends in the Dataset. Figure 2 below illustrates the website traffic through time. It can

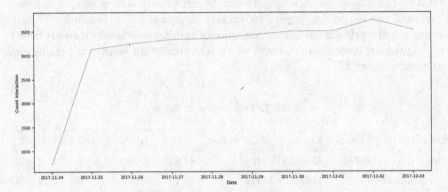

Fig. 2. Trends in user interaction

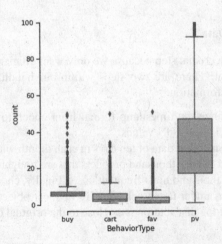

Fig. 3. Summary statistics of each behavior

be seen that the users' interactions fluctuate by date and sharply increase after November

---

[5] https://colab.research.google.com/drive/12M-RhrSprJphg6UvbIoo-q0DmhECl7OS?usp=sha ring.

24th, reaching peak in December 2nd. Note that this figure only shows dates having at least fifty interactions for convenience. Statistically, it is explainable in reality since there is a growing tendency for people to shop in last few months of the year. Therefore, this dataset is suitable for further analysis.

Summary Statistics. The summary statistics of each interaction of each user after cleaning data is shown in Fig. 3. It can be seen clearly that the average number of page views among users is the largest, following by buy behavior.

3 Methodology

3.1 Problem Formulation

Users of the online information system can engage with given items in a variety of ways in real-world circumstances, such as click, browse, add-to-favorite, and purchase. Among those behaviors, there is always one activity that immediately boosts the revenue of the business. As mentioned in the Introduction, we aim to make an improvement for a recommender system that takes advantage of multiple types of behavior, to model the target behavior. Our work can be formulated in the same manner as [9, 10]: ·

- **Input:** Set of the observed of each behavior user-item interaction: $A = \{A^1, A^2, \ldots, A^T\}$. Where, T is the number of behaviors; $A^t \in \mathbb{R}^{n_u \times n_i}$ where n_u is the number of users and n_i is the number of items, and defined as:

$$A_{u,i}^t = \begin{cases} 1, & \text{if user } u \text{ interact with item } i \text{ under behavior } t \\ 0, & \text{otherwise} \end{cases} \tag{1}$$

- **Output:** The probability that a user u interacts with an item i under the target behavior A^T

Similar to previous research [9], our method is the composed of three propagations followed by an aggregate layer. The architecture of our method is described in Fig. 4.

3.2 Building Heterogeneous Graph

For each behavior $t \in N_{behavior} = \{pv, cart, fav, buy\}$, the user-item interaction can be described as a heterogeneous graph $G_t = (V, E_t)$, where V is a set of user's node $u \in U$ and item's node $i \in I$. The edges in E_t contain the user-item interaction under behavior t. To represent graph G_t, an adjacency matrix $A^t \in \mathbb{R}^{n_u \times n_i}$ is built, $A_{u,i}^t = 1$ when there is an interaction between user u and item i under the behavior t. Besides user-item graphs, a graph between items is also built to further exploit item relevant information. Specifically, we define $B^t \in \mathbb{R}^{n_i \times n_i}$ as the item-item adjacency matrix where $B_{i,j}^t = 1$ when item i and item j are interacted together by users under behavior t.

3.3 Item-to-User Propagation and User-to-Item Propagation

Similar to previous research [3, 4, 9, 10], to describe users and items, the users embedding matrix $P \in \mathbb{R}^{n_u \times d}$ and the items embedding matrix $Q \in \mathbb{R}^{n_i \times d}$ are created, where d is embedding size. Those embedding matrices are considered as initialization features which are fed into each subsequent propagation.

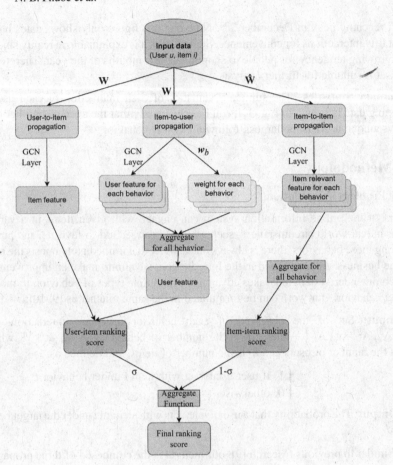

Fig. 4. Architecture illustration

3.3.1 Item-to-User Propagation

Users feature under a specific behavior can be determined through the items which the user had previously interacted with. Therefore, a graph convolutional operator [9, 11, 12] can be used to extract users' information:

$$\overline{\mathbf{p}}_u^t = \frac{1}{|N_{\mathbf{I}}^t(u)|} \sum_{i=1}^{|N_{\mathbf{I}}^t(u)|} \mathbf{q}_i \tag{2}$$

where $N_{\mathbf{I}}^t(u)$ is a set of items that are interacted by user u under the behavior t, $\overline{\mathbf{p}}_u^t$ is the behavior t's item-to-user embedding and $\mathbf{q}_i$ indicates the embedding for item i. Those embedding $\overline{\mathbf{p}}_u^t$ with $t \in N_{behavior}$ are hereafter aggregated together based on the parameter $\alpha \in \mathbb{R}^{n_u \times |N_{behavior}|}$, which is used to control the contribution of each behavior [9].

$$\alpha_{u,t} = \frac{w_t \times |N_{\mathbf{I}}^t(u)|}{\sum_{b=1}^{|N_{behavior}|} w_b \times |N_{\mathbf{I}}^b(u)|} \tag{3}$$

where w_t is a weight for behavior t, which is shared between users. The aggregate item-to-user is similar to existing method in [9]:

$$\overline{\mathbf{p}}_u = W \cdot \left(\frac{1}{|N_{behavior}|} \sum_{b=1}^{|N_{behavior}|} \alpha_{u,b} \overline{\mathbf{p}}_u^b \right) \tag{4}$$

where $W \in \mathbb{R}^{d \times d}$ which is used to further learn to represent user and item features in latent dimension.

3.3.2 User-to-Item Propagation

In contrast to users' feature, items' features are immutable under different behaviors. Therefore, behavior does not affect the representation of items in embedding space. The user-to-item propagation is defined as [9, 11, 12]:

$$\overline{\mathbf{q}}_i = W \cdot \left(\frac{1}{|N_U(i)|} \sum_{u=1}^{|N_U(i)|} \mathbf{p}_u \right) \tag{5}$$

where $|N_U(i)|$ is a set of users who interacted with item i under target behavior.

3.4 Item-to-Item Propagation

In reality, along with user-item relationship, the relationship between items also provides useful information for recommendation systems. Therefore, similar to the previous method in [9], we create an item-to-item propagation to further exploit the relationship between items. Specifically:

$$\tilde{\mathbf{q}}_i^t = \hat{W} \cdot \left(\frac{1}{|N_I^t(i)|} \sum_{j=1}^{|N_I^t(i)|} \mathbf{q}_j \right) \tag{6}$$

where $\hat{W} \in \mathbb{R}^{d \times d}$ is a parameter used to learn to represent relationship of items in latent space d, $N_I^t(i)$ is a set of items which are interacted together with item i by users under the behavior t.

3.5 Aggregated Prediction

In the last step, we proposed residual connection for user feature and item feature. This improvement helps the model to learn better from the residual function with reference to initialize embedding.

$$\begin{aligned} \overline{\mathbf{p}}_u &= \overline{\mathbf{p}}_u \| \mathbf{p}_u + \mathbf{p}_u \cdot W_u \\ \overline{\mathbf{q}}_i &= \overline{\mathbf{q}}_i \| \mathbf{q}_i + \mathbf{q}_i \cdot W_i \end{aligned} \tag{7}$$

where $\|$ denote concatenation operation, $W_u, W_i \in \mathbb{R}^{d \times 2d}$ is used to match the dimensions. With those feature, user-item ranking score can be calculated as follow [4, 9]:

$$\hat{y}_{user-item}(u, i) = \overline{\mathbf{p}}_u^T \cdot \overline{\mathbf{q}}_i \tag{8}$$

Although user-to-item propagation and item-to-user propagation can capture huge information between users and items, it cannot deal with the cold start problem [9]. Therefore, similar to [9], we use item-item score to overcoming cold start problem:

$$\hat{y}_{item-item}(u, i) = \sum_{b \in N_{behavior}} \sum_{j \in N_{\mathbf{I}}^t(u)} \frac{(\tilde{\mathbf{q}}_j^t)^T \cdot W_t \cdot \tilde{\mathbf{q}}_i^t}{|N_{\mathbf{I}}^t(u)|} \tag{9}$$

where $W_t \in \mathbb{R}^{2d \times 2d}$ which is used to learn the relationship between items.

In previous research [9], they ignore the personal dependency/weight that controls user-item score and item-item score by using a fixed hyperparameter to aggregate user-item and item-item score together. However, we found that using a fixed $\sigma \geq 0$ has some limitations due to two reasons: i) Each user has their own preference; ii) In reality, there are people who buy according to their personal preferences (meaning big σ), but there are also trend followers (meaning small σ). Therefore, we defined a learnable parameter $0 \leq \sigma \leq 1$ for each user to combine two above ranking score together to get the final score:

$$\hat{y}(u, i) = \sigma_u \cdot \hat{y}_{user-item}(u, i) + (1 - \sigma_u) \cdot \hat{y}_{item-item}(u, i) \tag{10}$$

where $\sigma_u = sigmoid\left(\overline{\mathbf{p}}_u \cdot w_{\sigma_u}\right)$ and w_{σ_u} is a weight for user u.

4 Experiment

4.1 Evaluation Metrics and Hyperparameter Setting

To evaluate the performance of each model, two metrics are used: Recall and Normalized Discounted Cumulative Gain (NDCG). Our model is implemented in Pytorch[6]. To learn the parameters, we optimized the model with BPR loss [7]. The idea behind BPR loss is that the observed interaction, which is the user's preference, should be assigned a higher score than the unobserved interactions. The BPR loss can be defined as:

$$Loss = \sum_{(u,i,j) \in O} - \ln\left(sigmoid\left(\hat{y}(u, i) - \hat{y}(u, j)\right)\right) + \lambda \cdot \|\Theta\|_2^2 \tag{11}$$

where $O = \{(u, i, j)|(u, i) \in \mathbb{R}^+, (u, j) \in \mathbb{R}^-\}$ is training pairwise target behavior, $\mathbb{R}^+$ denotes observed target behavior and $\mathbb{R}^-$ denotes unobserved target behavior. λ is a parameter used to control the effectiveness of regularization terms.

Hyperparameters settings are summarized in Table 2. To avoid overfitting, a scheduler is used to reduce learning rate after ten epochs without improvement. Early stop is also performed if Recall@10 on validation is not improved for fifty epochs.

---

[6] https://pytorch.org/.

Table 2. Hyperparameters settings

Hyperparameter	Value
Number of epochs	500
Embedding size	256
Learning rate	0.0001
Batch size	1024
Optimization	Adam [13]
Message dropout rate	0.1
Regularization weight (λ)	0.0001
Parameter initialization	Xavier [14]

4.2 Ablation Study

In this paper, two methods are introduced to improve performance of original research in [9]: i) residual for users and items feature; ii) Learnable score weight σ to merge user-item score and item-item score together. To understand the importance of each method, we create four different variants from baseline in [9] and compare their performance along with the Matrix factorization (MF) model [4]. The final result is shown in Table 3.

Table 3. Ablation study and final results on testing data

Approach	Recall@5	NDCG@5	Recall@10	NDCG@10	Recall@20	NDCG@20	Recall@40	NDCG@40
MF [4]	0.019	0.012	0.029	0.015	0.039	0.018	0.050	0.020
Baseline [9]	0.047	0.029	0.072	0.037	0.105	0.045	0.140	0.052
[9] with residual	0.056	0.037	0.078	0.044	0.107	0.052	0.136	0.057
[9] with learnable σ	0.052	0.032	0.081	0.042	0.114	0.050	0.156	0.058
[9] with residual and σ	**0.093**	**0.061**	**0.149**	**0.079**	**0.216**	**0.096**	**0.300**	**0.113**

It is shown that residual connection can be used to improve baseline model by 8.01% on Recall@10 and 20.11% on NDCG@10, while learnable σ improve baseline model by 12,62% on Recall@10 and 12.74% on NDCG@10. The model with both residual and learnable σ outperform the baseline model. This demonstrates that residual and learnable σ can help the baseline model learn much more effectively. The comparison between those five models is shown in Fig. 5.

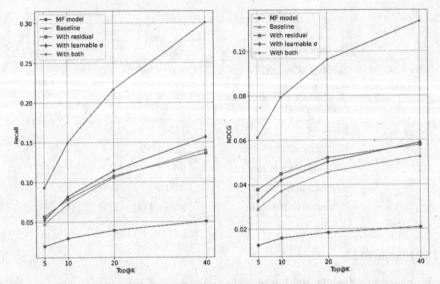

Fig. 5. Comparison between models on Taobao sub-dataset

5 Conclusion and Future Work

By diving deep into GCN and examining previous research [9], this work proposes an improvement of graph-based multi-behavior recommendation system by introducing two methods: residual connection and learnable parameter σ to improve performance of the model on the aggregate layer. Ablation studies demonstrate the effectiveness of those two methods in modeling the user's preference and semantic of different behavior.

For future work, we plan to experiment extensively over the entire dataset and other real-world datasets. In addition, we hypothesize that increasing embedding size may lead to better performance of the model. Finally, the three propagations described above only have one layer. By adding residual connection, increasing the number of layers as mentioned in [9] is one of the promising directions that we are aiming for. The work is also a good reference for research problems in recommender systems [15, 16].

References

1. Ricci, F., Rokach, L., Shapira, B.: Introduction to recommender systems handbook. In: Ricci, F., Rokach, L., Shapira, B., Kantor, P.B. (eds.) Recommender Systems Handbook, pp. 1–35. Springer, Boston (2011). https://doi.org/10.1007/978-0-387-85820-3_1
2. Sarwar, B., Karypis, G., Konstan, J., Riedl, J.: Item-based collaborative filtering recommendation algorithms. In: Proceedings of the 10th International Conference on World Wide Web, pp. 285–295 (2001)
3. Bobadilla, J., Ortega, F., Hernando, A., Gutiérrez, A.: Recommender systems survey. Knowl.-Based Syst. **46**, 109–132 (2013)
4. Koren, Y., Bell, R., Volinsky, C.: Matrix factorization techniques for recommender systems. Computer **42**, 30–37 (2009)

5. Chen, C., Zhang, M., Zhang, Y., Ma, W., Liu, Y., Ma, S.: Efficient heterogeneous collaborative filtering without negative sampling for recommendation. In: Proceedings of the AAAI Conference on Artificial Intelligence, pp. 19–26 (2020)
6. Gao, C., He, X., Gan, D., Chen, X., Feng, F., Li, Y., Jin, D.: Learning to recommend with multiple cascading behaviors. IEEE Trans. Knowl. Data Eng. **33**, 2588–2601 (2019)
7. Loni, B., Pagano, R., Larson, M., Hanjalic, A.: Bayesian personalized ranking with multi-channel user feedback. In: Proceedings of the 10th ACM Conference on Recommender Systems, pp. 361–364 (2016)
8. Ding, J., et al.: Improving implicit recommender systems with view data. In: IJCAI, pp. 3343–3349 (2018)
9. Jin, B., Gao, C., He, X., Jin, D., Li, Y.: Multi-behavior recommendation with graph convolutional networks. In: Proceedings of the 43rd International ACM SIGIR Conference on Research and Development in Information Retrieval, pp. 659–668 (2020)
10. Xia, L., Xu, Y., Huang, C., Dai, P., Bo, L.: Graph meta network for multi-behavior recommendation. In: Proceedings of the 44th International ACM SIGIR Conference on Research and Development in Information Retrieval, pp. 757–766 (2021)
11. Gao, H., Wang, Z., Ji, S.: Large-scale learnable graph convolutional networks. In: Proceedings of the 24th ACM SIGKDD International Conference on Knowledge Discovery & Data Mining, pp. 1416–1424 (2018)
12. Hamilton, W., Ying, Z., Leskovec, J.: Inductive representation learning on large graphs. In: Advances in Neural Information Processing Systems (2017)
13. Kingma, D. P., Ba, J.: Adam: a method for stochastic optimization. arXiv preprint arXiv (2014)
14. Glorot, X., Bengio, Y.: Understanding the difficulty of training deep feedforward neural networks. In: Proceedings of the Thirteenth International Conference on Artificial Intelligence and Statistics. JMLR Workshop and Conference Proceedings, pp. 249–256 (2010)
15. Quan, V.H., Hung, P.D.: Heterogeneous neural collaborative filtering for a business recommender system. In: Al-Emran, M., Al-Sharafi, M.A., Al-Kabi, M.N., Shaalan, K. (eds.) ICETIS 2021. LNNS, vol. 322, pp. 93–104. Springer, Cham (2022). https://doi.org/10.1007/978-3-030-85990-9_9
16. Hung, P.D., Huynh, L.D.: E-commerce recommendation system using mahout. In: Proceedings of the IEEE 4th International Conference on Computer and Communication Systems (ICCCS), Singapore, pp. 86–90 (2019)

Binary Matrix Factorization Discretization

Georges Spyrides[✉][ID], Marcus Poggi[ID], and Hélio Lopes[ID]

Potifícia Universidade Católica do Rio de Janeiro, Rio de Janeiro, Brazil
{gspyrides,poggi,lopes}@inf.puc-rio.br

Abstract. Binary Matrix Factorization can be used at the core of many data analysis pipelines. It is used for clustering items, categorical characteristics of observations, and recommendation systems for users interacting with itemsets. The most common algorithms approximate the factorization through gradient descent. However, the results are approximately binary. When thresholded, the reconstruction error is so high that the matrices are no longer representative of the original. Therefore, the analyst must always choose between precision and explainability. We achieved theoretical results that greatly improve solving the exact subproblem of this factorization. These results enable a backtracking approach that can solve the linearized formulation of the subproblem in large binary matrices taking advantage of their sparsity in real settings. Finally, we test this new approach post-processing matrices yielded by gradient descent algorithms using the new backtracking to obtain actually binary factorized matrices with a diminished reconstruction error, close the level of what gradient descent is capable of finding. We tested our algorithm using gene expression datasets, and could find a error rate comparable to the relaxed continuous problem before discretization. The discretized matrices allow for domain experts to question biclusters of gene-expressions and samples taken.

Keywords: Binary matrix factorization · Gene Expression · Algorithms

1 Introduction

Recent progress in smartphones, internet-of-things devices and their use of sensors, precision medicine, and the social media use brought to the public a vast range of datasets. Frequently the data is about relationship between consumers and products, entities to another entity, observations to some features. Even in unusual settings such as text mining, we are used in transforming data to vector representations, such as the count of specific words (bag-of-words) or the presence of words in binary vectors, often called one-hot encoding.

An approach to discovering the underlying structure of these datasets is by matrix factorization. The most common method is the principal component analysis (PCA). Newer methods change the unconstrained setting of the PCA,

L. Rutkowski et al. (Eds.): ICAISC 2023, LNAI 14126, pp. 388–401, 2023.
https://doi.org/10.1007/978-3-031-42508-0_35

in order to obtain decomposed matrices with new properties. Popular methods combine the introduction of sparseness-inducing mechanisms or relax the orthogonality for just searching for independence between components. A particularly powerful constraint is allowing the factorized matrices just positive entries. The non-negative contraint forces the reconstruction to rely only on basic addition, therefore each of the components are forced to assume parts of the objects expressed in given matrices, Lee and Seung [10] explain this effect in greater detail, and how these matrices produce explainable results in real settings.

In an even more constrained setting, some authors such as Zhang et al. [37,38] and Miettinen et al. [14] describe a binary matrix factorization for binary matrices. Binary matrices can be used to encode a myriad of problems. Binary vectors can be used to represent the presence of an item into a set. The resulting matrices of the decomposition reveal common subsets and mixing of subsets to approximate each original set in the decomposed matrix. Applications that benefit from this form of interpreting the decomposition are: market basket analysis, topic modelling in text mining, microarray gene expression for sample and genes biclustering, any problem using categorical features for many observations, recommendation systems based of discrete features of user behaviour, the relationship between entities such as friendships in social networks. Given a matrix with binary (or boolean) entries $A_{[m \times n]}$, the binary matrix factorization obtains ideally two also binary matrices $W_{[m \times g]}$ and $H_{[g \times n]}$ that when multiplied together are a rank g approximation to A.

A Binary Matrix can be interpreted as a table with observations in the rows and binary features in the columns, such as presence of a specific word in a document, or purchase of an item in one shopping cart, or the presence of a category in a categorical variable. We can interpret the rows of matrix H as a common subsets of features and matrix W as a mixing matrix that shows which subsets combined give a approximation to a specific observation. Common subsets of features obtained in matrix H can be used later to decide which products to place together in a real store or web interface, common words in a topic inside a text corpus. The mixing matrix W can give statistics of most common subsets, clustering of observation based on common subsets.

Therefore, we believe that there is a great benefit of analyzing the structure of binary matrices through the lens of the binary matrix factorization. What limits it's wide adoption in a real setting is the practical trade-off of current approaches. Approaches that can handle real-world sized problems such as described in Zhang et al. [38] and implemented by Zitnik and Zupan in their software package Nimfa [39], are based on gradient descent methods, and their response is almost binary, but still fractional. These matrices obtained by gradient descent, when thresholded to obtain truly binary matrices the reconstruction errors practically greatly increase to a point that the matrices do not represent the original matrices any longer. For real settings where interpreting the problem as subsets of elements are lost to this approach. Other approaches such as described by Miettinen et al. [14] are truly binary but do not scale outside of matrices in a few hundreds of rows and columns for ranks G under 10.

Our contribution is a post-processing procedure for discretizing matrices obtained by gradient descent. In our experimental setting, this algorithm recovers the reconstruction error after the thresholding. We were able to process in reasonable time matrices with thousands of rows and columns and a rank of up to 100.

2   Related Work

There are two main approaches for decomposing the binary matrices. The first approach by Zhang [38] relaxes the problem such that the entries can assume any values between 0 and 1 by alternating gradient descent. Thus it approximates the problem by navigating a continuous space between 0 and 1. A problem to this approach arises when discretizing the variables by a threshold. The reconstruction error falls to a level that deems the matrices useless in practice. There is a newer approach, that are constant-factor approximation algorithms with guarantees to the problem, presented by Kumar et al. [8].

Another approach is through heuristics and formulation, more closely related to classic combinatorial optimization approaches. A pioneer work of [14] describes the ASSO algorithm. This algorithm uses pairwise distance between rows to decide which position should be rounded to one, managing to maximize coverage of the target matrix and minimize overlapping positions. In the same paper, the authors briefly present alternatives for the ASSO, including using k-means and exhaustive search.

Mirisaee et al. in [15] propose a neighborhood for searching improvements in each row. Additionally, the authors presents different versions of the search by linearizing the objective function, which is an idea explored by us. Also, there is a work using genetic algorithms in order to search for solutions introduced by Snášel et al. in [28] and [27].

3   Method

Our approach is to combine ideas from the heuristic exact methods to post-process the results given by the gradient descent approach. We use a linearized objective function as a surrogate for the reconstruction objective error, usually calculated with the Frobenius norm. The linearized objective function allows for rewriting the problem into set notation and operations, which will be the foundation for the algorithm presented later in this section.

3.1   Formulation and the Discrete Basis Subproblem

In our setting, the matrix $A \in \{0, 1\}^{|\mathcal{M}|, |\mathcal{G}|}$ is given as input and the stochastic gradient descent outputs two matrices $W \in [0, 1]^{|\mathcal{M}|, |\mathcal{G}|}$ and $H \in [0, 1]^{|\mathcal{G}|, |\mathcal{N}|}$, such that the multiplication $W \cdot H$ is an stable (local optimum) approximation for A. Notice that the entries of W and H are real values between 0 and 1, and for many applications, we want to discretize these entries without losing too much of the reconstruction error, which measures the distance of approximation between A and the reconstruction $W \cdot H$.

One common way to measure this approximation error is to measure how much of the variance was captured. Thus, we measure how close to zero is the difference $A - W \cdot H$. We can calculate this by measuring the norm of this difference relative to the norm of the original matrix A, as shown in Eq. 1.

$$\text{minimize } \|A - W \cdot H\|_2 = \sum_{m \in \mathcal{M}} \sum_{n \in \mathcal{N}} (a_{mn} - (\sum_{g \in \mathcal{G}} w_{mg} \cdot h_{gn}))^2 \qquad (1)$$

Using this equation as an optimization problem we observe some characteristics that suggest hardness even for approximations: binary decision variables, bilinearity and quadratic objective. Therefore, we decided approximate the problem using a linearized surrogate objective function using the ℓ_1-norm, as shown in Eq. 2.

$$\text{minimize } \|A - W \cdot H\|_1 = \sum_{m \in \mathcal{M}} \sum_{n \in \mathcal{N}} |a_{mn} - (\sum_{g \in \mathcal{G}} w_{mg} \cdot h_{gn})| \qquad (2)$$

Many matrix decomposition algorithms rely on alternating optimization such as in Zhang et al. [38]. Which means fixating an approximation of one of the matrices, optimizing one side, then fixating the optimized side and solving the previously fixated matrix, and repeat until achieving solution stability. Our intent is to apply a exact binary optimization as the last step of the alternating minimization. Therefore, the algorithm presented can be used as a post-processing step to many approaches. In the present work we tested it as post-processing step for the gradient descent binary decomposition presented by Zhang et al. in [38] and implementation released in the package Nimfa [39].

In our approach, given any approximation to one of the matrices, preferably W first, we solve a subproblem of approximating each column of the given matrix A as a mixing of columns of W, obtaining matrix H. Then, fixing the value of matrix H and solving the transposed view of the first step, approximating each row of A as a sum of a subset of rows of H, obtaining a new value for W.

3.2   The Discrete Basis Problem

Assuming a first approximation for W as fixed, a simple rearrangement of Eq. 2 shows that we can treat the summation over rows in $\mathcal{M}$ separately for each column in set $\mathcal{N}$.

$$\text{minimize } \sum_{m \in \mathcal{M}} \sum_{n \in \mathcal{N}} |a_{mn} - (\sum_{g \in \mathcal{G}} w_{mg} \cdot h_{gn})| = \sum_{n \in \mathcal{N}} \left[\text{minimize } \sum_{m \in \mathcal{M}} |a_{mn} - (\sum_{g \in \mathcal{G}} w_{mg} \cdot h_{gn})| \right] \qquad (3)$$

Another way of thinking about this subproblem is a problem of choosing a subset of a binary basis to represent a given binary vector. We show this interpretation in Eq. 4. In this equation we have to approximate the column a_n using the binary decision variables h_{gn} to choose from a set of fixed basis, the columns of W.

$$\begin{bmatrix} | \\ a_n \\ | \end{bmatrix} \approx \begin{bmatrix} | \\ w_1 \\ | \end{bmatrix} h_{1n} + \begin{bmatrix} | \\ w_2 \\ | \end{bmatrix} h_{2n} + \cdots + \begin{bmatrix} | \\ w_g \\ | \end{bmatrix} h_{gn} + \cdots + \begin{bmatrix} | \\ w_{\mathcal{G}} \\ | \end{bmatrix} h_{\mathcal{G}n} \quad (4)$$

We can also run an similar procedure fixating H and optimizing matrix W, one row of A at a time, by just transposing the multiplication.

$$A_{[m \times n]} \approx W_{[m \times g]} \cdot H_{[g \times n]} \rightarrow A^T_{[n \times m]} \approx H^T_{[n \times g]} \cdot W^T_{[g \times m]} \quad (5)$$

Therefore, the discrete basis in this transposed view becomes a selection of rows of H to approximate each row t of matrix A.

Consequently, a single algorithm for this subproblem can be used to optimally solve the linearized optimization formulation described in Eq. 3 looping through each columns then through each row.

3.3   The Set Representation

For dealing with really large matrices, we can take advantage of the structure of the problem transforming the many binary vectors into sets that contain the positions in which this vectors are equal to one. Let $\mathcal{I}$ a function that transforms vectors to a set of positions equal to one. We can apply this function to any rows or columns of matrices A, W, or H during the discrete basis subproblem solve.

Definition 1 (Function $\mathcal{I}$ that translates sparse vectors to sets). *Let $x \in \{0,1\}^n$. Then the function $\mathcal{I}(x) : \{0,1\}^n \rightarrow 2^n$ is the set of indices of the positions of x which are greater or equal to 1.*

Examples of usage of function $\mathcal{I}$. Let $x = [0, 1, 1]$. Then $\mathcal{I}(x) = \{2, 3\}$. Or let $y = [1, 1, 0]$. Then $\mathcal{I}(y) = \{1, 2\}$.

An algorithm for the discrete basis subproblem using a fixed W, has to decide which positions of vector h_n should be explored fixating to 1. The algorithm starts with the trivial solution such that all positions assigned to zero. The vector h_n has size $|\mathcal{G}|$. Therefore, using the set representation, we begin the algorithm with:

$$\mathcal{I}(h_n) = \varnothing$$

since all positions initially are zero.

We add $g \in \mathcal{G}$ to $\mathcal{I}(h_n)$ whenever we are investigating assigning position g in vector h_n to 1. As the algorithm takes steps t it inserts into the current solution some basis g from $\mathcal{G}$

$$\mathcal{I}(h_n) \subset \mathcal{G}$$

Definition 2 (Set $\mathcal{Q}$ of remaining positions to cover in the target vector). *The algorithm keeps track of the set $\mathcal{Q}$ of uncovered positions of the target vector a_n. The set $\mathcal{Q}$ is a subset of $\mathcal{M}$.*

$$\mathcal{Q} = \mathcal{I}(a_n) - \left(\bigcup_g^{\mathcal{I}(h_n)} \mathcal{I}(w_g) \right)$$

If a new g is added to solution set $\mathcal{I}(h_n)$ then we can update $\mathcal{Q}$ in the following manner:

$$\mathcal{Q} := \mathcal{Q} - \mathcal{I}(w_g)$$

Using these definitions, we can also use the following theoretical framework of proven by Spyrides et al. in [30].

Lemma 1 (Gain calculation using set representation). *When solving for a_n, the increment Δ_{gn} of adding g to a solution $\mathcal{I}(h_n)$ is calculated as:*

$$\Delta_{gn} = |\mathcal{I}(w_g) \cap \mathcal{Q}| - |\mathcal{I}(w_g) - \mathcal{Q}|$$

This lemma, sets the foundation for the following theorem. It will allow for an efficient search in practice.

Theorem 1 (Contribution decreasing monotonicity). *Whenever adding g to solution $\mathcal{I}(h_n)$, all the gains of adding any other element in the solution in next steps can only stay the same or decrease. Which means when recalculating all other $\Delta_{g'n}$ of g' not yet in the solution set $\mathcal{I}(h_n)$, the new value is lesser or equal than it was before.*

Theorem 1 has many interesting consequences. The monotonicity can be used to define local optima and to eliminate positions to search during a recursive enumeration. This enables the design of a backtracking algorithm which finds the global optimum for the sub-problem and only explores a small subset of the combinatorial decision space.

Corollary 1 (Local optimum and Negative contributing candidates skipping). *If $\Delta_{g'n}$ associated with any remaining $g' \notin \mathcal{I}(h_n)$ is negative, then g' will never be in any local optimum solution with the g that belong to the current solution set $\mathcal{I}(h_n)$.*

Corollary 1 shows that we have to search though all possible local optimum, and that we can know beforehand if a candidate g will ever be needed in a current solution, given it's current contribution Δ.

Corollary 2 (Early stopping upper-bound). *The solution set $\mathcal{I}(h_n)$ is a subset of $\mathcal{G}$. Any subset $\mathcal{P}$ of $\mathcal{G}$ disjoint from $\mathcal{I}(h_n)$ can have it's overall upper-bound calculated as.*

$$\Delta_{UB} = \sum_{g \in \mathcal{P}} max(\Delta_{gn}, 0)$$

Which means if any subset of $\mathcal{P}$ is added to the solution set $\mathcal{I}(h_n)$ in any order, the overall contribution to the objective function is bounded by Δ_{UB}.

If we assume a sequential inclusion of candidate bases to the solution, at any given point during the search, we can sum positive deltas remaining to explore and calculate an upper-bound of the contribution of any combination of insertions of the associated bases. This means that if we already know any solution, this fact can be used to prove that we don't need to further explore a significant part of the decision space.

3.4   The Backtracking Algorithm for the Discrete Basis Subproblem

We have introduced the sufficient elements to design a recursive procedure that efficiently explores the decision space of the discrete basis subproblem. The main ideas are to calculate the individual contributions of all bases, consider only the ones with positive contribution, begin adding the one with the greatest contribution.

In a recursive scheme, our idea is to design a procedure that only controls one inclusion step. In further recursive calls, the Δ's tend to rapidly diminish to negative values, and we can loop through the decision space efficiently. We provide a pseudo-code for this procedure in Algorithm 3.4.

---

function column_solve(W, $\mathcal{G}$, $\mathcal{Q}$, $\mathcal{I}(h_n)$, OF):

 Let $PQ :=$ empty priority queue
 Let $\mathcal{I}(h_n)^* := \mathcal{I}(h_n)$
 Let $OF^* := OF$
 for g **in** $(\mathcal{G} - \mathcal{I}(h_n))$:
  $\Delta_{gn} = |\mathcal{I}(w_g) \cap \mathcal{Q}| - |\mathcal{I}(w_g) - \mathcal{Q}|$ // *From Theorem 1*
  if $\Delta_{gn} > 0$: // *From Corollary 1*
   add g with priority Δ_{gn} to PQ
 while PQ **is not** empty queue:
  Let $g, \Delta_{gn} :=$ remove first priority item from PQ
  $\mathcal{I}(h_n)_{rec}, OF_{rec} :=$ column_solve(W,
        $\mathcal{G} := \{g | g \in PQ\}$,
        $\mathcal{Q} := \mathcal{Q} - \mathcal{I}(w_g)$,
        $\mathcal{I}(h_n) := \mathcal{I}(h_n) \cup \{g\}$,
        $OF := OF - \Delta_{gn}$)
  if $OF_{rec} < OF^*$:
   $OF^* := OF_{rec}$; $\mathcal{I}(h_n)^* := \mathcal{I}(h_n)_{rec}$
  $\Delta_{UB} := \sum_{g \in PQ} \Delta_{gn}$
  if $OF - OF^* > \Delta_{UB}$ **break** // *From Corollary 2*
 return $\mathcal{I}(h_n)^*, OF^*$
column_solve(W, $\mathcal{G} := \mathcal{G}$, $\mathcal{Q} := \mathcal{I}(a_n)$, $\mathcal{I}(h_n) := \varnothing$, $OF := |\mathcal{I}(a_n)|$)

The algorithm's inputs are the fixed matrix W and four other data structures that describe the state of a exhaustive search. The state of the search can be controlled using three sets and one integer. Internally the algorithm keeps a priority queue PQ of candidate positions to include in the solution set. In a loop, the algorithm makes a recursive call to itself updating the data structures which represent the subproblem of searching once a candidate basis g is added to solution set $\mathcal{I}(h_n)$.

The set $\mathcal{G}$ represents remaining positions to explore. At the root of the recursive calls, we assign $\mathcal{G}$ to the set of all possible indexes we can add to the solution set $\mathcal{I}(h_n)$. At the beginning of the step we filter indexes $g \in \mathcal{G}$ with positive contributions $\Delta_{gn} > 0$ to a priority-queue PQ. The algorithm loops through all positions greedily, choosing the greatest contribution in the priority queue and then calling recursively the same procedure. The recursive call narrows the space of remaining candidates to those remaining in the priority queue, that is, those with positive contributions and are not yet explored in the loop. Thus we assign to $\mathcal{G}$ in the recursive call just the elements in PQ.

The set $\mathcal{Q}$ represents the uncovered positions of the original target vector a_n. The set $\mathcal{Q}$ is initialized as the original positions in a_n, which are equal to one. This set allows calculating the contributions Δ_{gn} efficiently. In the recursive call, when we add g to the solution set $\mathcal{I}(h_n)$, we must update what are the positions left to cover by subtracting the set $\mathcal{I}(w_g)$ of positions covered this basis.

Also, we have the current objective function represented as a floating-point variable OF. In the recursive call we simply update the OF by subtracting the contribution Δ_{gn} associated with the candidate g added to the solution set. Finally, the algorithm will keep track of the best solution found in each recursion made in each loop. If the solution $\mathcal{I}(h_n)_{rec}$ found in the recursion is better than the best solution $\mathcal{I}(h_n)^*$ found previously, the algorithm will store its value.

3.5   A Simple Post-processing for Discretizing Near-Binary Decompositions

Any binary matrix factorization algorithm yields two matrices, W and H. As we discussed before, the previous approaches can either: (1) obtain matrices with almost binary entries that, when are thresholded, have a great loss in precision or (2) obtain matrices with truly entries but with small sizes. As we showed in Eq. 4, the linearized version of the problem, in addition to fixating some of the matrices, can be algebraically divided into solving a the discrete basis subproblem for each of the columns of the original matrices and, in the transposed view, each of the rows of the original matrix.

Our main contribution is using a now scalable approach for solving thousands of discrete basis problems to post-process matrices factorized by gradient-descent approaches. Gradient-based methods can deal with large matrices and can provide a first approximation needed to solve these problems. Internally, they use alternating minimization until they converge in two almost binary matrices with low reconstruction error.

Thus we loop through the rows of a given matrix A and the approximations yielded by gradient descent algorithms W and H. We fixate W, use its columns as basis to recalculate each row of H by looping through the columns of A. Then we run a similar procedure for the transposed view.

We show the pseudo-code for this procedure in Algorithm 3.5.

---

function backtracking_discretization(A, W):
    Let $|\mathcal{M}|, |\mathcal{N}| :=$ dimensions of target matrix A
    Let $|\mathcal{M}|, |\mathcal{G}| :=$ dimensions of approximation matrix W
    Let $H :=$ matrix of zeros with dimensions $|\mathcal{G}|, |\mathcal{N}|$
    for v **in** $\mathcal{N}$:
        $\mathcal{I}(h_n)^*, OF^* :=$ column_solve(a_n, W, $\mathcal{G}$, $\mathcal{Q} := \mathcal{I}(a_n)$,
                    $\mathcal{I}(h_n) := \varnothing$, $OF := |\mathcal{I}(a_n)|$)
        $h_n :=$ reconstruct column h_n of H assigning values 1 to positions $\mathcal{I}(h_n)^*$
    Let $W :=$ matrix of zeros with dimensions $|\mathcal{M}|, |\mathcal{G}|$
    for t **in** $\mathcal{M}$:
        $\mathcal{I}(w_m)^*, OF^* :=$ column_solve(a_m, H, $\mathcal{G}$, $\mathcal{Q} := \mathcal{I}(a_m)$,
                    $\mathcal{I}(w_m) := \varnothing$, $OF := |\mathcal{I}(a_m)|$)
        $w_m :=$ reconstruct rows w_m of W assigning values 1 to positions $\mathcal{I}(w_m)^*$
    return W, H

---

4   Results for Large Gene Expression Datasets

The application of Binary Matrix Factorization for Gene expression data was introduced also by Zhang et al. [37] for analysing gene expression data following their main paper in [38]. These datasets come from a innovation in mapping the genome, introduced by the DNA microarrays and the Serial Analysis of Gene Expression. This allowed scientists to analyze thousands of genes in the same study [24].

We used the Gene Expression Omnibus Dataset Browser [5] and [1] as the source for our tests. The datasets gather gene expression over specific diseases or conditions. Diseases range from colitis, to maternal use of tobacco, to a variety of leukemia and cancer diseases. Our choice criteria was selecting datasets related diseases with the largest amount of samples.

We used the 31 datasets found in the National Center for Biotechnology Information Gene Expression Omnibus Dataset Browser [5] and [1]: GSE11223 [19]; GSE1133-GPL1073, GSE1133-GPL1074, GSE1133-GPL96 [31]; GSE12417-GPL570, GSE12417-GPL96, GSE12417-GPL97 [12]; GSE13355 [18]; GSE13576 [13]; GSE1726 [16]; GSE1888 [4]; GSE19392 [26]; GSE19429 [21]; GSE21521 [6], GSE22845 [34]; GSE27272 [36]; GSE27567-GPL1261, GSE27567-GPL570 [9]; GSE30310 [17]; GSE30999 [32]; GSE32474 [22]; GSE3578 [7]; GSE4115 [29]; GSE4290 [33]; GSE50948 [23]; GSE54514 [20]; GSE6919-GPL8300, GSE6919-GPL92, GSE6919-GPL93 [2]; GSE755 [35]; GSE9820 [25].

In these datasets, the expressions are real valued entries. In Creighton and Hanash [3] and in Liu et al. [11] have a discretization procedure based on the distribution of the entries for each gene. For values in a higher end of the distribution, they considered that a specific sample was up-regulated in that gene. In contrast, an entry in the lower-end was down-regulated. Their data had a log normal distribution, and they picked a threshold under which they would consider that specific gene as down-regulated and another threshold over which the expression would be considered up-regulated.

In our tests datasets coming from a more diverse source from different studies. We verified that some datasets were already normalized, others were not log-normally distributed. Then we have adapted their approach to an affine-invariant approach, choosing up-regulated expressions from the fourth quartile of their respective distribution and similarly choosing down-regulated for expressions in the first quartile. Consequently, we could standardize our tests safely.

Therefore, we preprocessed these 31 instances. The resulting binary matrices ranged from 4776 to 54765 rows representing each gene expression and ranged from 158 to 416 columns because instances ranged number of samples from 79 to 208. Consequently, when our backtracking discretization algorithm (BackDisc) was looping through rows, it had to solve tens of thousands of discrete basis problem using the first procedure in each instance.

Each experiment followed these steps: (0) using the pre-processing steps explained previously, (1) decomposing the matrix using Zhang's [38] algorithm implemented by the python package Nimfa [39], (2) searching for the combinations of thresholding of the matrices W and H which minimized the quadratic reconstruction error given by 1, (3) ran the algorithm described in Algorithm 3.5.

We compare each step of the algorithm with a lower bound calculated using the matrix's principal component analysis (PCA). The PCA is an algorithm for obtaining the truncated singular value decomposition (SVD), given the desired rank G. The SVD has an interesting property that it has the best reconstruction possible using a given rank G. Thus it serves as a deterministic and unique lower bound of a given instance, sometimes denoting if the instance has a low rank structure even expressible by any factorizations.

We run our experiment in each of these datasets, varying only the rank of the factorization, using ranks $G \in \{10, 20, 50, 100\}$. Also, we defined a time-out parameter because, in some cases, when the rank was set to 100, the procedure ran for a long time.

We can also observe the deterioration caused by the thresholding procedure is accompanied by not tackling the sparsity of reconstruction at the same level of the original. We believe the thresholding tends to leave entries equal to zero frequently. Fortunately, our approach recovers the sparsity and the level of reconstruction error (Fig. 1).

However when comparing the error, we first notice that the lower bound set by the principal component analysis (PCA) is very low, even with a very low rank of $G = 10$, for instance. This shows that the data has some inherent low rank-structure. The error of the gradient descent method is around 50%,

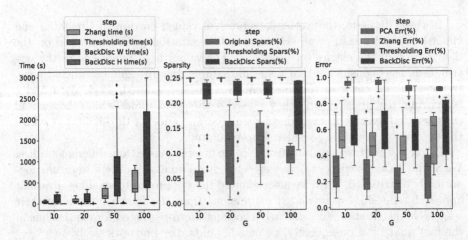

Fig. 1. Results showing time, sparsity and reconstruction error of the tests across the 31 instances. In our test we compare the PCA lower bound in blue, the gradient descent approach described in [38] and implemented by [39] in yellow, the thresholding with the minimum reconstruction error found in red, and our backtracking discretization algorithm (BackDisc) in green. The main result is that we can discretize the matrices while maintaining the reconstruction error in the same level as the gradient descent approach, the alternative was to threshold matrices with a significant loss. (Color figure online)

that arises to 90% when thresholded and then recovered back to 50% using our approach.

Instances have tens of thousands of rows, for each instance the time for reconstructing W has to solve tens of thousands discrete basis problems. Even though, for ranks $G \in \{10, 20\}$, time was under 600 s (10 min) for all instances, and for ranks of $G \in \{50, 100\}$ our algorithm ran under 3000 s (50 min).

5   Discussion

Binary matrices are explainable when the user has truly binary entries. Binary rows and columns of the factorization can be interpreted as frequent subsets that serve as a basis for the original matrix, and this introduces a powerful way of interpreting the problem. For real setting matrices with tens of thousands of observations and maybe thousands of elements that could be present or absent, the only viable approach was to use the gradient descent approach presented by Zhang in [38], and hope to achieve a good approximation without too many mid-level entries such as .4 or .5.

Often, matrices obtained by these approaches do not strongly indicate the belonging of a element to a group. Moreover the thresholding approach deteriorates the accuracy of reconstruction by a tendency to assume entries are equal to zero. We observed that the thresholding greatly affects the sparsity of the reconstruction. Therefore, it loses the power to capture inner structures of the original matrices. In our results, original matrices had a sparsity by construction very close to 25%, the reconstruction of the thresholding seemed to not even tackle aa fraction of these positions.

Our approach processes in a reasonable time matrices with thousands of rows and columns and a selection of up to 50 as the rank of the factorization. We demonstrated that this approach has more error than Zhang's [38] gradient descent, although it solves the problem of fixating the entries of resulting matrices W and H truly to zero or one. The alternative approach by thresholding tends to significantly increase the reconstruction error relative to the original matrix.

Truly binary solutions to these problems can be a tool for discovering structure in data and even leveraging a practitioner's knowledge. In a real setting, emerging groups of observations in the represented in columns of matrix W and groups of features represented in the rows H can be suggested by the algorithm and then corrected by human knowledge, and a new factorization recalculated using our backtracking discretization approach.

References

1. Barrett, T., et al.: NCBI GEO: archive for functional genomics data sets-update. Nucleic Acids Res. **41**(D1), D991–D995 (2012)
2. Chandran, U.R., et al.: Gene expression profiles of prostate cancer reveal involvement of multiple molecular pathways in the metastatic process. BMC Cancer **7**(1), 1–21 (2007)
3. Creighton, C., Hanash, S.: Mining gene expression databases for association rules. Bioinformatics **19**(1), 79–86 (2003)
4. Dillman, J.F., et al.: Genomic analysis of rodent pulmonary tissue following Bis-(2-chloroethyl) sulfide exposure. Chem. Res. Toxicol. **18**(1), 28–34 (2005)
5. Edgar, R., Domrachev, M., Lash, A.E.: Gene expression omnibus: NCBI gene expression and hybridization array data repository. Nucleic Acids Res. **30**(1), 207–210 (2002)
6. Hinze, C.H., et al.: Immature cell populations and an erythropoiesis gene-expression signature in systemic juvenile idiopathic arthritis: implications for pathogenesis. Arthritis Res. Ther. **12**, 1–13 (2010)
7. Iwakawa, M., et al.: The radiation-induced cell-death signaling pathway is activated by concurrent use of cisplatin in sequential biopsy specimens from patients with cervical cancer. Cancer Biol. Ther. **6**(6), 905–911 (2007)
8. Kumar, R., Panigrahy, R., Rahimi, A., Woodruff, D.: Faster algorithms for binary matrix factorization. In: International Conference on Machine Learning, pp. 3551–3559. PMLR (2019)
9. LaBreche, H.G., Nevins, J.R., Huang, E.: Integrating factor analysis and a transgenic mouse model to reveal a peripheral blood predictor of breast tumors. BMC Med. Genomics **4**(1), 1–14 (2011)
10. Lee, D.D., Seung, H.S.: Learning the parts of objects by non-negative matrix factorization. Nature **401**(6755), 788–791 (1999)
11. Liu, Y.C., Cheng, C.P., Tseng, V.S.: Mining differential top-k co-expression patterns from time course comparative gene expression datasets. BMC Bioinformatics **14**, 1–13 (2013)

12. Metzeler, K.H., et al.: An 86-probe-set gene-expression signature predicts survival in cytogenetically normal acute myeloid leukemia. Blood J. Am. Soc. Hematol. **112**(10), 4193–4201 (2008)
13. Meyer, L.H., et al.: Early relapse in all is identified by time to leukemia in NOD/SCID mice and is characterized by a gene signature involving survival pathways. Cancer Cell **19**(2), 206–217 (2011)
14. Miettinen, P., Mielikäinen, T., Gionis, A., Das, G., Mannila, H.: The discrete basis problem. IEEE Trans. Knowl. Data Eng. **20**(10), 1348–1362 (2008)
15. Mirisaee, H., Gaussier, E., Termier, A.: Efficient local search for L1 and L2 binary matrix factorization. Intell. Data Anal. 783–807 (2016)
16. Monks, S., et al.: Genetic inheritance of gene expression in human cell lines. Am. J. Hum. Genet. **75**(6), 1094–1105 (2004)
17. Morse, C.G., et al.: HIV infection and antiretroviral therapy have divergent effects on mitochondria in adipose tissue. J. Infect. Dis. **205**(12), 1778–1787 (2012)
18. Nair, R.P., et al.: Genome-wide scan reveals association of psoriasis with IL-23 and NF-κB pathways. Nat. Genet. **41**(2), 199–204 (2009)
19. Noble, C.L., et al.: Regional variation in gene expression in the healthy colon is dysregulated in ulcerative colitis. Gut **57**(10), 1398–1405 (2008)
20. Parnell, G.P., et al.: Identifying key regulatory genes in the whole blood of septic patients to monitor underlying immune dysfunctions. Shock **40**(3), 166–174 (2013)
21. Pellagatti, A., et al.: Deregulated gene expression pathways in myelodysplastic syndrome hematopoietic stem cells. Leukemia **24**(4), 756–764 (2010)
22. Pfister, T.D., et al.: Topoisomerase i levels in the NCI-60 cancer cell line panel determined by validated ELISA and microarray analysis and correlation with indenoisoquinoline sensitivity. Mol. Cancer Ther. **8**(7), 1878–1884 (2009)
23. Prat, A., et al.: Research-based PAM50 subtype predictor identifies higher responses and improved survival outcomes in HER2-positive breast cancer in the NOAH study. Clin. Cancer Res. **20**(2), 511–521 (2014)
24. Schena, M., Shalon, D., Davis, R.W., Brown, P.O.: Quantitative monitoring of gene expression patterns with a complementary DNA microarray. Science **270**(5235), 467–470 (1995)
25. Schirmer, S.H., et al.: Suppression of inflammatory signaling in monocytes from patients with coronary artery disease. J. Mol. Cell. Cardiol. **46**(2), 177–185 (2009)
26. Shapira, S.D., et al.: A physical and regulatory map of host-influenza interactions reveals pathways in H1N1 infection. Cell **139**(7), 1255–1267 (2009)
27. SnÃÅel, V., PlatoÅ, J., KrÃmer, P.: Developing genetic algorithms for boolean matrix factorization. In: CEUR Workshop Proceedings, pp. 61–70. CEUR-WS (2008)
28. SnÃÅel, V., PlatoÅ, J., KrÃmer, P., HÃsek, D., Frolov, A.: On the road to genetic boolean matrix factorization. Neural Netw. World **17**, 675–688 (2007)
29. Spira, A., et al.: Airway epithelial gene expression in the diagnostic evaluation of smokers with suspect lung cancer. Nat. Med. **13**(3), 361–366 (2007)
30. Spyrides, G., Poggi, M., Lopes, H.: Towards efficient searches for the discrete basis problem. Technical report, 02/2023, PUC-Rio, Departamento de Informática (2023)
31. Su, A.I., et al.: A gene atlas of the mouse and human protein-encoding transcriptomes. Proc. Natl. Acad. Sci. **101**(16), 6062–6067 (2004)
32. Suárez-Farinas, M., Li, K., Fuentes-Duculan, J., Hayden, K., Brodmerkel, C., Krueger, J.G.: Expanding the psoriasis disease profile: interrogation of the skin and serum of patients with moderate-to-severe psoriasis. J. Investig. Dermatol. **132**(11), 2552–2564 (2012)

33. Sun, L., et al.: Neuronal and glioma-derived stem cell factor induces angiogenesis within the brain. Cancer Cell **9**(4), 287–300 (2006)
34. Taskesen, E., et al.: Prognostic impact, concurrent genetic mutations, and gene expression features of AML with CEBPA mutations in a cohort of 1182 cytogenetically normal AML patients: further evidence for CEBPA double mutant AML as a distinctive disease entity. Blood J. Am. Soc. Hematol. **117**(8), 2469–2475 (2011)
35. Tian, E., et al.: The role of the WNT-signaling antagonist DKK1 in the development of osteolytic lesions in multiple myeloma. N. Engl. J. Med. **349**(26), 2483–2494 (2003)
36. Votavova, H., et al.: Transcriptome alterations in maternal and fetal cells induced by tobacco smoke. Placenta **32**(10), 763–770 (2011)
37. Zhang, Z.Y., Li, T., Ding, C., Ren, X.W., Zhang, X.S.: Binary matrix factorization for analyzing gene expression data. Data Min. Knowl. Disc. **20**, 28–52 (2010)
38. Zhang, Z., Li, T., Ding, C., Zhang, X.: Binary matrix factorization with applications. In: Seventh IEEE International Conference on Data Mining (ICDM 2007), pp. 391–400. IEEE (2007)
39. Zitnik, M., Zupan, B.: NIMFA: a python library for nonnegative matrix factorization. J. Mach. Learn. Res. **13**, 849–853 (2012)

Combining Linear Classifiers Using Score Function Based on Distance to Decision Boundary

Pawel Trajdos⬤, Robert Burduk$^{(\boxtimes)}$⬤, and Andrzej Kasprzak⬤

Department of Systems and Computer Networks, Wroclaw University of Science and Technology, Wroclaw, Poland
`robert.burduk@pwr.edu.pl`

Abstract. In this work, we addressed the issue of combining linear classifiers in the geometrical space. In other words, it means that linear classifiers are combined via the combination of their decision hyperplanes. For this purpose, an approach based on the potential functions is proposed. The potential function spans a potential field around each decision plane. The potential fields coming from decision planes are superposed, and the resultant decision field is used as an aggregated model of the ensemble classifier. During the experimental study, the proposed approach was applied to an ensemble built on heterogeneous base classifiers, and it was compared to two reference methods – majority voting and soft voting, respectively. The result shows that the proposed method can improve classification performance metrics compared to soft voting.

Keywords: Linear classifier · Classifiers fusion · Ensemble method

1 Introduction

The supervised classification algorithm builds a mathematical model based on training data. This model makes predictions or decisions for a new object not belonging to the training set. Thus, the final effect of the recognition system uses the previously learned model to indicate the class label for the new object. In this general scenario, a classifier maps the feature space into class label space. This mapping process can be decomposed into three stages. The first is to determine the value of the scoring function. The second one is the calibration of the scoring function, and the last is the conversion of the calibrated scoring function into a class label. For example, the scoring function of a linear SVM classifier is the object's distance from the decision boundary. Then, Platt scaling [12] computes the probability that a given object belongs to a particular class label.

The purpose of classifier calibration is an approximation of the predicted scores to the actual probabilities. The calibration converts scores function into probabilities or, more precisely, transforms classifier outputs into values that can be interpreted as probabilities. The calibration methods can be generally

© The Author(s), under exclusive license to Springer Nature Switzerland AG 2023
L. Rutkowski et al. (Eds.): ICAISC 2023, LNAI 14126, pp. 402–411, 2023.
https://doi.org/10.1007/978-3-031-42508-0_36

divided into two groups: parametric and non-parametric methods. The sigmoidal transformation maps the score of a classifier to a calibrated probability output as proposed by Platt [12]. The non-parametric methods are based on binning [17] or isotopic regression [18].

Ensemble methods are a popular approach in building a classification model that is more stable and a model that uses a set of many individual classifiers (base classifiers) and combine them to classify new data [13]. The main concept behind the ensemble technique is to create a classification method that outperforms every one of the base classifiers. As was previously mentioned, the outputs of the base classifiers can be used in various ways to determine the decision of a classifiers committee.

Different base classifiers have different definitions of their scoring functions. For this reason, in this paper, we present the concept of a scoring function, which is the same for all base classifiers and depends on the object's distance from the decision boundary of a given base classifier. Therefore, the proposed method's advantage is unifying the scoring function for all base classifiers. The research presented in the article has some limitations because it applies only to linear classifiers.

This paper is organized as follows: Sect. 2 presents the necessary terms connected with the linear classifiers and the proposed method for calculating the score function. In the next section, experimental studies are presented. Finally, some conclusions are presented.

2   Proposed Method

In this section, the proposed approach is explained. Additionally, this section introduces the notation used in this paper.

2.1   Linear Binary Classifier

In this paper, it is assumed that the input space $\mathbb{X}$ is d − dimensional Euclidean space $\mathbb{X} = \mathbb{R}^d$. Each object from the input space $x \in \mathbb{X}$ belongs to one of the two available classes, so the output space is: $\mathbb{M} = \{-1; 1\}$. It is assumed that there exists an unknown mapping $f : \mathbb{X} \mapsto \mathbb{M}$ that assigns each input space coordinates into a proper class. A classifier $\psi : \mathbb{X} \mapsto \mathbb{M}$ is a function that is designed to provide an approximation of the unknown mapping f. In this paper, only linear classifiers are considered. A linear classifier separates the classes using a hyperplane D defined by the following equation:

$$D : \langle n; x \rangle + b = 0, \tag{1}$$

where n is a unit normal vector of the decision hyperplane ($\|n\| = 1$), b is the distance from the hyperplane to the origin and $\langle \cdot; \cdot \rangle$ is a dot product defined as follows:

$$\langle a; b \rangle = \sum_{i=1}^{d} a_i b_i, \; \forall a, b \in \mathbb{X}. \tag{2}$$

In this paper, we use a norm of the vector x defined using the dot product:

$$\|x\| = \sqrt{\langle x; x \rangle}. \tag{3}$$

The linear classifier makes its decision according to the following rule:

$$\psi(x) = \text{sign}\left(\omega(x)\right), \tag{4}$$

where $\omega(x) = \langle n; x \rangle + b$ is the so called *discriminant function* of classifier ψ [9]. When the normal vector of the plane is a unit vector, the absolute value of the discriminant function equals to the distance from the decision hyperplane to point x. The sign of the discriminant function depends on the site of the plane where instance x lies.

Now, let us define an ensemble classifier:

$$\Psi = \left\{ \psi^{(1)}, \psi^{(2)}, \cdots, \psi^{(N)} \right\} \tag{5}$$

that is a set of N classifiers that work together in order to produce a more robust result [9]. There are multiple strategies to combine the classifiers constituting the ensemble. The simplest strategy to combine the outcomes of multiple classifiers is to apply the majority voting scheme [9]:

$$\omega(x) = \sum_{i=1}^{N} \text{sign}(\omega^{(i)}(x)), \tag{6}$$

where $\omega^{(i)}(x)$ is the value of the discriminant function provided by the classifier $\psi^{(i)}$ for point x. However, this simple yet effective strategy completely ignores the distance of instance x from the decision planes.

Another strategy is model averaging [14]. The output of the averaged model may be calculated by simply averaging the values of the discriminant functions:

$$\omega(x) = \frac{1}{N} \sum_{i=1}^{N} \omega^{(i)}(x) \tag{7}$$

An alternative strategy is to normalize the discriminant function within interval $[0, 1]$. The normalization may be done using a sigmoid function – the *softmax* function for example [9]:

$$\widetilde{\omega}^{(i)}(x) = \left(1 + \exp(-\omega^{(i)}(x))\right)^{-1}. \tag{8}$$

The value of the discriminant function may also be used to estimate the conditional probability of a class given instance x [12,18]. The normalized outputs are then simply averaged:

$$\omega(x) = \frac{1}{N} \sum_{i=1}^{N} \widetilde{\omega}^{(i)}(x). \tag{9}$$

After combining the base classifiers, the final prediction of the ensemble is obtained according to the rule (4).

2.2   The Proposed Method

In this paper, an approach similar to the softmax normalization is proposed. Contrary to the softmax normalization, our goal is not to provide a probabilistic interpretation of the linear classifier but to provide a fusion technique that works in the geometrical space. The idea is to span a potential field around the decision plane. The value of the potential function should be 0 at the surface of the decision plane. The sign of the potential depends on which side of the hyperplane the investigated point x is, whereas the absolute value of the potential depends on the distance to the decision plane. The value of the potential should also be bounded. The potential field may be constructed by applying some kind of transformation to the value of the discriminant function. The transformation must meet the following properties:

$$\text{sign}(g(\omega^{(i)}(x))) = \text{sign}(\omega^{(i)}(x)) \forall x \in \mathbb{X}, \tag{10}$$

$$g(z) \in [-1; 1] \forall z \in \mathbb{R}, \tag{11}$$

$$g(0) = 0. \tag{12}$$

Property (10) assures that the crisp decision based on the transformed value is the same as the decision based on the unmodified discriminant function. Property (11) bounds g interval $[-1; 1]$. However, contrary to the softmax normalization the transformation does not have to be a sigmoid function.

When the transformation is applied, the discriminant function of the ensemble is calculated using the following formula:

$$\omega(x) = \sum_{i=1}^{N} g(\omega^{(i)}(x)), \tag{13}$$

The properties of the transformation change in the way that the soft outputs are combined. During the combination stage, the potentials coming from different hyperplanes are summed up, and the decision depends on the sign of the sum.

In this paper, two transformations are proposed. The first one is a sigmoid function based on tanh function:

$$g_1(z) = \tanh(\gamma z), \tag{14}$$

where γ is a coefficient thats determine the steepness of the slope.

The second transformation is based on the exponential function:

$$g_2(z) = z \exp(-\gamma z^2 + 0.5)\sqrt{2\gamma}, \tag{15}$$

where γ is a coefficient that determines the position and steepness of the peak. The translation constants 0.5 and the scaling factor $\sqrt{2\gamma}$ guarantee that the maximum and minimum values are 1 and -1 respectively.

All models in the ensemble share the same shape coefficient γ. The shape coefficient is tuned in order to achieve the best classification performance metric of the entire ensemble.

The proposed algorithm is able to deal only with binary classification problems. However, any multi-class problem can be decomposed into multiple binary problems. In the experimental stage the One-vs-One strategy was used [8]. This strategy builds a separate binary classifier for each pair of classes. In our method, a single pair-specific is replaced by the above-described ensemble classifier.

3   Experimental Setup

In the conducted experimental study, the proposed approach was used to combine classifiers in heterogeneous and homogeneous ensemble of classifiers. The following base classifiers were employed:

- Fisher LDA – ψ_{FLDA},
- single layer MLP classifier – ψ_{MLP},
- nearest centroid (Nearest Prototype) – ψ_{NC},
- SVM classifier with linear kernel (no kernel) – ψ_{SVM},

The classifiers implemented in WEKA framework [5] were used. The classifier's parameters were set to their defaults. The multi-class problems were dealt with using One-vs-One decomposition [8]. The experimental code was implemented using WEKA framework [5]. The source code of the algorithms is available online[1].

During the experimental evaluation the following classifiers were compared:

1. the ensemble combined using the sigmoid normalization approach – Ψ_{SM},
2. the ensemble combined using the majority voting approach – Ψ_{MV},
3. the ensemble combined using g_1 transformation – Ψ_{g_1},
4. the ensemble combined using g_2 transformation – Ψ_{g_2}.

The normalized values for the Ψ_{SM} ensemble were obtained using the following techniques:

- ψ_{FLDA} – softmax
- ψ_{MLP} – softmax
- ψ_{NC} – the value of the discriminant function is inversely proportional to the distance from class prototypes. The values were normalized using the softmax approach
- ψ_{SVM} – the normalized values of the discriminant function is obtained using logistic regression [12].

The heterogeneous ensemble employs one copy of each of the abovementioned base classifiers. Each classifier is learned using the entire dataset. The homogeneous ensemble is built using 10 copies of each classifier. Training data sets for each of the classifiers are generated using the bagging approach [1]. The percentage of the training dataset is set to 66%.

---

[1] https://github.com/ptrajdos/piecewiseLinearClassifiers/tree/master.

Coefficient γ for transformations g_1 and g_2 was tuned using the grid search approach. The following set of parameter values were investigated:

$$\{\gamma = \exp(i) | i \in \{2, \cdots, 10\}\}.$$

The parameter is chosen in such a way that it provides the maximum value of the macro-averaged F_1 criterion.

To evaluate the proposed methods the following classification performance metrics are used [10]:

- Zero-one loss (Accuracy),
- Macro-averaged FDR, FNR, F_1,
- Micro-averaged FDR, FNR, F_1,

Following the recommendations of [2] and [4], the statistical significance of the obtained results was assessed using the two-step procedure. The first step is to perform the Friedman test [3] for each classification performance metrics separately. Since the multiple criteria were employed, the familywise errors (FWER) should be controlled [16]. To do so, the Holm's [7] procedure of controlling FWER of the conducted Friedman tests was employed. When the Friedman test shows that there is a significant difference within the group of classifiers, the pairwise tests using the Wilcoxon signed-rank test [2, 15] test were employed. To control FWER of the Wilcoxon-testing procedure, the Holm approach was employed [7]. For all tests the significance level was set to $\alpha = 0.05$.

Table 1 displays the collection of the 64 benchmark sets that were used during the experimental evaluation of the proposed algorithms. The table is divided into two columns. Each column is organized as follows. The first column contains the names of the datasets. The remaining ones contain the set-specific characteristics of the benchmark sets.

- The number of instances in the dataset ($|S|$).
- Dimensionality of the input space (d).
- The number of classes (C).
- Average imbalance ratio (IR)

The datasets come from the Keel[2] repository or are generated by us.

During the dataset-preprocessing stage, a few transformations on datasets were applied. That is, features are selected using the correlation-based approach [6]. Then, the PCA method was applied [11] and the percentage of variance was set to 0.95. The attributes were also scaled to fit the interval $[0; 1]$. Additionally, in order to ensure the dot product to be in the interval $[-1; 1]$, vectors in each dataset were scaled using the factor $\frac{1}{d^2}$. This normalization makes it easier to find a proper γ for transformations g_1 and g_2.

---

[2] https://sci2s.ugr.es/keel/category.php?cat=clas.

Table 1. The characteristics of the benchmark sets

Name	$|S|$	d	C	IR	Name	$|S|$	d	C	IR
appendicitis	106	7	2	2.52	optdigits	5620	62	10	1.02
australian	690	14	2	1.12	page-blocks	5472	10	5	58.12
balance	625	4	3	2.63	penbased	10992	16	10	1.04
banana2D	2000	2	2	1.00	phoneme	5404	5	2	1.70
bands	539	19	2	1.19	pima	767	8	2	1.44
Breast_Tissue	105	9	6	1.29	ring2D	4000	2	2	1.00
check2D	800	2	2	1.00	ring	7400	20	2	1.01
cleveland	303	13	5	5.17	saheart	462	9	2	1.44
coil2000	9822	85	2	8.38	satimage	6435	36	6	1.66
dermatology	366	34	6	2.41	Seeds	210	7	3	1.00
diabetes	768	8	2	1.43	segment	2310	19	7	1.00
Faults	1940	27	7	4.83	shuttle	57999	9	7	1326.03
gauss2DV	800	2	2	1.00	sonar	208	60	2	1.07
gauss2D	4000	2	2	1.00	spambase	4597	57	2	1.27
gaussSand2	600	2	2	1.50	spectfheart	267	44	2	2.43
gaussSand	600	2	2	1.50	spirals1	2000	2	2	1.00
glass	214	9	6	3.91	spirals2	2000	2	2	1.00
haberman	306	3	2	1.89	spirals3	2000	2	2	1.00
halfRings1	400	2	2	1.00	texture	5500	40	11	1.00
halfRings2	600	2	2	1.50	thyroid	7200	21	3	19.76
hepatitis	155	19	2	2.42	titanic	2201	3	2	1.55
HillVall	1212	100	2	1.01	twonorm	7400	20	2	1.00
housevotes	435	16	2	1.29	ULC	675	146	9	2.17
ionosphere	351	34	2	1.39	vehicle	846	18	4	1.03
iris	150	4	3	1.00	Vertebral_Column	310	6	3	1.67
led7digit	500	7	10	1.16	wdbc	569	30	2	1.34
lin1	1000	2	2	1.01	wine	178	13	3	1.23
lin2	1000	2	2	1.83	winequality-red	1599	11	6	20.71
lin3	1000	2	2	2.26	winequality-white	4898	11	7	82.94
magic	19020	10	2	1.42	wisconsin	699	9	2	1.45
mfdig_fac	2000	216	10	1.00	yeast	1484	8	10	17.08
movement_libras	360	90	15	1.00					
newthyroid	215	5	3	3.43					

4 Results and Discussion

The numerical results are given in Table 2. Each table is structured as follows. The first row contains numbers assigned to algorithms in Sect. 3. Then, the table is divided into eleven sections – one section is related to a single evaluation criterion. The first row of each section is the name of the classification performance metric. The second row shows the p-value of the Friedman test. The third one shows the average ranks achieved by algorithms. The following rows show p-values resulting from the pairwise Wilcoxon test. The p-value equal to 0.000 informs that the p-values are lower than 10^{-3} and p-value equal to 1.000 informs that the value is higher than 0.999.

The results of the Friedman test show that, for all classification performance metrics, there are significant differences between classifiers. The average ranks and the results of the post-hoc Wilcoxon test show that the classifier based on

Table 2. Statistical evaluation. The Wilcoxon test for the heterogeneous ensemble – p-values for paired comparisons of the investigated methods.

	1	2	3	4	1	2	3	4
Nam.	Zero-One				MaFDR			
Frd.	3.040e-02				3.040e-02			
Rank	2.885	2.238	2.269	2.608	2.931	2.346	2.438	2.285
1		0.013	0.018	0.220		0.018	0.014	0.020
2			1.000	1.000			1.000	1.000
3				0.468				1.000
Nam.	MaFNR				MaF1			
Frd.	4.702e-07				5.323e-07			
Rank	3.254	2.462	2.131	2.154	3.285	2.269	2.192	2.254
1		0.000	0.000	0.000		0.000	0.000	0.000
2			0.078	0.342			1.000	1.000
3				1.000				1.000
Nam.	MiFDR				MiFNR			
Frd.	3.040e-02				3.040e-02			
Rank	2.885	2.238	2.269	2.608	2.885	2.238	2.269	2.608
1		0.013	0.018	0.220		0.013	0.018	0.220
2			1.000	1.000			1.000	1.000
3				0.468				0.468
Nam.	MiF1							
Frd.	3.040e-02							
Rank	2.885	2.238	2.269	2.608				
1		0.013	0.018	0.220				
2			1.000	1.000				
3				0.468				

output averaging is significantly worse than the classifiers based on majority voting and the g_1 transformation in terms of all classification performance metrics. The between-ranks differences are greater for the macro-averaged classification performance metric. For the macro-averaged criteria also the classifier based on the g_2 transformation performs better than the soft voting approach. It means that the approach based on simple averaging of the classifier soft-outputs performs worse on the imbalanced datasets. This is a consequence of the a fact that the macro-averaged measures are more sensitive to the minority-class performance.

On the other hand, for all criteria, there are no significant differences between the proposed algorithms and the majority-voting classifier. In terms of micro averaged and zero-one classification performance metric, there are also no significant differences between the classifier based on g_2 transformation and the

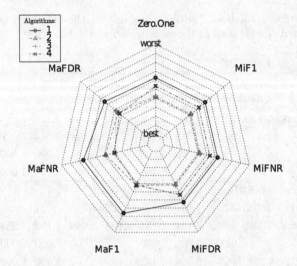

Fig. 1. Average ranks of for the heterogeneous ensemble

classifier based on simple output averaging. Despite the lack of significant differences between the transformations based on g_1 and g_2 functions, the average ranks may suggest that, in terms of the micro-averaged measures and zero-one measure, the classifier based on g_2 transformation is slightly worse than the classifier based on transformation g_1. Due to the properties of micro-averaged measures, these results may suggest that the classifier based on g_2 may prefer a minority class (Fig. 1).

5   Conclusions

In this paper, a combination linear base classifiers scheme was proposed. The proposed approach was tested with two different potential functions. The results showed that, for heterogeneous base classifiers used in the ensembles, the proposed method is significantly better than the simple-averaging approach and is comparable with the majority-voting combiner.

The proposed method's main advantage is that the form of the scoring function is identical for all base classifiers. This function depends on the object's distance from the decision boundary of a given base classifier.

The proposed approach needs a proper setting of the potential function parameters, and finding those parameters using the grid-search method is computationally expensive. The next step in this research should be to propose an effective heuristic way to find proper values of the potential function without such a great computational burden.

References

1. Breiman, L.: Bagging predictors. Mach. Learn. **24**(2), 123–140 (1996). https://doi.org/10.1007/bf00058655
2. Demšar, J.: Statistical comparisons of classifiers over multiple data sets. J. Mach. Learn. Res. **7**, 1–30 (2006)
3. Friedman, M.: A comparison of alternative tests of significance for the problem of m rankings. Ann. Math. Statist. **11**(1), 86–92 (1940). https://doi.org/10.1214/aoms/1177731944
4. Garcia, S., Herrera, F.: An extension on "statistical comparisons of classifiers over multiple data sets" for all pairwise comparisons. J. Mach. Learn. Res. **9**, 2677–2694 (2008)
5. Hall, M., Frank, E., Holmes, G., Pfahringer, B., Reutemann, P., Witten, I.H.: The WEKA data mining software. SIGKDD Explor. Newsl. **11**(1), 10 (2009). https://doi.org/10.1145/1656274.1656278
6. Hall, M.A.: Correlation-based feature selection for machine learning. Ph.D. thesis, The University of Waikato (1999)
7. Holm, S.: A simple sequentially rejective multiple test procedure. Scand. J. Stat. **6**(2), 65–70 (1979). https://doi.org/10.2307/4615733
8. Hüllermeier, E., Fürnkranz, J.: On predictive accuracy and risk minimization in pairwise label ranking. J. Comput. Syst. Sci. **76**(1), 49–62 (2010). https://doi.org/10.1016/j.jcss.2009.05.005
9. Kuncheva, L.I.: Combining Pattern Classifiers: Methods and Algorithms, 1 edn. Wiley-Interscience (2004)
10. Luaces, O., Díez, J., Barranquero, J., del Coz, J.J., Bahamonde, A.: Binary relevance efficacy for multilabel classification. Prog. Artif. Intell. **1**(4), 303–313 (2012). https://doi.org/10.1007/s13748-012-0030-x
11. Pearson, K.: LIII. on lines and planes of closest fit to systems of points in space. London Edinburgh Dublin Philos. Mag. J. Sci. **2**(11), 559–572 (1901). https://doi.org/10.1080/14786440109462720
12. Platt, J., et al.: Probabilistic outputs for support vector machines and comparisons to regularized likelihood methods. Adv. Large Margin Classif. **10**(3), 61–74 (1999)
13. Rokach, L.: Pattern classification using ensemble methods, vol. 75. World Scientific (2010)
14. Skurichina, M., Duin, R.P.: Bagging for linear classifiers. Pattern Recognit. **31**(7), 909–930 (1998). https://doi.org/10.1016/s0031-3203(97)00110-6
15. Wilcoxon, F.: Individual comparisons by ranking methods. Biom. Bull. **1**(6), 80 (1945). https://doi.org/10.2307/3001968
16. Yekutieli, D., Benjamini, Y.: The control of the false discovery rate in multiple testing under dependency. Ann. Statist. **29**(4), 1165–1188 (2001). https://doi.org/10.1214/aos/1013699998
17. Zadrozny, B., Elkan, C.: Learning and making decisions when costs and probabilities are both unknown. In: Proceedings of the Seventh ACM SIGKDD International Conference on Knowledge Discovery and Data Mining (2001). https://doi.org/10.1145/502512.502540
18. Zadrozny, B., Elkan, C.: Transforming classifier scores into accurate multiclass probability estimates. In: Proceedings of the Eighth ACM SIGKDD International Conference on Knowledge Discovery and Data Mining - KDD 2002. ACM Press (2002). https://doi.org/10.1145/775047.775151

Author Index

A

Abdelkefi, Fatma II-48
Abdollahzadeh, Fatemeh II-145
Agarwal, Pooja II-78
Al Osman, Hussein II-331
Alaya Cheikh, Faouzi I-274
Aleksandra, Klos-Witkowska II-239
Alfarano, Andrea II-3
Ambros, Maximilian I-570
Andonie, Răzvan I-167
Andrii, Semenets II-239
Angryk, Rafal A. I-475
Argasiński, Jan K. II-258
Arya, Arti II-78

B

Bartczuk, Łukasz I-363
Belkacem, Soundes II-17
Beshley, Halyna II-26, II-281
Beshley, Mykola II-26, II-281
Bieniek-Kobuszewska, Martyna II-123
Bilski, Jarosław I-3, I-12
Biru, Tibebu I-570
Blanco, Rosmary II-258
Bouguila, Nizar II-320
Brandt-Pook, Hans II-91
Bujok, Petr I-352
Burduk, Robert II-402

C

Cabani, Adnane II-48
Chalmers, Eric I-23
Charaf, Hassan I-157
Chen, Yang I-475
Cherukuri, Aswani Kumar II-353
Chun-Wei Lin, Jerry I-193
Cierniak, Robert II-269
Contreras, Rodrigo Colnago II-291
Coulter, Duncan I-56

Cpałka, Krzysztof I-385
Crimi, Alessandro II-207, II-258
Csorba, Kristof I-157
Czerwinski, Dariusz I-68

D

Dagner, Tizian I-35
de Araujo, Thiago Giachetto I-339
De Magistris, Giorgio II-3
Del Monaco, Daniel II-145
Del-Moral-Hernandez, Emilio I-286
Do, Thai Thanh II-102
Draguns, Andis I-304
Duda, Piotr I-46
Dünnweber, Jan I-236
Duy, Huynh Anh II-307
Dziwiński, Piotr I-363

F

Falck, Tristan I-56
Falcó-Roget, Joan II-258
Fernández-Martínez, Juan Luis II-228
Fernández-Muñiz, Zulima II-228
Ferreira, Heitor F. I-487
Forouzanfar, Darya II-320
Freivalds, Karlis I-304

G

Gabryel, Marcin I-522
Gadekallu, Thippa Reddy I-560
Gaile, Eliza I-304
Gałka, Łukasz I-68
García-Piquer, Álvaro I-375
García-Sánchez, Juan Manuel I-375
Georg, Peter I-236
Giang, Pham Hong II-102
Gordienko, Yuri I-251
Grabowski, Dariusz I-510
Gregus Jr., Michal II-26

L. Rutkowski et al. (Eds.): ICAISC 2023, LNAI 14126, pp. 413–416, 2023.
https://doi.org/10.1007/978-3-031-42508-0

Grela, Radoslaw   I-463
Gronau, Norbert   I-570
Grum, Marcus   I-78, I-570
Grycuk, Rafał   II-58
Grzeszczak, Jakub   I-497
Guido, Rodrigo Capobianco   II-291

H

H. Bugatti, Pedro   I-226
Hamada, Samir   II-145
Hao, Pei-Yi   I-101
Hordiichuk-Bublivska, Olena   II-281
Hung, Phan Duy   II-102, II-307, II-377

I

Ibrahim, Doaa   II-331
Iddrisu, Khadija   II-207
Inkpen, Diana   II-331
Itano, Fernando   I-286
Ivanochko, Iryna   II-281

J

Jimenes-Vargas, Karina   II-219

K

Kalina, Jan   II-343
Kamalov, Firuz   II-353
Karczmarek, Paweł   I-68
Karpiel, Ilona   II-176
Kasprzak, Andrzej   II-402
Kempton, Dustin J.   I-475
Kesler, Selin   I-35
Khoa, Huynh Anh   II-307
Kiersztyn, Adam   II-123
Kiersztyn, Krystyna   II-123
Kierzkowski, Jakub   I-181
Klimas, Maciej   I-510
Kloczkowski, Andrzej   II-228
Kobielnik, Martyna   II-112
Kocić, Eliza   I-522
Kocić, Milan   I-522
Kolenovský, Patrik   I-352
Komorowski, Jacek   I-325
Korzeń, Marcin   II-69
Kowalczyk, Barosz   I-12
Kowalczyk, Bartosz   I-3
Krallmann, Hermann   I-570
Krishnan, Sivarama   I-560

Kryvinska, Natalia   I-463
Krzyżak, Adam   I-530
Kucharski, Daniel   I-385
Kwenda, Clopas   II-37
Kwolek, Bogdan   I-112

L

Lacko, Martin   I-352
Łada-Tondyra, Ewa   II-58
Łapa, Krystian   I-399
László Galata, Dorián   I-157
LaTorre, Antonio   I-439
Lerma-Martín, Alexandre   I-375
Leś, Michał   I-122
Loni, Mohammad   I-203
Lopes, Hélio   II-388
Luczak, Artur   I-23

M

Machacuay, Javier   I-215
Malec, Sylwia   II-207
Mańdziuk, Jacek   II-134
Manouchehri, Narges   II-320
Martins, Luiz G. A.   I-487
Mastalerczyk, Mateusz   II-251
Mavathur, Anusha   II-78
Mazurek, Szymon   II-258
McConnell, Benjamin   II-145
Messaoud, Walid   II-48
Mikitiuk, Artur   I-497
Mirjalili, Seyedali   I-427
Mohannazadeh Bakhtiari, M.   I-134, I-145
Mojeed, Hammed A.   I-415
Mongelli, Leonardo   II-3
Moreno, Hugo   I-439
Morkowski, Jakub   I-542
Mrad, Mohamed Azouz   I-157
Munteanu, Cristian R.   II-219
Muşat, Bogdan   I-167
Mzyk, Grzegorz   II-366

N

Nagy, Zsombor Kristóf   I-157
Naharro, Pablo S.   I-439
Najgebauer, Patryk   II-58
Nallakaruppan, M. K.   I-560
Napoli, Christian   II-3

Nega Tarekegn, Adane   I-274
Niewiadomski, Szymon   II-366

O

Oliveira, Gina M. B.   I-487
Ozolins, Emils   I-304

P

Panasiewicz, Grzegorz   II-123
Parzeller, Rafael   I-35
Peña, José-María   I-439
Penna, Puca Huachi Vaz   I-339
Perełkiewicz, Michał   I-181
Perez-Castillo, Yunierkis   II-219
Peštová, Barbora   II-343
Phuoc, Nguyen Bao   II-377
Pluta, Piotr   II-269
Poggi, Marcus   II-388
Poláková, Radka   I-451
Połap, Dawid   I-193
Polap, Dawid   I-560
Poniszewska-Marańda, Aneta   I-463
Poświata, Rafał   I-181
Pothumarthi, Apurva   II-78
Praveen, Anjali   II-78
Prokop, Katarzyna   I-193

Q

Quinde, Mario   I-215

R

Rafajłowicz, Ewaryst   I-530
Rafajłowicz, Wojciech   I-530
Raza Moosavi, Syed Kumayl   I-427
Reddy, Praveen Kumar   I-560
Reichhuber, Simon   II-192
Rodziewicz-Bielewicz, Jan   II-69
Rojahn, Marcel   I-570
Russo, Samuele   II-3
Rutkowski, Leszek   I-46

S

S. M. Silva, William   I-226
Sajjad, Muhammad   I-274
Salimi, Maghsood   I-203
Sanchez, Sergio   I-215
Sanfilippo, Filippo   I-427
Sawant, Pradnya   II-158
Schäfer, Andreas   I-236

Scherer, Magdalena   II-170
Scherer, Rafał   II-58
Shinji, Sako   I-112
Siłka, Jakub   II-112
Sirjani, Marjan   I-203
Smoląg, Jacek   I-12
Sonawane, Kavita   II-158
Souza, Marcone Jamilson Freitas   I-339
Spyrides, Georges   II-388
Srinivasa, Anagha   II-78
Srivastava, Gautam   I-193, I-560
Stadler, Timo   I-236
Starcevic, Ana   II-176
Starczewski, Janusz   II-3
Statkevych, Roman   I-251
Stecker, Benjamin   II-91
Stirenko, Sergii   I-251
Sulieman, Hana   II-353
Surówka, Grzegorz   I-263
Szczepanik, Tomasz   II-251
Szlapczynski, Rafal   I-415

T

T. M. Saito, Priscila   I-226
Tejera, Eduardo   II-219
Tinoco, Claudiney R.   I-487
Tomforde, Sven   II-192
Trabelsi, Rim   II-48
Trajdos, Pawel   II-402
Trang, Duong Thuy   II-377
Trojanowski, Krzysztof   I-497
Tung, Pham Son   II-102

U

Ullah, Mohib   I-274
Urbinate, Eder   I-286

V

Valenta, Daniel   I-451
Vasyl, Martsenyuk   II-239
Viana, Monique Simplicio   II-291
Victor Gwetu, Mandlenkosi   II-37
Vilasís-Cardona, Xavier   I-375
Villmann, A.   I-134
Villmann, T.   I-134, I-145
Vincent Fonou-Dombeu, Jean   II-37
Volodymyr, Pastukh   II-26
Vucinic, Boris   II-176

W

Walczak, Jakub   II-58
Walczak, Patryk   II-134
Walkowiak, Tomasz   I-296
Weikl, Sandra   I-236
Wein, Simon   I-236
Weiss, Tobias   II-192
Wieczorek, Michał   II-112
Wojciechowski, Adam   II-58
Wojtulewicz, Mateusz   I-46

Woźniak, Marcin   II-112
Woźniak, Michał   I-122

Z

Zabihimayvan, Mahdieh   II-145
Zafar, Muhammad Hamza   I-427
Zakovskis, Ronalds   I-304
Zalasiński, Marcin   II-251
Żebrowski, Michał   I-325

Printed in the United States
by Baker & Taylor Publisher Services

Printed in the United States
by Baker & Taylor Publisher Services